S0-ATC-081

Forging Alberta's Constitutional Framework

Forging Alberta's Constitutional Framework

RICHARD CONNORS AND JOHN M. LAW,
EDITORS

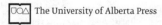 The University of Alberta Press

in association with

 Centre for Constitutional Studies
Centre d'études constitutionnelles

University of Alberta

Published by

The University of Alberta Press
Ring House 2
Edmonton, Alberta, Canada T6G 2E1

Copyright © The University of Alberta Press 2005

Library and Archives Canada Cataloguing in Publication

Forging Alberta's constitutional framework / Richard Connors and
John M.Law, editors.

Includes bibliographical references and index.
ISBN 0–88864–457–4 (bound) ISBN 0–88864–458–2 (pbk.)

1. Constitutional history—Alberta. 2. Civil rights—Alberta—History.
3. Federal-provincial relations—Alberta—History. 4. Law—Alberta—History.
I. Connors, Richard Travanion, 1964– II. Law, John M III. University of
Alberta. Centre for Constitutional Studies IV. Title.

KEA454.F67 2005   342.7123   C2005-905707-6
KF4482.F67 2005

Printed and bound in Canada by
Houghton Boston Printers, Saskatoon, Saskatchewan.
First edition, first printing, 2005
All rights reserved.

No part of this publication may be produced, stored in a retrieval system, or transmitted in
any forms or by any means, electronic, mechanical, photocopying, recording, or otherwise,
without the prior written consent of the copyright owner or a licence from The Canadian
Copyright Licensing Agency (Access Copyright). For an Access Copyright license, visit
www.accesscopyright.ca or call toll free: 1–800–893–5777.

The University of Alberta Press is committed to protecting our natural environment. As part
of our efforts, this book is printed on stock produced by New Leaf Paper: it contains 100% post
consumer recycled fibres and is acid- and chlorine-free.

The University of Alberta Press gratefully acknowledges the support received for its publishing
program from The Canada Council for the Arts. The University of Alberta Press also gratefully
acknowledges the financial support of the Government of Canada through the Book Publishing
Industry Development Program (BPDIP) and from the Alberta Foundation for the Arts for our
publishing activities.

Canada Council   Conseil des Arts
for the Arts   du Canada

Canadä

Contents

ix Acknowledgements

xi About the Contributors

xvii Preface

xix Introduction

A Legal and Constitutional History of Alberta
RICHARD CONNORS AND JOHN M. LAW

1 One

In the Mind's Eye
Law and British Colonial Expansion in Rupert's Land in the Age of Empire
RICHARD CONNORS

25 Two

Ambiguous Authority
The Development of Criminal Law in the Canadian North-West and Alberta
DESMOND BROWN

61 Three

Venerable Rights
Constitutionalizing Alberta's Schools, 1869–1905
SANDRA M. ANDERSON

103 Four

One Language and One Nationality
The Forcible Constitution of a Unilingual Province in a Bilingual Country, 1870–2005
EDMUND A. AUNGER

137 Five

Out of the West: History, Memory, and the "Persons" Case, 1919–2000
CATHERINE CAVANAUGH

165 Six

Alberta's Real Constitution
The Natural Resources Transfer Agreement
THOMAS FLANAGAN AND MARK MILKE

191 Seven

Bible Bill and the Money Barons
The Social Credit Court References and their Constitutional Consequences
DALE GIBSON

237 Eight

Not Like the Others
The Regulation of Indian Hunting and Fishing in Alberta
ROBERT IRWIN

267 Nine

Justices of the Peace in Alberta
ROD MACLEOD AND NANCY PARKER

289 Ten

Alberta's Crowning Glory
The Office of Lieutenant-Governor
KENNETH MUNRO

315 Eleven

Federal-Provincial Tensions and the Evolution of a Province
PRESTON MANNING

345 Twelve

Alberta Métis Settlements
A Brief History
FRED V. MARTIN

391 Thirteen

The Perfect Storm
The National Energy Program and the Failure of Federal-Provincial Relations
DOUGLAS OWRAM

411 Fourteen

Premiere Peter Lougheed, Alberta and the Transformation of Constitutionalism in Canada, 1971–1985
MICHAEL D. BEHIELS

459 Fifteen

Equality and Women's Political Identity in Post-1970s Alberta
LOIS HARDER

479 Sixteen

Uncertain Future
Alberta in the Canadian Community
ALLAN TUPPER

497 Selected Bibliography

517 Index

Acknowledgements

A collaborative project of this nature would be impossible without the contributions and assistance of many. Our greatest debt is owed to the authors of the various chapters. Each of their contributions adds to our understanding of Alberta's complex evolution as a political entity with a unique identity. Their enthusiasm for the project was infectious. We would also to thank those who participated in the Alberta's Constitutional History project colloquium held at the University of Alberta in October 2003, especially David Hall, Department of History and Classics, Julian Martin, Department of History and Classics, and Robert Chambers, Faculty of Law.

The project would not have been possible without the generous financial support of the Alberta Law Foundation whose continued commitment to public legal education is greatly appreciated. We are also grateful for the financial support provided by Fraser, Milner, Casgrain L.L.P., a law firm whose roots are deeply embedded in the legal history of Alberta, the Office of the Vice President, Research, University of Alberta, and the Faculty of Law, University of Alberta. This support has greatly assisted the publication of the volume by the University of Alberta Press.

We are grateful to our editor, Mary Mahoney-Robson, at the University of Alberta Press, for her patience and enthusiastic assistance in seeing this book through the publication process. In addition we thank Peter Midgley who copy-edited the manuscript, Peter Paz who prepared the Bibliography, Marvin Harder who designed the book and cover and did the page layout, and Judy Dunlop who prepared the final index. The editors would like to thank the academic reviewers for their comments.

Finally, we acknowledge the support of the chairs of the Management Board, Centre for Constitutional Studies, University of Alberta, current chair, Richard Bauman and former chairs, Bruce Elman and Allan Tupper, and the assistance of its administration staff.

About the Contributors

SANDRA M. ANDERSON is a partner in the Edmonton office of Field, where she conducts a general litigation practice in the areas of employment, education, and privacy law before Alberta courts and tribunals at all levels. She has a B.A. from Duke University, an M.A. and a Ph.D. from Northwestern University in Evanston, Illinois, and an LL.B. from the University of Calgary. Prior to obtaining her law degree, she helped found an alternative public school in Calgary and served for two terms as a trustee on the Calgary Board of Education, where she became chairperson. Her longstanding interest in Alberta's history, in particular its schools, was put to further practical use while researching the early education and social service infrastructure of the Province to prepare the case for the plaintiffs in the wrongful sterilization lawsuits against the government of Alberta.

EDMUND A. AUNGER is Professor of Political Science at the Faculté Saint-Jean at the University of Alberta. His research focuses on the governance of divided societies, particularly multilingual societies, and he has published extensively on official language policies in Canada and Europe. He is especially interested in Canada's French-speaking minority communities.

MICHAEL D. BEHIELS is Professor of Canadian History, former chair of University of Ottawa's Department of History, and writer, commentator, and consultant on contemporary Canadian political, ideological, and constitutional developments. He has been invited to submit briefs to and give testimony before committees of the Parliament of Canada and the Ontario Legislature on Constitutional renewal and the *Clarity Act*. He is the author of two books, including the seminal *Canada's Francophone Minority Communities, Constitutional Renewal and the Winning of School Governance* (2004), French version with University of Ottawa Press (2005) and *Prelude to Quebec's Quiet Revolution: Liberalism versus Neo-Nationalism, 1945–1960* (1985) as well as the author, editor and co-editor of ten books including *Nation, Ideas, Identities: Essays in Honour of Ramsay Cook* (2000) and *The Meech Lake Primer: Conflicting Views on the 1987 Constitutional Accord* (1987). Professor Behiels has taught at the University of Toronto (1973–75), Acadia University (1975–86) and the University of Ottawa since 1986. He has been a visiting Professor at the University of Alberta, at the Institute for Canadian Studies, University of Augsburg, Germany, and in the Department of Intercultural Studies, City University of Nagoya, Japan.

DESMOND BROWN is Adjunct Professor in the Department of History and Classics at the University of Alberta. He has published numerous articles on the criminal law in early Britain and Canada in scholarly journals and law reviews. He is author of *The Genesis of the Canadian Criminal Code of 1892* (1989) and *The Birth of a Criminal Code: the Evolution of Canada's Justice System* (1995). He is currently working on a history of Canadian Criminal Law.

CATHERINE CAVANAUGH is Associate Professor at Athabasca University where she teaches history and women's studies. She is co-editor of *Standing on New Ground: Women in Alberta* (1993), *Making Western Canada: Essays on European Colonization and Settlement* (1996) and *Telling Tales: Essays in Western Women's History* (2000). Her article "'No Place for a Woman': Engendering Western Canadian Settlement" garnered the O.O. Winther Prize and the Joan Jenson-Darlis Miller Prize. She is a co-editor of the two-volume centennial history of Alberta, *Alberta Formed, Alberta Transformed* (2005).

RICHARD CONNORS is Assistant Professor of History at the University of Ottawa since 2002. He has also taught history at the University of Essex and the University of Alberta and from 1999 to 2002, he taught in the Faculty of Law at the University of Alberta. He has published numerous articles and edited books on early modern British and Imperial history. He is completing a book for Palgrave-Macmillan Press on the nature of the state in Hanoverian Britain. His current research concentrates upon the political and constitutional history of 18th century Britain and its Empire.

THOMAS FLANAGAN is Professor of Political Science at the University of Calgary. His publications include *Metis Lands in Manitoba* (1991); *The Collected Writings of Louis Riel*, Vol. 3 (1985); *Riel and the Rebellion: 1885 Reconsidered* (2nd ed.,

2000); *Louis "David" Riel: 'Prophet of the New World'* (2nd ed., 1996); *Waiting for the Wave: The Reform Party and Preston Manning* (1995); *Game Theory and Canadian Politics (1998);* and *First Nations? Second Thoughts* (2000). He was Director of Research for the Reform Party of Canada 1991–92, Chief of Staff in the Office of the Leader of the Opposition, House of Commons, 2002–03 and Manager of the National Campaign of the Conservative Party of Canada, 2004. Dr. Flanagan is a Fellow of the Royal Society of Canada.

DALE GIBSON graduated in Arts from what is now the University of Winnipeg in 1954, and in Law from the University of Manitoba as gold medalist in 1958. After obtaining an LL.M. degree from Harvard University, he taught law at the University of Manitoba from 1959 to 1991 and at the University of Alberta from 1991 until 2001. Since retiring from the University of Alberta he continues to write and to practice as a consulting barrister in the area of public law. Professor Gibson is the author of several books and many articles, chiefly about constitutional law and legal history. His public service includes a lengthy term with the Manitoba Law Reform Commission, Chairmanship of the Manitoba Human Rights Commission, and service as constitutional advisor to several governments, as well as to the Royal Commission on Aboriginal Peoples. Mr. Gibson is a Fellow of the Royal Society of Canada.

LOIS HARDER is Associate Professor of Political Science at the University of Alberta. She has written extensively on women and politics in Alberta and Canada, including the book *State of Struggle: Feminism and Politics in Alberta* (2003). Her current research focuses on the politics of marriage and the family in Canada and the United States.

ROBERT IRWIN teaches history at Grant MacEwan College. His current research projects examine both Canadian Indian policy and Canadian Indian treaties.

JOHN M. LAW is Professor of Law at the University of Alberta. He teaches and has research interests and publications in administrative law, legal history, the legal profession and professional responsibility. Prior to joining the Faculty of Law in 1984, he practiced law with an Edmonton firm, acted as Board Counsel and Director of Licensing with the Alberta Liquor Control Board and served as Associate Director and Executive Director of the Legal Education Society of Alberta. Professor Law has served as Associate Dean and is presently a member of the Board of Trustees of the Law School Admission Council. He has served on several Law Society committees and was the Executive Director of the Canadian Institute for the Administration of Justice. He currently serves on the University's Board of Governors.

ROD MACLEOD is Professor Emeritus in the Department of History and Classics at the University of Alberta. He has authored books, articles and edited collections on a variety of subjects including criminal justice, the Canadian West, and Canadian military history. He is currently researching and writing the official history of the University of Alberta for their centennial in 2008.

PRESTON MANNING was one of the principal founders and subsequently the leader of the Reform Party, and a founder of the Canadian Reform Conservative Alliance. He was first elected to the House of Commons in 1993, became Leader of the Opposition in 1997, and resigned his seat in January 2002. He has been a Distinguished Visitor at the University of Calgary and currently holds such a title at the University of Toronto. His publications include *Think Big: My Adventures in Life and Democracy* (2002).

FRED V. MARTIN is a lawyer in Edmonton with a practice related to energy, utilities and aboriginal communities. He has worked with the Métis Settlements of Alberta since 1975. In that capacity he participated in the development of the Federation of Métis Settlements, the negotiation of the Alberta-Metis Settlements Accord, and the drafting of related legislation. He has also advised First Nations and the Government of Nunavut on energy and utility related matters.

MARK MILKE is a former director with the Canadian Taxpayers Federation and author of two books. He is currently completing his Ph.D. in Political Science at the University of Calgary.

KENNETH MUNRO is Professor of History in the Department of History and Classics at the University of Alberta. Dr. Munro received his Ph.D. in history from the University of Ottawa in 1973. Since 1972, he has taught at the University of Alberta. Dr. Munro specializes in political biography in late nineteenth century French Canada and also studies and writes on the Canadian Crown.

DOUGLAS OWRAM is Professor of History and Classics at the University of Alberta. He has previously written on Canadian expansion into the West, the rise of planning in government between the wars and a history of the baby boom in Canada, *Born at the Right Time* (1996). He is also co-author with Ken Norrie and Herb Emery of *A History of the Canadian Economy* (1990; 2nd ed. 1996). Professor Owram served as Provost and Vice-President Academic of the University of Alberta and President of the Canadian Federation of Humanities and Social Sciences.

NANCY PARKER works in external relations at Athabasca University and conducts research in the fields of higher education policy and criminal justice history. She earned her Ph.D. in History from York University.

ALLAN TUPPER is Associate Vice President (Government Relations) and Professor of Political Science at the University of British Columbia. Dr. Tupper is a graduate of Carleton University (B.A., D.P.A., M.A.) and Queen's University where he received his Ph.D. in Political Studies in 1977. For more than 20 years, he was Professor of Political Science at the University of Alberta. He served as Chair of the Department of Political Science, Associate Dean of Arts and Associate Vice President (Government Relations). He was also Vice President (Academic) at Acadia University. His major teaching and research interests are Canadian politics, western Canadian politics, public policy and public administration. He has published extensively on these topics and has authored or edited six books and many articles and chapters. Dr. Tupper is actively involved as an instructor in the Senior Executive Development Program of the Government of Alberta.

Preface

Forging Alberta's Constitutional Framework was conceived five years ago, as a special project of the Centre for Constitutional Studies at the University of Alberta, to mark Alberta's centenary as a province in the Canadian Confederation in 2005. This collection of essays seeks to make a contribution to a specialized but growing body of work on the legal history of the Canadian west through an examination of Alberta's constitutional development from historical, political and legal perspectives. Given the broad scope of the work, it cannot claim to be a comprehensive treatment of Alberta's constitutional legal history. Rather, the authors of the various essays, drawn from a number of disciplines, have sought to address the central role played by law in the development of Alberta as a province through an examination of some of the ways that law, legal institutions, legal processes and ideology shaped and influenced the evolution of Alberta from a colonial, settler society to its current status as one of the key players, economically and politically, in the Canadian Confederation. In many ways, the resulting stories are unique and hopefully will prompt further research and investigation.

In its original conception, the project entailed an examination of Alberta's constitutional development through a largely chronological analysis of a number of defined periods: the territorial period, the early years of provincehood, the Great Depression, Alberta in an increasingly centralized federation and finally Alberta in an era of Canadian constitutional reform. This approach would also involve research into some of the issues and themes that cut across the last 100 years, such Alberta's unique contributions to Canadian constitutional development and its well-publicized struggles with Ottawa to gain and maintain full province status. However, the project evolved as the participation of contributing authors from a variety of backgrounds and disciplines was settled. Within the general framework of the original conception, it became a collection of essays that reflected the varied interests of the contributors. The different stages of constitutional development were respected but dealt with in the context of a collection of essays that addressed events, issues, struggles and aspirations rather than simply change and continuity through defined time periods. The research undertaken by the contributing authors involves the exploration of new areas but also the reconsideration of well-known events from new perspectives. The end result better reveals the richness and diversity of Alberta's constitutional development than a more traditional collection that simply traces changes in political and legal institutions or the changing course of federal provincial relations over time. It is our expectation that this volume will make a significant contribution to our understanding of Alberta's legal history by shedding light on subjects and issues, little or not explored in previous works, and by prompting others to further study.

The essays in this volume are the tangible product of a colloquium held at the University of Alberta under the auspices of the Centre for Constitutional Studies in October 2003. Over the course of two days, the participants had the opportunity to collectively reflect on the project and to constructively consider their own and their colleagues' contributions. As a result, the project gained greater cohesion and a sense of purpose.

Introduction

A Legal and Constitutional History of Alberta
RICHARD CONNORS AND JOHN M. LAW

In the last two decades, Canadian legal scholars have done an impressive job of redefining the legal and historical experiences of people before and after Confederation. A steady stream of literature can be found in a growing number of monographs, volumes of collected essays, specialist historical journals and university law reviews.[1] Collectively, this disparate though burgeoning scholarship reflects an academic vitality that needs to be relished by those tilling and toiling in the field. These academic developments come at a time when our population, the legal profession and the Bench clearly require a deeper knowledge of history and of legal history in particular to understand and tackle the legal questions and constitutional challenges Alberta faces as it celebrates its centenary. Amongst other processes, this need has been driven by two inter-related legal developments: the repatriation of the *British North America Act* (1867) and the subsequent development of the Charter of 1982, and the ongoing land and treaty claims of Canada's First Nations. Such tendencies are best embodied in, and reflected by, the Supreme Court of Canada's recent judgement in *Delgamuukw v. British Columbia* that oral histories and indigenous interpretations of the past be recognized in law.[2] These judicial and constitutional developments, as well as the issues that have devolved out of them, have done much to remind Canadians that many of today's legal questions can only be appreciated, if not answered, by coming to terms with our past, or more precisely, our pasts.[3]

While academics continue to debate the scholarly and methodological similarities and uniqueness of the study of law and of history, it is clear that the two are necessarily pre-occupied with, and bedevilled by, the past.[4] For the law, the past provides continuity through precedent; for history, the past potentially offers much more, but rarely surrenders enough to be quite so definitive.[5] This wave of recent work on Canadian legal history has produced

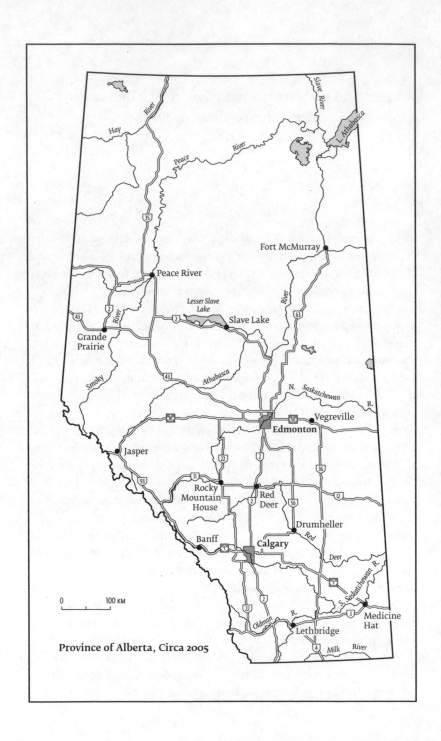

Hay River

Slave River

Peace River

L. Athabasca

35

River

Fort McMurray

Peace River

River

63

Lesser Slave Lake

2

Slave Lake

43

2

Grande Prairie

River

43

Athabasca

Smoky

N. Saskatchewan R.

16

Vegreville

16

Edmonton

Jasper

22

2

11

93

Rocky Mountain House

2

Red Deer

56

36

12

Drumheller

Banff

1

Calgary

Red

Deer

S. Saskatchewan R.

1

3

Medicine Hat

22

2

Oldman R.

Lethbridge

4

Milk River

0   100 KM

Province of Alberta, Circa 2005

a rich body of work that has ambitiously examined not only the institutional structures of the law and state, but also the role of the nation's legal system in the development of the structures of modern Canadian society. Such scholarship has drawn methodological inspiration from sociology and the founding fathers of the social sciences, from social (and more recently, cultural) history and from the "critical legal studies" school.[6] Collectively, these approaches have given depth and breadth to legal history and have offered scholars the opportunity to integrate traditional areas of study, which concentrated upon "legal doctrine, legal institutions and legal personnel," with more recent revelations that the law was not so much an institution, but a process through which, or a forum within which, structures of authority were disputed, contested, negotiated, reconfigured and resolved.[7] As Peter Coss has noted, nuanced and critical legal histories are more than merely "the juxtaposition of 'law and society' 'law and economy'...; more than the setting of text within context."[8] They cast light upon "broad themes that critically and meaningfully explain the historical role of the legal system in social context," and the legacy those historical developments have upon our existing structures of, and experiences with, authority, the constitution, the state and our contemporary legal mores and culture.

Forging Alberta's Constitutional Framework seeks to contribute to these revivified and reinvigorated fields. It does so by analyzing some of the principal events and processes that precipitated the emergence and formation of the law and legal culture of Alberta from the foundation of the Hudson's Bay Company in 1670 until the eve of the centenary of the Province in 2005. Amongst other things, the volume illustrates the fact that the formation of Alberta's constitution and legal institutions was by no means a simple process by which English, and later Canadian, law was imposed upon a receptive and passive population.[9] Challenges to authority, latent lawlessness, interaction between indigenous and settler societies, periods (pre- and post-1905) of jurisdictional confusion and conflict, and demands for individual, group, regional and provincial rights and recognitions are as much part of Alberta's legal history as the heroic and mythic images of an emergent and orderly Canadian west patrolled from the outset by red-coated mounted police and peopled by peaceful and law-abiding subjects of the Crown.[10]

Avoiding a whiggish portrayal of legal and constitutional accumulation and acculturation, *Forging Alberta's Constitutional Framework* illustrates the important point that Alberta's constitution is the product of decades, even centuries, of contest, debate, division, negotiation and compromise. By offering an analysis of some of these vicissitudes, we can gain an appreciation not only of the organic nature of our constitution, but also of the uniqueness of Alberta's legal and constitutional history, and of the vital contributions the province has made to Canada's current constitutional arrangements. Many of the chapters offer particular insights into specific aspects of Alberta's historical experiences and cast light upon issues of national and even international importance. They share the goal of revealing the plethora of social, political, economic and cultural influences on the development of the province. Our approach to the legal history of Alberta is, in part, informed by recent research in American legal history that has benefited from a conceptual framework that considers "legalities" rather than merely formal law and allows us to incorporate into our understanding of legal history "the myriad ways in which people ordered their relations with one another, whether as individuals, groups, classes, communities or states." There are "many legalities" at work in the development of any polity and adopting such an approach to contextualize Alberta's legal and constitutional formation provides us with the opportunity to develop a comprehensive and inclusive legal history by considering such themes as the aspirations, experiences and interaction of individuals, peoples and institutions as well as the implications of places and property, rights and responsibilities.[11]

The fact that scholars can trace "many legalities" from the historical experiences of peoples and places is also significant, for Alberta's history is also a story of the aspirations of many different peoples. It could be argued that Alberta's constitutional history is as much about the search in law for acknowledgement, recognition and entitlement. At the provincial level, Alberta has aspired to cast off the legacy that it entered Confederation with second-class status. Repeated conflicts with Ottawa over resources and jurisdictional prerogatives have their genesis in the fact that Alberta did not enjoy clearly-recognized control of them when it became a province in 1905. As a result, Alberta and Albertans (as individuals and groups) have repeatedly turned to the courts and to the law to substantiate and clarify their rights and desire for full status within the Federation. Many of the chapters in this book address specific instances where those legal and constitutional aspirations or demands for provincial, individual and group recognitions were resolved.

Thus, Alberta has, in part, forged its own Constitution and its place within Canada's Constitution. "Forge" is a thoroughly appropriate term to use when describing the legal and constitutional history of Alberta. A trip to either Heritage Park in Calgary or Fort Edmonton in the provincial capital helps to remind us of the centrality of the blacksmith, his forge, his hammer and his anvil in pioneering communities. As the blacksmith used his craftsmanship to hammer out manufactured goods, so the peoples of the Colonial (1670–1870), Territorial (1870–1905) and Provincial (1905–2005) periods have hammered out a way of life in the Canadian west. Moreover, just as they crafted and framed their society, so too did they hammer out disputes, both legal and constitutional, with the same enthusiasm, intensity, sweat and determination. At the same time, Albertans realized, and should still realize, that the template and constitutional blueprint they used, and use, derive from constitutional conventions that Alberta inherited with its transnational and colonial history. Central to this constitutional experience is, of course, Canada's British imperial past, for it remains crucial in the idea of sovereignty, the concept of the Crown, and in the structure and nature of courts and offices of state. Though inherited, these foundations of Alberta's constitution were quite literally copied, or "forged," from British blueprints. Nevertheless, generations of Canadians and Albertans have altered and adapted these constitutional principles beyond British recognition and for our own specific needs. Alberta's constitutional history was, therefore, forged by debate and contest, by hammering out difficult and complex questions of rights and responsibilities through negotiation, accommodation and, over time, the recognition that all peoples deserved to be heard.

Our historical analysis begins with a discussion of the Hudson's Bay Company Charter and the establishment of Rupert's Land in 1670, nearly two and a half centuries before the creation of the province of Alberta. Aspects of this imperial project will be familiar to specialists, but we begin here to remind our readers that the genesis of these Canadian legal experiences has indigenous, imperial and transatlantic contexts.[12] From this perspective, the emergence of Canadian law, legal institutions, jurisdictions and legal culture was inextricably connected to the related processes of European and British imperial expansion, and of cross-cultural interaction between Anglo-European and indigenous American peoples.[13] Yet without the vestiges of state, the legal institutional apparatus or the clearly-defined structures of authority that delineated social relations and the social order in the old world, the fur traders and Hudson's Bay Company representatives faced the daunting task of re-inventing, as they were obligated by their trade monopoly to do, the legal framework of Britain in the new world.[14] Desmond Brown's concept of "Ambiguous Authority" shows that the inescapable questions of conflicting and vague jurisdictions and lawlessness repeatedly compromised those attempts, as did the realities of environment, geography and competition between fur-trading companies, colonizers, free-spirited individuals and the indigenous peoples into whose space, and upon whom, these ideas and institutions were imposed.[15] The realization and exercise of this authority and legal culture was also informed by the particular imperial mindsets of those Company officers to whom that daunting responsibility passed.

While historians have shown that the First Nations did not passively accept these interactions, they regularly experienced these processes at the behest of others and often at distinct disadvantages to their European counterparts, for theirs has been, until recently (Delgamuukw and Nisga'a), a story of retreat—resilient and defiant, but retreat nonetheless.[16] The implications of these interactions are currently contested in the courts and communities throughout Canada. While they do not receive detailed attention here, the experiences of indigenous Albertans have, and continue to attract, scholarly interest, much of which is shortly due for publication.[17] From this research we are only now coming to appreciate fully the degree to which these processes were not in the first instance based only upon extortion, eradication and expropriation, but also upon accommodation, acquiescence and acceptance.

Throughout the nineteenth century, the perspective that emerges is one of a gradual legal acculturation. This was reflected by the growth of a legal order as manifested by the Magistracy, by increasingly organized jurisdictional divisions, by processes of centralization and by the development of responsible government. This recent scholarship casts light upon a cross-cultural discourse that is not based upon teleological assertions of an emergent and prosperous Anglo-Canadian ascendancy. Instead, research into the emergence of law and legality in the Canadian west, the North-West Territories and eventually the provinces of Alberta and Saskatchewan illustrate that these protracted and complex processes were negotiated, moderated, evaded, challenged, defied and violently resisted by indigenous and Métis peoples from Hudson's Bay to the Pacific coast for much of the period under consideration. Therefore, the compelling and subtle story offered here of the legal history of Alberta and the Canadian west is one that accentuates its uniqueness. The legal codes and legal culture that the British, and later the Canadian, state imposed upon the west, were avoided, altered, and adapted by the protagonists who populate the pages of this book and produced a distinct legal history.

A number of features loom large in explaining why Alberta has developed the way it did. These features go far in accounting for the distinctive individualistic qualities and identity for which the province is recognized and that it reflects to the rest of Canada. Perhaps most importantly, from the 1700s onwards the territory that is now Alberta has witnessed periods of remarkably rapid, and often unsettling, change.[18] For instance, the intense fur trade rivalry in the early nineteenth century throughout the region first opened it to the forces of transnational commercial competition.[19] Later, during the 1860s and 1870s, westward expansion by central and eastern Canadian interests ensured that the Canadian west was inexorably drawn into their orbit.[20] The tensions that these processes precipitated led directly to the development of the North-West Territories and to tragic hostilities that reached their apogee with the Riel Rebellion.[21] By the late nineteenth century, the completion of the transcontinental railway and the subsequent migration of an ethnically diverse and increasingly large number of settlers did much to solidify the multicultural personality of the future province.[22] As a fledgling province in the early twentieth century, Alberta experienced further waves of immigration that accelerated and altered forever the economic, social, cultural and demographic characteristics of the province. The upheavals of Depression and the expectations of two World Wars also left an indelible mark on the province and propelled it towards an urban and natural resource based economy.[23] The discovery of vast oil deposits within the province since the late 1940s has ensured that Alberta's economy, population, and economic power continue to grow—sometimes at hardly sustainable and uncertain rates, and at times in the face of economic challenge or crisis.[24]

Secondly, Alberta's particular and peculiar economic development was strikingly influenced by her distinct topography and each of her principal regions: woodland and parkland, foothills and cordillera, prairie and grasslands, and northern Precambrian shield.[25] Thus, the eighteenth and nineteenth century fur trade drew heavily on the fur-bearing mammals (beaver, martin, and fox) that inhabited the northern woodlands of Rupert's Land or what is now northern Alberta and Saskatchewan. The forestry industry then, and now, still relies on the same regions to stimulate their sector of the economy. Later, from the 1870s onwards, as settlers flocked to Alberta, the intensive agricultural and ranching potential of parkland, prairie, plains and foothills were realized and harnessed, and helped drive the economic engine of the province until the dustbowl days of the Depression in the 1930s. Agricultural revitalization in the post-war world has been impressive despite the fact that it has been eclipsed, at least in the popular imagination, since 1947 by the emergence and the development of petroleum reserves that have drawn the northern shield regions near Fort McMurray and the eastern slopes of the

Rocky Mountains into the modern fossil fuel-driven economic engine that has propelled Alberta into the twenty-first century. Geographical and geological diversity have done much to shape the development of Alberta.

Furthermore, there is the diversity of peoples—from the numerous First Nations peoples (Blackfoot, Sarcee, Cree, Ojibwa, Stoney, Beaver, Slavey, Chipewyan)[26] and then Métis[27] to the waves of immigrants from first western and then eastern Europe, and subsequently from Asia, Latin America and Africa—who have all brought with them social mores, cultural conventions, religious beliefs, political perspectives and multifarious experiences and expectations of what life could and should be like for them, their families, their communities, their province and their country. Collectively, these ethnically diverse peoples have produced a complex society and political culture that has repeatedly turned to law and the constitution to address the periodic dispute and division that has arisen amongst them. It is a testament to those people and to our constitution that much of this discord has been dealt with through peaceful negotiation and accommodation. It is also a reflection of the determination and will of the peoples who populated, and now populate, Alberta that the historical legal, moral, economic, religious, linguistic, ethnic and social divisions, which will be considered in greater detail in the essays in this volume, have not torn the province asunder, but have actually made it much stronger and richer as a society. We do not wish to suggest that these processes have been experienced without difficulty and suffering for some (and at times many), for there has been plenty of that, but we do wish to suggest that our forebears often sought redress of grievance through the law and its processes. Thus, to better "understand ourselves in time," we need to reflect upon some of the key instances where those vicissitudes were confronted and settled.[28]

Collectively, these unique historical, geographical, social, political, and economic circumstances profoundly affected the development of the province and have deeply influenced the attitudes and expectations of Albertans. This book considers some of the most significant legal and constitutional circumstances that were shaped by, and helped shape, Alberta and Albertans.

Finally, what do we mean by "constitution" in the context of this work? Like the phrase "many legalities," we see the opportunity here to consider the concept of constitution in numerous instances as a means of revealing the historic irony that underlines our constitution, both in its simplicity and its sheer complexity.[29] This paradox is perhaps best explained by noting that constitutions can be reduced to a number of general principles, even singular documents, but that they possess a spirit, an essence or, as the rather confused Australian lawyer Dennis Denuto suggested in the celebrated film, *The Castle*, "a vibe," as in "the vibes of the constitution," that embraces all potential circumstances.[30]

Forging Alberta's Constitutional Framework explores the nature and development of Alberta's constitution by examining a number of celebrated cases and themes that have shaped and reflected the aspirations of Albertans and altered legal, social, economic, political and cultural rights and responsibilities within Alberta and Canada. Amongst other things, like formal rule and the dispensation of governance and authority, constitutions lie at the intersection of law, politics and society. Formal constitutions set down the organization and structure of powers of government of the Canadian state and its provinces.[31] Indeed, the powers of the government are clarified and constrained by the terms laid down in the constitution.[32] In Canada's case, the Constitution sets out the jurisdiction and the powers of the federal government and of its provincial counterparts. Dispute over the exact nature of those terms, and subsequent demands to revisit and revise federal and provincial rights and responsibilities within the constitution lie at the heart of many of the chapters that follow. These themes are well illustrated in the studies that concentrate upon the development of criminal law in the Canadian west in the nineteenth century, upon the Natural Resources Transfer Agreement of 1930, upon the National Energy Program of the 1980s, upon federal-provincial relations, and upon the role and responsibilities of the offices of Justices of the Peace, and of the Lieutenant-Governor.[33]

Moreover, constitutions address the question of sovereignty, powers of government, and the limits to the powers of those who govern. Constitutions in modern western societies privilege individual rights, autonomy and liberty. Most often, constitutions seek to constrain governmental power to protect individual liberties and preserve the rule of law.[34] Such issues are embodied in our discussions on the Alberta Press Act Case, The Person's Case, and the *Alberta Metis Settlements Act*.[35] Tied closely to these expectations of the constitution is the recognition that it speaks to the political and legal culture of our society. Thus, organic constitutions like ours evolve over time to reflect different and changing cultural and religious values and social mores.[36] This theme is considered in the essays that concentrate on popular concepts of sovereignty, legal thought and empire in the seventeenth and eighteenth centuries, on the nature of legal authority in the nineteenth century, and on the schools question in the late nineteenth century.[37] Similarly, contest emerges over whose voices are heard on these cultural and social matters, for the right to be heard is at times crucial to gaining and maintaining rights and responsibilities within the polity. Peoples who demanded access to, and recognition from, the constitution are considered here in an analysis of French language rights from the 1870s to the present, in an examination of the Person's Case and our memory of the "famous five," in a consideration of Indigenous and Métis peoples' hunting, fishing and property rights and in recent years, women's challenges to successive Conservative governments for redress of numerous grievances and their manifest recognitions of rights.[38]

Ideally, the constitution and the political institutions of state that derive their authority from it will operate effectively enough to provide stability in the political arrangements of society. Moreover, the constitution provides a template for the fundamental ordering necessary for the stability and longevity of a political society. Yet, at the same time, constitutions must be capable of growth and alteration. This often occurs through formal amendment or, in the Canadian case, through judicial interpretation.[39] These dimensions to our understanding of constitutionalism are given thorough consideration in the examination of the Lougheed years and constitutional transformation and renewal, through an examination of the constitution in the Klein years, and through our consideration of the Person's Case.[40]

These issues are rarely settled without protracted debate and after years of discord. Our constitution has proven so durable because it provides opportunities for conflict resolution. The allocation of authority or sovereignty in the hands of those who govern, at various levels, is particularly important in a liberal, capitalist society where legal, political and economic arrangements do not remain static. In Canada, the conflict has often been between the founding provinces of central and eastern Canada (arguably British Columbia also), which were until Confederation semi-autonomous colonies of the British crown, and the newer Prairie Provinces, particularly Alberta, which were colonies of the federal government.[41] In these contexts, it has proven clear that constitutional changes were, and some would still argue, are, necessary—if only to reflect the changing demographic and economic realities of the last century and to allow for the alteration of institutions and structures of government to give the newer provinces a stronger voice that mirrors the aspirations of their populace. The essays by Michael Behiels and Preston Manning both speak to the significance of these themes of contest and re-negotiation in modern Canadian and Alberta history. In those essays the tensions between nation and province, federalism and regionalism, centralization and devolution are considered within specific historical contexts. It is against the backdrop and memory of those set-piece constitutional debates that contemporary arguments about taxation, jurisdiction, Senate reform and federal-provincial funding arrangements continue to be discussed. Furthermore, the constitution offers an arena for conflict between governments (federal and provincial) and individuals and groups with "constitutional identities" as identified most recently by the *Canadian Charter of Rights and Freedoms*.[42] The demand of individuals and groups for rights lie at the heart of many issues considered in the pages that follow in *Forging Alberta's Constitutional Framework* and are central to the papers on Indigenous rights, the *Metis Settlements Act*, the rights of women, freedom of the Press, language rights and recognition of religious communities. What is unique about all of these crucial constitutional debates—debates that had not only provincial, but national and even Commonwealth and international repercussions—is that they were initiated, championed and settled at the behest of the peoples of Alberta. We suggest here that the legal and constitutional issues at stake in the pages of this volume did much to shape modern Alberta and Canada. Indeed, it could be argued that Alberta and Albertans have done as much, if not more, in the last century to reconfigure the modern constitution in Canada than any other jurisdiction save Quebec.

At the same time, these constitutional and legal struggles in which Albertans have been key players and active participants have ensured that our constitution provides the nation with transcendent symbolic values that retain significance across the centuries. Albertans and Canadians invest much confidence and faith in the "rule of law," popular sovereignty, the legitimacy of authority, the Crown and the Courts, individual and group rights, and the over-arching principle of "Peace, Order and Good Government."[43] As the history of the province reveals, Albertans have contributed much to the historical decisions that give those terms meaning today. In these processes, Alberta has developed amongst other Canadians the reputation of a maverick province and Albertans the distinction of being a confident, brash, individualistic, self-reliant and determined people.[44] And just as they have produced a unique and important, if understudied and misunderstood, constitutional history, it is clear too that those historical experiences have produced the Albertan and the Alberta that we embody today.

Notes

1. See for example, B. Wright, "Towards a New Canadian Legal History," *Osgoode Hall Law Journal* 22 (1984): 349–74; L.A. Knafla and S.W.S. Binnie, "Beyond the State: Law and Legal Pluralism in the Making of Modern Societies," in L.A. Knafla and S.W.S. Binnie, eds., *Law, Society and the State: Essays in Modern Legal History* (Toronto: University of Toronto Press, 1995), 3–33; M.H. Ogilvie, "Recent Developments in the History of Canadian Law: Legal History," *Ottawa Law Review* 19 (1987): 223–54; and the numerous volumes edited by various scholars in the Osgoode Society for Canadian Legal History series, particularly the eight volumes entitled *Essays in the History of Canadian Law* (Toronto: Osgoode Society, 1981–1999).

2. See *Delgamuukw v. British Columbia* [1997] 3 S.C.R. 1010. See also S. Persky, ed., *Delgamuukw: The Supreme Court of Canada Decision on Aboriginal Title* (Vancouver: Greystone Books, 1998), 76–77. For discussions of the broader legal, historical and political implications of this protracted case, see the contributions to "Native peoples and Colonialism: a special double issue," *BC Studies* 115 & 116 (1997/98); and H. Foster, "Law, History and Aboriginal Title: *Calder v. The Attorney General of British Columbia*," in B. Hesketh and C. Hackett, eds., *Canada, Confederation to Present* (Edmonton: Chinook Multimedia, 2002), CD-ROM.

3. Amongst many others, see J. Tully, *Strange Multiplicity: Constitutionalism in an Age of Diversity* (Cambridge: Cambridge University Press, 1995); D. Schneiderman and K. Sutherland, eds., *Charting the Consequences: The Impact of Charter Rights on Canadian Law and Politics* (Toronto: University of Toronto Press, 1997); A. Cairns, *Charter versus Federalism: The Dilemmas of Constitutional Reform* (Kingston and Montreal: McGill Queen's University Press, 1992); M. Ignatieff, *The Rights Revolution* (Toronto: Anansi Press, 2000), 33–126; J. Tully, "Aboriginal Property and Western Theory: Recovering the Middle Ground," *Social Philosophy and Policy* XI (1994): 153–80; and P.H. McHugh, "The Common-Law Status of Colonies and Aboriginal 'Rights': How Lawyers and Historians Treat the Past," *Saskatchewan Law Review* 61 (1998): 393–429.

4. On this voluminous subject see R.W. Gordon, "Critical Legal Histories," *Stanford Law Review* 6 (1984): 57–125; G.E. White, *Intervention and Detachment, Essays on Legal History and Detachment* (Oxford: Oxford University Press, 1994); J.P. Reid, "Law and History," *Loyola of Los Angeles Law Review* 27 (1993): 193–223; W.W. Fisher III, "Texts and Contexts: The Application to American Legal History of the Methodologies of Intellectual History," *Stanford Law Review* 49 (1997): 1065–110; D. Sugarman, "Writing 'Law and Society' Histories," *Modern Law Review* 55 (1992): 292–308; J.H. Zammito, "Are we being theoretical yet? The new historicism, the new philosophy of history, and 'practicing historians'," *Journal of Modern History* 65 (1993): 783–814; L. Lessig, "Fidelity in Transition," *Texas Law Review* 71 (1993): 1165–268; M.S. Flaherty, "History 'Lite' in Modern American Constitutionalism," *Columbia Law Review* 95 (1995): 523–90; R.A. Epstein, "History Lean: The Reconciliation of Private Property and Representative Government," *Columbia Law Review* 95 (1995): 591–600; and C.R. Sustein, "The Idea of a Useable Past," *Columbia Law Review* 95 (1995): 601–8. For historiographical debates on this theme, also see P. Novick, *That Noble Dream: The "Objectivity Question" and the American Historical Profession* (Cambridge: Cambridge University Press, 1988); T.L. Haskell, "Objectivity is not Neutrality: Rhetoric vs. Practice in Peter Novick's *That Noble Dream*," *History and Theory* 29 (1990): 129–57; H. Butterfield, *The Whig Interpretation of History* (New York: W.W. Norton, 1965); J. Appleby, L. Hunt and M. Jacob, *Telling the Truth About History* (New York: W.W. Norton, 1994); and for useful discussions of a specific legal-historical period, see the

contributions to "Forum: Explaining the Law in Early American History—A Symposium," *William and Mary Quarterly* L (1993): 3–50; "Forum: American Law and the American Revolution," *William and Mary Quarterly* L (1993): 123–80; and J.R. Pole, "Further Reflections on Law and the American Revolution: A Comment on the Comments," *William and Mary Quarterly* L (1993): 594–99.

5.   Historians have written extensively on these and related historiographical issues, therefore, the following select references are offered as illustrative of work that is particularly valuable for socially contextualising early modern legal history: C. Ginzburg, *The Cheese and the Worms* (London: Routledge and Kegan Paul, 1982); C. Ginzburg, "Monter et citer: La Verite de l'histoire," *Le Debat* 56 (1989): 43–54; C. Ginzburg, "Checking the Evidence: The Judge and the Historian," *Critical Inquiry* 18 (1991): 79–92; C. Ginzburg, "Proofs and Possibilities: In the Margins of Natalie Zemon Davis' *The Return of Martin Guerre*," *Yearbook of Comparative and General Literature* 37 (1988): 114–27; N. Zemon Davis, *The Return of Martin Guerre* (Cambridge, MA., Harvard University Press, 1983); and R. Finlay, "The Refashioning of Martin Guerre," *American Historical Review* 93 (1988): 553–71.

6.   See for example, K.J.M. Snell and J.P.S. McLaren, "History's Living Legacy: An Outline of Modern Historiography of the Common Law," *Legal Studies* 21 (2001): 251–324.

7.   B. Wright, "An Introduction to Canadian Law in History," in W.W. Pue and B. Wright, eds., *Canadian Perspectives on Law and Society: Issues in Legal History* (Ottawa: Carleton University Press, 1988), 8. On law as process see, for example, S. Hindle, *The State and Social Change in Early Modern England, c.1550–1640* (London: Macmillan, 2000), and P. King, *Crime, Justice and Discretion in England, 1740–1820* (Oxford: Oxford University Press, 2000).

8.   P. Coss, "Introduction," in P. Coss, ed., *The Moral World of the Law* (Cambridge: Cambridge University Press, 2000), 1–16, at 1.

9.   On this subject see G. Parker, "Canadian Legal Culture," in L. Knafla ed., *Law and Justice in a New Land: Essays in Western Canadian Legal History* (Toronto: Carswell, 1986), 3–29; L. Knafla, "From Oral to Written Memory: The Common Law Tradition in Western Canada," in Knafla, ed., *Law and Justice*, 31–77; and J.E. Coté, "The Reception of English Law," *Alberta Law Review* 15 (1977): 29–92.

10. These themes are considered in C. Betke, "Pioneers and Police on the Canadian Prairies, 1885–1914," in R. Macleod, ed., *Lawful Authority: Readings on the History of Criminal Justice in Canada* (Toronto: Copp Clark Pitman, 1988), 98–119; D. Morton, "Cavalry or Police: Keeping the Peace on Two Adjacent Frontiers, 1870–1900," *Journal of Canadian Studies* 12 (1977): 27–37; H. Foster, "Shooting the Elephant: Historians and the Problem of Frontier Lawlessness," in R. Eales and D. Sullivan eds., *The Political Context of Law* (London: Hambledon Press, 1987), 135–44.; J.P. Reid, "Principles of Vengeance: Fur Trappers, Indians, and Retaliation for Homicide in the Transboundary North American West," in T. Loo and L.R. Mclean, eds., *Historical Perspectives on Law and Society in Canada* (Toronto: Copp Clark Longman, 1994), 14–34; and the essays in J. Mclaren, H. Foster and C. Orloff, eds., *Law for the Elephant, Law for the Beaver: Essays in the Legal History of the North American West* (Regina: Canadian Plains Research Centre, 1992).

11. On this important subject consult C.L. Tomlins, and B.H. Mann, eds., *The Many Legalities of Early America* (Chapel Hill: University of North Carolina Press, 2001), quotations at 447; and J.P. Greene, "'By Their Laws Shall Ye Know Them': Law and Identity in Colonial British America," *Journal of Interdisciplinary History* 33, no. 2 (2002): 247–60.

12. See for example A. McFarlane, *The British in the Americas, 1400–1815* (London: Longman, 1994); I. Steele, *The English Atlantic, 1675–1740: An Exploration of Communication and Community* (Oxford: Oxford University Press, 1986); and P. Lawson, ed., *Parliament and the Atlantic Empire* (Edinburgh: Edinburgh University Press, 1995).

13. See L. Colley, *Britons: Forging the Nation, 1707–1837* (New Haven: Yale University Press, 1992); A. Pagden, *Lords of all the World: Ideologies of Empire in Britain, France and Spain 1400–1800* (New Haven: Yale University Press, 1995); and M. Daunton and R. Halpern, eds., *Empire and Others: British Encounters with Indigenous Peoples, 1600–1850* (Philadelphia: University of Pennsylvania Press, 1999).

14. See the essays in G. Smith, A. May and S. Devereaux, eds., *Criminal Justice in the Old World and the New* (Toronto: Centre for Criminology, 1998); and L. Knafla, ed., *Crime and Criminal Justice in Europe and Canada* (Waterloo: Wilfrid Laurier University Press, 1981). For a brilliant analysis of custom and law in a colonial context see J. Bannister, *The Rule of the Admirals: Law, Custom and Naval Government in Newfoundland, 1699–1832* (Toronto: University of Toronto Press, 2003).

15. The nature of this interaction is considered in K. McNeil, *Common Law Aboriginal Title* (Oxford: Clarendon Press, 1989); A.J. Ray, *I Have Lived Here Since the World Began: An Illustrated History of Canada's Native People* (Toronto: Key Porter Books, 1996), 69–111; J.H. Thompson, *Forging the Prairie West: The Illustrated History of Canada* (Toronto: Oxford University Press, 1998), 7–42; G. Friesen, *The Canadian Prairies: A History* (Toronto: University of Toronto Press, 1987), 10–90; R. White, *The Middle Ground: Indians, Empires and Republics in the Great Lakes Region, 1650–1815* (Cambridge: Cambridge University Press, 1991); and J. Axtell, *Beyond 1492: Encounters in Colonial North America* (Oxford: Oxford University Press, 1992).

16. This literature is summarized in S. Harring, *White Man's Law: Native People in Nineteenth-Century Canadian Jurisprudence* (Toronto: Osgoode Society, 1998). Also see and H. Foster, "Law, History and Aboriginal Title: Calder v. the Attorney General of British Columbia," and the contributions to "Special Issue: The Nisga'a Treaty," *BC Studies* 120 (1998/99); D. Culhane, *The Pleasure of the Crown: Anthropology, Law and First Nations* (Vancouver: Talon Books, 1998); T.R. Berger, *A Long and Terrible Shadow: White Values, Native Rights in the Americas Since 1492* (Vancouver: Douglas and McIntyre, 1999 ed.); C. Denis, "The Nisga'a Treaty: What Future for the Inherent Right to Aboriginal Self Government?" *Review of Constitutional Studies* 7 (2002): 35–54; the essays in "Special Issue: Advocacy and Claims Research," *Native Studies Review* 6, no. 2 (1990); and essays in "Special Issue on Aboriginal People," *Prairie Forum* 17, no. 2 (1992).

17. On this growing subject see J. Borrows, *Recovering Canada: The Resurgence of Indigenous Law* (Toronto: University of Toronto Press, 2002); M. Asch, ed., *Aboriginal and Treaty Rights in Canada: Essays on Law, Equity, and Respect for Difference* (Vancouver: University of British Columbia Press, 1997); J. Borrows, "A Genealogy of Law: Inherent Sovereignty and First Nations Self-Government," *Osgoode Hall Law Journal* 30 (1992), 291–353; J.B. Promislow, "Towards a Legal History of the Fur Trade: Looking for Law at York Factory, 1714–1763" (LL.M. Diss., York University, 2004); J. Borrows, "Contemporary Traditional Equality: The Effect of the Charter on First Nations Politics," in D. Schneiderman and K. Sutherland, eds., *Charting the Consequences*, 169–199; P. Macklem, *Indigenous Difference and the Constitution of Canada* (Toronto: University of Toronto Press, 2001), and P.H. Russell, *Recognizing Aboriginal Title: The Mabo Case and Indigenous Resistance to English-Settler Colonialism* (Toronto: University of Toronto Press, 2005).

18. On the history of Alberta see H. and T. Palmer, *Alberta: A New History* (Edmonton: Hurtig Publishers, 1990); A.S. Morton, *A History of the Canadian West to 1870–71*, 2nd ed. (Toronto: University of Toronto Press, 1973); and J.H. Thompson, *Forging the Prairie West*, 7–42.

19. D. Francis, *Battle for the West: The Fur Traders and the Birth of Western Canada* (Edmonton: Hurtig Publishers, 1983); J.M. Bumsted, *Fur Trade Wars: The Founding of Western Canada* (Winnipeg: Great Plains Publications, 1999); H.A. Innes, *The Fur Trade in Canada: An Introduction to Canadian Economic History: with a New Introductory Essay by A.J. Ray* (Toronto: University of Toronto Press, 1999); and M. Payne, "Fur Trade Historiography: Past Conditions, Present Circumstances

and a Hint of Future Prospects," in T. Binnema, G.J. Ens, and R.C. Macleod, eds., *From Rupert's Land to Canada* (Edmonton: University of Alberta Press, 2001), 3–22.

20. D. Owram, *The Promise of Eden: The Canadian Expansionist Movement and the Idea of the West, 1856–1900* (Toronto: University of Toronto Press, 1980); A.A. den Otter, *Civilizing the West: The Galts and the Development of Western Canada* (Edmonton: University of Alberta Press, 1982); L.H. Thomas, *The Struggle for Responsible Government in the North West Territories, 1870–1897* (Toronto: University of Toronto Press, 1978); and H. Palmer, ed., *The Settlement of the West* (Calgary: University of Calgary Comprint Press, 1977).

21. B. Beal and R.C. Macleod, *Prairie Fire: The 1885 North-West Rebellion* (Edmonton: Hurtig Publishers, 1984); D.N. Sprague, *Canada and the Métis, 1869–1885* (Waterloo: Wilfrid Laurier University Press, 1988); F. Pannekoek, *A Snug Little Flock: The Social Origins of the Riel Resistance 1869–70* (Winnipeg: Watson and Dwyer, 1991); G.J. Ens, *Homeland to Hinterland: Changing Worlds of the Red River Métis in the Nineteenth Century* (Toronto: University of Toronto Press, 1996); J.M. Bumsted, *Louis Riel v. Canada: The Making of a Rebel* (Winnipeg: Great Plains Publications, 2001); T. Flanagan, *Riel and the Rebellion: 1885 Reconsidered*, 2nd ed. (Toronto: University of Toronto Press, 2000); and A.R. Braz, *A False Traitor: Louis Riel in Canadian Culture* (Toronto: University of Toronto Press, 2003).

22. See H. and T. Palmer, eds., *Peoples of Alberta* (Saskatoon: Western Producers, 1985); G. Friesen, "Immigrant Communities," in *The Canadian Prairies: a History* (Toronto: University of Toronto Press, 1984), chapter 11; N. Macdonald, *Canada: Immigration and Colonization 1842–1908* (Toronto: Macmillan, 1966); J. Burnet and H. Palmer, *"Coming Canadians": An Introduction to the History of Canada's Peoples* (Toronto: McClelland and Stewart, 1988); J.H. Thompson, *Forging the Prairie West*, 43–70; and for an historiographical overview of work on immigration history see H. Palmer, "Canadian Immigration and Ethnic History in the 1970s and 1980s," *Journal of Canadian Studies* 17, no. 1 (1982): 35–50.

23. H.C. Klassen, ed., *The Canadian West: Social Change and Economic Development* (Calgary: University of Calgary Press, 1977); D. Breen, *The Canadian Prairie West and the Ranching Frontier 1874–1924* (Toronto: University of Toronto Press, 1982); V.C. Fowke, *The National Economy and the Wheat Economy* (Toronto: University of Toronto Press, 1973); H.A. Dempsey, *The CPR West: The Iron Road and the Making of a Nation* (Vancouver: Douglas and McIntyre, 1984); J.A. Eagle, *The Canadian Pacific Railway and the Development of Western Canada, 1896–1918* (Montreal: McGill Queen's University Press, 1989); and H. and T. Palmer, *Alberta: A New History*, 106–243. On the Depression see: J.H. Thompson and A. Seager, *Canada 1922–39: Decades of Discord* (Toronto: McClelland and Stewart, 1985); D. Francis and H. Ganzevoort, eds., *The Dirty Thirties in Prairie Canada* (Vancouver: Tantalus, 1980); M. Horn, *The Dirty Thirties* (Toronto: Copp Clark Pitman, 1972); J. Gray, *The Winter Years* (Toronto: Macmillan, 1966); J. Gray, *Men Against the Desert* (Saskatoon: Western Producer, 1967); and D.C. Jones, *Empire of Dust: Settling and Abandoning the Prairie Dry Belt* (Calgary: University of Calgary Press, 2002).

24. On this voluminous subject see J.H. Thompson, *Forging the Prairie West*, 137–187; H. and T. Palmer, *Alberta: A History*, 281–370, as well as the numerous sources they suggest in their detailed bibliography of the post-war period.

25. See for example, L.D. Cordes and D.J. Pennock, "Biophysical Constraints of the Natural Environment on Settlement," in B.M. Barr and P.J. Smith, *Environment and Economy: Essays on the Human Geography of Alberta* (Edmonton: Pica Pica Press, 1984); W.G. Hardy, *Alberta, A Natural History* (Edmonton: Hurtig Publishers, 1967); R. Griebel, *Landscapes: An Annotated Bibliography on the Natural History of Alberta* (Edmonton: Alberta Culture, 1986); and A. Nikiforuk, *The Land Before Us: A Geological History of Alberta* (Red Deer: Red Deer College Press, 1994).

26. On the vast history of indigenous peoples see for example: A.J. Ray, *I Have Lived Here*, 69–111; G. Friesen, *The Canadian Prairies*, 10–90; O.P. Dickason, *Canada's First Nations: A History of the Founding Peoples from Earliest Times* (Toronto: McClelland and Stewart, 1992); L. Peers, *The Ojibwa of Western Canada, 1780–1870* (Winnipeg: University of Manitoba Press, 1994); R. White, *The Middle Ground*; A.J. Ray, *Indians in the Fur Trade: Their Role as Trappers, Hunters and Middlemen in the Lands Southwest of Hudson's Bay, 1660–1870* (Toronto: University of Toronto Press, 1974); R. Wilson, *Native Peoples: the Canadian Experience* (Toronto: Oxford University Press, 1995); J.R. Miller, *Skyscrapers hide the Heavens: a history of Indian-white relations in Canada*, 3rd ed. (Toronto: University of Toronto Press, 2000); and B.G. Trigger and W.E. Washburn, eds., *The Cambridge History of the Native Peoples of the Americas*, Vol. 1, *North America* (Cambridge: Cambridge University Press, 1997), chapter 11 and 13—the chapters by R.A. Fisher and A.J. Ray respectively.

27. For a recent discussion of the Métis consult "Section II: Métis History," in T. Binnema, G.J. Ens and R.C. Macleod, eds., *From Rupert's Land to Canada*, 111–192; D. Payment, "Plains Métis," in R.J. DeMallie, ed., *Plains* (Washington: Smithsonian Institution, 2001), 661–76; P. Drieksen, *We Are Métis: The Ethnography of a Halfbreed Community in Northern Alberta* (New York: AMS Press, 1985); J.E. Foster, "The Plains Métis," in R.B. Morrison and C.R. Wilson, eds., *Native Peoples: The Canadian Experience*, 2nd ed. (Toronto: McClelland and Stewart, 1985), 388–94; J. Brown and J. Peterson, eds., *The New Peoples: Being and Becoming Métis in North America* (Winnipeg: University of Manitoba Press, 1986); and N. St-Onge, *Saint-Laurent, Manitoba: Evolving Métis Identities, 1850–1914* (Regina: Canadian Plains Research Centre, 2004).

28. P. Laslett, *The World We Have Lost—Further Explored* 3rd ed. (London: Methuen, 1983), 274–86.

29. For recent scholarly discussions on the historic meaning of constitution see: G. Maddox, "Constitution" in T. Ball, J. Farr and R.L. Hanson, *Political Innovation and Conceptual Change* (Cambridge: Cambridge University Press, 1989), 50–67; T. Ball and J.G.A. Pocock, eds., *Conceptual Change and the Constitution* (Lawrence: University Press of Kansas, 1988); R. Bellamy and D. Castiglione, eds., *Constitutionalism in Transformation: European and Theoretical Perspectives* (Oxford: Blackwell's, 1996); and R.C. Van Caenegem, *An Historical Introduction to Western Constitutional Law* (Cambridge: Cambridge University Press, 1995).

30. Dennis Denuto's phrase fully entered the legal sphere when cited in the New South Wales Court of Appeal on 31 July 2002. See *Harris v. Digital Pulse PTY LTD* [2003] NSWCA 10. This source can be accessed electronically at www.austlii.edu.au/au/cases/nsw/NSWCA/2003/10/html. We would like to thank Professor Robert Chambers for drawing this legal case to our attention.

31. See for instance R.L. Watts, *Intrastate Federalism in Canada* (Toronto: University of Toronto Press, 1985); R. Simeon, *Federal-Provincial Diplomacy: The Making of Recent Policy in Canada* (Toronto: University of Toronto Press, 1972); D.V. Smiley, *The Federal Condition in Canada* (Toronto: McGraw-Hill Ryerson, 1987); D. Shugarman and R. Whitaker, eds., *Federalism and Political Community: Essays in Honour of Donald Smiley* (Peterborough: Broadview Press, 1989). For alternative perspectives that are arguably more fully grounded in historical contexts and are germane to discussions of the division of power in the constitution, see R. Cook, *The Maple Leaf Forever: Essays on Nationalism and Politics in Canada* (Toronto: Macmillan, 1971); P. Romney, *Getting it Wrong: How Canadians Forgot Their Past and Imperilled Confederation* (Toronto: University of Toronto Press, 1999); F. Vaughan, *The Canadian Federalist Experiment: from Defiant Monarchy to Reluctant Republic* (Montreal: McGill Queen's University Press, 2003).

32. J.E. Hodgetts, "Constitution of Canada," in G. Hallowell, ed., *The Oxford Companion to Canadian History* (Toronto: Oxford University Press, 2004), 152–53; P.W. Hogg, *Constitutional Law of Canada*, 3rd ed. (Toronto: Carswell, 1992); D.M. Beatty, *Constitutional Law in Theory and*

Practice (Toronto: University of Toronto Press, 1995); G.-A., Beaudin, *La Constitution du Canada: Institutions, partage des pouvoir, droits et libertes* (Montreal: Wilson and Lafleur, 1990); H. Brun and G. Trembley, *Droit Constitutionnelle*, 2nd ed. (Cowansville: Yvon Blais, 1990); J.R. Mallory, *The Structure of Canadian Government* (Toronto: Gage, 1984); A.C. Cairns, *Constitution, Government and Society in Canada* (Toronto: McClelland and Stewart, 1988); M.S. Whittington and R.J. Van Loon, *Canadian Government and Politics: Institutions and Processes* (Toronto: McGraw-Hill Ryerson, 1996); and M. Dorland and M. Charland, *Law, Rhetoric and Irony in the Formation of Canadian Civil Culture* (Toronto: University of Toronto Press, 2002).

33. See the following essays in this volume: D. Brown, "Ambiguous Authority: The Development of Criminal Law in the Canadian North-West and Alberta"; T. Flanagan and M. Milke, "Alberta's Real Constitution: The Natural Resources Transfer Agreement"; D. Owram, "The Perfect Storm: The National Energy Program and the Failure of Federal-Provincial Relations"; P. Manning, "Centralization and Reaction in Federal-Provincial Relations"; R. Macleod and N. Parker, "Justices of the Peace in Alberta"; K. Munro, "The Lieutenant-Governor and the Maple Crown in Alberta."

34. T.R.S. Allen, *Constitutional Justice: A Liberal Theory of the Rule of Law* (Oxford: Oxford University Press, 2001); J. Rawls, "The Law of Peoples," in S. Shute and S. Hurley, eds., *On Human Rights: The Oxford Amnesty Lectures 1993* (London: Basic Books, 1993), 41–82; H.L.A. Hart, *The Concept of Law* 2nd ed. (Oxford: Clarendon, 1994); R. Dworkin, *Law's Empire* (Harvard: Belknap Press, 1986); J. Rawls, *A Theory of Justice* (Oxford: Oxford University Press, 1972); and F. DeCoste, *On Coming to Law: An Introduction to Law in Liberal Societies* (Markham: Butterworths, 2001).

35. See the following essays in this volume: D. Gibson, "Bible Bill and the Money Barons: The Social Credit Court References and their Constitutional Consequences"; C. Cavanaugh, "Out of the West: History, Memory and the 'Person's' Case, 1919–2000"; and F.V. Martin, "A Brief History of Alberta's Métis Settlements Legislation."

36. In its Western European contexts see H. Berman, *Law and Revolution: The Formation of the Western Legal Tradition* (Harvard: Harvard University Press, 1983); H. Berman, *Law and Revolution II: The Impact of the Protestant Reformation on the Western Legal Tradition* (Harvard: Harvard University Press, 2003); P. Collinson, "Religion and Human Rights: The Case of and for Protestantism," in O. Hufton, ed., *Historical Change and Human Rights: The Oxford Amnesty Lectures 1994* (London: Basic Books, 1994), 21–54; D. Lyons, *Moral Aspects of Legal Theory: Essays on Law, Justice and Political Responsibility* (Cambridge: Cambridge University Press, 1993). In specific Canadian contexts see W. Kymlicka, *Finding our Way: Rethinking Ethnocultural Relations in Canada* (Toronto: Oxford University Press, 1998); W. Kymlicka, *Multicultural Citizenship: A Liberal Theory of Minority Rights* (Oxford: Oxford University Press, 1996); J. Tully, *Strange Multiplicity*; A.C. Cairns and C. Williams, eds., *Constitutionalism, Citizenship and Society in Canada* (Toronto: University of Toronto Press, 1985).

37. See the following essays in this volume: R. Connors, "In the Mind's Eye: Legal Thought and Rupert's Land in the Age of Empire"; D. Brown, "Ambiguous Authority"; and S. Anderson, "Venerable Rights—Constitutionalizing Alberta's Schools 1869–1905."

38. See the following essays in this volume: E. Aunger, "One Language and One Nationality: The Forcible Constitution of a Unilingual Province in a Bilingual Country"; C. Cavanaugh, "Out of the West"; R. Irwin, "Not Like the Others: The Regulation of Indian Hunting and Fishing in Alberta"; F.V. Martin, "Métis Settlements Act"; and L. Harder, "Equality and Women's Political Identity in Post 1970s Alberta."

39. On these matters see for example J.T. Saywell, *The Lawmakers: Judicial Power and the Shaping of Canadian Federalism* (Toronto: The Osgoode Society, 2002); A.A. Peacock, ed., *Rethinking the Constitution: Perspectives on Canadian Constitutional Reform, Interpretation, and Theory* (Toronto: Oxford University Press, 1996); D. Schneiderman and K. Sutherland, eds., *Charting the Consequences*; M. Behiels, ed., *The Meech Lake Primer: Conflicting Views of the 1987 Constitutional Accord* (Ottawa: University of Ottawa Press, 1989); C.P. Manfredi, *Judicial Power and the Charter* (Toronto: McClelland and Stewart, 1993); A.C. Cairns, *Disruptions: Constitutional Struggles from the Charter to Meech Lake* (Toronto: McClelland and Stewart, 1991); A.C. Cairns, *Charter verses Federalism: The Dilemmas of Constitutional Reform* (Montreal: McGill Queen's University Press, 1992).

40. See the following essays in this volume: M. Behiels, "Premier Peter Lougheed, Alberta and the Transformation of Constitutionalism in Canada, 1971–1985"; A. Tupper, "Uncertain Future: Alberta in the Canadian Community"; and C. Cavanaugh, "Out of the West: History, Memory and the 'Persons' Case."

41. A. Bramley-Moore, *Canada and Her Colonies: or Home Rule for Alberta* (London: W. Stewart and Co., 1911).

42. See for example, A.C. Cairns, "The past and future of the Canadian administrative state," *University of Toronto Law Journal* XL (1990): 320–61; and E.R. Alexander, "The Supreme Court of Canada and the Canadian Charter of Rights and Freedoms," *University of Toronto Law Journal* XL (1990): 1–73.

43. See the aforementioned works cited in nn. 31 and 38, as well as P.H. Russell, *Constitutional Odyssey*, 3rd ed. (Toronto: University of Toronto Press, 2004) and P.H. Russell, *Federalism and the Charter: Leading Constitutional Decisions: a New Edition* (Montreal: McGill Queen's University Press, 2003).

44. H. and T. Palmer, *Alberta: A New History*; and A. van Herk, *Mavericks: An Incorrigible History of Alberta* (Toronto: Viking Books, 2001).

One

In the Mind's Eye
Law and British Colonial Expansion in Rupert's Land in the Age of Empire

RICHARD CONNORS

"Thus in the beginning all the world was America, and more so than that is now."[1] With these words, John Locke, the seventeenth-century English philosopher and theorist of state, concluded his observations about property in his work on contractarian governance, *Two Treatises of Government*. Locke's chapter "Of Property" was, in part, a justification for English imperial expansion during the seventeenth century. For Locke, the appropriation of land was a timeless process; one that had transformed common land into private property. This process had taken place over centuries in England and in Europe, but in the late seventeenth century it had yet to take place on a vast scale in North America. For Locke and his fellow Englishmen and -women, the prospect of making America their private property proved powerful. Thus, Locke's views embodied a moral and philosophical rationalization throughout the eighteenth century for the British accumulation of a global empire. While historians continue to debate whether or not this expanding British Empire was acquired, as the famous Victorian scholar J.R. Seeley suggested, in "an absence of mind," there can be no doubt that British imperial ambitions were championed to a considerable degree by Chartered Companies and the pursuit of profit.[2]

After 1670, English interest in the western regions of North America, the area they named and thereby claimed as Rupert's Land, fell under the direction and control of the newly-formed Hudson's Bay Company. With the creation of Rupert's Land, even if only in the imagination of merchants and ministers in London, the fate, the fortunes and the future of northwestern North America became inextricably connected to those of the English, and later, the British Empire. For that region 1670 was, in many ways, the dawn of a new era despite the fact that the aforementioned *Two Treatises of Government* had yet to be written, yet to be read, and yet to be realized. For most

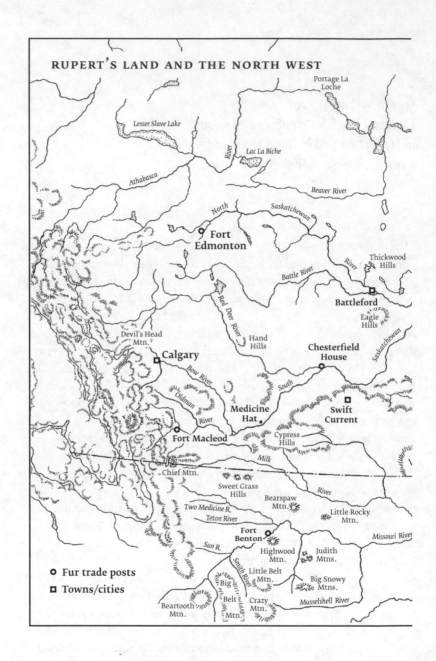

RUPERT'S LAND AND THE NORTH WEST

Portage La Loche

Lesser Slave Lake

Lac La Biche

Athabasca *River*

Beaver River

North Saskatchewan

Fort Edmonton

River Thickwood Hills

Battle River

Battleford

Eagle Hills

Red Deer River

Devil's Head Mtn.

Hand Hills

Calgary

Chesterfield House

Saskatchewan

Bow River

South

Oldman

River

Medicine Hat

Swift Current

Cypress Hills

Fort Macleod

Chief Mtn.

Milk *River*

Sweet Grass Hills

Bearspaw Mtn.

Little Rocky Mtn.

Two Medicine R.

Teton River

Fort Benton

Missouri River

Sun R.

Highwood Mtn.

Judith Mtns.

Smith River

Little Belt Mtn.

Big Snowy Mtns.

Big Belt Mtn.

Crazy Mtn.

Musselshell River

Beartooth Mtn.

○ **Fur trade posts**

□ **Towns/cities**

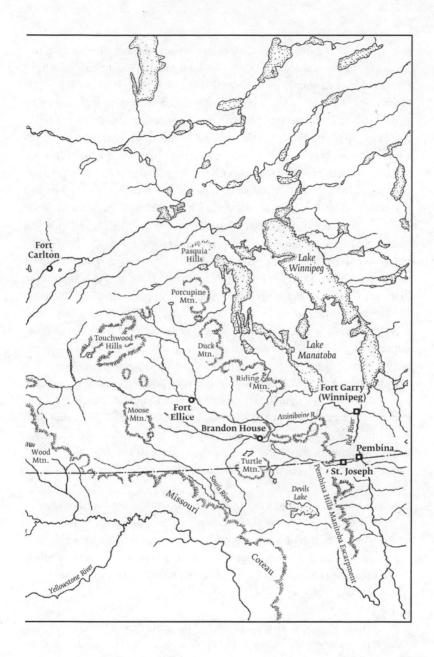

inhabitants of the British Isles, all the world was not America, but for the fledgling Hudson's Bay Company it was, and more so than they could have imagined in their mind's eyes. Nevertheless, even though most of the merchants and investors who received the Royal Charter of 1670 entitling them to the lands that drained into the Hudson's Bay—the right to Rupert's Land— could not have appreciated its size, they did have an inkling of its potential. It could be argued that it was this imagination that drove them into the interior of western North America. A more cynical interpretation of the appropriation of Rupert's Land by the English would repeatedly remind readers of greed and the desire for profit amongst investors, since these were powerful motives too. The merchant venturers did envisage commercial success, and Europe's seemingly insatiable desire for late seventeenth-century or "Cavalier" fashions ensured that the fur and pelt trade would inexorably draw Rupert's Land and its resources into an Anglo-European commercial orbit. This chapter provides an explanation of how the appropriation of Rupert's Land was justified, legitimized and rationalized in the minds of early modern Britons. Moreover, it pays particular attention to the legal and constitutional foundations upon which Rupert's Land, and thereafter, the Canadian west and later Alberta were built.

In justifying the wholesale appropriation of an empire during the early modern period, the English (and after the Anglo-Scottish Union of 1707, the British) drew in the first instance upon a number of arguments that possessed medieval British archipelagic roots and, in the second, on a number of assumptions about empire that they shared with their principal European imperial rivals. As the noted historian, A.F. McC. Madden, reminds us,

> before ever Elizabethan adventurer set foot in the New World there were five centuries (or more) of precedent stored away in the minds and archives of English officials. Issues had been joined, questions asked, expedients found, a system formed; and such experience was not irrelevant to the subsequent history of the British empire, and indeed it was crucial.[3]

It is crucial for modern historians, even those considering the creation and appropriation of Rupert's Land by the English empire to remember that "the history of governance overseas...began near at home in the British Isles and in Europe: an English medieval empire was the seedbed of forms used later."[4] Medieval experience established a number of colonial conventions that passed directly into early modern and modern imperial practice.[5] first it was recognized that the monarchy was sovereign and that "dominions" were possessions of the English Crown. Moreover, these dominions would "retain their own laws and customs, except so far as common law, ordnance and statute might be imposed upon them."[6] Furthermore, it was established that the monarch and Parliament could legislate for "dominions" and that Acts of the English Parliament were binding on subjects of those dominions. In return, the monarch-in-council could hear and adjudicate petitions and appeals from dominions. Collectively, these developments provided a measure of imperial authority to England's medieval empire. At the same time, it was also recognized by medieval monarchs that the maintenance of a disparate or far-flung empire lay beyond their control, and that "dominions" required a considerable degree of local self-governance and discretion. In practical terms, local latitude granted to "dominions" depended on the strength of the English state, the proximity of imperial rivals, and the distance it lay from the metropole (London). Throughout the medieval and into the modern period, the Crown was content to govern at a distance and as cheaply as possible. As McC. Madden further reminds us,

> Long before the grant of powers of government to merchant companies (like those of Virginia or the East Indies) in identical phrases to those of guilds, or to proprietors (like Baltimore of Maryland or Carlisle for the Caribbees) of fiefs similar to those for Man or Durham, England had a "colonial" system in embryo. Moreover she had the experience of the crucial and universal dilemma of empire: how to secure a reasonable and inexpensive balance between local diversity and central unity, between independence and interdependence, between freedom and a continuing association.[7]

These constitutional precedents informed early modern English imperial minds and provided the blueprint that guided imperial expansion in the Americas from the late sixteenth century onwards. But how those thinkers resolved the "dilemmas of empire" that they also inherited forced them, in turn, to articulate precisely how they could claim rightful possession of America and vast regions of it such as Rupert's Land.

Before the English set their sights on North America, they focused upon Ireland and from that sixteenth- and early seventeenth-century experience gained powerful motivations and justifications for the expansion of an empire. In subduing and subsequently establishing "plantations" in Ireland, the Elizabethan English claimed not only the "right of conquest," but also a responsibility to civilize and to Christianize. Edmund Spencer noted that though, as Roman Catholics, the Irish were theoretically Christian, they were "all papists by their profession, but in the same so blindly and brutishly informed for the most part as that you would rather think them atheists or infidels." As another suggested, the Irish lived like "beastes, void of lawe and all good order...more uncivill, more uncleanly, more barbarous and more brutish in their customs and demeaneurs, than in any other part of the world that is known."[8] Armed with these observations and assertions, the English found it easy to justify bringing Ireland under their rule, for their God, a Protestant God, had vested in Protestant England that responsibility. It was, therefore, only a stretch of their imagination, as well as imperial ambition, to contemplate the creation of more colonies across the Atlantic in the seventeenth century.[9]

The English arrived late on the transatlantic imperial scene and took up the challenge of establishing colonies in places not already claimed by the Portuguese and Spanish and recognized, thereafter, by Papal Bulls in the Treaty of Tordesillas in 1494 and Saragossa in 1542–1543.[10] As is well known, this expediency and pragmatism drove the English into the North Atlantic along the American seaboard and further afield in search of the Northwest Passage. Once it became clear that they would find neither a northern route to Cathay, nor the sort of riches that the Spanish had encountered in the bullion-rich regions of Mexico and Peru, English imperial interests turned to colonies of settlement. While there would be no immediate financial rewards in North America like there were for the Spanish in New Spain, English imperial interest in the Americas in the seventeenth century reinforced and fed Albion's appetite for produce, power and profit. From the restoration of monarchical rule in 1660, English ambitions in the Atlantic world propelled them not only into conflict over colonies with their European rivals, but also into providing themselves and others with a complex constitutional establishment for their colonies and coherent philosophical justification for their imperial enterprise.

On the eastern seaboard, a number of colonies were established in short order, particularly Carolina (1663) and Delaware (1664); New York and New Jersey were seized from the Dutch (1664 and 1665); and in the West Indies, the Cayman Islands and the Bahamas were acquired between 1655 and 1670.[11] With the creation of the Hudson's Bay Company in the same year, English interests stretched from the Artic Circle to the Caribbean and provided the metropole with a bewildering assortment of commodities and new colonial markets at the same time that its domestic economy was recovering from the dislocation caused by decades of civil war and political instability.[12] Combined with increased trade from Asia, growing consumer demand in Britain, and protectionist legislation such as the Navigation Acts (1651, 1660, 1663, and 1673), imports from the fledgling empire arriving at the port of London between 1634 and 1669 soared by nearly 20%.[13] Just as Englishmen and -women were developing a taste for the fruits of empire, so too was the emerging English "fiscal-military" and "imperial state" for the taxes and tariffs that could be drawn from a late seventeenth-century "consumer revolution" precipitated by colonial trade.[14]

Government involvement in the management of the economy and colonial expansion waxed and waned during the later seventeenth century and this owed something not only to the interests of specific ministers and ministries, but also to the loose oversight that London and Whitehall provided during the period. From 1660 onward, the Privy Council relied upon two advisory councils, one for trade and one for foreign plantations. Both sought to enable the exchange of information between mercantile interests, members of Parliament and officials of state. This ad hoc structure proved limited in its success, was disbanded, and then briefly reconstituted in the 1670s. It was not until 1696 that a permanent office, the Board of Trade and Plantations, was created by William III's royal prerogative to provide control over colonial affairs. Founded by letters patent in that year, it was made up of "eight full time professional councillors, with the nominal membership of the principal officers of state, and a staff which effectively established it as a government department."[15] Even then, the formal structures of governance within the English empire were still weak and ineffectual. This condition continued until the early nineteenth century. Until colonial affairs were transferred to the office of Secretary of State for War and Colonies in 1801, there was really "no central machinery for the government of the first British Empire."[16] In place of an integrated and co-ordinated structure for colonial administration, a number of government departments held some, though not exclusive, colonial obligations and often maintained overlapping and, at times, contradictory jurisdiction over specific imperial matters. Instead of creating new structures of state and executive machinery to oversee and govern an emerging global empire, officials recorded the details of colonial administration in the same ledger books and decisions were made by the same ministers as dealt with the internal affairs of the nation. There was, as A.F.McC. Madden aptly notes, "no new blue print for the New World" and the "relics of the medieval empire were still a conscious part of the English constitutional heritage: they constituted the only ready model, which the 'realm' had available, of extended extra-territorial control."[17] Thus, the Board of Trade spent much of its time dealing with, and collecting information about, colonial matters, but it held limited authority when dealing with issues that came to its attention. That power rested in the hands of the Secretary of State for the Southern Department, for he held formal responsibility for colonies. However, this was but one portfolio of many that required his constant oversight. At the top of this loosely-held administrative apparatus, the Privy Council held ultimate authority over the colonies. Further complicating this rather bewildering bureaucratic labyrinth was the fact that the colonies themselves had considerable latitude over how they actually implemented London's directives and colonial administrators depended on the nature of the colonies themselves.[18]

Constitutionally, many of the colonies established during the seventeenth century were "proprietary" or "chartered" and were thereby controlled by an individual or group in a form of feudal tenure provided by the Crown. By the turn of the eighteenth century, most of the English-held Caribbean colonies had become royal provinces with governors appointed by the monarch. On the mainland of North America there were essentially two types of colonies, royal/crown or proprietary/chartered. Both were created at the behest of the Crown and not Parliament. In the case of Crown or Royal colonies, the monarch granted commissions to a governor and these commissions were often regarded as constitutional blueprints for the colony since they usually laid out the terms of its governance.[19] By 1690 many of the mainland American colonies such as Virginia, Massachusetts, Carolina, New York, New Jersey and Delaware also fell under royal control, though some were able to exercise some influence over colonial matters through councils or assemblies. Only four colonies—Rhode Island, Connecticut, Maryland and Pennsylvania—retained their chartered or proprietary status into the eighteenth century.[20] Later, in the eighteenth century, Nova Scotia, New Brunswick and Prince Edward Island were all made royal colonies, with a governor whose commission contained standard provisions for the creation of an Assembly or Legislature, an Executive Council and courts of law.[21] Even in royal colonies in the Americas, the governor's ability to carry out London's instructions was limited by local circumstances and increasingly during the eighteenth century by the expectations of colonial assemblies and their colonial populations.[22] In the absence of thoroughly-trained bureaucrats or civil servants in London and in the colonies, the administration of the Atlantic empire relied as much on colonial acceptance and accommodation as it did on imperial and imperious instruction from Whitehall. Alongside these colonies also developed trading companies chartered by the Crown to conduct business under monopoly rights within certain regions. The primary goal in the development of Chartered Companies like the East India (1600), the Royal Africa (1663 and 1672) and the Hudson's Bay (1670) was for the promotion of trade and commerce. Boards of Directors appointed the Governors and Councils who administered these companies, but in the last analysis they were all as accountable to their shareholders as they were to the English state. The extensive territorial possessions that fell under their control were also their responsibility. Trade and commerce were their established goals, while territorial aggrandizement and settlement were of secondary importance and were frequently discouraged by Company Directors and Government officials in London.[23]

In the case of the Hudson's Bay Company, the Governor and Company of Adventurers of England trading into Hudson's Bay were granted by Royal Charter on 2 May 1670 the vast tract of North America that Charles II named Rupert's Land. Granted "in free and common socage and not in Capite or by Knightes Service" (freehold tenure), the Charter paid tacit recognition to older medieval notions of kingship and property, but also reflected contemporary legal thinking about property and the nature of early modern English sovereignty with the restoration of royal power in the wake of the English Civil Wars.[24] In 1660, the Statute of Tenures had abolished antiquated and financially or personally burdensome tenures, such as knight's tenure, in favour of free and common socage, which required regular but merely symbolic rent or tribute to the Monarch. In the case of the HBC Charter, the Company was expected annually to pay the Crown "two elkces and two black beavers whensoever and as often as Wee our heires and successors shall happen to enter into the said Countryes Territoryes and Regions hereby granted."[25] The incorporation of the Company and the creation of Rupert's Land drew inspiration from the only legal relationship to land that was conceivable for the English, and post-1707 British, empire. The "law of the empire was that of personal land-holding from the Crown on the analogy of feudal tenure, and that of the delegated use of the crown's powers within regulated limits to adventuring proprietors or merchant companies."[26]

Initially, the Hudson's Bay Company may have wished to find a route to the Pacific, as the preamble to the Charter notes, but from 1670 onwards its essential business lay in a network of factories or trading forts that sought out furs and pelts from the regions drained by the Hudson's Bay watershed.[27] The Charter stated that the Governor and his Company had the

> Sole Trade and Commerce of all those Seas Streightes Bayes Rivers Lakes Creekes and Soundes in whatsoever latitude they shall bee that lies within the entrance of the Steightes commonly called Hudsons Streightes together with all the Landes and Territoryes upon the Countryes Coastes and confines...that are not already actually possessed by or granted to any of our Subjectes or possessed by the Subjectes of any other Christian Prince or State...and that the said Land bee from henceforth reckoned and reputed as one of our Plantacions or Colonyes in America called Ruperts Land.[28]

Theoretically, therefore, the Crown recognized prior claims of other Christian powers to northeastern North America, but between 1670 and the fall of Quebec in 1759, the British government repeatedly challenged the rights of France to conduct business in the region. Moreover, Charles II and his ministers ignored entirely the rights and pre-existing claims of the indigenous inhabitants of the continent.[29] To accomplish this task, the Charter not only incorporated the Company and gave it exclusive fur-trading privileges in Rupert's Land, but also gave it the capacity to control and dispose of land, and to govern. In the first instance, the Company had permission to protect its interest, and that of the Crown, in Rupert's Land through armed force if necessary. Thus, the Governor and Company were given

> free Liberty and Lycence in case they conceive it necessary to send either Shippes of War Men or Ammunicion unto any theire Plantacions Fortes Factoryes...for the security and defence of the same...to continue or make peace or Warre with any Prince or People whatsoever that are not Christians in any places where the said Company shall have any Plantacions Fortes or factoryes.[30]

Rupert's Land may have been appropriated by the stroke of a pen, but it was to be retained by the might of the sword. Though the Charter did not claim Rupert's Land by the right of conquest, the English state did recognize her right to keep it through the principle of just war.

While the Charter provided for measures to deal with non-Christian indigenous peoples in America, it also made provision for the regulation and discipline of Company employees. The Charter conferred upon the Company the authority to make laws for the preservation of order in Rupert's Land, to maintain order amongst HBC employees and to ensure the advancement of commerce. Thus, it was enacted that the Governor or his officials could

> Make ordyne and constitute such and soe many reasonable Lawes Constitucions Orders and Ordinances...for the good Government of the said Company and of all Governors of Colonyes Fortes and Plantacions Factors Masters Mariners and other Officers employed or too bee employed in any of the [Company] Territories and Landes. The said Governor and Company soe often as they shall make ordeyne or establish any such Lawes Constitucions orders and Ordinances in such forme as aforesaid shall and may lawfully impose ordeyne limit and provide such paines penaltyes and punishments upon all Offenders contrary to such Lawes.[31]

The terms of the Charter further provided for the administration of law, and it was this responsibility that proved so important for the Hudson's Bay Company and for the jurisdictions that eventually emerged out of Rupert's Land (the North-West Territories, and Manitoba, Saskatchewan and Alberta). The Charter noted that

> the Governor and his Councill of the several and respective places where the said Company shall have Plantacions Fortes Factoryes Colonyes or Places of Trade within any the Counrtyes Landes or Territoryes hereby granted may have power to judge all persons belonging to the said Governor and Company or that shall live under them in all Causes whether Civil or Criminall according to the Lawes of this Kingdome and to execute Justice accordingly And in case any crime or misdemeanor shall bee committed in any of the said Companyes Plantacions Fortes Factoryes or Places of Trade within the Lymittes aforesaid where Judicature cannot bee executed for want of a Governor and Councill there then itt shall bee lawfull for the chiefe factor of that place and his Councill to transmit the party together with the offence to such other Plantacion Factory or Fort where there shall bee a Governor and Councill where Justice may bee executed or into this Kingdome of England as shall bee thought most

convenient there to receive such punishment as the nature of his offence shall deserve.[32]

With the stroke of a quill pen, the entire region covered by the Charter was now not only governed by the Hudson's Bay Company, but also fell under English law and, via Company officials, the authority of London. Henceforth, HBC officials were expected to dispense English law as it existed in 1670. Even though they were now armed with extra-territorial authority and the powers of extradition to England, the Company found that imposing English Law upon Rupert's Land proved a more challenging responsibility than any Briton could have imagined at the outset of the venture in 1670. A plethora of jurisdictional questions remained to be answered, and many remained unanswered until the passage of the *Canada Jurisdiction Act* of 1803.[33] The Charter took no account of those indigenous peoples already living in western North America under their own legal, social and cultural mores.[34] Nor did the Crown recognize Amerindian claims to a territory they asserted was now theirs. It was not until the Royal Proclamation of 1763 that the British state sought a comprehensive settlement over land and questions of sovereignty with many of the First Nations of North America.[35] Furthermore, English authorities in London did not realistically recognize the claims of other Europeans—especially the French—to the region. The Charter implicitly noted the possibility that the French had some presence, but most Company officials assumed that the French had not formally laid claim to the territory west of Hudson's Bay. These disingenuous claims were contested, disputed, negotiated and re-negotiated by the two imperial powers until the French empire in Canada fell with Quebec and was surrendered at the Treaty of Paris in 1763.[36]

Armed with the terms of its Charter, the Company set out to expand its commercial enterprise across the Hudson's Bay watershed and to prosper in the face of foreign competition. Though it had been granted Rupert's Land, it was clear that little permanent settlement was originally envisaged for the region and it did not therefore develop in the same manner as the settlement colonies along the eastern seaboard. In the absence of a quickly-growing settlement colony, the immediate need to establish resident magistrates and a legal apparatus of courts that could offer freeborn Englishmen their law did not materialize. When the need did arise in the mid to late eighteenth century, the Company proved incapable of dealing with the situation and it took direct intervention by the Crown and the British parliament, with the passage of the *Canada Jurisdiction Act* in 1803, to galvanize colonial officials into action.[37] Despite the promulgation of statute to bring Rupert's Land under greater legal oversight, lawlessness and recourse to self-help remained characteristic of the region well into the nineteenth century. Most important for our understanding of the English imperial mind in the seventeenth and eighteenth centuries is the fact that the English so strenuously articulated the need for law in Rupert's Land and also in their other imperial possessions.

From the outset of this imperial experience, the people of the British Isles and Europe who fanned out across Rupert's Land and later the Indian Territory of the north and west did so not only armed with the "benefits" of European civilization, but also with English law. It was based on the premise that the HBC Charter had expected and required the Company (as Master) to dispense English law to its employees (as servants) and to the inhabitants of Rupert's Land.[38] How exactly that was to be accomplished by merchants and businessmen operating across the vast reach of Rupert's Land was undoubtedly a problem, but that was left to the Company's discretion. Such a principle rested upon contemporary thinking that the propertied were responsible for upholding and administering the law, and for law to work in the "British" shires and localities such as Cornwall, Cumberland and the Cotswolds, let alone the Canadas, it had to be discretionary.[39] That said, there could be no doubt that Britons, wherever they happened to be, were entitled to their law. Such a philosophical perspective—the birthright of freeborn Englishmen to their law—was a concept that few Britons tired of discussing among themselves or of reminding their European neighbours during the long eighteenth century. As William Blackstone noted in the 1760s in his famous *Commentaries on the Laws of England*, "it is held, that if an uninhabited country be discovered and planted by English subjects, all the English laws are immediately there in force. For as the law is the birth-right of every subject, so wherever they go they carry their laws with them."[40] In the long shadow of the Seven Years War (1756–1763), which witnessed British victories over their traditional and imperial adversary, France, in Canada, the Caribbean and the Indian subcontinent, Blackstone qualified this confidence by noting that "in conquered or ceded countries, that have already laws of their own, the king may indeed alter them and change those laws; but, till he does actually change them, the antient (*sic*) laws of that country remain, unless such as are against the law of God, as in the case of an infidel country."[41] Under these strictures, and those offered by John Locke in his *Two Treatises of Government* (which also nullified indigenous sovereignty on the assertion that Indians possessed neither a sense of property nor political society), Britons saw it as their duty to bring western Canada under their law.[42] These eighteenth-century perspectives therefore ensured that even if those Britons and other employees of the Hudson's Bay Company who arrived in Rupert's Land without an intimate knowledge of the Common Law or Statute Books, without wigs and robes, or without the rituals and regulations of the Bench at Quarter Sessions or Assizes, they still brought with them the legal culture, the legal mores and obligations of early modern Britain.[43] At the heart of this imperial ethos lay the law. It was drawn upon to justify the right of the Crown to create colonies, relied upon to dignify the appropriation of land from others, and to formalize its redistribution into the hands of Britons (individuals, proprietors and chartered companies) as property. Scholars such as John Locke gave the law legitimacy by providing it, and Hanoverian Britons, with the intellectual underpinning needed to dispossess Amerindians of their territory and space. His observations about the inadequacy of indigenous political organization and their incapacity to turn common property into improved, enclosed and valuable private property gained its inspiration, in part, from earlier Iberian debates about the morality of "dispossessing the barbarian."[44] It most certainly inspired imperial Britons, British North Americans, and their American colonial and post-revolutionary brethren, to claim America as theirs and mould it for their own interests. That legacy of dispossession is one that subsequent jurisdictions—Canada and Alberta—also inherited from the age of empire in Rupert's Land. But not everyone read nor agreed with Locke and his disciples, and the morality of imperial expansion precipitated disagreement even as the British Empire was finding its stride in the mid to late eighteenth century.

Thus, it should not be too surprising that the expansion of the Hudson's Bay Company into Rupert's Land raised questions that still perplex scholars of European and British imperial history. Recent research on the early modern period (1500–1800) has shown that the expansion of European powers into the Americas and around the globe were complex processes of cross-cultural interaction that confirmed, but also challenged, many of the cherished assumptions that people had of their world.[45] We are only now coming to appreciate the fact that these interactions profoundly influenced the ways that Europeans understood themselves and those with whom they came into contact. It is well known that during the early modern period a number of European states developed economic, political, social, religious and cultural ties to the Americas and that these processes had profound implications for the development of the distinctive nation-states of North

America.[46] These seventeenth and eighteenth century Northern American developments were tied to broader British expansionary interests in the Atlantic and transoceanic world.

Everywhere the British went, they took with them their law and legal culture and sought to establish it wherever they established imperial interests.[47] Historians would do well to remember that Britons did so in the first instance to regulate and benefit themselves (as the HBC Charter reveals) and only thereafter did they "benevolently" share it with those whom they made their colonial subjects.

While the process of British colonial aggrandizement and appropriation took place on a global scale and numerous continents and peoples experienced similar authority at the hands of the English, all colonial encounters were unique. Rupert's Land and the "western Canadian legal experience" is no exception. This chapter has concentrated on early modern English legal conventions and imperial expansion, but it is necessarily, therefore, a reflection on aspects of emergent "Canadian" law too. If anything else, the historical and imperial experiences considered here remind the reader that Canadian and Albertan legal history necessarily embraces and encompasses the legal histories of numerous peoples and nations. This observation by no means diminishes the importance of the study of "Canada" and Canadian legal institutions in these processes. Instead, it reveals quite the opposite— namely, that the study of seventeenth, eighteenth and nineteenth century Rupert's Land offers scholars the opportunity to study, analyze and understand the interactions of numerous legal cultures and traditions. The majority of those who came to Rupert's Land in the seventeenth and eighteenth century were British, or peoples who had immigrated to the British Empire. They brought with them not only a set of legal codes and institutions, but also a legal culture contemporaries argued made them the envy of other Europeans and indigenous peoples. It is worth remembering that by the late seventeenth century, when Charles II granted the Hudson's Bay Company its Charter and monopoly rights to Rupert's Land, the English had already been an imperial power for centuries and had considerable experience with colonization. This included imposing their law and will upon peoples in the Atlantic archipelago and other regions of the Americas. Furthermore, since 1600 their chartered companies had been plying the global seas in search of profitable goods and markets.[48] Despite these imperial experiences, the English presence in Canada and western North America was different from that in Ireland, the Caribbean or for that matter the seaboard colonies on the American mainland. There are a number of reasons for this uniqueness. First, the indigenous peoples and nations of western North America were different than those the English encountered elsewhere. Also by the early eighteenth century, the "British empire was a ragged and conflict-ridden community of separate interests: English speaking creoles—people born in the colonies but retaining English culture; virtually self-governing colonies of settlement; antique trading corporations, colonial land speculators and peasant farmers."[49] Moreover, the Royal chartered companies were given considerable latitude over how they conducted themselves and their employees in the lands they literally ruled. Enjoying broad privileges, the Hudson's Bay Company had the authority to "raise money, conduct courts, negotiate trading concessions, develop colonies, and initiate wars."[50] Thus, the peoples and the specific circumstances of commercial and colonial expansion ensured that the legal and imperial experience in the Canadian west would be unique. Finally, the geography and vast expanse of Rupert's Land and the Indian Territory ensured that English institutional structures would be stretched beyond comprehension and imagination.

For those imperializing Britons bolstered by Locke's *Two Treatises of Government* and burdened with Blackstone's *Commentaries of the Laws of England* and his adage about their law, the crucial question of how to forge law and jurisdiction in a land that stretched beyond the mind's eye was of paramount importance.[51] How we understand that process and how we reconfigure for the twenty-first century that early modern legal world we have inherited in the foundations of Alberta's modern legal system will prove equally challenging and equally important.

Notes

1. J. Locke, *Two Treatises of Government*, ed. P. Laslett, revised ed. (Cambridge: Cambridge University Press, 1988), 301.
2. J.R. Seeley, *The Expansion of England: Two Courses of Lectures* (London: Macmillan, 1883). Also see B. Porter, *Absent-Minded Imperialists: What the British Really Thought about Empire* (Oxford: Oxford University Press, 2004); D. Cannadine, *Ornamentalism: How the British Saw their Empire* (Oxford: Oxford University Press, 2001); numerous essays in R. Winks, ed., *Historiography*, vol. 5, *Oxford History of the British Empire* (Oxford: Oxford University Press, 1999); and D. Peers, "Is Humpty Dumpty Back Together Again?: The Revival of Imperial History and the Oxford History of the British Empire," *Journal of World History* 13 (2002): 451–68.

3. A.F. McC. Madden, "1066, 1776 and All That: The Relevance of English Medieval Experiences of 'Empire' to later Imperial Constitutional Issues," in J.E. Flint and G. Williams, eds., *Perspectives of Empire: Essays Presented to Gerald S. Graham* (London: Longman, 1973), 9–26, at 10.

4. Ibid.

5. On this issue also see J. Gillingham, "The Beginnings of English Imperialism," *Journal of Historical Sociology* 5 (1992): 392–409; R. Davies, "The English State and the 'Celtic' Peoples 1100–1400," *Journal of Historical Sociology* 6 (1993): 1–14; S. Reynolds, *Kingdoms and Communities in Western Europe, 900–1300*, 2 ed. (Oxford: Oxford University Press, 1997); J. Muldoon, *Empire and Order: The Concept of Empire, 800–1800* (London: Macmillan Ltd., 1999); and R. Bartlett, *The Making of Europe: Conquest, Colonization and Cultural Change, 950–1350* (Princeton: Princeton University Press, 1993).

6. A.F. McC. Madden, "1066, 1776 and All That," 10. On this subject also see J.G.A. Pocock, *The Ancient Constitution and the Feudal Law: A Study of English Historical Thought in the Seventeenth Century* (Cambridge: Cambridge University Press, 1987); E. Kantorowicz, *The King's Two Bodies: A Study of Mediaeval Political Theology* (Princeton: Princeton University Press, 1997); E. Sandoz, ed., *The Roots of Liberty: Magna Carta, Ancient Constitution, and the Anglo-American Tradition of the Rule of Law* (Columbia: University of Missouri Press, 1993); and J. Nelson, "Kingship and Empire," in J.H. Burns, ed., *The Cambridge History of Medieval Political Thought c.350–c.1450* (Cambridge: Cambridge University Press, 1988), 211–51.

7. A.F. McC. Madden, "1066, 1776 and All That," 11.

8. These quotations are drawn from T.R. Metcalf, *Ideologies of the Raj* (Cambridge: Cambridge University Press, 1994), 2. On the subject of the English colonization of Ireland see: N. Canny, "The Ideology of English Colonization: From Ireland to America," *William and Mary Quarterly* 30 (1973): 575–98; S.G. Ellis and S. Barber, eds., *Conquest and Union: Fashioning a British State, 1485–1725* (London: Longmans, 1995); B. Bradshaw and P. Roberts, eds., *British Consciousness and Identity: The Making of Britain, 1533–1707* (Cambridge: Cambridge University Press, 1998); J.H. Ohlmeyer, "'Civilizinge of those Rude Partes': Colonization within Britain and Ireland, 1580s–1640s," in N. Canny, ed., *The Origins of Empire: British Overseas Enterprise to the Close of the Seventeenth Century*, Vol. I, *Oxford History of the British Empire* (Oxford: Oxford University Press, 1998), 124–47; and N. Canny, *Making Ireland British* (Oxford: Oxford University Press, 2003).

9. On this theme see K.R. Andrews, *Trade, Plunder and Settlement: Maritime Enterprise and the Genesis of the British Empire, 1480–1630* (Cambridge: Cambridge University Press, 1984); D. Loades, *England's Maritime Empire: Seapower, Commerce and Policy, 1490–1690* (London: Pearson, 2000), and N. Canny, "The Origins of Empire: An Introduction," in N. Canny, ed., *The Origins of Empire*, 1–33. On America in the imagination see the essays in P.J. Marshall and G. Williams, *The Great Map of Mankind: Perceptions of New Worlds in the Age of Enlightenment* (Harvard: Harvard University Press, 1982), 1–63 and 187–226; K. Kupperman, ed., *America in European Consciousness 1493–1750* (Chapel Hill: University of North Carolina Press, 1995); and J.P. Greene, *The Intellectual Construction of America: Exceptionalism and Identity from 1492 to 1800* (Chapel Hill: University of North Carolina Press, 1993).

10. See R.A. Williams, Jr., *The American Indian in Western Legal Thought: The Discourses of Conquest* (Oxford: Oxford University Press, 1990), 71–118; L.C. Green and O.P. Dickason, *The Law of Nations and the New World* (Edmonton: University of Alberta Press, 1989), 3–34 and 175–84; O.P. Dickason, "Old World Law, New World Peoples, and Concepts of Sovereignty," in D.B. Quinn et. al., *Essays on the History of North American Discovery and Exploration* (Arlington: Texas A & M University Press, 1988), 52–63; A. Pagden, *Spanish Imperialism and the Political Imagination*

(New Haven: Yale University Press, 1990); A. Pagden, *Lords of All the Worlds: Ideologies of Empire in Spain, Britain and France c.1500–c.1800* (New Haven: Yale University Press, 1995), 24–62; and J. Muldoon, "Discovery, Grant, Charter, Conquest, or Purchase: John Adams on the Legal Basis for English Possession of North America," in C.L. Tomlins and B.H. Mann, eds., *The Many Legalities of Early America* (Chapel Hill: University of North Carolina Press, 2001), 25–46.

11. On the development of American colonies see A. McFarlane, *The British in the Americas, 1480–1815* (London: Longmans, 1994); R. Middleton, *Colonial America: A History, 1585–1776*, 2 ed. (Oxford: Blackwell's, 1996); and R.C. Simmons, *The American Colonies: From Settlement to Independence* (New York, W.W. Norton and Co.), 1981, 20–121.

12. C.G.A. Clay, *Economic Expansion and Social Change: England 1500–1700*, Vol. II, *Industry, Trade and Government* (Cambridge: Cambridge University Press, 1984), 141–222; and K. Wrightson, *Earthly Necessities: Economic Lives in Early Modern Britain* (New Haven: Yale University Press, 2000), 227–68.

13. These calculations and general observations are drawn from D. Loades, *England's Maritime Empire*, 219; N. Zahedieh, "Overseas Expansion and Trade in the Seventeenth Century," in N. Canny, ed., *The Origins of Empire*, 398–422; R. Brenner, *Merchants and Revolutionaries: Commercial Change, Political Conflict and London's Overseas Traders, 1550–1653* (Princeton: Princeton University Press, 1993); N. Zahedieh, "Economy," in D. Armitage and M.J. Braddick, eds., *The British Atlantic World, 1500–1800* (London: Palgrave Macmillan, 2002), 51–68; and C.G. Pestana, *The English Atlantic in an Age of Revolution, 1640–1661* (Harvard: Harvard University Press, 2004).

14. On the emergence of the a fiscal military state see J. Brewer, *Sinews of Power: War, Money and the English State, 1688–1783* (London: Unwin Hyman, 1989); L. Stone, ed., *An Imperial State at War: Britain from 1689 to 1815* (London: Routledge, 1994); P. Corrigan and D. Sayer, *The Great Arch: English State Formation as Cultural Revolution* (Oxford: Blackwell's, 1985); and M. Braddick, *The Nerves of State: Taxation and the Financing of the English State, 1558–1714* (Manchester: Manchester University Press, 1996). For discussions of the "consumer revolution" see N. McKendrick, J. Brewer and J.H. Plumb, *The Birth of a Consumer Society* (London: Europa, 1982); J. Brewer and R. Porter eds., *Consumption and the World of Goods* (London: Routledge, 1993); J. Brewer and A. Bermingham, eds., *The Consumption of Culture 1600–1800: Image, Object, Text* (London: Routledge, 1995); and T.H. Breen, *The Marketplace of Revolution: How Consumer Politics Shaped American Independence* (Oxford: Oxford University Press, 2004), 1–147.

15. D. Loades, *England's Maritime Empire*, 231.

16. P.D.G. Thomas, *British Politics and the Stamp Act Crisis: The First Phase of the American Revolution, 1763–1767* (Oxford: Clarendon Press, 1975), 27. Also see I.K. Steele, "The Anointed, the Appointed, and the Elected: Governance of the British Empire, 1689–1784," in P.J. Marshall, ed., *The Eighteenth Century*, Vol. II, *Oxford History of the British Empire* (Oxford: Oxford University Press, 1998), 105–27; P. Lawson, ed., *Parliament and the Atlantic Empire* (Edinburgh: Edinburgh University Press, 1995); and E. Mancke, "Negotiating an Empire: Britain and Its Overseas Peripheries, c.1550–1780," in C. Daniels and M.V. Kennedy, eds., *Negotiated Empires: Centers and Peripheries in the Americas, 1500–1820* (New York: Routledge, 2002), 235–65.

17. A.F. McC. Madden, "1066, 1776 and All That," 22.

18. In addition to the aforementioned volumes I and II of the *Oxford History of the British Empire* that consider the governance of the empire from various perspectives, see also: H.V. Bowen, "British Conceptions of Global Empire, 1756–83," *Journal of Imperial and Commonwealth History* 26 (1988): 1–27; E. Mancke, "Empire and State," in D. Armitage and M.J. Braddick, eds., *The British Atlantic World, 1500–1800* (Pearson Macmillan, 2002), 175–95; P.J. Marshall, "Britain and the World in the Eighteenth Century, I: Reshaping the Empire," *Transactions of the Royal*

Historical Society 8 (1998): 1–18; and P.J. Marshall, "Britain and the World in the Eighteenth Century, II: Britons and Americans," *Transactions of the Royal Historical Society* 9 (1999), 1–16.

19. On the legal nature of colonies see J.E. Coté, "The Reception of English Law," *Alberta Law Review* 15 (1977): 37–53.

20. F.N. Thorpe, ed., *The Federal and State Constitutions, Colonial Charters, and other Organic Laws of the States, Territories, and Colonies Now or Heretofore forming the United States of America* (Washington, D.C.: Government Printing Office, 1909); J.P. Greene, ed., *Settlement to Society, 1607–1763: A Documentary History of Colonial America* (New York: W.W. Norton, 1975); and J.P. Greene, *Peripheries and Center: Constitutional Development in the Extended Polities of the British Empire and the United States 1607–1788* (Athens: University of Georgia, 1986).

21. J. Read, "Early Provincial Constitutions," *Canadian Bar Review* 26 (1948): 621–70; M. Conrad and A. Finkel, *History of the Canadian Peoples: Beginnings to 1867*, 2 vols. (Toronto: Copp Clark, 1998), 1: 179–85; P. Buckner and J.H. Reid, eds. *The Atlantic Region to Confederation: A History* (Toronto: University of Toronto Press, 1994).

22. R.M. Bliss, *Revolution and Empire: English Politics and the American Colonies in the Seventeenth Century* (Manchester: Manchester University Press, 1990); J.M. Sosin, *English America and Imperial Inconstancy: The Rise of Provincial Autonomy, 1696–1715* (Lincoln: University of Nebraska Press, 1985); J.M. Sosin, *English America and the Revolution of 1688: Royal Administration and the Structure of Provincial Government* (Lincoln: University of Nebraska Press, 1982); J.M. Sosin, *English America and the Restoration Monarchy of Charles II: Transatlantic Politics, Commerce and Kinship* (Lincoln: University of Nebraska Press, 1980); and J.P. Greene, *Negotiated Authorities: Essays in Colonial Politics and Constitutional History* (Athens: University of Virginia Press, 1994).

23. P. Lawson, *The East India Company: A History* (London: Longmans, 1993); E.E. Rich, *Hudson's Bay Company 1670–1870*, 3 vols. (Toronto: McClelland and Stewart, 1960); J.S. Galbraith, *The Hudson's Bay Company as an Imperial Factor* (Berkeley: University of California Press, 1957).

24. On "free and common socage" see: A. W. B. Simpson, *An Introduction to the History of Land Law* (Oxford: Oxford University Press, 1961), 1–23; and J.H. Baker, *An Introduction to English Legal History*, 2 ed. (London: Butterworths, 1979), 193–219. For an understanding of the immediate influence these decisions had in Anglo-Indigenous relations see A.J. Ray, J. Miller and F.J. Tough, *Bounty and Benevolence: A History of Saskatchewan Treaties* (Kingston: McGill-Queen's University Press, 2000), 1–10. The Statute of Tenures and the nature of "free and common socage" were discussed in 1953 when the Privy Council considered the Alberta case (*A.G. for Alberta v. Huggard* [1953] A.C. 420). At stake in this case over Oil and Gas rights was the question of whether or not the Statute of Tenures applied to Rupert's Land.

25. For a copy of the Charter see *Charters, Statutes and Orders in Council relating to the Hudson's Bay Company* (London: Hudson's Bay Company, 1931). Also see E.H. Oliver, *The Canadian North-West—Its Early Development and Legislative Records* (Ottawa: Government Printing Bureau, 1914), I:1735. For an online copy of the H.B.C. Charter see: www.solon.org/Constitutions/Canada. All subsequent quotations from the H.B.C. Charter are drawn from this source.

26. A.F. McC. Madden, "1066, 1776 and All That," 21–2.

27. On the voluminous literature on the Hudson's Bay Company see amongst others, M. Payne, "Fur Trade Historiography: Past Conditions, Present Circumstances and a Hint at Future Prospects," in T. Binnema, G. Ens and R.C. Macleod, eds., *From Rupert's Land to Canada: Essays in Honour of J. E. Foster* (Edmonton: University of Alberta Press, 2001), 3–22; J.M. Bumsted, *Fur Trade Wars: The Founding of Western Canada* (Winnipeg: Great Plains Publications, 1999); E. Mancke, *A Company of Businessmen: The Hudson's Bay Company and Long Distance Trade, 1670–1730* (Winnipeg: Rupert's Land Research Centre, 1988); A.S. Morton, *A History of the Canadian West*

to *1870–71*, 2 ed. (Toronto: University of Toronto Press, 1973); F. Pannekoek, *The Fur Trade and Western Canadian Society* (Ottawa: Canadian Historical Association, 1987); D. Francis, *Battle for the West: Fur Traders and the Birth of Western Canada* (Edmonton: Hurtig Press, 1982); E.E. Rich, *The Fur Trade and the Northwest to 1857* (Toronto: McClelland and Stewart, 1967); H.A. Innes, *The Fur Trade in Canada: An Introduction to Canadian Economic History, with a New Introductory Essay by A.J. Ray* (Toronto: University of Toronto Press, 1999); and E. Burley, *Servants of the Honourable Company: Work, Discipline and Conflict in the Hudson's Bay Company, 1770–1870* (Toronto: Oxford University Press, 1997).

28. The Hudson's Bay Company Charter can be conveniently accessed online via www.solon.org or via the website of the Centre for Constitutional Studies, Faculty of Law, University of Alberta at www.uofaweb.ualberta.ca/ccs/Canadian/cfm. Also see *Charter, Statutes and Orders in Council Relating to the Hudson's Bay Company* (London: Hudson's Bay Company, 1963).

29 . On the voluminous subject of indigenous legal history, dispute resolution and Aboriginal rights see K. McNeil, *Common Law Aboriginal Title* (Oxford: Oxford University Press, 1989); J. Borrows, *Recovering Canada: The Resurgence of Indigenous Law* (Toronto: University of Toronto Press, 2002); B. Slattery, "Aboriginal Sovereignty and Imperial Claims," *Osgoode Hall Law Journal* 29 (1991): 681–703; M. Walters, "British Imperial Constitutional Law and Aboriginal Rights: A Comment on *Delgamuukw v. British Columbia*," *Queen's Law Journal* 17 (1995): 350; the essays in M. Asch, ed., *Aboriginal and Treaty Rights in Canada* (Vancouver: University of British Columbia Press, 1997); H. Foster, "Forgotten Arguments: Aboriginal Title and Sovereignty in Canada Jurisdiction Act Cases," *Manitoba Law Journal* 21 (1992): 343–45; J. Borrows, "Constitutional Law from a First Nations Perspective: Self Government and the Royal Proclamation," *University of British Columbia Law Review* 28 (1994): 1–47; T. Isaac, "Discarding the Rose-Coloured Glasses: A Commentary on Asch and Macklem," *Alberta Law Review* 30 (1992): 708–12; M. Asch and P. Macklem, "Aboriginal Rights and Canadian Sovereignty: An essay on *R. v. Sparrow*," *Alberta Law Review* 29 (1991): 498–517; P.G. McHugh, "The Common-Law Status of Colonies and Aboriginal 'Rights': How Lawyers and Historians Treat the Past," *Saskatchewan Law Review* 61 (1998): 393–429; S.L. Harring, *White Man's Law: Native People in Nineteenth-Century Canadian Jurisprudence* (Toronto: Osgoode Society, 1998); D. Johnston, *The Taking of Indian Lands in Canada: Consent or Coercion?* (Saskatoon: University of Saskatchewan Native Law Centre, 1989); D. Culhane, *The Pleasure of the Crown: Anthropology, Law and First Nations* (Vancouver: Talon Books, 1998); the essays in F. Cassidy, ed., *Aboriginal Self-Determination* (Halifax: Institute for Research on Public Policy, 1991); and K. McNeil, "Sovereignty and the Aboriginal Nations of Rupert's Land," *Manitoba History* 37 (1999): 2–8.

30. www.uofaweb.ualberta.ca/ccs/Canadian/cfm or *Charter, Statutes and Orders in Council Relating to the Hudson's Bay Company*.

31. Ibid.

32. Ibid.

33. On the ambiguity of law in Rupert's Land and the difficulties that "long-distance justice" presented see: H. Foster, "Long-Distance Justice: The Criminal Jurisdiction of Canadian Courts West of the Canadas, 1763–1859," *American Journal of Legal History* XXXIV (1990): 1–48; D. Gibson, "Company Justice: Origins of Legal Institutions in Pre-Confederation Manitoba," *Manitoba Law Journal* 23, nos. 1 & 2 (1995): 247–292; H. Harvey, "The Early Administration of Justice in the North West," *Alberta Law Quarterly* 1 (1934–36): 1–15; D. Gibson and L. Gibson, *Substantial Justice: Law and Lawyers in Manitoba, 1670–1870* (Winnipeg: Pegius, 1970); R. Smandych and R. Lindon, "Administering Justice Without the State: A Study of the Private Justice System of the Hudson's Bay Company to 1800," *Canadian Journal of Law and Society* 11 (1996): 21–61; D. Brown, "Unpredictable and Uncertain: Criminal Law in the Canadian Northwest

Before 1886," *Alberta Law Review* 17 (1979): 497–512; L. Knafla, "From Oral to Written Memory: The Common Law Tradition in Western Canada," in L. Knafla ed., *Law and Justice in a New Land: Essays in Western Canadian Legal History* (Toronto: Carswell Press, 1986), 31–77; R.C. Macleod, "Law and Order on the Western Canadian Frontier," in J. Mclaren, H. Foster and C. Orloff, eds., *Law for the Elephant, Law for the Beaver: Essays in the Legal History of the North American West* (Regina: Canadian Plains Research Centre, 1992), 90–105; K. Bindon, "Hudson's Bay Company Law: Adam Thom and the Institution of Order in Rupert's Land, 1839–54," in D. Flaherty ed., *Essays in the History of Canadian Law: Volume I* (Toronto: Osgoode Society, 1981), 43–78; H. Robert Baker, "Creating Order in the Wilderness: Transplanting the English Law to Rupert's Land, 1835–51," *Law and History Review* 17 (1999): 209–46; H. Robert Baker, "Law Transplanted, Justice Invented: Sources of Law for the Hudson's Bay Company in Rupert's Land, 1670–1870" (M.A. Diss., University of Manitoba, 1996); P.C. Nigol, "Discipline, Discretion and Control: The Private Justice System of the Hudson's Bay Company in Rupert's Land, 1670–1770" (Ph.D. Diss., University of Calgary, 2001); J. Swainger and C. Backhouse, eds., *People and Places: Historical Influences on Legal Culture* (Vancouver: University of British Columbia Press, 2003); and H. Foster, "Law and Necessity in Western Rupert's Land and Beyond, 1670–1870," in L.A. Knafla and J. Swainger eds., *Essays in the History of Canadian Law—The Middle Kingdom: The Northwest Territories and Prairie Provinces, 1670–1945* (Vancouver: University of British Columbia Press, forthcoming). I would like to thank Professor Foster for allowing me to use this important paper in advance of publication.

34. For an analysis of social relations between European and Indigenous peoples see R. White, *The Middle Ground: Indians, Empires, and Republics in the Great Lakes Region, 1650–1815* (Cambridge: Cambridge University Press, 1991); S. Van Kirk, *Many Tender Ties: Women in Fur-Trade Society, 1670–1870* (Winnipeg: Watson and Dwyer, 1980); J. Brown, *Strangers in Blood: Fur Trade Families in Indian Country* (Vancouver: University of British Columbia Press, 1980); A.J. Ray, *I Have Lived here Since the World Began: An Illustrated History Of Canada's Native Peoples* (Toronto: Key Porter Books, 1996), 69–111; and J.E. Foster, "Wintering, the Outsider Male and Ethnogenisis of the Western Plains Metis," *Prairie Forum* 19 (1994): 1–13. For a detailed analysis of the socio-economic relations between the Company and Indigenous people see: A.J. Ray and D. Freeman, *"Give us Good Measure": An Economic Analysis of Relations Between the Indians and the Hudson's Bay Company before 1763* (Toronto: University of Toronto Press, 1978); A.J. Ray, *Indians in the Fur Trade: Their Role as Hunters, Trappers and Middlemen in the Lands Southwest of Hudson's Bay, 1660–1870* (Toronto: University of Toronto Press, 1974); B. White, "'Give Us a little Milk': The Social and Cultural Meaning of Gift Giving in the Lake Superior Fur Trade," *Minnesota History* 48 (1982): 60–71; A.J. Ray, "The Northern Interior, 1600 to Modern Times," in B.G. Trigger and W.E. Washburn, eds., *The Cambridge History of the Native Peoples of the Americas*, Vol. I, *North America, Part 2* (Cambridge: Cambridge University Press, 1996), 267–300.

35. The full text of the Proclamation is printed in A.L. Getty and A.S. Lussier, eds., *As Long as the Sun Shines and Water Flows: A Reader in Canadian Native Studies* (Vancouver: University of British Columbia Press, 1983), 29–37. For an analysis of the Royal Proclamation see J. Stagg, *Anglo-Indian Relations in North America to 1763 and an Analysis of the Royal Proclamation of 7 October 1763* (Ottawa: Department of Indian Affairs and Northern Development, 1981); R.A. Williams, Jr., *The American Indian in Western Legal Thought*, 228–302; and for its continental implications R.N. Clinton, "The Proclamation of 1763: Colonial Prelude to Two Centuries of Federal-State Management of Indian Affairs," *Boston University Law Review* 69 (1989):

329–85; W.R. Jacobs, "British Indian Policies to 1783," in W.E. Washburn ed., *History of Indian-White Relations*, Vol. 4 (Washington: Smithsonian Institution, 1988), 5–12; and R.J. Surtees, "Canadian Indian Treaties," in W.E. Washburn, *History of Indian-White Relations*, 202–10; D.K. Richter, "Native Peoples of North America and the Eighteenth Century British Empire," in P.J. Marshall, ed., *The Eighteenth Century*, 363–69.

36. See W.J. Eccles, "Sovereignty-Association, 1500–1783," *Canadian Historical Review* LXV (1984): 475–510; H.V. Nelles, *A Little History of Canada* (Oxford: Oxford University Press, 2004), 54–74.

37. 43 Geo. III, c. 138. See A.S. Morton, "The Canada Jurisdiction Act and the North West," *Proceedings and Transactions of the Royal Society of Canada*, 3 series (1939), sec. II at 121; also H. Foster, "Long Distance Justice," 4–11 and 14.

38. D. Hay and P. Craven, eds., *Masters, Servants, and Magistrates in Britain and the Empire, 1562–1955* (Chapel Hill: University of North Carolina Press, 2004), esp. chapters 1–5.

39. On these matters see P. Langford, *Public Life and the Propertied Englishman, 1689–1798* (Oxford: Oxford University Press, 1993); N. Landau, ed., *Law, Crime and English Society, 1660–1830* (Cambridge: Cambridge University Press, 2002); M.J. Braddick and J. Walter, eds., *Negotiating Power in Early Modern Society: Order, Hierarchy and Subordination in Britain and Ireland* (Cambridge: Cambridge University Press, 2001); and P. King, *Crime, Justice and Discretion in England, 1740–1820* (Oxford: Oxford University Press, 2000).

40. W. Blackstone, *Commentaries on the Laws of England*, 4 vols. (Oxford: Clarendon Press, 1765), I:104–5.

41. Ibid.

42. J. Locke, *Two Treatises of Government*. On the subject of Locke's views on America and Indigenous societies consult B. Arneil, *John Locke and America* (Oxford: Clarendon Press, 1996); J. Tully, *An Approach to Political Philosophy: Locke in Contexts* (Cambridge: Cambridge University Press, 1993); D. Armitage, *The Ideological Origins of the British Empire* (Cambridge: Cambridge University Press, 2000); J. Tully, *Strange Multiplicity: Constitutionalism in an Age of Diversity* (Cambridge: Cambridge University Press, 1995), 71–78; P. Miller, *Defining the Common Good: Empire, Religion and Philosophy in Eighteenth Century Britain* (Cambridge: Cambridge University Press, 1994).

43. Recent works that discuss these themes include P. Griffiths, A. Fox and S. Hindle, eds., *The Experience of Authority in Early Modern England* (Basingstoke: Macmillan, 1996); and M. Gaskill, *Crime and Mentalities in Early Modern England* (Cambridge: Cambridge University Press, 2000).

44. See A. Pagden, "Dispossessing the Barbarian: the Language of Spanish Thomism and the Debate over the Property Rights of the American Indians," in A. Pagden ed., *The Languages of Political Theory in Early-Modern Europe* (Cambridge: Cambridge University Press, 1987), 79–98; A. Pagden, *Lords of All the World*, 63–102; and P. Seed, *Ceremonies of Possession in Europe's Conquest of the New World, 1492–1640* (Cambridge: Cambridge University Press, 1995).

45. On this subject see L. Colley, *Captives: Britain, Empire and the World 1600–1850* (London: Jonathan Cape, 2002); P.J. Marshall, and G. Williams, *The Great Map of Mankind*; P.J. Marshall, ed., *The Cambridge Illustrated History of the British Empire* (Cambridge: Cambridge University Press, 1996); C. Bayly, *Imperial Meridian: The British Empire and the World, 1780–1830* (London: Longmans, 1989); L. Russell, ed., *Colonial Frontiers: Indigenous-European Encounters in Settler Societies* (Manchester: Manchester University Press, 2001); M. Daunton and R. Halpern, *Empire and Others: British Encounters with Indigenous Peoples, 1600–1850* (Philadelphia: University of Pennsylvania Press, 1999); and C. Hall, *Civilizing Subjects: Metropole and Colony in the English Imagination, 1830–1867* (Cambridge: Polity Press, 2002).

46. See B. Trigger, *Natives and Newcomers: Canada's "Heroic Age" Reconsidered* (Montreal: McGill-Queen's University Press, 1985); D. Delage, *Amerindians and Europeans in the American Northeast, 1600–1664*

(Vancouver: University of British Columbia Press 1993); L.C. Green and O.P. Dickason, *The Law of Nations and the New World*; O.P. Dickason, *The Myth of the Savage and the Beginnings of French Colonialism in the Americas* (Edmonton: University of Alberta Press, 1984); A. Pagden, *European Encounters with the New World* (New Haven: Yale University Press, 1991); A. Pagden, *The Fall of Natural Man: The American Indian and the Origins of Comparative Ethnology* (Cambridge: Cambridge University Press, 1982); and J.H. Elliott, "Part I: The American World," in J.H. Elliott, *Spain and its World, 1500–1700* (New Haven: Yale University Press, 1989), 3–64.

47. This area of research is only now attracting the attention it deserves. On this emerging theme see the essays in D. Kirkby and C. Coleborne, eds., *Law, History, Colonialism: The Reach of Empire* (Manchester: Manchester University Press, 2001). Also see P. Karsten, *Between Law and Custom: High and Low Legal Cultures in the Lands of the British Diaspora—The United States, Canada, Australia, and New Zealand, 1600–1900* (Cambridge: Cambridge University Press, 2002); and J.C. Weaver, *The Great Land Rush and the Making of the Modern World, 1650–1900* (Kingston: McGill-Queen's University Press, 2003).

48. On this voluminous subject see H. Bowen, *Elites, Enterprise and the Making of the British Overseas Empire, 1688–1775* (Basingstoke: Macmillan Press, 1996); D. Hancock, *Citizens of the World: London Merchants and the Integration of the British Atlantic Community, 1735–1785* (Cambridge: Cambridge University Press, 1995); J. Tracy, ed., *The Rise of Merchant Empires: Long-Distance Trade in the Early Modern World, 1350–1750* (Cambridge: Cambridge University Press, 1990); and J. Tracy, ed., *The Political Economy of Merchant Empires: State Power and World Trade, 1350–1750* (Cambridge: Cambridge University Press, 1991).

49. C. Bayly, *Imperial Meridian*, 76.

50. I. Steele, "The Anointed, the Appointed, and the Elected: Governance of the British Empire, 1689–1784," in *The Oxford History of the British Empire*, vol. 2, *The Eighteenth Century* (Oxford: Oxford University Press, 1998), 105–27 at 106.

51. This subject has been explored by a number of historians. See for example H. Foster, "Sins Against the Great Spirit: The Law, the Hudson's Bay Company, and the Mackenzie's River Murders, 1835–1839," *Criminal Justice History* X (1989): 23–76; H. Foster, "Long-Distance Justice: The Criminal Jurisdiction of Canadian Courts West of the Canadas, 1763–1859," *American Journal of Legal History* XXXIV (1990): 1–48.

Two

Ambiguous Authority
The Development of Criminal Law
in the Canadian North-West and Alberta

DESMOND BROWN

After much testy negotiation, the rejection and humiliation of a Canadian governor-to-be, and an insurrection that fathered the Province of Manitoba, Rupert's Land and the Indian Territory[1] were admitted to the Canadian Union on June 23, 1870. These events were by no means the only problems that Canada had with the North-West before and after union: the criminal law in those parts was ambiguous and indeterminate even though some of the lands had been a colony[2] of the Crown for 200 years. To begin with, the number of jurisdictions within the specified area was a question that engaged the attention of legislators and lawyers before and after Union. For example, in 1814 five eminent English counsel gave it as their opinion that, in effect, there were two jurisdictions in the North-West at that time: the Indian Territories and Rupert's Land.[3] After Union, David Mills, a future minister of justice, argued that there had been three separate jurisdictions before Union: the District of Assiniboia, Rupert's Land, and the Indian Territory.[4] Not so, said C.C. McCaul, a leading barrister in the North-West Territories, who argued that Rupert's Land, including the District of Assiniboia and the Indian Territory, together formed one large jurisdiction.[5] But there was even greater disagreement concerning the specific body of criminal law that was in effect in a given jurisdiction at Union. Opinion ranged from McCaul's assertion that the law throughout the entire region at Union was that of Upper Canada,[6] to a judgement of Mr. Justice Albert Killam of the Manitoba Court of Queen's Bench in 1886 in which he said that the law of 1670 England was in force in Rupert's Land, including the District of Assinibioa, until these jurisdictions were ceded to Canada.[7] A hundred years later the question had still not been answered definitively, and yet another body of law was adduced—that of Rupert's Land subsequent to 1803. E.E. Rich, the official biographer of the Hudson's Bay Company, maintained that Rupert's Land was included in the

Indian Territories and therefore was subject to the law of Lower Canada laid down by statute in 1803.[8] In short, the criminal law of the North-West was the very antithesis of what good law should be: it was ambiguous when Rupert's Land and the Indian Territories were ceded to Canada, and it remained so for some years after that.[9] What is of interest here, are the questions and challenges contemporaries faced in bringing the North-West under their control and under "good law" in the nineteenth century. As such, the task at hand is to chart the steps taken during the nineteenth century to create a legal culture that was explicable and enforceable in a period of imperial expansion, but also of jurisdictional confusion.

The events that caused the confused situation evident in 1870 and, to some extent, the extraterritorial jurisdictional problems that came to plague the British in North America, appear to have been the result of the initial pattern of settlement on the continent. Typically, English settlers created a colony on the coast that later settlers extended along the eastern seaboard. This was in contradistinction to the French practice of penetrating the hinterland. Over time, various types of colony were founded. The earliest was that organized by a joint stock company whose aim was to procure land, populate it and cultivate it, and so to create commercial wealth for its stockholders. Virginia, the first English colony, was of this type. Its Charter was a royal grant of 1607 from James I to the Virginia Company, whose governor and Court sat in the permanent headquarters in London, and whose members had purchased stock in the company.[10] The first colonists (all male) were considered to have taken peaceful possession of virgin land, the approximate and vague extent of which was specified in the Charter.[11] By the terms of the Charter, English law compatible with local conditions in force on the date of the Charter's proclamation explicitly became the law of the colony.[12] Thereafter the London Company enacted ordinances to suit the colonial conditions, since English statutes enacted after the Charter came into force would not bind the colony unless the specific Charter was named in the legislation.[13] When women, wives and children came to join the first settlers and conditions began to resemble those in England, a Legislature was convened. The Virginia House of Burgesses whose first session was held in 1619, twelve years after the first settlers arrived, was such a Legislature, and thus law-making in Virginia became similar to law-making in England. Very evidently, this system of government suited the settlers because they grew in numbers and wealth and, with neighbouring colonies, began to penetrate the hinterland in search of new land for settlement. There was, of course, opposition from the indigenous peoples to this westward wave of settlement. They were understandably angered and dismayed at being forced to give up their ancestral lands, and they exacted a heavy toll from the settlers. But they were steadily forced to retreat by the increasing number of Europeans and their superior weaponry. Hence, it was not until the last years of the seventeenth century, when the English came into abrasive contact with the outposts of the French Empire in North America, that the English advance was halted. Subsequently, after years of friction and bloodshed between the two powers, undeclared war in North America ensued in 1754, and two years later merged with the global conflict between France and Britain and their several allies. Seven years later, in 1763, the Treaty of Paris extinguished French dominion in North America.

If there was any rejoicing over this settlement among settlers and land agents waiting to trek west, it was short-lived because soon after the Treaty of Paris came into force, the Royal Proclamation of 1763 caused a border to be drawn along the western reaches of the Atlantic colonies.[14] Extending this "proclamation line" to the north was the border of the new colony of Quebec, while to the west and southwest an immense area of land designated "Indian Territory" was set aside as tribal hunting grounds, and was thus outside the jurisdiction of any European system of law. Entry into the Indian Territory was prohibited absolutely to all Europeans, excepting those licensed by the British authority to trade with the tribes at military posts, whose personnel enforced the provisions of the Royal Proclamation. That this prohibition was not wholly effective is demonstrated by the fact that within two years it became necessary to include legislation in the annual *Mutiny Act* for the apprehension of persons suspected of having committed offences in the Indian Territory and for their transport to and trial in the nearest British colony, according to the law of that jurisdiction.[15] This inconvenient, costly and time-consuming procedure was not welcomed by the military and other authorities, who were required to transport the accused, witnesses and evidence to the jurisdiction that would try the accused—and that could be hundreds of miles distant. General Thomas Gage, the British commander-in-chief, and his superintendent of Indian Affairs, Sir William Johnson, would have preferred to try such offenders on the spot by court marshal, but their preference was overruled. However, Johnson accurately predicted that accused persons subject to this procedure would be acquitted "for want (as it may be said) of all the necessary Law proofs."[16] It is obvious that this provision failed to bring the problem under control, since it was subsequently necessary to amplify and re-enact the legislation, with the final version being the most ample and definitive.[17] In part, it was laid down that:

> If any Person, not being a Soldier, shall commit any Crime or Offence in any [place] within His Majesty's Dominions in *America*, which [is] not within the...Jurisdiction of any Civil Government hitherto established, it shall...be lawful for any Person to apprehend such Offender, and to carry him...before the Commanding Officer for the Time being of his Majesty's forces there [who] shall convey and deliver with all convenient Speed, every such offender to the civil magistrate of the next adjoining Colony, together with the cause of his...Detainer [where] it shall be lawful to prosecute and try every such Offence in the Court of suc...Colony where Crimes...of the like Nature are usually tried, and where the same would be properly tried, in case such Crime...had been committed within the Jurisdiction of such Court; and such Court shall proceed therein to Trial, Judgement, and Execution, in the same manner as if such Crime...had really been committed within the Jurisdiction of such Court.[18]

This Act was due to expire in 1777, but by this time events had been overtaken by war and the legislation had lapsed. However, some 25 years later similar legislation was enacted in an attempt to correct a similar problem, with similar antecedents, in the newly-defined British North America.

Apart from the fact that the coastline of Rupert's Land's territorial grant did not front on the Atlantic, the origin and early development of the Government and Company of Adventurers trading into Hudson's Bay followed a similar course to that of its sister joint stock colonies on the eastern seaboard. However, while the latter welcomed settlers, the Hudson's Bay Company, as it became known, did not. It was a strictly commercial venture to monopolize the trade in fur, with an all-male work force that did grow, but not by natural increase. Hence, although it was a colony of Great Britain's for 200 years, no Legislature ever sat in Rupert's Land. The Company was brought into existence in 1670 by a Royal Charter that, inter alia, gave vague definition to Rupert's Land (all the territory within the height of land surrounding Hudson's Bay[19]), gave it monopoly of trade in the area and over Hudson's Bay itself, introduced English law as of the date of the Charter, empowered the governor and court in London to enact laws "for the good government of the said Company" and gave the Company jurisdiction to s and installment is

September 2010 to September 2012
Lethbridge, AB

October 2012 to January 8, 2013
Lethbridge, AB

Sales
Lethbridge, AB
September 2010 to September 2012

ided the same are reasonable and
In Rupert's Land, the appointed
to judge company personnel "in
ng to the laws of this Kingdom."[21]
n of the Privy Council,[22] unless
governor and court in London,
ngland of 1670. Again, as in the
pread along the shoreline of the
s bartered trade goods for pelts
ped to England relatively quickly
Bay. But here the similarity with
because it was not land hunger
posts in the interior; rather, it
npany had to meet the compe-
ence who, by long and devious
villages and camps of western

and the Treaty of Paris in 1763 ended rivalry at the national level, but ushered in a period of even more intense competition for pelts as British capital in Montreal-backed independent and aggressive fur trading companies who took over the old French routes and tactics. Initially the contest was among the independents themselves, since the Hudson's Bay Company posts, being far to the north, offered no challenge to the independents. In addition, employees of the Company were salaried personnel who had no share in the profits and who, from an early date, were under orders to avoid conflict with the indigenous peoples and other Europeans.[24] As the competition for pelts intensified, friction among the independents increased. In an attempt to obviate the problem, several independents combined to form the North West Company in 1787.[25] Nevertheless, friction with the remaining independents increased and the problem of law enforcement became acute. Moreover, as personnel of the smaller companies pushed further to the west, they entered regions that were clearly outside the vague boundary of Rupert's Land. Crimes committed there were outside the jurisdiction of whatever law-enforcement machinery the Company might possess, as the murder of John Ross in 1787 demonstrates. Ross, a partner in an independent company, was in charge of its operation along the Athabasca River. Peter Pond, a partner in the North West Company, and an individual already infamous for murdering Jean Etienne Wadden at

Lac La Ronge in 1782, had his post nearby.[26] In the spring of 1787 Pond ordered three of his men to rob Ross of a load of pelts. In the ensuing altercation, one Péché shot and killed Ross. Péché remained at large, but in some unexplained manner his two accomplices were arrested and transported to Montreal, over 2,000 miles away, where they were charged with the crime. There they were released by a committee of privy councillors convened in 1788 by the governor-general, Lord Dorchester, on the grounds that there was not enough evidence to send them to trial.[27]

Dorchester's committee had not been formed to deal only with the murder of Ross; rather, it sat to determine how to prosecute several prisoners who had been sent to Montreal from areas outside the jurisdiction of Quebec courts and from former British possessions that were now in unorganized United States territory. Several expedients were proposed, including prosecution pursuant to a statute of Henry VIII that provided for the trial in England of certain offences committed abroad. Interim measures were taken, but no firm decisions were made. Hence, Dorchester sent the committee's report to Lord Sydney, the home secretary, with a letter in which he requested "his Majesty's commands on this important subject as soon as may be."[28] He went on to give a sketch of the lucrative fur trade in the northwest, and the considerable number of persons involved that would no doubt be the source of further problems. Dorchester was prescient in this respect because when, in 1800, the remaining independent fur companies united as the XY Company, the conflict between the North West Company and the XY Company became a bitter and bloody feud, and they both began to take on the Hudson's Bay Company, whose personnel now vied for pelts with the two new companies from posts ever deeper to the south and west.[29] In the meantime, Lord Sydney said that he had not been able to "receive His Majesty's commands" in respect of Dorchester's request, but that he had received advice from the Attorney General and the Solicitor General that Dorchester did not have the authority to authorize the measures taken provisionally by his committee. They went on to suggest that the only solution was that "some provision must be made by [the Imperial] Parliament" to give the courts of the province the necessary jurisdiction, and there the matter rested.[30] After more bloodshed among the Montreal companies,[31] Robert Milnes, lieutenant-governor of Lower Canada, was moved late in 1802 to summarize the situation, stressing the "the growing importance of the [fur trade] to the Mother country." He suggested that, in accordance with advice from the Bench, a likely solution of the problem would be for the Imperial Parliament to enact legislation similar to that of 1775, whereby persons accused of crime in the Indian Territories would be transported to Lower Canada for trial and punishment.[32] Since it was evident from Milnes's submission that the problem was far worse than that which had prevailed in the Indian Territory created by the Royal Proclamation of 1763, Prime Minister Henry Addington's administration decided to respond to the situation, and the result was the *Canada Jurisdiction Act* of August 11, 1803.[33]

The *Canada Jurisdiction Act* combined aspects of both the Royal Proclamation of 1763 and the legislation of 1775. It defined a new territorial entity, the "Indian Territories," and erected a competent jurisdiction for that entity.[34] However, in attempting to combine a relatively complex definition with an administrative procedure in a short piece of legal writing, those who drafted the Act did neither task well, and so provided material for a controversy that is still not settled and that has generated considerable legal fees.[35] This was not surprising when it is considered that in 1837 Lord Melbourne, then prime minister, could say "How could one expect to show interest in a country like Canada where a salmon would not rise to a fly?"[36] If his interest in Canada was so low then, one wonders how Prime Minister Addington would have characterized Canada three decades earlier, in 1803, when there is not even mention of Canada, the fur trade or the Hudson's Bay Company in his two biographies? The problem was that Westminster was 6,000 miles distant from the seat of the problem, and neither of the individuals who were responsible for the legislation, Attorney General Spencer Percival and Solicitor General Thomas Manners-Sutton, had ever been further afield than France. Moreover, it is unlikely that they or their draftsmen had any conception of the distance between Montreal and Lake Winnipeg or the Peace River, the extreme weather conditions that prevailed in the North-West, or the modes of transportation in use there. They were all, no doubt, eminent barristers (and the jargon of the law permeates the Act), but they knew little or nothing about the Hudson's Bay Company or its jurisdiction in British North America. Furthermore, while the legislation may have been of consuming interest to Montreal fur-trading companies, it was unlikely that it was even on the horizon of many British members of Parliament, for Britain had declared war on France three months earlier. The immediate concerns of Parliament were to provide manpower for the ships of the Royal Navy and to re-enlist the battalions of the army, both of which had been decimated by Prime Minister Addison's administration in the previous three years.[37] Understandably, the legislation for British North America got short shrift.

In summary: on Saturday, July 30, 1803 it was *ordered* that leave be given to bring in a Bill for extending the Jurisdiction of the Courts of Justice, in the Provinces of *Lower* and *Upper Canada*, to the trial and punishment of persons guilty of crimes and offences out of the limits of the said Provinces: And that Mr. Attorney General and Mr. Solicitor General do prepare, and bring in, the same."[38] The bill was given first reading on August 2 and second reading and committal on August 3; the Committee of the Whole House considered it on August 4, and third reading was held on August 5. On August 10 the Lords agreed to the bill, and it was given royal assent on August 11.[39]

The preamble to the resulting Act that defines the Indian Territories by implication only is as follows:

> Whereas Crimes and Offences have been committed in the *Indian* Territories, and other parts of *America*, not within the Limits of the Provinces of *Lower* or *Upper Canada*...or of the Jurisdiction of any of the courts established in those Provinces, or within the Limits of any Civil Government of the United States of *America*, and are therefore not cognizable by any Jurisdiction whatever....[40]

Nowhere, it will be noted, is there mention of Rupert's Land, nor is it alluded to in the remainder of the text. Therefore it would seem that it is included in the "*Indian* Territories and other parts of *America*." On the other hand, it is stated that "Crimes and Offences" in those parts "are therefore not cognizable by any jurisdiction whatever." Yet, it is an undeniable fact that the Charter of the Hudson's Bay Company gave it jurisdiction in Rupert's Land and that it had managed its affairs there tolerably well for over 100 years. Therefore Rupert's Land could not be included in "*Indian* Territories, and other parts of *America*."[41] If a lay reader can arrive at these two mutually exclusive propositions before the end of the first clause of the preamble, it is not difficult to imagine what a skilled legal mind could do with these words in court. One of the main provisions of the Act vested authority in the governor of Lower Canada to appoint "Civil Magistrates and Justices of the Peace for any of the Indian Territories...for the purpose only of hearing crimes and offences, and committing any person guilty...of any crimes or offences, in order to his... being conveyed to the said Province of Lower Canada to be dealt with according to law,"[42] and such justices could be resident in the Indian Territories or in Upper or Lower Canada. Additionally, the governor of Lower Canada could authorize the trial of the accused in Upper Canada.[43] Much of this is reminiscent of the 1775 legislation, but the situation in 1803 was quite different. Whereas the committing authorities in former years were military commanders who would have been relatively impartial where civil offenders were concerned, the only men of the necessary stature and authority to be appointed justices of the peace in the Indian Territories would of necessity be senior partners of the competing fur-trading companies. In view of the events of the past years, the impartiality of such men was questionable. Moreover, the Act contained another clause that was almost a direct quotation from the previous legislation, to the effect that "any person or persons" were authorized to apprehend a suspected lawbreaker and hand him over to a justice of the peace, or to take him directly to Lower Canada for trial.

The Act of 1803 did nothing to stop the conflict in the North-West. The following years were a sad record of murder, mayhem and theft, even though Lieutenant-Governor Milnes commissioned five justices of the peace from the two Montreal companies.[44] The situation deteriorated further when the Montreal companies settled their differences and merged in 1804 to do business thereafter in the name of the North West Company. Their hitherto divided depredations were thus concentrated and in an attempt to monopolize the fur trade all the effort of the new concern was directed against the Hudson's Bay Company.[45] With the merger of the two trouble makers, the Canada Jurisdiction Act was a dead letter until 1809, when the Nor'Westers learned what an advantage it gave them.

During a dispute over the ownership of furs at the Hudson's Bay Company post at Eagle Lake (west of Lake Nipigon) in the autumn of 1809, a hostile party of Nor'Westers made an unprovoked attack on personnel of the London company. Aeneas Macdonell, a Nor'Wester, attacked and wounded John Mowat and others of the Hudson's Bay Company with his sword. Mowat and his companions were unarmed, but Mowat then procured a pistol and when the Nor'Wester made to attack him again, Mowat shot and killed Macdonell. News soon reached the North West Company and John Haldane, a partner in that company, and a large group of armed Nor'Westers came to arrest Mowat, but did not have a warrant to authorize the arrest. Evidently Haldane and his party overawed the men at Eagle Lake and it was agreed that they would take Mowat to Montreal for his trial and that two of his co-workers would accompany him as witnesses on his behalf. But the party did not go directly to Montreal. They stopped for the winter at the North West Company Post at Rainy River, where Mowat was kept in the irons of a convicted felon, and then moved on to Nor'Wester headquarters at Fort William. There,

A.S. Morton tells us, we would not want to know "the harrowing details of the treatment of Mowat after his appearance before Mr. Angus Morris, Justice of the Peace" and a senior partner in the North West Company, who charged him with murder, pursuant to the *Canada Justice Act*.[46] Mowat and his companions were not sent to Montreal until August 1810. In that city his companions were arrested and charged with aiding and abetting McDonnell's murder and, as the Hudson's Bay Company then had no agent in Montreal, all three were kept in jail for a further six months. Ultimately, justice did prevail, in part, and may have prevailed totally if the trial judge had disqualified himself from sitting.[47] The Montreal grand jury declined to indict Mowat's companions, but Mowat was convicted of manslaughter and was sentenced to six month's imprisonment and to be branded on the thumb.[48] Mowat was not released until September 1811, two years after the death of Macdonell. Throughout the proceedings, the men of the London company had undergone a harrowing experience and the Hudson's Bay Company was deprived of their services for a long period.

Legal opposition to the *Canada Jurisdiction Act* took some time to develop, and came about in a curious manner. In the first years of the century, Thomas Douglas, Lord Selkirk, became interested in encouraging emigration from Scotland and Ireland to British North America, and came to favour the area at the confluence of the Red and Assiniboine rivers in the south of Rupert's Land as a suitable location for an agricultural colony. He worked toward this end by becoming a large shareholder in the Hudson's Bay Company and in June 1811, by a vote of the governor and court, was granted 116,000 square miles of Rupert's Land that became known as the District of Assiniboia, an area that was more than twice the size of any of the Atlantic seaboard colonies.[49] Under the governance of Miles Macdonell, an army officer and a protégé of Selkirk's, no time was wasted in setting up and peopling the Red River colony, as it came to be called. Macdonell was appointed by Selkirk: he was commissioned governor of Assiniboia in the summer of 1811 by the governor of the Hudson's Bay Company, and in December of that year he was appointed justice of the peace by the governor-general in Quebec, as were eight other governors and senior officers of the Hudson's Bay Company in the North-West.[50] In 1812 the first settlers, all men, arrived at Red River to build housing for the settlement and to plant the first crops; more settlers, including women and children, arrived later that year and in the summer of 1813.[51] In 1814, Selkirk directed Governor Macdonell to create a court and to appoint a sheriff and constables, as well as a council to assist him on the bench.[52] To inform their joint deliberations on the bench, Selkirk sent Macdonell a document titled "Instructions Relative to Judicial Proceedings" and, perhaps, copies of William Blackstone's *Commentaries on the Laws of England* and Richard Burn's *Justice of the Peace*, both of which were referred to in the "Instructions" and were later found in the Red River library.[53]

At this time Rupert's Land had been an English colony for 140 years, and for that period had been without a Legislature and remained so for several more years. However, with the arrival of agricultural settlers in Assiniboia the instruments of civilization were being set in place for that jurisdiction in much the same manner as in the colonies on the eastern seaboard. While there was no gift of self-government, as such, it was pointed out in testimony before a committee of the Imperial House of Commons in 1857 that "The Principle inhabitants of Red River are themselves the councillors of Assiniboia, with the Governor" and that "they are appointed by the Company at the suggestion of the Governor, or on the application of any of the inhabitants."[54]

The grant to Selkirk in June 1811 occurred about two months after the trial of Mowat, so that there is little doubt that Selkirk, if he had not known of it before, soon became aware of the jurisdictional conflict between the Charter of the Hudson's Bay Company and the *Canada Jurisdiction Act*. If he had not done so previously, he then sought legal advice as to whether or not the Charter gave the Company sound title to jurisdiction in Rupert's Land. Whatever advice he got convinced him that the Company did have jurisdiction in Rupert's Land, and he therefore proceeded "to make the requisite arrangements for the proposed settlement."[55] In all probability, Selkirk's actions and the further deterioration in relations with the Nor'Westers caused the Hudson's Bay Company also to seek advice about its legal right to the territory of Rupert's Land and to jurisdiction within it. This would account for the opinions the Hudson's Bay Company solicited from George Holroyd and William Cruise in 1812, and from their colleague, James Scarlett, in 1813. The barristers all agreed that the Hudson's Bay Company did have civil and criminal jurisdiction in Rupert's Land, but they said so in different words and made different minor provisos.[56] The most definitive opinion was given in 1814 by five eminent counsel, including Holroyd, Cruise and Scarlett, who considered the Company's title to be well founded and, in part, stated that "We do not think this Act [the *Canada Jurisdiction Act*] gives jurisdiction within the territories of Hudson's Bay Company the same being within the jurisdiction of their own Governor and Council."[57] Their opinion suggested that there were therefore two jurisdictions in the North-West: Rupert's Land and the Indian Territories. This opinion gathers added weight from the fact that in the following year the Company published a code of penal laws for its Southern Department that was applicable to its employees and to "foreigners of whatever nation" and that laid down that "all Crimes, Offences or misdemeanours, that are cognizable by the Laws of England, will in future be punished according to the said Laws," and, presumably, would be enforced by the justices of the peace appointed in 1811.[58]

The justice of the peace who committed Mowat for trial in Lower Canada was a partner in the North West Company and following the precedent he set, committals pursuant to the *Canada Jurisdiction Act* were often made as a matter of company policy.[59] For example, in 1814 the sheriff of the Red River colony, John Spencer, was arrested on the order of Archibald McLeod, justice of the peace and a partner in the North West Company, for impounding Nor'Wester pemmican, as was Governor Macdonell the next year, and both were sent to Montreal for trial on a charge of larceny. On arrival at Montreal, the charges were dropped and both men were released.[60] If all committals and outcomes had been similar to this, the situation might have continued indefinitely, but they were not. Theft, assault and murder were committed.[61] The situation was brought to a head at Seven Oaks in 1816 when Macdonell's successor, Governor Semple, and 20 men of the Red River Colony were killed by Nor'Wester personnel, some of whom were apprehended, charged under the *Canada Jurisdiction Act* and sent to Montreal for trial. The outcome was predictable: all but one were acquitted.[62] The exception was Charles de Reinhard, a Nor'Wester, who was accused of murdering Owen Keveny of the Hudson's Bay Company in the aftermath of the killings at Red River. Reinhard was tried in Quebec City, found guilty and sentenced to be executed. But even he cheated the gallows because the question of where the murder took place was a bone of contention at the trial and the matter was therefore referred to the prince regent-in-council.[63] The decision was that the crime had taken place in the territory of Rupert's Land and that the *Canada Jurisdiction Act* was not in force in Rupert's Land because it was not named in the statute; so in the end, de Reinhard also went free.[64] Law was indeed ambiguous in the North West.

All these events caused a lengthy and voluminous correspondence between the governor-general of Canada, Sir John Sherbrooke, his successor, Lord Dalhousie, and the secretary for war and colonies, Lord Bathurst. However, in the end the spate of letter-writing did lead to some positive results.[65]

While the correspondence reflected many concerns—from anxiety over the perverted use of the Statute of 1803 to fear that the United States might interest itself in the North-West[66]—it is clear that the focus of their attention was on the continuing rivalry between the fur traders and on measures to bring this rivalry to an end.[67] The outcome was that Sherbrooke struck a Commission of Enquiry in October 1816, appointed its members as justices of the peace, and revoked the commissions of all magistrates appointed under the authority of the *Canada Jurisdiction Act* before that time. In his instructions to the commissioners, Sherbrooke specified that when reporting on recent events they were to "communicate the fullest information that [they could] obtain as to the circumstances there and of the persons implicated in them,"[68] but, strangely, he did not ask them to make recommendations for the prevention of further troubles. He was taken at his word, because the Commissioner's Report, which is 98 pages long, is confined to a comprehensive and factual review of the conflict between the two companies from 1810 on, and to the part played by the partisan magistrates. It was tabled in Parliament on July 12, 1819.

Since the Report was largely a recital of the conflict in the North-West between the London and the Montreal companies, it comes as no surprise to learn that Parliament's response, two years later, was the enactment of a bill entitled *An Act for Regulating the Fur Trade, and Establishing a Criminal and Civil Jurisdiction within Certain Parts of North America*.[69] The future regulation of the fur trade was settled clearly and unequivocally in the first two sections of the statute. These reserved to the Crown the right to grant monopolistic trading rights in any area of North America outside the territories of Britain, the United States, or the Hudson's Bay Company, to a single individual or company, for a period not to exceed 21 years.

The same clarity extends to several of the sections that amplify the provisions of the *Canada Jurisdiction Act* in respect of criminal and civil jurisdiction. In particular, section III spells out the responsibility of the Hudson's Bay Company in the execution of all civil and criminal procedures in Rupert's Land and in any future land grant. In order to ensure compliance with this provision, both the Company and any other future recipient of a grant to trade were required under a bond, later set at £5,000, to produce for trial any employee or person acting under company authority who was charged with a criminal offence. Thus, the responsibility for law enforcement was laid on the grantee. Furthermore, in a completely new departure, the Crown in England assumed the direct right to appoint justices of the peace in addition to those commissioned by the governor of Lower Canada. The jurisdiction of these Crown-appointed justices of the peace would extend "as well within any territories heretofore granted to the Company of Adventurers of *England* trading to *Hudson's Bay*, as within the *Indian* Territories of such other parts of *America* as aforesaid."[70] In addition, such magistrates could be authorized to hold courts of record within their jurisdictions, but they were not authorized to try criminal actions that could result in punishments of death, life imprisonment, transportation, or civil suits that involved property worth more than £200.[71]

While all these provisions are clear and straightforward, the parts of the Act that dealt with the question of whether the *Canada Jurisdiction Act* was in force in Rupert's Land are not. Section 5 laid down that

> the said Act...entitled An Act for extending the Jurisdiction of the Courts of Justice in the Provinces of Lower and Upper Canada, to the Trial and Punishment of Persons guilty of Crimes and Offences within certain Parts of North America adjoining to the said Provinces, and all the Clauses and Provisos therein contained, shall be...construed...to extend to and over, and to be in full force in and through all the Territories heretofore granted to the Company of Adventurers of England trading to Hudson's Bay; anything in any Act or Acts of Parliament, or this Act, or in any Grant or Charter to the Company, to the contrary notwithstanding.

The intention of this section seems evident—to include the maintenance of law in Rupert's Land within the scope of the current Act. However, the matter proved not to be that simple, for section 14 read:

> nothing in this Act contained shall be...construed to affect any Right, Privilege, Authority or Jurisdiction that the Governor and Company of...Hudson's Bay are by Law entitled to claim and exercise under their Charter; but that all such Rights, Privileges, Authorities and Jurisdictions shall remain in as full force, virtue and effect, as if this Act had never been made; anything in this Act to the contrary notwithstanding.

Obviously, there is a contradiction. Was the law of Rupert's Land to be the current law of Upper or Lower Canada as set out in section 5, or the English law specified in the Charter of 1670, as laid down in section 14? The question of what criminal law ran in Rupert's Land remained as ambiguous as ever. The question that arises is: who was responsible for the ambiguity? Apparently, it was Edward Ellice, a very wealthy Englishman who was a senior partner in Ellice, Inglis and Company, the London agents of the North West Company. Edward Ellice later became a senior official of the North West Company and of the Hudson' Bay Company in his own right. From his childhood on, Ellice had frequently visited North America for long periods and in 1803 he was actually employed in the Ellice office in Montreal. He was elected to the Imperial Parliament in 1818 and it was he who was the *eminence grise* in the negotiations that solved the problem of the warring fur trade companies.[72]

After the Red River Commissioner's Report had been tabled in Parliament in 1819, Bathurst exerted great pressure on the fur-trading companies to settle their differences and to bring about a union that would eliminate the intense competition. As an inducement, government sources let it be known that such an arrangement would meet with official approbation and concessions, whereas continued mayhem would result in drastic governmental action against both companies.[73] Behind the scenes, Ellice quietly offered to purchase Lord Selkirk's shares in the Hudson's Bay Company in 1819. If the offer had been accepted, this would have given Ellice a controlling interest in the company so that the North West Company could engross the fur trade and Ellice could arrange for the North West Company to use the shorter and faster route to the North-West through Hudson's Bay.[74] When the offer was refused, Ellice immediately turned his attention to arranging a merger of the two companies. Negotiations toward this end, in which Ellice acted for the North West Company, began in the winter of 1819 and were successfully concluded in March 1821 when the North West Company was merged with the Hudson's Bay Company and all interested parties did business thereafter in the name and under the Charter of the latter.[75] In so doing Ellice, to guard his considerable investment and to take maximum advantage of the 1670 Charter, threw all his considerable weight behind the proposition that the Hudson's Bay Company was sovereign in its jurisdiction. His intention was to undercut the *Canada Jurisdiction Act*, as his own account of events demonstrates. According to his testimony before the Select Committee on the Hudson's Bay Company in 1857, Ellice said that some time during 1819, Bathurst had sent for him and asked him to promote a union between the two companies.[76] Furthermore, Ellice asserted that at this time, he had "suggested to Lord Bathurst to propose a Bill to Parliament, which should enable the Crown to grant a license of exclusive trade [saving the right of the

Hudson's Bay Company over their territory], as well over the country to the east as over that beyond the Rocky Mountains, and extending to the Pacific Ocean, so that any competition that was likely to be injurious to the peace of the country should be thereafter prevented."[77] This, of course, became the *Act of 1821 for Regulation of the Fur Trade*. Ellice maintained that this Act did not extend Canadian jurisdiction over Rupert's Land, an interpretation he stuck to under further questioning, during which he said that had been instrumental in drafting the bill.[78] When Ellice discussed the clauses that provided for the appointment of justices of the peace by the Crown, he was explicit: "I put in those clauses myself, in order that the Crown or Canada might have the power of appointing justices under it; but it has never appointed any, therefore the clause is inoperative."[79]

It was fortunate that Ellice was still alive in 1857 and able to inform the Committee about what had transpired in Parliament in 1821 because they would not have found any information in parliamentary sources if he had been dead. While the account of the passage of the Bill of 1803 in Parliament was brief and uninformative, there was nonetheless a record. There was no record at all of the passage of the bill of 1821 in *Hansard's Parliamentary Debates*. Although Ellice and Bathurst both spoke at length to several Bills during the session of 1821, a page-by-page review of *Hansard* for 1821 failed to find any mention of fur, the fur trade, any allied enterprise, or the Hudson's Bay Company.[80] What it did reveal is that Parliament and the public were excised over the Bill of Pains and Punishments against Queen Charlotte, and that several hundred columns were devoted to this subject. As Ernest Woodward writes of this period, "the [colonies] were out of mind as well as out of sight."[81] Nevertheless, those who were in the know had no doubt as to who the author and promoter of the Bill to merge the fur companies was, as John Richardson—an old friend of Ellice's and a partner in the firm that contracted for the North West Company in Montreal—made clear in a letter to Ellice: "In respect to the negotiation and arrangements with the H.B. Co. none can be more disposed than I to give you full credit for your zeal and ability therein, and particularly in getting the Act of Parliament passed."[82]

In December 1821, after the amalgamation of the two companies, an exclusive grant to trade in the Indian Territories was made to the new version of the Hudson's Bay Company. Perhaps the best evidence of Ellice's veracity is the Company's almost immediate move to reform the administration of justice in Assiniboia, which it was enabled to do without let or hindrance since the moving force behind the settlement, Lord Selkirk, had died in 1820. In May 1822, the General Court of the Company in London passed an Ordinance which provided that the governor of Assiniboia and two councillors would, in addition to the administrative and legislative functions they had begun to exercise,[83] sit as a law court and try offences with the aid of the customary petit jury of twelve men.[84] This tribunal eventually came to be known as the General Court. Bathurst gave his blessing to this enactment in a letter in which he also said that the Crown would not at that time appoint magistrates under the provisions of the Act of 1821 and until the Crown moved, "the Resolutions of the 29th instant appear well calculated to preserve the peace and good government of that part of North America, under the jurisdiction of the Hudson's Bay Company."[85] Moreover, there was no doubt about what law was to run in that jurisdiction, at least not in the minds of the Governor and Court of the Company, because in the instructions to Andrew Bulger, the newly-appointed governor of Assiniboia, it was directed that he "administer justice according to the law of England under the provisions of the Charter;"[86] that is, pursuant to the law of 1670.

After a lapse of thirty years, this opinion was again confirmed by the Law Amendment Committee of the Council of Assiniboia in 1851. While deploring the fact that the law was outdated, the Committee nevertheless confirmed that it was the law of England of 1670, and it suggested adoption of English law of a later date.[87] This opinion must have raised some doubts in Governor William Caldwell's mind because he wrote to London questioning his competency to try cases where the judgement would involve sums exceeding £200. In answer he was informed that the "court being held under the authority of the charter within the Limits of Rupert's Land, its powers are not restricted as to the amount upon which the adjudication may be made, the rights held under the charter being reserved by the last clause of the Act [1 and 2] Geo. 4, c. 66."[88]

The final legislation enacted by the Imperial Parliament concerning criminal jurisdiction in British North America did not alter the position of the Company in any way, since Rupert's Land was specifically excluded from its provisions.[89] It was enacted to fill the gap left when the Company's exclusive right to trade in the Indian Territories expired in 1859 and with it, the responsibility of the Company to apprehend and produce lawbreakers for trial. The Act enlarged the powers of justices of the peace in the Indian Territories by authorizing them to set up courts of record wherein they could try any criminal charge by the law of the Colony of Canada, excepting those for which the penalty was death. Persons accused of such crimes were to be sent for trial to Canada or British

Columbia.[90] Thus, by the time the Hudson's Bay Company surrendered title of its lands and grants to the Crown in 1868, the jurisdictional tangle caused by Imperial enactments was acute. However, this was only one of three elements that comprised the law in the North-West at the time.

A second element of the law in the North-West lay in the fact that, pursuant to its Charter, the Hudson's Bay Company was enabled to make laws for the governance of its personnel, and that such laws had been enacted by the governor and council of Rupert's Land in 1815. Legislative activity may have occurred in the Red River settlement about the same time, but the record does not appear to have survived, and the earliest very brief and obscure account of such activity is in the minutes of the Council of Assiniboia for December 2, 1822.[91] It was not until 10 years later, in 1832, that the governor and council began to concern themselves with enacting local law and, in effect, began the creation of a municipal civil and criminal code. Naturally, they first concerned themselves with offences peculiar to the place and time and, among other things, took notice of rooting pigs on the loose, and provided that the owners of such animals were to be fined two shillings. Punitive fines of £10, or banishment from the settlement would be incurred for persons who set fires in the open, while a similar fine, or two months' hard labour, was specified for persons who committed "the felonious practice of taking horses away from their grazing without the consent of the owners, and riding or driving them in harness to a distance."[92] Since some offences came to be punished with imprisonment, a jail was built in 1835 to house those so convicted.

As the population of Red River increased, and after Assiniboia came under the direct control of the Hudson's Bay Company in 1836 when the then Lord Selkirk re-conveyed the property to the London Company, the Council of Assiniboia increased its legislative and legal activity.[93] In 1839, the municipality was divided into districts, each to have a court of two magistrates, with appeals and some cases of first instance heard by the General Court that would now sit quarterly with petit juries chosen according to a procedure laid down in the Council minutes. Although the governor and council were steadily increasing the body of municipal law in Red River and gave substantial justice to litigants that emphasized conciliation rather than the adversarial procedure favoured by common law advocates, no governor or councillor had been educated to the law, and so could have been vulnerable to a challenge from a common lawyer.

This was evident to George Simpson, the HBC's governor in North America; he therefore appointed Adam Thom to the judicial appointment of Recorder of Red River in 1839. Thom was a Scot who had been educated in the formal and adversarial style of the common law, and he had drafted much of Lord Durham's Report of 1838; perhaps more to the point, he was a friend of Simpson's.[94] Thom was a stickler for the letter of the law and under his direction the General Court lost its characteristic informality and became more decorous and formal and he introduced elements of the common law that were, in his opinion, lacking. For example, from the first year of his tenure Thom convened a grand jury, an institution of English common law that needed no formal proclamation, to approve or negate the bill of indictment laid against a person accused of a felony.[95] Thom was also the senior member of the governor's council and under his influence successive Councils gave a great deal of attention to unsatisfactory local conduct, and enacted longer and more comprehensive codes to encompass such behaviour and to provide appropriate penalties. Hence, in 1841,[96] 1851[97] and 1852[98] revised codes that were largely Thom's work came into force. The last revision by the Council of Assiniboia, that of 1862,[99] while not compiled by Thom, was based on his general plan. Moreover, Thom not only influenced the Council members to vote for new codes of municipal law, he also made them, as well as his superiors in the Company, the grand and petit jurors, and all and sundry in Red River whom he could reach, aware of the fact that the law of Rupert's Land, and thus of Assiniboia, was the English law of 1670, and that such law was inadequate.[100] Accordingly, the Council expressed its dissatisfaction with the existing law at length in the preamble to the 1851 Code and, following this line of reasoning in 1862, enacted that

> In place of the laws of England of the date of the Hudson's Bay Company's Charter, the Laws of England of the date of Her Majesty's accession so far as they may be applicable to the condition of this Colony shall regulate the proceedings of the General Court till some higher authority or this Council shall have expressly provided either in whole or in part to the contrary.[101]

Thus, the law of 1670 was substituted by that of 1837. But as the years went by this would have deprived the jurisdiction of the tremendous amelioration of English criminal law that was in the process of enactment in the years following 1837.[102] Accordingly, in 1864 the Council provided that "the proceedings of the General court shall be regulated by the laws of

England, not only of the date of her present Majesty's accession so far as they may apply to the condition of the Colony, but also by all such laws of England of subsequent date as may be applicable to the same."[103] Hence, if a person had been accused of a serious criminal offence in Assiniboia after January 7, 1864, he or she would have been tried under the criminal law then in force in England.

Thom also practiced what he preached. There was not much serious crime in Red River or, indeed, in the North-West after the merger of the Hudson's Bay and the North West Companies in 1821, and in only one case, in 1837, was an accused person sent to Lower Canada for trial.[104] However, after Thom's arrival in 1839, trials of those accused of felonies or misdemeanours in the North-West were held in Red River before Mr. Recorder Thom and the governor, notwithstanding the fact that pursuant to the Acts of 1803 and 1821 magistrates in the Rupert's Land and the Indian Territories were required to send to the Canadas any person charged with a capital offence. Thom's reasons for assuming jurisdiction in such cases are perhaps best expressed in the Opinion he delivered in *The Public Interest* v. *Calder*,[105] a case of murder committed near the Peace River in 1848.[106] Moreover, Roy St. George Stubbs, who quotes extensively and with approval from Thom's Opinion, informs us that Mr. Justice Killam of the Manitoba Queen's bench endorsed Thom's decision on jurisdiction in his judgement in *Sinclair* v. *Mulligan* and that Killam's judgement was affirmed by the Manitoba Court of Appeal.[107] It should also be observed that, like Edward Ellice's machinations in the 1820s, Thom, the good servant of the Hudson's Bay Company, made an unstated case for the proposition that the jurisdiction of his court was as good or better than that of the Province of Canada. It also undoubtedly saved the company a good deal of money because no accused persons, food, equipment or guards had to make the long journey to Canada. The case citation of *Calder* may cause some surprise, but it can be explained by the fact that Thom was also an innovator. His court was not a Crown tribunal and it had been made clear to him by Governor Simpson that he was first and foremost a employee of the Hudson's Bay Company; so Thom faced a problem when an indictment was drafted against a person charged with a felony. He could not use the familiar "*The Queen* v. *Roe*" or "*R.* v *Doe*," nor would he have chosen "*The Hudson's Bay Company* v. *Doe*"—not only because civil cases were cited in the latter style, but also because of the adverse publicity it would attract from the enemies of the Company who could then complain that the Company was usurping the prerogative of the Crown. Instead he chose the colourless but expressive phrase "The Public Interest." Thus we find "*The Public Interest vs. Kapenesweet*," a case of murder in 1845, and "*The Public Interest* v. *Peter Hayden*," another murder case heard in 1846.[108]

The third element of the criminal law was a number of Imperial statutes that were in force in all British colonial possessions. These covered a broad spectrum, ranging from homicide on the high seas to the validity of Imperial writs of *habeas corpus* in the colonies. [109] While many of these statutes were inapplicable in the North-West by reason of being offences committed on the high seas, several could have been enforced there, particularly those relating to coinage offences.

It is therefore evident that no definitive answer can be given to the question: What system of criminal law was in force in the North-West when it was admitted to the Canadian Union? Moreover, since a diverse group of learned men, including judges, lawyers and historians have subsequently disagreed in answering the question, it is equally apparent that the question is unlikely ever to receive a definitive answer. In line with this reasoning, the sole purpose of the following summary is to demonstrate that reasonable men, arguing from a basis of authoritative documentary evidence, could arrive at contradictory conclusions as to what system of criminal law was in force.

From the theoretical viewpoint, the lawyer C.C. McCaul argued that Assiniboia, the remainder of Rupert's Land, and the Indian Territories comprised one large jurisdiction that was subject to the law of Upper Canada, and based his argument on an interpretation of the Acts of 1803 and 1821.[110] It was the opinion of Edward Ellice that there were two jurisdictions in the North-West: Rupert's Land and the Indian Territories, and that the English law of 1670 governed the former and the law of Upper Canada the latter.[111] The statutes of 1803 and 1821 are also the basis for this interpretation and that is also the way Mr. Justice Killam viewed the situation, although his Judgement was based on the provisions of the Charter.[112] In debate in the Commons with Sir John A. Macdonald, David Mills argued that there were three jurisdictions: the two recognized by Ellice and Killam, and the District of Assiniboia. However, he did not specify what law was in force there and since his remarks were paraphrased in the *Debates* it is difficult to follow his argument, but there is no doubt that it is based on constitutional stepping stones.[113] Finally, there is E.E. Rich's contention that, as of 1803, the criminal law of Rupert's Land and the Indian Territories was that of Lower Canada.[114] This then was the state of the criminal law as interpreted by these authoritative individuals when the North-West became part of Canada on July 15, 1870.

If this situation was known in Ottawa, it is a fair question to ask why the Dominion Government took many years to rectify the situation and why Parliament did not at once proclaim the criminal law of Canada to extend throughout the North-West Territories.[115] No evidence has as yet been found to answer this question directly, but there appear to be several reasons why the government proceeded with caution. Perhaps the first, although not the most obvious, is that parts of the relatively sophisticated system resulting from the process of amendment and consolidation of the criminal law of the former colonies would have been inappropriate in a western setting.[116] To introduce Canadian Law without first determining what the western situation was might have been extremely foolhardy; it might even have stirred up a hornet's nest, as the unfortunate William McDougall had done in the winter of 1869 at Red River, when he had attempted to enforce Canadian legislation for the temporary government of Rupert's Land.[117] Moreover, at that time, Ottawa had no means of enforcing criminal law in the Territories for there was neither a police force to bring offenders to book, nor a judiciary competent to administer the new law. In any case and whatever the cause, the Dominion Government chose to move slowly.

In fact, in its first legislation in 1869 concerning the Territories, Parliament did not appear to move at all, because it stipulated that all laws in force in the North-West Territories at Union were to remain in force, and that all judicial personnel were to remain in office.[118] Thus magistrates appointed during the regime of the Company continued to dispense the local law while that law was frozen in the form it had held on Union. This was so because the Imperial Act that ceded the Territories to Canada gave Ottawa the exclusive right to legislate for the Territories in all matters without reservation.[119] Since Ottawa did not choose to exercise its powers and continued to maintain the *status quo*,[120] the move that began the resolution of the legal tangle in the North-West had the effect of confirming the position always held by the Hudson's Bay Company; that is to say, there were two jurisdictions in the North-West. This move was made by the enactment of the Imperial statute of 1872[121] that repealed the *Canada Jurisdiction Act*. Thus, until Ottawa made a move, there was no doubt that the English criminal law of 1670, supplemented by local municipal ordinances, ran in Rupert's Land because this measure also invalidated the fifth clause of the 1821 Act providing that the *Canada Jurisdiction* Act was to be enforced within the Company's boundaries. The Indian Territories did not thereby lose its criminal law, since the 1859 Act that provided for the administration of justice in those parts remained in force.[122] That British legislators became aware of the anomaly caused by their Act of 1872 there is no doubt, because two years later they repealed c. 5 of the 1821 Act and that clause alone.[123] However, this state of affairs did not last long, for in 1873 the Canadian Parliament passed amending legislation to the *Territories' Government Act* that completely changed the situation in the North-West. In effect, this short, two-page statute created a single jurisdiction by enacting that almost the whole body of Canadian criminal law—20 separate acts covering 270 pages—was to apply and be enforced in the North-West Territories.[124] That it completely superseded the English law of 1670 there can be no doubt, because a section-by-section comparison of Lord Chief Justice Hale's *Pleas of the Crown* that expounds the criminal law of England c.a. 1670[125] and Ottawa's legislation reveals that the latter is far more comprehensive and detailed than the former. For example, when a prisoner stood mute in Hale's day when asked to plead, he was subjected to *peine fort et dure*; that is to say, to having weights piled on his body until he either entered a plea or he died.[126] In a specific subsection, the Canadian legislation lays down that for a prisoner who refuses to plead, a plea of "not guilty"[127] must be entered on the record. Again, Hale discusses benefit of clergy at great length—who may claim it and under what circumstances.[128] In one line, the Canadian enactment abolished benefit of clergy.[129] In addition, the Act of 1873 also superseded English statutes relating to coinage offences that were in force in the colonies.

Furthermore, if by any chance some part of the boundaries of the old District of Assiniboia projected beyond the borders of the new Province of Manitoba (David Mills maintained that there was such a projection[130]) and thus extended the reach of the few pre-1870 criminal ordinances into a part of the Territories, the Canadian statutes would have superseded all of these. In short, the effect of the Dominion legislation of 1873 would have been to cause a person accused of a criminal offence in the North-West Territories to be charged and sentenced in accordance with the provisions of Canadian legislation, provided that the offence was comprehended in the statutes. If it was not, it would go unpunished, or the offender would be dealt with according to local custom. This anomaly was caused by the fact that a small number of criminal statutes had not been extended to the Territories.

The statutes that had not been extended to the Territories were of three types: legislation that at that time had no application in the Territories, such as an act that laid down penalties for attempting to persuade soldiers and sailors to desert; measures that were framed for only one province; and statutes that were drafted for enforcement in a social milieu different from that which prevailed in the West, such as the act respecting vagrancy.[131] Enforcing such a law in the conditions then prevailing could have been extremely dangerous since, by definition, many Aboriginals would have qualified as vagrants.[132] Moreover, the cost of enforcement would have been high in both money and the manpower of the magistrates and police officers also provided for by legislation in 1873.

It was this legislation and the promptness with which it was enforced that made the eventual Canadian response so much superior to any made before. All previous legislation had provided only for the appointment of magistrates who were invariably officers of the fur-trading companies and thus far from impartial, and had laid the onus of police work on local initiative or a private company. Ottawa's enactment, on the other hand, had not only provided for the appointment of stipendiary magistrates but it also authorized the raising of a police force for the North-West.[133] Moreover, the North West Mounted Police force was formed and on its way west in little more than a year, by which time further legislation had made its commissioner a stipendiary magistrate and all his officers *ex officio* justices of the peace.[134] In a very real sense, the law and its enforcers went west together in 1874.

During the next decade, statute criminal law in the Territories kept pace with the rest of Canada, as Ottawa put in force new statutes and amending legislation to old ones by means of acts applicable only to the Territories. These acts also continually enlarged the powers of stipendiary magistrates who, by 1876, included not only the new Commissioner of the North West Mounted Police, but also his predecessor and two civilian appointees.[135] Each of the latter three men was based in one of the incipient jurisdictions of the Territories (Alberta, Saskatchewan and Assiniboia) and travelled on circuit to hear cases at various locations.[136] With these additions, the North-West Territories had, in comparison with anything that had gone before, a coherent body of criminal law and an efficient and practical system by which to administer it. There were also some innovations: since there was no senior tribunal in the Territories, appeals from judgements there were to be heard by the Court of Queen's Bench in Manitoba; there was to be a jury of six in criminal cases, and the grand jury was abolished.[137]

At the time Adam Thom convened the first grand jury at Red River in 1839, it was coming under intense criticism in England.[138] It was a venerable common law institution whose antecedents stretched back to Anglo-Saxon times and whose first appearance in statutory form was as the jury of presentment defined in the Assizes of Clarendon and Northampton.[139] Its function was to name the persons of the jurisdiction who, by common repute, were suspected of having committed felonies and to "present" this information to the royal judiciary in what came to be known as a bill of indictment. Over the years it came to be known as the grand jury because it consisted of 23 jurors, and its duty was enlarged to include the investigation of many aspects of life at first hand, as required by the king's justices. For example, it could be instructed to find out why many individuals complained of short measure in the market. The grand jury investigated and then "presented" to the bench that Alfred, the keeper of the measures, needed a new set of scales. Eventually, and in addition to its criminal role, which was becoming increasingly redundant, the institution came to be influential in many of the activities now performed by local government, such as the building and repair of roads, bridges, and municipal buildings. As an editorial in the *Canadian Law Journal* remarked, this system was "a sort of county council and a local executive body."[140] Since civil government is funded by the taxpayer of the municipality and the grand jury was an unpaid institution, the taxpayer was not eager to see either the non-criminal functions of the grand jury scaled down nor the institution abolished. It was in this form that the grand jury came to the old provinces of Canada.

Needless to say, grand jurors and municipal taxpayers in Canada were no more inclined to see the decline or demise of the institution than those in England, and woe betide any provincial government that made any serious attempt to achieve this end.[141] The first public criticism of the institution in Canada came from Mr. Justice Gwynne of the Ontario bench in an address to the grand jury of Kingston in 1869. The judge argued that, in effect, the criminal side of the grand jury had become redundant with the enactment of the *County Attorney Act* in 1857, which provided for what are now known as Crown prosecutors to aid the magistrate in his preliminary investigation.[142] Now, said Gwynne, before the grand jury even heard of the case, "the charges [had] already undergone a preliminary examination before magistrates, aided in most cases by counsel of the Crown Attorney."[143] What was the point, Gwynne asked, of repeating the process before the grand jury? Thereafter, the question was taken up and debated in the media and in government. In 1877 the Attorney General in Ottawa intimated in correspondence with the Oliver Mowat, the Ontario Attorney General and premier, that the Dominion government was contemplating legislation to cut down or abolish the grand jury. However, this initiative was complicated by a constitutional question: who had jurisdiction over the grand jury? Mowat, a former lawyer and judge who had introduced bills to amend jury legislation in Upper Canada and Ontario since 1859,[144] contended that "the abolition of Grand Juries is not within the authority of the Dominion Government; that the Grand Jury is part of the constitution of the court and is not a matter of mere procedure."[145] Ottawa dissented and the parties agreed to refer the question to the Supreme Court. But this was never done and, by default, the constitution of all juries in provincial courts is part of the constitution of the court. However, in 1875 when the public debate about the grand jury was in full swing, the North-West Territories was a dependent of the Dominion government. Taking advantage of this fact, Ottawa abolished the grand jury in the Territories and after Alberta became a province in 1905 no action was taken by the Legislature to revive the institution.

A somewhat similar development took place respecting the petit jury; it too was a venerable common law institution that had developed out of the grand jury. It was composed of 12 jurors, which was also the norm for petit juries in the provinces of Canada. The function of the petit jury was to render a verdict of guilty or not guilty in a trial that came about as a result of the grand jury finding a bill of indictment against an accused. However, after Union, and with the lure of free land, immigration from the east increased and by 1880 immigrants were spread thinly across a land area about the size of Alberta today to form a population of about 17,000.[146] With such a dearth of inhabitants it would be difficult, if not impossible, to find 12 persons suitably qualified to form a jury in any given location in the Territories, except Red River. Provision for this shortcoming was made in the Dominion legislation of 1880, which provided that if punishment for an offence would exceed five years, a magistrate sitting with a justice of the peace was to try the accused with a jury not exceeding six persons.[147] Six was the number of jurors specified in an early Ordinance of the North-West Territories Legislature and in the Ordinances of the Territories adopted by Alberta in 1905[148] by virtue of the section in the Criminal Code that specified that its provision for a 12-person jury was superseded by that of the North-West Territories Act of 1880.[149] In the first Alberta legislation respecting juries in 1921, it is stated that "Every jury shall consist of six persons." This was enforced in all cases; there is no mention of criminal or civil juries. The wording remained unchanged in several amendments to the Jury Act over the next 45 years, until 1966 when it was enacted that "In civil proceedings a jury shall consist of six persons;"[150] there was no mention of criminal juries.

Hence, from 1880 to 1966, the trial jury in the area that is now Alberta was a jury of six persons, and it was the only province to retain that distinction.[151]

However, there was a theoretical fly in the ointment in the 1880s that became all too apparent during the trial of Louis Riel. Only statute law had been extended to the Territories. Nothing had been said about the common law in which statutes are enmeshed.[152] It will be recalled that Canadian criminal statutes were a consolidation of all the similar enactments of the several colonies that confederated.[153] Each of these colonies had, in one way or another, received English law as of a certain date. From that point on, colonial legislators had abolished, changed or otherwise amended this basic body of law as required by conditions in North America. In the courts, judges had interpreted this law as necessary for the administration of justice, during which process they had drawn on common law not only from their own jurisdiction, but also from other common law jurisdictions. [154] Their decisions became precedents for the future, and in this way a body of case law was generated. Thus, after Confederation, a judge in any of the provinces could rest his decision on a coherent and unbroken line of statutes and common law dating back through the reception of English law to the earliest English decisions. In theory, the body of common law after 1670 was denied to Territorial magistrates because it did not form part of the legal development of the North-West Territories. [155] Moreover, it will be recalled that David Mills had attempted to rectify this situation with a bill that would have brought into effect in the Territories the common law of 1878, but no legislation had resulted.[156] Nevertheless, case law was used to arrive at decisions by the bench in the Territories. Perhaps the most obvious example was in 1885 during the Riel trial in Regina when several references were made to *M'Naghten's Case*, which had been tried in 1843.[157]

With the impetus caused by the wide publicity given to the Riel trial, the bench received rapid and retroactive sanction for its use of case law in a statute enacted in 1886. The Bill was introduced to Parliament by the minister of justice, John Thompson, himself a lawyer and a former judge of the Supreme Court of Nova Scotia, "to bring in force there the common law at any rate."[158] His objective was attained when it was enacted that "the laws of England relating to civil and criminal matters, as the same existed on the fifteenth day of July, in the year of our Lord one thousand eight hundred and seventy, shall be in force in the Territories, in so far as the same are applicable to the Territories.[159] Now, in matters that Ottawa had not legislated on, English statutes could be resorted to, and the whole body of case law that subsumedthatoftheCanadianUnionwouldbeatthedisposalofthemagistrates. A further provision of the 1886 Act put the Territories on the same footing as the rest of the Dominion in terms of the applicability of statute law by enacting that all general statutes then in force, and all those to be proclaimed hence-forth, were to apply to the North-West Territories.[160] When this legislation came into effect, the criminal law in the Territories became the most com-prehensive and up-to-date in Canada. Finally, the administration of justice was made to keep pace with the enlarged body of law, the rapidly increasing population and the creation of three electoral districts by the newly-erected Legislature of the Territories, by providing for the creation of a supreme court for the North-West Territories.[161]

With the passage of this Act, Parliament put the finishing touches to a process that had been completed for all practical purposes in 1873. All the ambiguity that had been caused by the fumbling attempts by British admin-istrators in the eighteenth century to deal with lawlessness in the North-West, the enactment of the ill-conceived *Canada Jurisdiction Act* in 1803, the compounding of the ambiguity by the machinations of both Edward Ellice in 1821 and Adam Thom in the 1840s, the rudimentary law-making at Red River, and the piecemeal introduction of Canadian criminal law was at an end. The criminal law was now as certain and as predictable as statutes and a growing case law could make it and, with the exception of the grand and petit juries, it was the same as that in the other provinces of Canada. This is the body of law that became the criminal law of Alberta in 1905.

Notes

1. Order-in-Council, June 23, 1870; *Charters, Statutes, Orders in Council Relating to the Hudson's Bay Company* (London: Hudson's Bay Company, 1963), II:171–77. For all practical purposes the Indian Territory was the land to the north and west of Rupert's Land.
2. A colony is a settlement in a foreign country possessed by settlers who have a political connection with, and are subordinate to, their mother country. John Burke, ed., *Jowitt's Dictionary of English Law*, 2 vols, 2 ed. (London: Maxwell, 1977), II:375.
3. See text to nn. 103–07.
4. Canada, House of Commons, *Debates* (March 24, 1879), p. 679 (hereafter, *Debates*).
5. C.C. McCaul, "The Constitutional Status of the North-West Territories of Canada," *Canadian Law Times* 4 (1884): 49–61.
6. McCaul, "Constitutional Status," 15.

7. *Sinclair v. Mulligan*, *Manitoba Law Report* 3 (1886), p. 485. At the time of the Judgement, Mr. Justice Killam was judge of the Manitoba Court of Queen's Bench. He later (in 1899) became chief justice of Manitoba and was elevated to the Supreme Court of Canada in 1903.

8. E.E. Rich, *The History of the Hudson's Bay Company 1670–1770*, 2 vols. (London: Hudson's Bay Record Society, 1959), 230.

9. *Sinclair v. Mulligan*, *Manitoba Law Report*, vol. 3 (1886), p. 485.

10. Alexander Brown, *The Genesis of the United States* (1890; New York: Russell and Russell, 1964), 52–64.

11 . "Peaceful possession," as opposed to settlement after conquest as occurred, for example, in Nova Scotia after 1713. See *Campbell v. Hall*, 98 *English Reports*, 1045–50, (1774) for a full discussion of the question of how British possessions were perceived to have received English law. For a recent analysis of this case and the two cases quoted in nn. 11 and 12 see R. MacGregor Dawson, *The Government of Canada*, 5 ed. (Toronto: University of Toronto Press, 1970), 4–6.

12. *Blankard v. Goldy*, 91 *English Reports*, 356, (1694).

13. *Case 15—Anonymous*, 24 *English Reports*, 646, (1722). The relevant passage reads as follows: "If there be a new and uninhabited country found out by English subjects, as the law is the birthright of every subject, so, wherever they go, they carry their laws with them, and therefore such new found country is to be governed by the laws of England, though after such country is inhabited by the English, acts of parliament made in England, without naming the foreign plantations, will not bind them."

14. Adam Shortt and Arthur G. Doughty, eds., *Documents Relating to the Constitutional History of Canada*, 3 vols. (Ottawa: King's Printer, 1918), I:163–69.

15. 5 Geo. III, c. 33, s. 25 (1765). In 1773, one Dué was convicted in Quebec of murdering his employer in the Indian Territory and executed pursuant to this statute; George Chalmers, *Opinions of Eminent Lawyers* (1814; Farnbrough, England: Gregg International, 1971), 204. See also Gage to Secretary at War, Welbore Ellis, January 2, 1765, in Clarence Edwin Carter, *The Correspondence of General Thomas Gage*, 2 vols. (New Haven: Yale University Press, 1931), I:266; Gage to Johnson, June 16, 1766, in Milton W. Hamilton, et al., eds., *The Papers of Sir William Johnson*, 14 vols. (Albany: University of New York, 1965), V:272; and Johnson to Gage, June 27, 1766, in *The Papers of Sir William Johnson*, XII:115. For commentary see Frederick Bernays Wiener, *Civilians Under Military Justice* (Chicago: Chicago University Press, 1967), 68.

16. Hamilton, et al., *Papers of Sir William Johnson*, XII:115.

17. Wiener, *Civilians Under Military Justice*, 68, n. 22.

18. 16 Geo III, c. 15, s. 29 (1775). Plurals such as "or persons," "or soldiers," and "or crimes," have been omitted from this quotation.

19. E.H. Oliver, *The Canadian West; Its Early Development and Legislative Records*, 2 vols. (Ottawa: Government Printing Bureau, 1914), I:136.

20. Oliver, *The Canadian West*, I:145.

21. Oliver, *The Canadian West*, I:135–53.

22. See n. 12 above.

23. For detail see Arthur S. Morton, *A History of the Canadian West to 1870*, 2nd ed. (Toronto: University of Toronto Press, 1973), 125–256.

24. Morton, *A History*, 146–50; 320–24.

25. Morton, *A History*, 342.

26. Morton, *A History*, 334.

27. Dorchester to Sydney, June 9, 1788, appended report of May 29, National Archives of Canada, microfilm B 44. (Hereafter NAC.)

28. Dorchester to Sydney, June 9, 1788, NAC, microfilm B 44.

29. Morton, *A History*, 508–10, ff. For details of the many crimes committed over the years and the legal efforts to bring malefactors to justice see Hamer Foster, "Long Distance Justice: the Jurisdiction of Canadian Courts West of the Canadas, 1763–1859," *American Journal of Legal History* XXXIV, no. 1 (January 1990): 1–48.

30. Sydney to Dorchester, November 6, 1788, appended opinion of the law officers, NAC, microfilm B 44. The law officers made the same remark concerning the proposal to prefer charges pursuant to the statute of Henry VIII, and said that even if it were within Dorchester's power, they did not think the time, effort and money expended in transporting accused, witnesses and evidence to England would result in justice being done.

31. Morton, *A History*, 513–16. For more detail see Thomas, Lord Selkirk, *A Sketch of the British Fur Trade in North America* in J.M. Bumsted, ed. *The Collected Writings of Lord Selkirk*, 2 vols. (Winnipeg: Manitoba Record Society, 1998), 66–67; 70–75; 83–84.

32. Milnes to Lord Hobart, Colonial Secretary, October 30, 1802, Canada, Parliament, *Sessional Papers*, 1893, no. XXVI, pp. 136–46.

33. Imperial, Geo. III, c. 138 (1803).

34. The territorial situation in 1803 was as follows: The border of Quebec, as defined after the Peace of Paris in 1783, and now the provinces of Upper and Lower Canada, marched with the border of Rupert's Land, from northern Labrador to the west of Lake Superior then south to the border of Louisiana. Between Rupert's Land and the Indian Territories the border ran from north of Hudson Bay, southwest to the Rocky Mountains and thence south to Louisiana.

35. See text to nn. 56 and 57.

36. Quoted in James Morris, *Heavens Command: An Imperial Progress* (London: Faber and Faber, 1973), 30.

37. J. Steven Watson, *The Reign of George III 1760–1815*. (Oxford: Clarendon Press, 1960), 407–16.

38. United Kingdom, Parliament, House of Commons, *Journals of the House of Commons*, vol. 58, p. 652.

39. Geo. III, c. 138 (1803). *Journals of the House of Commons*, vol. 58, pp. 670, 675, 679, 683, 687, 690. While the *Journal* records the detail of the various steps in this bill's process, it does so in pro forma sentences that contain no sense of the debate, if there was any. William Woodfall's *Parliamentary Register* (vol. IV, London, 1803) is even more brief in that it omits mention of the first, second and third readings. On the contrary, the report of the debate on the Army bill on August 11 in this volume runs to 40 pages (pp. 812–52). At least there was mention of the *Canada Jurisdiction Act* in these publications. There is no mention at all in biographical works such Spencer Walpole, *Life of the Rt. Hon. Spencer Perceval* (London: Hurst and Blackett, 1874); Edward Foss, *The Judges of England* (1848; New York: AMS Press, 1966); or in contemporary British newspapers that have been consulted.

40. *Imperial Act for extending the Jurisdiction of the Courts of Justice in the Provinces of Lower and Upper Canada to the Trial and Punishment of Persons guilty of Crimes and Offences within Certain Parts of North America adjoining to the said Provinces*, 43 Geo. III, c. 138 (1803).

41. See the able argument of Lord Selkirk in support of this statement. *A Sketch of the British Fur Trade*, 93–95.

42. Geo. III, c. 138, s. 2 (1803). This drafting slip drew a tart comment from Adam Thom: "Guilty [is a] slovenly substitute for accused." *R. v. Calder*, *Western Law Times* 2 (April 1891): 10. Thom

was the first legally trained magistrate in Red River. For detail see Roy St. George Stubbs, *Four Recorders of Rupert's Land* (Winnipeg: Peguis, 1967), 1–47.

43. 43 Geo. III, c. 138, s. 3.

44. A.S. Morton, "The Canada Jurisdiction Act (1803) and the North-West," *Proceedings and Transactions of the Royal Society of Canada*, 3 series [1938, section II], 129.

45. Morton, *A History*, 518–25.

46. Morton, "Canada Jurisdiction Act," 131–32. Lord Selkirk was not as reticent as Morton and provides chapter and verse about Mowat's treatment at Fort William. Selkirk, *A Sketch of the British Fur Trade*, 87–88. It will also be noted that Fort William was in Upper Canada where the Act of 1803 was in force, as was Angus Morris. It could not therefore be alleged that Morris had acted illegally.

47. Foster, "Long Distance Justice, 21–22.

48. Morton, *A History*, 25–26.

49. Morton, *A History*, 534.

50. Morton, *A History*, 537–38; Oliver, *Canadian North West* I:176.

51. Morton, *A History*, 539–57.

52. Selkirk to Macdonell, 1814, in Oliver, *Canadian North West*, 186–88.

53. Dale and Lee Gibson, *Substantial Justice* (Winnipeg: Peguis Publishers, 1972), 7. The two publications may also have been brought by Macdonell himself in 1811, or sent in 1813 with a letter similar in content to that of 1814, but suggestive in tone rather than peremptory; Oliver, *Canadian North-West*, I:178, I:182, I:186, II:1291.

54. United Kingdom, Parliament, House of Commons, *Parliamentary Papers*. Report of Select Committee on British Possessions in North America, 1857. Colonies, Canada, vol. 3, 74. In Irish University Press Series, Shannon, Ireland. (Hereafter cited as *Report of Select Committee, 1857*.) Selkirk and then his heirs appointed the councillors until 1835, when Assiniboia reverted to the direct rule of the governor and court in London, and from then on they were appointed by the latter.

55. [John Halkett], *Statement Respecting The Earl of Selkirk's Settlement upon the Red River in North America* (1817; New York: Johnson Reprint, 1968), 2. Halkett, Selkirk's brother-in-law, wrote the book to counteract the publications of the North West Company that were winning the press war in England at the time. Naturally, he put forward the best evidence for his case and thus created a problem for researchers. In view of Mowat's trial, there is little doubt that Selkirk took legal advice about the right of jurisdiction in Rupert's Land before he made arrangements to send his settlers there, as explained by Halkett. However, Halkett may not have known who gave the advice to Selkirk or, if he did, did not consider that the person was of sufficient eminence. He therefore substituted the text of eminent counsel (as Appendix A) who wrote the definitive opinion at the request of the Hudson's Bay Company, but omitted to print the date of the document, June 10, 1814. See also Morton, *A History*, 537–38.

56. Legal opinions of George Holroyd, October 1, 1812, William Cruise, March 18, 1812, and James Scarlett, January 2, 1813, Hudson's Bay Company Archives, A 39/2 folio 118, folio 109, folio 124.

57. Opinion, August 4, 1814, Hudson's Bay Company Archives, A 39/2, folio 170. It would seem that counsel gave opinions that their clients wanted to hear. See the opinions of equally eminent counsel who were consulted by the North West Company: [Samuel Hall Willcocke], *A Narrative of Occurrences in the Indian Countries of North America* (1817; New York: Johnson Reprint, 1968), Appendixes 4, 5 and 6.

58. Oliver, *Canadian West*, II:1285–87.

59. For details of wholescale arrests by made by both companies see United Kingdom, Parliament, House of Commons, "Papers Relating to the Red River Settlement; 1815–1819" (1819), 206, 232. (Hereafter "Red River Commissioner's Report.")

60. Morton, *A History*, 566; 570–71.

61. Rich, *History of the Hudson's Bay Company*, II:366; Morton, *A History*, 581.

62. A. Amos, ed., *Report of Trials in the Courts of Canada, Relative to the Destruction of the Earl of Selkirk's Settlement on the Red River* (London: John Murray, 1820); Foster, "Long Distance Justice," 27–29. See also the summary of all the trials for murder and other offences conducted in the Canadas in Rich, *History of the Hudson's Bay Company*, II:338.

63. The prosecution argued that the crime was committed in the Indian Territories and the defence said it took place in Upper Canada. William S. Simpson, *Report at large of the trial of Charles de Reinhard, for murder (committed in the Indian territories), at a court of oyer and terminer, held at Quebec, May 1818: to which is annexed a summary of Archibald McLellan's [evidence], indicted as an accessory* (Montreal: James Lane, 1819), xii; 173–92; 194–95.

64. de Reinhard languished in jail until December 19, 1821, when he received an unconditional pardon and was released. NAC, RG 4, B 20, pp. 2483–85.

65. While Dorchester and Sherbrooke monopolized the authority to act, they did not monopolize the right to express their opinion in writing. See the many communications to Dorchester and to Sherbrooke and Dalhousie from all and sundry, including the London and Montreal companies and Selkirk. Douglas Brymer, ed., *Report on Canadian Archives 1896* (Ottawa: Queen's Printer, 1897), 161–64; 296; 218; 222; 234–36; 249–51; and Brymer, ed., *Report on Canadian Archives 1897* (Ottawa: Queen's Printer, 1890), 296–98; 304; 353.

66. "Red River Commissioners Report," 63.

67. "Red River Commissioners Report," 55–56.

68. "Red River Commissioners Report," 64.

69. 1 and 2 Geo. IV, c. 66 (1821).

70. 1 and 2 Geo. IV, c. 66, ss. 10, 11. In passing, it is worth noting that although the latter provision made a clear distinction between Rupert's Land and the Indian Territories, it was a distinction by implication because, as with the Act of 1803, the Indian Territories were not defined in terms of boundaries.

71. 1 and 2 Geo. IV, c. 66, s. 12.

72. Ellice, whose influence on Canadian history is little known, came from a family that had long been connected with the fur trade. He worked in both the London and Montreal offices of the family company that, in the early years of the nineteenth century, had become the agent for both the North West and the XY companies. Ellice became head of the firm on the death of his father in 1805, at which time the gross worth of his North American inheritance was well over £125,000. His interests were wide-ranging: he was Secretary to the Treasury and Whip in Lord Grey's Reform administration in 1830 and Secretary at War in 1833, and he was influential in the appointment of Lord Durham as commissioner and governor-general of Canada in 1838. Above all, Ellice was the parliamentary expert on Canada, which is why Bathurst turned to him in 1821. James M. Colthart, "Edward Ellice," *Dictionary of Canadian Biography*, vol. IX (Toronto: University of Toronto Press, 1976), 233–39(hereafter DCB). See also D.E.T. Long, "The Elusive Mr. Ellice," *The Canadian Historical Review* XXIII, no. 1 (1942): 42–57.

73. Rich, *History of the Hudson's Bay Company*, II:385; II:389–93.

74. Morton, *A History*, 614.

75. Rich, *History of the Hudson's Bay Company*, II:397.
76. *Report of Select Committee, 1857*, 324.
77. *Report of Select Committee, 1857*, 324.
78. The reason Ellice was able to draft the 1821 Act was that at that time many bills that today "could not be carried except as Government measures, were in the [seventeenth century] and in the earlier part of [the eighteenth century], introduced and carried by private members," Courtenay Ilbert, *Legislative Methods and Forms* (Oxford: Clarendon Press, 1901), 82.
79. *Report of Select Committee, 1857*, 338.
80. As in 1803, there is no mention of Canada, the fur trade or the Hudson's Bay Company in the several biographies of Lord Liverpool, the prime minister at the time.
81. Ernest L. Woodward, *The Age of Reform 1815–1870* (Oxford: Clarendon Press, 1954), 350.
82. Richardson to Ellice, October 25, 1821. Quoted in Long, "The Elusive Mr. Ellice," 53.
83. The first Council of Assiniboia sat December 4, 1822. Oliver, *Canadian West*, I:226.
84. Oliver, *Canadian West*, I:219–223. Although no commission has been discovered, it is probable that Andrew Bulger, the governor of Assiniboia (1822–1823), was gazetted as a justice of the peace, as was his predecessor, Miles Macdonnell.
85. Letter Bathurst to Joseph Berens, Governor of Rupert's Land, May 31, 1822, in Oliver, *Canadian West*, I:222.
86. Letter Andrew Colville, Deputy Governor of Rupert's Land, to Bulger, May 31, 1822, in Oliver, *Canadian West*, I:222.
87. Oliver, *Canadian West*, I:369.
88. Letter W. G. Smith, Secretary of the Hudson's Bay Company, to William Caldwell, Governor of Assiniboia, April 5, 1854, in Oliver, *Canadian West*, II:1309.
89. Imperial, 22 and 23 Vic. c. 26, s. 4 (1859).
90. Imperial, 22 and 23 Vic. c. 26, s. 1 (1859).
91. Oliver, *Canadian West*, I:226.
92. Oliver, *Canadian West*, I:264–65.
93. The population of Red River increased from 2,417 in 1831 to 3,972 in 1838 and the jurisdiction was defined to extend over a circular area 100 miles in diameter, centred on the confluence of the Red and Assiniboine Rivers; Oliver, *Canadian West*, I:74; I:296; and *Charters Relating to the Hudson's Bay Company*, 231–34.
94. Stubbs, *Four Recorders*, 7, 8.
95. Stubbs, *Four Recorders*, 19–20.
96. Stubbs, *Four Recorders*, 15.
97. Oliver, *Canadian West*, I:369–75.
98. Oliver, *Canadian West*, II:1317, n. 14.
99. The Code of 1862, with later amendments, is printed in the *Consolidated Statutes of Manitoba*, 44 Vic., liv–lxxx (1880–1881).
100. *R. v. Calder*, *Western Law Times* 2 (April 1891): 2–10. Thom's learned and able exposition in 1851 of the state of the law in Assiniboia and how it got to be that way is an instructive and interesting read; Oliver, *Canadian West*, I:369–73.
101. Oliver, *Canadian West*, I, 369–75. Since the Red River Council was a creature of the Hudson's Bay Company and not a legislative body of the Crown, the enactment of this Ordinance was beyond its authority, as its closing words indicate. In effect, the Quarterly Court could administer the law of 1837 so long as no person objected to the practice.
102. Desmond H. Brown, "Abortive Efforts to Codify English Criminal Law," *Parliamentary History* 11, part I (1992): 17–22.

103. Oliver, *Canadian West*, I:534; *Consolidated Statutes of Manitoba, 1880–1881*, lxxix.

104. This was Baptiste Cadien; for detail see Foster, "Long Distance Justice," 39.

105. Records of the Quarterly Court, August 18, 1848, Red River, Public Archives of Manitoba, MG2 B4, 4–1, District of Assiniboia, Court Records, Minutes of the General Quarterly Court 1844–1872; hereafter, Red River Court Records.

106. *R. v. Calder*, *Western Law Times* 2 (April 1891): 1–11. In passing, Thom made the case that the Acts of 1803 and 1821 were not specifically carried over to the Province of Canada in 1841 and therefore null and void in that jurisdiction; ibid., 9.

107. Stubbs, *Four Recorders*, 13–15.

108. Red River Court Records, September 4, 1845 and February 19, 1846. For other cases cited in this style, see Gibson, *Substantial Justice*, 323–24. The style was discontinued in 1864, when the Code of 1862 was amended to adopt the use of current English criminal law, and long after Thom had returned to Britain. Frederick Read, "Early History of the Manitoba Courts," *Manitoba Bar News* 10, no. 2 (1937): 468–69. Extensive research has failed to turn up any similar case citations in the jurisdictions of the British Empire.

109. F.T. Piggot, *Imperial Statutes Applicable to the Colonies* (London: William Clowes, 1902), I:102–03.

110. McCaul, "Constitutional Status," 15.

111. *Report of Select Committee, 1857*, 324.

112. *Sinclair v. Mulligan*, *Manitoba Law Report* 3 (1886): 487–88.

113. *Debates*, March 24, 1879, pp. 675–80. The subject of the debate was a bill proposed by David Mills that would have introduced in the Territories the criminal law of Ontario at the time of Confederation and the civil law of Ontario of January 1, 1873. Mills led off with the remark that "with regard to the North-West Territories, it was very difficult to state what law was in force." The truth of this statement was amply demonstrated by the participants in the ensuing debate.

114. Rich, *History of the Hudson's Bay Company*, 230.

115. Since the Province of Manitoba was separated from the North-West Territories on July 15, 1870, and since Manitoba followed a separate constitutional development thereafter, it will not treated in the following discussion.

116. Desmond H. Brown, *The Genesis of the Canadian Criminal Code of 1892* (Toronto: University of Toronto Press, 1989), 92–98.

117. William McDougall was appointed lieutenant-governor of Rupert's Land and the North-West Territories in 1869, prior to its cession by the British Crown to Canada. It was McDougall's attempt to enter Rupert's Land from the south to assume his appointment that, in large part, caused the insurrection at Red River in 1869–1870.

118. Canada, 32–33 Vic., c. 3, ss. 5 and 6 (1869). This Act was extended by 33 Vic., c. 3, s. 36 (1870), and continued to have force until 1871.

119. United Kingdom, 31–32 Vic., c. 105 (1868).

120. Canada, 34 Vic., c. 16 (1871).

121. United Kingdom, 35 and 36 Vic., c. 63 (1872),

122. Imperial, 22 and 23 Vic. c. 26 (1859).

123. United Kingdom, 37 and 38 Vic., c. 35 (1874). For the discussion of 1 and 2 Geo. IV, c. 66 (1821) see above, n. 73.

124. Canada, 36 Vic., c. 34 (1873).

125. Matthew Hale, *History of the Pleas of the Crown*, 2 vols. (London: E. and R. Gosling, 1736), I:xv ff.

126. Hale, *Pleas of the Crown*, 314 ff.

127. Canada, 32 and 33 Vic., c. 29, s. 34 (1869).

128. Hale, *Pleas of the Crown*, II:323–82.

129. Canada, 32 and 33 Vic., c. 29, s. 16 (1869). It may seem curious that the Canadian Parliament should concern itself with legislation that the Imperial Parliament had abolished several years before [26 and 27 Vic., c. 125 (1863)]. The explanation is that English law that came to a colony with the first settlers became the law of that colony and was not affected by repeal or amendment by the Imperial Parliament. If the colony wanted to follow the British lead or to otherwise alter the law, such change had to be effected in the Colonial Legislature. This was one of the ramifications of the case decided by the Privy Council in 1722 (see n. 12).

130. *Debates*, March 24, 1879, p. 678.

131. Canada, 32 and 33 Vic., c. 28 (1869). Laws concerning vagrancy were on the statute books in 1670 [39 Eliz. I, c. 4 (1597); I Jas., c. 7 (1604)]. However, Hale does not discuss them because they were not looked upon as criminal statutes, as such, but rather as legislation to keep labourers at their place of work. Moreover, they were inapplicable both in the colonies that formed the Dominion and the territories, because of the differences between social conditions in Elizabethan England and those that obtained in the northern part of North America.

132. Canada, 32 and 33 Vic., c. 28 (1869).

133. Canada, *Act Respecting the Administration of Justice, and for the Establishment of a Police Force in the North-West Territories*, 36 Vic., c. 35, s. 10, 15 (1873).

134. Canada, *Act to Amend the Act Respecting the Administration of Justice, and for the Establishment of a Police Force in the North-West Territories*, 37 Vic., c. 22, s. 15 (1874).

135. The force was so designated by Canada, 42 Vic., c. 36, s. 3 (1879).

136. Alexander Begg, *History of the North-West*, 3 vols. (Toronto: Hunter, Rose & Co., 1894–1895), II:245. Lewis H. Thomas, *The Struggle for Responsible Government in the North-West Territories* (Toronto: University of Toronto Press, 1956), 114.

137. Canada, 38 Vic., c. 64, (5), (6); (1875); 43 Vic., c. 25, s. 76, (5), (1880).

138. For detail of the development and decline of the grand jury see Desmond H. Brown, "The Canadian Criminal Code 1892: A Comparative Study in Codification," (Ph.D. Diss., University of Alberta, 1986), 71–82; 210–16.

139. Imperial, 12 Hen. II, c. 1 (1166); 22 Hen. II, c. 7 (1176).

140. "Grand Juries," *Canadian Law Journal* 27 (1891): 6. This excellent article presents the case against the criminal side of the grand jury and finds that "the grand jury is a useless and very often a dangerous incumbrance to our system of administering criminal justice" (9).

141. An attempt to cut down the functions of the grand jury was a major factor in the defeat of Premier John Thompson's government in Nova Scotia in 1882. Brown, *Genesis of the Canadian Criminal Code*, 61.

142. Upper Canada, *Act for the Appointment of County Attorneys*, 20 Vic., c. 59 (1857).

143. Quoted in John Kains, *How Say You?* (St. Thomas [Ont.]: *The Journal*, 1893), 11.

144. A. Margaret Evans, *Sir Oliver Mowat* (Toronto: University of Toronto Press, 1992), 31; 37; 184; 187–88.

145. Quoted in Kains, *How Say You?*, 63–64.

146. Thomas, *Struggle for Responsible Government*, 98; 104; 114.

147. Canada, 43 Vic., c. 76, s. 5. If the punishment for an accused person would not exceed five year's imprisonment, he or she was to be tried summarily by a magistrate.

148. *Ordinances of the North-West Territories*, 1886. Ordinance Respecting Juries, c. 6, s.16. *Consolidated Ordinances of the North-West Territories of 1898 and Amendments and Substitutions up to and Including 1915*. Ordinance Respecting Juries, c. 28, s. 16.

149. *Revised Statutes of Canada*, 1927, Criminal Code, c. 36, s. 9 (c). See also *R v. Browne, Alberta Law Review* 24 (1930): 421.

150. Alberta, *Act to Amend the Jury Act*, 15 Eliz. II, c. 45 (1966). Alberta is the only provincial jurisdiction with a six-person jury in civil actions.

151. Both Saskatchewan and Manitoba adopted the common law jury of 12 persons in the early years of the twentieth century, went back to six, and then back again to 12. *Tremeer's Annotated Criminal Code*, 5 ed. (Toronto: Carswell, 1944), 1160.

152. The Legislative Council of the North-West Territories enacted an ordinance in 1884 that would have made July 15, 1870, the date of the reception of English common law in the jurisdiction. But it was of no effect because it was in conflict with the Canadian statute 32–33 Vic., c. 3, s. 5 (1869). For detail see Jean Côté, "The Introduction of English Law into Alberta," *Alberta Law Review* 3 (1964): 264.

153. Desmond H. Brown, *Genesis of the Canadian Criminal Code*, 73–91.

154. "Common law" is here defined as being that law that had its source in England, as opposed to the "code" jurisdictions such as France and Germany.

155. This theory must not be pushed too far. It has never been the subject of a definitive legal decision, but it is the subject of a long and on-going debate that has filled many pages in legal journals. See Jean Côté, "The Reception of English Law," *Alberta Law Review* 15 (1977): 62–70, for a recent interpretation.

156. Canada, House of Commons, *Debates*, March 24, 1879, p. 676.

157. See D. Morton, *The Queen v. Louis Riel* (Toronto: University of Toronto Press, 1974), 305–06.

158. Canada, House of Commons, *Debates*, May 19, 1886, p. 1382.

159. Canada, 49 Vic., c. 25, s. 3 (1886).

160. Canada, 49 Vic., c. 25, s. 2 (1886).

161. Canada, 49 Vic., c. 25, s. 4 (1886). For the increase in population, the electoral districts and the creation of the Legislature, see Thomas, *Struggle for Responsible Government*, 104; 114.

Three

Venerable Rights
Constitutionalizing Alberta's Schools 1869–1905
SANDRA M. ANDERSON

Introduction

In 1905, when the provinces of Alberta and Saskatchewan were carved out from the North-West Territories and entered Confederation, the constitutional status of their schools was complex and resonated with the echoes of historic battles over denominational and separate schools that had animated the early years of the country. In the 1905 autonomy debates in Parliament, no subject took up more time and energy than the school bill for the new provinces, and Catholics and Protestants clashed in the backrooms and sometimes openly over whether the more equitable provisions for separate schools that had been enshrined in the British North America Act, 1867 and in the North-West Territories Act of 1875 should prevail, or whether those guarantees should yield to the national school model introduced into the North-West Territories Ordinances between 1884 and 1901 by Western[1] "progressives," who resented the yoke of the central Canadian regime of denominational schools and the domination of the Roman Catholic Church in Western affairs.

The subject required profound examination. A great deal of work went into reconciling the governance of North-West Territories schools, with their early sporadic and sectarian and local character, and the fervour for forging the national identity and cultural conformity through schooling—a concern that occupied the minds of early twentieth-century Canadian leaders. During the last quarter of the nineteenth century, the interests of religious leaders, in particular those of the Roman Catholic Church, collided head-on with growing public confidence in the importance and efficacy of state control over schools as a civilizing force in society.

The Parliamentary and public controversy over the place of separate schools in the new province of Alberta was primarily a re-enactment of the 1867 compromise between Ontario and Quebec on the schools question, leavened by the Manitoba schools controversy of the 1880s and 1890s. Hundreds of petitions opposed to separate schools in the new provinces flowed into Parliament. The majority of these petitions came from Ontario and were based on an opposition to limiting provincial power over education.[2]

The subjects of the controversy, the inhabitants of the new province itself, seem largely to have thought it a tempest in an Eastern teapot.[3] In response to a purported telegram from Calgary that was published in Toronto and warned that "should the autonomy legislation reaffirm the clause in the Northwest Territories Act guaranteeing separate schools to the minority, the turmoil will be precipitated, and the fiery cross will be carried through the length and breadth of the territories," the *Calgary Herald* scoffed on February 9, 1905:

Well, isn't that the limit! Just what reason a sane person would have for talking about "furious turmoil in the west" is not clear to us. "The fiery cross" may be carried through the length and breadth of the hair trigger brains of some eastern enthusiasts but that the virile, fair-minded people of the west can be dragged into such a controversy, or stampeded by the shout of people two thousand miles removed from Alberta, who are absolutely uninformed as to what are the true conditions existing here, is entirely unlikely.[4]

Seeing that there was no abatement of the furor, the *Calgary Herald* returned to the theme in its editorial of March 2, 1905:

Rival gangs of politicians are shouting themselves hoarse in Ontario over the educational affairs of Alberta. While each cries: "Hands off the west," they urge, with singular unanimity that the views of their particular crowd should be enforced in the new province.... The west has not spoken on the subject of separate schools. Not one single utterance from a public man of the west has thus far been made on this subject, yet, in spite of the complacency of the very people who are most concerned, Ontario is being inflamed by orators who display amazing zeal in the affairs of the country 2,000 miles removed.

It is just possible that Alberta would be more thankful to these enthusiasts if they would urge more even-handed justice for the west in the way of distribution of the natural resources of the country, a more equitable boundary division, capital location, and other features of substantial value in the new provinces.... Just now the people of Alberta at least are more interested in the other phases of the autonomy bill than education.[5]

In July 1905, as Alberta moved towards provincehood, the parliamentary debaters invoked the constitution at every turn. Clifford Sifton, Sir Wilfrid Laurier's Manitoba-based minister of the interior, had spent much time in the Territories and possessed a practical Western bent. He deserves to be quoted:

> It seems to me that almost everybody will agree with my hon. Friend the Minister of Finance that the man in the street, hearing the hon. Gentleman who leads the opposition say that he stands by the constitution, and hearing the right hon. Gentleman who leads the government say that upon the rock of the constitution he stands, and seeing these two gentlemen both standing on the rock of the constitution but coming to diametrically opposite conclusions will be likely to say: "I cannot hope to understand the law or the constitution, but I do want to know what kind of schools they are going to have in the North-West Territories...."[6]

The *British North America Act, 1867*

The "great compromise" over schools had been a key factor in creating the original Dominion. When the *British North America Act* came into effect for the four original Canadian provinces in 1867, it contained a hard-fought provision, section 93, which carved out of the general grant to the provinces of plenary power over education a special constitutional protection for denominational rights. Section 93 read:

> In and for each Province the Legislature may exclusively make Laws in relation to Education, subject and according to the following Provisions:

> > (1) Nothing in any such Law shall prejudicially affect any Right or Privilege with respect to Denominational Schools which any Class of Persons have by Law in the Province at the Union:
> > (2) All the Powers, Privileges, and Duties at the Union by Law conferred and imposed in Upper Canada on the Separate Schools and School Trustees of the Queen's Roman Catholic Subjects shall be and the same are hereby extended to the Dissentient Schools of the Queen's Protestant and Roman Catholic Subjects in Quebec:
> > (3) Where in any Province a System of Separate or Dissentient Schools exists by Law at the Union or is thereafter established by the Legislature

of the Province, an Appeal shall lie to the Governor General in Council from any Act or Decision of any Provincial Authority affecting any Right or Privilege of the Protestant or Roman Catholic Minority of the Queen's Subjects in relation to Education:

(4) In case any such Provincial Law as from Time to Time seems to the Governor General in Council requisite for the due Execution of the Provisions of this Section is not made, or in case any Decision of the Governor General in Council on any Appeal under this Section is not duly executed by the proper Provincial Authority in that Behalf, then and in every such Case, and as far only as the Circumstances of each Case require, the Parliament of Canada may made remedial Laws for the due Execution of the Provisions of this Section and of any Decision of the Governor General in Council under this Section.

Four policy principles were embedded in section 93: (1) each province was to be entirely responsible for education within its own boundaries; (2) pre-existing legal rights to denominational schools of whichever group was the minority in a given province were to be protected, whether this minority was Roman Catholic or Protestant; (3) the minority group was to have at all times the right to appeal; and (4) the federal government could resort to remedial legislation if the circumstances warranted.[7]

However, in 1867, no one was looking to section 93 for the governing framework for Alberta's schools. Alberta, then part of Rupert's Land and the North-Western Territory (as it was then known), was owned by the Hudson's Bay Company, and the *British North America Act* only made provision for entry into Canada "on Address from the Houses of the Parliament of Canada to admit Rupert's Land and the North-western Territory, or either of them, into the Union, on such Terms and Conditions in each Case as are in the Addresses expressed and as the Queen thinks fit to approve, subject to the Provisions of this Act."[8]

The *Temporary Government of Rupert's Land Act, 1869*

After the Hudson's Bay Company sold Rupert's Land, including the territory that is now Alberta, and it came into hands of the government of Canada,[9] there was no pressing need for a legislative framework for schools in the territory. At the time, there were isolated schools here and there, established by missionary orders (in the main, Catholic and French[10]), but no concerted government policy for establishing or maintaining schools.

There was, however, provision in the *Temporary Government of Rupert's Land Act, 1869* for continuation of existing statutes that contained an important proviso, which suggests that section 93 could well have been in force in the North-Western Territory and Rupert's Land until 1875:

> All of the Laws in force in Rupert's Land and the North-Western Territory, at the time of their admission into the Union, shall so far as they are consistent with "The British North America Act, 1867,"—with the terms and conditions of such admission approved of by the Queen under the 146th section thereof,—and with this Act, remain in force until altered by the Parliament of Canada, or by the Lieutenant Governor under the authority of this Act.[11]

Nevertheless, in the next 35 years to 1905, as those schools multiplied into 560 school districts[12] established for the burgeoning population of the North-West Territories, the struggles over the character of and protection for schools in the lands west of Manitoba, including Saskatchewan and Alberta, were destined to play a central role in the development of the Territorial and later provincial consciousness. It is no exaggeration to say that to understand the development of education policy and its legal and constitutional framework in those years is to understand the origins of the Province of Alberta.

The *North-West Territories Act* of 1875

The Order-in-Council of June 23, 1870[13] that admitted Rupert's Land and the North-Western Territory into the Union granted "to the Parliament of Canada authority to legislate for their future welfare and good government." In 1875, Parliament enacted an *Act to Amend and Consolidate the Laws Respecting the North-West Territories*,[14] which set up a five-person governing council and, in section 11, narrowly adopted[15] the principle of territorial (provincial) control over education, along with the minority-rights exception that had been enshrined in section 93 of the *Constitution Act 1867*:

> When, and so soon as any system of taxation shall be adopted in any district or portion of the North-West Territories, the Lieutenant-Governor,

by and with the consent of the Council or Assembly, as the case may be, shall pass all necessary ordinances in respect to education; but it shall therein be always provided, that a majority of the ratepayers of any district or portion of the North-West Territories, or any lesser portion or sub-division thereof, by whatever name the same may be known, may establish such schools therein as they may think fit, and make the necessary assessment and collection of rates therefore; and further, that the minority of the rate-payers therein, whether Protestant or Roman Catholic, may establish separate schools therein, and that, in such latter case, the rate-payers establishing such Protestant or Roman Catholic separate schools shall be liable only to assessments of such rates as they may impose upon themselves in respect thereof.

In this way, the initial federal constitutional policy that had protected Protestants in Quebec and Catholics in Ontario was grafted onto the North-West Territories,[16] but, as was the case in Manitoba, the almost completely dual system of sectarian separate schools that section 11 provided for was shortly to meet with opposition.

"All Necessary Ordinances"—1884–1904

After the enactment of the *North-West Territories Act* in 1875, the small number of white settlers in the Territory and general absence of municipal institutions meant that there were no immediate attempts to make government funding or governance arrangements for schools until 1883,[17] when the member for Edmonton, Frank Oliver, introduced a bill in the North-West Council for the organization of "Public and Separate School Districts." The bill was circulated to interested parties after second reading, and the tireless defenders of separate schools in the North-West Territories, Bishops Grandin and Taché, worked to fend off legislation that would weaken clerical surveillance and control over Catholic schools and so foster the feared *étatisme*, the elevation of state over religious interests. This time they succeeded in obtaining a school ordinance that brought in a dual confessional system acceptable to them and which was already familiar from the Confederation compromise.[18]

Their satisfaction was short-lived. Nearly every year between 1884 and 1904, the Territorial government, under its plenary power over education, enacted an Ordinance respecting schools. The main provisions of these Ordinances have been set out in table 3.1 (See Appendix 1). The table shows that the provisions[19] reflect the increasing influence of a series of powerful school administrators,[20] imported mainly from Ontario, who managed and directed the establishment of schools for the new Territorial government and shifted control over them from the churches and missionary orders to the Territorial government by means of centrally-controlled regulation, inspection, and funding. This trend towards "national schools" reflected the waning influence of the Catholic hierarchy[21] on North-West Territories schools, a process that was hastened by the decline in number of Métis as a percentage of the population and further fuelled by the controversy and cultural tension created by the Northwest Rebellion and the 1885 hanging of Louis Riel.

The deciding factor in this shift of power over schools from the Catholic hierarchy to the Territorial government during the last quarter of the nineteenth century was the growth in size and influence of the non-Catholic population throughout the North-West Territories,[22] accompanied by the autonomy movement and its assertion of independence from Central Canadian ways and, on school questions, from the Manitoba and Eastern Canadian experience. Autonomy and provincial status for the West provided powerful support for the principle of "national schools"; that is, schools that were non-sectarian and under governmental control.

Frederick William Gordon Haultain, Chairman of the North-West Executive Committee and, after 1901, commissioner of education, was the standard-bearer for these developments, determined as he was that the North-West was to take its rightful place as an English-speaking country. On March 16, 1893, he wrote to the *Winnipeg Tribune*:

The English speaking people were now, and always would be, in the ascendancy in the North-West, and there was no danger that the separate school question would be engrafted on the Territories.[23]

An influential politician almost from the time he came from Ontario to Fort Macleod to practice law, Haultain's public opposition to the separate school clauses of the Autonomy Bill in 1905 eventually cost him the opportunity to be premier of either of the new provinces of Alberta or Saskatchewan.[24] His capable deputy, David James Goggin, superintendent of education from 1893 to 1902, shared his views.[25]

Between 1881 and 1885, the federal government paid steadily-increasing grants in aid from the appropriated funds for the North-West Territories to teachers who turned in satisfactory statistics, and thereafter, the Ordinances also reflect the attempts to put funding for schools on an acceptable basis as the Territorial Assembly struggled to wrest control over school grants from the federal government.[26]

Each new or amended Ordinance represented a step forward to central Territorial control and a step away from the dual-system principle of permitting the minority's separate schools to be operated as the minority ratepayers "may think fit." It was inevitable that a unitary system of control with limited separate school guarantees would narrow the scope of the constitutional entrenchment of denominational school rights in the new provinces of Alberta and Saskatchewan.

By 1892, it was obvious, at least to Catholic leaders, that separate school rights had been intolerably eroded by the continuing series of school Ordinances. Father Hippolyte Leduc started a campaign against the 1892 Ordinance, saying that separate schools did not really exist,

> for [they] are really abolished in what constitutes their essential difference from all others Public, Atheistic or Protestant schools. ...For how can the Catholics recognize, as separate and theirs, Schools over which they have no longer any control? Choice of books, examinations, inspectors and inspections, qualifications and diplomas of teachers, all has been taken away from them.[27]

Instead of the blunt instrument of the Manitoba legislation, Leduc saw Superintendent Goggin, "Tzar of education in the North West," as the instrument of Haultain and others who had adopted a superficially neutral Ordinance "for the Catholic schools which he will kill by inches."[28] Father Leduc was not far off the mark, since Haultain boasted much later that Goggin "had administered all the separateness out of them."[29] Even Goggin's appointment as superintendent had been carried out surreptitiously by Haultain without consultation with Catholic members of the Council of Public Instruction when he acted as "a subcommittee of one for the transaction of all ordinary business under the new Ordinance."[30]

Father Leduc has left a vivid description of his trip to Regina in August 1894, where he developed a "plan of campaign" with his co-religionist ally on the former Board of Education and the two Catholic members of the Territorial Assembly to bring his own and others' petitions before the Standing School Committee of the North-West Legislative Assembly, where he complained that the 1892 Ordinance was "so cleverly fashioned that it allows good as well as evil, and authorizes the existence or the complete destruction of our schools."[31] Candidly admitting he did not have the support for repeal, he sought amendments to deal with such immediate problems as the rules that required teachers to come to Regina for training, a rule that was impossible for the teaching orders of nuns in convents to observe and which drew his particular ire;[32] the lack of Catholic vote and representation on the Council of Public Instruction; allowances for use of French in the schools where necessary; and the freedom to use Catholic textbooks. Father Leduc also gave an account of the unsatisfactory response to their petition from the Territorial Assembly.[33] Not surprisingly, the federal government did nothing to assist the minority, caught as it was between the views of Ontario and Quebec.[34] However, the petitions resonated in the Territorial Assembly, where the 1894 Ordinance introduced minor ameliorations.[35]

The 1901 Ordinance has been called "the formal end of a period of transition in school control from a board constituted along denomination lines to a governmental department responsible to the [Territorial] Assembly."[36] Separate school supporters had lost control over teacher certification, inspection and textbooks; even though they could establish their own schools and school districts, their distinctive character was submerged in the "efficient, non-partisan"[37] national school principles espoused by leaders such as Haultain, whose Anglophile bias found expression in lofty pronouncements about how a single system of common schools, where all children pursue the same course of study, would foster Canadian sentiment among the citizenry, however disparate their backgrounds, and assimilate them into a united people. With such noble and popular principles, it was easy to paint the bifurcated dual system of separate and public schools as an anachronism of foreign and narrow religious interests. The mission of British imperialism threatened to engulf the mission schools of the old North-Western Territory.

Nevertheless, Bishop Legal of St. Albert reported in June 1902 that the advantages of the school system in the North-West Territories included the formation of Catholic separate and public school districts, the right to Catholic school taxes, trustees and teachers, and government grants to Catholic schools. Still to be attained, he said, was an end to the suppression of the word "Catholic" in the title of Catholic public school districts and a share of the school taxes paid by companies.[38]

Although there is a noticeable tendency towards centralization in the evolution of the school ordinances of the North-West Territories after 1875, there is historical evidence that this tendency was an expression of what the central authorities found desirable, not what actually took place.[39] Indeed, the issue of what school governance actually existed in 1905 that conferred constitutional protection for separate or public schools at the time Alberta entered Confederation is so vexed that it has become the centrepiece of a long legal battle nearly a century later.[40]

After 1892, the main legislative privilege remaining to separate schools consisted of the right of minority ratepayers to assess themselves for support of their own schools instead of the public schools and the right, given to public and separate schools alike, to provide religious instruction during the last half hour of the school day. Otherwise, the Ordinances of 1892 brought a uniform system of governance to both separate and public schools. This shift has been described as:

> a sharp distinction between the clerically controlled ecclesiastical schools made possible in earlier ordinances, and the government supervised separate schools as they existed from 1892, although authority for all was derived from the 1875 federal Act.[41]

Thus, when the question of preserving the existing school arrangements in Alberta's constitution was being debated in 1905, it emerged that the perspective of what "existed" was quite different for the prime minister, Wilfrid Laurier, who derived his Bill from the 1875 *North-West Territories Act*, and for those who applauded the Haultain- and Goggin-inspired evolution in North-West Territories legislation to the government-controlled system of the 1892 Ordinances. The clash was inevitable.

Autonomy for the North-West Territories—Alberta Becomes a Province

Laurier established a cabinet committee to meet with Haultain and A.L. Sifton, the representatives of the North-West Territories. Haultain rejected special representation from French Canadians with a curt comment that the French had special rights, but special representation was not one of them; the interests to be represented were Territorial interests, not those of "any special race or creed."[42]

Laurier asked Haultain to submit the Territorial case in writing. Haultain's draft Autonomy Bill, presented on December 7, 1901, made no explicit reference to education, but specified that the *British North America Act*[43] would apply to the new province as if the latter "had been one of the Provinces originally united by the said Act," except such sections as applied only to Ontario and Quebec. Although this could have meant that section 93(1) would apply, restricting the power of the Legislature from passing legislation that would "prejudicially affect any Right or Privilege with respect to Denominational Schools which any Class of Persons have by Law in the Province at the Union," Haultain took the position later with respect to education that:

> The question is one of Provincial rights. It is not a question of the rights of a religious minority which must be properly and may be safely left to the Provincial Legislatures to deal with subject to the general constitutional provisions in that regard.[44]

In the delicate negotiations over autonomy for Alberta and Saskatchewan and with tension building once again over the school question, Laurier asked the Catholic hierarchy not to take an active and public role in the elections in the fall of 1904 and, in exchange, he would negotiate the school question himself. When Laurier and the Liberals carried the nation, including taking seven of the 10 Territorial seats, the Catholic hierarchy set out to secure the minority's educational interests.[45] For a time, in Laurier's initial proposals to Parliament for education in the new provinces, they appeared to have succeeded.

The Catholic Hierarchy and the Education Provisions of the Autonomy Bill

Apart from peppering Laurier with observations about the language of the school provisions from the outset,[46] Mgr. Donatus Sbaretti, Archbishop Delegate of the Holy See in Ottawa, took it upon himself to lecture Laurier on the nature of existing North-West Territories' school legislation. For example, on February 15, 1905, he wrote to Laurier about the latter's proposal to remove the words "whether a public school has been established or not:"

> The words mentioned are useful as showing more clearly that the rights of the minority are not to be dependent upon the activity or inactivity of the majority. Besides it has to be noticed that by the present school ordinance in the Territories (Section 36, Chap. 70, Consolidated Ordinances

N.W.T. 1898), a separate school can be established only in an organized Public school district. That provision seems not to be in harmony with the Dominion Statute consolidating the North West Territories.... I should prefer to see the clause inserted [despite] the extra trouble which might be caused by its insertion.[47]

Sbaretti wasted no time in responding to the new draft of the education provisions of the Autonomy Bill:

Conscious of the awful responsibility resting on me at this crucial moment, I have studied with the greatest diligence possible Chapters 29, 30 and 31 of the Ordinances of the N.W.T. 1901, in relation especially to the first sub-section of the clause presented to me on the 5th of March by you and the Hon. R.W. Scott....[48] I am sorry to say that I find that the principle of Separate Schools is not guaranteed by that sub-section against the act of a hostile Legislature.... The Legislature can change this system and do away with the method of districts by establishing, let us suppose, provincial or municipal schools. The right to separate schools would be imperilled as hypothetically depending upon the system of erecting school districts. What we want is that the right to separate schools be guaranteed beyond any doubt....The clause in its present form is practically useless...."[49]

Sbaretti hit the nub of the problem: the constitutional right to establish separate schools was a derivative of the continued existence of public school districts.[50]

Increasingly frantic, Sbaretti reminded Laurier of their "deal" by which Laurier achieved Catholic support for his Bill:

First by the Hon. R.W. Scott, the Secretary of State, in person, and afterwards by you in your letter of March 7, 1904,[51] confirmed by another on the 12th of the same month, I was solemnly promised that the right of the minority to separate schools in the North West Territories would be guaranteed in the Constitution of the Provinces, to be erected therein, *as in the Provinces of Ontario and Quebec*. [emphasis in original]

In the elections of last November on the strength of your promise, I exercised my influence with the Prelates and Catholics of this country that no excitement or agitation would be created on the question of schools in the North West Territories, and in a letter to the Honourable Secretary of State on October 13th, I promised that the same question would not be discussed in the Catholic papers. And my efforts were successful, as you are well aware. I am extremely sorry to say that the clause read to me last evening does not fulfil the promised security.[52]

When Sbaretti continued to offer suggestions for amendment, Laurier relied on the weight of the political forces arrayed against the Bill to resist them:

The position of the minority in all these respects seems to me absolutely secure, yet I recognize that it may be advisable, under certain circumstances, to make doubly sure what is already sure. On the other hand, I have very serious misgivings as to the possibility of obtaining any changes, however slight, in the draft as it now stands.

The confident tone with which you express the hope that the improvements which you suggest would be accepted, leads me to think that you have no adequate conception of the intent forces which oppose this legislation, and of the efforts which are necessary to overcome them.[53]

The warnings had the necessary effect on Sbaretti. After advising Laurier that he had met with the Bishops of the Catholic Church in Canada and that they were all in agreement with Sbaretti on the school clause; that is, that they were satisfied with the original draft, but not the present one, he wrote:

At the same time, although in view of the circumstances as they are represented to them, they do not intend to oppose the clause, they trust that some improvement will be made in favour of the Catholics. Let me express the hope then that you will still see your way to do something to better the clause along the lines I suggested....[54]

This exchange, with its tacit acknowledgement that Catholic power was not sufficient to win the day,[55] was a reprise of the petitions against the 1892 Ordinance submitted by the separate boards and the Church hierarchy in the North-West Territories calling for its disallowance or a formal order to the Legislative Assembly and Council of Public Instruction in the North-West Territories to repeal or to amend the 1892 Ordinance in such a way as to restore Catholic rights to control their own schools. When the government declined to disallow the legislation, based largely on a report of the Executive Committee of the North-West Territories that had been prepared by Haultain and forwarded by C.H. Mackintosh, lieutenant-governor of the North-West Territories,[56] Archbishop Taché wrote an eloquent rebuttal, the memorial of 1894, which was presented to Parliament.[57] In it, Archbishop Taché reviewed not only the school conditions in the North-West Territories, but also, as a warning not to repeat recent Manitoba history in the North-West Territories, the broken promises to the Red River inhabitants when Manitoba entered into confederation and that ultimately resulted in the extinction of Catholic school rights in Manitoba.[58] The failure of the Privy Council to disallow the 1892 Ordinance, in "commend[ing] us to the mercy, to the generosity of the avowed enemies of our religious institutions, of our schools, of our convents,"[59] was a bitter pill for Catholics to swallow, particularly after their humiliation in Manitoba. From the Catholic point of view, both the purpose and the result of the 1892 Ordinance was "the abolition of all distinct character of our schools."[60]

How could the result have been otherwise? The power of disallowance provided in section 93 was a direct affront to the autonomy of provincial and territorial Legislatures. Its use would have upset the balance of power so profoundly that it has remained a recourse destined to remain moribund.

The Education Provisions of Laurier's Autonomy Bill[61]
The First Draft

Laurier explained on more than one occasion what his intention was for the constitutional regime for education in the new provinces of Alberta and Saskatchewan:

> The education clause of the B.N.A. Act [s. 93(1)] was the most remarkable of all and in that clause George Brown, who was a most determined opponent of separate schools, agreed not only to admit the system in his own province, but to make its continuance part of the Constitution. Nor is this all, but a similar provision was made for the minority of any Province which might enter the Dominion with a system of separate schools. Can you doubt that if the Provinces of Alberta and Saskatchewan had been admitted into the Dominion in 1867 instead of 1905, they would have received the same treatment as was given to Ontario and Quebec? I do not think this can be denied.

The proposition in the Bill is to give the minority the guarantee of the continuance of their system of schools as they would have had it in 1867.... If this is refused, the minority of the North West Territories will smart under a sense of wrong and injustice.... I am well aware that the idea of having schools partaking of ecclesiastical domination is repugnant to the spirit of our age. Even such an objection could not hold against the spirit of the Constitution; but I truly relieve the true character of the schools in the North West Territories is not known; under the name of separate schools, they are really national.[62]

When he introduced the draft Bill in the House of Commons on February 21, 1905, after having been heavily lobbied by Mgr. Donatus Sbaretti to guarantee protection for separate schools and explicit inclusion of section 93(1),[63] Laurier explained the principle that guided him in the draft Bill even in areas in which he was of the view that unsound compromises had been made in 1867:

...it is the duty of everybody in this House and in the country to take confederation as we find it, with its good points and its blemishes, and carry it to the end of the principle upon which it was established.[64]

On the same occasion, Laurier spoke of the education question as "perhaps under existing circumstances the most important of all that we have to deal with." His next sentences revealed the pressures that had been applied to him:

There are evidences not a few coming to us from all directions, that the old passions which such a subject has always aroused are not, unfortunately, buried; indeed, already, before the policy of the government has been known, before the subject is fairly before the people, the government has been warned as to its duty in this matter, and not only warned but threatened as well. The government has been warned, threatened from both sides of this question, from those who believe in separate schools and from those who oppose separate schools. These violent appeals are not a surprise to me.... We have known by the experience of the past, within the short life of this confederation, that public opinion is always inflammable whenever questions arise which ever so remotely touch upon the religious convictions of the people. It behooves us therefore all the more at this solemn moment to approach this subject with care, with calmness and deliberation....[65]

Laurier's answer to the pressures was to hark back to the great compromises that had been made in 1867 to achieve Confederation, referring to George Brown ("who with Sir John Macdonald was the central figure") and the "sacrifice" Brown had made of his opposition to separate schools for Ontario "upon the altar of the new country which it was his ambition to establish on this portion of the North American continent." He called for more compromise in the same spirit and along the same lines because "the work of confederation is not yet finished...we are now engaged in advancing it."[66]

Having noted that Nova Scotia and New Brunswick had no separate schools "by law," and that it had been determined judicially that Manitoba had no separate schools either "by law or by practice," Laurier went on to describe the situation in the North West Territories:

> In 1875...Mr. Mackenzie introduced an Act for the government of the North-west Territories, and in this Act, the parliament of Canada, which, at that time, had among its members some of the ablest men who ever sat in a Canadian parliament—Sir John Macdonald, Mr. Mackenzie, Mr. Blake, Sir Charles Tupper and a score of others—unanimously, deliberately and with their eyes open, introduced into the North-west Territories the system of separate schools. And not only that, but the parliament of Canada, four times successively—in 1880, in 1885, in 1886 and in 1898—deliberately and with their eyes open, ratified the system of separate schools in the Territories.[67]

Laurier stated that "we have to decide this problem upon the very terms of the legislation which was introduced in 1875."[68] Accordingly, the original draft of the Autonomy Bill provided that:

> 1. The provisions of Section 93 of the British North America Act, 1867, shall apply to the said Provinces as if, at the date upon which this Act comes into force, the Territory comprised therein were already a Province, the expression "the Union" in the said section being taken to mean the said date.
>
> 2. Subject to the provisions of the said Section 93, and in continuance of the principles heretofore sanctioned under the North-West Territories Act, it is enacted that the Legislature of the said Province shall pass all necessary laws in respect of education and that it shall therein always be provided

(a) that a majority of the ratepayers of any district or portion whatever name it is known, may establish such schools therein as they think fit, and make the necessary assessments and collection of rates therefor, and

(b) that the minority of the ratepayers therein, whether Protestant or Roman Catholic, may establish separate schools therein, and make the necessary assessment and collection of rates therefor, and

(c) that in such case the ratepayers establishing such Protestant or Roman Catholic separate schools shall be liable only to assessment of such rates as they impose upon themselves with respect thereto.

3. In the appropriation of public moneys by the Legislature in aid of education, and in the distribution of any moneys paid to the Government of the said Province arising from the school fund, established by the Dominion Lands Act, there shall be no discrimination between the public schools and the separate schools, and such moneys shall be applied to the support of public and separate schools in equitable shares or proportion.[69]

To say the least, not everybody agreed with Laurier's proposal for the Autonomy Bill to continue the application of section 93(1) to Alberta and Saskatchewan and to constitutionalize the education provisions of the *North-West Territories Act*. First, there were Haultain's comments in an interview published by the *Toronto Globe* on February 25, 1905:

I take exception to Sir Wilfrid Laurier's argument in regard to constitutional guarantees. At the time to which he refers the Dominion Parliament was the only body exercising a Government jurisdiction over the Territories, and they had to make provision for everything.... But to say that because the Dominion Parliament passed an act with regard to the educational or any other matter in 1875 it stands forever, that it be imposed upon the Province and perpetuated, is a position which if applied with equal fairness to anything else they did it is very rapidly brought to the reductio ad absurdum.[70]

This passage cannot be understood apart from Haultain's more extensive comments to Laurier in a published letter[71] dated March 11, 1905, in which, after chiding the prime minister for not consulting with him about the draft Autonomy Bill prior to introducing it for first reading, he wrote:

With regard to the question of education generally, you are no doubt aware that the position taken by us was that the Provinces should be left to deal with the subject exclusively subject to the provisions of The British North America Act, thus putting them on the same footing in this regard as all the other Provinces in the Dominion except Ontario and Quebec. I submit that Parliament is bound by the provisions of The British North America Act, 1867, in passing legislation of this kind. The power of the King in Council, exercising in effect the legislative functions of the Parliament of the United Kingdom under the authority of section 146 of The British North America Act, 1867, is restricted by the words "subject to the provisions of this Act." This restriction must equally apply to Parliament exercising the powers conferred on it by The British North America Act, 1871, which by section 3 of The British North America Act, 1886, must be "construed together" with The British North America Act, 1867. If the King in Council is bound by the provisions of the Act in admitting an independent and consenting Colony into the Union, it can hardly be contended that Parliament has the power to create an unwilling, inferior and imperfect organization. As was pointed out in June, 1869, by the Honourable Edward Blake in the House of Commons in the discussion upon a proposal to rearrange the terms of Confederation with respect to Nova Scotia: "It is perfectly clear, on great and obvious principles, that the basis of Union settled by The British North America Act is not capable of alteration 'by Parliament." If the Provincial jurisdiction can be invaded by positive Federal legislation such as is proposed in this case, what limit is there to the exercise of such a power? Similar restrictions might be imposed with respect to any or all of the matters in relation to which, under The British North America Act, 1867, the Provincial Legislature possess exclusive power.

The only jurisdiction possessed by Parliament in this respect is the remedial jurisdiction conferred by sub-section 4 of section 93 of The British North America Act, 1867. The proposed attempt to legislate in advance on this subject is beyond the power of Parliament and is an unwarrantable and unconstitutional anticipation of the remedial jurisdiction. It has, further, the effect of petrifying the positive law of the Province with regard to a subject coming within its exclusive jurisdiction and necessitating requests for Imperial legislation whenever the rapidly changing conditions of a new country may require them. On the fifteenth of July, 1870, the North-West Territories were "admitted into the Union,"[72] in the express terms of section 146 of The British North America Act, 1867. To speak of the Provinces of Alberta and Saskatchewan being "admitted into the Union" on the first July, 1905, is an improper and indefensible use of the expression. The territory included within the boundaries of these proposed Provinces was "admitted into the Union" on July 15, 1870, and immediately upon the creation of these Provinces the provisions of section 93 of The British North America Act, 1867, become, as a matter of indefeasible right, a part of their Constitution. On the creation of the Provinces, the term "Provinces" in that section interprets itself and the term "Union" bears the unmistakable meaning which is given to it with regard to the area included in the Provinces by the actual language of section 146.

The first sub-section of section 16 [later, section 17] of the Bills is drawn in direct contradiction of this principle. It is an attempt to create a Province retroactively. It declares Territorial school laws passed under the restriction imposed by The North-West Territories Act to be provincial school laws. It clothes laws imposed by the Federal Parliament withal the attributes of laws voluntarily made by a free Province. It ignores Territorial limitations and conditions. It denies facts and abolished time. It declares what was not to have been, and seeks to perpetuate as existing what never was nor is....

The fact that since the acquisition of the North-West Territories Parliament has passed certain laws affecting those Territories does not involve the principle that those laws must be perpetuated in the Constitution of the proposed Provinces. In this respect laws relating to education do not differ from laws relating to any other subject. To state that the law passed in 1875 with regard to education must forever limit the power of the Province with regard to a very important Provincial right involves the theory that Parliament might practically take away all the jurisdiction of a Province and leave it shorn of every power which it is supposed to possess under the Constitution.

I wish to lay great stress on the fact that this is a purely constitutional question and is not concerned in any sense with the discussion of the relative merits of any system of education. The question is one of Provincial rights. It is not a question of the rights of a religious minority which must be properly and may be safely left to the Provincial Legislatures to deal with subject to the general constitutional provisions in that regard. It is the question of the right of a minority of

Canadians in the wider arena of the Dominion to the same rights, and the same privileges, the same powers and the same constitution as are enjoyed by the rest of their fellow citizens and which they claim to be their inalienable possession under the one and only Canadian charter, The British North America Act.[73]

From this passage, it appears that Haultain was, at least initially, of the view that section 93 of the 1867 *British North America Act* was the only constitutional imperative for education in any of the provinces, including his own.[74] Moreover, he found it acceptable for Alberta, more acceptable than constitutionalizing the 1875 *North-West Territories Act*. What must he have made of Laurier's later amendment to the Autonomy Bill, which instead constitutionalized certain of the Ordinances of his own Legislature!

A different and ultimately more consequential and influential position was taken by Clifford Sifton,[75] Laurier's minister of the interior, who would have preferred to see total provincial control over education without even the limitations imposed by section 93. Sifton returned from six weeks away in the United States to find that the school part of the new constitutional provisions had taken an unexpected twist. On February 25, 1905, he wrote to J.W. Dafoe, editor of the *Manitoba Free Press*, in words that illuminate both Laurier's character and that of his lieutenants:

> Respecting the school matter, what I agreed to was that the present system of separate schools in the North West Territories should be perpetuated.... [F]rom every standpoint I regard it as most desirable that the question should be settled by simply adopting the principles of the system as it exists now.... As I understand it the North West members are unanimously of the same opinion.... As the clause in the Bill is drawn, however, it seems to go further and it seems to be vague. I do not myself with all my experience in construing and arguing clauses of this kind profess to know what it means, and the fact that it was drawn by Fitzpatrick does not add anything to my confidence that the draftsman had in mind the same intention that we had. I do not accuse him of intentionally deceiving anyone, but he makes no secret of the fact that he is desirous of meeting the views of the Church..... I am just sending you this letter as an advance bulletin so that you will know what is going on. I have not discussed the matter with Sir Wilfrid at all further than that he called me into his room yesterday and spoke at some length of the difficulties which he had had. He did not ask

me my opinion or what my views were. Sir Wilfrid's proceeding in matters of this kind is always to assume that everyone agrees with him until they insist upon quarrelling. He finds this much the easiest way of getting on. He will not seek for an opportunity of allowing me to raise a dispute about it, but I shall of course be compelled to bring the subject up very soon. I will have another talk with the Western Members on Monday or Tuesday.[76]

Those who opposed maintaining a dual system of schools in the new province were concerned that there was to be a wholesale sell-out to Papal interests. After Laurier told Sifton, who had been out of the country for his health and was taken by surprise by the education clause,[77] that he would not be set off course by Sifton's warnings, Sifton offered his resignation to Laurier, the reason for which he described to Dafoe in a letter dated February 27, 1905:

> The first part of the clause relating to the establishment of a school system does not make explicit provision for complete regulation and control by the Legislature. I perhaps might bring myself to support the continuance of the present school system of the North West Territories, provided it is absolutely clear, as I believe it is, under the ordinance that the Legislature has the power to control all schools, control them and prescribe the conditions upon which the public money is to be distributed. These safeguards are absent in the proposed clause although Sir Wilfrid stoutly asserts that this is not the case.... [A]s to the last clause, it constitutes a division of the proceeds of the enormous land subsidy for school purposes in the North West. The Dominion Lands Act reserves these lands for public schools. Laurier proposes to divert a portion of the amount, which in the whole will probably amount to from twenty to forty million dollars to endow the separate schools of the Roman Catholic church. I am unalterably opposed to such a proposition. I cannot conceive of any serious minded man in the present state of the history of Canada contemplating the possibility of such a measure.[78]

Sifton feared that giving the Catholics a "vested interest" in the proceeds of school lands would be "an inducement to the Catholic people to organize as many separate schools as possible."[79]

The draft wording precipitated Sifton's immediate resignation because he was not prepared to have any words in the Bill "which will give the minority one iota beyond the limits of their present rights."[80] Moreover, he said:

The form of the clause as drawn seems to me to be ambiguous. I do not feel at all confident that I or in fact anyone else can be certain what it means, but I am quite satisfied that it does not safeguard the right of the legislature to fully regulate and control all the schools.[81]

Sifton's resignation created a crisis for Laurier, as Sifton had undoubtedly hoped it would. In early March, caucuses of MPs were debating an education clause drafted by Sifton, hoping to find a compromise. By March 11, 1905, Sifton was reporting to Dafoe about the still-confidential draft amendment:

The final draft has followed the suggestion contained in your telegram of yesterday, that is to say it follows the first subsection as shown in the draft sent to you except that Chapter 31 of the North West Ordinances is not mentioned. Chapter 31 provides for the distribution of the Legislative Grant and instead of confirming it we added a short provision to the effect that in distributing monies appropriated by the legislature for the aid of schools organized under the School Ordinance there shall be no discrimination against any particular class of schools. Then a Section is added to make Subsections 3 and 4 applicable by the necessary verbal changes.... The point to be made in discussing it with our friends is to show that the Church is absolutely eliminated. There is no possibility of the Church getting its finger on the schools known as "separate schools" under the present North West Ordinances, and the result is that they are shut out forever unless they can get the people of the North West Territories to give them something more.[82]

The Second Draft

Whether or not Laurier had deliberately set out initially to revoke the Ordinances of recent years by harking back to the *North-West Territories Act* for separate school guarantees, the second draft (the Sifton clause) was profoundly different. It made no mention of the *North-West Territories Act*, with its phrase "a majority...may establish such schools therein as they think fit." The new clause made the rights of the minority wholly dependent on the prior establishment of a public school district and this frustrated Catholics in those areas where they still formed the majority. Religious instruction was to be limited to the last half hour of the day for all schools. Most immediately alarming for the

Catholics was the failure to guarantee separate schools a share in the school-lands fund. The clause confined separate school rights and privileges to the terms of chapters 29 and 30 of the *North-west Territories Ordinances* of 1901.

The terms of what is now Section 17 of the *Alberta Act* were made public by Laurier on March 20 and substituted for the original wording when he proposed second reading on March 22. It was termed the "compromise clause," but by eliminating all reference to the 1875 *North-West Territories Act*, the western members and Sifton achieved their goals fully, a continuation of the school system as it had evolved legislatively to 1901, rather than a return to older system enshrined in 1867.[83] Laurier introduced the amended provisions in a lengthy peroration.[84] Some have analysed his remarks as naïvely premised upon the guarantees contained in the 1875 Act, the basis for Laurier's promises to the Catholic hierarchy, without realizing what he had done by making Ordinances 29 and 30 the reference point for section 17.[85]

Those who supported the amended Bill, but feared reaction to it (like Sifton) minimized the differences between it and Laurier's draft. However, Frank Oliver, the Edmonton member who succeeded Sifton as minister of the interior, pulled no punches. Describing himself as "one who knows something of this matter, as one who has had experience in regard to school legislation, as one of those members of the North-West Assembly who made the change in the North-West school law between what it was before 1891 and what it is today," he saw it (rightly) as "the difference between clerical control of schools and national control of schools."[86]

On May 3, 1905, after Conservative leader Sir Robert Borden's amendment to give the provincial Legislature "full powers of provincial self government including power to exclusively make laws in relation to education" failed on a 140 to 59 vote, Laurier's motion for second reading of the Sifton clause passed.[87]

The Alberta Act, Section 17

The constitutional framework for Alberta's schools was provided for in *The Alberta Act*,[88] which included as section 3 the incorporation of existing constitutional provisions:

> The provisions of The British North America Acts, 1867 to 1886, shall apply to the province of Alberta in the same way and to the like extent as they apply to the provinces heretofore comprised in the Dominion, as

if the said province of Alberta had been one of the provinces originally united, except in so far as varied by this Act and except such provisions as in terms made, or by reasonably intendment may be held to be, specially applicable to or only to affect one or more and not the whole of the said provinces.

Thus the constitutional framework that had existed in 1867 was indubitably erected over the new province, but with an important exception in section 17 for education:

Section 93 of The British North America Act, 1867, shall apply to the said province, with the substitution for paragraph (1) of the said section 93, of the following paragraph:-

(1) Nothing in any such law shall prejudicially affect any right or privilege with respect to separate schools which any class of persons have at the date of the passing of this Act, under the terms of chapters 29 and 30 of the Ordinances of the North-West Territories, passed in the year 1901, or with respect to religious instruction in any public or separate school as provided for in the said ordinances.

(2) In the appropriation by the Legislature or distribution by the Government of the province of any moneys for the support of schools organized and carried on in accordance with the said chapter 29 or any Act passed in amendment thereof, or in substitution therefore, there shall be no discrimination against schools of any class described in the said chapter 29.[89]

(3) Where the expression "by law" is employed in paragraph 3 of the said section 93, it shall be held to mean the law as set out in the said chapters 29 and 30, and where the expression "at the Union" is employed, in the said paragraph 3, it shall be held to mean the date at which this Act comes into force.

In 2000, Mr. Justice Major, writing for the Supreme Court of Canada in *Public School Boards Association v. Alberta*, succinctly described the effect of section 17 and its analogous purpose to that of section 93(1):

In the same manner as s. 93(1), s. 17(1) "freezes in time" the rights and privileges of separate schools and the rights to religious instruction of both public and separate schools as they existed in 1905.[90]

Conclusion

As was said by the Royal Commission on Education in Alberta nearly 50 years ago:

> Discussion of the organization and administration of education must... be predicated upon the fact that *the separate schools are part of the public school system*. Their welfare contributes to the welfare of education in Alberta. Whereas the Commission cannot accede to all recommendations, it has sought ways and means whereby the educational aspirations of Roman Catholics might be attained more fully within the framework of existing statutory authority.[91] (emphasis in original)

Nevertheless, this view was predicated on two principles: (a) that separate schools, as part of the public school system, must abide by the standards and regulations applicable to the public school system as a whole, and (b) that apart from the unique constitutional right to establish a tax-supported separate school system in any school district where a minority, either Protestant or Catholic, desires it, their rights are identical to those of public school supporters, as specified in provincial legislation.[92] In light of aggressively assimilationist policies of provincial authorities, exemplified in the school Ordinances of the North-West Territories, the stage was set for future battles over the content of those constitutionally entrenched minority rights. It was left to a later future, and primarily to the Courts, to redefine separate school rights as guaranteeing more than the right to organize a school, but also as protecting the right to maintain the essence of Catholic dogma[93] in curriculum and special requirements for teachers to conform with Catholic teaching.[94]

The Alberta Legislature enjoys plenary power over schools except only as limited by section 17 of the *Alberta Act*. Therefore, rather than examining the extent of the rights and privileges of separate schools as they existed under section 93 of the *Constitution Act 1867* in the school laws of the original provinces, or as they existed in 1875 under the *North-West Territories Act*, Albertans must have recourse to chapters 29 and 30 of the *Ordinances of the North-West Territories*, passed in the year 1901, to determine the constitutional status of their education system.

Since 1982, however, the *Canadian Charter of Rights and Freedoms* has introduced a new layer of constitutional protections into school law, protections that must be reconciled with the venerable constitutional imperatives without doing violence to either.[95] The considerable body of jurisprudence on separate school rights in Alberta shows that, ironically, these rights have been interpreted expansively,[96] as indeed they have in other Canadian provinces.[97] Nearly a century of legislation and litigation since 1905 has strengthened the commitment to a broad interpretation of the constitutional position of Alberta's separate schools to the point where their legal position is as strong as if they were protected by the earlier, more friendly principles contained in the 1875 *North-West Territories Act*. Perhaps because that is so, separate school supporters have not for a long time felt it necessary to test their right to petition the lieutenant-governor-in-council for redress or to obtain remediation of provincial education laws from the federal Parliament, rights they appear still to have under sections 93(3) and 93(4) of the *Constitution Act, 1867*.

However, in *Public School Boards Association v. Alberta*, the Supreme Court of Canada stressed the "malleability" of Alberta's education institutions and the fact that the right to dissent does not guarantee the specific means and framework in which the dissent is exercised, so that "the Province of Alberta may alter educational institutions within its borders as it sees fit, subject only to those rights afforded through the combined effect of s. 93 and s. 17."[98] Ultimately, separate school supporters may not only have to analyze those provisions and the "snapshots" of chapters 29 and 30 of the 1901 *Ordinances of the North-West Territories*, but also the more subtle intrusions of today's school legislation on the forms in which they exercise their venerable rights.

Appendix 1

Table 3.1 Summary of NWT School Ordinances—1884–1901

Appendix 1: Table 3.1 Summary of NWT School Ordinances—1884–1901

	1884[99]	1885[100]	1886[101]
School Districts	An area of not more than 36 square miles, with four resident heads of families and 10 children (s. 11); the owner of land outside a district could petition to have his land included in an adjacent district when the latter was of his faith (s. 37).	An area of not more than 36 square miles, with four resident heads of families and 10 children (s. 9); the owner of land outside a district could petition to have his land included in an adjacent district when the latter was of his faith (s. 40).	°The terms "Protestant" and "Catholic" need no longer be included in school district names; name of district to be chosen by the people of the district (majority) (ss. 8–9).
Establishment of separate school district	°Dual public system;[107] with each school district declaring whether it is Protestant or Catholic, public or separate (ss. 10, 25).	S. 25 continued as s. 31.	°Limited to the minority, either Protestant or Roman Catholic, in the area of an already-established public school district (s. 31), as determined to the satisfaction of LGIC (s. 35).
Disestablishment of separate school district			
Governance	12-man Board of Education, divided into Protestant and Catholic sections (s. 1) (never appointed[108]).	Board of Education reduced to five—two Protestants and two Roman Catholics, chaired by the LGIC (s. 1); divided into Protestant and Roman Catholic sections (s. 6).	Board of Education and sections continued.
Administration			
Make regulations	Controlled by section (s. 5).	Controlled by Board (s. 4).	Controlled by section, but by Board if school is not designated either Protestant or Roman Catholic (s. 6).

1887[102,103]	1887[104,105]	1901[106]
Name of district may be proposed by petitioning ratepayers, but LGIC sets the name (ss. 15, 19).	Name of district may be proposed by petitioning ratepayers (s. 15), and Council recommends proclamation to LGIC (s. 30); district names to be numbered consecutively in order of proclamation (s. 12); any person not living in a district may petition to have his land included in it (s. 13).	Any area may be erected into a public school district, with Commissioner able to expand its size beyond five square miles (s. 12); Commissioner can alter name of district, but change does not affect existing obligations, rights (s. 35); Commissioner can take action in respect of areas without school districts (s. 7(3)) and order a district erected (s. 39); the owner of land outside a district may petition to have his land included in any district (s.164).
Minority, either Protestant or Roman Catholic, within any organized public school district (s. 36).	Minority, either Protestant or Roman Catholic, within any organized public school district (s. 32).	*Minority in any district, whether Protestant or Roman Catholic, may establish a separate school therein (s. 41) and petition to erect a separate school district (s. 42) on same terms as for public districts (s. 44).
		Ratepayers in contiguous public and separate districts may resolve to unite both districts into one public district (s. 52).
Board of Education (five Protestants; three Catholics), limited to 2-year terms (s. 1) and who elect a voting chair from among themselves (s. 6); divided into Protestant and Catholic sections (s. 8).	Council of Public Instruction (consisting of all members of the Executive Committee, with four advisors—two Protestant and two Catholic)[109] replaces Board of Education (s. 5).	Department of Education presided over by Commissioner of Education replaces Council of Public Instruction (ss. 3-5). Five-person Education Council (at least two Catholics) to consider matters referred to it for discussion and report (ss. 8, 10).
Secretary appointed by LGIC to call all meetings of the Board and of sections (s. 12).	Superintendent appointed by LGIC serves as Secretary to Council (s. 5)—until 1896, when administration and funding were separated from other functions.	Commissioner (became Minister in 1909) is the political head of the department, with permanent professional deputy commissioner.
Controlled by section, but by Board if school is not designated either Protestant or Roman Catholic (ss. 7–8).	Controlled by Council.	Controlled by Commissioner (s. 6).

	1884[99]	1885[100]	1886[101]
Control and Manage Schools of its section	Controlled by section (s. 5).	Controlled by section (s. 6).	Controlled by section, but by Board if school is not designated either Protestant or Roman Catholic (s. 6).
Teacher grading and certification	Controlled by section; suitable teachers to be engaged by trustees (s. 79).	Controlled by whole Board (s. 5); teachers to be engaged by trustees (s. 69).	Controlled by section, but by Board if school is not designated either Protestant or Roman Catholic (s. 6).
Appoint examiners of teachers	Appointed by LGIC according to faith and free to grant certification (s. 88).	Controlled by Board.	Controlled by section, but by Board if school is not designated either Protestant or Roman Catholic (s. 6).
Teacher decertification	Controlled by section.	Controlled by section (s. 6).	Controlled by section, but by Board if school is not designated either Protestant or Roman Catholic (s. 6).
Text books	Controlled by section (s. 5), except Catholic districts to use books selected by the Catholic section of the Board in Manitoba (s. 75(6)).	Controlled by section (s. 6(3)).	Controlled by whole Board if a school is not designated either Protestant or Roman Catholic (s. 5); otherwise by section (s. 6).
Religious observances	Controlled by section; trustees could adopt a form of opening prayer (s. 83) and religious instruction approved by them after 3 P.M.; no child to be forced to remain (s. 84).	Opening prayer provision omitted, but separate schools exempted from the restrictions, leaving them free to teach religion as they saw fit (s. 78).	Previous provisions continued.
Language of instruction			

1887[102,103]	1887[104,105]	1901[106]
Controlled by section (s. 8).	Controlled by Council.	No sections.
Controlled by general Board of Examiners, one half of which is nominated by each section (s. 9), but textbooks for examining and teachers in history and science selected by sections (s. 10); certificate to be endorsed by member of Board and registered with Secretary (s. 167).	Controlled by Council of Public Instruction (s. 7); certificate to be endorsed by Council and registered with Superintendent (s. 168).	Controlled by Commissioner (s. 6); certified by single Board of Examiners appt. by LGIC; certificate to be issued under the regulations (s. 149).
Each section appointed two members of a General Board of four Examiners.	Controlled by Council.	Controlled by Commissioner (s. 6).
Controlled by section, but by Board if school is not designated either Protestant or Roman Catholic (ss. 7–8).	Controlled by Superintendent; appointed by LGIC (s. 9).	Controlled by Commissioner (s. 7(4).
Undesignated districts to choose textbooks authorized by one section, so "public" schools could select Protestant textbooks.[110]	Controlled by Council for both public and separate schools (s. 7).	Controlled by Commissioner (s. 6)
Opening prayer restored for public schools, if trustees so choose (s. 86(1)); otherwise, separate schools exempted from the restrictions (s. 86).	Restricted to the last half hour of the school day, and no child to be forced to remain (ss. 85–86).	Opening prayer, if trustees so choose, but no religious instruction in any district until last half hour, and no child to be forced to remain (ss. 137–38).
Still optional; trustees could authorize additional courses of instruction besides the 8 compulsory ones (s. 83)	All schools to teach elements of an English and commercial education (s. 4(b)); to be taught in English (s. 83); trustees of any school permitted to cause a primary course to be taught in French (s. 83(1)).[111]	All schools to teach in English, but trustees of any school permitted to cause a primary course to be taught in French; or upon agreement by parents and their payment of costs, any language (s. 136).

	1884[99]	1885[100]	1886[101]
Inspection	Inspectors appointed by section (s. 5), and by LGIC for districts, according to faith (s. 88).	Inspectors appointed by whole Board (s. 5(3–5)).	Controlled by whole Board, which hears appeals from their decisions; appointed by whole Board for schools not designated Protestant or Roman Catholic (s. 1).
Grants	Paid to organized districts, but aid paid in accordance with the 1881 Regulations to unorganized schools with 15 or more pupils (s. 91).	Paid according to the class of teaching certificate, daily average attendance, number of additional teachers, inspectors' reports, number of children in advanced classes (ss. 85–87).	Provisions continued, with minor adjustments to grant amounts.
Assessment	Assessed according to faith of owner, or in case of joint holding by Protestant and Catholic, in proportion to share (s. 99), unless owner elects to pay taxes to another school district not of his faith (s. 119).	Assessed according to faith of owner, or in case of joint holding by Protestant and Catholic, in proportion to share (ss. 89–90), unless owner elects to pay taxes to another school district not of his faith (s. 111).	No change.
School Types			
Fees			

1887[102,103]	1887[104,105]	1901[106]
Controlled by whole Board.	Appointed by LGIC (s. 11); under the control of the Council of Public Instruction (s. 7).	Controlled by Commissioner (s. 6), who appoints person to hear appeals from their decisions (s. 7).
Paid according to the class of teaching certificate, daily average attendance, number of additional teachers, inspectors' reports (s. 91).	70% of an amount consisting of: (1) $420 for schools with daily average attendance of 6–10 pupils; (2) $5 for each pupil over minimum; (3) $18 for each pupil over Standard III; (4) $50 for 1st class teacher certificate, or $25 if second class (s. 92).	Grants based on amount of assessable land in the district; incentives for longer school year, transportation, boarding students, number of students, and for high school classes (Ch. 31).
Assessed according to faith of owner, or in case of joint holding by Protestant and Catholic, in proportion to share (ss. 95–96); the ability to make election to pay taxes to another school district deleted.	Assessed according to faith of owner, or in case of joint holding by Protestant and Catholic, in proportion to share (ss. 98–99).	Assessed according to faith of owner (Ch. 30, s. 94), or in case of joint holding by Protestant and Catholic, in proportion to share of property or land of a company (Ch. 30, ss. 8–9).
	Public, Separate, Kindergarten, Night, Normal, Teachers' Institutes (s. 3).	Definitions removed. [112]
All schools free, unless parents or guardians are not ratepayers for that school (s. 89).	All schools free except high schools, i.e., Union Schools (s. 88), kindergarten (s. 89), and night school (s. 90).	Fees may be charged if a district maintains pupils above Standard V (s. 132), kindergarten (s. 140), and night school (s. 141).

Notes

1. Ironically, these Ordinances were influenced by the "national school" model developed by Ontarians such as Frederick William Gordon Haultain, chief executive of the North-West Territories and chairman of the Council of Public Instruction, and David Goggin, superintendent of education between 1893 and 1902, who followed the principles espoused by Egerton Ryerson, who was superintendent of education in Upper Canada and Ontario from 1844 to 1876, and the architect of non-sectarian, publicly-supported, centrally-controlled schools designed to bolster conformity, social harmony, and assimilation of the immigrant masses through uniform learning experiences for all. For a summary of Ryerson's achievements and the origins of Ontario's public and separate schools against the background of the rise of ultramontaine tendencies in the Roman Catholic hierarchy, see J. Donald Wilson, "The Ryerson Years in Canada West," in J. Donald Wilson, Robert M. Stamp, and Louis-Phillipe Audet, eds., *Canadian Education: A History* (Scarborough: Prentice Hall, 1970).

2. Numbers in Manoly R. Lupul, *The Roman Catholic Church and the North-West School Question: A Study in Church-State Relations in Western Canada, 1875–1905* (Toronto: University of Toronto Press, 1974), 183.

3. For quotations from the press, see Lupul, *The Roman Catholic Church and the North-West School Question*, 182–83.

4. Reproduced in: Douglas R. Owram, ed., *The Formation of Alberta: A Documentary History* (Calgary: Alberta Records Publication Board; Historical Society of Alberta, 1979), 274–75.

5. Reproduced in Owram, ed., *The Formation of Alberta*, 299–300.

6. House of Commons Debates (HCD) 3099.

7. For discussion, see M.P. Toombs, "The Control and Support of Public Education in Rupert's Land and the North-West Territories to 1905 and in Saskatchewan to 1960" (Ph.D. Diss., University of Minnesota, 1962), 72ff.

8. Section 146, *British North America Act, 1867*, 30 & 31 Victoria, c. 3 (U.K,). Rupert's Land and the North-Western Territory (subsequently designated the North-West Territories) became part of Canada, pursuant to section 146 and the *Rupert's Land Act, 1868*, 31–32 Vict., c. 105 (U.K.) by Order-in-Council of June 23, 1870. The power of the Parliament of Canada to establish provinces in territories other than the original provinces was reaffirmed by the *British North America Act, 1871*, 34–35 Vict., c. 28 (U.K.). The Province of Alberta was established, pursuant to the *British North America Act, 1871*, by the *Alberta Act* (July 20, 1905) 4–5 Edw. VII, c. 3 (Canada). These statutes are conveniently collected in *Revised Statutes of Canada*, 1970, Appendices, and described on p. 231.

9. Upon payment of £300,000 and on terms set out in Order-in-Council of June 23, 1870, *Revised Statutes of Canada*, 1970, Appendices, p. 257ff.

10. For example, Roman Catholic schools were established at Lac Ste. Anne in 1842, at Edmonton in 1860, at St. Paul de Cris, near Duvernay, in 1865, and at St. Paul in the 1890s. See John C. Chalmers, *Schools of the Foothills Province: The Story of Public Education in Alberta* (Toronto: University of Toronto Press, 1967), 10–11. For details about early Catholic schools and their leaders in Alberta, see Lupul, *The Roman Catholic Church and the North-West School Question*.

11. Section 5 of *An Act for the temporary Government of Rupert's Land and the North-Western Territory when united with Canada, 1869*, 32–33 Victoria, c. 3 (Canada) (*Revised Statutes of Canada*, 1970, Appendices, p. 244); repealed as a "Schedule A" Act by section 76 of the *North-West Territories*

Act 1875 which nevertheless provided that "such repeal shall not affect any duty accrued, right acquired, or penalty, forfeiture or liability incurred under the said Acts, or any of them...." (*Revised Statutes of Canada*, 1970, Appendices, p. 257ff.)

12. On September 1, 1905, there were 560 school districts in the new province. To illustrate the rate of growth in those days, in 1881 the entire non-Indian population in the North-West Territories was 6,974; by contrast, there were 24,254 pupils in the organized school districts on the date of union, a figure which rose to 28,784 in 1906, representing an increase of 18 per cent. See Province of Alberta, Dept. of Education, *Annual Report 1906* (Edmonton, 1907), 12. In a December 30, 1893, answer by Haultain to a petition for disallowance of the 1892 Ordinance, he stated that there were 44 Roman Catholic and 286 Protestant schools in the North-West Territories. See *Sessional Papers*, 4th Session of the 7th Parliment, 1894, no. 17, p. 13.

13. *Revised Statutes of Canada*, 1970, Appendices, p. 257ff.

14. 38 Vict. 1875, c. 49.

15. The opposition to it is described by Robert Carney, "'Hostility Unmasked' Catholic Schooling in Territorial Alberta," in Nick Kach and Kas Mazurek, eds., *Exploring Our Educational Past—Schooling in the North-West Territories and Alberta* (Calgary: Detselig, 1992), 23; and Lupul, *The Roman Catholic Church and the North-West School Question*, 14–17.

16. Toombs, "The Control and Support of Public Education in Rupert's Land," 89, 111. For background on the debates in Parliament over the school clause in the *North-West Territories Act*, see Lupul, *The Roman Catholic Church and the North-West School Question*, 13–16.

17. Lupul, *The Roman Catholic Church and the North-West School Question*, 8–10, 17–20; Toombs, "The Control and Support of Public Education in Rupert's Land," 86. Toombs adds that "the limitation clauses of section 93 of the British North America Act could not apply."

18. Robert Carney, "'Hostility Unmasked'," 23; Sister L.A. Hochstein, F.C.J., "Roman Catholic Separate and Public Schools in Alberta" (M.Ed. Diss., University of Alberta, 1954), 13.

19. Described in useful detail in F.C.J. Hochstein, "Roman Catholic Separate and Public Schools," 13 48.

20. For example, Frederick William Gordon Haultain, Chairman of the North-West Executive Committeee; David James Goggin, Superindendent of Education for the Territories, 1893–1902, an administrator who was Haultain's right-hand man, described by Neil McDonald as "a Canadian nationalist imperialist who identified strongly with the Anglo-Saxon WASP community of nineteenth-century Canada." Neil McDonald, "Canadian Nationalism and North-West Schools, 1884–1905" in Alf Chaiton and Neil McDonald, eds., *Canadian Schools and Canadian Identity* (Toronto: Gage Educational, 1977), 19. All of these men were influenced by Egerton Ryerson, superintendent of education in Ontario from 1844 to 1876.

21. E.g., Oblates Bishop Vital Grandin of St. Albert, Bishop Emile Grouard of Athabaska-McKenzie, E. Legal, Father Albert Lacombe, Father Leduc, and Adelard Langevin, Archbishop of St. Boniface, who brought papal perspectives on the importance of educating Catholic children in Catholic schools to bear on their school activities. See Lupul, *The Catholic Church and the North-West School Question*, chap. 1; Annette Ramrattan, "The Theory of Catholic Schooling in the Archdiocese of Edmonton, 1884–1960" (M.Ed. Diss., University of Alberta, 1982).

22. By 1885, Roman Catholics were in the minority in the Territories. See Ramrattan, "The Theory of Catholic Schooling," 91. For a discussion of how important the changing population distribution between Roman Catholics and Protestants was to the movement away from the initial Protestant support for the dual system with which their Quebec counterparts protected themselves, see Toombs, "The Control and Support of Public Education in Rupert's Land," 153–61.

23. F.W.G. Haultain, quoted in Neil McDonald, "Canadian Nationalism and North-West Schools, 1884–1905," in Alf Chaiton and Neil McDonald, eds., *Canadian Schools and Canadian Identity*, 63.

24. Haultain became leader of the Provincial Rights Party, the official opposition, and later became chief justice of Saskatchewan in 1912. See McDonald, "Canadian Nationalism and North-West Schools," 61. On Haultain's background, see Lupul, *The Roman Catholic Church and the North-West School Question*, 82–83.

25. See McDonald, "Canadian Nationalism and North-West Schools," 66–73; and Neil McDonald, "David J. Goggin: Promoter of National Schools," in David C. Jones, Nancy M. Sheehan, Robert M. Stamp, eds., *Shaping the Schools of the Canadian West* (Calgary: Detselig, 1979), 14–36; Lupul, *The Roman Catholic Church and the North-West School Question*, 83–85.

26. For a description of this struggle for control of the schools, see Toombs, "The Control and Support of Public Education in Rupert's Land," 94ff.

27. Father Hippolyte Leduc, *Hostility Unmasked: School Ordinance of 1892 of the North-West Territories and its Disastrous Results* (Montreal: C.O. Beauchemin and Sons, 1896), 2, 4.

28. Leduc, *Hostility Unmasked*, 7.

29. From an unpublished interview with Haultain at the Assiniboia Club, Regina, August 8, 1931. Quoted in Neil McDonald, "Canadian Nationalism and North-West Schools," 82.

30. Lupul, *The Roman Catholic Church and the North-West School Question*, 81.

31. Leduc, *Hostility Unmasked*, 31. See Lupul, *The Roman Catholic Church and the North-West School Question*, 88–102, for a review of the petitions and their outcome and political impact.

32. Teacher certification was a continuing battleground for the Catholic hierarchy, who resented the implication that Catholic teachers, in particular, the established teaching orders who ran many of the earliest schools, were inferior to Protestant teachers increasingly favoured in the North-West Territories. See Lupul, *The Roman Catholic Church and the North-West School Question*, 32–35, 87–88. Inspectors' reports were full of references to the "difficulties" of teachers not properly trained to assimilate the foreign elements in the population to the "national sentiment." Therefore, the inspectors recommended a session in the Normal School as a prerequisite to being given authority to teach. These sessions were supervised by Goggin as Director of Normal Schools, who was the chief instructor in Regina. In this way, Goggin wrote, teachers who did not "understand our conditions, [were] ignorant of our school laws, [and failed] to appreciate our aims" could be retrained. Quoted in McDonald, "Canadian Nationalism and North-West Schools," 81–82.

33. The petitions, contained in *Sessional Papers of Canada*, 1894, Vol. XXVII, No. 40C, are described in detail in Toombs, "The Control and Support of Public Education in Rupert's Land," 135–38. By 1893, there were 47 petitions to disallow the Ordinance. See Lupul, *The Roman Catholic Church and the North-West School Question*, 80–81.

34. Lupul, *The Roman Catholic Church and the North-West School Question*, 103–15.

35. See Table 3.1. See also Lupul, *The Roman Catholic Church and the North-West School Question*, 118.

36. Robert Steven Patterson, "F.W.G. Haultain and Education in the Early West" (M.Ed. Diss., University of Alberta, 1961), 65.

37. A contemporary description quoted in Patterson, "F.W.G. Haultain and Education in the Early West," 68.

38. Lupul, *The Roman Catholic Church and the North-West School Question*, 167.

39. For work done in relation to nineteenth-century education administration in Ontario, see the work of R.D. Gidney. In particular, see: R.D. Gidney and D.A. Lawr, "The Development of an Administrative System for the Public Schools: The First Stage, 1841–50," in Neil

McDonald and Alf Chaiton, eds., *Egerton Ryerson and His Times* (Toronto: MacMillan, 1978), 160–83; R.D. Gidney, "Centralization and Education: The Origins of an Ontario Tradition," *Journal of Canadian Studies* 7, no. 4 (Nov. 1972): 33–48; R.D. Gidney and W.P.J. Millar, "Rural Schools and the Decline of Community Control in Nineteenth Century Ontario," in *Fourth Annual Agricultural History of Ontario Seminar Proceedings*, October 28, 1979 (Guelph: University of Guelph, 1979), 70–91; R.D. Gidney and W.P.J. Millar, *Inventing Secondary Education: The Rise of the High School in Nineteenth Century Ontario* (Kingston: McGill-Queen's University Press, 1990); and R.D. Gidney and D.A. Lawr, "Who Ran the Schools? Local Influence on Education Policy in Nineteenth Century Ontario," *Ontario History* LXXII, no. 2 (1980): 3–13. See also Chad Gaffield, "Children, Schooling, and Family Reproduction in Nineteenth-Century Ontario," *Canadian Historical Review* LXXII, no. 2 (1991): 157–91.

40. *Public School Boards Association of Alberta v. Alberta* (2000) 191 DLR (4th) 513 (SCC), in which Major J. concluded, without intervention from municipal organizations, that municipal institutions and school boards do not have an independent constitutional status, a sphere of reasonable autonomy based on implicit legal norms derived from s. 92(8) and s. 93 of the *Constitution Act, 1867* and from s. 17 of the *Alberta Act*, but are mere creatures of provincial legislation. School boards are the "vehicles through which the constitutionally entrenched denominational rights of individuals are realized" (p. 530). The author has had the benefit of access to the historical evidence before the Court and to the views of counsel for PSBAA, Dale Gibson, the author's husband.

41. Evelyn Eager, "Separate Schools and the Cabinet Crisis of 1905," *Lakehead University Review* 2, no. 2 (Fall 1969): 91–115, at 96.

42. Quoted in Lupul, *The Roman Catholic Church and the North-West School Question*, 162–63.

43. Since 1982 referred to as the *Constitution Act, 1867*.

44. Quoted in Lupul, *The Roman Catholic Church and the North-West School Question*, 163; see p. 171 for a contrary view expressed by a legal advisor to the Catholics.

45. Lupul, *The Roman Catholic Church and the North-West School Question*, 169–70.

46. For example, on February 7, 1905, he wrote to Laurier and included amended wording of the draft he had received from the minister of justice (Laurier Papers, vol. 354, pp. 94549–94551, MG 26 G 1(a), National Archives of Canada). For an account of Sbaretti's and Legal's efforts at an earlier stage to influence the bill from the outset, see Lupul, *The Roman Catholic Church and the North-West School Question*, 166–79.

47. Laurier Papers, vol. 355, pp. 94822–94823, MG 26 G 1(a), National Archives of Canada. Laurier rejected the words as likely to cause a great deal of trouble.

48. Laurier's Secretary of State.

49. Sbaretti to Laurier, March 11, 1905, Laurier Papers, vol. 359, pp. 95661–95663, MG 26 G 1(a), National Archives of Canada.

50. As the Alberta Legislature has never attempted to abolish public school districts altogether, the proposition that the derivative right of the minority in any school district ensures that public school districts must continue to exist has not been tested. However, if a constitutionally-protected separate school right can only be exercised if there is a public school district within which to exert it, then there may be a right to secure the bare existence of a public school district vested in separate school supporters. The PSBAA case was concerned with protecting the implicit constitutional right to local government from intrusive provincial control, not the existence of school districts.

51. Laurier's letter to Sbaretti, March 7, 1904, Laurier Papers, 82982, is reproduced in Owram, ed., *The Formation of Alberta*, 267.

52. Sbaretti to Laurier, March 13, 1905, Laurier Papers, vol. 359, pp. 35718–35720, MG 26 G 1(a), National Archives of Canada, reproduced in Owram, ed., *The Formation of Alberta*, 311–12.

53. Laurier to Sbaretti, May 2, 1905, Laurier Papers, vol. 364, pp. 97194–97195, MG 26 G 1(a), National Archives of Canada.

54. Sbaretti to Laurier, May 7, 1905, Laurier Papers, vol. 365, pp. 97249–97250, MG 26 G 1(a), National Archives of Canada.

55. For a detailed survey of Catholic differences over the degree to which opposition to the Sifton clause should be made public, see Lupul, *The Roman Catholic Church and the North-West School Question*, 180–212.

56. Reproduced in *Sessional Papers*, 4th Session of the 7th Parliament, 1894, vol. 17, pp. 12–15.

57. The petitions and the memorial comprise pp. 1–66 of *Sessional Papers*, 4th Session of the 7th Parliament, 1894, vol. 17.

58. See especially *Sessional Papers*, 1894, vol. 17, pp. 44–49. On the Manitoba School Question, see Toombs, "The Control and Support of Public Education in Rupert's Land," 72–85.

59. Father H. Leduc, O.M.I., letter dated February 17, 1894, Appendix A to the Memorial of Archbishop Taché, *Sessional Papers*, 4th Session of the 7th Parliament, 1894, vol. 17, p. 58.

60. A.E. Forget, secretary to the lieutenant-governor, letter dated March 1, 1894, Appendix D to the Memorial of Archbishop Taché, *Sessional Papers*, 4th Session of the 7th Parliament, 1894, vol. 17, p. 62.

61. Evelyn Eager, "Separate Schools and the Cabinet Crisis," 96–97; see Lupul, *The Roman Catholic Church and the North-West School Question*, 170ff.

62. Laurier to J.R. Dougall, "The Witness," March 4, 1905, Laurier Papers, vol. 358, pp. 95478–95480, MG 26 G 1(a). It has been suggested that Laurier was not fully aware of what he was doing with his proposal, not having had opportunity to discuss the matter with Sifton prior to its introduction in the Commons, but that proposition is rejected by J.W. Dafoe, *Laurier, A Study in Canadian Politics* (Toronto: McLelland and Stewart, 1963), 77, who attributes the wording to an attempt to appease his Quebec supporters who were still resentful over the settlement of the Manitoba school question. Dafoe goes so far as to say (on pp. 78–79) that it had already been decided within the government to continue in the provincial constitution the precise rights enjoyed by the minority under the territorial school ordinances of 1901. Laurier and his minister of justice, Charles Fitzpatrick, contended that the autonomy bill did just that, while Sifton, absent at the time the education portion of the autonomy bill was drafted, obviously felt that it did not embody what had been agreed upon and tendered his resignation. Both Laurier's Ontario and Quebec Party factions felt betrayed at the end of the day.

63. See Lupul, *The Roman Catholic Church and the North-West School Question*, 170–75.

64. HCD 1435.

65. HCD 1441–42.

66. HCD 1448–51.

67. HCD 1452.

68. HCD 1453.

69. Reproduced in Owram, ed., *The Formation of Alberta*, 290–91.

70. Reproduced in Owram, ed., *The Formation of Alberta*, 294.

71. Published in the *Toronto Globe* on March 13, 1905, according to Lupul, *The Roman Catholic Church and the North-West School Question*, 187.

72. Order of Her Majesty–in–Council Admitting Rupert's Land and the North-Western Territory into the Union, June 23, 1870, in RS 1906.

73. Reproduced in Owram, ed., *The Formation of Alberta*, 303–05.

74. The debate over whether section 93(1) is operative in Alberta has continued. In *Public School Boards Association of Alberta v. Alberta* (2000) 191 DLR (4th) 513 (SCC), Major J. assumed it does: "The Province of Alberta may alter educational institutions within its borders as it sees fit, subject only to those rights afforded through the combined effect of s. 93 and s. 17" (at p. 530).

75. See Lupul, *The Roman Catholic Church and the North-West School Question*, 180ff.

76. Sifton Papers, vol. 263, pp. 209–12, reproduced in Owram, ed., *The Formation of Alberta*, 294–95.

77. Lupul, *The Roman Catholic Church and the North-West School Question*, 176.

78. Sifton Papers, vol. 263, pp. 228–29. Sifton announced his resignation in the House of Commons on March 1, 1905, assigning the reason exclusively to his differences with Laurier over the school question (HCD 1851–1853). In a letter to Laurier written the previous day, he had expressed himself at least as strongly, saying: "The school lands endowment of the Territories will amount to some millions of acres—the proceeds will be many millions of dollars. The proposition made would constitute a most colossal endowment of sectarian education from public property," Sifton Papers, vol. 263, pp. 213–15.

79. Sifton to Dafoe, March 11, 1905, quoted in Evelyn Eager, "Separate Schools and the Cabinet Crisis," 100–01.

80. Lord Grey to Laurier, March 2, 1905, Laurier Papers, pp. 202922–29, quoted in Evelyn Eager, "Separate Schools and the Cabinet Crisis," 98.

81. Sifton to Laurier, February 26, 1905, Sifton Papers, vol. 263, pp. 213–15, reproduced in Owram, ed., *The Formation of Alberta*, 296.

82. Sifton to Dafoe, March 11, 1905, Sifton Papers, vol. 263, pp. 660–63, reproduced in Owram, ed., *The Formation of Alberta*, 309–10.

83. Sifton acknowledged in the House of Commons on March 24, 1905, in reply to Opposition taunts that the amendment was substantially the same as the original education clause, that the amendment was "in accordance with the views I had formed in the course of my administration of that country," HCD 3093.

84. HCD 2915–2926.

85. Evelyn Eager, "Separate Schools and the Cabinet Crisis of 1905," 104–08.

86. HCD 3153. Lupul described Oliver as the most open opponent of separate schools. See Lupul, *The Roman Catholic Church and the North-West School Question*, 189–90.

87. HCD 5400–5401, 5423.

88. 4–5 Edward VII, c. 3 (Canada) (*Revised Statutes of Canada*, 1970, Appendices, pp. 317 ff., reprinted in R.S.C. 1985, App. II, No. 20.)

89. This has been held not to require "formalistic equality," but fairness in proportionality between public and separate educational opportunities: *Public School Boards Association of Alberta v. Alberta* (2000) 191 DLR (4th) 513 at 534 (SCC).

90. (2000) 191 DLR (4th) 513 at 537 (SCC).

91. Report of the Royal Commission on Education in Alberta, 1959 (Edmonton: 1959), 269.

92. Report of the Royal Commission on Education in Alberta, 1959 (Edmonton: 1959), 270.

93. *Caldwell v. Stuart* (1985) 1 WWR 620 (SCC).

94. E.g. *Casagrande v. Hinton Roman Catholic Separate School District No 155* (1987) 51 Alta. L.R. (2d) 349 (QB).

95. See *Reference re Bill 30, An Act to Amend the Education Act* (Ont.) (1987) 40 DLR (4th) 18 (SCC).

96. See, for example, *Casagrande v. Hinton Roman Catholic Separate School District No 155* (1987) 51 Alta. L.R. (2d) 349 (QB) and *Calgary Board of Education v. A.-G. Alberta* (1980) 106 DLR (3d) 415 (Alta. QB); affirmed (1981) 122 DLR (3d) 249 (CA); leave to appeal refused (1981) 122 DLR (3d) 249fn. (SCC).

97. See, for example, *Caldwell v. Stuart* (1985) 1 WWR 620 (SCC), but the rights have not transferred to other minority religions: e.g. *Adler v. Ontario* (1996) 140 DLR (4th) 385 (SCC).

98. (2000) 191 DLR (4th) 513 at 530 (SCC), after citing *Reference re Education Act* (Que.) (1993) 105 DLR (4th) 266, in which Justice Gonthier said: "What s. 93 of the Constitution guarantees...is the right to dissent itself, not the form of the institutions which have made it possible to exercise that right since 1867."

99. No. 5 of 1884: *An Ordinance providing for the organization of Schools in the North-West Territories*.

100. No. 3 of 1885: *An Ordinance to amend and consolidate as amended the School Ordinance of 1884*, which by section 168 came into force on February 1, 1886, repealing the School Ordinance of 1884.

101. No. 10 of 1886: *An Ordinance to Amend the School Ordinance of 1885*, amendments enacted November 16, 1886.

102. No. 2 of 1887: *An Ordinance Respecting Schools*, enacted November 18, 1887, by section 182, repealing the Ordinances of 1885 and 1886, and by section 174, continuing all schools heretofore established subject to this Ordinance.

103. There were further ordinances between 1887 and 1892: No. 59 of 1888, No. 20 of 1889, No. 15 of 1890 (which provided for "Union Schools" to be established in adjacent school districts for high school purposes), No. 28 of 1891–92 (which provided that the LGIC could appoint school inspectors).

104. No. 22 of 1892: *Ordinance to Amend and Consolidate as amended the Ordinances Respecting Schools*, by section 193, repealing the Ordinances of 1888, 1889, 1890, and 1891–92. For an account of Haultain's travails in having the School Ordinance of 1892 enacted, see: Robert Steven Patterson, "F.W.G. Haultain and Education in the Early West" (M.Ed. thesis, University of Alberta, 1961), 45–60.

105. There were further ordinances between 1892 and 1901: No. 23 of 1893 (expanding control of LGIC over appointing persons to carry out purposes of the ordinances; giving the Council power to suspend teachers for cause and to cancel certificates); No. 9 of 1994 (amending section 2 to require that any general regulations regarding schools, teachers, textbooks, or normal sessions be adopted only at a general meeting of the Council called for the purpose, and amending section 85 to permit any school to be opened with reciting the Lord's Prayer); No. 2 of 1896 (making by section 4 the two Protestants and two Roman Catholics full members of the Council of Public Instruction; making by section 107 the prohibition on religious instruction applicable to all schools, but any school can open with the Lord's Prayer; beginning with section 125, a new provision for dividing corporate taxes with separate boards), repealing in section 229 the Ordinance of 1892, No. 3 of 1897, No. 26 of 1900.

106. Section numbers refer to Chapter 29 of 1901: *An Ordinance respecting Schools*, in effect September 1, 1901, and repealing the Ordinances of 1898 and 1900, unless specific reference is made to the companion ordinances, Chapter 30 of 1901: *An Ordinance respecting Assessment and Taxation in School Districts*, in effect January 1, 1902; Chapter 31 of 1901: *An Ordinance to Regulate Public Aid to Schools*, in effect January 1, 1902.

107. The 1884 Ordinance provided that every school district was to be designated either Protestant or Roman Catholic, depending on the majority in the district. The minority had the right to form a Protestant or Roman Catholic separate school district. Under the 1884 Ordinance, therefore, there were 48 Protestant school districts, 10 Roman Catholic public school districts, and one Roman Catholic separate school district erected and, in addition, there were eight Roman Catholic and four Protestant schools receiving grants from the federal government but not yet formed into districts under the 1884 Ordinance. By 1888, there were 132 Protestant public school districts, 22 Roman Catholic public school

districts, and six Roman Catholic separate school districts: see M.P. Toombs, "The Control and Support of Public Education in Rupert's Land", 99 and 114. This regime explains the existence of what is now Greater St. Albert Catholic regional Division No. 35, the public school board, and St Albert Protestant Separate School District No. 6, since the Roman Catholic ratepayers were in the majority at the time the district was organized.

108. Lupul, *The Roman Catholic Church and the North-West School Question*, 25.

109. The advisors became members of the Council of Public Instruction by section 4 of the 1896 Ordinance.

110. See 1894 Regulations and Lupul, *The Roman Catholic Church and the North-West School Question*, 28.

111. McDonald describes the purpose of this provision as being to reduce French from a language of instruction to a subject of instruction and points out that the provision was included only after prolonged and bitter debate: "Canadian Nationalism and North-West Schools, 1884–1905," in Chaiton and McDonald, eds., *Canadian Schools and Canadian Identity*, 80. Lupul describes the split between French- and English-speaking Roman Catholics, compounded by divisions between Métis groups and among the clergy over French as the language of instruction: Lupul, *The Roman Catholic Church and the North-West School Question*, 31–32.

112. This paved the way for state support for Roman Catholic secondary schools, described as a distinguishing feature of the Alberta system, since high schools were not differentiated from elementary schools for purposes of the 1905 constitutionalization of separate schools: C.B. Sissons, *Church & State in Canadian Education* (Toronto: Ryerson, 1959), 341–43.

Four

One Language and One Nationality
The Forcible Constitution of a Unilingual Province
in a Bilingual Country, 1870–2005[1]

EDMUND A. AUNGER

Introduction

In 1870, Canada purchased the Hudson's Bay Company holdings known as Rupert's Land and joined them with the North-West Territory; it then redivided these newly consolidated lands, renaming them Manitoba and the North-West Territories. (In 1905, after further reorganization, it carved two large pieces out of the North-West Territories in order to create the provinces of Alberta and Saskatchewan.) Manitoba, encompassing the former District of Assiniboia, the most settled part of Rupert's Land, had used English and French in its government and courts for more than two decades and, as part of the Confederation bargain, the Canadian government agreed to constitutionally entrench this language regime. It followed suit, seven years later, by also providing for official bilingualism in the North-West Territories.

The 1870 annexation opened the floodgates to immigrants from the neighbouring province of Ontario and, in less than a decade, thousands of English-speaking colonists had swamped the North-West's original population. French-speakers, for example, who had numbered about three-quarters of the non-Native population in the 1870s, accounted for less than one-fifth by 1885. The new majority demanded an end to bilingualism and biculturalism—it sought, instead, exclusivity for the English language and supremacy for the British nationality. Thus began the forcible constitution of a unilingual region, initiated first by the government of the North-West Territories, then continued subsequently by the government of Alberta.

Political scientist Jean Laponce has argued convincingly that such efforts are the norm in situations of language contact: "Each language group strives to establish its domination and exclusivity in a given territory, goals much more easily achieved if a language has control of the machinery of government and in particular the control of an independent state."[2]

Historian Ramsay Cook concurs, observing that Canada's language debates have been shaped since the nineteenth century by Lord Durham's assumption that linguistic homogeneity is fundamental to nation-building. If British North America were to remain British, "its inhabitants would have to speak English. Francophones would have to accept assimilation."[3] However, as constitutionalist Joseph Eliot Magnet rightly points out with particular reference to the Western Canadian experience, attempts to legislate unilingualism have often borne bitter fruit: "The examples illustrate a vicious vein in Canada's history typified by bitter, dangerous conflict fought over language rights as a result of a stingy, vindictive spirit by provincial majorities. It is [a] history of explosive racial strife, full of dangers for the Canadian Federal State."[4]

This essay examines the history of language legislation in Alberta and the regional government's determined attempt to build a unilingual province in a bilingual country. Three distinct time periods are highlighted. The first, a relatively short period dating from 1870 until 1887, was a time of official bilingualism, when both English and French co-existed as languages of government and justice. The second, characterizing most of the next century, was a time of forcible unilingualism, as the government actively legislated the exclusive use of the English language. The third, beginning about 1988, has been a time of relative tolerance. English is now universal in Alberta, but the provincial government has permitted, and occasionally supported, the use of other languages.

Official Bilingualism in Canada's North-West, 1870–1887
Manitoba-based Bilingualism, 1870–1876

On May 12, 1870, Canada proclaimed the *Manitoba Act, 1870*, an act that provided primarily for the government of the newly created province of Manitoba, but also for the North-West Territories. Section 35 charged the lieutenant-governor of Manitoba with responsibility for the North-West Territories, thereby assuring them a bilingual administration. Section 23 had formally recognized English and French as Manitoba's official languages:

> Either the English or the French language may be used by any person in the debates of the Houses of the Legislature, and both these languages shall be used in the respective Records and Journals of those Houses;

and either of those languages may be used by any person, or in any Pleading or Process, in or issuing from any Court of Canada established under the British North America Act, 1867, or in or from all or any of the Courts of the Province. The Acts of the Legislature shall be printed and published in both those languages.

The first lieutenant-governor of Manitoba and the North-West Territories, Adams G. Archibald, was a Nova Scotian, and a Father of Confederation, who spoke both English and French. He appointed a North-West Executive and Legislative Council composed of three prominent Manitoba residents, Francis G. Johnson, Pascal Breland and Donald A. Smith, and reported that "my present Council gives a fair representation of the three great interests of the West, the English, the French & the Hudson's Bay interest."[5] Unfortunately, Archibald had exceeded his authority by making these appointments and although he subsequently submitted a new list of nominees to the Canadian government, he finished his term of office before it was approved.

Archibald's successor, Alexander Morris, the former chief justice of Manitoba, took office on December 2, 1872. The first North-West Council, appointed the same month, was composed of 11 members, although it increased a year later to 18. Five councillors were French-speaking: Marc Girard, Pascal Breland, Joseph Dubuc, Joseph Royal, and Pierre Delorme. Girard, Dubuc and Royal were French Canadians; Breland and Delorme, French-speaking Métis. Although a minority, they carried considerable political weight. Marc Girard, the senior councillor, had been called to the Canadian Senate in 1871 and was subsequently appointed premier of Manitoba in 1873. Joseph Dubuc and Joseph Royal were co-founders of Manitoba's French-language newspaper, Le Métis. Pascal Breland had been a member of the Council of Assiniboia; Pierre Delorme had served as a delegate to the provisional government's 1869 and 1870 conventions. All five held seats in the Manitoba Legislative Assembly.

The North-West Council apparently recognized two, and occasionally three, official languages. For example, on September 13, 1873, it directed its legislative committee "to see that all Acts of Council &c shall be published in the English, French, and Cree languages."[6] The following year, at its March 16, 1874 meeting, the Council requested that the clerk prepare a legal manual containing all its acts, and print a number "in both French and English" for use by public officials. On June 2, 1874, a council committee, chaired by Joseph Dubuc, reported two bills and instructed the secretary "to enlarge their

Preambles and have copies of the Bills printed (in English and French) for the use of Members."

The Assiniboia General Court, later the Manitoba Court of Queen's Bench, with its bilingual judges and mixed jury system, was the North-West's first supreme court.

Legislative Entrenchment of Official Bilingualism, 1877

In 1876, the Canadian government finally proclaimed an act adopted the previous year, the *North-West Territories Act, 1875*, thus establishing a separate North-West administration distinct from the Manitoba regime and without its French-language components. It also appointed an English-speaking government, led by Lieutenant-Governor David Laird, a Prince Edward Islander and former minister of the interior, and Magistrate-Councillors Hugh Richardson, Mathew Ryan and James F. Macleod. The French-language *Le Métis* expressed its bitter disappointment that

> la population métisse des territoires du Nord-Ouest, c'est-à-dire les trois quarts de la population n'a pas un seul représentant dans le Conseil Exécutif, législatif et judiciaire de son propre pays. On ignore sa langue, ses habitudes, son caractère; mais on lui fait des lois et on se prépare à le juger et d'une façon singulière comme on le voit.[7]

It called upon the minister of the interior to modify the *North-West Territories Act* and to restore the rights previously enjoyed by the French-speaking population.

Marc Girard, a former North-West Council member, now the only French-speaking Westerner in the Canadian parliament, echoed this complaint when in 1877 the Canadian government introduced an amending bill to repeal the council's legislative powers. He argued that the North-West had been better off under the Manitoba regime. Now, its affairs were "in the hands of strangers."[8] Further, "the French language seemed to have been totally ignored in the bill, although the majority of people of the territories were French, and they had as much right to have their language acknowledged there as they had in Quebec and Manitoba by having a translation of all the ordinances passed for their guidance." Ten days later, he successfully proposed an amendment that entrenched English and French as official languages in the North-West Territories, its council and its courts. Section 11 of the amended *North-West Territories Act, 1875* now provided that:

> Either the English or the French language may be used by any person in the debates of the said Council, and in the proceedings before the Courts, and both those languages shall be used in the records and journals of the said Council, and the ordinances of the said Council shall be printed in both those languages.

In 1880, this provision was altered to read "the Council or Legislative Assembly" in anticipation that an elected Assembly would soon replace the appointed council, and in 1886 it was renumbered, becoming section 110 of a revised statute.

Official Bilingualism in the North-West, 1878–1881

On July 1, 1878, in response to complaints that the French-speaking Métis had no representation on the North-West Council, the Canadian government added a fourth member, Pascal Breland. Breland had a long record of public service—he had been appointed to the Council of Assiniboia in 1857, elected to the Manitoba Legislative Assembly in 1870, and named to the first North-West Council in 1872. Several years later, in 1883, the government appointed a second French-speaker, Charles Rouleau, who also served as stipendiary magistrate.

The North-West Council met in Battleford, the new capital, in 1878, 1879 and 1881, and its clerk, Amédée Forget, faithfully recorded the minutes and ordinances in English, before translating them into French. P.G. Laurie, the government printer, then published the ordinances in separate volumes, by year and language. The North-West secretary reported a printing of 200 French-language copies of the 1878 and 1879 ordinances, "practically all" distributed.[9] The print-run was increased to 300 French-language copies for the 1881 ordinances.

Several ordinances required that public notices be printed and posted in both French and English. In 1881, for example, the *Ordinance Respecting Trespassing and Stray Animals*, section 9(2), directed the pound-keeper to insert notices about impounded animals in the nearest newspaper "in both English and French if apparently necessary." The same year, a *Proclamation relating to*

Electoral Districts and Elections in the North-West Territories, section 50, provided that: "In any Electoral District in which a number of the electors speak the French language, such proclamation and notices shall be issued in the English and French language." Three years later, the *Ordinance Providing for the Organization of Schools in the North-West Territories* issued more comprehensive directives. According to section 15(1), all notices advising electors of a proposed school district "must be in both the French and English languages." Further, in section 17(2), the returning officer was obliged to post, in the polling place, "a copy of the notice of voting in both languages." Finally, once the lieutenant-governor had proclaimed the election of a school district, section 41 required that: "This proclamation shall be printed and posted up in at least ten public and conspicuous places throughout the district, at least fourteen days before the day appointed therein for the nomination and election of trustees, and shall be in both the French and English languages."

Dewdney's Obstruction of Bilingualism, 1882–1887

The Canadian government's decision, on December 3, 1881, to appoint Edgar Dewdney, an English-born engineer, as lieutenant-governor, marked an important turning point in the North-West's official bilingualism. The population's linguistic composition was rapidly changing, and Dewdney's anti-French prejudices fitted the new environment. A year earlier, the census had shown that while French-speakers still constituted a majority of the non-Native population, their proportions were dwindling: there were 2,900 French and 2,500 British inhabitants.[10] Four years later, however, a special census conducted in three provisional districts—Alberta, Assiniboia, and Saskatchewan—counted 4,900 French, but 22,000 British inhabitants.[11] The government moved with the tide and in March 1883 the North-West capital settled in Regina.

In 1883, the North-West Council held its fourth legislative session and the new government printer, Nicholas Flood Davin, published both the English- and French-language ordinances promptly during the same year. Thereafter, however, the situation deteriorated. Although the English-language ordinances for 1884, 1885, 1886 and 1887 were printed almost immediately, at the end of the corresponding legislative session, the French language ordinances languished. They were neither translated nor printed. Finally, during the last year of his mandate, Lieutenant-Governor Dewdney apparently tried to make amends, contracting for the full printing of the backlog. Before this work could be completed, however, Dewdney's successor ordered that the North-West ordinances be revised and consolidated, thereby rendering the previous versions obsolete. In 1889, Frederick Haultain, a leading member of the North-West Assembly, reported disgustedly that "[l]ast year, just as the House had finished revising and consolidating the ordinances, large bales of French ordinances were being brought in from the east and deposited in the government buildings. The Territories were saddled with this large expense and the printing was altogether useless."[12]

The ordinances were not the only French-language publication, although they were the most important. The first issue of the *North-West Territories Gazette* appeared on December 8, 1883, and was printed in both English and French, in parallel columns. Seven issues appeared in 1884; this was increased to twelve issues in 1886. The council minutes were not published until 1886, at which time the complete series was printed *en bloc*, in both English and French.

The failure to print the French-language ordinances, except after a considerable delay, was a portent of things to come. The council was routinely eliminating, without fanfare, its various legislative provisions for French-language proclamations and notices. In 1885, for example, when the council amended and consolidated the *School Ordinance*, it systematically purged all bilingual requirements. The 1888 consolidation of North West legislation similarly omitted all references to language, whether English or French.

One Language and one Nationality in the North-West
and Alberta, 1888–1987
The Dual-Language Question, 1888–1904

On May 22, 1888, the Canadian parliament amended the *North-West Territories Act* and provided, in section 2, for a Legislative Assembly that "shall have the powers and shall perform the duties heretofore vested in and performed by the Council of the North-West Territories." The new Assembly would be composed of 22 elected members sitting for a three-year term, and three appointed members. The latter would be legal experts entitled to participate in debates, but with no voting rights. The executive power of the lieutenant-governor continued unchanged; however, he was to be assisted by an "advisory council on matters of finance" selected from among the Assembly members.

The new lieutenant-governor, Joseph Royal, had been a member of the first North-West Council from 1872 until 1876. He had also served as speaker of Manitoba's Legislative Assembly, as well as provincial secretary, minister of public works and attorney-general, before taking a seat in the Canadian House of Commons in 1879. Perhaps more significantly, Royal was the recognized leader of Western Canada's French-speaking population, both Métis and Canadian. His appointment had been widely anticipated, but not altogether welcomed. In the words of Lewis H. Thomas, it "aroused a considerable volume of adverse comment in the territorial press, much of it motivated by prejudice against French Canadians."[13] When, in 1887, Prime Minister John A. Macdonald advised Dewdney concerning his possible successor, Dewdney responded: "I shall be very sorry to see a Frenchman here and it will create a very bad feeling."[14]

The North-West Legislative Assembly, convened on October 31, 1888, was composed of 22 elected legislators returned in 19 electoral divisions. All were English-speakers of British origin and most were Ontario-born. They were nearly all recent arrivals; indeed, 15 had immigrated to the North-West between 1882 and 1884. More than half had just been elected to the North-West Legislature for the first time and the longest-serving member, James Ross, had been elected only five years earlier in 1883.[15] No French-speakers were returned to the Assembly until 1891 when Antonio Prince was elected in the newly-created riding of St. Albert, and Charles Nolin in the readjusted riding of Batoche.[16] The North-West's three Supreme Court judges, James Macleod, Hugh Richardson and Charles Rouleau, acted as legal advisors to the Assembly and non-voting members until 1891.

In all probability, very few of the newly elected legislators were aware that the *North-West Territories Act* recognized two official languages. The effects of this provision were often invisible, particularly since no French-language ordinances had been published for several years. Thus, the assembled parliamentarians reacted with shocked disbelief when, at the opening of the Legislative Assembly, Royal read his speech from the throne, first in English and then in French. William Perley, a former member of the North-West Council, blamed this event for "the agitation commenced by the people declaring that they did not want French as an official language":

When I was a member of the Assembly I never heard any fault found about the dual language. There was no question about it at all; I hardly knew that it was on the Statute-book, and there would not have been any fault found with it had it not been that Mr. Royal undertook to force the French language on the people of that country. There were 22 elected members representing the North-West Territories, and not one of them could speak the French language at all. Mr. Royal was conversant with that fact, yet he read his speech in French. Not one of the members of the House understood him, and the ceremony was neither edifying nor amusing.[17]

Senator Bellerose later reported that the North-West legislators had "warned Governor Royal that if he should [again] speak French at the opening he would be insulted."[18]

A year later, in 1889, Royal read the speech from the throne in English only. However, the speech was immediately followed by an unusual intervention: "Before the speech was replied to or any other business done, Mr. [Hugh] Cayley of Calgary gave notice of introducing a motion to have a committee appointed to draft a resolution to be submitted to the Governor-General, to have clause 110 of the Northwest Territories act expunged."[19] Two days later, Cayley moved the committee's appointment and explained that "owing to the unanimous opinion of the House on this question it was not necessary to make any comments."[20] His motion was carried. The committee immediately prepared its report, but deferred public discussion for several days in order that Judge Charles Rouleau, one of the Assembly's three legal experts, might be present.

On October 28, 1889, Cayley justified the committee's request for repeal "on the grounds that the needs of the Territories do not demand the official recognition of a dual language in the North-West, or the expenditure necessitated by the same."[21] Frederick Haultain (MacLeod), voiced his support "on the ground of convenience and on the ground of economy." While the proponents lauded the cost savings, they were, ironically, quite uncertain as to what these might be. Two years earlier, in response to a question from John Turriff (Moose Mountain) regarding the cost of the French-language ordinances, Edgar Dewdney, the previous lieutenant-governor, had responded:

Ordinances of 1884, 1885 and 1886 are now under contract for translation at a cost of $1,000; and the printing will probably cost as much more. The sum of three thousand dollars was voted for this purpose at the last session of the Dominion Parliament, and it is hoped that this amount will prove sufficient to cover also cost of translating and printing of the Ordinances of this [1887] session.[22]

Cayley cited this information, with some exaggeration, during the 1889 debate, describing the cost of the French-language ordinances as "about $1,000 a year." In fact, the cost was $605 per year over the three-year period, including $250 for translation and $355 for printing.[23] This exceeded, but only moderately, the thirteen-year average of $581 per year, including $185 for translation and $396 for printing.

Other legislators, however, gave a different explanation for abolishing the official use of the French language. Benjamin Richardson (Wolseley), for example, stated quite simply that "the sentiment of the country was strongly in favour of one language and one nationality."[24] Frank Oliver (Edmonton), publisher of the *Edmonton Bulletin*, expanded on this theme, editorializing that a single language was necessary "to build up a strong nation, having a national sentiment, that will be purely Canadian."[25] The Assembly adopted the Cayley motion, known thereafter as "the language resolution," by a vote of 17–2.

Three months later, in the Canadian House of Commons, D'Alton McCarthy, the Conservative member for Ontario's Simcoe North, moved the repeal of section 110 of the *North-West Territories Act* as a step "to create and build up in this country one race with one national life, and with a language common to us all."[26] McCarthy had already signalled his intentions several months earlier, arguing in Winnipeg that Canada would never be united unless it adopted English as its common language. If French-speakers could be assimilated, political violence would be avoided: "We have the power to save this country from fratricidal strife, the power to make this a British country in fact as it is in name."[27] McCarthy's conclusions were buttressed by the scholarly research of a contemporary, Edward A. Freeman, Regius Professor of Modern History at Oxford University.[28] Freeman held that language defined the nation ("where there is not community of language, there is no common nationality") and that "a government and a nation should coincide."[29] He reasoned that language diversity invariably led to political instability, since "the only way in which national feeling can show itself is by protesting, whether in arms or otherwise, against existing political arrangements."[30]

Although the motion was defeated on the second reading, the issue dominated the parliamentary agenda for several weeks and provoked a national crisis. The minister of justice, John Thompson, proposed a compromise solution: official bilingualism would be maintained in the North-West, but the Assembly could determine the language of its proceedings. The Canadian parliament adopted this proposal on September 30, 1891 by adding a qualifying clause to section 110:

Provided, however, that after the next general election of the Legislative Assembly, such Assembly may by ordinance or otherwise, regulate its proceedings, and the manner of recording and publishing the same; and the regulations so made shall be embodied in a proclamation which shall be forthwith made and published by the Lieutenant Governor in conformity with the law, and thereafter shall have full force and effect.[31]

The North-West welcomed the amendment with jubilation. Cayley's *Calgary Herald* bluntly revealed "the real issues" and called "a spade a spade."[32] It trumpeted: "The country knows, the French members know, that there has been administered a knock down blow to French pretensions, a great discouragement and mortification to the French race throughout Canada." The editorialist regretted, somewhat gallantly, that unity and patriotism required a winner and a loser. However:

Men may do this [express their regrets] while refusing to yield their conviction of the absolute necessity of securing for the English language in Canada that supremacy which British arms, British blood, British courage, British ideas, British institutions may fairly claim, at the close of this nineteenth century in a country over which the British flag has waved for a century and a quarter. The Northwest will part and part forever with a system which prevents national unity, encourages race strife, promotes national disintegration and is a standing menace to the integrity of British institutions and the permanence of British power in this half of the North American continent.[33]

Territorial elections were held about a month later, and the North-West Legislative Assembly convened on December 10, 1891. Shortly afterwards, the lieutenant-governor called upon Frederick Haultain to form a four-member executive committee. The committee met for the first time on January 4, 1892 and that same day, Haultain made an announcement to the Assembly:

With regard to the Journals he might say that they had not been printed in French for some time past and he could inform the House that it was the intention of the Executive Committee to bring a resolution before the House on this matter, at which time they hoped to be able to give full reasons for their policy of having the Journals printed only in English. (Applause).[34]

Two weeks later, on January 19, 1892, Haultain moved "that it is desirable that the proceedings of the Legislative Assembly shall be recorded and published hereafter in the English language only."[35]

Once again, Haultain cited the potential cost savings. He explained that "he brought up the question simply as one affecting expenditure and he commended the motion to them as reasonable from the point of economy, convenience and necessity."[36] James Clinkskill (Battleford) concurred, calling it "a question of economy and necessity," and Thomas Tweed (Medicine Hat) "one of necessity and economy." Others, of course, hinted at more nationalist motives. During the 1891 election campaign, Daniel Mowat (South Regina) had urged his electors: "With reference to languages, I say let this be an English speaking country and let us do away with having the Ordinances, etc. printed in any other language, and thereby save expense."[37]

The Haultain motion was debated and, later that same day, adopted by a vote of 20–4. The lieutenant-governor did not, as required, proclaim the resolution. Nonetheless, the government never again published a French-language version of the Assembly's proceedings; the 1890 edition of the North-West *Journals*, already in press, was the last to be printed in that language.

Later the same year, a closely-related issue reared its head when the North-West Assembly considered revisions to the *School Ordinance*. Daniel Mowat (South Regina) proposed that English be the sole language of instruction, arguing that "we would never have true patriotic feeling in the country until there was one language."[38] Nevertheless, he was persuaded to accept a compromise that permitted the teaching of a French-language primary course. Mowat justified this revised proposal by explaining that the "provision to make the teaching of English compulsory was rendered necessary on account of the large influx of foreigners. An exception was made in favor of teaching a primary course in French, as the French were fellow Canadians."[39] On December 29, 1892, the Legislature adopted the new school bill. Section 83 provided that "all schools shall be taught in the English language." An additional clause, section 83.1, allowed school trustees "to cause a primary course to be taught in the French language."

This "exception" allowed a course in reading and composition at the primary level, that is, during the first two years of schooling.[40] However, the prescribed text, a bilingual reader, was—perhaps by design—best suited for teaching English to the French-speaking population. When the course was offered, the allotted time generally varied between a half-hour and a full hour per day, strictly controlled by the local school inspector.[41]

With the adoption of the 1892 school bill, public debate on the dual-language question largely came to a close. However, the surreptitious suppression of the French language continued apace. The practice of publishing French-language regulations and reports ended in the 1891 fiscal year with the printing of 500 French-language copies of the Department of Public Works annual report, and 300 French-language copies of the Board of Education regulations.[42] The publication of the French-language ordinances ended in 1894 with the printing of the 1892 edition, although no formal announcement was made and no public explanation given.[43] Similarly, the *North-West Territories Gazette* published its last bilingual issue on August 15, 1895; thereafter, it appeared exclusively in English.

In 1901, the German-speaking community entered the political fray, petitioning the Legislative Assembly to allow school instruction in German. In response, the Assembly amended the *School Ordinance*, section 136, and permitted a school board to "employ one or more competent persons to give instructions in any language other than English" subject to the departmental regulations and on condition that this not interfere with the required school program and that the costs be collected directly from the parents concerned. The department of education regulations subsequently provided the necessary clarification: "Such instruction shall be given between the hours of three and four o'clock in the afternoon of such school days as may be selected by the board and shall be confined to the teaching of reading, composition and grammar. The text books used shall be those authorized by the Commissioner of Education."[44] Schools rarely took advantage of this possibility however, since, as the legislators had probably anticipated, the immigrant population lacked the necessary financial means.[45]

Alberta's Inherited Language Regime, 1905–1918

In 1905, the Canadian parliament created two new provinces, Alberta and Saskatchewan, and provided for their governance. The *Alberta Act*, section 14, stipulated that "all the provisions of the law with regard to the constitution of the Legislative Assembly of the Northwest Territories and the election of members thereof shall apply, *mutatis mutandis*, to the Legislative Assembly of the said province." Section 16, similarly, provided that "all laws and all orders and regulations" already in vigour in the Territories would continue in the new province of Alberta until such time as the provincial legislature (or the federal parliament, as appropriate) decided otherwise.[46]

The *Alberta Act* made no explicit provision for an official language in the province although, in introducing the act, the Canadian minister of justice, Charles Fitzpatrick, had explained that "we are perpetuating the rights, whatever they may be, in the North-West Territories with respect to language, leaving it to the legislature to determine hereafter to what extent these rights may be maintained."[47] This meant, first and foremost, that section 110 of the *North-West Territories Act*, recognizing English and French as the official languages of the legislature and courts, continued to have legal force in Alberta until amended by the provincial Legislature. Of course, the North-West Legislature had, in practice, completely (and illegally) abandoned the use of French more than a decade earlier. Provincial legislators and jurists, often recent immigrants to Western Canada and blissfully ignorant of the region's constitutional history, blindly conformed to this English-only regime. If they occasionally permitted the use of French, this was considered to be a temporary privilege rather than a legal right.

The Alberta Legislative Assembly, for example, published its statutes and regulations exclusively in English. However, in 1909, Alberta's first French-speaking cabinet minister, Prosper Edmond Lessard (Pakan), proudly announced that the government had translated all its statutes into French.[48] Two years later he backtracked somewhat, claiming simply that the most useful laws were available in French, "telles que celles concernant les Battages, les clôtures, les animaux errants, les Sociétés d'Agriculture, les Privilèges d'ouvriers, les mauvaises herbes, la fabrication du beurre et du Fromage, les feux de prairie, les Mines de charbon, les mariages, et décès, etc."[49] He also warned, furthermore, that the government was still not convinced that there was a real demand for this service.[50] In subsequent years, Lessard's newspaper, *Le Courrier de l'Ouest*, took over the job itself, occasionally reprinting translated statutes in its own pages.[51]

The North-West Territories' *School Ordinance* was also carried into the new province, including section 136, in slightly revised form, which stated that "All schools shall be taught in the English language but it shall be permissible for the board of any district to cause a primary course to be taught in the French language." Nevertheless, in 1913 the Liberal minister of education, John R. Boyle, boasted that in Alberta "we have no Bi-lingual schools.... English is the only language permitted to be used as a medium of instruction in our schools."[52] Two years later, during a by-election held in Whitford, he accused the Conservative opposition of catering to the immigrant vote by advocating the establishment of Ukrainian schools.[53] The opposition, eager to prove its innocence, immediately moved a resolution: "That this House place itself on record as being opposed to Bi-lingualism in any form in the School system of Alberta, and as in favour of the English language being the only language permitted to be used as the medium of instruction in the schools of Alberta, subject to the provisions of any law now in force in the Province in that effect."[54] The Liberal government, caught ignominiously in its own trap, voted with the opposition, and the resolution passed unanimously.

The Alberta Legislative Assembly, taking over where its territorial predecessor had left off, continued to legislate the use of the English language in public affairs. In 1909, for example, it adopted an *Alberta Election Act* requiring, in section 121, that the returning officer in each riding publish a proclamation "in the English language" listing the place and time for nominations and voting, and the boundaries of the polling subdivisions. Section 175 made provision for an interpreter: "If the person desiring to vote is unable to understand the English language the deputy returning officer shall enter a remark to that effect opposite his name in the poll book and may allow him to retire from the polling place until a competent interpreter can be procured." More disconcertingly, a second paragraph added: "If no such interpreter is found or presents himself at the polling place the voter shall not be allowed to vote."

Since English was, in practice, the sole language of the courts, the 1914 *Rules of Court*, section 404, similarly provided for an interpreter during the written interrogation of non-English-speaking witnesses:

> Where a witness does not understand the English language the order or commission shall, unless otherwise ordered, be executed with the aid of an interpreter nominated by the examiner or commissioner and sworn by him to interpret truly the questions to be put to the witness and his answers thereto, and the examination shall be taken in English.

The Legislative Assembly also imposed English as the official language of municipal government. The 1912 *Rural Municipality Act*, section 178(1), required the municipal secretary to "keep a full and correct record in the English language of the proceedings of every meeting of the council." The 1912 *Town Act*, sections 15 and 72, demanded that candidates for election as mayor or councillor be "able to read and write the English language." In the same vein, the 1913 *Edmonton Charter*, section 21, provided that "no person shall be eligible for election as mayor or alderman, unless he is…able to read and write the English language."

Provincial law similarly made English the required language for employment. The *Coal Mines Regulations Ordinance*, section 34, carried into Alberta from the North-West Territories, ordered that "no person unable to speak and read English shall be appointed to or shall occupy any position of trust or responsibility." The 1910 *Alberta Land Surveyors Act*, section 22(1), required that a person articling with a land surveyor first pass an examination in English grammar. The 1913 *Mines Act*, section 22, required that each applicant for a miner's certificate "satisfy the board that he is able to read and write in the English language." The 1917 *Alberta Provincial Police Act*, section 8, required that all constables be "able to read and write the English language legibly."

Few laws regulated commercial signage. Nevertheless, a 1917 statute requiring the City of Calgary to adopt an early-closing policy also ordered that exempted shops "expose in two prominent places in the front door, and in the front window, a card not less than two feet square on which there shall be printed in English, in type of not less than one inch high, the following words only: 'This shop is closed by law, except for the sale of (*here state the goods, or any of them, mentioned in this subsection*).'"[55] This obligation was later extended to all cities in Alberta.

Alberta's Official Language Provision, 1919

On April 17, 1919, the Alberta Legislature adopted an amendment to the *Interpretation Act*, affirming English as the province's official language: "Unless otherwise provided where any Act requires public records to be kept or any written process to be had or taken it shall be interpreted to mean that such records or such process shall be in the English language." The province had inherited some 124 ordinances from the North-West Territories, regulating a wide range of activities, including elections, government departments, public printing, public health, civil justice, marriage, professions and trades, companies, municipalities, schools, agriculture, liquor sales, tax assessment, and insurance—and the great majority did indeed require the keeping of public records or the taking of written process. The *Elections Ordinance*, for example, described in exquisite detail a plethora of required written records and procedures, including the issuing of writs, the publication and posting of notices, the taking of oaths and statements, the printing of ballots, the recording of electoral information, the keeping of poll books and record books, the certification of nominations and elections, the serving of summons, and the filing of appeals.

Oddly, the attorney-general, John R. Boyle (Sturgeon), buried the English-language amendment deeply within an omnibus housekeeping bill modifying 51 different statutes, and formally entitled *An Act to Amend The Factories Act, The Liquor Act, The Soldiers' Home Tax Exemption Act, and certain other Acts and Ordinances*. The bill made only a fleeting appearance in the Legislature, attracting little attention and no debate. Its second reading, late on a Monday afternoon, was completely upstaged by lengthy and heated exchanges concerning the practice of chiropractic. The legislative reporter's summary was revealingly brief and inarticulate: "The house agreed without discussion to the second readings of two acts introduced by the attorney general, one to amend the factories act, the liquor act, and other effected by the special revisions of certain measures; and the other to postpone the commencement of certain other acts."[56]

The Legislature's silent support for the English-language amendment contrasted dramatically with the outspoken stance of the Orange Order. A few weeks earlier, on March 20, 1919, at meetings addressed by the mayor of Edmonton and the lieutenant-governor of Alberta, the Grand Orange Lodge of Alberta had adopted the following resolution:

> That in the interests of a united Canada urgent representation be made to the federal and provincial governments, so far as their respective jurisdictions are concerned, (1) to enact legislation whereby the English language shall be the sole medium of instruction in every grade of every school under government control, and (2) to enforce the existing law of the land so that within the province of Alberta the English language only shall be read officially on any public form or document, or in any public office, school or assembly.[57]

The Orangemen also called upon the federal government to "enact legislation preventing the immigration of persons from alien enemy countries or of such extraction, for a period of twenty years and further, to deport all such aliens now in Canada unless they furnish ample proof of loyalty."

In 1922, when Alberta's statutes were consolidated, the English-language provision was labelled "English as official language." In 1958, the legislature adopted a new *Interpretation Act*, and section 27, now labelled "Public records," appeared in revised form: "Where by an enactment public records are required to be kept or any written process to be had or taken, the records or process shall be had or taken in the English language." The provision was repealed in 1980.

Alberta's Intrinsic Unilingualism, 1920–1967

During the next several decades, Alberta made no substantive changes to its official language regime. None were needed. The dominance of English was uncontested; competing languages had been vanquished. The legislative framework supporting English unilingualism was firmly in place, and the norms regulating language use were now intrinsic.

For many years, the French-speaking community had lobbied cautiously for the right to introduce French-language instruction in its schools. Knowing that the government would not modify the statutory provisions adopted in 1892, banishing languages other than English, its leaders astutely focused instead on the interpretation given the expression "a primary course." Instead of a single French-language course, they sought a complete French-language program, albeit for only the first two years of schooling. In 1925 these efforts finally paid off and the Department of Education discretely issued new instructions for the teaching of French:

> In all schools in which the board by resolution decides to offer a primary course in French, in accordance with Sec. 184 of the School Ordinance, French shall be for the French-speaking children one of the authorized subjects of study and may be used as medium of instruction for other subjects during the first school year. Oral English must, however, from the beginning be included in the curriculum as a subject of study. During the second year and after the child has learned to read in the mother tongue, the formal teaching of reading in English shall be begun. From Grade III on, a period not exceeding one hour each day may be allotted to the teaching of French.[58]

Some four decades later, the provincial government modified the *School Act* to formally confirm this practice. A 1964 amendment provided that French might be the language of instruction up to grade 9 on condition that in grades one and two "at least one hour a day shall be devoted to instruction in English;" in grade three "not more than two hours a day shall be devoted to instruction in French;" and, in grades four through nine "not more than one hour a day shall be devoted to instruction in French."[59]

No such concessions were made for language use in the Legislative Assembly. English continued to be the sole language of law-making and record-keeping. Indeed, in 1971, constitutionalist Claude-Armand Sheppard concluded (mistakenly) that "English has been the only language ever used in the legislature or in any of its committees."[60] In fact, French had been spoken on rare occasions, but its use was considered a privilege, to be reluctantly granted or rudely denied. In 1936, *La Survivance* reported that J. William Beaudry (St. Paul), a member of the governing Social Credit party, had delivered parts of his maiden speech in French.[61] His remarks, including praise for the contribution of the province's French-speaking pioneers, were warmly received. In 1952, the *Edmonton Journal* noted that the Liberal opposition leader, J. Harper Prowse (Edmonton), had spoken "in what the house assumed was French" to underline his opposition to the planned elimination of "foreign" languages taught in grade 10.[62] However, his speech met with a frosty response, and a government backbencher rising on a point of order questioned "whether members were allowed to speak French in the legislature." A decade later, a new Liberal opposition leader, Michael Maccagno (Lac La Biche), endured more blatant bigotry when commenting in French on Canadian bilingualism. A government member allegedly demanded: "Mr. Speaker, have the honourable member from Lac La Biche speak white."[63] Instead, the chair permitted Maccagno to continue in French, but requested an oral translation.

The provincial Legislature persisted in requiring the use of the English language in municipal affairs. The 1919 *Municipal Hospitals Act*, section 7(2) limited eligibility for election to a hospital board to those "who can read and write the English language." Although this condition was repealed in 1947, it resurfaced the following year in the *Lloydminster Hospital Act*, section 35(4)(b). The *Town and Village Act* and the *Municipal District Act*, as amended on April 6, 1945, also established English-language competence as a condition for eligibility to elected office. The 1951 *City Act*, section 95, added an oral requirement: "No person shall be qualified to be elected mayor or a member of the council of a city unless,—(a) he can speak, read and write the English language." A 1951 amendment to the *Irrigation Districts Act* required that district trustees be "able to read and write in the English language."

In at least once instance, the province also imposed the use of English in the business sector. The 1936 *Male Minimum Wage Act*, section 14(1), required that "every employer shall keep in his principal place of business in the Province a true and correct record in the English language of the wages paid to and the hours worked each day by each of his employees, together with a register in the English language of the names, nationalities, ages and residential addresses of all his employees." This same obligation also appeared in the 1936 *Hours of Work Act*, section 13(1), and the 1947 *Alberta Labour Act*, section 10(1).

Alberta's Unilingualism Is Breached, 1968–1987

In 1968, a tidal wave of official bilingualism, set off by the federal *Official Languages Act*, opened an important breach in Alberta's system of unilingual schooling. The provincial government amended its *School Act*, section 386, to permit the use of French for up to "50 per cent of the total period of time devoted to classroom instruction each day" in grades three through twelve. In 1971, it also amended section 150 so that other minority languages received similar status: "A board may authorize (a) that French be used as a language of instruction, or (b) that any other language be used as a language of instruction in addition to the English language, in all or any of its schools." The minister of education then authorized instruction in these languages, notably Ukrainian, during 50 per cent of each school day for grades one through three.[64] In 1976, this was extended to grades four through six; in 1980, to grades seven and eight; and, finally, in 1983, to grades 9 through 12.[65] In a 1988 report, the government declared: "Alberta Education supports the provision of opportunities for students who wish to acquire or maintain languages other than English or French so that they may have access to a partial immersion (bilingual) program or second language courses in languages other than English or French."[66] The same report noted that some 2,775 students were enrolled in these bilingual programs, chiefly in Ukrainian (1,362), but also in Hebrew (458), German (339), Arabic (265), Mandarin (234) and Polish (117).[67] They accounted for 1.5 per cent of all enrolments in provincial language programs or courses.

In 1976, the provincial government again expanded the number of hours available for French-language instruction by reducing the English-language minimum. As before, schools were obliged to offer at least one hour of English instruction per day in grades one and two, but they were now freed from the 50 per cent rule for subsequent grades. Instead, French-language schools could limit their English instruction to 190 hours per year in grades three through six, 150 hours in grades seven through nine, and 125 hours in grades 10 through 12.[68] This meant, in effect, that French-language instruction could occupy up to 80 per cent of regular class time.

On February 23, 1978, at a meeting of provincial leaders in St. Andrews, New Brunswick, Premier Peter Lougheed signed a national statement on minority language rights: "Each child of the French-speaking or English-speaking minority is entitled to an education in his or her language in the primary or secondary schools in each province wherever numbers warrant."[69] The following day, however, he issued a distinctly Albertan clarification:

> It should be recognized that the provision of French language instruction is not limited to those students whose mother tongue is French. In fact, because of Alberta's population mix and distribution, many boards must rely on large numbers of students whose mother tongue is other than French in establishing classes where French is used as the language of instruction. It will continue to be our policy to allow admission to French language programs regardless of mother-tongue.[70]

Alberta thereby diverged from the national consensus, refusing to distinguish between immersion schools designed for the English-speaking majority, and Francophone schools intended for the French-speaking minority.

This refusal took on added significance when, several years later, the *Constitution Act, 1982*, section 23, guaranteed the right of official language minorities to have their children instructed "in minority language educational facilities provided out of public funds." Since Alberta's French-language educational facilities were, in reality, immersion schools and not minority schools, they fell considerably short of the constitutional requirement. In 1982, a group of French-speaking parents, led by Jean-Claude Mahé, Angéline Martel and Paul Dubé, attempted to obtain French minority schooling for their children. First, they contacted the minister of education and then, on his advice, the Edmonton Public School Board and the Edmonton Catholic School Board. When their efforts failed, the parents took the province to court, claiming that the *School Act* contravened the Canadian constitution. In 1985, Purvis J. of the Alberta Court of Queen's Bench ruled in their favour and ordered the province to make specific provision for French minority schools.[71] Two years later, Kerans J., speaking for the Alberta Court of Appeal, confirmed this decision.[72]

In 1980, a spate of new laws further softened the province's unilingual face, discretely dropping legal references to longstanding English-language obligations. For example, the Alberta Legislature adopted a new *Interpretation Act*, but the provision recognizing English as an official language, first adopted in 1919, was nowhere to be found. The new bill, introduced by a government backbencher, slipped phantom-like through the Assembly, including committee of the whole, unquestioned and uncommented.[73] The new *Election Act* no longer specified, for the first time since 1909, that the electoral proclamation would be published "in the English language." Nor did it disenfranchise non-English-speaking electors if no interpreter could be found. Similarly, the *Municipal Election Act*, as amended in 1980, no longer required that prospective council members be "able to speak, read and write English."

Any illusion that the Legislature might be inclined to temper its own unilingualism was quickly dispelled, however, when it adopted a standing order, on November 27, 1987, providing that "the working language of the Assembly, its committees, and any official publications recording its proceedings shall be in English."[74] This "new" rule was the Legislature's heavy-handed response to a bizarre political crisis. Several months earlier, opposition member Leo Piquette (Athabasca–Lac La Biche) had spoken several words in French during question period: "Thank you, Mr. Speaker. To the Minister of Education, le ministre de l'éducation. Mr. Speaker, these questions are pertaining to section 23 of the Constitution Act signed by this province on April 19, 1982. Les franco-Albertains attendent impatiemment depuis 1982."[75] At this point, the Speaker intervened, called Piquette to order, and commanded: "The Chair directs that the questions will be in English or the member will forfeit the position." Piquette immediately contested the speaker's decision, claiming that "the language rights guaranteed in section 110 of the North West Territories Act were never extinguished and do still obtain in the Legislative Assembly of the Province of Alberta."[76] Subsequently, the Standing Committee on Privileges and Elections rejected Piquette's claim, and upheld the Speaker's ruling. It decided, moreover, that Piquette had breached the privileges of all members of the Assembly "by his failure to uphold the absolute authority of the Speaker to rule on points of order and to accept such rulings without debate or appeal."[77] For this, it recommended that he "unconditionally apologize to the Assembly."

A New Tolerance for Bilingualism in Alberta, 1988–2005
Alberta's Languages Act, 1988

A few months later, on February 25, 1988, the Supreme Court of Canada confirmed unequivocally, in the *Mercure* case, that section 110 was still in vigour in Saskatchewan and, by implication, Alberta. It noted that laws giving expression to language rights possess an almost constitutional nature, and could only be repealed by "clear legislative pronouncement."[78] Where there is a conflict between a fundamental law and other specific legislation, "the human rights legislation must govern."[79] Further, the long-standing practice of using English exclusively in the debates, statutes and court proceedings did not in any way change the statutory protection accorded the French language since "statutes do not, of course, cease to be law from mere disuse."[80] In sum:

> Section 110 of *The North-West Territories Act* was a law existing at the establishment of the province. Since no provision of the *Saskatchewan Act* was inconsistent with s.110 or was intended as a substitute for it, and since there was no amendment of the provisions of that section with respect to the language of the statutes and of the proceedings in the courts, it follows that s.110 continues in effect for that purpose and that the statutes of Saskatchewan must be enacted, printed and published in English and French and that both languages may be used in the Saskatchewan courts.[81]

Nevertheless, the court declared that the province could, if it wished, adopt a statute repealing this provision although, paradoxically, any such statute would have to "be enacted, printed and published in the English and French languages."[82] Thus, on June 22, 1988, Attorney-General James Horsman (Medicine Hat) introduced a bilingual bill entitled the *Languages Act*, providing that "section 110 of *The North-West Territories Act*, chapter 50 of the Revised Statutes of Canada, as it existed on September 1, 1905, does not apply to Alberta with respect to matters within the legislative authority of Alberta."[83] Horsman argued, without embarrassment or apology, that this measure was "fair and reasonable and practical and recognizes the reality of Alberta and the distinct nature of Alberta society."[84] He explained further:

Mr. Speaker, we are dealing with the reality of the fact that the Mercure decision has said that an Act passed in 1886—which had never been used in this province, never been implemented, had fallen into complete disuse in the Northwest Territories prior to Alberta becoming a province in 1905—is still the law because of a technicality....We have now been told by the Supreme Court of Canada how we must proceed in order to change that antiquated, unused piece of legislation which was a hangover from 1886.[85]

The Liberal leader, Nick Taylor (Westlock-Sturgeon), retorted that this was "nothing more than summoning up the prejudices of centuries past and taking a poke at a defenseless minority under the guise that it reflects Alberta's reality."[86] Attorney-General Horsman was the only member of the governing Conservative party to participate in the debate. Nine members of the 20-person opposition intervened, however, and several made comments in French. The speaker conducted the proceedings in both languages, announcing each reading and each vote in English and in French, as did the chairman in committee of the whole. In one particularly ironic turn of events, the chairman refused to accept an opposition amendment calling for the translation of selected laws into French, because the amendment itself had not been translated into French.[87]

The principal objective of the *Languages Act* was the suppression of section 110 and its requirement that all statutes be enacted and printed in French. This measure drew public attention, and was hotly debated. However, the act also provided, in section 5(1), that "members of the Assembly may use English and French in the Assembly." This resulted subsequently in a modest, largely symbolic, increase in French language use. For example, in 1999, Nancy MacBeth (Edmonton-McClung), the Liberal opposition leader, spoke in French when she congratulated the government on its creation of a Secrétariat aux affaires francophones, although she then repeated her remarks in English.[88] Two years later, the president of this secretariat, Denis Ducharme (Bonnyville-Cold Lake), also spoke in French when he announced that the Association canadianne-française de l'Alberta was celebrating its 75th anniversary.[89] Ducharme did not repeat his announcement in English, but he did provide a written translation, and this too was printed in *Hansard*.

The *Languages Act* also provided, in section 4(1), that "any person may use English or French in oral communication" in court proceedings. Nevertheless, French continues to get short shrift in civil matters before Alberta's courts, largely because the province has failed to provide the necessary resources, including bilingual judges. McIntosh J. Prov. Ct. unwittingly illustrated this problem when he admonished a French-speaking defendant:

> With respect, you can do all the talking in French that you like but in Alberta, with respect, Provincial matters are conducted in English, so if you're going to communicate with me you'll have to do it in English, or you will have to have somebody here that can assist you in English. But this trial is conducted in English. That's the law in Alberta, for Provincial Statutes.[90]

In criminal matters, of course, the government must comply with federal legislation that grants an accused, on application, the right to "be tried before a justice of the peace, provincial court judge, judge or judge and jury, as the case may be, who speak the official language of Canada that is the language of the accused or, if the circumstances warrant, who speak both official languages of Canada."[91]

Tolerance for the French Language in Alberta, 1988–2005

The movement to a more tolerant language regime was evident mainly in the area of French-language education. Ironically, this new tolerance was conceded under duress, often as a reluctant response to litigation. For example, in 1987, in the *Mahé* case, the Alberta Court of Appeal vindicated French-speaking parents who argued that the province's *School Act* was not constitutional. As a result, the provincial Legislature adopted a new act the following year that recognized in section 5(1), albeit awkwardly and ambiguously, the right to French minority schooling: "If an individual has rights under section 23 of the *Canadian Charter of Rights and Freedoms* to have his children receive school instruction in French, his children are entitled to receive that instruction in accordance with those rights wherever in the Province those rights apply." Unsatisfied, the parents appealed to the Supreme Court of Canada, claiming that the provincial legislation still failed to provide for minority schools, that is, schools managed and controlled by the French-speaking minority. The court agreed and, in 1990, ruled that the province must enact legislation granting exclusive authority to the French minority for decisions relating to the minority language instruction and facilities, including: (a) expenditures of funds provided for such instruction and facilities; (b) appointment and direction of those responsible for the administration of such instruction and facilities; (c) establishment of programs of instruction; (d) recruitment and assignment of teachers and other personnel; and (e) the making of agreements for education and services for minority language pupils.[92]

Three years later, the Legislative Assembly amended the *School Act* to provide for minority school boards, described formally as "Regional authorities for Francophone Education Regions." These authorities were responsible for the management and control of French minority schools in their region, including: tracking eligible students and facilitating their education in French, representing French-speaking parents, promoting French-language instruction in the province, maintaining links with other regional authorities, and developing rules and regulations for French education.[93] Further, as school boards, they were empowered to establish policies for the provision of educational services and programs; to employ teachers and non-teaching personnel, including administrators and supervisors; to maintain and furnish their real property; to make rules respecting the attendance and transportation of students; and, generally, to deal with all matters within their jurisdiction.

The *School Act* was further revised in 2000 with the introduction of a preamble that, for the first time, highlighted minority schooling. It proclaimed that:

> the Regional authority of a Francophone Education Region has a unique responsibility and the authority to ensure that both minority language educational rights and the rights and privileges with respect to separate schools guaranteed under the Constitution of Canada are protected in the Region, such that the principles of francophone educational governance are distinct from, not transferable to nor a precedent for, the English educational system.

Since 2001, section 255(3) has stipulated that "a Regional authority must designate each school either as a public school or as a separate school." In 2003–2004, the province could boast five regional authorities administering 18 French Catholic schools and seven French Public schools, with 3,638 registered students.[94]

The Alberta Legislature's decision to permit the use of French in corporate names also reveals a significant, if less momentous, break with the long-standing tradition of repressive unilingualism. For example, the current *Interpretation Act*, section 16(e), vests a corporation that has "a name consisting of an English and French form or a combined English and French form" with the power "to use either the English or French form of its name or both forms." The *Business Corporations Act*, section 10(6), similarly recognizes that the name of a corporation "may be in an English form or a French form or in a combined English and French form and the corporation may use and may be legally designated by any of those forms." The *Cooperatives Act*, section 16(2), the *Insurance Act*, section 21(2), and the *Loan and Trust Corporations Act*, sections 20(2) and 34(3), all include similar provisions.

The *Business Corporations Act*, section 10(1) also requires that corporations include, as the last part of their name, one of a select number of English or French words, or abbreviations: "Limited," "Limité," "Incorporated," "Incorporé," "Corporation," "Ltd.," "Lté," "Inc," or "Corp." The *Cooperatives Act*, section 16(2), contains a parallel provision, requiring that cooperatives include words such as "cooperative", "co-operative", or "coopérative," as does the *Loan and Trust Corporations Act*, section 20(1)(e), requiring that trust companies use "trust," or "fiducie." Similarly, the *Insurance Act*, section 213, stipulates that only an incorporated insurance company may use the words "insurance company" or "insurance corporation," or "the French equivalents of those words," in its name.

Conclusion

For more than a century, Alberta's legislators imposed the use of English in a wide variety of domains, including government, justice, education, business and commerce. Their goal was to suppress minority languages and to build a homogeneous English-speaking province, hence the rallying cry "one language and one nationality." This behaviour was fully consistent with Jean Laponce's "language war" thesis that languages in contact struggle for domination, seeking to drive their rivals out.[95] Governments, of course, are favoured instruments in this struggle since their language choices are critical and their social powers are formidable. They cannot remain neutral: a government cannot function without using a language for public affairs, that is, without choosing an official language. But they can intervene: a government has the power to regulate both individual and societal language use.

Nevertheless, the Alberta government's extensive and longstanding intervention in language matters runs counter to the avowed tenets of its present-day ideology, and to the widely-held perceptions of its past behaviour. In recent decades, Alberta has proclaimed its commitment to a free enterprise, market-driven economy, and a minimalist government. This neo-liberal philosophy is reflected in the province's declarations trumpeting freedom of language choice—unimpeded by political constraints and tempered only by market forces. For example, in a 1992 statement on Alberta's constitutional policy, former premier Don Getty called for the abolition of language legislation so that individuals could make free and independent decisions. Needless to say, this call was directed solely and quite unselfconsciously at the federal government: "I propose that in Canada, we recommit ourselves to the concept of bilingualism as a positive, fundamental characteristic of Canadian unity but, I believe the time has come when bilingualism should be removed from the force of law. This would be a fundamental change in Canada. Bilingualism by choice, not law."[96]

Today, the Alberta government intervenes no less often than in the past, but the nature of its intervention has changed, veering from generalized repression to selective tolerance. Provisions that impose English language usage are increasingly rare, provisions that tolerate minority languages increasingly common. Education provides a prime example. Whereas after 1892, the provincial government imposed a sole language of instruction, English, it has now, since 1971, permitted teaching in several minority languages, including French, Ukrainian, German and Hebrew. Further, since 1994, in a particularly dramatic breakthrough, the government has created a province-wide system of French minority schools managed by French school boards.

Nevertheless, the decisions that ended repressive unilingualism were often made with reluctance and under duress. Again, education provides a defining example. It was only after French-speaking parents had appealed to the Alberta Court of Queen's Bench and, in the *Mahé* case, successfully demonstrated that the *School Act* contravened section 23 of the *Constitution Act, 1982*, that the province recognized in a 1988 amendment that the French-speaking minority had a right to its own schools. Nevertheless, this recognition still fell considerably short of the standards set by the constitution, since it did not provide the minority with exclusive powers in matters pertaining to instruction in these schools. When, in 1990, the Supreme Court of Canada ordered Alberta to enact the necessary legislation, the provincial government threatened, ill-advisedly, to override this requirement. (Surprisingly, the government did not at first realize that the constitution's so-called "notwithstanding" clause was not applicable to section 23.) Finally, in 1993, the Legislative Assembly adopted an amendment to the *School Act* providing for French minority school boards and, in 1994, these were established.

Of course, repressive unilingualism, when successful, frequently sows the seeds of its own demise. Why legislate the use of English in a society composed overwhelmingly of English-speakers? In Alberta, English is now universal and unthreatened: 99 per cent of the province's population is able to converse in English, and 94 per cent speak it in their homes. If there ever was a reason to forcibly impose a common language, it has long since disappeared.

Notes

1. This essay draws extensively on previously published research dealing with the history of language law in Alberta. See, for example: Edmund A. Aunger, "Language and Law in the Province of Alberta," in *Language and Law*, eds. Paul Pupier and José Woehrling (Montreal: Wilson & Lafleur, 1989), 203–29; Edmund A. Aunger, "The Mystery of the French Language Ordinances: An Investigation into Official Bilingualism and the Canadian North-West, 1870 to 1895," *Canadian Journal of Law and Society* 13 (1998): 89–124; Edmund A. Aunger, "Justifying the End of Official Bilingualism: Canada's North-West Assembly and the Dual-Language Question, 1889–1892," *Canadian Journal of Political Science* 34 (2001): 451–86; Edmund A. Aunger, "Legislating Language Use in Alberta: A Century of Incidental Provisions for a Fundamental Matter," *Alberta Law Review* 42 (2004): 463–97; Edmund A. Aunger, "De la répression à la tolérance: Les contrariétés du néolibéralisme linguistique en Alberta," in *La gouvernance linguistique: Le Canada en perspective*, ed. Jean-Pierre Wallot (Ottawa: Presses de l'Université d'Ottawa, 2005), 111–26.
2. Jean Laponce, *Languages and Their Territories* (Toronto: University of Toronto Press, 1987), i. This is the English translation of *Langue et territoire* (Quebec: Presses de l'Université Laval, 1984).
3. Ramsay Cook, "Language Policy and the Glossophagic State," in *Language and the State*, ed. David Schneiderman (Cowansville, Quebec: Éditions Yvon Blais, 1991), 75.
4. Joseph Eliot Magnet, *Official Languages of Canada* (Cowansville, Quebec: Éditions Yvon Blais, 1995), 20–21.
5. Adams G. Archibald, lieutenant-governor, Rupert's Land and the North West Territory, to Joseph Howe, secretary of state for the provinces (22 October 1870) reprinted in Edmund H. Oliver, ed., *The Canadian North-West: Its Early Development and Legislative Records*, vol. 2 (Ottawa: Government Printing Bureau, 1915), 976.
6. This quotation, and subsequent references to the council minutes, are taken from the original minute book "North-West Territories Council Minutes, 1873–1875," found in

the collection of the Saskatchewan Archives Board, Saskatoon, file NWT I.1. Oliver has conveniently reprinted these minutes, but his hand-copied source contained occasional errors. See Oliver, *The Canadian North-West*, 990–1075.

7. "Le Gouvernement du Nord-Ouest, " *Le Métis* (Saint-Boniface, Manitoba), April 12, 1877, 2.

8. *Senate Debates* (April 9, 1877), p. 319.

9. "Return Showing, by Years, the Cost of Printing the Ordinances and Other Official Papers and Publications in the French language from the Time of Passage of the North-West Territories Act of 1877," in Canada, House of Commons, *Sessional Papers*, 1890, no. 1890–33, p. 3.

10. Canada, Department of Agriculture, *Census of Canada, 1880–81*, vol. 1 (Ottawa: Maclean, Roger, 1882), 300.

11. Canada, Department of Agriculture, *Census of the Three Provisional Districts of the North-West Territories, 1884–5* (Ottawa: Maclean, 1886), 10–11.

12. "Legislative Assembly," *The Regina Leader* (November 1, 1889), 1.

13. Lewis H. Thomas, *The Struggle for Responsible Government in the North-West Territories, 1870–97*, 2 ed. (Toronto: University of Toronto Press, 1978), 160.

14. Edgar Dewdney, lieutenant-governor, to John A. Macdonald, prime minister (April 11, 1887), quoted in Thomas, *Struggle for Responsible Government*, 160.

15. This information is drawn from "Sketches of the Members," *The Regina Leader* (October 30, 1888), 4–5.

16. Nolin's election was subsequently declared void and the following year he was replaced by Charles Boucher.

17. *Senate Debates* (April 29, 1890), p. 632.

18. *Senate Debates* (September 3, 1891), p. 547.

19. "Assembly Notes," *Edmonton Bulletin*, November 2, 1889. The article continued: "Most of the Territorial papers are clamoring for the abolition of the separate schools, and use of the French [language] as an official language. One significant fact was that the governor's speech was read in English only, while last year it was read in both French and English."

20. "Legislative Assembly," *The Regina Leader* (October 22, 1889).

21. "Legislative Assembly," *The Regina Leader* (November 1, 1889).

22. North-West Territories Legislative Assembly, "Return showing number of Ordinances printed in French since 1883, number distributed, number on hand, and cost of said printing," *Journals of the Council of the North-West Territories of Canada, Session 1887* (Regina: Amédée E. Forget, Printer to the Government of the North-West Territories, 1887), 101.

23. Aunger, "Justifying the End of Official Bilingualism," 469.

24. "Legislative Assembly," *The Regina Leader* (November 1, 1889).

25. "School Question," *Edmonton Bulletin* (December 7, 1889).

26. Canada, House of Commons, *Debates* (January 22, 1890), col. 51.

27. "McCarthy's Speech," *Manitoba Weekly Free Press* [Winnipeg] (August 8, 1889).

28. J.R. Miller, "'As a Politician He is a Great Enigma': The Social and Political Ideas of D'Alton McCarthy," *Canadian Historical Review* 58 (1977): 43.

29. Edward A. Freeman, "Race and Language," in *Historical Essays*, 3rd series, 2nd ed. (London: Macmillan, 1892), 206. These essays were first published in 1879. See also, Edward A. Freeman, *Comparative Politics*, 2nd ed. (London: Macmillan, 1896).

30. Ibid., 226.

31. *North-West Territories Act*, R.S.C. 1886, c. 50, s. 110, as amended by S.C. 1891, c. 22, s. 18.

32. "The Commons Debate," *Calgary Daily Herald* (February 24, 1890).

33. Ibid.

34. "N.W. Parliament," *The [Regina] Leader* (January 12, 1892).

35. *Journals of the Second Legislative Assembly of the North-West Territories, Session 1891–92* (Regina, NWT: R. B. Gordon, Printer to the Government of the North-West Territories, 1892), 110.

36. "The Assembly!" *The [Regina] Leader* (January 26, 1892).

37. "Elections," *The [Regina] Leader* (November 3, 1891).

38. "The Legislature," *The [Regina] Leader* (August 18,1892), 1.

39. "Legislative Assembly," *The Edmonton Bulletin* (August 22, 1892), 2.

40. Y.T.M. Mahé, "L'enseignement du français dans les districts scolaires bilingues albertains, 1885–1939," *Cahiers franco-canadiens de l'Ouest* 4 (1992): 294–95.

41. *Ibid.*, 295.

42. Canada, *Report of the Auditor General for the Year ended 30th June 1891* (Ottawa: S.E. Dawson, Queen's Printer, 1892), D226, D229.

43. Aunger, "The Mystery of the French Language Ordinances," 121.

44. *Regulations of the Department of Education* (Regina: John A. Reid, 1903), s. 25.

45. In 1916, Bishop Legal received legal advice that this regulation conflicted with the provision for a French-language primary course taught during school hours. His solicitors also noted that "no other language other than French has been taught between the hours of three and four in the afternoon limited to grammar, reading, and composition, except perhaps in some isolated districts where the teacher had taken the liberty to do as she pleased." See S.T. Rusak, *Relations in Education between Bishop Legal and the Alberta Government, 1905–1920* (M.Ed. Diss., University of Alberta, 1966), 94–95.

46. *Alberta Act*, S.C. 1905, c. 3 (reprinted R.S.C. 1970, App. II, No. 19), s. 16. One of the new government's first priorities, then, was to consolidate the existing laws. See Alberta, Department of the Attorney-General, *The Ordinances of the North West Territories, Being an official consolidation of the Ordinances of the North-West Territories in force on August 31st, 1905* (Edmonton: J.E. Richards, 1907).

47. House of Commons, *Debates* (30 June 1905), p. 8634.

48. "Le problème français de l'Ouest," *Le Courrier de l'Ouest* [Edmonton] (June 17, 1909), 4.

49. P.E. Lessard, Editor of *Le Courrier de l'Ouest*, to A. Turgeon, Attorney-General of Saskatchewan (September 29, 1911), Saskatchewan Archives Board, File M3-17K.

50. "Les ordonnances en français," *Le Courrier de l'Ouest* [Edmonton] (October 19, 1911), 1.

51. See for example "Acte des liqueurs," *Le Courrier de l'Ouest* [Edmonton] (May 20, 1915), 6.

52. *Canadian Annual Review of Public Affairs, 1913* (Toronto: Annual Review Publishing Company, 1914), 655.

53. "La question bilingue à la législature d'Alberta," *Le Courrier de l'Ouest* [Edmonton] (April 8, 1915), 1.

54. *Canadian Annual Review of Public Affairs*, 1915 (Toronto: Annual Review Publishing Company, 1916), 702.

55. *Act to amend the Acts and Ordinances constituting the Charter of the City of Calgary, and to validate Certain By-laws of the said city*, S.A. 1917, c. 45, s. 19(4).

56. "Chiropractic Bill removed from Agenda," *The [Edmonton] Morning Bulletin* (April 15, 1919), 5.

57. "Resolutions passed by the Orange Lodge," *The [Edmonton] Morning Bulletin* (April 21, 1919), 1.

58. Alberta, Legislative Assembly, "Instructions concerning the Teaching of French in the Elementary Schools of the Province of Alberta," in *Sessional Papers* (1925), Vol. 20, Paper No. 4-e, 1.

59. *An Act to Amend the School Act*, S.A. 1964, c. 82, s. 43, amending R.S.A. 1955, c. 297, s. 386.

60. Claude-Armand Sheppard, *The Law of Languages in Canada* (Ottawa: Information Canada, 1971), 297.

61. "Premier discours du député de St-Paul à la Législature," *La Survivance* [Edmonton] (February 26, 1936), 1.

62. "Language Courses Questioned As Education Budget Studied," *Edmonton Journal* (March 20, 1952), 1.

63. Michael Maccagno, "Excerpt from unpublished memoirs." See Alberta, Legislative Assembly, Standing Committee on Privileges and Elections, Standing Orders and Printing, *Minutes* (June 22, 1987), exhibit 12.

64. P. Lamoureux, *Bilingual Schooling in Alberta* (Edmonton: Alberta Education, c. 1984), 3–4.

65. Ibid.

66. Alberta, Government of Alberta, *Language Education Policy for Alberta* (Edmonton, 1988), 16.

67. Ibid., 22.

68. *French Language Regulations*, Alta. Reg. 250/76.

69. Canada, Premiers' Conference, "Statement on Language" (February 23, 1978).

70. Alberta, Government of Alberta, "Statement by Premier Peter Lougheed and Education Minister Julian Koziak RE: Minority Language Instruction" (February 24, 1978).

71. *Mahé v. Alberta* (1985), 39 Alta. L.R. (2d) 215.

72. *Mahé v. Alberta* (1987), 54 Alta. L.R. (2d) 212.

73. *Alberta Hansard* (November 26, 1980), 1751.

74. *Alberta Hansard* (November 27, 1987), 2093.

75. *Alberta Hansard* (April 7, 1987), 631.

76. L. Piquette, MLA Athabasca-Lac La Biche, to D.J. Carter, Speaker, Legislative Assembly of Alberta (April 8, 1987). See Alberta, Legislative Assembly, Standing Committee on Privileges and Elections, Standing Orders and Printing, *Minutes* (6 May 1987), exhibit 2.

77. Alberta, Legislative Assembly, Standing Committee on Privileges and Elections, Standing Orders and Printing, *Minutes* (June 25, 1987), 212.

78. R. v. *Mercure*, [1988] 1 S.C.R., 237.

79. Ibid., 267.

80. Ibid., 255.

81. Ibid., 236.

82. Ibid., 280.

83. *Languages Act*, S.A. 1988, c. L-7.5, s. 7.

84. *Alberta Hansard* (June 30, 1988), 2170.

85. Ibid., 2171.

86. Ibid., 2170.

87. Ibid., 2153.

88. *Alberta Hansard* (March 16, 1999), 543.

89. *Alberta Hansard* (May 30, 2001), 933.

90. R. v. *Desgagné* (June 13, 1996), Peace River A 06115443 T (Alta. Prov. Ct.), 3; cited in Canada, Department of Justice and Department of Canadian Heritage, *Annotated Language Laws of Canada*, 2nd ed. (Ottawa: Department of Public Works and Government Services, 2000), 208.

91. *Criminal Code*, R.S.C. 1985, c. C-46, s. 530(1).

92. *Mahé v. Alberta* [1990] 1 S.C.R., 345.

93. Alberta, Alberta Education, *Guide de mise en oeuvre de la gestion scolaire francophone* (Edmonton: School Business Administration Services, March 4, 1994), 9.

94. Éric Batalla and Sandrine Griffon, *Écoles francophones, Alberta* (Edmonton: Le Franco et La Fédération des conseils scolaires francophones de l'Alberta, 2003).

95. Jean Laponce, *Languages and Their Territories* (Toronto: University of Toronto Press, 1987). See also: Louis-Jean Calvet, *La guerre des langues et les politiques linguistiques* (Paris: Hachette Littératures, 1999).

96. "Excerpts from Premier's speech on the Constitution," *The Edmonton Journal* (January 10, 1992), A2.

96. "Excerpts from Premier's speech on the Constitution," The Edmonton Journal (January 10, 1992), A2.

Nellie McClung holds up a front page headline announcing the high court's decision that "Women are Persons." Photograph by Paul Cavanaugh.

Five

Out of the West
History, Memory, and the "Persons" Case, 1919–2000

CATHERINE CAVANAUGH

October 18, 2000 marked the 71st anniversary of what has become known as the "Persons" case. In Ottawa it was a crisp, clear day. CBC's *Newsworld* cameras panned across the carefully manicured grounds of Parliament Hill, swept past its neo-gothic, grey stone buildings, capturing the glint of late morning sun reflected off the deep blue waters of the placid Ottawa River. The cameras lingered briefly on the graceful sweep of the distant Gatineau hills draped in their vivid autumn hues before coming to rest on an area just east of the Centre Block, home of the Senate Chambers. The voice of the network's senior anchor, Peter Mansbridge, broke into the scene. He welcomed viewers to a special, hour-long broadcast of the dedication of a bronze statue commemorating five women from Alberta who successfully petitioned Britain's Judicial Committee of the Privy Council (JCPC) for Canadian women's full rec ognition as "Persons" under section 24 of the *British North America Act* (*BNA Act*).[1] "They came out of the West," Mansbridge announced, reciting the name of each petitioner: "Murphy, Muir Edwards, Parlby, McKinney, McClung." His voice alone seemed to confer heroic status. "It was a remarkable time," he explained, recounting the Alberta women's collective achievement in 1929, a "very important time for the progress of women in this nation's history."[2]

This essay examines ways in which history and memory intersect to give the "Persons" case a privileged position within the telling of Anglo-Canadian women's history. Indeed, in the popular imagination and among some scholars the case, and the five Alberta women who were most closely associated with it, have come to represent an entire generation's political activism, including a nation-wide campaign for women's suffrage. But the case has also attracted controversy. While some see the "Famous Five" as a symbol of modernity, signifying an uninterrupted movement of women's political rebellion and progress,[3] others are critical—sometimes harshly critical—of the Alberta women as racist, elitist and tarnished by their associations with the eugenics movement of the 1920s and 30s.[4] By examining the case and the memorials to it created by women in the 1930s and at the end of the twentieth century, this essay argues that remembering the "Persons" case is to (re)present women's rebellions in ways that often overwrite such tensions and contradictions, offering a unified symbol of women's resistance and achievement that is made subordinate to the nation-state.[5] It argues that the case itself never should have been necessary, but, with the dedication of two statues, one in Calgary and another in Ottawa, it has entered public discourse as the singular achievement of "first wave" feminism.[6]

One reason why the "Persons" case has occupied such a prominent position in women's history is its importance for Canadian legal development. The case is known to every first-year law student as *Henrietta Muir Edwards v. Attorney-General for Canada*, a constitutional watershed that interpreted the BNA Act as a "living tree"—dynamic and open to change, and not narrowly bound by the intentions of the original framers. Following this line of argument, the members of Britain's Judicial Committee of the Privy Council, the highest court in Canada at the time, were able to overcome historical convention and find that women were fully included as "Persons" in the constitutional life of the nation.[7]

The question of women's capacity to hold public office had been decided in Alberta more than a decade earlier than the Privy Council decision in 1929. In that case the province's Supreme Court was asked to rule on a legal challenge to women's right to sit as magistrates. The charge that they were incompetent based on their sex was aimed directly at Emily Murphy and Alice J. Jamieson. Appointed in 1916 in Edmonton and Calgary respectively, they were the first two women magistrates in the British empire. Some members of the Alberta Bar would have none of it and on her first day in court Murphy's authority was called in question by the defence lawyer who argued that women were disqualified from holding public office because they were not "persons" within the meaning of the BNA Act.[8] The "persons" argument continued to hound the two women until 1918 when Justice Scott responded to an appeal from a conviction for vagrancy arising from the Calgary court in *Rex v. Cyr*.

The case involved a Calgary prostitute, Lizzie Cyr (alias Lizzie Waters) who was sentenced to six months of hard labour. In what would become only one of many ironies associated with the case, two of the grounds put forward in the appeal were that the accused, being a woman, was not within the definition of a vagrant in the Criminal Code of Canada and that the magistrate who convicted her, also a woman, was incompetent to exercise judicial office.[9] While Scott had no difficulty deciding that a woman vagrant was just as clearly a vagrant within the meaning of the Criminal Code as a male vagrant, he struggled with the second point. Declaring that he had "serious doubt whether a woman is qualified" for judicial appointment, he demurred, refusing to consider the question in the context of the case before him.[10] Only on further appeal did Chief Justice Stewart address the issue head on, finding that Alberta was not bound by the historical exclusions found at common law and therefore he concluded that there was "no legal disqualification for holding public office arising from any distinction of sex."[11] But legal developments in Alberta had no binding impact on the rest of the country so the matter remained contested.

The pressure for change came from organized women building on the significant political gains they had won in the late 1910s and early 20s in their push for greater political emancipation. Between 1916 and 1925 women won the right to sit in the federal House of Commons and in all of the provincial legislatures except New Brunswick and Quebec.[12] Alberta elected the first women legislators, Louise McKinney and Roberta MacAdams, in 1917, followed by Irene Parlby and Nellie McClung in 1921. In British Columbia, Mary Ellen Smith was elected in 1918, followed, in 1919 and 1920, by Mrs. M.O. Ramsland in Saskatchewan and Edith Rogers in Manitoba, respectively. In March 1921 Mary Ellen Smith was appointed to the cabinet in British Columbia, followed in August by Irene Parlby, who was named minister without portfolio in the newly elected United Farmers Government in Alberta, making them the first women cabinet members in the British empire. That same year, Agnes McPhail took her seat in the federal House of Commons as the first woman member of Parliament. With a growing number of women in public offices it became increasingly obvious that their continued exclusion from appointment to the Senate was clearly out of step with the times. When he connected the dots, one government member of Parliament put it succinctly: "since the government had...extended the suffrage to women and they are now entitled to sit in this Chamber as well as in the Provincial Legislatures, I see no reason why they should not be enabled to sit in the Upper Chamber of this Parliament."[13]

By the time the member from Kindersley rose in the House, women had already called repeatedly for just such an appointment, but were routinely ignored or rebuffed on the grounds that their admission to the Senate was constitutionally impossible.[14] Indeed, that same year, in a brief to the federal government that was clearly intended as a final word on the case, the long-time deputy minister of justice, Edmund Leslie Newcombe, expressed the opinion that women were not qualified for appointment to the Senate. In a hastily-written note in the margin of a Department memorandum on the topic, Newcombe noted that there was no "Latin word to describe a Senatress...[and] the...name Senator does not apply to a woman."[15]

Historically, the "Persons" case has been seen as a reflection of a more radically democratic politics associated with western Canada—a version of western exceptionalism—spearheaded by one of the West's most outspoken feminist crusaders, Emily Murphy, and backed by some of the leading activists in the newest of Canada's provinces.[16] While Murphy is rightly credited with much of the work of skilfully guiding the case through its long and often torturous legal and political path, the campaign also illustrates the crucial importance of women's developing national networks in the immediate post-suffrage period. The Federated Women's Institutes, presided over by Judge Murphy, first called for women's appointment to the Senate at their founding convention in 1919, and they continued to press for this change annually. In 1921, when a western seat in the Senate became available, 2,000 Quebec members of the Women's Christian Temperance Union signed petitions calling for a woman senator, University Women's Clubs added their voices, and the National Council of Women of Canada (NCWC), claiming to represent 450,000 women across the country, renewed their call, this time urging Murphy's appointment.[17]

Henrietta Muir Edwards later credited the NCWC as a crucial force behind the successful campaign.[18] But, according to Murphy, the idea of her nomination was first raised by the much smaller Montreal Women's Club. As a former Calgarian, the Club's secretary, Gertrude E. Budd, was familiar with Murphy's work and the advances made by Alberta women. The strategy of the Club members was clear. By putting forward the name of a prominent woman who was well qualified for appointment, the federal government should be compelled to act. With Agnes McPhail in the House of Commons and Emily Murphy in the Senate, it would be more difficult for the government of their own province to continue to oppose extending the franchise to Quebec women. Moreover, like Isabella Scott, the Club's President, many Canadian women saw the campaign as having significance far beyond the narrow question of women's access to the Senate. Rather, throughout the decade-long struggle, the "persons" argument took on symbolic meaning as the final barrier to Canadian women's full citizenship. As Scott explained to Nellie McClung, "How can 'persons' be denied the Provincial vote, the entrance to the liberal professions, including the church, the right to study architecture at McGill and so on?"[19]

When they recruited Murphy, organized women found the champion they needed to ensure success. A popular, seasoned campaigner for women's rights, who was also knowledgeable in the law, and who enjoyed close connections with women's networks across the country as well as links to members of Central Canada's legal and political elite, Murphy took up the cause with her characteristically fierce determination. When the government turned down the Montreal women's request, Murphy replied to the Club. Reiterating her experience with the "persons" argument in Alberta, she expressed confidence concerning the battle ahead. "After five years of quietude on the Saskatchewan," she wrote, "along comes the memorandum from the office of the Minister of Justice, with the same old rigmarole. It is almost unbelievable."[20] Ottawa's intransigence was not only "unbelievable;" with the possibility of her appointment, the campaign to change government opinion became personal for Murphy. Moreover, in 1921, the goal seemed within reach. Her brother, William Ferguson, a member of the Ontario Supreme Court, reassured Murphy that "there is nothing in the British North America Act to prevent your appointment to the Senate."[21]

Legal opinion would ultimately vindicate Judge Ferguson's view, but in the backlash climate of the 1920s the campaign met firm resistance from Ottawa. Indeed, the "persons" question would bedevil four prime ministers and five governments. Sir Robert Borden was the first to deny women's claim on the grounds that an appointment would require an amendment to the BNA Act, followed by Arthur Meighen, R.B. Bennett and W.L. Mackenzie King. King initially attempted to introduce reform through the Senate but when that failed, he acceded to the women's demands for a judicial ruling on the matter.[22] By 1927 Murphy realized that the question had become hopelessly stalled at the political level. It would take a reference to the Supreme Court of Canada to get clarity on the matter.

Faced with eight years of government foot-dragging and the open hostility of the all-male Senate, Murphy decided that a new strategy was necessary. She would initiate a direct appeal to the courts, including the JCPC, should that become necessary. It is likely that Murphy's brother William alerted her to Section 60 of the BNA Act that permitted any "interested persons" to request interpretation of any constitutional point raised by the Act. In addition, it provided that should the Department of Justice agree that the question was of sufficient public importance, the federal government would pay all reasonable expenses incurred by bringing a reference case. With annual calls from women's organizations behind her, it only remained for Murphy to enlist the support of a few others who were willing to add their names to the petition.

Given the critical importance of their alliances in the reform movement, it is reasonable to think that Murphy may have included several men as petitioners in the case. We do not know whether or not she considered this approach. But choosing four other prominent Alberta women with close ties to the women's movement carried powerful symbolic weight. It was a clear statement of women's ability to act on their own behalf and had the effect of pitting a small group of women against the entire resources of an all-male government. Under Murphy's guidance, organized women would use the full force of all that they had achieved in the early decades of the twentieth century to make a compelling second bid for the full recognition of their citizenship rights. Henrietta Muir Edwards of MacLeod was author of two books on women and the law and long-time Convenor of the NCWC's Laws Committee. Nellie McClung was a popular author, temperance campaigner, and one of the country's best-known suffragists, who had served a single term as a Liberal member of the Legislature of Alberta (MLA). Louise Crummy McKinney of Claresholm was also an activist, temperance organizer and former MLA, and Irene Parlby was a founding member and former President of the United Farm Women of Alberta (UFWA), a sitting member of the Alberta Legislature and government minister. Among them, the five had many years of active work in various campaigns for women's rights dating back to the 1880s and 90s and they all enjoyed a national and, particularly in the case of McClung, an international reputation.

None of these women had the financial resources necessary to mount a legal challenge in the Supreme Court, but Murphy reassured her co-petitioners that the *Act* gave them access to the public purse. She pointed out that Alberta had recently sought a constitutional interpretation concerning the Separate Schools question and their action "was without cost to this province." At the same time she explained that she was initiating the reference knowing that it had the full support of "Canadian women generally, they having already endorsed the principle." Alluding to King's abortive attempt to initiate reform through the Senate, she was steadfast: "We have now come to realize that the matter is one which cannot with any degree of fairness be submitted for decision to a body of male persons, many of whom have expressed themselves towards it in a manner that is distinctly hostile."[23] Indeed, a few months later she charged that the negative view held by "law officers of the crown" was allowed to insert itself into the proceedings and mislead the government.[24]

Drawing on more than 10 years of experience as a magistrate, Murphy determined that moving forward required a shift in strategy. She called a meeting of the group at her home in Edmonton, advising that they remove the question from the realm of partisan politics where it had floundered for so long and place it in the hands of the courts. Agreed, the group petitioned the Government, asking that the Supreme Court determine where power to appoint women to the Senate was vested and if it was "constitutionally possible" for Parliament to make such an appointment.[25] Later, Murphy added a third question, requesting that the court clarify whether or not special legislation was necessary to allow for women Senators and, if so, who was responsible for such legislation. As she explained to her co-petitioners, they did not want to have to go back to the court at some future date.[26]

It seemed to be an opportune moment to advance changes to the Senate in 1927. Progressives in particular were calling for its abolition and Senate reform was on the agenda of the Dominion-Provincial Conference when it met that year. At the very least, the women's petition raised questions about the procedure for amending the BNA Act. But the question of women's appointment to the Senate was never discussed during these meetings.[27] As editorial opinion pointed out, organized women were asking the government to do little more than complete the changes initiated by the extension of the franchise almost 10 years earlier. That their concerns failed to make it onto the Conference agenda seems a clear indication of the extent to which Ottawa was determined to stem the tide of women's emancipation. However, mounting pressure to act led to a sudden about-face and in October, Minister of Justice Ernest Lapointe announced that the government now felt that interpretation of section 24 was "of great public importance," recommending that the question be referred to the Supreme Court as "an act of justice to the women of Canada."[28] But the wording of the reference proposed by his department was precisely what Murphy had carefully avoided when she framed the Alberta women's petition.

The question stated by the government was "Does the word 'Persons' in section 24 of the British North America Act, 1867, include female persons?"[29] Murphy felt that stated this way, the reference would inevitably receive a negative reply. The Department had repeatedly expressed the view that sex determined eligibility for appointment to the Senate, and that sex was male. Murphy was aware that its opinion had not changed and she suspected further political shenanigans in the rewording. She immediately protested the change, pointing out that the question to be referred to the court was not the question asked by the petitioners and thus the government's action had caused "amazement and perturbation." She demanded that the petition, as revised by the government, be withdrawn and that the original wording, with the additional third question, be submitted to the court.[30] In an equally blunt rebuttal the Department insisted that the government's wording was the only "real and substantial point" raised by the petition, and that "no injustice has been done" to the women by the revision.[31] On the advice of their counsel, Newton Wesley Rowell, Murphy and her co-petitioners agreed to allow the question, as put by the Department, to go forward.[32]

At Murphy's request, Rowell had agreed to take the case. Once again her Ontario family connections came into play, helping her engage a prominent and highly respected member of the Canadian bar.[33] A former leader of the Liberal Party of Ontario and member of Borden's wartime government, Rowell was an experienced constitutional lawyer who was well connected in legal and political circles in Ottawa. He was also closely associated with progressive politics and sympathetic to the women's cause.[34] According to her biographer, Murphy met Rowell in Edmonton where he was speaking in support of the League of Nations.[35] By early November she had the agreement of the other four petitioners and notified the Federal Government of their intention to have Rowell represent them. Later that month, Rowell consulted with the Department of Justice and was reassured that, should he act for the Alberta women, all "reasonable expenses" would be paid by the minister of finance.[36] Clearly, Rowell was looking for just such assurances. He also asked if the Department objected to him taking the case since he was on retainer to them in a number of liquor cases. If anything, their long-standing relationship with Rowell likely allayed any concerns that the Department may have had about undertaking to cover the costs of the reference. The relationship between Murphy and the Department had become strained over the question of the nature of the wording of the petition, and Department lawyers were likely relieved to learn that the Alberta women would be ably represented. Rowell was well known to them and they could deal directly with him. Indeed, responding to Murphy's repeated protests over the terms of the reference, the Department reassured her and then urged that she seek Rowell's advice.[37]

Thus, the case brought together an impressive group of politically seasoned women with personal links to a national network of women's organizations and close associations to the political and legal establishment in Central Canada.[38] Yet, from the outset Murphy was adamant that the group should maintain a low profile as long as the matter was before the courts. Later, she pointed out that at no time had "recriminations, nor any spirit of bitterness been permitted to becloud the issue."[39] With organized women in full support and editorial opinion across the country firmly in their favour, she was careful to avoid controversy.

While it has received the most attention, *Henrietta Muir Edwards v. The Attorney-General of Canada* is only one of a number of "persons" cases brought by women seeking admission to the professions in the early decades of the twentieth century.[40] Debates over women's right to hold public office, however, had a much longer history and in his arguments before the Supreme Court counsel for the federal government, William Stuart Edwards, put forward a long stream of common law cases to support sex-based exclusion. At issue was whether or not women were included in section 24 of the *BNA Act*. Ignoring the earlier decision by the Alberta court, Edwards argued that they were not because

> the expression "qualified persons"...is to be interpreted in the sense it bore...when the Act was passed: in other words, that which it meant when enacted it means to-day, and its legal connotation has not been extended, and cannot be influenced by, recent innovations touching the political status of women, or by the more liberal conceptions respecting the sphere of women in politics and social life which may, perhaps, be assumed now to prevail.[41]

In other words, in his view, women's historical exclusions based on their sex prevailed unless otherwise specifically removed by the framers of the act.

All five justices hearing the case agreed, and on April 24, 1928 announced that "Women are not 'qualified persons' within the meaning of section 24 of the BNA Act, 1867, and therefore are not eligible for appointment by the Governor-General to the Senate of Canada."[42] Murphy had anticipated this negative decision and she immediately advised Rowell of the Alberta women's intention to appeal to London. In August, she advised her co-petitioners that the group was off to the Privy Council. She was pleased that the Federal Government would not oppose them but did not see this as any indication that Ottawa was backing away from their long-held view. Besides, she concluded, "they don't really need to [defend against the appeal] in that the Privy

Council will have the Factum and arguments they made before the Supreme Court of Canada."[43] Further good news awaited. At the last minute, the province of Quebec also withdrew its opposition; a decision that was especially welcomed by suffragists in that province.

In the aftermath of the Supreme Court's adverse decision, Lapointe indicated the government's intention to find some "means" around it. But Murphy was confident that an appeal to the Privy Council would bring a clear victory and she was skeptical of political interference. "It is well...that it has turned out this way," she wrote to the other petitioners, "for if a woman or women had been appointed [to the Senate] through 'means' Quebec would have most likely appealed against it, so we may as well get it settled now so far as the legal end is concerned."[44] "Of the ultimate results I have not the slightest doubt," Murphy confided to McClung. With the firm support of organized women and editorial opinion across the country squarely behind them, she was confident that "Nothing can prevent our winning."[45]

It is unclear why Murphy expected the British court to be any less conservative than their Canadian brethren, particularly as Margaret Haig, Viscountess Rhondda, a peer in her own right, had been denied the right to sit in the House of Lords just six years earlier, in 1922. Murphy may have been relying on her brother's advice that no sex bar existed in law to prevent women's appointment to the Senate, although, in the intervening years, she had come to believe that the issue turned on a constitutional interpretation and that Canadian jurisprudence must develop in response to changing circumstances. She was unconvinced by arguments concerning the original intent of the framers of the constitutional act and wrote to Isabella Scott in Montreal explaining that, "when you come to think it over, you'll find that sex, in itself, is no longer a disqualification."[46] But she also prepared for a negative result in London, confiding to Rowell that, should the appeal fail, "political means" would be pursued.[47] In the event, Murphy's confidence in the British court proved well placed. On October 18, 1929, Lord Chancellor Sankey took the unusual step of reading in full the decision in which the Privy Councillors overturned the Canadian Supreme Court, finding that exclusion was "a relic of days more barbarous than ours" and that women were "persons" under the meaning of the BNA Act and therefore eligible for appointment to the Senate.[48]

Sankey's actions ensured that the case which was seen to be "of exceptional interest, not only for the constitutional point involved, but because it also raised the question of the general status of women," received national and international attention.[49] Newspapers across Canada, in Britain and throughout the Dominions, as well as in the United States, announced the decision in bold headlines. As editorials were quick to point out, the court's interpretation had implications in Great Britain and all Commonwealth countries. Referring to the continued exclusion of women from the House of Lords, one paper trumpeted the news that "Canadian Women Beat Their English Sisters." With the Labour Party in power, another speculated that the case opened the way to the "remodelling of the upper house" in Britain.[50] "Senate Doors Swing Open To Women" one Canadian newspaper declared. *The Calgary Herald* took a more measured tone, calling the Privy Council's decision "a common sense view" of "an anomaly in the public life of the Dominion which is both striking and absurd."[51] Others thought that Ottawa had been caught unprepared and saw more trouble ahead as those "men lined up to receive political patronage will be forced to accept women into the competition."[52] Writing from the nation's capital, Charles Stewart easily predicted that the decision would "not be popular in the Senate because [Senators] have always brushed aside the suggestion and have even been disposed to look on women in the Commons as an enemy."[53]

It was widely felt that the decision would have implications well beyond the question of Senate appointments, even signalling a new chapter in the campaign to extend women's public role. And, indeed, the press later reported that, in Palestine, the lawyer Rosa Ginsberg had won the right to appear before the courts in the British-controlled territory in part because of the ruling in the "Persons" case. "That case helped my point a great deal," Ginsberg reported to Murphy, "I owe you my best gratitude not only for cheering me up when I was very much depressed, but also for the strong weapon which helped me to win my case."[54] But, coming as it did on the very day that prices on Wall Street began to fall precipitously, the optimism engendered by the decision would have little lasting effect.

At the time, however, no one could foresee the disaster that lay ahead and legal reiteration of their full citizenship gave organized women encouragement. Mrs. J.A. Wilson, President of the NCWC, welcomed the removal of an "anachronism" in law. She saw the decision as the culmination of decades of struggle, declaring that "one of the remaining disabilities for women had been removed."[55] The subsequent introduction of provincial legislation prohibiting sex as grounds for exclusion from public office known as the *Sex Disqualification (Removal) Act* suggests that she was right. But, as legal scholars have pointed out, up to and including *Henrietta Muir Edwards v. Attorney-General for Canada*, Canadian courts fell short of guaranteeing women's full equality. Rather, the courts had delivered a qualified interpretation, finding at best that the word "persons" only included women if they were not expressly excluded. Not even the Privy Council had decided that the word "persons" must always include both sexes.[56]

Nevertheless, in the autumn of 1929, women savoured an important victory. Letters of congratulations poured in from across the country, many expressing confidence that a Senate appointment for Murphy was assured.[57] Agnes Macphail, the only woman member of Parliament, considered the Senate "as a menace to the Government of the Country," but she praised the Alberta women on the success of their campaign, noting that "women have at last received the recognition they are entitled to and deserving of."[58] Henrietta Muir Edwards shared her view, arguing that the decision recognized women's "personal individuality and independence of sex."[59] McClung was "elated" and credited Murphy with much of the work of the campaign. "It was she who wrote all the letters and arranged every detail of the controversy," McClung reported, "assuming all the expenses and labor involved... her handling of the whole matter has been a master stroke of diplomacy."[60] Speaking by telephone from her home in Alix, Alberta, Irene Parlby stated that "we always felt that we had a very just appeal." [61] She did not expect that women would rush to enter the Senate but that an important principle had been established by the decision: "women felt that if they desired to [become Senators] the privilege should be theirs.[62]

All five women expressed gratification at the outcome of what was a "long and sometimes arduous struggle," but Murphy downplayed the element of sex victory. "I am not one who looks for radical, and far-reaching reforms from the appointment of women to the Senate," she wrote in an article published in *The Chatelaine* in December, 1929. Addressing the charge that women would be a disruptive force in the Upper Chamber—"perverse and refractory...with brickbats under their blouses and terrible chips on their shoulders"—she argued that women were experienced in public service and would "easily fall into the habit of saying 'we' instead of 'you' in all affairs of state." [63] In Montreal, Isabella Scott was especially moved. "I can't write coherently to-night," she confided to McClung on the evening of the decision, "I don't remember being so stirred in my emotions since Armistice night. I really did not expect this decision.... You have certainly covered yourselves with glory and your names should go down in the history of Canada as the liberators of your sex."[64]

Following an initial flurry of press attention, the case soon disappeared from the front pages of Canadian newspapers. But, determined that an important chapter of women's history should not be lost, the Canadian Federation of Business and Professional Women's Club commissioned a bronze plaque commemorating the "Persons" case and the five petitioners from Alberta, who, in the intervening years, had become popularly known as the "Famous Five." The club had a special interest in the decision because the "persons" argument was frequently used to block women's entry into the professions. On June 11, 1938 between three and four hundred dignitaries assembled outside the entrance to the Senate chambers to witness the unveiling, including the prime minister, Mackenzie King, members of the House of Commons and the Senate, two women Senators, Cairine Wilson and the recently appointed Iva Fallis, and Thérèse Casgrain, President of the Quebec League for Women's Rights, who had recently presided over yet another defeat of female suffrage in her province. They were joined by a large delegation of club members from Eastern Canada and Ontario as well as other invited guests. Of the two surviving members of the original five, only Nellie McClung was present.

The ceremonies in Ottawa reflected the extent to which the significance of the case was contested. Earlier close associations with Alberta and the West were recognized but also subordinated to nationalist themes that linked the "new" West and the older provinces in a common project of nation building. In the summer of 1938, economic crisis at home and the looming spectre of war in Europe must have given an added sense of urgency to the crucial importance of shoring up national unity. Far from opening up a "direct route" to public office that some envisioned, formal recognition of women as "Persons" had done little to expand women's participation in politics. Indeed, the movement that had been so hopeful in 1929 was now stalled. Beginning in the early 1930s, the number of women on public boards and at all levels of government registered a sharp decline. Economic opportunities that had seemed so bright in the 1920s, particularly for women in the professions, were steadily disappearing. A question on many people's minds at the time must have been what would women's role in the war be? In this climate, the dedication of a plaque commemorating a final victory in the women's movement of the 1910s and 20s had several purposes for business and professional women: first, by honouring an earlier generation of leaders, it ensured that their history would not be forgotten, second, it reiterated women's claim to a public space that was rapidly shrinking. A permanent memorial to women's successful activism, installed on the stone walls just outside the entrance to the Senate, would ensure

Unveiling of a plaque commemorating the five Alberta women whose efforts resulted in the Persons Case, which established the rights of women to hold public office in Canada. (Front row, left to right): Mrs. Muir Edwards, daughter-in-law of Henrietta Muir Edwards; Mrs. J.C. Kenwood, daughter of Judge Emily Murphy; Hon. Mackenzie King; Mrs. Nellie McClung. (Rear row, left to right): Senators Iva Campbell Fallis, Cairine Wilson. Library and Archives Canada C-054523.

that "As long as these parliament buildings stand the path to its door will be beaten by the feet of eager travelers who know the history of the women's movement in Canada." [65]

But women claiming public space that was assumed to be an exclusively male domain was full of contradiction. The regional, class, and gendered tensions inherent in the "Persons" case were evident in the dedication ceremonies and in the plaque itself. Simple in its construction, the plaque bears the names of each of the petitioners and the city or town in which they were living in 1929, noting that "All [were] of The Province of Alberta." Underscoring their western connections, the plaque or tablet describes the five as "outstanding pioneer women" acting in the "cause of womankind." While recognizing the feminist objectives of the campaign to extend women's citizenship rights, the memorial linked the case with the aims and objectives of the Business and Professional Women's Club whose green and gold crest appears at its head while the entire inscription is tightly ringed by a chain of embossed maple leaves, a national symbol of Canada.

Opening the dedication ceremonies, President Dr. Ellen C. Douglas of Winnipeg dropped the usual reference to Alberta, choosing instead to describe the petitioners as "five Canadian women" and citizens of "the Dominion at large."[66] She praised the five for their "doubtless courage and leadership," but, adhering closely to a widely-held view of separate spheres, she reassured her listeners that the public role of the five did not compromise their femininity. On the contrary, it was, she said, the "well rounded nature of these women's lives, as wives and mothers" that underpinned their contributions to the life of the nation. No mention was made of the many setbacks that women had experienced during the 1930s. Rather, Douglas saw the case as ushering in a period of uninterrupted progress for women in the "field of public service." Echoing the call of the immediate post-suffrage period, she urged women at the end of the decade to follow the example set by Murphy and her colleagues and take up the challenges of full citizenship that had been extended to them.[67]

The prime minister was next to speak. In sketching a brief outline of the events leading up to the Privy Council decision, King gave no hint of the political opposition the five women petitioners and their supporters had encountered. He shed little light on why his government suddenly reversed its opposition to women's appointment to the Senate and decided instead to allow the appeal to the British courts to go forward. Indeed, he erroneously implied that his administration had initiated the appeal. He may have been the gatekeeper, but he was not the initiator. By 1927, pressure on the gate was more than could be legitimately resisted. He also took full credit for Wilson's appointment as the first woman Senator, but failed to recognize the continued disappointment felt in some quarters that Murphy was passed over, although it was Bennett, himself a westerner, who had failed to act in that instance.[68] King too saw a narrowly circumscribed role for women in government. The singular achievement of the Alberta women, he said, was that they "helped to throw into bold relief the special gifts which it is within the power of woman to bring to the organized life of the community and of the nation."[69] In a rhetorical move that had the effect of domesticating women's recently-expanded public political authority, he welcomed their special maternal qualities in government. "Endowed with special powers of intuition," he explained, "a keen insight into human values, and in most cases an abiding loyalty to cherished institutions and principles, woman possesses and has revealed in public and in private life a quite exceptional capacity for sustained and unselfish service."[70] By calling on the deeply rooted notion or female loyalty to man-made institutions King effectively reined in sex rebellion, subordinating it to the state. In a climate of diminishing opportunities for women, King placed their activism firmly in the domestic realm, pointing out that

> Today, when the problems of government the world over are essentially human problems and our very homes and all that we hold most sacred are threatened by appalling dangers from without and by subversive forces from within, it is well that our national existence should be fortified by the participation in its affairs of those who are so exceptionally qualified to contribute to human well being and to the preservation of the foundations of home and family life. [71]

Senator Louis Coté also spoke, cautioning women on their role in government. Speaking directly to organized women who had so vigorously supported the campaign for appointment, and well aware of the continuing struggle for suffrage in Quebec, Coté warned against an "ardent" or "exaggerated feminism" in public affairs. He firmly rejected the notion of sex-based representation and praised the two recent women appointees for their "intelligent and active collaboration" with their male counterparts.[72] His views reflected the anti-feminist sentiment that had dogged the campaign from the outset. They also give added weight to the earlier explanation of one male Senator as to why Canadian women failed in their bid to get Murphy appointed. "She would have caused too much trouble," he is reported to have said.[73] Two women sat in the Upper House—what Senator Fallis described as "the last exclusive stronghold of the male"—but they remained politically marginalized.[74]

It was left to the seasoned campaigner, Nellie McClung, to reassert women's radical feminist purposes. Speaking for the five petitioners, she said, "the circle was complete." But she reminded those gathered outside the entrance to the Senate and the radio audience at home that there was much more at stake then the public recognition of five Alberta women. In dedicating the tablet they were also honouring the many women across Canada who fought to advance the cause of all women: "the great unnumbered, unremembered and unknown people...whose names will never appear in the papers, people whose names we will never know. Women," she reminded her audience, "had to begin from so far down...[they] had first to convince the world that they had souls and then that they had minds. And then it came to this matter of political entity." [75] In a mild rebuke to Coté and his like-minded fellows, she cautioned that the battle was far from over: "there are people who would sign a minority report."

It must have been a bittersweet moment for McClung, with so many of her friends and colleagues gone. She read a message from Irene Parlby, who was listening to the radio broadcast from her home in Alix, and thanked the four others for their "loyalty, for their love, and for their steadfastness. For their wonderful companionship." She was especially mindful of the group's "undaunted and indomitable, incomparable leader," Emily Murphy who had died suddenly in 1933. Clearly, the fact that Murphy was denied a Senate appointment continued to rankle. Knowing that much had been made of Murphy's ambition, which some saw as unseemly in a woman, McClung insisted that the person who had done so much to win the right to appointment "didn't care who got the honour. She was never one to care who got the vote of thanks. She would joyfully pin a medal anytime on somebody else." McClung's tribute to Murphy reflected more than her interest in guarding the reputation of her deceased friend and colleague. For her the notion of sex unity remained paramount to success in women's political struggles.[76]

By the end of the twentieth century the diversity of women's lives was much more apparent, reflecting the increased social diversity of Canada generally. As a "third wave" of the women's movement emerged, few feminists would agree with this earlier generation's idea of a unity of women. With the approach of the millennium, a small group of women in Calgary began to organize to remember the "Famous Five" and their achievements. As business and professional women they would use their resources and connections to mount the most ambitious project memorializing women to date, the construction of two bronze statues in the image of the Alberta five. Their objectives were similar to those of their counterparts in the Business and Professional Women's Club almost 60 years earlier. They too would work in a climate of backlash and an atmosphere of rapidly changing times.

The project that would culminate in the largest, most costly, privately-funded public monument built by women honouring women's political activism began with a simple question. When her friend Nancy Millar completed a history of Canada as seen through tombstones, *Once Upon A Tomb*, Francis Wright asked what was on the tombstones of the five Alberta women petitioners in the "Persons" case. She discovered that few traces remained of the campaign or the women who took their fight for Senate appointment to the Privy Council in London. With the seventieth anniversary of the decision

"Famous Five" monument by Edmonton sculptor Barbara Paterson, Ottawa, Ontario. Judge Emily Murphy greets the other four petitioners: (left to right) Nellie McClung, Irene Parlby, Henrietta Muir Edwards, Louise Crummy McKinney (seated) and Emily Murphy. Photograph by Paul Cavanaugh.

rapidly approaching, Wright and a committee of four other women launched the Famous Five Foundation. "We wanted Canadians to know and appreciate the achievements of the 'Famous Five,'" Wright explains, "and through them, other female Canadian achievers, thus providing inspiration for others to follow their own dreams."[77]

The group deliberately decided to follow in the tradition of monuments to political leaders and commissioned a bronze statue representing the five women from Alberta. Ultimately, two statues were erected, one in the Olympic Plaza in downtown Calgary and the second on Parliament Hill at a cost of more than one million dollars. In addition to a series of fundraising luncheons and other activities, the foundation sought out five prominent Canadian women willing to donate two hundred thousand dollars each.[78] Although they faced many critics, the Foundation also attracted a large number of people ready to support the project. Thirty-six major public events were held in two years and, by October 2000, "more than 1,000 volunteers—private and corporate volunteers, funders, politicians and government officials—in 12 cities" had contributed.[79]

Opposition to the project was especially strong in Calgary, a city that was home to the majority of the private and corporate donors, but where, according to Wright, anti-feminist sentiment is especially strong. The situation was

Detail. Louise Crummy McKinney and Henrietta Muir Edwards raising a tea cup. Photograph by Paul Cavanaugh.

very different in Ottawa where the Foundation found a climate of co-operation. Wright says that "Ottawa wanted to find ways to do this." She recalls that no one in Ottawa asked if these women were feminist, but the question came up repeatedly in Calgary and by one male member of the Reform Party. That one-man opposition became crucial because the group had to gain all-party support in both the House of Commons and the Senate for a special resolution permitting the installation of the memorial on Parliament Hill.

The rules limit statues on the Hill to three categories of persons: (1) deceased prime ministers, (2) fathers of confederation, and (3) monarchs of Canada. After three defeats, unanimity was achieved when a deal was struck to allow the Reform Party to speak on a separate matter that was before the House in exchange for all-party support.

In the face of anti-feminism, Wright made a strategic decision to empha- sise the achievements of the "Famous Five" as nation builders and to downplay their feminism. But, from the outset, she was determined that the project should be the work of women remembering and honouring women. Aware that success required a broad coalition of supporters, women and men from all political persuasions, working in a manner similar to Murphy and her colleagues, Wright quickly learned to represent the objectives of the group in "images" and "language" that would garner wide acceptance. The central message of the monument became one of civic activism, strength and leadership in a female form.[80]

To realize their vision, the group commissioned Edmonton sculptor Barbara Paterson. Responding to criticism that a representational bronze statue was old-fashioned and therefore inappropriate, Paterson proposed an interactive element in the form of an empty chair. The larger-than-life-size figure of Emily Murphy stands slightly behind and to the side of the chair, her arm raised in greeting, welcoming visitors. The other four women form a circle around Murphy. Muir Edwards and McKinney are seated, drinking tea. Parlby and McClung appear in street dress. As if in response to the nearby statue of John A. Macdonald, in which the former prime minister is repre- sented with a raised copy of the *British North America Act*, McClung holds up a bronze copy of a newspaper announcing the Privy Council's reinterpretation declaring women as "Persons." The scene is reminiscent of the moment in 1927 when Murphy invited the four to her home to discuss launching the reference case. As one observer put it, it is as if Murphy is inviting the others in from the "political cold."[81]

In sharp contrast to traditional bronze monuments in which the figure, usually a national hero or prominent politician, is positioned high above the ground on a stone pedestal, the "Famous Five" are intentionally placed at ground level, closer to the viewer. Moreover, working from photographs taken at the time, Paterson represented the five as they were, five older women with very different personalities and backgrounds. Herself a mother and grandmother, Paterson sought to represent individual strength, courage and love in the figures of the five Alberta women who were all in their fifties and sixties in 1929, with the exception of Henrietta Muir Edwards, the eldest at eighty years of age.[82] According to Wright, the Foundation wanted a realistic portrayal. "We want people to know what they looked like," she says, "to know that people at any age can make a difference to our national life."[83]

In October 2000, the theme of nation building predominated at the ceremonies dedicating the first and only monument to Canadian women to grace Parliament Hill. Only Adrienne Clarkson, the recently-appointed Governor-General, directly mentioned the group's feminism. In her remarks, Clarkson underscored the radical politics of this earlier generation of women, drawing a direct link between them and the women's movement of the late 1960s and early 70s. Moreover, as if to silence critics, Clarkson deftly negotiated aspects of class and social background reflected in the case that is closely associated with a small, but influential, group of middle-class women and their male supporters. Referring to Nellie McClung's suffrage activism, Clarkson recounted how McClung stood up to the rebuke of Manitoba's Premier, Sir Rodmond Roblin, when he roundly dismissed women's political claims as betraying the respectability of their sex. "Nice women," he charged, "were not interested in voting." The quick-witted McClung countered that

> by nice women you probably mean selfish women who have no more thought for the underpaid, overworked woman than a pussy cat in a sunny window has with a starving kitten on the street. Now, in that sense, I am not a nice woman for I do care. I care about those factory women in ill smelling halls and we intend to do something about it. And when I say we, I'm talking for a great many women of whom you are going to hear more as the days go on.

Clarkson clearly intended that her audience identify their own political struggles with the battles of the so-called first wave of feminism. Clarkson reminded her audience that, in her day, Emily Murphy was an outspoken critic of social conditions that put women at risk and had warned her contemporaries that "while any woman, any single woman anywhere is downgraded or degraded in our society no woman should feel comfortable." Having established their radical feminist political credentials, the Governor-General went on to place the Alberta women at the heart of Canada's nation building enterprise. Again drawing on their words, she reminded the viewers and those in attendance on the Hill of Murphy's claim to a special place for Canadians in the twentieth century's women's movement, declaring that "never was a country better adapted to produce a great race than this Canada of ours; nor a race of women better adapted to make a great country."[84]

It was a day to celebrate; a day of significant personal achievement for those who had successfully seen the million-dollar project to completion; a day of remembering an important event in Canadian history, and women's history in particular. It was also a day of carefully staged, classical Canadian political theatre that included among others a chorus of school children, women who held powerful positions in government and industry, First Nations dancers, a few descendants of the "Famous Five," dramatic re-enactments linking the past and the present, all captured against the colourful and dramatic back-drop of an Ottawa autumn and broadcast to a nation-wide audience.

What no one mentioned on that crisp fall day was that the "Persons" case should never have been brought. It was necessary because of the anti-feminist backlash in the mid- to late-1920s. But the creation of the monu-ments virtually guarantees the continued prominence of the case in the telling of Canadian history. It also reshapes the narrative to realign feminist activism in relation to the state. Once seen as western radicals and a threat to existing political institutions, the statues in Ottawa and Calgary recast the "Famous Five" as nation builders, effectively muting their feminism, and subordinating their objectives to the interests of the state. The monuments glorify a particular group, thus underwriting a specific model of change-making, one that is peaceful and works in collaboration with the state. Its message is pan-Canadian, emphasizing unity in citizenship and symbolically bridging regional differences, while reinforcing a popular notion of Canada as progressive and liberal. Moreover, with the introduction of a new fifty-dollar bill bearing its image in October 2004, the statue comes to stand in for the women themselves.

But for others the monuments take on different meanings. Of particular significance to many is the idea that these women pushed the boundaries of what was considered acceptable for their sex, and in the process altered the possibilities for all Canadian women. In Ottawa, for example, the annual protest against male-violence against women, Take Back the Night, frequently begins or ends at the statue. Security guards on the Hill report that some people, mainly women, come in the night seeking refuge and comfort.[85] For these people the statue has become sacred ground, a permanent public space demarcated as a women's space.

For others the "Persons" case has taken on larger meaning, representing the fight for human rights generally. A typical view was expressed during the recent campaign for same-sex marriage. Speaking in support of legislative change, Reverend Brian Kopke of the First Unitarian Congregation in Ottawa drew a direct comparison with the case, saying that the word "marriage" would be redefined just as the word "persons" was redefined to include women in 1929. "If you go back and read the editorials of the time people had a real problem with the word 'person' being changed," Kopke explained. "There was a lot of hysteria. But we've come to live with it; men and women have come to live side-by-side and share power in this society. The same will happen in terms of marriage."[86] Reactions to the monument suggest that the significance of the case rests with Canadians and what they make of their history in the day-to-day struggles for equality.

Acknowledgements

The author wishes to thank Patricia Prestwich for many lengthy discussions in the preparation of this essay. Her constant encouragement and thoughtful comments are greatly appreciated.

Notes

1. Section 24 states that "The Governor General shall from Time to Time, in the Queen's Name, by Instrument under the Great Seal of Canada, summon qualified Persons to the Senate; and, subject to the Provisions of this Act, every Person so summoned shall become and be a Member of the Senate and a Senator." The qualifications of a Senator are set out in Section 23, including that "He shall be of full age Thirty Years," a citizen, and owning property of at least four thousand dollars in value. Arguments against admitting women pointed to the use of the expression "qualified Persons" in section 24 together with the use of the pronoun "he" throughout section 23. National Archives of Canada [hereafter referred to as NAC], RG 125, vol. 563, "Factum on Behalf of the Attorney-General For Canada", Ottawa: 1928. But the *Interpretation Act*, also known as *Lord Broughton's Act*, Cap. 21, s. 4, in force in Britain in 1867, stipulated that "in all Acts words importing the Masculine Gender shall be deemed and taken to include Females, and the Singular to include the Plural, and the Plural the Singular, unless the contrary as to Gender or Number is expressly provided..." Ibid., "Petitioners' Factum," Toronto: 1928.
2. CBC Archives, Toronto, NNL, SPEC-1203, 2000–10–18.
3. For example, Eleanor Harman, "Five Persons From Alberta," in Mary Quayle Innis, ed., *The Clear Spirit* (Toronto: University of Toronto Press, 1966), 158–78.

4. For a recent example see "She started the war on weed," *The Ottawa Citizen*, March 8, 2004, A4.

5. On nationalism and memorials to women, see Colin M. Coates and Cecilia Morgan, *Heroines & History* (Toronto: University of Toronto Press, 2002). This paper also owes an intellectual debt to Laura E. Nym Mayhall, "Domesticating Emmeline: Representing the Suffragette, 1930–1993," *National Women's Studies Association Journal* 11, no. 2 (1999): 1–24.

6. The memorial in Calgary was installed in 1999.

7. "Henrietta Muir Edwards and others v. Attorney-General for Canada," *Supreme Court Reports* (1928), 276.

8. City of Edmonton Archives [hereafter referred to as CEA], Murphy papers, MS-2, scrapbook 4, "Alberta Women Leading In Struggle for Senate," 247; and Byrne Hope Sanders, *Emily Murphy—Crusader* (Toronto: MacMillan, 1945), 214. It should be noted that this was only one of a number of "persons" cases fought by women in Canada and other common-law countries. See Beverly Baines, "Law, Gender, Equality," in Sandra Burt, Lorraine Code, Lindsay Dorney, eds. *Changing Patterns: Women in Canada* (Toronto: McClelland and Stewart, 1993), 243–78.

9. Olive M. Stone, "Canadian Women as Legal Persons: How Alberta Combined Judicial Executive and Legislative Powers to Win Full Legal Personality for all Canadian Women," *Alberta Law Review* 17, no. 3 (1979): 331–71, and David Bright, "The Other Woman: Lizzie Cyr and the Origins of the 'Persons' Case," *Canadian Journal of Legal Studies* 13, no. 2 (1998): 99–115.

10. "Rex v. Cyr," *Alberta Law Reports* 12 (1917), 320.

11. Stone, "Canadian Women as Legal Persons," 332–33; and *Alberta Law Reports* 12 (1917), 320.

12. In New Brunswick women became eligible to sit in the provincial legislature by special legislation that came into force on March 9, 1934, although they had been able to vote since 1919. Quebec women had to wait until 1940 before winning the dual rights of voting and office-holding. It would take another 20 years, until 1960, before these rights were extended to Canada's First Nations women and men. Catherine Lyle Cleverdon, *The Woman Suffrage Movement in Canada* (Toronto: University of Toronto Press, 1950).

13. Ruby G. Marchildon, "The 'Persons' Controversy: The Legal Aspects of the Fight for Women Senators," *Atlantis* 6, no. 2 (Spring 1981): 102–03; and Dominion of Canada, *Debates of the House of Commons 1921*, vol. 1 (Ottawa: 1921), 389.

14. Historians have tended to accept the notion that special legislation was necessary to enable the appointment of women Senators and that this would require agreement of both Houses of Parliament and unanimous agreement of the provinces. However, in 1981 the Supreme Court of Canada decided that constitutional amendment did not require unanimity. Moreover, the appointment of a woman had no impact on the distribution of Senate seats among the provinces, suggesting that the federal government could, in law, act alone. It was, of course, also possible for Britain to act alone. I am grateful to David P. Jones for discussions on this point.

15. NAC, Department of Justice Fonds, RG 13, vol. 2524, "Memorandum for the Deputy Minister," May 18, 1921 and "Reference re Eligibility of Women to be Summoned to the Senate," February 2, 1928. Later, as a member of the Supreme Court of Canada, Newcombe signed the order setting the reference down for hearing in 1928. British Columbia Archives [hereafter referred to as BCA], Nellie McClung's papers, MS-0010, box 11, file 10, letter to McClung from Stewart Edwards, November 2, 1927. Newcombe's opinion was taken very seriously at the time. He was deputy minister of justice for more than 30 years before being appointed to the Supreme Court in 1924. Newcombe did not sit on the "Persons" Case, but his view of the

case found its way into the arguments presented by the federal government and the province of Quebec. "Mr. Justice Newcombe," retrieved from Supreme Court of Canada Online, April 10, 2004. http://www.scc-csc.gc.ca/aboutcourt/judges/newcombe/index_e.asp.

16. A typical example is Stone's conclusion that "in the great battles for women's emancipation, Western Canada, and Alberta in particular, were in the forefront and carried the standard for less favoured women elsewhere to see and follow," "Canadian Women as Legal Persons," 371.

17. NAC, Department of Justice Fonds, RG13 vol. 2524, letter to H.C.J. Doherty, Minister of Justice from Elizabeth B. Price, Publicity Convener Federated Women's Institutes of Canada, June 18, 1921.

18. The Council had put forward Edwards's name as a Senate nominee in 1921. Patricia Roome, *Henrietta Muir Edwards: The Journey of a Canadian Feminist* (PhD Diss., Simon Fraser University, 1996), 293.

19. BCA, McClung Papers, MS-0010, box 11, file 12, letter to McClung from Scott, October 18, 1929.

20. Sanders, *Emily Murphy—Crusader*, 217.

21. NAC, RG 13, vol. 2524, letter to Murphy from Ferguson, June 7, 1921.

22. In a somewhat bizarre episode, King had Senator McCoig from Chatham, Ontario bring forward an amendment in the Upper Chamber, but McCoig failed to speak to the matter that day and it was not reinstated.

23. BCA, Nellie McClung papers, MS-0010, box 11, file 10, letter to McClung from Murphy, August 5, 1927. Indeed, Murphy was aware that "hostile opinion" could be found in the Commons and particularly in the Senate. But at least one member of the Supreme Court had also expressed his view in the negative (See n. 7.)

24. NAC, Department of Justice Fonds, RG 13, vol. 2524, letter from Murphy to Stewart Edwards, November 9, 1927.

25. NAC, Department of Justice Fonds, RG 13, vol. 2524, letter from Murphy to the Governor-General-in-Council, August 27, 1927.

26. BCA, Nellie McClung Papers, MS-0010, box 11, file 10, letter from Murphy to McClung, November 5, 1927.

27. Marchildon, "The 'Persons' Controversy," 102.

28. BCA, McClung Papers, MS-0010, "Copy of a Minute of a Meeting of the Committee of the Privy Council," P.C. 2034.

29. BCA, McClung papers, MS-0010, box 11, no. 10, letter from Thomas Mulvey, Under-Secretary of State, to Murphy November 8, 1917.

30. NAC, Department of Justice Fonds, RG 13, vol. 2524, letter from Murphy to Stuart Edwards, November 9, 1927.

31. NAC, Department of Justice Fonds, RG 13, vol. 2524, letter from Stewart Edwards to Murphy, December 14, 1927.

32. Ibid., letters from Stewart Edwards to Murphy, December 14 and November 30, 1927.

33. As has already been mentioned, Murphy's brother, William Nassau, was a member of the Ontario Supreme Court. Her youngest brother, Harcourt, was also a lawyer practicing in Toronto and a third brother, Thomas Roberts, had a law practice in Winnipeg. In a tragic footnote to the case, T.R. died suddenly in 1923 and Harcourt died in 1927, followed by William a year later, in the fall of 1928. Sanders, *Emily Murphy—Crusader*, 140.

34. Margaret Prang, *N.W. Rowell: Ontario Nationalist* (Toronto: University of Toronto Press, 1975). Rowell is perhaps best know as chair of the Rowell-Sirois Commission on Federal-Provincial relations.

35. Sanders, *Emily Murphy—Crusader*, 225.

36. NAC, Department of Justice Fonds, RG 13, vol. 2524, letter from Stewart Edwards to Rowell, November 28, 1927.

37. Ibid., letter from Stewart Edwards to Murphy, December 14, 1927.

38. William Stuart Edwards, deputy minister of justice, in the late 1920s, and the person who argued the case before the Supreme Court of Canada in 1928, was related to Henrietta Muir Edwards by marriage. This may have had some influence on the Department's decision to allow the case to be heard, but it had no positive effect on the government's view of the matter. *Henrietta Muir Edwards*, 224.

39. CEA, Murphy papers, "Canada Soon to Appoint Women to Senate," *Edmonton Bulletin*, April 25, 1928, MS-2, Scrapbook 3, p. 48.

40. Baines, "Law, Gender, Equality," esp. 246–53.

41. NAC, RG 125, vol. 563, "Factum on Behalf of the Attorney-General of Canada," 4.

42. "Henrietta Muir Edwards and others v. Attorney-General for Canada," 278.

43. BCA, McClung papers, MS-0010, box 11, file No. 11, letter from Murphy to McClung, August 16, 1928.

44. Ibid.

45. Ibid., letter from Murphy to McClung, May 2, 1928.

46. Sanders, *Emily Murphy—Crusader*, 231.

47. Ibid., 242.

48. BCA, McClung papers, MS-0010, box 11, file 12, "Privy Council Appeal No. 121 of 1928."

49. CEA, Murphy papers, MS-2, scrapbook 1, p. 128.

50. Ibid., "Women Are 'Persons'," *Edmonton Bulletin*, October 18, 1929, 35.

51. Ibid., scrapbook 4, p. 24.

52. Ibid.

53. Ibid.

54. Ibid., pp. 128 and 140.

55. *The Montreal Gazette*, October 19, 1929, 1.

56. Baines, "Law, Gender, Equality," 257. As Baines points out, "Women are not yet perceived [in law] as persons, always and everywhere," (258).

57. Murphy was passed over for appointment. Cairine Wilson of Ontario was the first woman appointed to the Senate in 1930. When Edmonton Senator E.P. Lessard died in January 1931, women's groups urged the prime minister, R.B. Bennett, to appoint Murphy. But her former political ally chose to appoint on the basis of religion. Lessard was Catholic and the appointment would go to a Catholic. Murphy was Anglican and married to a former minister. This effectively ended her Senate ambitions. See Sanders, *Emily Murphy—Crusader*, 256–57.

58. *Ottawa Citizen (The Evening Citizen)*, October 18, 1929, 1.

59. Ibid.

60. Ibid.

61. Ibid.

62. Ibid.

63. "Now That Women Are Persons What's Ahead?" *The Chatelaine*, 2, no. 12 (Dec 1929): 5.

64. BCA, McClung papers, MS-0010, box 11, file 12, letter from Scott to McClung, October 18, 1929.

65. CEA, Murphy Papers, MS-2, scrapbook 3, "Tablet is Unveiled by Prime Minister," *Montreal Gazette*, June 13, 1938, 138.

66. Ibid. Douglas was a decorated veteran of the Great War, serving in France as an officer of the Royal Army Medical Corps, with the rank of Major.

67. CBC Archives, Toronto, "Special—Tablet to Pioneer Women in the Senate," Ottawa, June 11, 1938.

68. King makes no mention in his diaries of the reference case or the appeal to the JCPC.

69. CEA, Murphy Papers, MS-2, scrapbook 3, "Historical Occasion When Plaque In Honour of Five Women is Unveiled," *The Citizen,* June 13, 1938, 136–37.

70. Ibid.

71. Ibid.

72. Ibid.

73. Sanders, *Emily Murphy—Crusader*, 259.

74. CEA, Murphy Papers, MS-2, scrapbook 3, "Historical Occasion When Plaque In Honour of Five Women is Unveiled," *The Citizen,* June 13, 1938, 137.

75. CBC Archives, Toronto, "Special—Tablet to Pioneer Women in the Senate," Ottawa, June 11, 1938.

76. Ibid.

77. Interview with Frances Wright, Calgary, April 14, 2004.

78. The donors were Senator Vivienne Poy, a fashion designer and sister-in-law of Governor-General Adrienne Clarkson, Heather Reisman, who was at the time president of Indigo Books and Music Inc., Toronto-based financier Kiki Delaney, Maria Eriksen, owner of a Calgary corporate psychology firm, who donated along with her sister-in-law, author Ayala Manolson, and former University of Calgary Chancellor, Ann McCaig, who contributed along with her daughters, Roxanne and Jane. *Maclean's*, 112 (October, 18, 1999): 12.

79. Corporate sponsors included Petro-Canada, Alberta Energy Company, PanCanadian Petroleum and Nova. Francis Wright, "Lessons from the Famous 5," unpublished manuscript, p. 8.

80. Interview with Francis Wright.

81. Interview with Barbara Paterson, Edmonton, March 25, 2004.

82. Murphy, McKinney and Parlby were all born in 1868. McClung was the youngest of the group, born in 1873.

83. Interview with Frances Wright.

84. CBC Archives, Toronto, NNL, SPEC-1203, 2000–10–18.

85. Interview with Frances Wright.

86. CBC, "The World at Six," July 18, 2004.

Six

Alberta's Real Constitution
The Natural Resources Transfer Agreement

THOMAS FLANAGAN AND MARK MILKE

The modern economy of Alberta, which depends so much on oil and gas, coal, and forest products, is legally underpinned by the Natural Resources Transfer Agreement of 1930 (NRTA), which transferred the province's cornucopia of resource wealth from federal to provincial jurisdiction. Curiously, however, the Agreement has received little attention from scholars. This essay explains why Alberta started its provincial life without control of its lands and resources, and then tells the story of how the NRTA was negotiated and approved.

Although the story ended more than 70 years ago, readers will see much in it that is still of interest. It was, above all, a protracted but ultimately successful example of constitutional amendment through executive federalism, i.e., direct consultations between the prime minister of Canada and the premiers of several provinces. The story, moreover, included many elements that seem to recur endlessly in Canadian politics:

- Conflict between Ottawa and the western provinces over control of natural resources;
- Subordination, at least at times, of western priorities to those of Quebec;
- Spillover of political conflict into the courts;
- Recourse to a Royal Commission headed by a judge, which in this case proved successful in finding a solution to the political conflict.

Plus ça change....

Public Lands in Canada

At the beginning of colonization in British North America, the Imperial Crown retained ownership of public lands as part of the royal prerogative. In practice, this meant that public lands were controlled, not by the locally elected Legislature, but by the governor and his appointed council, subject to instructions from the Colonial Office in London. Under these circumstances, the demand for local control of public lands inevitably became part of the movement for responsible government in the colonies.

The demand was conceded in the *Act of Union, 1840*. The historian Chester Martin described it as an exchange: the Province of Canada received its public lands in return for a Civil List of £75,000, i.e., undertaking to bear the costs of self-government.[1] There was still a measure of Imperial control because bills relating to public lands had to be laid before the British parliament before receiving royal assent, but that restriction was lifted in 1854 by the *Union Act Amendment Act*.[2]

Building upon these developments, provincial control of public lands became a fixed principle of Canadian Confederation, enshrined in section 109 of the *Constitution (British North America) Act, 1867*:

> 109. All Lands, Mines, Mineral, and royalties belonging to the several Provinces of Canada, Nova Scotia, and New Brunswick at the Union, and all Sums then due or payable for such Lands, Mines, Minerals, or Royalties, shall belong to the several Provinces of Ontario, Quebec, Nova Scotia, and New Brunswick in which the same are situate or arise, subject to any Trusts existing in respect thereof, and to any Interest other than that of the Province in the same.

Control of public lands and natural resources was at least as crucial to the provinces in the nineteenth century as it is today. At the time there were no income and sales taxes, and the provinces, which could only levy direct taxes, were shut out of the lucrative fields of customs and excise. Apart from fees, licences, and federal subsidies, the main sources of provincial revenue were resource royalties, property taxes, and the sale and lease of public lands.

British Columbia retained its ownership of public lands when that province joined Confederation in 1871. Indeed, under section 11 of the Terms of Union, the Dominion agreed to pay British Columbia $100,000 a year as compensation for the lands in the "Railway Belt" that the province conveyed to the Dominion to help fund a transcontinental railway.[3] Prince Edward Island was treated even more generously when it joined Confederation in 1873. The public lands of that province had been alienated a century earlier by Crown grants to large estates, so the Dominion agreed to pay a subsidy of $45,000 a year because the province "enjoys no revenue from that source for the construction and maintenance of local works." The Dominion also loaned Prince Edward Island $800,000 at 5% interest—money that the province used to purchase lands from large proprietors and resell them at a profit to small landholders.[4] The only provinces without the beneficial ownership of their public lands and natural resources were Manitoba when it entered Confederation in 1870, and Alberta and Saskatchewan when they were created out of the North-West Territories in 1905. The reasons for this different treatment lie in the unique historical circumstances under which Canada acquired Rupert's Land and Manitoba entered Confederation.

Entry of Manitoba into Confederation

On May 2, 1670, Charles II issued the Hudson's Bay Company charter, which made the Company "the true and absolute Lordes and Proprietors" of the lands lying along the waters draining into Hudson Bay.[5] This grant, known as Rupert's Land, included what are now the three prairie provinces. For 200 years after 1870, the Company governed Rupert's Land as a colony for the primary purpose of trading for furs.

Section 146 of the *Constitution (British North America) Act, 1867*, provided for the eventual admission of Rupert's Land into Canada:

> 146. It shall be lawful for the Queen, by and with the Advice of Her Majesty's Most Honourable Privy Council, on Addresses from the Houses of Parliament of Canada, and from the Houses of the respective Legislatures of the Colonies or Provinces of Newfoundland, Prince Edward Island, and British Columbia, to admit those Colonies or Provinces, or any of them into the Union, and on Address from the Houses of the Parliament of Canada to admit Rupert's Land and the North-Western Territory, or either of them, into the Union, on such Terms and Conditions in each Case as are in the Addresses expressed and as the Queen thinks fit to approve, subject to the Provisions of this Act; and the Provisions of any Order in Council in that Behalf shall have effect

as if they had been enacted by the Parliament of the United Kingdom of Great Britain and Ireland.

On December 17, 1867, the Senate and House of Commons sent a joint address to the Queen asking that Canada be "extended westward to the shores of the Pacific Ocean," and in particular "to unite Rupert's Land and the North-Western territory with this Dominion." The address promised "that the legal rights of any corporation, company, or individual within [Rupert's Land] shall be respected," and

> furthermore that, upon the transference of the territories in question to the Canadian Government, the claims of the Indian tribes to compensation for lands required for purposes of settlement will be considered and settled in conformity with the equitable principles which have uniformly governed the British Crown in its dealings with the aborigines.[6]

The British government decided that legislation was necessary to create a framework for the transfer. The Imperial Parliament, therefore, passed the *Rupert's Land Act, 1868*, which received royal assent on July 31 of that year.[7] The Act provided that the Hudson's Bay Company could surrender to the Queen "all or any of the Lands, Territories, Rights, Privileges, Liberties, Franchises, Powers, and Authorities whatsoever granted or purported to be granted by [the charter of 1670],"[8] and that the Queen could then by Order-in-Council transfer Rupert's Land to Canada.[9]

After passage of the Act, Canada sent two cabinet ministers, George-Etienne Cartier and William McDougall, to London to negotiate terms for the transfer. Agreement was reached in March 1869. In return for surrendering all its land rights, the Hudson's Bay Company would receive £300,000 from Canada. The Company would be allowed to retain tracts of land around its trading posts, and would receive one-twentieth of the land in the so-called "Fertile Belt" south of the North Saskatchewan River. It would be at liberty to continue trading in the surrendered territory.[10]

On April 10, 1869, the Earl Granville, the Colonial Secretary, wrote to the Governor-General of Canada that the British authorities would take measures to effect the transfer, "provided that the acceptance of the terms by the Government and Parliament of Canada is duly signified to them within six months."[11] Canada accepted the negotiated terms in a joint address approved by the House of Commons on May 29 and the Senate on May 31, 1869,[12] and shortly thereafter passed *An Act for the Temporary Government of Rupert's Land,* which received royal assent on June 22.[13] The Hudson's Bay Company signed the Deed of Surrender on November 19, 1869. Louis Riel's insurrection and demands for provincial status culminated in passage of the *Manitoba Act, 1870;* and Section 30 of that Act created a new type of partner in Confederation—a province with responsible government but without control of its own public lands and natural resources:

> 30. All ungranted or waste lands in the Province shall be, from and after the date of the said transfer, vested in the Crown, and administered by the Government of Canada for the purposes of the Dominion, subject to, and except and so far as the same may be affected by, the conditions and stipulations contained in the agreement for the surrender of Rupert's Land by the Hudson's Bay Company to Her Majesty.[14]

In the absence of revenue from land and resources, Manitoba would be supported by federal subsidies[15] (a precedent that would be followed for Alberta and Saskatchewan after their assent to provincial status 35 years later). After the *Manitoba Act* passed through Parliament and received royal assent on May 12, 1870, the Queen accepted the surrender from the Hudson's Bay Company on June 22 and the Imperial cabinet passed an Order-in-Council on June 23 that made the transfer of Rupert's Land to Canadian jurisdiction effective July 15, 1870.[16] As of that date, Canada received "full power and authority to legislate for the future welfare and good government of the said Territory."

Western Grievances

Canada's leaders had intended to acquire Rupert's Land as a territory, out of which provinces would later be constructed. To deal with Riel's insurrection, they had accepted immediate provincial status for a scaled-down province of Manitoba, but they still wanted to keep control of affairs in the West because major issues of policy were involved. Canada had acquired Rupert's Land to build a nation *a mari usque ad mare.* Federal leaders felt they could not afford to leave such a huge territory under the control of 12,000 people concentrated at the forks of the Red and Assiniboine Rivers. Macdonald explained in the House of Commons the reasons why he had refused Manitoba's demands for ownership of its public lands:

Hon. Sir John A. Macdonald said the object of the residents had been to obtain possession of the whole country. They wished Rupert's Land made into one Province and to have all the land within the boundary as in other Provinces.... It was pointed out that it was impossible to hand over the country, to be legislated for by the present inhabitants. He pointed out that the Territory had been purchased for a large sum from the H.B. Co., that settlement had to be made with the Indians, the guardianship of whom was involved, that the land could not be handed over to them, as it was of the greatest importance to the Dominion to have possession of it, for the Pacific Railway must be built by means of the land through which it had to pass.[17]

And again:

He considered it would be injudicious to have a large province which would have control over lands, and might interfere with the general policy of the Government in opening up communication to the Pacific, besides the land legislation of the Province might be obstructive to immigration. All that vast Territory should be for purposes of settlement under one control, and that the Dominion Legislature. Another consideration was that by obtaining the control of these lands they would be able to obtain means by which they would be in a position to obtain repayment of the disbursement of the £300,000 for the purchase and of the expenditure which they might be hereafter put to.[18]

In other words, the Dominion had to retain ownership of western public lands in order to finance railway construction through land grants, control the flow of immigration through homestead policy, and recoup its investment by selling lands to settlers and developers.

The Dominion's policy left Manitoba with diminished revenue, leading to incessant agitation for "Better Terms." In 1876, the Dominion agreed to increase its annual subsidy by $26,746.96 on condition that the Manitoba government save money by abolishing the upper house of the Provincial Legislature.[19] In 1882, the province secured an additional annual subsidy of $45,000 "in lieu of lands," on the model of Prince Edward Island. The amount was then increased to $100,000 a year in 1885, on the model of British Columbia. Manitoba was also given about 2,000,000 acres of "swamp lands" in the province that it could reclaim and sell, as well as 150,000 acres of land "of fair average quality" as an endowment for the University of Manitoba.[20] The Dominion forced the Manitoba Legislature to accept a so-called "finality clause" in 1885, but a sense of injustice continued to rankle.[21]

The Dominion owned the public lands in the neighbouring North-West Territories, but this ownership also came under challenge after May 2, 1900, when the NWT premier, Frederick Haultain, started a campaign for provincial status.[22] Haultain drew up an eight-point list of demands including "transfer of the public domain with all territorial rights and beneficial interests."[23] Prime Minister Wilfrid Laurier was slow to respond, but he finally promised in the federal election campaign of 1904 that he would grant provincial autonomy to the Territories.[24]

Pressure for status as a province and its attendant rights had been building for some time in the western portion of the North-West Territories (the area later to become the province of Alberta). An 1882 Order-in-Council had divided the North-West territories into provisional districts. Present-day Alberta was divided into Athabasca in the northern half, about 122,000 square miles in all, and Alberta, about 100,000 square miles, in what now constitutes the southern half of the province of the same name.[25]

The drive for provincial status began first as a demand for a separate territory. The *Calgary Herald* broached the topic in 1890 with a call for the division of the North-West Territories, "which will throw together those portions of the vast country that have interests in common as a country for ranching, mining and mixed farming."[26] The *Herald* proposed a district encompassing the districts of Alberta and Athabasca. The call for provincial status was not as yet explicit, though hinted at. At this stage, the explicit demand was for a self-governing territory separate from that which then existed and was governed from Regina.

Not everyone agreed with the call for a separate territory. The *Lethbridge News*[27] disagreed, for example. The *Regina Leader* was also opposed, though the *Herald* dismissively put down opposition from the territorial capital as derived from a desire to "keep things centralized in Regina."[28]

By 1891, the *Calgary Herald* stated its case more clearly: "We will be content...to accept nothing short of the responsibilities and privileges which have fallen to the Provinces of Canada."[29] The issue of provincial status then languished for several years while more attention was paid to responsible government for the territories rather than to division.[30] By 1895, however, interest was rekindled in part because of Manitoba's demands for a better deal, something that a new editor at the *Calgary Herald* took as a cue to press the issue of provincial status for Alberta:

So the Province of Manitoba is again sending a delegation to Ottawa to ask for "Better Terms." The horseleech hath two daughters, crying "give, give"—and so it is with that political Oliver Twist, the prairie province. It has been a succession of "Better terms." Those of 1894, in which the Farmers' Union agitation culminated were supposed to have finally settled its financial arrangements with the Dominion. And, on the whole, Manitoba was very liberally dealt with. There is no legitimate excuse for an attempt to re-open the matter at this juncture. But the Greenway government is getting hard up for political capital, and an agitation on this line is always something to conjure with in a community of such cupidity as Manitoba.... The particular bearing of all this on Alberta is that Alberta had better obtain provincial status and endowment before Manitoba succeeds in draining the Dominion treasury dry.[31]

The *Herald's* position was not unopposed. The *Edmonton Bulletin* differed on the grounds that the desire for provincial status from Calgary (where proponents also assumed the provincial capital should be located) was driven by "hog-like propensities" and concern not for Alberta but "simply the little patch of about one mile by two miles simply known as the city of Calgary."[32] The *Macleod Gazette* argued that it had no quarrel with the idea of provincial autonomy, merely that the time was not yet ripe for such a change.[33] Still, there could be no denying that there was popular interest in the idea, especially in southern Alberta. For example, an 1895 pamphlet claimed the following:

On the 22nd of March, 1895, advantage was taken of the presence in Calgary of a large number of representative men from all parts of Alberta to hold a mass meeting to consider the propriety of taking action to obtain the early constitution of the western portion of the Northwest Territories into a Province, and so secure for its people their full rights as Canadian subjects, a number of which they do not now enjoy.[34]

The anonymous author of the pamphlet enunciated the justification of such rights:

The birthright of a British subject is self-government. This principle, hammered out by centuries of conflict in Great Britain, has been extended to every corner of the Empire in a greater or lesser degree. It is based on the common sense notion that every ordinarily reasonable human being knows best what he wants himself, and can best point out the method of attaining it, either by himself or in concert with others in like circumstances.

The British subject who leaves the settled haunts of civilization and goes forth to open up fresh tracts and add new provinces to the Empire, never imagines for a moment that in so doing he is relinquishing one jot or tittle of this right.[35]

Alberta was governed by a lieutenant-governor who resided nearly 500 miles away in Regina, and such powers as existed did not include the ability to borrow money, to regulate any local works, incorporate any railway, steamboat, canal, transportation, telegraph, irrigation, or insurance company, nor any power with regards to immigration.[36] In addition, the subsidy from the federal government was only $30,000. The writer complained that the Legislature, to which the western portion of the territory furnished 10 out of 29 representatives, had to take whatever sum was offered it and was thus no better than a "legal minor."[37] The say of citizens in this part of the British empire as it concerned their own affairs, argued the pamphleteer, was no more substantial than that exercised by Russian peasants at "the court of St. Petersburg."[38]

Despite this public pressure, most politicians were not yet on board; the North-West's premier, F.W.G. Haultain, still opposed provincial status and the separation of Alberta into a distinct territorial region.[39] His views changed later only after repeated requests for more extensive funding for the territories were not met to the degree that he desired.[40]

The issue of provincial status waxed and waned over the next several years. On one occasion in 1896, when the Herald openly mused about an Alberta-British Columbia province instead of its original Alberta province idea, the Regina Leader noticed and took the occasion to declare the idea of an autonomous province of Alberta to be a "fad" and "dead."[41] Continued irritation in the Territories, including a series of 1899 memoranda on the subject of necessary increases in the federal grant to the region by Premier Haultain to Clifford Sifton, the minister of the interior, eventually converted Haultain to the idea of provincial status, albeit as one province for all the territories that then encompassed the North-West Territories.[42]

When provincial status eventually did come, with separate provinces for Saskatchewan and Alberta, and an enlarged Manitoba, it was after the federal Liberals returned to office in 1905, and after negotiations over provincial status began early that year. The Alberta Act was presented to the House of

Commons on February 21 of that year.[43] However, as with Manitoba's initial entry into Confederation in 1870, the *Alberta Act* provided for the Dominion to retain control of public lands.[44] The prime minister of the day, Wilfred Laurier, might have yielded on the land question; but Clifford Sifton, still the leading western member of cabinet and the minister responsible for Canada's booming immigration program, was adamant that such a transfer not occur. He wrote to Laurier that

> giving [public lands] to the Provinces would be ruinous to our settlement policy and would be disastrous to the whole Dominion. The mere report that the lands had been handed over and that there might be a change in the policy of administering them would cost us tens of thousands of settlers in the next two years to say nothing of the more distant future— the continued progress of Canada for the next five years depends almost entirely on the flow of immigration.[45]

Land grants to railways were a thing of the past, but immigration was still important enough to Ottawa to be used as a justification for retaining public lands under the federal Crown.

The federal government compensated Alberta and Saskatchewan with subsidies in lieu of lands. Each province was to receive $375,000 a year, to rise to a maximum of $1,125,000 with population growth.[46] This amount of money temporarily led western Liberals to reverse their previous demand for provincial control of public lands; but the Conservatives, led by Haultain and R.B. Bennett in the west and by Robert Borden nationally, continued to press for the transfer of ownership. The financial compensation paid to Alberta and Saskatchewan also led to demands from Manitoba for equal treatment, but that province's Conservative premier, Rodmond Roblin, did not succeed in getting increased federal subsidies until 1912, after Robert Borden had become prime minister.[47]

Negotiating the Natural Resources Transfer Agreement

Following the election of the Conservative government of Prime Minister Robert Borden in 1911, another effort was made to extend beneficial resource rights to Alberta, Saskatchewan and Manitoba. The Borden government took steps in 1913 to deal with the natural resources question by proposing a Dominion-Provincial Conference. Borden had already stated in 1905:

The people of the north west, when they are granted Provincial rights...
are entitled to the control of these lands just as much as the people of
the eastern provinces of Canada are entitled to control their provincial
domain. I see no distinction. We beg to submit that any permanent
settlement of the Natural Resources Question must be based upon the
ample recognition on the part of the Dominion [of] the inherent British
rights of the prairie provinces to their natural resources as from the date
of provincial organization or responsible government; the restoration of
full provincial beneficial control of these which remain unalienated, and
compensation upon a fiduciary basis for those which have been alienated
by Canada for the purpose of the Dominion.[48]

Wilfred Laurier's government's policy had been to consider separate agreements between the prairie provinces and the Dominion.[49] Borden, in contrast,
resolved that the question had to be negotiated collectively since any agreement with one province would necessarily affect the other two. In a letter
to Saskatchewan premier, Walter Scott, he stated in 1913: "In regard to
natural resources, the Provinces of Manitoba and Alberta occupy a similar
position to that of Saskatchewan and thus it would be not only useless but
undesirable to arrange a conference with the Government of only one of
these Provinces."[50]

A Dominion-Provincial conference was held on October 27, 1913. As a
result, Premiers R.P. Roblin of Manitoba, Walter Scott of Saskatchewan, and
Arthur Sifton of Alberta drafted a proposal to Borden:

After having an interview with you in regard to the questions in respect
of which the Prairie Provinces have received different treatment from
the other Provinces of Canada, and at your suggestion a meeting of the
Premiers of Manitoba, Saskatchewan and Alberta, it has been agreed
between us to make to you, on behalf of the said Provinces, the proposal
that the financial terms already arranged between the Provinces and
the Dominion as compensation for lands should stand as compensation
for lands already alienated for the general benefit of Canada, and that
all lands remaining within the boundaries of the respective Provinces,
with all natural resources included, be transferred to the said Provinces,
the Provinces accepting respectively the responsibility of administering
the same.[51]

Borden dismissed this proposal since it neither protected homesteading and immigration nor took account of compensation provided by the *Alberta* and *Saskatchewan Acts*, as well as by the 1912 Act extending Manitoba's borders.[52] After 1914, progress toward a natural resources transfer was blocked by the demands of the First World War.

Throughout the war, the governments of the prairie provinces petitioned for the transfer of school lands and of the fund created from the sale of school lands in the past. They agreed that the provinces could administer more "economically and satisfactorily" and serve settlers' educational needs more effectively by investing part of the funds in school bonds and debentures.[53] Borden dismissed this suggestion, stating that "the trust was created by the Dominion Parliament, that the subject matter of the trust was among the assets of the Dominion and that the administration of the trust was committed by Parliament to His Majesty's Governor in Council."[54] Borden also reiterated his objections to the transfer of any powers to the provinces until a negotiation process was established and agreed upon by the premiers.[55]

In November 1918, the three provinces submitted another draft proposal, demanding a settlement based on the right of the prairie provinces to their natural resources and the right to compensation for resources already alienated for the general benefit of Canada.[56] Presentation of this resolution at the Dominion-Provincial Conference of November 1918 resulted in the other Canadian premiers requesting subsidies for all the provinces comparable to the subsidies paid to the prairie provinces. Throughout this period, the premiers of Manitoba, Saskatchewan and Alberta had not altered the terms of the proposal of 1913 and had maintained that it was the only acceptable means to reach an agreement.

In 1920, another round of negotiations opened between the governments of the prairie provinces and the Dominion, now represented by Prime Minster Arthur Meighen. Meighen offered the provinces a straight transfer without any additional subsidy, and requested Premiers Norris of Manitoba, Martin of Saskatchewan and Stewart of Alberta to make the best offer possible on the basis of an abatement of the present subsidy in lieu of lands.[57] This proposal was followed by another conference in December 1920, where Norris withdrew the proposal of 1913 and suggested that the accounting of compensation must be "an account upon fiduciary basis of actual resources of the Province alienated 'by the Government of Canada for the purpose of the Dominion.'"[58] In response, Meighen accused Norris of hampering negotiations by refusing to make a realistic proposal.[59] Meighen's view was that strict accountability on a fiduciary basis would require the Dominion government to compensate the prairie provinces for lands given away as free homesteads,[60] and he was against providing subsidies in lieu of lands alienated.

Under the Liberal government of Prime Minister William Lyon Mackenzie King, a new phase in the resolution of the agreement ensued. The Liberals had stated their position on the transfer at their national convention of 1919: "Resolved that the Provinces of Manitoba, Saskatchewan and Alberta should be granted the ownership and control of natural resources within their respective boundaries on terms that are fair and equitable to all other Provinces of the Dominion."[61] King initially repeated Meighen's policy that, upon transfer of the lands, the prairie provinces would have to surrender the subsidy they were being paid in lieu of lands:[62]

> It is suggested that whatever sums have been received by the Dominion Government from these lands are probably fully balanced by the sums expended by the Government in one way or another in the management of the lands. If there is a fair ground for this belief, would it be advisable to enter upon an accounting which would necessarily be a lengthy affair? If the Provinces could accept this short and swift method of adjustment, the whole transaction might be quickly arranged and the lands could without further delay be handed over to the Provinces.[63]

In 1922, the Manitoba Legislature passed a resolution for the immediate negotiation of transfer of "all Lands and Natural Resources within the Province hitherto unalienated, and to effect an accounting to the Province by the Dominion upon a fiduciary basis" with respect to lands and resources alienated since 1870.[64] Premier Norris had demanded not a credit and debit statement but "the kind of accounting due from a trustee to his beneficiary."[65] Charles Dunning, the premier of Saskatchewan, concurred on these issues, pointing to the burden that Saskatchewan had carried for 20 years because of the Canadian Pacific Railway Company's property-tax exemptions. Dunning also pointed out that it was impossible to negotiate without acknowledging the past transactions between the provinces and the Dominion with respect to subsidies in lieu of land and the constitutional basis of provincial control of the public domain.[66]

A Natural Resources Conference was convened in November 1922, where it was agreed that if negotiations between Manitoba and the Dominion failed, the issue would be settled by arbitration.[67] At this conference the Dominion put forward four options, all of which Bracken, as well as the other prairie premiers, found unacceptable:

1. To return the unalienated resources and discontinue the "subsidy in lieu of lands";
2. To return the unalienated resources, to discontinue the annual "subsidy in lieu of lands" and to make a cash payment to the province (no sum was mentioned in this connection except the amount of two or three years' subsidy);
3. To return the unalienated resources with an accounting of receipts and expenditures in respect to Dominion Lands;
4. To modify such accounting by taking into consideration certain alienations of land made for that purpose outside the provinces.[68]

After the conference, it was apparent to Bracken that the process of negotiation had broken down, so he requested arbitration to resolve the issue. Alberta's premier, Herbert Greenfield, also expressed his disappointment in the offer made by the Dominion government since it was "considerably less" than the estimate calculated by the Department of Natural Resources for the accounting of the fiduciary compensation for unalienated resources as well as compensation for land alienated for Dominion purposes.[69] Alberta would be willing to forego compensation for land alienated for federal purposes if a one-time transfer of 6,400,000 acres of land alienated for subsidizing railways constructed outside of Alberta reverted back to the Province along with an adjustment in the subsidy.[70]

Provincial politics in Alberta also played a role in the negotiations. A letter to Mackenzie King from Edmonton mayor, K.A. Blatchford, suggested the "Mayors of the Western Cities," most of whom were Liberals, be invited to the negotiations. Blatchford pointed out that the interests of resource investment capital were not represented by the United Farmers' government, and that it was a good opportunity for the Liberals of Alberta to receive credit for the transfer.[71]

In 1924 another Natural Resources Conference was convened, and Manitoba again called for the transfer of natural resources to the prairie provinces, commencing with unsold school lands as well as the Dominion-administered trust fund created from the sale of school lands.[72] Prime Minister King dismissed this claim because it departed from the negotiation agreement of 1922, and because it did not deal with the whole matter but would require repeated reference to Parliament and the Provincial Legislature for ratification as different aspects of the transfer agreement were resolved piecemeal.[73] In April 1924, Manitoba's Legislature passed a resolution requesting arbitration to resolve the transfer question.[74] Also, Manitoba's government solicited legal opinions on the matter and commissioned Dr. Chester Martin, a history professor at the University of Manitoba, to write a historical summary of the issue from 1870 to 1922.

Alberta, on the other hand, was prepared to accept a Dominion offer of a fixed sum in lieu of accounting going back to 1905, plus an annual subsidy for three years. This agreement, however, was stalled on the issue of how much the subsidy would be. Premier Greenfield also raised the question of how services would be divided with regard to forests and national parks. Alberta did not want to absorb the cost of administering national parks and forests that were of no benefit to the province in terms of natural resources. Greenfield attributed the high expenditure charged against the province to the fact that "certain items have been included which we do not think can fairly be charged to the administration of natural resources."[75]

The Hudson's Bay Company (HBC) was also interested in the disposition of western lands because its claim was guaranteed in the *Deed of Surrender* and the *Dominion Lands Act,* and the Company was operating a land business within the Fertile Belt. According to the Company's management, their concern was that if the land reverted back to the provinces, "our rights under the original surrender and under this agreement might be prejudiced.... [W]e would ask that in any agreement between the Dominion and the Province, a clause be inserted similar to that in the Alberta Act, with the addition of the agreement of the 23rd December, 1924, between his Majesty and the Company."[76]

At a conference in 1925, a draft agreement was reached between the Dominion and Alberta. Premier Greenfield was anxious to have the agreement concluded in order to regain the support of the United Farmers of Alberta prior to the provincial election. The agreement, however, was not finalized until after a year of federal stalling and the resignation of Greenfield.[77] In early 1926, Premier John Brownlee of Alberta made a deal with the Dominion government for the transfer of natural resources that repealed the subsidy provided by the *Alberta Act,* and replaced it with an annual sum of $562,500 for three years after the repeal in order to meet the outlay necessary for the implementation of the agreement and the administration of public lands.[78] Brownlee was anxious to campaign with at least one concession to the province. At the time, Alberta was suffering from an agricultural recession and the provincial budget needed balancing.

In February 1926, a number of changes were made to the bill prior to Mackenzie King's introducing it in the House of Commons. These changes included the continued administration of schools and the school lands fund in accordance with Section 17 of the *Alberta Act*.[79] Brownlee initially approved the change without fully understanding that its effect was to reaffirm the guarantee of public support for Catholic schools as a concession for Quebec's support. When he realized this, he saw it as an attempt of the federal government to meddle in Alberta's affairs, since education fell under provincial jurisdiction. He suggested that the reference to section 17 of the *Alberta Act* be dropped. According to Brownlee's biographer, Franklin Foster:

> The federal Cabinet, having gained the change which Ernest Lapointe wanted in order to disarm potential objections from French-Canadian Nationalist leader, Henri Bourassa, refused to allow the Alberta Government to retract that change. The political reality was that the majority of King's seats were in Quebec. The inclusion of the reference to Section 17 was thought necessary to reassure French-Canada that, in transferring the control of the natural resources, the rights of the Catholic minority to separate schools had been protected.[80]

To avoid whipping up religious hostility on the eve of the provincial election, Brownlee and Mackenzie King suspended negotiations for the transfer.[81] The question was then referred to the Supreme Court of Canada in 1927, which concluded that section 17 of the *Alberta Act* was valid:

> [Varying] the provisions of s. 93 of the B.N.A. Act, 1867, in their application to the province of Alberta, and enacted to perpetuate under the Union the rights and privileges with respect to separate schools and with respect to religious instruction in the public or separate schools, as provided under the terms of chapters 29 and 30 of the Ordinances of the North-West Territories passed in the year 1901, and to prevent discrimination in the appropriation and distribution of moneys for support of schools, was within the powers of the Dominion Parliament, and is wholly *intra vires*.[82]

According to Justice Newcombe, who rendered the judgement on April 20, 1927, "s. 17 of the Alberta Act is not, in whole or in part, *ultra vires* of the Parliament of Canada."[83] This meant that the federal government had a constitutional right to order the province to provide support for Catholic education even though the BNA Act placed education under provincial control.[84]

This "Catholic Clause" rendered the agreement unacceptable to the Alberta government. Subsequently, the case was referred to the Judicial Committee of the Privy Council, which "expressed the view that there should be an appellant other than the Dominion government, whose contentions had been upheld by the unanimous judgement of the Supreme Court of Canada."[85] The province declined to act as the appellant in this case, however. This was indeed a vintage piece of political manipulation of the reference power. Alberta declined to appeal because it knew that it would probably lose; the Dominion appealed, even though it knew it was the wrong appellant, in order to create a face-saving ending for Alberta, in which the Privy Council would not explicitly uphold the Supreme Court of Canada.

In the following year, the Dominion and Alberta reached a compromise over schools, according to which the resources would be turned over, as well as the administration of schools, provided Alberta kept within the "letter and spirit of the constitution," thereby providing funding provisions for separate schools and accommodating Mackenzie King's Quebec ministers.[86] Brownlee also proposed a sliding scale to increase the subsidy as the population increased, thereby stalling the negotiations for another year.

Public opinion was also affected by the school question. To some, it was a question of allowing a province to provide the education it saw fit to provide. For others, it was a direct attack on a constitutional guarantee that protected minority rights.

At the Dominion-Provincial Conference of 1927, it seemed that a deal was in the making. The other provinces, while making no claim for compensation from the transfer, maintained, according to Premier John Baxter of New Brunswick, that the West should have "a brotherly consideration for those who had shared the load so that those lands could be made valuable by railways and other developments."[87] The Maritime provinces' claim was that they, "for geographical reasons cannot be given any equivalent in territory on account of gifts of portions of the public domain made, or which may be made, to other Provinces, a state of inequality thus being created."[88] The Maritime provinces emphasized that the provinces of Manitoba, Ontario and Quebec had had their territories enlarged in 1912 and the prairie provinces had received subsidies, while the Atlantic portion of the Dominion had to accept the terms of Confederation. The Duncan Commission was appointed in 1927 to deal with Maritime claims, and special bonuses, subsidies and favourable freight rates were subsequently granted to the Maritime provinces. According to Premier J.G. Gardiner of Saskatchewan, the prairie premiers saw no reason why the West should be indebted to any other part of the Dominion for its public lands.[89] The Maritime premiers generally accepted the transfer, but echoed the argument advanced since Confederation, that because the original provinces shared in the acquisition of Rupert's Land, they were entitled to compensation, or at least the same subsidy, if natural resources were transferred to the prairie provinces. Ontario and Quebec, on the other hand, were now prepared to allow the prairie provinces their resources and their full subsidies.[90]

In 1928, another round of negotiations began with a natural resources conference held July 3 and 4. It was agreed between the Dominion and Manitoba that the latter would be "placed in a position of equality with the other provinces of Confederation with respect to the administration and control of its natural resources, as if exercised from its entrance into Confederation in 1870."[91] To arbitrate the issue, a three-man commission was appointed in 1928, chaired by Justice W.F.A. Turgeon of the Saskatchewan Court of Appeal. The other members were T.A. Crerar of Manitoba and Charles Bowman, director of the Mutual Life Assurance Company of Canada.[92] The commission's purpose was to place Manitoba in a position of equality with the other provinces of Confederation and to transfer to the province the natural resources that had not been alienated by the Crown. As well, the commission was charged with devising a schedule of compensation for Crown lands alienated since July 15, 1870.[93]

The commission presented its report in May 1929, stating,

> The purposes for which the Dominion retained the agricultural lands of the Province have now been achieved; the railways have been built and the lands settled.... The time has no doubt come in Manitoba when, Dominion necessities having been satisfied, and the resources set apart having been practically exhausted, the Dominion Government should pay in full for the value it has received and leave to the Province the responsibility of administering what is left.[94]

Reasonable compromise, the commissioners suggested, was the only solution for the transfer, because "the various arrangements devoid of any clear principle which have been entered into, from time to time, have complicated the situation almost beyond the possibility of clear unanswerable solution."[95]

While the Commission held hearings, Alberta and Saskatchewan also began negotiating an agreement in December 1928, following a meeting held in Ottawa between Premiers Brownlee of Alberta and Anderson of Saskatchewan. To resolve the school-lands issue, Prime Minister King proposed the transfer of the school lands and the school-land fund to the province of Alberta, to "be administered by the Province for the support of schools organized and carried on therein in accordance with the laws of the Province, but in compliance with the letter and spirit of the constitution."[96] In addition, Alberta was to continue receiving its present annual subsidy of $562,500, while a commission consisting of Turgeon, Bowman and Fred Osborne, the Mayor of Calgary, would also be appointed to "consider the question whether any and, if any, what consideration, in addition to annual sums equal to those specified in Section 21 of the Alberta Act, should be paid to the Province in order that it may be placed in a position of equality with the other Provinces of Confederation."[97]

Saskatchewan received a similar offer from the Dominion government, including the appointment of a third person to the commission to add representation for Saskatchewan. In the case of Saskatchewan, reference was made to special terms that fell outside the purview of the other two agreements. Saskatchewan claimed that part of the *Saskatchewan Act* of 1905 was not within the competence of Parliament and therefore subject to a claim for compensation between the years 1870 and 1905. In a letter to Premier Anderson, Mackenzie King stated:

> We find it difficult to appreciate the nature of the legal arguments upon which this claim is founded, but these are obviously, in any event, a matter for the consideration of the Courts. Accordingly, if the Government of the Province desires to present its contentions on this head, our Government is quite ready to co-operate in obtaining a decision upon them by referring appropriate questions to the Supreme Court of Canada, whose decision would according to the usual practice, be subject to appeal to the Judicial Committee of the Privy Council. In case such a reference was made, the matter of agreement with the Province would, of course, have to stand in abeyance pending the final disposition of the questions submitted.[98]

Saskatchewan's demand resulted from political pressure placed on Anderson during the provincial election of 1929. According to T.C. Davis, a

Prince Albert lawyer, Anderson made a number of "extravagant statements" during the campaign, calling for an annual subsidy of four or five million dollars per year in perpetuity.[99] In the end, Anderson, after defeating Gardiner in the provincial election, was willing to accept the current subsidy, a reference to the Supreme Court of Canada over the claim to compensation for land alienated between 1870 and 1905, and an amendment to the constitution regarding certain provisions in the *Saskatchewan Act* that the provincial government thought were "not within the Legislative competence of the Parliament of Canada."[100] Alberta echoed the sentiment of Saskatchewan by demanding a single lump-sum payment similar to that recommended for Manitoba to compensate for land alienated between 1870 and 1905.[101]

On December 14, 1929, Alberta and Manitoba signed the agreement for the transfer of natural resources. It was based on the recommendations of the Turgeon Commission for the full transfer of natural resources and included a guarantee for the possession of Hudson's Bay Company land and railway land and rights of way. The matter of providing any additional subsidy for Alberta, as well as Brownlee's reservations about the Dominion government developing resources in the national parks, was to be left to the commission. Alberta was to receive an annual subsidy of $562,500 until the population of the province reached 800,000, when the subsidy would increase to $750,000. When the population reached 1,200,000, the province would receive $1,125,000. The Dominion transferred the lands and the school-lands fund with the condition that they be administered in accordance with the provisions of the *Dominion Lands Act* and the law of the province.[102] Indian land was to remain under the control of the Dominion, and the province would be required to surrender land from time to time to fulfil federal treaty obligations.

In Manitoba, the transfer bill received assent on 19 February, 1930. What distinguished it from the Alberta agreement was that it included compensation for the diminished subsidy that existed between 1870 and 1905, consisting of $4,584,212.49, "with interest thereon at the rate of five per cent per annum from the first day of July, 1929."[103] Saskatchewan followed this and accepted the agreement, in the same form as the *Alberta Transfer Act* on March 20, 1930.[104]

Royal assent was granted on July 1, 1930, for Manitoba and on October 1, 1930, for Saskatchewan and Alberta.[105] With the transfer, the prairie provinces took control of the unalienated public lands within their boundaries and began to staff provincial departments of natural resources. Initially, these positions were filled with the employees of the federal Department of the Interior who had become redundant as a result of the transfer. Eventually, many of these civil servants were absorbed into the provincial administrations. Thus concluded the negotiations that spanned more than two decades and occupied every Dominion-Provincial conference over that period. The prairie provinces had finally achieved legal equality with the other provinces with respect to public lands and natural resources.

The Natural Resources Transfer Agreement and Alberta's Place within Confederation

It is worth pondering what an Alberta without natural resource control might have looked like. Absent the transfer of resource control to Alberta in 1930, the province known for its budget surpluses and periodic boom-and-bust economic cycles might well have been closer to Saskatchewan and Manitoba's status, both in terms of its economic status and in terms of its political clout vis-à-vis the federal government. Also, the existence of natural resource revenues contributed to the province's overall standard of living and economic competitiveness and also allowed Alberta to develop its public infrastructure —roads, schools, higher educational institutions—along with regulations for Crown land use, in a manner thought appropriate by the province's citizens themselves. From the available and actual results for the fiscal years 1985–1986 to 2001–2002 inclusive (17 years in total), it is possible to ascertain that Alberta's natural resource revenues were $61.292 billion (in unadjusted dollars).[106] Those revenues would have gone to federal coffers, with amounts returned to Alberta to be determined at the prerogative of that government.

The National Energy Program, initiated by Pierre Trudeau's government in the 1980s as a way to provide below-market oil to other provinces, might well have become a permanent fact of western life. Nor should it be assumed that Alberta's energy industry would have developed as it did; federal tax, regulation, and environmental policies and legislation could have led to a very different energy sector (perhaps smaller and less efficient) than the one that was created.

The existence of natural resources is not itself a guarantor of prosperity, as shown by resource-rich jurisdictions in Central and South America and in Africa that co-exist with much poverty and squalor. In that sense, the Natural Resources Transfer Agreement of 1930 was Alberta's Constitution and one that—while it did not guarantee future prosperity—was a necessary component of later success.

Notes

1. Chester Martin, *"The Natural Resources Question": The Historical Basis of Provincial Claims* (Winnipeg: Philip Purcell, 1920), 20.

2. Martin, *Natural Resources Question*, 21.

3. Martin, *Natural Resources Question*, 58–59.

4. Martin, *Natural Resources Question*, 72.

5. Quoted in Peter A. Cumming and Neil H. Mickenberg, *Native Rights in Canada*, 2nd ed. (Toronto: General Publishing, 1972), 139.

6. Address to Her Majesty the Queen from the Senate and House of Commons of the Dominion of Canada, December 17, 1867, Schedule A to the Imperial Order-in-Council, June 23, 1870, R.S.C. 1970, Appendix, p. 264–65.

7. 31–21 Victoria, c. 105 (U.K.).

8. Ibid., s. 3.

9. Ibid., s. 5.

10. "Terms, as stated in the Letter from Sir Frederic Rogers, of 9th March, 1869," R.S.C., 1870, Appendix, pp. 266–67.

11. The Earl Granville to John Young, April 10, 1869, in Papers Relating to Rupert's Land, printed August 11, 1869, by order of the House of Commons, 14.

12. Address to the Queen's Most Excellent Majesty," May 29–31, 1869, R.S.C. 1970, p. 269–71.

13. S.C., 1869, c.3.

14. Ibid., s. 30.

15. Ibid., ss. 24–26.

16. Order of Her Majesty–in–Council Admitting Rupert's Land and the North-Western Territory into the Union, June 23, 1870, R.S.C. 1970, Appendix, p. 257–63.

17. *House of Commons Debates*, May 2, 1870, 1319.

18. Ibid., 1328.

19. Martin, *Natural Resources Question*, 82.

20. Chester Martin, *"Dominion Lands'" Policy*, ed. Lewis H. Thomas (Toronto: McClelland and Stewart, 1973), 177; 208–09.

21. Martin, *Natural Resources Question*, 83–85.

22. Grant MacEwan, *Frederick Haultain: Frontier Statesman of the Canadian Northwest* (Saskatoon: Western Producer Prairie Books, 1985), 122–23.

23. Ibid.

24. James G. MacGregor, *A History of Alberta* (Edmonton: Hurtig, 1972), 187.

25. Owram, Douglas R, *The Formation of Alberta: A Documentary History* (Calgary: Historical Society of Alberta, 1979), 52–53.

26. Owram, *The Formation of Alberta*, 76.

27. Owram, *The Formation of Alberta*, 78.

28. Owram, *The Formation of Alberta*, 81.

29. Owram, *The Formation of Alberta*, 81.

30. Owram, *The Formation of Alberta*, 82.

31. Owram, *The Formation of Alberta*, 83.

32. Owram, *The Formation of Alberta*, 95.

33. Owram, *The Formation of Alberta*, 99.

34. Owram, *The Formation of Alberta*, 89.

35. Owram, *The Formation of Alberta*, 89.
36. Owram, *The Formation of Alberta*, 90.
37. Owram, *The Formation of Alberta*, 91.
38. Owram, *The Formation of Alberta*, 91.
39. Owram, *The Formation of Alberta*, 99.
40. Owram, *The Formation of Alberta*, 114–23.
41. Owram, *The Formation of Alberta*, 111.
42. Owram, *The Formation of Alberta*, 121–23.
43. Evelyn Eager, *Saskatchewan Government: Politics and Pragmatism* (Saskatoon: Western Producer Prairie Books, 1980), 27.
44. *Alberta Act*, S.C., 1905, c. 3, s. 21; *Saskatchewan Act*, S.C., c. 42, s. 21.
45. Quoted in Eager, *Saskatchewan Government*, 29.
46. Ibid., 31; Martin, *"Dominion Lands" Policy*, 211–12.
47. Murray Donnelly, *The Government of Manitoba* (Toronto: University of Toronto Press, 1963), 43.
48. Quoted in Arthur Meighen to T.C. Norris, December 24, 1920 PAM, Executive Council Records, Bracken Files, GR 1661 G666, Natural Resources Papers, 164.
49. Wilfred Laurier to Arthur Sifton, August 11, 1911, PAM, Executive Council Records, Bracken Files, GR 1661 G666, Natural Resources Papers, 20.
50. Robert Borden to Walter Scott, January 9, 1913, PAM, Executive Council Records, Bracken Files, GR 1661 G666, Natural Resources Papers, 48.
51. Walter Scott, R.P. Roblin, and Arthur Sifton to Robert Borden, December 22, 1913, PAM, Dept. Natural Resources Records, GR 1599 Vol. G 1060 File 2, Natural Resources Agreement, 64.
52. Robert Borden to R.P. Roblin, Walter Scott, and A.L. Sifton, March 5, 1914, PAM, Executive Council Records, Bracken Files, GR 1661 G666, Natural Resources Papers, 66.
53. Arthur Sifton to Robert Borden, February 9, 1916, PAM, Executive Council Records, Bracken Files, GR 1661 G666, Natural Resources Papers, 76.
54. Robert Borden to T. C. Norris, April 17, 1916, PAM, Executive Council Records, Bracken Files, GR 1661 G666, Natural Resources Papers, 87.
55. Robert Borden to T.C. Norris, Walter Scott, and A.L Sifton, March 10, 1916, PAM, Executive Council Records, Bracken Files, GR 1661 G666, Natural Resources Papers, 81.
56. Draft joint submissions by representatives of the prairie provinces, November 1918, PAM, Executive Council Records, Bracken Files, GR 1661 G666, Natural Resources Papers, 112.
57. Arthur Meighen to T.C. Norris, December 7, 1920. PAM, Executive Council Records, Bracken Files, GR 1661 G666, Natural Resources Papers, 134.
58. T.C. Norris to Arthur Meighen, March 10, 1921, PAM, Executive Council Records, Bracken Files, GR 1661, G666, Natural Resources Papers, 171.
59. Arthur Meighen to T.C. Norris, April 27, 1921, PAM, Executive Council Records, Bracken Files, GR 1661 G666, Natural Resources Papers, 177.
60. Ibid., 174.
61. Quoted in ibid., 174–75.
62. William L. Mackenzie King to T.C. Norris, February 20, 1921, PAM, Executive Council Records, Bracken Files, GR 1661 G666, Natural Resources Papers, 190.
63. Ibid.
64. Resolution passed unanimously by the Legislative Assembly of Manitoba, March 28, 1922, PAM, Executive Council Records, Bracken Files, GR 1661, G666, Natural Resources Papers, 198.
65. T.C. Norris to Arthur Meighen, March 10, 1921, PAM, Department of Natural Resources Records, GR 1599 Vol. G 1060 File 2, Natural Resources Transfer Agreement, Correspondence, 167.

66. C.A. Dunning to W.L. Mackenzie King, April 10, 1922, NAC, W.L. Mackenzie King Papers, MG 26J, Reel C-2244, vol. B-72.

67. Memorandum for Natural Resources Conference, November 14, 1922, PAM, Executive Council Records, Bracken Files, GR 1661, G666, Natural Resources Papers, 204.

68. John Bracken to W.L. Mackenzie King, November 17, 1922, PAM, Executive Council Records, Bracken Files, GR 1661, G666, Natural Resources Papers, 212.

69. Herbert Greenfield to W.L. Mackenzie King, December 29, 1923, NAC, Mackenzie King Papers, MG 26J, File Greenfield, Reel C2253, p. 2, Vol. B-89.

70. Ibid.

71. K.A. Blatchford to W.L. Mackenzie King, December 30, 1923, NAC, W.L. Mackenzie King Papers, MG 26J, File Blatchford, Reel C-2251, Vol. B-84.

72. Memorandum of the Government of Manitoba for the Natural Resources Conference, January 4, 1924, PAM, Executive Council Records, Bracken Files, GR 1661, G666, Natural Resources Papers, 225–28.

73. W.L. Mackenzie King to John Bracken, January 29, 1924, PAM, Executive Council Records, Bracken Files, GR 1661, G666, Natural Resources Papers, 230.

74. Resolution Unanimously Passed by Legislative Assembly of Manitoba, April 5, 1924, PAM, Executive Council Records, Bracken Files, GR 1661, G666, Natural Resources Papers, 245.

75. Herbert Greenfield to W.L. Mackenzie King, May 28, 1924, NAC, W.L. Mackenzie King Papers, MG 26J, File Greenfield, Reel C-2265, Vol. B-101, 2–3.

76. Edward Fitzgerald to W.L. Mackenzie King, January 20, 1925, NAC, W.L. Mackenzie King Papers, MG 26J, File Hudson's Bay Company, Reel C-2276, Vol. B-114.

77. Franklin Foster, *John E. Brownlee: A Biography* (Lloydminster: Foster Learning Inc., 1996), 114–15.

78. Memorandum of Agreement, January 9, 1926. PAM, Department of Natural Resources Records, GR 1599 Vol. G 1060, file 14.

79. Foster, *John E. Brownlee,* 124–25.

80. Ibid., 125.

81. Ted Byfield, ed., *Brownlee and the Triumph of Populism 1920–1930,* vol. 5 *Alberta in the 20th Century* ·(Edmonton: United Western Communication, 1996), 81.

82. [1927] S.C.R. 364.

83. Ibid.

84. Byfield, *Brownlee and the Triumph of Populism,* 91.

85. W.L. Mackenzie King to Brownlee, December 17, 1928, NAC, W.L. Mackenzie King Papers, MG 26J1, Reel C-2302, vol. 151.

86. Ibid.; Byfield, *Brownlee and the Triumph of Populism,* 91.

87. Official Précis of Dominion Provincial Conference, November 8, 1927, PAM, Executive Council Records, Bracken Files, GR 1661, G666, Natural Resources Papers, 336.

88. In re Claims of Maritime Provinces for compensation in connection with grants made from public domain to the other Provinces, April 18, 1921, PAM, Executive Council Records, Premier Bracken's Files, GR 1661 G 550 File 232, Natural Resources, 10.

89. Official Précis of Dominion Provincial Conference, November 8, 1927, PAM, Executive Council Records, Bracken Files, GR 1661, G666, Natural Resources Papers, 337.

90. Extracts from Notes Taken by Mr. R.M. Pearson, Deputy Provincial Treasurer at Dominion Provincial Conference held in Ottawa in November 1927, November 9, 1927, Official Précis of Dominion Provincial Conference, November 8, 1927, PAM, Executive Council Records, Bracken Files, GR 1661, G666, Natural Resources Papers, 339.

91. Manitoba Natural Resources, July 4, 1928, PAM Executive Council Records, Bracken Files, GR 1661, G550, File 232, Natural Resources Papers, 4.

92. Manitoba Natural Resources Supplementary Announcement, July 7, 1928, PAM Executive Council Records, Bracken Files, GR 1661, G550, File 232, Natural Resources Papers.

93. Martin, *"Dominion Lands" Policy*, 218.

94. *Report of the Royal Commission on the Transfer of the Natural Resources of Manitoba*, 1929, 49–50.

95. Ibid., 55.

96. Mackenzie King to Brownlee, December 17, 1928, NAC, W.L. Mackenzie King Papers, MG 26J1, Reel C-2302, vol. 151.

97. Mackenzie King to Anderson, December 31, 1929, NAC, W.L. Mackenzie King Papers, MG 26J1, Reel C-2307, Vol. 158, 159.

98. Ibid.

99. T.C. Davis to Mackenzie King, December 12, 1929, NAC, W.L. Mackenzie King Papers, MG 26J1, Reel C-2309, Vol. 161, 162.

100. Anderson to Mackenzie King, February 14, 1930, NAC, W.L. Mackenzie King Papers, MG 26J1, Reel C-2315, Vol. 160, 170.

101. Foster, *John E. Brownlee*, 166.

102. Agreement for the Transfer of Natural Resources of Alberta, December 14, 1929, PAA, Acc. No. 69.289, Reel No. 60, File/Item No. 620.

103. An Act respecting the Transfer of the Natural Resources of Manitoba, February 19, 1930, PAM, Department of Natural Resources Records, GR 1599, Vol. G1060, File 1.

104. Agreement for the Transfer of Natural Resources of Saskatchewan, March 20, 1930, PAC, Indian Affairs, RG 10, Vol. 6820, File 492-4-2, Pt. 1.

105. Martin, *"Dominion Lands" Policy*, 221–22.

106. Alberta Finance, Alberta Budget 2003, Fiscal Plan Tables 2003–06, 61.

Seven

Bible Bill and the Money Barons
The Social Credit Court References
and their Constitutional Consequences
DALE GIBSON

The sudden born-again conversion of grass-roots Albertans to the radical economic/political principles of social credit in the mid-1930s is a story that has been told many times by historians, political scientists and economists. What has been less studied is the long-term impact of Alberta's social credit political revolution on the legal evolution of the Canadian Constitution.

Early attempts by the provincial government of Premier William Aberhart to enact legislation that would put in place a social credit economic regime in Alberta were held by the Supreme Court of Canada to be constitutionally impermissible, and the reasoning upon which the Court's conclusions were based continues to influence constitutional adjudication to this day. My purpose is to evaluate that reasoning process and some of its consequences. Before turning to constitutional analysis, however, it will be useful to summarize the remarkable events of the summer of 1935 and the politically tumultuous years that followed.

The "Dirty Thirties" hit Albertans and other prairie Canadians especially hard. On top the worldwide economic depression that followed the calamitous market crash of November 1929 came several years of drought, dust storms, grasshopper infestations, and crop failures. Barry Broadfoot's moving book, *Ten Lost Years, 1929–1939: Memories of Canadians Who Survived the Depression*[1] notes that the price of wheat plummeted from $1.60 to 38 cents a bushel in two and a half years. A prime steer *cost* one producer $6.00 to sell. In the cities, even people with clear title to their homes were in danger of losing them for property tax defaults, or of being forced to sell them for a fraction of their value. Unemployed workers sometimes offered their services free in the hope that doing so might lead to paid work, or at least "keep their hand in." "Relief" was eventually made available for the absolutely destitute, but the amounts provided were paltry, and the demeaning application process left permanent psychological scars on some recipients. A widow with three children had her $10 monthly relief payment cut off because her unemployed brother came to live on her farm, even though the farm was incapable of producing income.

What was to be done? The government of Canada, led by Calgary lawyer R.B. Bennett, had been of little assistance, and although Bennett would, on the brink of the 1935 general election, undergo something akin to a political deathbed repentance by leading Parliament to enact a package of mildly socialistic, economy-stimulating legislation that was inspired by F.D. Roosevelt's "New Deal" reforms south of the border, most of that legislation would be struck down by the courts as unconstitutional. Bennett's regime would be chiefly remembered for "Bennett buggies"—horse-drawn automobiles with their engines removed because their owners were unable to afford gasoline.[2] In Alberta, the once-radical UFA (United Farmers of Alberta) government, crippled by ideological fissures, near-bankruptcy, and sexual scandals that would result in the resignations of both Public Works Minister O.L. McPherson and Premier John Brownlee,[3] was also unable to deal effectively with the crisis.

William Aberhart thought he knew what should be done. Aberhart was a Calgary high school principal by profession and a fundamentalist preacher and pioneer radio evangelist by avocation.[4] Both his teaching and preaching careers were highly successful, but it was his immensely popular "Back to the Bible" broadcasts over Calgary's radio station CFCN that first brought "Bible Bill" wide public attention. Although the focus of his fiery sermons was theological, Aberhart was a practical-minded and caring man, well aware of and concerned about the day-to-day circumstances of his flock. For the first year or two of the Depression, he made little reference to it from the pulpit, except as an illustration or "foreshadow" of the misfortunes that befall those who fail to accept Christianity into their lives. But as the situation worsened, he was increasingly moved by reports from across Alberta about the severe practical hardships his followers were suffering. A particularly devastating blow was the news that one of his former students had taken his own life after a period of extended unemployment.[5]

In the summer of 1932, Aberhart was lent a book describing a radical scheme of economic reform called "social credit," devised by an obscure English writer, Major C.H. Douglas. Aberhart was so taken by the theory that he sat up all night to finish the book and announced to colleagues the next morning that he believed he had come upon a solution to the world's current economic ills.[6] Not long thereafter, on August 21, 1932, having obtained permission from the executive board of his radio sponsor, the Calgary Prophetic Bible Institute, Aberhart began to insert into his sermons ideas for economic redemption based on his interpretation of Major Douglas's social credit theories.[7]

Precisely what economic measures he had in mind was not altogether clear at that point. He undoubtedly believed, however, in common with proponents of both social credit and socialism alike (and indeed with most of those who advocated economic solutions for the ills of the times), that the stagnant economy needed to be jolted into motion by some form of external stimulus. The differences that divided the various political camps related largely to the nature of the stimulus considered appropriate and to the point in the complex machinery of production and consumption where it would be most usefully applied. While the socialists, whose 1933 *Regina Manifesto* would lead to the creation of the CCF (Co-operative Commonwealth Federation), and eventually to the New Democratic Party, urged the importance of placing the major means of production, transportation and communications under public ownership, Douglas, Aberhart and their supporters concentrated on attempts to relieve the consumers' severe shortage of purchasing power.

Douglas claimed that a lack of sufficient purchasing power was inherent to the orthodox economic system. He explained this phenomenon by means of what he called the "A + B Theorem."[8] In a healthy economy, he said, the total cost of producing all goods and services should be paid to individuals in the form of wages, dividends and profits. This would give them purchasing power that, when exercised, would keep the system fully operational by continuing to stimulate production and employment. However, he claimed, the full cost of production is never so distributed. If all the wages, dividends and profits expended in the production of a given product were added up, he said, the total, which he designated "A," would be significantly less than the full price of the product. The discrepancy, which he called "B," was made up of such other costs of production as raw materials, bank charges, and taxes. Since the purchasing power benefits paid to individuals (A) would always be less that the total cost of production (A + B), he concluded that the existing economic system was doomed to experience a chronic shortfall of purchasing power. The solution Douglas proposed was that the government should distribute to individuals as "social credit"—money equivalent to the "B" component of the equation—payments to keep the economy moving.

The fallacy in Douglas's theory was his assumption that the "B" factors are not distributed to individuals. Directly or indirectly, one way or another, the benefits flowing from "B" costs all find their way into people's hands: owners or producers of raw materials are paid for them; bank earnings are distributed to their employees and shareholders; tax revenues are used to pay public servants and the suppliers of public goods and services.

However, William Aberhart detected no fallacy in social credit theory as he understood it.[9] As his enthusiasm mounted, and that of his followers grew apace, he increased the economic content of his radio sermons, and began, with the help of others, to organize social credit study groups throughout Alberta.[10] The study groups eventually coalesced as the Social Credit League, which by 1934 was publishing a newspaper, the *Social Credit Chronicle*.[11] With his teacher's gift of simplified explanation and his organizational genius, William Aberhart was beginning to convince Albertans that the ideas of an obscure British amateur economist held the key to their economic salvation.

This fact did not escape the attention of Alberta's UFA government. As the prospect of a provincial election drew nearer, the UFA began flirting with social credit itself. In the spring of 1934, the Agriculture Committee of the Alberta Legislature conducted an inquiry into social credit principles, and invited both Major Douglas and William Aberhart, among others, to appear before it. Although their radical ideas were consistently rejected by the UFA leadership, growing numbers of its rank and file members were attracted. The matter came to a head at the UFA convention in February 1935, when a resolution to make the introduction of a social credit scheme to Alberta part of the party's platform was narrowly defeated. However, the dissatisfaction of those who had voted for the proposal was sufficiently disturbing to the government that it invited Douglas to come back to Alberta and engaged him as an economic consultant.[12]

The UFA's nervousness about the popularity of social credit was intensified by the fact that 1935 was an election year. Although Aberhart had no political ambitions when he first introduced Albertans to social credit thinking, and scoffed at the prospect of his running for office when it was initially suggested to him,[13] the UFA's refusal to embrace a social credit plank in its election platform convinced him that he had no acceptable alternative. On the day after the UFA convention, Aberhart announced to a friend that he intended to form a political party to contest the upcoming provincial election,[14] and he did so with characteristic energy and organizational brilliance. By the time the election was announced on July 16, a full slate of Social Credit candidates had been selected and a Social Credit campaign juggernaut was rolling across the province. Although Social Creditors continued to assert that their organization was a social movement rather than a political party, everyone knew that was a distinction without a difference.

Oddly (and cannily) enough, William Aberhart was not a candidate himself. Claiming that "I'm not seeking office. No sir, I am not,"[15] he cast himself as the spiritual leader of a grass-roots revolution. This left him free to stump the province on behalf of Social Credit candidates in every riding, while the leaders of other parties had to devote considerable time and effort to getting elected in their home constituencies. It also forestalled any attempt by the other parties to gang up on Aberhart and defeat him personally in whatever riding he might choose; and it protected him from the possibility that if he personally won at the polls, but Social Credit failed to win overall, he would become a mere opposition voice in the legislative wilderness. There was never any doubt, however, that if Social Credit formed a government, William Aberhart would be its premier.

The campaign was astonishing. Bolstered by an unprecedented number of volunteers across the province, the strong editorial support of the *Social Credit Chronicle*, and virtually unrestricted access to "Back to the Bible" audiences of about 300,000 weekly,[16] Aberhart and his disciples seemed to be everywhere at once, attracting large and boisterous crowds to pot-luck suppers, socials, picnics and lectures. Economic ideology was served up with scriptural side-dishes, rousing hymn-sings, and great draughts of down-home good-humoured fellowship and long-forgotten optimism. To emphasize the ludicrousness of an economic situation in which the world starved because willing workers were idle, Aberhart introduced to his program an oddly-accented "Man from Mars" to whom he purported to explain, in mock-serious tones, the reasons given for this predicament by bankers—the "50 eastern big-shots" and "high mucky mucks" to whom he attributed the real blame.[17] Before long, to the delight of all, the "Man from Mars" was appearing in person at Social Credit gatherings, complete with outlandish space-suit.[18]

To a depression-drained electorate, the most seductive aspect of the Social Credit campaign must have been the promise of monthly dividends for every Alberta resident. These dividends were intended to replace the "missing" purchasing power represented by the "B" part of Douglas's "A+B Theorem," and thus restore momentum to the stalled economy. A pamphlet authored by Aberhart described the promised payments as follows:

Basic dividends should be $25 a month for every bona fide citizen, male or female, 21 years or more. Children of bona fide citizens, 16 years old, will receive $5 a month. Those 17 and 18 years will receive $10 a month. Those 19, $15 and those 20, $20 a month.[19]

One of those who contributed to Barry Broadfoot's collection of depression-era stories assessed the 1935 Alberta election like this:

Along comes Bible Bill. Down with the bankers, down with high inter-est, down with everything the people were against. Everybody would get twenty-five bucks a month and that would stir up the economy. Do you know what twenty-five dollars a month meant in 1935?
...
It would have been goddamned surprising if Old Aberhart and his wild bunch of Social Credit hadn't got in that year. In '35.[20]

They did get in. In a big way. Social Credit, not one of whose candidates had held provincial elected office before, won 56 of the Legislature's 63 seats. Not a single UFA candidate was successful.

Two years would pass before the Alberta Legislature enacted the social credit legislation upon which the Supreme Court of Canada would be asked to rule. They were two very eventful and controversial years, during which Aberhart arranged loans from the government of Canada to avoid the looming provincial bankruptcy of which the UFA government had failed to warn, and to prevent the Alberta government from defaulting on a provincial bond issue.[21]

Social Credit's first legislative session—from February 6 to April 7, 1936—was busy. Members dealt with an ambitious legislative agenda, including Acts to establish a minimum wage, to impose a provincial sales tax, to expand the powers and revenues of the Liquor Control Board, to amend Alberta's educa-tion laws in important ways, and to permit voters to "recall" elected MLAs.[22] The only social credit measure enacted, however, was a vague statute that merely authorized a social credit scheme to be established by regulation.[23] The Aberhart government was clearly not yet ready to put its economic theo-ries into practice. It would have been surprising if it had been ready, given the enormity of the task, the novelty of the proposed means, and the scarcity of time. Aberhart had warned that "15 or 18 months might be required" to intro-duce social credit to Alberta,[24] and the task was complicated after the election by the refusal of Major Douglas to help implement the scheme, other than to criticize from afar.[25]

Many members of the Social Credit caucus, and large numbers of the general public, were becoming impatient. Aberhart had said at an unguarded moment during the election campaign that economic reform, which most construed to include dividend payments, could be brought about by "the stroke of a pen," and a growing number of Albertans were demanding that he set his pen in motion. Two things deterred him. First, despite the glib assurances he had given on the hustings, he really had no idea where the money to fund dividend payments would come from. Second, he was fully aware that prevailing legal opinion, including that of his own Attorney General, John Hugill, considered the scheme to be beyond the legislative competence of the provincial Legislature because it involved matters that fell within the exclusive constitutional jurisdiction of the Parliament of Canada. Even Douglas acknowledged the constitutional problem. Aberhart published a pamphlet expressing a contrary view on the constitutional question,[26] but he could not have expected, as a non-lawyer, to persuade any court.

As a stop-gap, and as a first step toward the realization of its larger goal, the Alberta government announced, in April 1936, that it would soon be issuing, under the regulatory authority granted by the general social credit enabling statute enacted that spring, what it called "Prosperity Certificates" (popularly referred to as "scrip" or "funny money"), designed to stimulate the provincial economy. Although social credit purists sneered at the scrip project, Aberhart loyalists saw it as a possible way to achieve some interim relief from Alberta's financial hardships, or at least as a way of appearing to be doing something.

Scrip was based on the widely-accepted premise that measures that increase the circulation of money are beneficial for a stagnant economy. The Alberta government proposed to put into circulation 500,000 certificates, each of which would be redeemable from the Province of Alberta in two years' time for $1.00 in Canadian currency. What made the certificates unique, and prevented their being either a true social credit device or a threat to the federal monetary system,[27] was a "perishability" feature. Each certificate would become void unless validated every week by affixing to its obverse side a 1 cent stamp purchased from the government. By the redemption date two years later, any certificate, to be redeemable, would thus have to bear $1.04 worth of stamps. Therefore, no new monetary credit would be created by the scheme. The 4 cent surplus would presumably cover the government's administration costs. Because the certificates would, by reason of the stamping requirement, effectively diminish in value with each passing week, it was hoped that they would pass rapidly from hand to hand, thereby stimulating the sluggish economy. It is difficult, though, to understand why anyone would have accepted scrip toward the end of its life cycle, when there would be a chance of getting stuck with it and having to pay the surplus 4 cents just to maintain its face value until the redemption date. The first certificates were issued in August 1936 as partial wages for workers employed on provincial road-building relief projects, and some general circulation ensued. However, both the chartered banks and the business community generally refused to accept the "funny money" and the scheme fizzled before the end of the year.[28]

About the same time that it began to circulate scrip, the Alberta government started registering citizens for distribution of the proposed monthly dividend.[29] The registration process was highly intrusive, prying into personal matters such as income, assets and liabilities. It also required the signature of an extraordinary "Covenant" agreeing, among other things, to "co-operate most heartily with the Alberta government," to "accept my remuneration in Alberta Credit [presumably scrip] as far as I can reasonably do so," to "exchange as much...as is convenient" of one's "Canadian Currency" income for Alberta Credit, but *not* to pay in Alberta Credit anything owing to the Alberta government, and *not* to demand that the Alberta government redeem Alberta Credit for Canadian currency.[30]

Neither these initiatives nor the enactment of more extensive social credit legislation at the 1936 fall session of the Alberta Legislature[31] satisfied the more impatient members of Aberhart's caucus. Catalyzed by a visiting British social credit firebrand named John Hargrave, dissidents began to mutter about their leader, and then to plot against him. Aberhart's confession, as the spring 1937 session of the Legislature opened, that he was not yet able to provide the promised dividend,[32] was unacceptable to a growing number of caucus members. Attorney General Hugill's warning to caucus that the proposals of Hargrave and others for realizing the dividend would be beyond the constitutional authority of a province was hooted down.[33]

The introduction in the provincial Legislature in March 1937 of the Aberhart government's annual budget, containing no social credit measures, was the final straw for the malcontents. They filibustered the budget bill and soon demonstrated that they had enough votes to defeat it. A caucus compromise, by which approval of an interim budget was traded off for Aberhart's agreement to introduce full-bore social credit legislation immediately, averted disaster for the premier, though it temporarily left him with seriously weakened political powers.[34]

The resulting statute, the *Alberta Social Credit Act*,[35] was the most thorough-going of the Alberta social credit measures to date. Embracing the main features of the previous legislation, though without the unpopular registration covenants, it authorized the immediate creation of a Commission of experts to advise on and administer the desired new fiscal regime. The key "experts" appointed to the Commission were two close associates of Major Douglas.[36] Although the new Act did not lead directly to implementation of the scheme, it provided a basis for detailed implementing legislation that was later enacted at a special session of the Legislature in early August 1937.[37]

When Aberhart and Attorney General Hugill delivered the implementing bills to Lieutenant-Governor J.C. Bowen for Royal Assent, the latter asked Hugill whether he considered them to be constitutionally valid. To Aberhart's dismay, Hugill's reply was in the negative.[38] At Aberhart's insistence, Bowen nevertheless signed the bills into law, but they were soon to be disallowed by the government of Canada.[39] In the meantime, John Hugill resigned as Attorney General, and let it be known that when the Legislature resumed he would cross the floor to sit as an independent MLA.

Federal disallowance of provincial legislation was a rare occurrence by that point in Canada's constitutional history.[40] The process, which is still a feature of the Canadian Constitution in theory, had colonial roots. When in 1867 the British North American colonies of Nova Scotia, New Brunswick and Canada were welded into a federal union, with provision for others to be added, they lost none of their former status as colonial possessions of the United Kingdom. Although the new, larger Canada would gain gradual independence by a complex combination of *de facto* and *de jure* measures, its constituting document—called the *British North America Act* then, and the *Constitution Act, 1867* now—retained strong legal ties to the mother country.

One of those legal ties was the power of the British government to annul Canadian legislation of which it did not approve. Section 56 of the *Constitution Act, 1867* required the Governor-General to send the British government a copy of every Act of the Parliament of Canada to which Royal Assent was granted at "the first convenient opportunity," and went on to provide that "if the Queen in Council within two years after receipt thereof by the Secretary of State thinks fit to disallow the Act, such disallowance...shall annul the Act." Section 90 created a parallel power by which the government of Canada could annul provincial legislation.

British disallowance of federal legislation occurred only once, in 1873. The treatment of provincial laws under s. 90 was a different story, however.

Although the federal power to disallow provincial legislation was proposed at the crucial Quebec Conference of 1864 by Oliver Mowat, a champion of provincial autonomy who claimed that the power was intended to be used as sparingly as British disallowance of federal legislation,[41] the government of Canada annulled 101 provincial statutes between 1867 and 1924.[42] Attitudes about the propriety of exercising the disallowance power had changed markedly by 1937, however. No provincial legislation had been disallowed in the 13 years since 1924, and when it was agreed at the Imperial Conferences leading up to British enactment of the *Statute of Westminster, 1930* (a major step toward Canadian independence) that the British should never again disallow federal legislation,[43] many felt that the federal government's equivalent veto power over provincial laws had impliedly been abandoned, too, or should have been.

Despite the controversial nature of the veto power over provincial laws, Mackenzie King's government chose to disallow the three social credit statutes enacted at the 1937 special summer session of the Alberta Legislature on the ground that the legislation was "not merely *ultra vires*, but constitutes an unmistakable invasion of the legislative field assigned to Parliament by the B.N.A. Act. It conflicts with Dominion laws and virtually supplants Dominion, institutions designed by Parliament to facilitate the trade and commerce of the whole Dominion."[44] William Aberhart and his followers were understandably outraged. The anger of some of the more rabid Social Credit supporters seemed to be leavened by a degree of satisfaction that the federal intervention would feed a sense of frustration on the part of the electorate that could help pave the way to a political Armageddon. Major Douglas's reaction, for example, was that the federal move was "magnificent," and that Aberhart was to be congratulated for having provoked it.[45] One of the "experts" Douglas had dispatched to Alberta later acknowledged that "the disallowed Acts had been drawn up mainly to show the people of Alberta who were their *real* enemies, and in that respect they succeeded admirably."[46]

Aberhart was not prepared to buckle under to pressure from Ottawa. When, in the autumn of 1937, his government convened a third session of the Alberta Legislature for that year, the House passed a resolution declaring that the federal disallowance power no longer existed, and urging the Alberta government to implement the statutes in spite of disallowance.[47] Aberhart also introduced at that session a more controversial social credit legislative agenda than ever before, this time without the assistance of a legally-trained Attorney General. There being no other lawyer in his caucus after Hugill's resignation, Aberhart had decided, in spite of his lack of legal qualifications, to undertake the responsibilities of Attorney General himself.[48] The most important social credit measures he introduced were a somewhat modified version of the disallowed *Credit of Alberta Regulation Act*,[49] and two bills that targeted Social Credit's chief *bêtes noirs*: the banks and the newspapers.

The banks had always been portrayed as villains by social credit theorists. It was the banks that were blamed for sucking the lion's share of the "B" component from the economy. Although Aberhart showed no sign of agreeing with Douglas's anti-Semitic view that this was the fault of an "international Jewish conspiracy,"[50] there is no doubt that he believed the "money barons"[51] had to be suppressed. If banks were removed from the scene and replaced by socially-responsible State Credit Houses, he and his followers believed that a healthier economy would result. Since "banking" is a subject assigned exclusively to the Parliament of Canada by s. 91(15) of the *Constitution Act, 1867*, the Alberta Legislature could not directly ban banks from the province. Provincial authority does extend to "direct taxation within the province" (s. 92(2)), however, so the Aberhart government decided to put indirect pressure on Alberta banks by means of lethally high taxation. The *Bank Taxation Act* bill[52] imposed taxes on the paid-up capital, the reserves, and the undistributed profits of banks operating in Alberta, at rates many believed were calculated to drive banks out of the province.

Newspapers were also anathema to Aberhart and his supporters. Although adroit use of radio had contributed immensely to Social Credit's 1935 landslide, the news media, especially newspapers, were now criticizing and lampooning the Aberhart government relentlessly. Little wonder: the economic theories of social credit were risible; the new government had accomplished very little during its first two years in office except its failed experiment with "funny money," and "Bible Bill" was a caricaturist's dream. Editorial cartoons treated the rotund Premier viciously, often portraying him as a fascist. A notorious example was a *Calgary Herald* illustration of fascist salutes: Mussolini's arm rigidly upright, Hitler's slanted forward at an angle, Aberhart's extended palm up, in a panhandling gesture.[53]

The provincial government's response to press criticism was to introduce in the Legislature a draconian newspaper censorship bill entitled the *Accurate News and Information Act*.[54] The *Press Act*, as it was commonly known, empowered the government to commandeer newspaper publication of official responses to criticism,[55] and to demand the disclosure of journalistic sources and the identification of writers.[56] Non-compliance could be punished by large fines,[57] by closing down newspapers, and by prohibiting the publication of information obtained from specified persons or written by specified persons.[58]

All three bills received the necessary three readings in the Legislative Assembly, but Royal Assent was not granted by Lieutenant-Governor Bowen, who reserved the bills "for the signification of the Governor-General's pleasure," in accordance with sections 55, 57 and 90 of the *British North America Act*.[59] Reservation is a process half-way between granting and withholding Royal Assent. It enables a provincial lieutenant-governor to pass legislative hot potatoes to the federal government for determination. Reserved bills have no legislative force unless granted Royal Assent by the Governor-General within a year of being originally brought to the lieutenant-governor for Assent. Like federal disallowance of provincial legislation, reservation was very unpopular with the provinces by 1937, and had not been exercised much since the turn of the century.[60]

Frantic negotiations ensued between the governments of Canada and Alberta, resulting in agreement that the governor-general-in-council (the federal Cabinet) would send two constitutional References to the Supreme Court of Canada in accordance with its power to do so under the *Supreme Court Act*. The first Reference would deal with Alberta's contention that federal use of the disallowance and reservation powers had been unconstitutional; the second would deal with Canada's assertion that the three reserved bills were unconstitutional. The Orders-in-Council placing these issues before the Supreme Court were swiftly issued.[61] There were interventions by the chartered banks and by two news organizations, the Canadian Press and a group of newspapers led by the *Edmonton Journal*. Large legal teams on both sides began preparations for what would be the Court's most important constitutional assignment until then.

The legal counsel were of the highest calibre. Leading for the banks and the Canadian Press was W.N. Tilley, K.C., a gruff Toronto barrister nearing the end of an illustrious career. A biographer described him as possessing "single-mindedness of purpose, an inability to suffer fools gladly," and a "well-grounded confidence that he knew more law than anyone else."[62] Tilley's no-nonsense approach was reflected in his fact-specific *Press Act* factum (pre-hearing written argument), couched in plain English, which cited authority sparingly and stated his arguments persuasively in seven closely-reasoned pages.[63]

The *Edmonton Journal* and other Alberta newspapers were represented by a group of lawyers headed by J.L. Ralston, K.C., an extremely able Montreal-based lawyer and politician, whose distinguished service in World War I had earned him the post of minister of national defence between 1926 and 1930, and who was destined to fill the same role during World War II.[64] His factum, although much fuller than Tilley's (40 pages), was also tightly structured, and a model of clarity.

On behalf of the Attorney General of Canada on all issues, including disallowance and reservation, appeared another titan of the Canadian bar, Aimé Geoffrion, K.C. of Montreal,[65] leading a powerful legal team. A biographer of both men suggested that if Tilley was not "alone at the top" of the Canadian bar at this time he shared that position with Aimé Geoffrion.[66] With "a foot in both the English culture and the French, favouring neither one nor the other," Geoffrion has been described as "a Canadian nationalist in the best sense."[67] The same attributes (along with strong Liberal connections) equipped him well to represent the Attorney General of Canada in numerous constitutional disputes, of which this case was one of his most important. Called to the bar the same year as Tilley, though four years his junior, Geoffrion had worked with Tilley, as both ally and opponent, on much landmark litigation over the years. Although their styles contrasted sharply— "one used the broad-sword, the other the rapier"[68]—they exhibited equal mastery of the barrister's art. While Tilley may well have known more law than most lawyers, Geoffrion's legal erudition was also massive, spanning as it did both the civil law and common law traditions. The latter's advocacy was nourished, moreover, by a profound reservoir of general learning, and was leavened by wit.

These qualities found expression in the Attorney General of Canada's long, unorthodox, but compelling factum. Wanting the Court to have a full understanding of the "new economic order" the Aberhart government acknowledged it was attempting to bring about, Geoffrion and his colleagues prepared a 138-page[69] "Brandeis brief"[70] type of factum, discursively written, and containing, in addition to orthodox legal submissions, lengthy quotations from legislative debates, news releases, radio scripts, books and other publications concerning the nature of Social Credit theory in general, and the intentions of the Alberta government in particular.

Defending the Aberhart government on all issues against this intimidating array of challengers was another impressive group of lawyers led by O.M. Biggar, K.C., of Ottawa. Although a highly-regarded counsel, Biggar was probably better known as an advisor to the federal government and an occasional public servant, having filled the posts, among others, of judge advocate general (1918–1919), prime minister's advisor at the 1919 Paris Peace Conference, vice-chairman of the Air Board (1919–1922), and federal negotiator of the 1930 Natural Resources Transfer Agreements with the prairie provinces.[71] Biggar, like Tilley, was a man of measured words, and filed a factum on the *Press Act* issue that was a mere four pages—13 short paragraphs—in length.

But what was he to do about Geoffrion's massive brief? Because all factums were filed simultaneously—a practice that would rarely occur today—Biggar had not had a chance to respond to Geoffrion in his own factum. He decided to attack the "irrelevance" of much of the material contained in the federal factum to the narrow legal issues before the Court, and made a preliminary motion to strike out 52 pages of it.[72] Geoffrion responded that in order to appreciate the significance of the legislation they were asked to rule upon it was necessary for the judges to understand the meaning of the terms and concepts it contained. Despite some reservations as to its usefulness, the Court declined to strike most of the impugned material, and although it took time to consider the question again during Geoffrion's main argument on the economic issues, in the end he was allowed to proceed.[73]

In 1938, the Supreme Court of Canada consisted of seven judges. Due to the fact that Justice Rinfret was in Florida recuperating from an illness, only six sat on this occasion. Chief Justice Sir Lyman Poore Duff had Olympian stature among Commonwealth jurists, in spite of one or two personal foibles. He had been a member of this Court for almost 32 years, six as chief justice, and was destined to serve for six more.[74] His colleagues were Justices Cannon, Davis, Crocket, Kerwin, and Hudson—the latter, from Manitoba, being the sole prairie representative. Since the chief justice did not exercise his option to complete the panel by adding an *ad hoc* judge from another court, some thought that a majority had already made up its mind.

The Reference concerning disallowance and reservation was argued first. Biggar, leading for the Province, must have known it would be an uphill battle. The federal powers of reservation and disallowance had been exercised many times, and had never before been challenged. Biggar was equal to the task, however, and presented an argument that Chief Justice Duff labelled "novel," observing that "everything that could be said for it with any degree of plausibility was lucidly put before us by Mr. Biggar."[75]

Section 90 is not a model of legislative clarity,[76] and the elasticity of its language left room for Biggar's submission that, in light of the autonomous nature of provincial Legislatures, s. 90 should be construed to mean that any disallowance of provincial legislation must, as in the case of federal legislation, be exercised by the British Crown directly rather than by the Governor-General; and that reservation of provincial legislation must be performed by the Governor-General for the signification of the King's pleasure.

The Court was unanimous in rejecting this submission, holding that the wording of s. 90 is sufficiently clear to establish that the governor-general is empowered to disallow and deal with reservations of provincial legislation. It also refused to accept Alberta's alternative arguments that disuse of those powers for the past 13 years, and Britain's implied promise to bring them to an end, somehow precluded the federal government's use of them on this occasion. Until formally amended, s. 90 carried the same meaning it had when enacted in 1867.[77]

Justice Cannon was especially blunt in rejecting the provincial autonomy subtext of Biggar's arguments:

An additional reason for the preservation of this power of disallowance of provincial statutes is its necessity, more than ever evident, in order to safeguard the unity of the nation. It may become essential, for the proper working of the constitution, to use in practice the principle of an absolute central control which seems to have been considered an essential part of the scheme of Confederation; this control is found in the Lieutenant-governor's power of reservation and the Governor-general in Council's power of disallowance.[78]

Cannon's invocation of constitutional "necessity" anticipated by 47 years the Supreme Court of Canada's first plenary reliance on that principle in the *Manitoba Language Reference*,[79] and his assertion of a "more than ever evident" need for "an absolute central control" in this case contrasts startlingly with the unwavering provincialist stance he had exhibited only two years previously in the "Bennett New Deal" References.[80] What can explain his radical change of approach in the Alberta case? Was he prescient enough to sense the surge of centralist thought, political and judicial, that would soon swing the constitutional pendulum in the direction of increased federal authority? Or did he simply consider the Aberhart phenomenon too dangerous to tolerate? We will probably never know; Justice Cannon died soon after the Alberta References were decided.[81]

When the Court's attention turned to the economic issues—the constitutional validity of the *Credit of Alberta Regulation Act*, and the *Bank Taxation*

Act—the onus of persuasion shifted from Mr. Biggar's shoulders to those of Canada's lead counsel, Aimé Geoffrion. After beating back the bulk of a renewed assault by Biggar on the politico-economic material contained in Canada's factum (he was denied only the right to refer to Aberhart's radio broadcasts),[82] Geoffrion first explained to the Court, with frequent references to that illustrative material, why the basic social credit scheme invaded the realms of banking and currency regulation, over which the Constitution bestowed exclusive jurisdiction on the Parliament of Canada.[83]

Because the legislation that created the basic structure of Alberta Social Credit was not before the Court, he outlined it and related policies and practices as a backdrop against which to examine the reserved *Credit of Alberta Regulation Act*. "The scheme of which [that Act] forms a part," Geoffrion contended, "[does] everything possible to make 'Alberta credit' the currency of the province, short of declaring it legal tender. It [has been] made a substitute for money in transactions within the province."[84] According to the newspaper report from which the foregoing quotation was drawn, he claimed that the Alberta Credit Houses were designed to "perform functions similar to banks," and that there were "difficulties placed in the way of those who refused to accept Alberta Credit," and "money and advantages conferred on those who did."[85]

Geoffrion's attack on the constitutionality of the *Bank Taxation Act* took less time to present, but was telling. While acknowledging that provinces had the right, under s. 92(2) of the Constitution, to impose "direct taxation within the province in order to the raising of a revenue," he submitted that this measure, which levied an annual tax of 0.05 per cent on the paid-up capital of banks doing business in Alberta, and 1 per cent on their reserve funds and undivided profits, was neither "direct" nor "within the province," and was not even a "tax" aimed at "raising a revenue." His final argument was the most powerful. Because the levy would amount to an unbearable burden on Alberta banks of some $2,000,000 annually, he submitted that "It [is] not a true tax for the raising of revenue. Its aim [is] to coerce the banks into submitting to provincial government control."[86] Besides, he argued, even if the tax bill were not invalid on its own, it would be so as an integral part of the overall scheme to establish an unconstitutional monetary scheme in Alberta.[87]

Biggar's reply to all these challenges began by insisting that the Court should restrict itself to questions of law and that it should concern itself with only the statutes referred to in the Reference, not with the entire social credit panoply.[88] Neither that plea nor his replies to his opponents' points about the two individual economic bills persuaded the Court. When the Supreme

·Court's unanimous decision was pronounced less than two months later, Chief Justice Duff's lengthy leading reasons for judgment opened with the statement that although "it is no part of our duty...to consider the wisdom of these measures":

> The three Bills referred to us are part of a general scheme of legisla-
> tion and in order ascertain the object and effect of them it is proper
> to look at the history of the legislation passed in furtherance of the
> general design.[89]

There followed eight pages of close and lucid analysis of what Duff called "the central measure...*The Alberta Social Credit Act*,"[90] that Biggar had tried so hard to persuade the Court was "irrelevant," and a further eight pages examin-ing the constitutional validity of that measure, before the chief justice finally turned to consider the bills actually submitted to the Court in the References. "In order to test the validity of the legislation," he said, "we must, we think, envisage the plan in practice as the statute contemplates it."[91]

His analysis appears to have been as fair as it was thorough. Some of his remarks seemed, in fact, mildly sympathetic to the aims of the scheme, and even to hint that, with wide public acceptance, it might work.[92] However, having found that "the substitution generally in internal commerce of Alberta credit for bank credit and legal tender as the circulating medium is of the very essence of the plan,"[93] he concluded that the overall scheme was clearly beyond the constitutional reach of the provincial Legislature because it involved three areas of exclusive federal competence: "currency," "banking," and "trade and commerce."[94]

Turning then to the specific economic statutes that were the subject of the References, the chief justice found that, in addition to the invalidity with which they were infected by the unconstitutionality of the general scheme of which they were a part, they were also *ultra vires* for reasons of their own. *The Credit of Alberta Regulation Act* was beyond provincial competence, he held, because it related in substance to the federal fields of "banking" and "trade and commerce."[95] With respect to *The Bank Taxation Act*, he agreed with the chal-lengers that the Act was not "taxation...in order to the raising of a revenue":

> [I]t requires no demonstration to show that such a rate of taxation must
> be prohibitive in fact and must be known to the Alberta Legislature to
> be prohibitive. It is our duty as judges, to take judicial notice of facts

which are known to intelligent persons generally; and any suggestion that the profits of banking as carried on in Canada could be such as to enable banks to pay taxes to the provinces of such magnitude...would be incontinently rejected by anybody possessing the most rudimentary acquaintance with affairs.[96]

It is not competent to the provinces of Canada, by the exercise of their power of taxation, to force banks which are carrying on business under the authority of the *Bank Act* to discontinue business; and taxation by one province on a scale which, in a practical business sense, is manifestly prohibitive is not a valid exercise of provincial legislative authority.... Such legislation, though in the form of a taxing statute, is "directed to" the frustration of the system of banking established by the *Bank Act*, and to the controlling of banks in the conduct of their business.[97]

Justice Davis shared Chief Justice Duff's reasons, and although Justices Cannon, Kerwin (for himself and Justice Crocket) and Hudson wrote separate reasons, they concurred completely in those of the chief justice.

Although the newspaper censorship imposed by the third Alberta bill under review—*The Accurate News and Information Act*, or *Press Act*—elicited much moral outrage, especially from news media,[98] it was the most difficult of the three to attack from a legal perspective. The constitutional and quasi-constitutional guarantees of "freedom of the press" that are now enshrined in the *Canadian Charter of Rights and Freedoms, 1982*, and the *Canadian Bill of Rights, 1960*, did not exist at the time, and it was widely accepted by lawyers that if a particular activity, such as the publication of newspapers, fell within the jurisdictional competence of the enacting legislative body, there were no legal constraints on the extent to which that activity could be regulated or restricted by the appropriate legislative body. Democratic ideals like freedom of expression were thought to be enforceable through the political process alone—not through the courts.

Those who sought to attack the legal validity of the *Press Act* were therefore obliged to argue either that press censorship generally, or this particular exercise of it, was a legislative topic within the exclusive purview of Parliament; or alternatively that some heretofore unrecognized constitutional principle protected freedom of the press in Canada. While it would appear from an examination of the parties' factums and newspaper accounts of oral submissions that the counsel who challenged the validity of the *Press Act* intended only to make arguments of the first type, their rhetoric, adopted and re-phrased by

Chief Justice Duff and Justice Cannon, contained seeds from which sprouted, in later years, a much more radical and portentous constitutional concept.

The most extensive oral assault on the bill came from J.L. Ralston on behalf of Alberta newspapers, though strong presentations to the same effect were also made by W.N. Tilley for the Canadian Press and federal counsel Aimé Geoffrion. Doubtless because they knew the Press Act presented a less obvious target for legal attack than the economic bills, these counsel came up with eight distinct lines of constitutional challenge. Beginning with the assertion that the bill must fall as an integral part of an invalid economic scheme, they also contended that it encroached, on its own, on the federal domains of criminal law, interprovincial undertakings, federally-incorporated companies, trade and commerce, and the appointment of superior court judges; and that commandeering free newspaper space for government statements amounted to confiscation of property, which they submitted could not be taken without compensation.[99]

The most creative line of argument, originally developed in Geoffrion's submissions[100] and elaborated orally by both Geoffrion and Ralston,[101] involved the interplay of Parliament's authority under the introductory words of s. 91 to make laws for the "peace, order and good government" of Canada in matters not within provincial jurisdiction, and the statement in the Preamble of the Constitution that Canada is to have "a Constitution similar in principle to that of the United Kingdom." Canada's factum asserted that the Press Act "deals with a matter, namely freedom of the press, which is, in substance, not local or provincial but is unquestionably a matter of national concern and importance affecting the body politic of the Dominion."[102]

To demonstrate that this was so, the factum referred to the preambular statement about Canada's Constitution being similar to Britain's, inferring from it that the establishment of "democratic institutions" in Canada was "the cardinal object of the British North America Act,"[103] and contending that:

> The policies and activities of any provincial government...are matters of concern to the whole of Canada, to the people not merely of Alberta but of every other province.... If the government for the time being in power in any province has the authority to dictate what the public will learn through the newspapers, the public's ability to judge, influence and, possibly, dismiss that government will be destroyed or at any rate impaired. The Central government, the Central Parliament, and the people of every part of Canada, have also an interest in this matter.[104]

Geoffrion and Ralston expanded orally on this "interconnectedness" theme by pointing out that censorship in one province could deprive that province's citizens of information they needed to participate in national elections and other national matters.[105] Although the argument would not be decisive in the Reference itself, it would turn out to be the most significant legal legacy of the litigation.

Biggar, for Alberta, must have felt blind-sided by all these submissions. His sparse factum on the censorship issue, filed, it will be remembered, simultaneously with those of the challengers, shows that he was completely unprepared for such novel arguments. He did his best to address them in oral submissions, and he seems to have been successful with respect to the bulk of them, to which the Court made no reference in its reasons for judgment. He was unable, however, to deflect three fatal lines of attack, one or more of which persuaded every judge to rule against the *Press Act*.

Common ground for the entire Court was that the *Press Act* was, in Chief Justice Duff's words, "a part of the general scheme of social credit legislation, the basis of which is *The Alberta Social Credit Act*... [And], since that Act is *ultra vires*, the ancillary and dependent legislation must fall with it."[106] To illustrate the close linkage between the *Press Act* and Alberta's substantive economic reforms, the federal factum had pounced upon statements in a Social Credit Board press release which, after referring to "the money barons—and their influenced press," baldly acknowledged that "the control of news and the control of credit are concentric."[107] Justice Cannon underlined that point:

> It seems obvious that this kind of credit cannot succeed unless every one should be induced to believe in it and help it along. The word "credit" comes from the Latin: *credere*, to believe. It is, therefore, essential to control the sources of information of the people of Alberta, in order to keep them immune from any vacillation in their absolute faith in the plan of the government. The Social Credit doctrine must become, for the people of Alberta, a sort of religious dogma of which a free and uncontrolled discussion is not permissible.[108]

Justice Cannon also agreed with the challengers that the *Press Act* was beyond the jurisdiction of the Alberta Legislature because it amounted to "criminal law," a topic that is constitutionally reserved for the Parliament of Canada:

[T]his bill deals with the regulation of the press of Alberta, not from the viewpoint of private wrongs or civil injuries...but from the viewpoint of public wrongs or crimes, i.e., involving a violation of the public rights and duties of the whole community, considered as a community, in its social aggregate capacity.... [T]he Alberta Legislature by this retrograde bill is attempting to revive the old theory of the crime of seditious libel.... It is an attempt by the Legislature to amend the *Criminal Code* in this respect.[109]

Although Justice Cannon was alone in invoking the federal criminal law power in this case, his analysis provided a model in later years for reliance by the Court on the criminal law power to strike down repressive provincial statutes.[110]

The third ground for striking down the *Press Act* which found judicial favour was Canada's argument that the Act intruded into exclusive federal jurisdiction, as a matter of "peace, order and good government" of Canada, to legislate with respect to freedom of the press, at least with respect to federal institutions like Parliament. Three of the six justices—Duff, Davis and Cannon—adopted the argument, and although that was not enough to make it a formal basis for the Courts' decision, it is the principal reason for which history remembers the case. Chief Justice Duff, writing for Justice Davis and supported by Justice Cannon's concurring reasons, expressed the argument with great eloquence:

Under the constitution by *The British North America Act*, legislative power for Canada is vested in one Parliament.... [T]hese provisions manifestly contemplate a House of Commons which is to be, as the name itself implies, a representative body; constituted, that is to say, by members elected by such of the population of the united provinces as may be qualified to vote. The preamble of the statute, moreover, shows plainly enough that the constitution of the Dominion is to be similar in principle to that of the United Kingdom. The statute contemplates a Parliament working under the influence of public opinion and public discussion. There can be no controversy that such institutions derive their efficacy from the free public discussion of affairs, from criticism and answer and counter-criticism, from attack upon policy and administration and defence and counter-attack; from the freest and fullest analysis and examination from every point of view of political proposals. This is signally true in respect of the discharge by Ministers of the Crown of their responsibility to

Parliament, by member of Parliament of their duty to the electors, and by the electors themselves of their responsibilities in the election of their representatives.

The right of public discussion is, of course, subject to legal restrictions; those based upon considerations of decency and public order, and other conceived for the protection of various private and public interests with which, for example, the laws of defamation and sedition are concerned. In a word, freedom of discussion means, to quote the words of Lord Wright in *James v. Commonwealth* ... "freedom governed by law."

Even within its legal limits, it is liable to abuse and grave abuse, and such abuse is constantly exemplified before our eyes; but it is axiomatic that the practice of this right of free public discussion of public affairs, notwithstanding its incidental mischiefs, is the breath of life for parliamentary institutions.

We do not doubt that...the Parliament of Canada possess authority to legislate for the protection of this right. That authority rests upon the principle that the powers requisite for the protection of the constitution itself arise by necessary implication from *The British North America Act* as a whole; and since the subject-matter in relation to which the power is exercised is not exclusively a provincial matter, it is necessarily vested in Parliament.

But this by no means exhausts the matter. Any attempt to abrogate this right of public debate or to suppress the traditional forms of the exercise of the right (in public meeting and through the press) would, in our opinion, be incompetent to the Legislatures of the provinces, or to the Legislature of any one of the provinces, as repugnant to the provisions of *The British North America Act*, by which the Parliament of Canada is established as the legislative organ of the people of Canada...

...Some degree of regulation of newspapers everybody would concede to the provinces. Indeed, there is a very wide field in which the provinces undoubtedly are invested with legislative authority over newspapers; but the limit, in our opinion, is reached when the legislation effects such a curtailment of the exercise of the right of public discussion as substantially to interfere with the working of the parliamentary institutions of Canada as contemplated by the provisions of *The British North America Act* and the statutes of the Dominion of Canada. Such a limitation is necessary, in our opinion, "in order," to adapt the words quoted above from the judgement in *Bank of Toronto v. Lambe*...to afford scope" for the working of such parliamentary institutions.[111]

Chief Justice Duff was well aware that his comments about the *Press Act* were not legally binding, but were just incidental remarks of the type lawyers call *obiter dicta*. He acknowledged that the other grounds upon which he relied were "sufficient for disposing of the question referred to us."[112] Then, after adding, "but we think there some further observations upon the bill which may properly be made," he launched on the foregoing commentary. In a letter written only a week after the Court's decision was released, Duff gave the impression that his purpose in making the comments was extra-legal:

> We thought...that the statement of the principle would be of some value for two reasons: first, it would probably appeal to moderately sensible people as indicating a restraint which provincial Legislatures ought to impose upon themselves; and, second, it might fortify the Dominion in respect of disallowance if any flagrant case arose.[113]

Whatever its author's intention might have been, the "Duff Doctrine" as it was first called, or the "Implied Bill of Rights" principle as it later came to be known, was treated from the first as a radical new legal concept by most lawyers, academics and judges who considered it and commented upon it.

The government of Alberta appealed the Supreme Court of Canada's decisions in both References to the Judicial Committee of the (British) Privy Council, which was at the time the tribunal of last resort for Canada. Alberta's appeal from the *Disallowance and Reservation Reference* ruling was withdrawn before argument, however, when Alberta's British counsel, Cyril Radcliffe, K.C., refused to participate in that part of the appeal and recommended its abandonment on the ground that "an attempt to argue this appeal, which has only political consideration to support it, will have the most undesirable effect upon the arguments and consideration of the Province's appeal in the other case."[114]

After the Supreme Court's ruling in the *Statutes Reference*, the Legislature of Alberta had repealed the *Alberta Social Credit Act*, the invalidity of which, although not included in the *Reference* directly, had been so influential to the Supreme Court's decision about the referred bills. The reason for repealing that Act appears to have been the hope of side-stepping the Supreme Court's first, and unanimous, ground by eliminating the crucial linkage between the referred bills and the overall Social Credit monetary scheme.[115] The manoeuvre backfired. When the hearing before the Judicial Committee opened, the panel asked counsel whether the validity of the *Credit of Alberta Regulation Act* and the *Press Act*, which both depended for their operation on agencies created by the repealed legislation, had not now become a moot issue because of the repeal of that legislation. Although both Biggar for Alberta and Geoffrion for Canada urged the Judicial Committee to deal with all three bills,[116] it declined to do so, ruling that:

> In these circumstances the two bills...cannot now be brought into opera-
> tion, and, since nothing can be done thereunder, the appeal from the
> order of the Supreme Court is one of no practical interest. It is contrary
> to the long-established practice of this Board to entertain appeals which
> have no relation to existing rights..., and their Lordships have, therefore,
> found it necessary to decline to hear arguments of this appeal insofar as
> it relates to...[the *Press Act* and *Credit of Alberta Regulation Act* bills].[117]

This was a serious blow to Alberta's cause, especially in relation to the *Press Act*, which the Supreme Court had nullified on grounds that the legally ortho-dox Judicial Committee might well have rejected.

Only the *Bank Taxation Act* was left to be considered by the Privy Council, which adopted the same approach the Supreme Court of Canada had taken on that issue. The Privy Council observed that "it is strange to find the Province singling out...banks...and not other wealthy corporations, body or persons,"[118] and noted that the proposed tax would increase Alberta's levies on banks from $72,200 to $2,081,925 per annum.[119] It also agreed with Chief Justice Duff that "this gigantic increase in the taxation of banks within the Province would be, and must have been known by the Alberta Legislature to be 'prohibitive'...in a practical business sense"[120] and found that the "legislative history" of the measure showed it to be part of "the attempt to create a new economic era in the Province."[121] The Privy Council concluded:

> [T]here is no escape from the conclusion that, instead of being in any true
> sense taxation in order to the raising of a revenue..., the bill...is merely
> "part of a legislative plan to prevent the operation within the Province
> of those banking institutions which have been called into existence and
> given the necessary powers to conduct their business by...Parliament
> of Canada."[122]

This decision brought an end, for the time being, to Alberta's Social Credit economic experimentation. World War II, which erupted less than a year after the Privy Council's ruling, diverted everyone's attention to national and international events. The war also, incidentally, solved the economic problems that Premier Aberhart's social credit reforms had attempted to target. The Social Credit government of Alberta was not seriously hurt by the defeat, however. It continued to reign for many years thereafter, first under the leadership of Aberhart until his death in 1943, then of his brilliant young protégé, Ernest Manning, and finally of Harry Strom, providing Albertans with good, conservative government until it was displaced by Peter Lougheed's Progressive Conservatives in 1971.

The social credit economic revolution did not quite end with the Privy Council's decision in the *Bank Taxation Act* appeal, however. In 1946, shortly after World War II ended, the Legislature of Alberta enacted a statute called the *Alberta Bill of Rights Act*.[123] Civil liberties were in the air in that immediate post-war era. The atrocities of Nazi Germany and its allies were on everyone's mind, and the new United Nations Organization was generating dreams of a more humane and tolerant future. Discussions that would result in the 1948 promulgation of the *Universal Declaration of Human Rights* were underway. Canadians, conscious of the discriminatory excesses that had been practiced in the name of national security by their own governments, federal and provincial, during the war years, were talking about passing a national Bill of Rights.[124] The new socialist CCF government of Saskatchewan was considering the enactment of a provincial Bill of Rights.[125] Alberta's *Bill of Rights Act* led the way, or tried to.

It was a Bill of Rights with a difference, though the difference may not have been immediately obvious. The *Alberta Bill of Rights Act* opened with a long Preamble referring to the fact that two world wars had been fought to defend freedom and to the duty of Canadians to now "win the peace." It asserted the province's "constitutional responsibility of providing its citizens with an opportunity to realize and enjoy their property and civil rights." There were hints, though, even in the Preamble, that the measure would include a distinctive social credit approach to these matters. The Preamble spoke of "so ordering their internal economy that the freedom and security for which they fought may be experienced in reality by all of our citizens," and its final recital proclaimed that "the control of policy with respect to the issue, use, and withdrawal of credit primarily determines the extent to which the citizens of Alberta may develop and enjoy the use of their resources...."

The substantive portions of the Act were divided into two parts, and although much of Part I was in a form that would soon become familiar in other jurisdictions—declaring the existence of the fundamental freedoms of speech, conscience, religion and so on—it concluded with four sections declaring the right of Albertans to certain economic benefits: either "gainful employment" or "the necessities of life," "educational benefits," "medical benefits," and "a social security pension."[126] The guarantee of such economic benefits was not a goal unique to social credit principles; it was shared by the CCF party, the Liberals, and probably even by the Conservatives at the time. However, it was a feature not found in the declarations of rights that were then under consideration elsewhere.

If Part I was unusual, Part II was dramatically distinctive. It was headed "Constitution and Functions of Board of Credit Commissioners," and it set out mechanisms for establishing a restructured social credit monetary scheme, complete with the issuance of "Alberta Credit Certificates,"[127] licensing of banks,[128] and the regulation of bank deposits.[129] The rationale for connecting these provisions to the rights declared in Part I was presumably that they would create a method of funding the economic rights referred to therein.

The statute stipulated that it would not come into force until it was certified to be constitutionally valid.[130] The Alberta government accordingly referred the Act to the Appellate Division of the Supreme Court of Alberta for an opinion as to its constitutionality. That Court found Part II to be *ultra vires* on the ground that it dealt in substance with the federal "banking" power. It held, however, that Part I fell properly within the province's jurisdiction over "property and civil rights in the province," and was sufficiently "severable" from the invalid Part II to exist on its own.[131] Both sides appealed directly to the Privy Council, employing a procedure that permitted the Supreme Court of Canada to be leapfrogged. Alberta appealed the decision that Part II was invalid; Canada cross-appealed the ruling that the two Parts were severable.

The Privy Council dismissed Alberta's appeal. It had no difficulty agreeing with the Alberta Court that Part II related to "banking":

It cannot be disputed that the object and effect of Part II are to interfere with and control the business carried on by a chartered bank in the Province.... Their Lordships entertain no doubt that such operations are covered by the term "banking" in s. 91.[132]

Finding that the declarations of liberties and rights in Part I were too closely connected to the social credit apparatus contained in Part II to be severed from them, the Privy Council disagreed with the Alberta Court on that issue, and so allowed Canada's cross-appeal. Its reasons for so holding were not as persuasive as they were with respect to Part II. Viscount Simon, who wrote for the Board, made much of the reference in the Preamble's final recital to "the control of policy with respect to...credit": "The final recital will be found to express the effective purpose of the Bill which, when it is read as a whole, seems plainly to be an application of the economic theory of what is called social credit."[133] Viscount Simon's description of the more orthodox rights declared by Part I was dismissive:

> Part I...consists of twelve sections, the first ten of which were all introduced by the words "it is hereby declared." Sections 3 to 8 appear to be mere declarations of common law rights. The language employed might, perhaps, raise questions as to their precise application—for example how does s. 7 apply to the case where a man's property is requisitioned or acquired on compensation terms for a public work or railway? But it is unnecessary to delay over these sections since nobody can suppose that the purpose of the Alberta Legislature in passing this legislation would justify the view that they would intend these sections to stand if the clauses which carried out the main purpose of the Bill had to be regarded as a nullity.[134]

Apart from merely asserting, rather than demonstrating, that it was the sole purpose of Part I as well as of Part II to achieve social credit economic reforms, these remarks reflect the view, common among British and British-oriented lawyers at the time, that declarations of rights were empty exercises on which no legislative body ought to waste its time. That point of view was also evident in some of Viscount Simon's closing words:

> Their Lordships have already indicated that they cannot suppose that sections 3 to 8 in Part I are other than preliminaries to what follows, and while it is true that sections 9 to 12 include a declaration that citizens of Alberta in certain circumstances are entitled to social security pensions, these declarations remain mere aspirations unless Part II operates to provide how it is to be done.... *The whole thing hangs together, and if Part II goes there is nothing left to be added to the statute law of Alberta which would have any effective operation.*[135]

One wonders whether a tribunal more sympathetic to the usefulness of statutory declarations of rights and liberties might have been willing, as the Alberta Appellate Division had been, to leave Part I of the *Alberta Bill of Rights Act* intact. That was not to be, however, and it fell to the Saskatchewan Legislature to pass Canada's first operational Bill of Rights the following year.[136] The federal government of John Diefenbaker followed suit in 1960.[137] Alberta did not successfully enact its own Bill (under the same name as the abortive 1946 Bill) until 1972.[138]

The only lasting governmental legacies of Alberta's social credit experimentation are the institutions now known as Alberta Treasury Branches, into which the original "State Credit Houses" evolved. Functioning collectively as a massive provincial "near bank," and performing most if not all the activities of chartered banks, the ATBs are major components of today's Alberta economy.

The constitutional validity of the ATBs has been questioned from time to time, but has never been conclusively determined. The Supreme Court of Canada was asked to rule on the question in 1969, and two of the nine justices did so, finding that the provincial statute establishing the branches is "banking" legislation beyond the jurisdictional scope of the Province. The majority of the Court held, however, that it did not have to deal with the constitutional question because it was raised by a defaulting ATB borrower who was legally obligated to repay the loan whether or not the legislation was valid.[139] There the constitutional question has lain, unanswered, for the past 36 years.

The "Bible Bill" Court References had major long-term consequences for the Constitution of Canada. These will be discussed in relation to three main areas: erosion of provincial autonomy, protection of civil liberties, and the unwritten Constitution.

The Social Credit References were decided at the end of a long period in which the courts, led by the provincialist orientation of Lord Chancellors Watson and Haldane in the Privy Council, had displayed a strong tendency to favour the provinces in contests between federal and provincial jurisdictional claims. The pendulum swung sharply in the other direction shortly thereafter, introducing several decades of strong central government. It may be asked, therefore, whether the rulings of the Supreme Court of Canada and the Privy Council in the Social Credit References played a significant role in causing that shift.

With one exception it is doubtful that they did. The constitutional tide turned because of forces much greater than any desire to quash Alberta's economic experimentation. The courts' refusal in the "Bennett New Deal" References, not long before, to permit the Parliament of Canada to take effective steps to deal with the country's crippling depression generated a groundswell of public frustration and indignation that was especially strong among the young intellectuals and community activists who would be leading the nation in the next decade. The exigencies of World War II were about to demand great governmental centralization. The left-leaning idealism that blossomed in the War's wake would bring major social welfare initiatives at the national level, requiring muscular government in Ottawa. Canada's large and distinctive military contribution to Allied victory, and the nationalism it bred, would soon make the federally-appointed and increasingly national-minded Supreme Court of Canada our court of final resort.

This is not to say that the extremity of the Aberhart revolution might not have influenced particular judges' perceptions of Canadian federalism. It is difficult to find any other explanation for Justice Cannon's remarkable about-face and centralist outburst, for example.[140] There is, however, little else in the Supreme Court's decision, or in the subsequent Privy Council ruling, to indicate any softening of judicial attitudes toward the federal order of government at that point.

The Supreme Court was certainly lenient in agreeing to consider most of the government of Canada's "Brandeis Brief" type factum, but the reference form of the litigation almost required that. Normal litigation commences with a trial, or at least affidavits, in which the factual background of the dispute is set out and tested, if necessary, by cross-examination. References are different. They are presented directly to appellate courts, often without the benefit of evidence. Since it is very difficult for courts to determine legal questions in a factual vacuum, "it is not uncommon," as Professor Hogg states, "in references...for the 'case,' or the factums...of counsel, to include social-science data, occasionally in affidavit form, but more often in the form of unsworn statements by experts or unsworn extracts from books, articles and reports."[141] The Supreme Court's tolerance of Geoffrion's fact-filled brief is therefore probably not attributable to favouritism, but to the Court's desire to be as fully informed as possible about the questions placed before it.

There was one aspect of the Supreme Court's reasons in the *Alberta Statutes Reference* that would contribute materially to the judicial expansion of federal jurisdiction in the years to come: Justice Cannon's reliance on Parliament's "criminal law" power as an alternative ground for striking down the *Press Act*. That development will be discussed in relation to "civil liberties."

The Supreme Court of Canada's nullification of the *Press Act* attracted far more attention, both from the news media and from legal commentators, than its other Reference rulings. Neither the Court's upholding of the federal disallowance and reservation powers nor its invalidation of the social credit and bank taxation measures came as a surprise to well-informed observers. But its finding that the Constitution could somehow protect freedom of the press by providing a basis for striking down a statute imposing press censorship was both newsworthy and legally noteworthy at a time when Canada possessed no such explicit constitutional protections.

As a legal precedent, the decision lay dormant for several years, though it was often discussed in academic circles. During the 1950s, however, it became the inspiration for a celebrated series of rulings by the now truly "supreme" Supreme Court of Canada, invalidating provincial statutes, chiefly from the Province of Quebec, that were considered to violate citizens' fundamental freedoms.[142] As in the original *Press Act* decision, the Court's formal reason for striking down the laws in question was not that they infringed freedoms, but that they intruded into some sphere of federal constitutional jurisdiction. The period might be described as one of "incidental" judicial protection of civil liberties.

The head of federal jurisdiction that was most often relied on for this purpose was that which Justice Cannon invoked in the *Alberta Statutes Reference*: "criminal law."[143] The first attempt to use "criminal law" for that purpose was not quite successful. In *Saumur v. Quebec*,[144] a Jehovah's Witness was prosecuted for distributing the literature of his faith on the streets of Quebec City, contrary to a city bylaw that prohibited the dissemination of any written material without permission from the Chief of Police. Saumur's counsel argued that because the bylaw interfered with freedom of religion and freedom of speech it was, in accordance with Justice Cannon's *Press Act* reasons, "criminal law," concerning which only the Parliament of Canada could legislate. Four of the nine Supreme Court judges[145] accepted that submission and found the bylaw invalid for that reason. Four others[146] disagreed, however, holding that the bylaw fell squarely within provincial jurisdiction with respect to "property and civil rights in the province,"[147] and voted to uphold it for that reason. The tie was broken by Justice Kerwin, who agreed with the latter group that the bylaw was not about "criminal law," but found it to be invalid for the non-constitutional reason that it offended an existing provincial statute guaranteeing freedom of worship.

The next time the Supreme Court was asked to determine whether a provincial restriction to religious freedom was "criminal" legislation, it reached a different—and unanimous—conclusion. The case was *Henry Birks and Sons v. Montreal*,[148] in which a Montreal retailer took issue with a City bylaw requiring businesses to close on major Roman Catholic holidays. Although there had been just one change in the Court's membership since the *Saumur* case,[149] all nine judges now agreed that the bylaw was beyond provincial jurisdiction because it dealt with criminal law. It was a less radical ruling than the Rand/Kellock/Estey/Locke analysis would have been if adopted by a majority in *Saumur*, because (a) the bylaw in the earlier case involved not just religious expression but all forms of writing; and (b) there was existing jurisprudence to the effect that Sunday observance laws, to which this bylaw was equated, were within the reach of Parliament's criminal law power. Only Justice Rand made express reference to the rulings he and his colleagues had made in the *Saumur* case.

A year and a half later, however, in *Switzman v. Elbling*,[150] the reasoning upon which those *Saumur* rulings was based was adopted by eight of the Supreme Court of Canada's nine members. The *Switzman* decision is often referred to as the *Padlock Law Case* because it struck down a Quebec statute commonly called the "Padlock Law." Enacted in 1937 as the *Communistic Propaganda Act*,[151] the statute made it unlawful to print, publish or distribute any writing "propagating or tending to propagate communism or bolshevism," or using or allowing the use of any house "to propagate communism or bolshevism by any means whatsoever." Upon satisfactory proof that a house had been used for such purposes, the Attorney General could order it to be closed. With only one dissent,[152] the Supreme Court held this statute to be unconstitutional, primarily on the ground that it was "criminal law." Justice Rand held, for example, that:

> freedom of discussion in Canada, as a subject matter of legislation, has a unity of interest and significance extending equally to every part of the Dominion.... This constitutional fact is the political expression of the primary condition of social life, thought, and its communication by language. Liberty is no less vital to a man's mind and spirit than breathing is to his physical existence.... Prohibition of any part of this activity as an evil would be within the scope of criminal law.[153]

While many applauded, in the absence of direct constitutional guarantees, this "incidental" type of judicial protection of civil liberties by means of the criminal law power and other heads of federal jurisdiction, it was far from a satisfactory technique. For one thing, it offered no protection against oppressive *federal* laws. For another, it tended to aggrandize federal powers in a manner unrelated to the functional needs of federalism. Professor Paul Weiler was prominent among those who cogently criticized the process,[154] and such critiques as his may well have contributed to diminishing judicial use of the criminal law power for that purpose by the late 1970s.[155] Another factor may have been judicial awareness that the enactment of an explicit constitutionally-entrenched guarantee of rights was under vigorous consideration in the political arena.

The Duff/Davis/Cannon "implied bill of rights" theorem also received considerable judicial attention during the 1950s, though it never became the primary basis for any court's decision. The development of the concept reached its zenith—and received a radical restatement—in the *Padlock Law Case* discussed above. Justices Rand, Kellock and Abbott all appeared to approve the "implied bill of rights" approach in that case. Justice Rand, speaking for Justice Kellock as well, eloquently re-articulated Chief Justice Duff's thoughts from the *Press Act* case:

> Indicated by the opening words of the preamble in the Act of 1867, reciting the desire of the four Provinces to be united in a federal union with a Constitution "similar in principle to that of the United Kingdom," the political theory which the Act embodies is that of parliamentary government, with all its social implications, and the provisions of the statute elaborate that principle in the institutional apparatus which they create or contemplate.... This means ultimately government by the free public opinion of an open society.
>
> But public opinion, in order to meet such a responsibility, demands the condition of a virtually unobstructed access to and diffusion of ideas. Parliamentary government postulates a capacity in men, acting freely and under self-restraints, to govern themselves; and that advance is best served in the degree achieved of individual liberation from subjective as well as objective shackles.[156]

Justice Rand stopped just short of extending the implications of that reasoning beyond Parliament's authority over criminal law. After observing that any prohibitions on free speech fall within criminal law he continued, tantalizingly but inconclusively:

Bearing in mind that the endowment of parliamentary institutions is one and entire for the Dominion, that Legislatures and Parliament are permanent features of our constitutional structure, and that the body of discussion is indivisible, apart from the incidence of criminal law and civil rights, and incidental effects of legislation in relation to other matters, the degree and nature of its regulation must await future consideration; for the purposes here it is sufficient to say that it is not a matter within the regulation of a Province.[157]

Justice Abbott pulled no punches. Eschewing the criminal law argument, he held the *Padlock Law* to be unconstitutional *solely* on the basis of the implied bill of rights principle, which he quoted at length from Chief Justice Duff's reasons in the *Alberta Statutes Reference*.[158] He then proceeded, by way of *obiter dictum*, to address the question left open by Justice Rand's closing words:

Although it is not necessary, of course, to determine this question for the purposes of the present appeal, the Canadian Constitution being declared to be similar in principle to that of the United Kingdom, I am also of opinion that as our constitutional Act now stands, Parliament itself could not abrogate this right of discussion and debate. The power of Parliament to limit it is, in my view, restricted to such powers as may be exercisable under its exclusive legislative jurisdiction with respect to criminal law and to make laws for the peace, order and good government of the nation.[159]

Here, at last, was recognition that the implied bill of rights concept was not just a basis for the incidental protection of rights from provincial encroachment by means of the federal criminal law power or other heads of federal jurisdiction. Justice Abbott recognized that it was not a federal/provincial division of powers argument at all. It was a much more fundamental notion that postulated a constitutional restriction on the power of *all* Legislatures, *federal and provincial*, to suppress or foul the basic well-springs of Canadian democracy.

The principle is one of interpretation, but it has massive substantive significance. It begins with the fact that the *Constitution Act, 1867* created and continues to mandate parliamentary institutions, both federal and provincial. While Chief Justice Duff mentioned only the federal Parliament, Justice Rand pointed out in the *Padlock Law Case* that provincial Legislatures are equally entrenched: "[T]he endowment of parliamentary institutions is one and entire for the Dominion,...Legislatures and Parliament are permanent features of our constitutional structure."[160]

Asking themselves what *type* of parliamentary institutions the drafters of the Constitution intended Canada to have, Chief Justice Duff and Justices Rand and Abbott concluded, in light of the Preamble's reference to British experience, that they must be interpreted to be *democratic* legislative bodies operating under the influence of free public debate and discussion. Implicit, therefore, in the constitutional imperative of parliamentary apparatus is a guarantee of democratic freedoms.[161]

This reasoning has often been criticized.[162] The use of the Preamble as a basis for adding radically new provisions to the document is sometimes objected to, for instance, on the ground that preambles are not intended to have substantive meaning. But Chief Justice Duff and his disciples never tried to give *substantive* effect to the preamble; they merely used it as an *aid to the interpretation* of the words "Parliament" and "Legislature" in the body of the *Constitution Act*. That is a perfectly orthodox function for preambles to play.[163]

A more serious objection is that the *most* fundamental principle Constitution of the United Kingdom—its *only* legal principle in 1867 in fact—is the notion of parliamentary supremacy, according to which the will of the majority of elected representatives is absolutely unfettered by law. If Canada's Constitution is really modelled on that of the United Kingdom, why have we not inherited that most basic feature of British constitutionalism, which is antithetical to any theory of guaranteed civil liberties?

The answer is that Canada's Constitution cannot possibly resemble that of the United Kingdom *completely*. It can only do so *to the extent* that British constitutional principles are *consistent* with the written constitutional instrument—the *Constitution Act*—that the Parliament of the United Kingdom bestowed on Canada in 1867. The differences between the British and Canadian constitutional models are necessarily great, starting with the elemental distinction between written and unwritten systems. The constitution of a federal state like Canada simply cannot resemble very closely that of a unitary state. A federal state must possess the elaborate judicially-enforceable machinery required to effectuate a division of legislative powers between the central and provincial Legislatures. This necessitates the existence of an express constitutional allocation of federal and provincial jurisdiction that cannot be altered by the ordinary legislative process. Once that exists, the theory of unlimited legislative supremacy has been displaced.

Moreover, Canada's written Constitution contains certain express limitations to the doctrine of legislative supremacy that are altogether unrelated to its federal nature. In addition to sections 91 and 92, which distribute legislative powers between the provincial and federal orders of government, there have been, ever since 1867, provisions that place beyond the reach of any Legislature such questions as separate schools,[164] the need for an annual session of Parliament,[165] the requirement of a federal election at least every five years,[166] and Canada's dual official languages.[167] Legislative supremacy is, therefore, a principle of Canadian constitutionalism only insofar as other requirements of the Constitution permit it to operate. Since the framers of that Constitution overrode the principle with numerous *explicit* constitutional provisions of major significance, it should not be surprising that the courts have found other displacements *implicit* in the meaning of other provisions.

Did the judges who advanced the democratically-steeped definitions of "Parliament" and "Legislature" in the *Press Act* and *Padlock Law* cases really intend to go this far? Did they really mean to postulate an "implied bill of rights"? Whatever Chief Justice Duff and his colleagues might have intended in the former case, I believe it is clear that in the latter one Justice Rand understood the long-range implications of the principle,[168] and Justice Abbott intended it to operate as a "bill of rights." When the Supreme Court's decision in the *Padlock Law* case was released, the writer was in his final year of law studies. Intrigued by Justice Abbott's application and re-interpretation of the Duff theorem, and interested in how it might tie in to a paper I was writing at the time, I wrote to him to confirm my understanding that his conclusions, like those of Chief Justice Duff, resulted from interpretation of the terms "Parliament" and "Legislature." I also asked Justice Abbott how his analysis, if generally accepted, might affect the then current controversy about whether Canada should enact a written Bill of Rights. His response on the latter point left no doubt that he appreciated how significant the principle could be: "I agree with you that the implications of this doctrine are far reaching and if it is correct, as I believe it is, it does go a long way to confute the arguments of those who contend that Canada should have a written Bill of Rights."[169]

That point of view did not prevent passage of the Diefenbaker government's *Canadian Bill of Rights* in 1960. In fact, it is probable that both the Diefenbaker *Bill* and the subsequent political pressure for a fully constitutional written guarantee of rights that culminated in the *Canadian Charter of Rights and Freedoms* in 1982, contributed to a gradual lessening of enthusiasm for the implied bill of rights concept among lawyers and judges.

The principle certainly did not fare well on the next occasion it was argued before the Supreme Court of Canada. *Attorney General of Canada v. Dupond*[170] was a challenge to a bylaw of the City of Montreal that authorized the prohibition of parades and other public gatherings. Relying heavily on the *Birks* and *Padlock Law* decisions, the challenger submitted that the bylaw was *ultra vires* because (a) it constituted criminal law, and (b) it violated the implied bill of rights. Both arguments failed. Justice Beetz, who wrote for the majority of the Court, showed no sympathy, or even patience, for the implied bill of rights:

> I find it exceedingly difficult to deal with a submission couched in such general terms. What is it that distinguishes a right from a freedom and a fundamental freedom from a freedom which is not fundamental? Is there a correlation between freedom of speech and freedom of assembly on the one hand and, on the other, the right, if any, to hold a public meeting on a highway or in a park as opposed to a meeting open to the public on private land? How like or unlike each other are an assembly, a parade, a gathering, a demonstration, a procession? Modern parlance has fostered loose language upon lawyers. As was said by Sir Ivor Jennings, the English at least have no written constitution and so they may divide their law logically.[171]

Among the several reasons Justice Beetz gave for not accepting the argument in this case, the most sweeping, and dispiriting for advocates of the theory, was his opinion that "None of the freedoms referred to is so enshrined in the Constitution as to be above the reach of competent legislation."

The dissenting reasons of Justice Laskin, for himself and Justices Spence and Dickson, while stating that "the bylaw goes much beyond what was invalidated" in the *Birks* and *Padlock* cases,[172] relied on those cases solely for their criminal law rulings, and made no reference to the implied bill of rights.

The implied bill of rights has not been much heard of since the *Dupond* decision. "However," Professor Hogg comments, "like freeway proposals and snakes, the theory does not die easily."[173] Justice Beetz himself had occasion, despite his scathing remarks in *Dupond*, to refer favourably to the principle in a subsequent decision,[174] and it continues to attract sporadic support from other judges. Whether it will ever attract majority approval in some appropriate situation[175] is doubtful, though not impossible. However, even if the implied bill of rights never achieves full acceptance, the interpretational process that led to its conception has already altered Canadian constitutional law fundamentally.

The most significant contribution that the *Alberta Statutes Reference* made to the evolution of Canada's Constitution, in my opinion, was the forthright reliance by Chief Justice Duff and his colleagues on unwritten constitutional values.[176] Although several years would elapse before that approach achieved full respectability, it eventually won unequivocal support from the Supreme Court of Canada.

The Supreme Court unanimously adopted it when, in the 1985 *Manitoba Language Reference*, it relied upon the "unwritten postulate" of "the rule of law" to help it craft a creative method of avoiding the "legal chaos" that it feared would otherwise have followed its ruling that most Manitoba statutes were void for not having been enacted in both English and French, as Manitoba's Constitution required.[177] In 1993, in the *Nova Scotia Speaker's* case,[178] a majority of the Court relied on the Preamble of the Constitution and British historical experience to bestow "inherent privileges" on provincial Legislatures and in the 1997 *Provincial Judges' Reference* Chief Justice Lamer stated on behalf of a majority of the Court that "By implication, the jurisdiction of the provinces over 'courts', as that term is used in s. 92(14)....contains within it an implied limitation that the independence of those courts cannot be undermined."[179]

Any possible doubt about the legitimacy and importance of the unwritten Constitution was laid to rest by the unanimous 1998 decision of the Supreme Court of Canada in the *Quebec Secession Reference*.[180] In the course of determining that Quebec would not be lawfully capable of seceding from Confederation unilaterally, the Court consulted four specific "unwritten organizing principles" of the Constitution—federalism, democracy, the rule of law, and respect for minorities[181]—as well as explaining, more fully than ever before, the significance of looking behind the Constitution's written text:

> Our Constitution is primarily a written one, the product of 131 years of evolution. Behind the written word is an historical lineage stretching back though the ages, which aids in the consideration of the underlying constitutional principles. These principles inform and sustain the constitutional text: they are the vital unstated assumptions upon which the text is based....
>
> Although these underlying principles are not explicitly made part of the Constitution by any written provision, other than in some respects by the oblique reference in the preamble to the *Constitution Act, 1867*, it

would be impossible to conceive of our constitutional structure without them. The principles dictate major elements of the architecture of the Constitution itself and are, as such, its lifeblood.[182]

It might not seem, at first blush, an earth-shaking discovery that the Canadian Constitution contains unwritten components, given that in 1867 the *entire* Constitution of the United Kingdom, whose former colony we are, was unwritten. There is a colossal difference, however, between the unwritten British Constitution and the unwritten portions of ours. In the United Kingdom, most unwritten principles have only political significance; they are not enforceable by the courts.[183] In Canada, by contrast, the unwritten constitutional norms uncovered by Chief Justice Duff and those who have since followed his lead are directly *enforceable by the courts*. As the Supreme Court pointed out in the *Secession Reference*:

> Underlying constitutional principles may in certain circumstances give rise to *substantive* legal obligations.... The principles are not merely descriptive, but are also invested with a powerful normative force, and are *binding* upon both courts and governments.[184]

William Aberhart deserves to be remembered as more than a colourful long-ago character who fashioned an outlandish and unsuccessful economic experiment out of the desperation of Albertans and the half-baked ideas of an amateur British economist. In addition to the concrete legacy of Alberta Treasury Branches, a strong case can be made for the proposition that Aberhart's political evangelism and stubborn determination had a powerful formative influence on the distinctive collective character of Albertans that even today causes them to suspect the blandishments of eastern Canada, and to insist on doing things their own way.

Although Aberhart's legacy to Canadian constitutional law was unwitting and unwanted on his part, it was nevertheless important. The Courts' rejection of his challenge to the federal disallowance and reservation powers may not have been very significant in view of Canada's virtual abandonment of those powers in future years. The centralist sentiments expressed by Justice Cannon in that Reference, and his use of the federal "criminal law" power in the *Statutes Reference* were, however, early harbingers of the sharp swing in the direction of federal authority that the Court was soon to take. The "implied bill of rights" principle might never have been invented without the provocation of Aberhart's repressive *Press Act*, and without that initiative, it is hard to know whether or how Canadian courts would have discovered Canada's judicially enforceable "unwritten Constitution."

If Premier Aberhart were able, from his seat in eternity, to read these words over the writer's shoulder, he would, of course, be shaking his head. He would not want to be given credit for causing the courts to develop legal principles by which they could strike down measures like those he laboured so hard to fashion. That realization does not, however, lessen my desire to give Mr. Aberhart back-handed credit for stimulating what I consider to have been positive and important developments in the evolution of the Canadian Constitution. To borrow, and supplement, Emerson's words: "He builded better than he knew—or desired."

Notes

1. Barry Broadfoot, *Ten Lost Years, 1929–1939: Memories of Canadians Who Survived the Depression* (Toronto: Doubleday Canada, 1973). The examples given in this paragraph are all drawn from that source.

2. See W.H. McConnell, "The Judicial Review of Prime Minister Bennett's New Deal," *Osgoode Hall Law Journal* 6 (1968): 39.

3. See John A. Irving, *The Social Credit Movement in Alberta* (Toronto: University of Toronto Press, 1959), 95–96; David R. Elliott and Iris Miller, *Bible Bill: A Biography of William Aberhart* (Edmonton: Reidmore Books, 1987), 127–28; T.C. Byrne, *Alberta's Revolutionary Leaders* (Calgary: Detselig, 1991). The press made much of the McPherson and Brownlee stories. See for example *Calgary Herald*, May 9, 1933, p. 1; May 10, 1933, p. 2; Sept. 22, 1933, p. 1; Sept. 23, 1933, p. 17; Nov. 14, 1933, p. 2; April 27, 1934, p. 1.

4. See generally Elliott and Miller, *Bible Bill*.

5. Elliott and Miller, *Bible Bill*, 104.

6. Elliott and Miller, *Bible Bill*, 106–07. Although the writings of Douglas himself, a professional engineer and amateur economist, were not easy to follow, and had failed to capture Aberhart's interest in the past, the description of Douglas's ideas in the book he read on this occasion—M.D. Colbourne, *Unemployment or War* (New York: Coward-McCann, 1928)—was a simplified version that he found thoroughly persuasive. Either that simplification or Aberhart's misunderstanding of it would later lead to difficulties with Douglas himself.

7. Elliott and Miller, *Bible Bill*, 108.

8. For an excellent explanation and critique, see C.B. MacPherson, *Democracy in Alberta: Social Credit and the Party System*, 2nd ed. (Toronto: University of Toronto Press, 1962), 107ff, see also Irving, *The Social Credit Movement*, 5ff; and Byrne, *Alberta's Revolutionary Leaders*, 90–91.

9. Byrne writes: "[H]e appeared incapable of analysis. He could comprehend ideas, arrange them in order, and translate them into graphic design. He seemed, however unable or unwilling to test their validity, examine their implications, or determine their relationships within broader patterns of thought. He did not analyze ideas; he accepted or rejected them according to patterns of belief that had become firmly fixed in his youth," (*Alberta's Revolutionary Leaders*, 81). Douglas complained that Aberhart misunderstood his ideas in some respects. It is difficult, however, to disagree with Byrne's assessment that "Despite the criticism of purists in Douglas' Social Credit theory, Aberhart appears to have grasped its quintessence" (*Alberta's Revolutionary Leaders*, 98).

10. Byrne, *Alberta's Revolutionary Leaders*, 91–95.

11. Byrne, *Alberta's Revolutionary Leaders*, 101.

12. Byrne, *Alberta's Revolutionary Leaders*, 96–104. See also Elliott and Miller, *Bible Bill*, 129–30 and 134–35.

13. Byrne, *Alberta's Revolutionary Leaders*, 114–15, quoting from a letter from Aberhart to his niece, July 31, 1933.

14. Byrne, *Alberta's Revolutionary Leaders*, 165, quoting from unpublished memoirs of Aberhart's friend H.B. Hill.

15. Byrne, *Alberta's Revolutionary Leaders*, 183, quoting from a radio broadcast April 7, 1935.

16. Byrne, *Alberta's Revolutionary Leaders*, 191.

17. Byrne, *Alberta's Revolutionary Leaders*, 99; Elliott and Miller, *Bible Bill*, 191. Foremost among these villains were the bankers, who were said to have absconded with much of the "B" portion of Social Credit's A+B equation. While Douglas referred to them as members of an international Jewish banking conspiracy, Aberhart's own analysis was free from anti-Semitic overtones.

18. Elliott and Miller, *Bible Bill*, 167.

19. Byrne, *Alberta's Revolutionary Leaders*, 188, quoting from W. Aberhart, *Social Credit Manual: Social Credit as Applied to Alberta* (n.p.: n.d., 1932), 19—the so-called "Yellow Manual." He cautioned, though, that the amounts listed were "illustrative," and that the payments would be in "credit," rather than money.

20. Broadfoot, *Ten Lost Years*, 312–13.

21. See Robert Ascah, *Politics and Public Debt: The Dominion, the Banks and Alberta's Social Credit* (Edmonton: University of Alberta Press, 1999).

22. The final measure was hastily repealed in 1937 (S.A. 1937, 3rd Sess., c. 7) when voters in Aberhart's own constituency began to invoke the procedure to unseat the premier himself.

23. *Social Credit Measures Act*, S.A. 1936, c. 5.

24. W. Aberhart, *Social Credit Manual*, 62.

25. Douglas, who possessed a rather prickly personality, felt from an early stage that Aberhart was distorting his theories. See Elliott and Miller, *Bible Bill*, 133–45. Aberhart's protracted efforts to have Douglas come to Alberta to assist with the project on reasonable terms, which Elliott and Miller describe at length (204–28), ended after a letter of refusal from Douglas, dated Mar. 24, 1936, which the latter eventually published in his account of the "experiment." See C.H. Douglas, *The Alberta Experiment: An Interim Survey* (London: Eyre and Spottiswoode, 1937), 197–98.

26. W. Aberhart, *The B.N.A. Act and Social Credit* (Calgary: Prophetic Bible Institute, 1934).

27. The *Edmonton Journal* reported on August 8, 1936, p. 1, that the government of Canada had declined to interfere because it considered scrip to be an internal provincial matter. Robert Ascah refers, however, to the Bank of Canada's quiet but effective background opposition by advising chartered banks not to accept scrip (*Politics and Public Debt*, 66).

28. *Edmonton Journal*, Aug. 5, 1936, p. 1.; Elliott and Miller, *Bible Bill*, 249.

29. *Edmonton Journal*, Aug. 3, 1936, p. 4; *Albertan*, July 31, 1936.

30. A copy of the "Alberta Citizens Registration Covenant" is reproduced in Elliott and Miller, *Bible Bill*, 242.

31. Including the establishment of "State Credit Houses," which would end up being one of the Aberhart government's few lasting legacies, in the form of today's Alberta Treasury Branches. See S.A. 1936 (2nd sess.), c. 1. See below, text associated with n. 139.

32. *Calgary Herald*, Mar. 1, 1937, p. 1.

33. Elliott and Miller, *Bible Bill*, 253. Hugill's constitutional concerns were underlined by judicial rulings in February (trial) and June (appeal) that the *Alberta Debt Reduction and Settlement of Debts Act*, passed at the last session of the Legislature to reduce or eliminate interest on debts the government did not declare to be exempt from the legislation, was unconstitutional. See *Credit Foncier Franco-Canadian v. Ross et al.*, [1937] 3 D.L.R. 365 (Alta. S.C.A.D.). These decisions would eventually be upheld by the Judicial Committee of the U.K. Privy Council, then the ultimate court of appeal for Canada. See *Lethbridge Northern Irrigation District v. I.O.O.F.*, [1940] A.C. 513 (P.C.). See also J.R. Mallory, *Social Credit and the Federal Power* (Toronto: Univeristy of Toronto Press, 1954), chap. 6. This was not a uniquely social credit measure; several provinces, of varying political persuasions, had enacted similar legislation in an attempt to alleviate the financial hardships of the depression. Its inability to pass constitutional muster buttressed the view of Hugill and others that more radical social credit devices were constitutionally doomed.

34. Elliott and Miller, *Bible Bill*, 257–60.

35. S.A. 1937, c. 10.

36. Elliott and Miller, *Bible Bill*, 261–64.

37. S.A. 1937 (2nd sess.), c. 1, 2, and 5.

38. Hugill's account of the incident was later given in an address to the Legislature, February 28, 1939, published in a pamphlet: John W. Hugill, *Constitutional Principle #1, In Re Office of His Majesty's Attorney General. Speech Delivered in the Legislative Assembly at Edmonton, Alberta, on Tuesday February 28th, 1939* (Calgary: The Author, 1939).

39. Government of Canada, P.C. 1985 & 1986, Aug. 17, 1937.

40. See: G.V. La Forest, *Disallowance and Reservation of Provincial Legislation* (Canada: Department of Justice, 1955); Eugene Forsey, "Canada and Alberta: The Revival of Dominion Control Over the Provinces," *Politica* 4 (1939): 95, reprinted in Eugene Forsey, *Freedom and Order: Collected Essays* (Toronto: McClelland and Stewart, 1974), 177; John Saywell, "Reservation Revisited: Alberta 1937," *Canadian Journal of Economics and Political Science* 27, no. 3 (1961): 367–72.

41. See Paul Romney, *Mr. Attorney* (Toronto: Osgoode, 1986), 248.

42. La Forest, note 41, 83ff.

43. Peter W. Hogg, *Constitutional Law of Canada*, looseleaf, para. 3.1, note 4.

44. La Forest, *Disallowance and Reservation*, 99–100.

45. Elliott and Miller, *Bible Bill*, 269.

46. Elliott and Miller, *Bible Bill*, 269, emphasis in original.

47. La Forest, *Disallowance and Reservation*, 16.

48. Lieutenant-Governor Bowen asked that in view of Aberhart's lack of legal expertise, proposed legislation should be vetted by a lawyer, but Aberhart refused. See Bowen to Aberhart, Oct. 1, 1937 and Aberhart to Bowen, Oct. 1, 1937; Provincial Archives of Alberta, Premiers' Papers, #774.

49. Provincial Archives of Alberta, Premiers' Papers, Bill #8.

50. Elliot and Miller, *Bible Bill*, 99.

51. The phrase "money barons" comes from a Social Credit press release quoted in the factum of the Attorney General of Canada, p. 65. It was also used by E.C. Manning in dialogue with Aberhart in a radio broadcast of the Edmonton Prophetic Bible Conference, Feb. 11, 1940, tape recording in possession of the writer.

52. S.A. 1937 (3rd sess.), Bill. #1.

53. Stewart Cameron, *Calgary Herald*, June 26, 1937.

54. S.A. 1937 (3rd sess.), Bill. #9.

55. S.A. 1937 (3rd sess.), Bill. #9, s. 3(1).

56. S.A. 1937 (3rd sess.), Bill. #9, s. 4.

57. S.A. 1937 (3rd sess.), Bill. #9, s. 7.

58. S.A. 1937 (3rd sess.), Bill. #9, s. 6.

59. Bowen to Lapointe, Oct. 9, 1937, Provincial Archives of Alberta, Bowen Papers.

60. La Forest, *Disallowance and Reservation*, 52.

61. Government of Canada, P.C. 2715/37 (disallowance), supplemented by P.C. 2802/37 (reservation); P.C. 2749/37 (Alberta Bills). The linkage of the issues was noted in paragraph 6 of the latter document.

62. David R. Williams, *Just Lawyers: Seven Portraits* (Toronto: Osgoode, 1995), 57. Tilley was 70 when he appeared before the Supreme Court of Canada in this case. In representing the banks on the economic aspects of the *Reference*, Tilley was assisted by three lawyers: R.C. McMichael, K.C. of Montreal, W.F. Chipman, K.C., and A.W. Rogers, K.C. In representing the Canadian Press, his associate counsel was H.P. Duchemin, K.C. of Sydney, Nova Scotia. A.J. Thompson of Toronto also contributed to the Canadian Press factum, but seems not to have been gowned.

63. The factums and Case on Appeal, which are still in the possession of the Supreme Court of Canada, were made available to the writer through the courtesy of the Honourable Mr. Justice John Major.

64. *The Canadian Encyclopedia* (Edmonton: Hurtig, 1985), 1546. Ralston was 57 at the time of the *Press Act* argument. Assisting him were S.W. Field, K.C. and R. de W. MacKay, K.C., of the Alberta bar. S.B. Woods, also of the Alberta bar, was first signatory of the factum (Ralston was last), but does not appear to have been present in court.

65. See Williams, *Just Lawyers*, 90ff. With Mr. Geoffrion were J. Boyd McBride K.C., an Alberta lawyer, and C.P. Plaxton, K.C., of the federal Department of Justice in Ottawa.

66. Williams, *Just Lawyers*, 59.

67. Williams, *Just Lawyers*, 125.

68. Williams, *Just Lawyers*, 102.

69. Eighty-two pages of text, plus a 56-page Appendix. Rule 42(4) of the current *Rules of the Supreme Court of Canada* places a 40-page limit on factums without special dispensation.

70. The Brandeis brief is a "Form of appellate brief in which economic and social surveys and studies are included along with legal principles and citations and which takes its name from Louis D. Brandeis, former Associate Justice of Supreme Court, who used such briefs while practising law": *Black's Law Dictionary*, 5th ed, s.v. "Brandeis brief." In 1938 Brandeis briefs were still uncommon in the United States, and rare in Canada.

71. *The Canadian Encyclopedia* (Edmonton: Hurtig, 1985), 171. Biggar was 62. His co-counsel were W.S. Gray, K.C. and J.J. Frawley, K.C., both of the provincial Attorney General's Department, Edmonton.

72. *Edmonton Journal*, January 11, 1938, p. 1. A story in the previous day's *Journal* had claimed that 66 pages were under attack.

73. *Edmonton Journal*, January 11, 1938, p. 1; January 12, 1938, p. 3, p. 10.

74. See David R. Williams, *Duff: A Life in the Law* (Vancouver: U.B.C. Press, 1984). Duff's role in this case is described at pp. 193–99. He was 73 at the time.

75. *Reference Re Powers of Disallowance and Reservation* [1938] S.C.R. 71 (Quicklaw version, p. 1).

76. La Forest, *Disallowance and Reservation*, 14, says: "The economy in words resulting from the drafting device adopted in section 90 was not achieved without some sacrifice of clarity, at least so far as the power of disallowance is concerned...."

77. *Reference Re Powers of Disallowance and Reservation* [1938] S.C.R. 71, pp. 3–6, 8, 15.

78. *Reference Re Powers of Disallowance and Reservation* [1938] S.C.R. 71, p. 9.

79. (1985) 19 D.L.R. (4th) 1, pp. 29–37.

80. *Reference Re Unemployment Insurance*, [1936] S.C.R. 427; *Reference Re Natural Products Marketing Act*, [1936] S.C.R. 398; *Reference Re Dominion Trade and Industry Commission Act*, [1936] S.C.R. 379.

82. See Wallace, *Dictionary of Canadian Biography*, Vol. 1, pp. 97–98.

82. *Edmonton Journal*, January 11, 1938, p. 1; January 12, 1938, p. 3, p. 10.

83. Section 14 ("currency and coinage"); 15 ("banking, incorporation of banks, and the issue of paper money"); 16 ("savings banks"); 18 ("bills of exchange and promissory notes"); 19 ("interest"); and 20 ("legal tender").

84. *Edomonton Journal* January 12, 1939, p. 2, tense altered.

85. *Edomonton Journal* January 12, 1939, p. 2.

86. *Edmonton Journal* January 12, 1939, p. 2, tense altered. W.N. Tilley, for the banks, made the same point even more bluntly: "It is not a tax at all. It is a discrimination against the banks for some ulterior purpose," *Edmonton Journal*, January 13, 1938, p. 2.

87. *Edmonton Journal*, January 12, 1938, p. 2.

88. *Edmonton Journal*, January 14, 1938, p. 9.

89. *Reference Re Alberta Statutes*, [1938] S.C.R. 100, p. 106.

90. *Reference Re Alberta Statutes*, [1938] S.C.R. 100, p. 107.

91. *Reference Re Alberta Statutes*, [1938] S.C.R. 100, p. 116.

92. *Reference Re Alberta Statutes*, [1938] S.C.R. 100, pp. 115–16.

93. *Reference Re Alberta Statutes*, [1938] S.C.R. 100, p. 113.

94. *Reference Re Alberta Statutes*, [1938] S.C.R. 100, p. 116.

95. *Reference Re Alberta Statutes*, [1938] S.C.R. 100, p. 123.

96. *Reference Re Alberta Statutes*, [1938] S.C.R. 100, pp. 128–29.

97. *Reference Re Alberta Statutes*, [1938] S.C.R. 100, pp. 131–32.

98. For example, on the first day of argument before the Supreme Court of Canada, newspapers across Canada carried a prominent story from Washington, D.C., which the *Edmonton Journal* (January 11, 1938, p. 2) headlined "PRESS FREEDOM FIGHT LAUDED: U.S. Leaders Back Stand Taken by Publishers in Alberta." The first paragraph read as follows: "Leaders on Capitol hill, official Washington in the world of journalism and in the field of education as well as Canadian-American bigwigs joined today in expressing their enthusiastic and wholehearted support of the press freedom fight being waged by Alberta newspapers against the Alberta press bill which would violate the centuries-old right of freedom of the press," and the article went on to quote statements by many prominent Americans, including the near-legendary Senator William Borah, in strong opposition to the Alberta's *Press Act*.

99. To the latter argument, made by Mr. Tilley, Chief Justice Duff commented, perhaps wistfully: "I wish I could agree with you, but I cannot see that," *Edmonton Journal*, January 13, 1938, p. 3.

100. Factum of Attorney General of Canada, pp. 73–78; *Edmonton Journal*, January 13, 1938, p. 13.

101. *Edmonton Journal*, January 14, 1938, p. 15.

102. Factum of Attorney General of Canada, p. 73.

103. Factum of Attorney General of Canada, pp. 75–76.

104. Factum of Attorney General of Canada, p. 75.

105. *Edmonton Journal*, January 13, 1938, p. 15; January 14, 1938, p. 19.

106. *Reference Re Alberta Statutes*, [1938] S.C.R. 100, p. 132.

107. Factum of Attorney General of Canada, p. 65.

108. *Reference Re Alberta Statutes*, [1938] S.C.R. 100, p. 144.

109. *Reference Re Alberta Statutes*, [1938] S.C.R. 100, pp. 144–45.

110. See below, text associated with n. 143ff.

111. *Reference Re Alberta Statutes*, [1938] S.C.R. 100, pp. 132–35. Chief Justice Duff also mentioned, at p. 135, that s. 129 of the Constitution calls for a continuation of laws in force at the moment of Confederation subject only to alteration by either federal or provincial legislation, as appropriate. He then stated that "The law by which the right of public discussion is protected existed" at the time of Confederation and "the Legislature of Alberta has not the capacity...to alter that law by legislation obnoxious to the principle...."

112. *Reference Re Alberta Statutes*, [1938] S.C.R. 100, p. 132.

113. Public Archives of Canada, Duff Papers, Q-R, Duff to Rowell, March 11, 1938. Duff also pointed out that his decision did not go so far as to find that the *Press Act* actually violated freedom of the press sufficiently to "interfere with the working of the parliamentary institutions of Canada," as he put it in his reasons: "Davis and I...express no opinion on the point whether the Alberta bill offends against this principle. The application of the principle in particular cases, if they arise, might be a very difficult and delicate job."

114. Radcliffe Memorandum, June 3, 1938, quoted from files of the Attorney General of Alberta by E. Tollefson in "Freedom of the Press," in O.E. Lang, ed., *Contemporary Problems of Public Law in Canada* (Toronto: University of Toronto Press, 1968), 63–64.

115. Lang, ed., *Contemporary Problems of Public Law*, 64.

116. Lang, ed., *Contemporary Problems of Public Law*, 64.

117. *Attorney General for Alberta v. Attorney General for Canada* [1939] A.C. 117, at p. 128 (P.C.).

118. *Attorney General for Alberta v. Attorney General for Canada* [1939] A.C. 117, p. 131.

119. *Attorney General for Alberta v. Attorney General for Canada* [1939] A.C. 117, p. 131.

120. *Attorney General for Alberta v. Attorney General for Canada* [1939] A.C. 117, p. 132.

121. *Attorney General for Alberta v. Attorney General for Canada* [1939] A.C. 117, p. 132.

122. *Attorney General for Alberta v. Attorney General for Canada* [1939] A.C. 117, p. 133.

123. S.A. 1946, c. 11.

124. See W.S. Tarnopolsky, *The Canadian Bill of Rights*, 2nd ed. (Toronto: Carleton Library, 1975), 3–7 and 11–12.

125. It did so in 1947. See *Saskatchewan Bill of Rights Act*, S.S. 1947, c. 35.

126. S.A. 1946, c. 11, s. 9–12.

127. S.A. 1946, c. 11, s. 15(a).

128. S.A. 1946, c. 11, s. 17(1). The term used was "credit institutions," but the definition of that term in s. 15(f) left little doubt that banks were included.

129. S.A. 1946, c. 11, s. 20(2); s. 24.

130. S.A. 1946, c. 11, s. 28.

131. *Reference Re Alberta Bill of Rights Act* [1946] 3 W.W.R. 772 (Alta. S.C., App. D.).

132. *Attorney General for Alberta v. Attorney General for Canada* [1947] A.C. 503, at p. 516 (P.C.).

133. *Attorney General for Alberta v. Attorney General for Canada* [1947] A.C. 503, p. 511.

134. *Attorney General for Alberta v. Attorney General for Canada* [1947] A.C. 503, p. 512.

135. *Attorney General for Alberta v. Attorney General for Canada* [1947] A.C. 503, p. 520, emphasis added.

136. S.S. 1946, c. 11, s. 9–12.

137. *The Canadian Bill of Rights, 1960*, S.C. 1960, c. 44.

138. Currently R.S.A., c. A-14.

139. *Breckenridge Speedway Ltd. v. Alberta* (1969) 9 D.L.R. (3d) 142 (S.C.C.). See P.N. McDonald, "The B.N.A. Act and Near Banks: A Case Study on Federalism," *Alberta Law Review* 10 (1972): 155. The question was revisited in 1973 by Chief Justice Milvain of the Alberta Supreme Court, Trial Division, in *Provincial Treasurer of Alberta v. Long* (1975) (sic) 49 D.L.R. (3d) 695. The case arose in the same way the *Breckenridge* case had, and Milvain C.J. disposed of it in the same manner as the Supreme Court, finding that "it is not necessary to determine the constitutionality of the *Treasury Branches Act*" (p. 700). He went on, however, by way of *obiter dicta*, to express the opinion, contrary to that of the two Supreme Court of Canada justices, that the legislation was valid.

140. *Reference Re Powers of Disallowance and Reservation* [1938] S.C.R. 71. It was almost literally a death-bed repentance, since Justice Cannon would be dead in less than a year.

141. P.W. Hogg, *Constitutional Law of Canada*, looseleaf, para. 57.2(c).

142. These decisions were the subject of favourable description in Professor F.R. Scott's book, *Civil Liberties and Canadian Federalism* (Toronto: University of Toronto Press, 1959).

143. *Constitution Act, 1867*, s. 91(27).

144. [1953] 2 S.C.R. 299

145. Rand, Kellock, Estey, and Locke JJ.

146. Rinfret C.J., and Taschereau, Cartwright and Fauteux JJ.

147. *Constitution Act, 1867*, s. 92(13).

148. [1955] S.C.R. 799.

149. Chief Justice Rinfret had been replaced by Abbott, J.

150. (1957) 7 D.L.R. (3d) 337 (S.C.C.).

151. R.S.Q. 1941, c. 52, at the time of the decision.

152. Taschereau J.

153. (1957) 7 D.L.R. (3d) 337 (S.C.C.), p. 358.

154. "The Supreme Court and the Law of Canadian Federalism," *University of Toronto Law Journal* (1973): 307.

155. See, for example *Attorney General of Canada v. Dupond* (1978) 84 D.L.R. (3d) 420 (S.C.C.) and *Re Nova Scotia Board of Censors and McNeil* (1978) 84 D.L.R. (3d) 1 (S.C.C.).

156. (1957) 7 D.L.R. (3d), pp. 357–58.

157. Ibid., 358–59.

158. Ibid., 369–71.

159. Ibid., 371.

160. Ibid., 358.

161. See Dale Gibson, "Constitutional Amendment and the Implied Bill of Rights," *McGill Law Journal* 12 (1966–67): 497; and Dale Gibson, "Legislative Interference with Civil Liberties in Canada" (Bachelor's Thesis, Faculty of Law, University of Manitoba, 1958).

162. See, for example, Tollefson, "Freedom of Speech."

163. It will be noted, in fact, when Duff C.J.'s words are examined carefully, that he had already concluded that the House of Commons was intended to be a representative elected body before adding, almost as an afterthought, that "The preamble of the statute, *moreover*, shows plainly enough that the Constitution of the Dominion is to be similar in principle to that of Great Britain;" *Reference Re Alberta Statutes*, [1938] S.C.R. 100, pp. 132–35, emphasis added.

164. *Constitution Act, 1867*, s. 93.

165. Originally *Constitution Act, 1867*, s. 20, now *Canadian Charter of Rights and Freedoms*, s. 5.

166. Originally s. 50 of the 1867 Act, now also s. 4 of the *Charter*.

167. Originally s. 133 of the 1867 Act, now also sections 17 to 19 of the *Charter*.

168. See Justice Rand's commented quoted at note 158.

169. Abbott to Gibson, 1958, writer's records. The text of the letter was reproduced in Gibson, "Legislative Interference with Civil Liberties in Canada," 50.

170. (1978) 84 D.L.R. (3rd) 420 (S.C.C.). For a critical commentary by the present writer see Dale Gibson, "The High Court Leans to the Right—Again," *Canadian Lawyer* (1978): 16–17.

171. Gibson, "The High Court Leans to the Right," 438–39.

172. Gibson, "The High Court Leans to the Right," 428.

173. P.W. Hogg, *Constitutional Law of Canada*, looseleaf ed., para. 31,4(c).

174. *OPSEU v. Ontario* [1987] 1 S.C.R. 2, at 57. See also the remarks of Dickson J. in that decision, p. 25, and in *Fraser v. PSSRB* [1985] 2 S.C.R. 455, at 462–63; of McIntrye J. in *RWDSU v. Dolphin Delivery* [1986] 2 S.C.R. 573, at 584; and of Lamer C.J. in *Re Remuneration of Judges* [1997] 3 S.C.R. paras. 94–105.

175. It has been suggested that it might be available if Parliament or a Legislature were to use their power under s. 33 of the *Charter* to opt out of freedoms fundamental to democracy.

176. See Dale Gibson, "Constitutional Vibes: Reflections on the *Secession Reference* and the Unwritten Constitution," (1999–2000) 11 N.J.C.L. 49.

177. (1985) 19 D.L.R. (4th) 1, at p. 25 (S.C.C.). See Dale Gibson, "The Rule of Non-Law: Implications of the Manitoba Language Reference," *Transactions of the Royal Society of Canada* 5, vol. 1 (1986): 24; and "The Real Laws of the Constitution," *Alberta Law Review* 28 (1990): 371–73.

178. *New Brunswick Broadcasting Co. v. Nova Scotia (Speaker of the House of Assembly)* [1993] 1 S.C.R. 319, pp. 376–89.

179. [1997] 3 S.C.R. 3, para. 108.

180. [1998] 2 S.C.R. 217.

181. [1998] 2 S.C.R. 217, para. 32.

182. [1998] 2 S.C.R. 217, para. 49, 51.

183. This was the case, at least, with the exception of the judicially-enforceable principle of parliamentary supremacy, when Canada received its British constitutional inheritance in 1867. Modern British constitutional evolution, influenced by such factors as association with the European Union and devolution of central powers to Scotland and Wales, has no direct significance for Canada.

184. [1998] 2 S.C.R. 217, para. 54, emphasis added.

Eight

Not Like the Others
The Regulation of Indian Hunting and Fishing in Alberta

ROBERT IRWIN

Although the Natural Resource Transfer Agreements (NRTA) were intended to transfer control of Crown lands and resources to the three prairie provinces "as will give full recognition to the principle that in this respect they are entitled to be placed in a position of equality with the other Provinces of the Confederation," the NRTA placed particular restrictions upon the ability of Manitoba, Saskatchewan, and Alberta to regulate Indian hunting and fishing.[1] In section 12 of the Alberta Resources Transfer Agreement, the power of the province to regulate Indian hunting, fishing, and trapping is itemized:

> In order to secure to the Indians of the Province the continuance of the supply of game and fish for their support and subsistence, Canada agrees that the laws respecting game in force in the Province from time to time shall apply to the Indians within the boundaries thereof, provided, however, that the said Indians shall have the right, which the Province hereby assures to them, of hunting, trapping and fishing game and fish for food at all seasons of the year on all unoccupied Crown lands and on any other lands to which the said Indians may have a right of access.[2]

This distinctive regulatory environment emerged as a result of the efforts to fulfill the promises made in the Indian treaties, overlapping jurisdictional questions related to Indian hunting and fishing, and most importantly, the confusing and contradictory policies pursued by the Department of Indian Affairs (DIA) with regard to the regulation of hunting in the period prior to the 1930s. The consequences of the decisions made in the NRTA negotiations are far-reaching. The Canadian courts have been active in deciding the relationship between treaty hunting and fishing rights and the NRTA right, the application of the NRTA right to non-treaty aboriginal people, and the extent of the NRTA right with regard to the application of provincial regulations to Indian peoples.[3] Furthermore, Indian peoples have recently attempted to use hunting and fishing rights as the foundation for establishing co-management of resource development and wilderness resources.

The regulatory issues that eventually led to the inclusion of section 12 in the NRTA began with the treaty-making process. Alberta is covered by Treaties 6, 7, and 8. Each of these treaties contains a promise with regard to Indian hunting and fishing privileges. In Treaty 6, the promise reads:

> Her majesty further agrees with Her said Indians, that they, the said Indians, shall have right to pursue their avocations of hunting and fishing throughout the tract surrendered as hereinbefore described, subject to such regulations as may from time to time be made by Her Government of Her Dominion of Canada, and saving and excepting such tracts as may from time to time be required or taken up for settlement, mining, lumbering or other purposes, by Her said Government of the Dominion of Canada, or by any of the subjects thereof duly authorized therefor by the said Dominion.[4]

The clauses in Treaties 7 and 8 are slightly modified, but similar in intent. In Treaty 7, only hunting is mentioned as a protected avocation; in Treaty 8 trapping is itemized as a protected vocation along with hunting and fishing. In Treaty 8, "the government of the country" is substituted for "the Government of Her Dominion of Canada" as the regulatory authority. The Treaty right, as it appears in the written text of the treaty, contains a geographic limitation (the tract surrendered), exists only on lands not taken up for other purposes, and is subject to regulations prepared by the federal government.

The hunting and fishing privileges were an essential element in the negotiation of the treaties. In discussing the origin of these promises, historian Jean Friesen argues that "at treaty time the Indians heard nothing that would cause them to question their assumption of Indian open access to resources." This open access would include both subsistence and commercial rights.[5] Such an interpretation would seem to contradict the limitations placed on the privilege in the text of the treaty. A review of the negotiations, however, shows that the both the extent of the privilege and the limitations to be imposed by regulation and use of lands were discussed.

In the making of Treaties 1 and 2, Lieutenant-Governor Archibald mentioned the issue in his discussions with the Indian peoples, although the eventual treaty contained no explicit promises. He stated:

> When you have made your treaty you will still be free to hunt over much of the land included in the treaty. Much of it is rocky and unfit for cultivation, much of it that is wooded is beyond the places where the white man will require to go, at all events for some time to come. Till these lands are needed for use you will be free to hunt over them, and make all the use of them which you have made in the past. But when lands are needed to be tilled or occupied, you must not go on them any more. There will still be plenty of land that is neither tilled or occupied where you can go and roam and hunt as you have always done...[6]

Similarly, during negotiations for Treaty 4, Commissioner Alexander Morris discussed the promise the Queen was willing to make regarding hunting and fishing. He remarked to the Indians: "We have come through the country for many days and we have seen hills and but little wood and in many places little water, and it may be a long time before there are many white men settled upon this land, and you will have the right of hunting and fishing just as you have now until the land is actually taken up."[7]

In the Treaties specific to Alberta, the issue was raised by the Indian negotiators. At Treaty 6, Chief Tee-tee-quay-say remarked: "We want to be at liberty to hunt on any place as usual." Morris replied: "You want to be at liberty to hunt as before. I told you we did not want to take that means of living away from you, you have it the same as before, only this, if a man, whether Indian or Half-breed, had a good field of grain, you would not destroy it with your hunt."[8] The issue of regulations to conserve game were also discussed. In response to Chief Kah-mee-yis-too-way's request that the buffalo be protected, Morris replied: "it is a subject of great importance, it will be considered by the Lieutenant-Governor and Council of the North-West Territories to see if a wise law can be passed, one that will be a living law that can be carried out and obeyed. If such a law be passed it will be printed in Cree as well as in English and French; but what the law will be I cannot tell...." To Big Bear at Fort Pitt, Morris reiterated that "The North West Council is considering the framing of a law to protect the buffaloes, and when they make it, they will expect the Indian to obey it."[9]

At the making of Treaty 7, a similar understanding was communicated to the Indian peoples. Commissioner David Laird reported: "They were also assured that their liberty of hunting over the open prairie would not be interfered with, so long as they did not molest settlers and others in the country." In recounting the Treaty 7 Commission, the reports in the Toronto *Globe* quoted Laird as saying: "The Great Mother heard that the buffalo were being killed very fast, and to prevent them from being destroyed her Councillors have made a law to protect them. This law is for your own good. It says that the calves are not to be killed, so that they may grow and increase; that the cows are not to be killed in winter or spring, excepting by the Indians when they are in need of them as food. This will save the buffalo...."[10] Laird was also the Commissioner for Treaty 8. He remarked that the issue of hunting and fishing was central to the negotiations and he solemnly assured the Indians "that only such laws as to fishing and hunting as were in the interest of the Indians and were found necessary in order to protect the fish and fur-bearing animals would be made."[11]

Thus the treaty process clearly established that Indian peoples would have specific hunting and fishing privileges subject to the regulatory authority of the Canadian government. Regulating these privileges, however, proved to be complicated. The federal government utilized its authority under section 91.24 of the *Constitution Act, 1867* to fulfill its obligations to Indian peoples. The DIA consequently took significant interest in the development of regulations related to hunting and fishing. The first question addressed was which level of government had the ability to make regulations in the newly-acquired North-West Territories and Manitoba. Although fish and game were not mentioned in the *Manitoba Act*, the federal government had granted the power to manage game resources to the North-West Territorial Council in 1875, and Manitoba enacted its first hunting regulations in 1883.[12] The enforcement of these regulations against Indians in Manitoba produced an immediate reaction from the DIA.

Deputy Superintendent General Lawrence Vankoughnet informed John A. Macdonald that he had requested that Manitoba allow:

...certain indulgences in regard to the killing of game out of season to Indians, but that the [Manitoba] Minister of Agriculture, after careful consideration was compelled to adhere to his former opinions on the matter, which were to the effect that no exception could be made in favour of Indians in the administration of the game laws.[13]

Faced with the intransigence of the Manitoba government, the DIA requested that the Department of Justice provide them with an opinion regarding the application of the provincial regulations because "it is most important...that no restrictions be placed on Indians killing game at any time for their own use as they were assured by the Treaties they would be allowed to do so." The Department of Justice, however, rejected disallowance as a possible solution and suggested Vankoughnet continue his negotiations with Manitoba.[14] The power of Manitoba to regulate hunting was confirmed by the Court in 1886. The Manitoba court upheld the conviction of an Indian hunter and noted that the regulation of hunting and trapping fell within the exclusive domain of the provincial authority by virtue of section 92.13 "matter of a local concern," and section 92.16 "civil and property rights" of the Constitution Act, 1867.[15]

Manitoba continued to reject the DIA requests that the regulations consider the treaty obligation. New legislation passed in 1890 made no special provision for Indian hunting. Although no documentary connection exists, the passage of an amendment to the Indian Act in 1890 appears to be clearly linked to Manitoba's intransigence. The Indian Act is the expression of federal jurisdiction over Indian peoples, as provided by section 91.24 of the Constitution Act, 1867. Section 133 of the Indian Act read:

> The Superintendent General may, from time to time, by public notice, declare that, on and after the day therein named the laws respecting game in force in the province of Manitoba and the North-West Territories, or respecting such game as is specified in the notice, shall apply to Indians within said province or Territories, as the case may be, or to Indians in such parts thereof as to him seems expedient.[16]

The decision to include this section can be understood as an effort by the DIA to ensure that Indian treaty right of access to game on unoccupied Crown lands was respected in Manitoba.[17] Although Manitoba's subsequent legislation made no reference to the provisions of the Indian Act, the game ordinance in the North-West Territories eventually recognized this clause and applied only to "such Indians as it is specially made applicable to in pursuance and by virtue of the powers vested in the Superintendent General of Indian Affairs."[18] The DIA subsequently announced that a number of Indian bands in the North-West Territories and four bands in the Birtle agency within Manitoba "were brought under operation of the laws respecting game in the North West Territories, on and after, the 31st day of December 1893." The Stony Indians at

Morley were brought under the operation of the laws effective January 1, 1895, and the northern bands in the Treaty 6 area were brought under the North-West Territory laws effective July 1, 1903.[19] No notice bringing the Indians under the game laws of the province of Manitoba was ever made. The DIA nevertheless encouraged Indian peoples to obey the game regulations of the province if they were not enforced against subsistence hunting.

During the confrontations with Manitoba regarding the applicability of hunting regulations to Indians, the DIA was also involved in negotiating fisheries regulations with the federal Department of Marine and Fisheries. Although neither the ownership of fish and game nor the regulation of hunting was itemized in the Canadian constitution, the federal government has a clear regulatory power over the fishery by virtue of Section 91.12 of the *Constitution Act, 1867*. The provincial authorities also obtained an interest in the fishery through their ownership of Crown lands following the Privy Council decision in *Re Fisheries* in 1898.[20] Thus fishing is a critical subject in federal/provincial relations in Canada. Although section 9 of the Alberta Resources Transfer Agreement placed the Province on equal footing with other provinces as regards fisheries, prior to 1930 regulation of the fishery was the exclusive jurisdiction of the federal government.

The Department of Marine and Fisheries and the DIA had discussions as early as 1885 regarding the application of regulations to Indian peoples. Since the Department of Marine and Fisheries was a federal agency, questions related to the regulatory effect on the treaty right did not parallel the discussions related to hunting. The DIA never challenged the right of fisheries officials to enforce regulations, but instead requested special conditions for Indian fishing in light of the treaty privileges. Indian Affairs sought both exclusive fishing reserves for Indian peoples and an exemption from the licensing system developed by the Fisheries Department.[21] In return for assistance in enforcement of fisheries regulations on Indian peoples, the Department of Marine and Fisheries indicated it would consider setting apart certain waters for the exclusive use of Indian peoples.[22] As a result, the regulations of 1892 provided for a special "domestic license" to be made available to all local residents (with no distinction between Indian or white) for $2.00 and section 16 noted:

These regulations shall apply to Indians and half-breeds, as well as to settlers and all other persons; provided always that the Minister of Marine and Fisheries may from time to time set apart for the exclusive use of Indians, such waters as he may deem necessary, and may grant to Indians or their bands, free licenses to fish during the close seasons, for themselves, but not for the purpose of sale, barter or traffic.[23]

Over the course of the next three years, the two federal departments would battle over the implementation of these provisions.

Despite the provision for exclusive fishing waters and free licenses in section 16, no special provisions were made for the 1893 fishing season. Complaints regarding the enforcement of the fisheries regulations as regarding Indian subsistence fishing during the closed season emerged in the fall of 1893. Indian Agents immediately made enquiries on behalf of the local Indian fishermen. The DIA negotiated a free license for all settlers, residents, and Indian peoples in the vicinity of lakes "to permit fishing during the close season, in such cases where the local fishery officer is satisfied that the applicant for license intends to fish for the supply of local wants, and not for export out of the locality."[24] These free domestic licenses, therefore, were not particular to Indian peoples, but certainly addressed some of the concerns of DIA. The Department of Marine and Fisheries, however, was unsatisfied with the arrangements and desired to ensure that all fishermen obeyed the regulations.

The DIA was notified that the emergency measures made in the fall of 1893 would not be reconsidered. According to the deputy minister of fisheries:

> I have the honour to remind you during the past year, these people [Indians and Half-breeds in the North-West Territories] were at the request of the Department of Indian Affairs in certain cases allowed to fish during the close season for domestic consumption but not for trade or barter.
>
> The Minister of Marine and Fisheries is in receipt of further reports from his officers on this subject, and it appears that...over-fishing in the close season has worked great injury to the fisheries. The fishery officers have notified the Indian settlers and Half-breeds that the close season would be strictly enforced in 1894.[25]

The Department of Marine and Fisheries then requested the views of Indian Affairs regarding this subject. The correspondence that followed defined the perspectives of the DIA with regard not only to the regulation of Indian fishing, but also to the perspectives that would shape its response to provincial regulation of Indian hunting as well.

In his response, T. Mayne Daly, the superintendent general of Indian Affairs, provided an explicit statement related to the DIA understanding of the treaty right:

> It seems quite clear that all Indians have, through their Treaty stipulations, expressed and understood, the right to expect to be allowed to fish for their own consumption, sale, or barter, without being made to pay for the privilege.
>
> This right is universally asserted by them, and tenaciously clung to. It may doubtless be properly contended that such right was made or intended to be subject to regulation, and that in the interests of the Indians themselves, to say nothing of others, certain restrictions are necessary. While, therefore, there would appear to be good ground for insisting upon the observation of the close season, and other regulations calculated to preserve the Fisheries, and it is possible to get the Indians to recognise this necessity, there would appear to be the best reasons for not going a step further, in the case of Indians, than is absolutely necessary, or imposing a tax of the justice of which they cannot be persuaded.... I am of the opinion that they [licenses] should be issued free of charge....
>
> The issue of licenses during the close season should be restricted to fishing for domestic consumption, and confined to Indians who can support themselves by no other means.[26]

Daly offered further clarification of his position in response to Fisheries' concerns that allowing Indians to fish during the closed season was unwarranted.

> You will remember that I admitted the existence of good ground for insisting generally speaking upon the observance of the close season, and suggested that only such Indians as could not support themselves in any other way should be allowed to fish during such season, and then only under license, and for their domestic consumption, and still it appears to me that the waters which would be fished under such restrictions by the Indians (and not by the Half-breeds, H.B.Co. Officers, or white settlers) would not be seriously affected.
>
> As to the argument that it would be better to feed the Indians during the close season, until such time as they can prepare themselves for it, I referred in my letter already quoted to the expense which such course would involve....

To feed them, however,—and by this I mean Indians who are really not settled down and cultivating reserves—means simply to confirm them in the most pernicious habit of dependence upon the Government....

As to the question of making Indians pay for licenses...I may remind you, however, of what I have already said as to the extraction of a license fee involving a question of right, and of the importance attached to it by all the Indians.[27]

Although the Department of Marine and Fisheries granted free permits to fish during the closed season in 1894 to selected Indian bands in the Edmonton, Carlton, Duck Lake, Prince Albert, Hobbema, Clandeboye, Pas and Berens River Agencies, its field officers clearly disliked the policy.

In 1895, the Fisheries department once again rejected applications for permits to fish in the closed season. Further, free licenses to Indians were restricted to licenses to fish for domestic consumption only. The fisheries overseers demanded that Indian fishermen who desired to sell or barter fish purchase a license. Hayter Reed, the deputy superintendent general, responded that the Treaty promises had to be maintained.[28] After reviewing the provisions of the Robinson treaties made with Indian peoples in Upper Canada in the 1850s, Reed addressed the issue of Treaties 1 and 2:

In Treaties Nos. 1 & 2, (Manitoba and the North West Territories) mention of hunting and fishing privileges is omitted, but then it was acknowledged later on that verbal promises were made to the Indians which were not included in the written text of these Treaties, and the treaty was afterwards amended so as to put these Indians on a footing with those of Treaty No. 3, the terms of which governed Treaties subsequently made.

In the revision nothing was said about hunting and fishing, because no complaint was made about them, but the reason obviously is that at the time nothing had occurred to raise any question in the minds of the Indians as to the privilege (understood) being interfered with, and certainly it could never have been intended to treat them differently in this respect from Indians whom prior and subsequent Treaties were made.

Reed next reviewed the Treaty promise in other treaties, and then proceeded to offer the following interpretation:

...the commissioners never contemplated giving the Indians to understand, and consequently the latter never supposed, that regulations would involve the payment of any tax. *The understanding was free privilege, subject to necessary regulations*, and this is universally asserted and tenaciously clung to, *all the more so because the Department's officials* like the undersigned (who attended some of the Treaties) *have never had any doubt as to the intention and understanding of the stipulations, and consequently have never attempted to shake the Indians convictions.... The Department freely concedes that in the interests of Indians themselves, the issue of licensed fishing during the close season should be restricted to fishing for domestic consumption, and confined to Indians who can support themselves by no other means.*

The Fisheries Department accepted the position of the DIA in the 1896 regulations, but continued to express concern regarding local exchanges of fish, which it perceived as commercial exchange rather than subsistence. The DIA assured the Fisheries Department that "the exchange of food supplies are strictly non-commercial, without profit to either party concerned" and Fisheries officers, consequently, were instructed "to allow the Indians this privilege."[29]

After an inspection of the fisheries in the Edmonton district, E.E. Prince, the Dominion Commissioner of Fisheries, reported that some of the bands "should have special concessions based upon their conditions and lifestyle, but many should be required to obey the regulations."[30] This formulation, clearly expressed in a memorandum April 5, 1898, became the framework for fisheries management until 1910. Indian peoples would be granted free permits for subsistence fishing, given privilege to fish in the closed season in special circumstances, and purchase licenses and follow regulations in all other situations. The DIA would raise specific cases periodically, citing the agreements of 1896, in protecting Indian people's special privileges.[31] Most DIA concerns focused on Fisheries officials' refusal to provide free licenses to Indian peoples fishing for barter or sale and their failure to grant exclusive fishing privileges to select Indian bands. This emphasis on protecting Indian peoples' free access to fishing and provision for a subsistence-based fishing privilege even during closed seasons became a consistent feature of the DIA policy.

The provision of free licenses and subsistence privileges were also concerns with regard to Indian hunting. The superintendent general provided for the application of the game ordinances of the North-West Territories to select Indian bands in 1893, 1894, and 1903. These bands were primarily in the southern and central regions where the DIA was attempting to transform Indian lifestyles from hunting to agriculture. The Territorial ordinance, furthermore, reflected DIA emphasis on subsistence privileges providing for free access to game for food even in the closed season.[32] The creation of Saskatchewan and Alberta in 1905 brought the issue of hunting to the forefront once again. Although these two provinces did not receive control over Crown lands and, as a result, did not have any jurisdiction with regard to fisheries, they were responsible for game management and the regulation of hunting. Both of these provinces quickly developed game management legislation. According to the *Alberta Game Act*, all people hunting in Alberta, including Indians, had to pay for a license and respect the closed seasons. The legislation also began to emphasize the important role of sport hunting in the southern districts of the province and restricted special subsistence privileges to travellers and residents, including Indians, north of 55 degrees latitude (beaver, buffalo, and elk were prohibited).[33] Debates over the application of these game management regulations to Indians quickly emerged.

Game management advocates and officials increasingly expressed concern about Indian hunting habits in the period prior to 1905.[34] Indian peoples were often blamed for the wanton slaughter of game in violation of game regulations. In the response to requests regarding the application of game laws to Indian peoples, the DIA cited the notices of 1893, 1894, and 1903 and indicated that those bands listed in the notices had to follow the game laws. In 1907, controversy erupted when the Treaty 8 inspector, H. Conroy, informed Treaty 8 Indian peoples that they could take beaver for food in violation of the provincial game regulations. Responding to the Alberta Government protests, Conroy noted "that so far as he was aware the Provincial Game Ordinances had not been made applicable to Indians with Treaty No. 8." Deputy Superintendent General Frank Pedley then added:

> In this connection I beg to transmit herewith a list of the Bands which were brought under the operation of the Game Ordinance of the North West Territories, and it may probably be assumed that they are as a consequence subject to the provisions of the Game Ordinance of the provinces within which they respectively reside.[35]

Pedley then remarked that Alberta had apparently "overlooked the provisions" of the *Indian Act* and that he would be pleased to enter discussions related to bringing the Indians of Treaty 8 under the provisions of the Alberta game regulations.

Although both levels of government identified their positions in the succeeding correspondence, they failed to resolve the constitutional questions. The Alberta government noted:

> It is not my purpose to enter upon a constitutional discussion as to what the effect of Section 66 of the Indian Act is, if indeed, it has any effect, but if you are sufficiently interested in the matter to go closely into it I think you will find that it would not be at all difficult to sustain the position that inasmuch as the protection of game is, and has always been a matter regarded as one of the matters falling within the exclusive jurisdiction of the Provinces, legislation such as that embodied in Section 28 of the Alberta Game Act (not, you will please observe, The Game Ordinance of the North West Territories) is binding upon all persons, irrespective of "race, creed, or previous condition of servitude," within the Province, save only such persons as are by the Provincial law declared not to be within the purview of the law.[36]

The superintendent general, Frank Oliver, after consulting with Pedley, responded with reference to the treaty privileges and the DIA's obligation to protect Indian access to game for food. He ignored the primary constitutional issue:

> The Department agrees with the stand taken by you at any rate in so far as it holds the opinion that the time has not arrived for going into the constitutional aspect of the question of the powers of the province to legislate for Indians with respect to the killing of game and will confine itself for the present in that connection to remarking that it has taken so much an interest in the preservation of game that in making the Treaty concerned, it was at pains to secure such agreement from the Indians as would remove the constitutional question with regard to preceding Treaties, viz; as to how far Treaty stipulations might exempt Indians from the operation of game laws whether emanating from the Dominion or Provincial Governments
>
> This interest on the part of the Department in the preservation of game is mainly connected with its relation to protecting what constitutes, at any rate in certain districts, the main source of the food supply necessary

for the preservation of the lives of its wards, and if it has any good grounds for supposing that the ultimate supply is being insured unnecessarily at the danger of an immediate or intervening sacrifice of life, it would certainly appear to be its duty to intervene to the extent of its ability.[37]

The discussions with Alberta, and other problems in Manitoba, led several DIA officials to consider the effect of the *Indian Act* provisions. Although a general consensus emerged that these sections of the *Indian Act* were *ultra vires* of the Dominion government, the section was not revoked.[38] The failure to resolve the conflict opened the door to legal proceedings regarding the application of game laws to Indians.

The Stony Indian hunters at Morley were regarded as one of the most problematic bands. In 1894, the Stony had been brought under the Game Ordinance of the North-West Territory effective January 1, 1895. They were informed, and apparently agreed, that regulations to preserve game were in their interest. Still, they were constantly accused of violating the regulations not only of Alberta, but also of British Columbia. According to Indian Agent Sibbald, these hunters frequented the foothills and the Rocky Mountains during the open and closed seasons despite his best efforts to have them follow the Alberta regulations. Wild game remained their primary food source, and the band took as many as 900 big game animals in a year.[39] The Stony protested against the enforcement of the new Alberta game regulations, especially as it related to the payment of a license fee and the regulation of hunting for food.[40] The DIA tried to negotiate with the Alberta government regarding license fees, but insisted that it was in the interest of the Stony Indians themselves that they follow the Alberta game regulations.

The Stony hunting practices led to a conviction against one of the band members for selling a trophy head of an animal killed contrary to the *Alberta Game Act*. In *R v. Stoney Joe*, Alberta Supreme Court Justice Charles Stuart overturned the conviction and provided the only legal decision regarding the application of the provisions of the *Indian Act* to provincial game regulations. Stuart decided that federal government legislation with respect to Indians took precedence over provincial legislation with respect to game if there was a conflict. Since the federal government exercised its 91.24 constitutional authority with regard to Indians and placed the Stony Indians of Morley under the game laws of the North-West Territories effective January 1, 1895, only such laws as were in effect at that date applied. He also remarked that in the absence of a notice by the superintendent general under the provisions of the *Indian Act*, the provincial game laws applied.[41] The decision was filled with problems and contradictions. It meant that the Indian bands identified in the 1893 notice (those bands most involved in agriculture and in the most heavily-settled zones) were subject only to the 1892 Game Ordinance of the North-West Territories. That Ordinance permitted Indians to kill game at any time for food. Meanwhile, those Indian bands identified in the 1903 notice (bands in the more northern settled districts and more dependent upon game for food) were subject to the more restrictive closed season conditions of the 1903 Ordinance. Meanwhile, Indian peoples for whom the superintendent general had not given notice that the game laws applied to them (the bands most dependent upon game for food) had the restrictive 1907 provincial game laws applied to them.[42] Given the difficulties, the DIA chose not to communicate the decision to its Agents, but no appeal was launched by either level of government.

Instead, the DIA entered into negotiations with the provincial authorities regarding the provision of a notice bringing the Stony Indians at Morley under the game laws of Alberta. The Alberta legislation of 1907 made no special provisions for Indian peoples and even placed them at a disadvantage related to farmers with regard to the price of a license. The DIA insisted that the game laws of Alberta provided for free licenses to Indians in conformity with the policies it had obtained with regard to fisheries. The Alberta legislation made provision for subsistence hunting during the closed season north of 55 degrees latitude, and DIA accepted that Indian hunters in the southern part of the province would obey the closed season. The *Alberta Game Act* was amended to provide for the Lieutenant-Governor-in-Council to rebate the license charge to all Treaty Indians upon application by the Indian Agent.[43] Following this change, the superintendent general gave notice of the application of the game laws of Alberta to the Stony Indians at Morley in 1914. The issue with regard to other Indian peoples remained an open question even though the Department informed Indian peoples that they were subject to provincial regulations.[44]

Despite the concessions obtained by DIA, game management continued to be somewhat more restrictive than fisheries management as it related to Indian peoples in Alberta. Following the 1910 *Dominion Alberta Saskatchewan Fisheries Commission* recommendations, fisheries regulations allowed for free licensing of "Indian and Half-breed" subsistence fishing even during closed seasons. Fisheries officials, moreover, agreed not to enforce fisheries regulations against Indians in the northern regions of the province on lakes where no commercial fishing occurred.[45] The Alberta hunting regulations provided for free hunting licenses for treaty Indian peoples, but restricted subsistence privileges during the closed season to those living in the northern regions of the province and placed Indians on equal footing with other residents in that regard. The questions related to notification provided under the *Indian Act* as raised by *R. v. Stoney Joe* remained unresolved as tensions with the Manitoba government increased.

The expansion of Manitoba in 1912 had brought new regions within the scope of the Manitoba game regulations. Despite protests from the DIA that it was customary for provincial game laws "to exempt the northern Indians from the provisions of the Act or to grant them licenses free of charge," Manitoba refused to provide any special considerations for Indian hunters and trappers. Manitoba informed the superintendent general that "the rights and privileges of the Indians are in the same category as white men, as far as the trapping and taking of fur bearing animals, outside the limits of their reserves are concerned."[46] Faced with Manitoba's intransigence, the superintendent general agreed to assist the province in having Indian peoples accept the regulations.

By now, the position of the DIA with regard to the application of game laws to Indian hunters was contradictory and confusing. The Department informed its field officers and Indian peoples that they had to obey provincial game laws despite the lack of notices granted under the *Indian Act*. The ability of the federal government to legislate with regard to Indian hunting and fishing was not in question. In *St. Catherines Milling v. the Queen*, the Privy Council noted the Dominion retained the power to regulate Indian hunting and fishing privileges and the Department of Justice had informed DIA with respect to matters in Ontario that:

> It seems to me that it is for your Department to determine, having regard to the terms of the Indian treaties or otherwise, to what extent the Indians should be immune from the Provincial game laws and that then that immunity should be provided by legislation, either by the Province if the Province will yield to the Dominion, otherwise by legislation of the Dominion in the exercise of its paramount power with regard to Indians and lands reserved for Indians.[47]

The *Indian Act*, however, was not amended to remove or change the wording of the section despite the ruling in *R. v. Stoney Joe*. Deputy Superintendent

General Duncan Campbell Scott nevertheless informed the minister that "there can be no doubt that they [Manitoba game laws] would not apply...in view of the stipulation in the treaties covering the same, without a formal notice" under the *Indian Act*.[48] The Department considered the idea of giving notice on a couple of occasions, but none was made.[49] Instead, the minister of Indian Affairs, Arthur Meighen, informed the House of Commons that it was his position that Indians outside of their reserves had to comply with provincial game laws.[50] The problematic issues related to section 66 of the *Indian Act* surfaced in 1923 when the Manitoba court decided that the effect of section 66 was that Provincial game laws did not apply on Indian reserves, but remarked that off-reserve Indians had to comply with Provincial laws. Justice Dennistoun concluded that:

> I find nothing in the *Indian Act*, R.S.C. 1906, ch. 81 which permits an Indian when off his reserve to act in defiance of provincial game laws. Sec. 66 says that such game laws may be made applicable to Indians by public notice by the superintendent general, but does not say that in the absence of such notice they shall have no effect.[51]

By 1923, consequently, the Indians were subject to provincial game laws, except on their reserve, until the superintendent general gave notice to apply the provincial game laws to them.

In making its decision, the Manitoba court relied on decisions related to the application of provincial laws related to medical licensing and alcohol distribution to Indian peoples.[52] The issue of hunting and fishing, however, were treaty issues related to Indians *qua* Indians. Although the federal government retained the right to legislatively exempt Indians from the application of provincial game laws, the DIA believed that conservation laws served the interests of the Indian peoples and was unwilling to directly intervene. The deputy superintendent general was a member of the federal Advisory Board for Wildlife Conservation and participated in national events and conferences related to wildlife conservation. At these conferences, DIA asserted its desire to co-operate with provincial officials. At a national conference in 1919, Scott insisted that DIA endeavoured to induce Indian peoples to obey provincial laws, but would search to obtain concessions to meet special conditions.[53] Similarly, following criticism of Indian hunting habits at the Dominion and Provincial Game Conference in 1926, Indian Agents were told to "please explain to the Indians in your Agency that they must strictly comply with the Game

Laws."[54] Scott effectively summarized the Department's position in response to claims that the DIA was failing to protect Indian treaty rights in Manitoba:

> It is the duty of the Superintendent General to see that the Indians secure the fullest enjoyment of privilege provided for in the Treaties. It is recognized, however, that with the settlement of the country, the game is becoming scarce.... It would appear that the Dominion Government in the exercise of its paramount power with regard to Indians and lands reserved for Indians, would have the authority to legislate with reference to the taking of game and fish by Indians, but if such legislation were enacted the regulations passed thereunder would no doubt follow closely the principles embodied in the Provincial Game Laws, and it is accordingly considered that the interests of the Indians can be properly safeguarded by conforming to the Provincial Regulations, with such modifications as the Provincial Authorities may be disposed to make in favour of the Indian bands on representations which may be made by the DIA from time to time.[55]

Despite this position, Provincial officials continued to assert that they received insufficient support from the DIA with regard to the regulation of Indian hunting.

The problems related to the regulation of Indian hunting became an issue in the NRTA negotiations because of provincial intransigence with regard to making concessions to Indian bands dependent upon game for food. Federal officials had always recognized that the transfer would affect Indian rights. Their original concerns related to the maintenance of federal title to reserve lands, the residual rights to reserve lands after surrenders, and the need to ensure that provinces provided lands for future reserves as required.[56] As negotiations approached a culmination in 1925, however, the DIA also made an effort to clarify the situation with regard to the regulation of Indian hunting and fishing. The DIA noted that "While the Indians shall be subject to the game laws of the Province, provision should be made for hunting and fishing reserves, and for exemptions in favour of Indians who are hunting and fishing purely for their own sustenance."[57] This request to include Indian hunting rights in the transfer sparked a serious discussion with the federal government negotiator.

The federal negotiator, O.M. Biggar, had no difficulty including provisions related to the administration of Indian lands, but expressed concerns over the provisions related to Indian hunting rights. In a lengthy memorandum, Biggar noted that the subject was addressed by the *Indian Act* and the treaties:

> The diminution in the quantity of game presses hardly upon the hunting Indians, and it is not without importance that, notwithstanding the game laws, they should be allowed to hunt and fish out of season for their own food. The view of the effect of Section 66 of the Indian Act to which the Department has been inclined has been that it absolves the Indians from the necessity of observing the game laws within the reserves proper, but they are bound by them in the same way as other residents of the Province elsewhere than on the reserves. It seems to me, however, doubtful if the operation of the section is thus limited.
>
> If it is *intra vires* of the Dominion as legislation on the subject of Indians, then there would appear to be no reason why all Indians in respect of whom no public notice had been given by the Superintendent General should not be at liberty to hunt and fish notwithstanding the game laws on any lands to which they were entitled to have access, in other words, at present, to all Crown lands, and that this was the idea underlying the provision when originally adopted...is indicated by its being then applied to "Manitoba and the Western Territories" but not to any other of the then provinces of Confederation, Manitoba being at that time the only province in which Crown lands were the property of Canada....
>
> There are provisions about hunting and fishing in all of the Alberta treaties...[that give] the Indians a right to continue to hunt and fish on all unoccupied lands, subject only to such regulations as the Dominion may make on the subject.... Moreover, on the transfer of to the Province of the Crown lands, it might be argued that the permission the treaties give to enter upon unoccupied lands for the purpose of hunting and fishing came to an end, since these lands were no longer under the control of the authority by which the treaty was made.[58]

Biggar concluded his memorandum by indicating that a provision clearly protecting the treaty right of access to Crown lands could be added to the agreement, but that the agreement should not address the issue of Indian peoples' compliance with provincial game laws. To go beyond protecting anything more than the treaty right of access, Biggar later remarked, was "not only unnecessary but would also be dangerous." Any inclusion in the agreement of Indian compliance with game laws "has no relation to lands, but to legislative jurisdiction over Indians as such.... The only possible effect of a provision on this point would be to narrow unnecessarily the Dominion's present plenary power."[59]

Biggar's antagonism to any discussion related to Indian compliance with provincial game laws led to the inclusion of a narrowly defined clause in the draft agreement reached with Alberta in 1925. Section 9 of the agreement read:

> To all Indians who may be entitled to the benefit of any treaty between the Crown and any band or bands of Indians, whereby such Indians surrendered to the Crown any lands now included within the boundaries of the Province, the Province hereby assures the right to hunt and fish on all unoccupied Crown lands administered by the Province hereunder as fully and freely as such Indian might have been permitted to so hunt and fish if the said lands had continued to be administered by the Government of Canada.[60]

This clause clearly reflected the concerns raised by Biggar. It protected the treaty right of access to unoccupied Crown lands while making no statement with regard to the application of provincial game laws. Although it reserved the rights of the federal government to use its *Indian Act* powers to exempt Indians from game laws since the DIA policy had been to make treaty Indians comply with provincial regulations, it raised no concerns in Alberta.

The Alberta draft agreement, however, died in 1926 when concerns related to separate schools in the province became the focus of debate.[61] When negotiations related to the transfer of resources resumed, Manitoba became the focus of federal efforts. The situation with regard to treaty in Manitoba was different than in Alberta. While Treaties 6, 7, and 8 each contained provisions related to hunting and fishing rights, in Manitoba the situation was not as clear. Treaties 3, 4 and 5 contained promises similar to those in Alberta, but the texts of Treaties 1 and 2 made no reference to these issues. Despite Hayter Reed's 1895 insistence that hunting and fishing rights be read into these treaties, the DIA now accepted that Indian peoples under Treaties 1 and 2 had no special privileges. When Manitoba enquired as to the rights of Indians to hunt and fish in the province under Dominion laws, Scott responded in a deliberately provocative fashion. He remarked that while it was a question as to the application of game laws to people in Treaties 1 and 2 given the absence of a treaty promise, it was his position that in the absence of notice under the *Indian Act*, "the Game Laws of the Province could not prevail against the provisions of the Treaties."[62]

Scott's position is only understandable in the context of ongoing discussions with Manitoba regarding the application of stringent hunting and trapping regulations against Indians in the northern aspects of the province. In the period 1926–1929, the DIA's desire to establish exclusive hunting and fishing privileges to certain areas had resurfaced. This desire, first reflected in the fisheries disputes of the 1890s, had been established in areas of exclusive federal jurisdiction by 1927, but received limited support from the provinces. Alberta, Manitoba and Saskatchewan agreed that exclusive zones could be established only on the condition that all Indian hunting was to be restricted to those zones. The DIA recognized that such a change represented a unilateral change to the treaty promises and could not be accepted. Competition from white trappers, however, led to intense pressure from Indian Agents to reach some agreement with the provinces. Despite Biggar's earlier concerns, the new agreement reached with Manitoba thus addressed the issue of Indian compliance with provincial game laws.

The new clause became section 12 of the Alberta Resources Transfer Agreement. The clause clearly reflected the DIA perspective on regulation that had developed over the last 50 years. In the clause, the federal government agreed that Indian compliance with the provincial game laws was important for the purposes of conservation and in return for their agreement not to use their constitutional power to exempt Indians, provinces would ensure that Indians would have continued access to all unoccupied Crown lands at all seasons when hunting, fishing, and trapping for food. According to an explanatory memorandum that accompanied the Manitoba bill before Parliament, the clauses related to Indian Reserves and hunting and fishing rights were described:

> Section 13—Section 69 of the *Indian Act*, R.S.C. 98, empowers the Superintendent General of Indian Affairs to apply the Provincial game laws to the Indians in any of the three western Provinces, or any part of any of them. What is in effect Canada's agreement by this clause to apply the provincial game laws to the Indian in Manitoba is accordingly compensated for by the provisions of the agreement that the application of these laws shall not deprive the Indians of the right to hunt and fish for food.[63]

In the explanation of the Alberta agreement, it simply stated: "The rights of hunting, trapping, and fishing on unoccupied Crown lands are secured to the Indians."[64] It was an agreement, therefore, to enshrine the regulatory structure the DIA had insisted upon with regard to fisheries and provincial game laws in the period 1890 to 1920. It represents a quid pro quo between the two governments and it was clearly understood in that context by officials at the time.

In a series of legal opinions and correspondence, federal officials constantly asserted this interpretation of the clauses. In opinions given by the deputy minister of justice, W. Stuart Edwards, the federal government argued that unoccupied lands did not include such lands as parks or reserves; that the term Indian should be interpreted broadly and not be confined to the *Indian Act* definition of a status Indian or a treaty Indian; that the term game should be interpreted broadly; and that Canada retained the right to regulate all Indian hunting and fishing, including hunting and fishing for food, under section 91.24 of the *Constitution Act, 1867*.[65] The issues upon which Edwards was called to comment are among the most important considerations when dealing with the consequences of the NRTA.

According to Edwards, provincial regulations applied to Indians, except Indians hunting and fishing for food, who were subject only to federal regulations. This last position was emphasized by the federal NRTA negotiator, O.M. Biggar, and the Department of the Interior's solicitor. Biggar wrote: "The effect of the agreement with the Province is, of course, in no sense to surrender the right of regulation now possessed by the Dominion Parliament by which, indeed, any regulation power of Indians must of necessity remain vested."[66] This interpretation is consistent with the decision that the *Migratory Birds Convention Act* applies to Indian hunting despite the NRTA provision.[67]

The idea that Indian hunting and fishing rights, including the right to hunt and fish for food, remain subject to federal regulations has significant implications for fisheries management. Section 9 of the NRTA placed the fisheries of Alberta in the same position as in other Provinces by transferring ownership of the fish to the Province while Canada retained its regulatory authority under section 91.12 of the *Constitution Act, 1867*. Canada and the Province subsequently agreed upon the regulations and passed concurrent rules. Fisheries regulations, consequently, remained a federal legislation and, as such, binding on Indian peoples.[68] The interpretation given to section 12 of the NRTA by Biggar, Edwards and the Department of the Interior would result in Indian peoples having to follow the regulations related to closed seasons, catch limits, and licenses even when fishing for food. This interpretation has never been tested in the Courts, however, since the focus of litigation has been on the relationship between treaty rights and the NRTA right.

There is no indication that any of the negotiators considered the consequences that this section would entail for the interpretation of treaty rights. Although Duncan Campbell Scott referred to the "important privilege" conferred upon the Indians by the NRTA, the minister responsible "explained that by the Natural Resources Transfer Agreement no new rights were accorded to Indians, that they were merely confirmed in the rights they have had all along."[69] Premier Brownlee had a similar understanding about the meaning of the NRTA privileges. The *Edmonton Bulletin* reported that in his address to the Alberta Legislature he noted:

A variety of objections could be raised which would never present themselves in practical experience. He was convinced that the only intention of Clause 12 was to protect the rights of the Indians in the same manner as they had been safeguarded previously by the Dominion. If it appeared that the agreement ceded further rights which might be thought in excess of those properly theirs, it was then purely a matter of adjustment.[70]

Early court decisions similarly confirmed that the NRTA had simply confirmed the existing treaty rights.[71]

The Supreme Court's acceptance that the treaty right included commercial as well as subsistence hunting rights and that the treaty right was restricted to the surrendered territory rather than the entire province led to a different interpretation of the section. The Supreme Court decided that the treaty right had been merged and consolidated by the NRTA. It suggested that a *quid pro quo* had occurred in that the NRTA restricted the right to subsistence, but extended the territory over which it could be practiced. In its most recent decision on the issue, the Supreme Court indicated that where the NRTA conflicted with the treaty right—the right to hunt commercially for example—it extinguished the treaty right. Where no conflict exists, however, the treaty right continues.[72]

The fact that the NRTA did not enshrine the treaty right in the constitution meant that the identification of the people to whom the right applied became important. Although the draft 1925 Alberta agreement had used the term Treaty Indians, section 12 of the Alberta Resource Transfer Agreement specified that the privileges are bestowed upon Indians. But who is an Indian? The word is not clearly defined constitutionally.[73] In 1939, the Supreme Court accepted that Inuit were Indian and this decision has led to arguments that the term also includes the Métis.[74] It has been determined that a person with Indian bloodlines living an Indian lifestyle is an Indian within the meaning of the NRTA, but that the term does not include those people who were Métis.[75]

Finally, the realization that the NRTA right had changed the treaty rights has led to the application of treaty interpretation to section 12 of the NRTA. The constitutional protection offered to aboriginal and treaty rights by section 35.1 of the *Constitution Act, 1982* has led the Supreme Court to identify a number of important characteristics of treaty rights. First, a treaty is an exchange of solemn promises; it is an agreement whose nature is sacred. Second, any restriction of a treaty right must be narrowly construed and ambiguity must be interpreted in favour of the Indian peoples. Third, treaty rights can be extinguished or modified by the Crown, but there must be "strict proof of the fact of extinguishment" and the Crown must demonstrate a clear and plain intention to extinguish the right in consultation with the aboriginal group. Finally, the Crown's fiduciary duty to uphold the right must be construed in a modern context.[76] The so-called Sparrow test, therefore, is applicable to the NRTA. Summarizing this application in *R. v. Bagder*, Justice Cory noted:

> Any infringement of the rights guaranteed under the Treaty or the NRTA must be justified using the Sparrow test. This analysis provides a reasonable, flexible and current method of assessing the justifiability of conservation regulations and enactments. It must first be asked if there was a valid legislative objective, and if so, the analysis proceeds to a consideration of the special trust relationship and the responsibility of the government *vis-à-vis* the aboriginal people. Further questions might deal with whether the infringement was as little as was necessary to effect the objective, whether compensation was fair, and whether the aboriginal group was consulted with respect to the conservation measures.[77]

This interpretation of the NRTA hunting and fishing rights, in conjunction with the interpretation of their treaty rights, have led Indian peoples to assert rights in other areas of law.[78] In recent cases, for example, it was found that an Indian could cut down trees and build a cabin in a park against regulations in practicing his treaty and NRTA hunting rights, but found that the Cold Lake Air Weapons Range was occupied land and Indian peoples could not practice these rights in that area.[79] In another case, the Halfway River First Nation asserted their Treaty 8 hunting and fishing rights to force British

Columbia to consult with them on forestry policy. The Whitefish Lake First Nation has similarly asserted that its Treaty 6 and NRTA rights require consultation with regard to gas production before the Environmental Appeal Board in Alberta.[80]

Thus the regulation of Indian hunting and fishing remains complex and problematic. The Crown has made promises to Indian peoples in the Treaties and, through the insistence of the DIA, a constitutionally guaranteed privilege of hunting, trapping, and fishing for food has been granted to all Indian peoples. Indian peoples demanded these rights in the treaty process, and it was accepted that the constitutional privileges were necessary to their "support and subsistence." Today, the federal and provincial authorities responsible for fish and game management must consider both the Indian treaty rights and the NRTA subsistence rights when designing fish and game regulations. Aboriginal access to the resources must take priority over sport hunting and fishing. That is not to say that these rights cannot be regulated. The Sparrow test allows the government to infringe on the rights with justification and conservation is a legitimate reason for infringement. None of the government negotiators, however, understood that the issue would have such wide application. It was never intended by the government negotiators that hunting and fishing rights would provide Indian peoples with a voice in parks, timber, or oil and gas management, yet decisions appear to be shaped in that direction. New decisions with regard to water management are on the horizon. The complete implications of Indian hunting and fishing privileges are still not known. Much remains to be decided.

Notes

1. The principle of equality was first enunciated by the federal government on April 21, 1922. The three provinces accepted this principle as the foundation of the negotiations. For a look at the federal negotiating position see "Reports by John A. Reid," April 18, 1921, RG 15, D-II-1, vol. 1163, file 5308722. For the Manitoba response see Manitoba PC 902, 5 May 1923. *Unpublished Sessional Papers, 1926–27*, Paper No. 172, RG 14, D 2, vol. 160.

2. *Constitution Act, 1930*, 20–21; Geo. V., c. 3, s. 12; *Statutes of Alberta, 1930*, c. 21, s. 12.

3. For the NRTA and treaty hunting rights see *Frank v. The Queen* [1978] 1 S.C.R. 95; *Moosehunter v. The Queen* [1981] 1 S.C.R. 282; *R. v. Horseman* [1990] 1 S.C.R. 901; and *R. v. Badger* [1996] 1 S.C.R. 771. For treaty fishing rights see *R. v. Gladue* [1996] 1 C.N.L.R. 153; and *R. v. Lamouche* [2001] 1

C.N.L.R. 263. For the application of the NRTA right to non-treaty aboriginal people see R. v. Ferguson [1993] 2 C.N.L.R. 148; aff'd [1994] 1 C.N.L.R. 117 (Alta. Q. B.); R. v. Grumbo [1998] 3 C.N.L.R. 172; R. v. Blais [2003] 2 S.C.R. 236. On the application of provincial regulations with regard to hunting methods see Prince and Myron v. R. [1964] S.C.R. 81; Cardinal v. Alberta [1974] S.C.R. 695; and Myran v. R [1976] 2 S.C.R. 137. See Robert Irwin, "A Clear Intention to Effect Such Modification: The NRTA and Treaty Hunting and Fishing Rights," Native Studies Review 13, no. 2 (2000): 43–80 for an historical overview.

4. Alexander Morris, The Treaties of Canada with the Indians of Manitoba and the North-West Territories including the Negotiations on which they were based (Toronto: Belfords Clark, 1880; repr. Saskatoon: Fifth House, 1995) contains the text of Treaties 1 through 7. The clause in Treaties 3, 5, and 6 is identical. The clause in Treaty 7 is subtly different with regard to the taking up of lands. In Treaties 8 to 11, trapping is itemized as a protected right and the word "avocation" is replaced by "vocation." For the text of Treaties 8 and 11, the reader could consult Rene Fumoleau, As Long As This Land Shall Last (Toronto: McClelland and Stewart, 1975). The Department of Indian Affairs has excellent research reports available on each of the Treaties.

5. Jean Friesen, "Magnificent Gifts: The Treaties of Canada with the Indians of the Northwest, 1869–76," Transactions of the Royal Society of Canada V, no. 1 (1986): 50. For a reprint of this article and other interpretive works on the Treaties see Richard Price, ed., The Spirit of the Alberta Indian Treaties, 3rd ed., (Edmonton: University of Alberta Press, 2000). The most recent survey of the Treaty process in western Canada is Jim Miller, Arthur Ray, and Frank Tough, Bounty and Benevolence: A History of the Saskatchewan Treaties (Montreal and Kingston: McGill-Queen's University Press, 2000). For coverage of Indian treaties and resources see Jean Friesen, "Grant Me Wherewith to Make My Living," in Kerry Abel and Jean Friesen, eds., Aboriginal Resource Use in Canada (Winnipeg: University of Manitoba Press, 1991), 141–55; and A.J. Ray, "Commentary on the Economic History of the Treaty 8 Area," Native Studies Review 10, no. 2 (1995): 169–95.

6. Morris, Treaties of Canada, 29.

7. Morris, Treaties of Canada, 96.

8. Morris, Treaties of Canada, 215; 218.

9. Morris, Treaties of Canada, 226–28; 241.

10. Morris, Treaties of Canada, 257–58; 267.

11. "Report of the Commissioners for Treaty 8," Sessional Papers, 1900, no. 8, p. xxxvi.

12. Statutes of Canada, 1875, 38 Vic., c. 49, s. 7; Statutes of Manitoba, 1883, 46–47 Vic., c. 19.

13. Vankoughnet to Macdonald, Sept. 30, 1884, RG 10, vol. 3692, file 14069.

14. Vankoughnet to Deputy Min. of Justice, April 8, 1885, RG 10, vol. 3692, file 14069.

15. R. v. Robertson [1886] 3 Man. R. 613.

16. Statutes of Canada, 1890, 53 Vic., c. 29, s. 10. This clause, amended to include Saskatchewan and Alberta subsequent to their creation in 1905, remained an integral element of the Indian Act until the 1951 revisions. Its number changed to sec. 66 in R.S.C. 1906 and to section 69 in R.S.C. 1927, c. 98.

17. Memorandum for Deputy Minister, Dec. 17, 1903, RG 10, vol. 6732, file 420-2. The memorandum holds that only the federal government could enforce the regulation of rights protected by the treaty. This rationale, without understanding the particular intransigence of Manitoba and the federal control over crown lands, is not entirely convincing. The federal government understood that Treaty 3, for example, was clearly within the boundaries of Ontario, but that province was not included in the provisions of the Indian Act section. The federal negotiator during the resource transfer negotiations,

O.M. Biggar, believed it was the combination of treaty rights and federal control of lands that led to the passage of the clause. In this case, he noted that regulations could not be enforced against Indian peoples on lands to which they had right of access (unoccupied Crown lands) without the concurrence of the federal government. It was thus the federal role of administrator of lands that brought them into this jurisdictional arrangement. Memorandum of O.M. Biggar, Jan. 30, 1925, RG 10, vol. 6820, file 492–4–2 pt. 1.

18. *Territorial Ordinances*, 1893, No. 8, sec. 19. Saskatchewan maintained this clause in its game legislation until 1912–1913 when it reserved the right to exempt Indians from Saskatchewan regulations to the lieutenant-governor-in-council. Alberta's first game legislation followed in the Manitoba tradition and made no special provision for Indian peoples. See *Statutes of Saskatchewan*, 1912–13, c. 40 and *Statutes of Alberta*, 1907, c. 14.

19. Lists of the affected bands are found in numerous Indian Affairs files. See the copies of the notices given June 1, 1893 and May 1, 1903 and a list of the affected bands in RG 10, 6756, file 420–11 pt. 1 or RG 10, vol. 6732, file 420–2. No notice was ever made respecting the game laws of Manitoba or to any other bands in Manitoba. The Indian Agents in the various agencies were sent copies of the *North-West Territorial Game Ordinance* and informed that the Indians would be bound by its terms. Forget to Agents, Aug. 17, 1893, RG 10, vol. 3581, file 878 pt. A.

20. *Attorney General for the Dominion of Canada v. Attorneys General for the Provinces of Ontario, Quebec and Nova Scotia* [1898] A.C. 700 in Richard Olmsted, arr. *Decisions of the Judicial Council of the Privy Council relating to the British North America Act, 1867 and the Canadian Constitution, 1867–1954* (Ottawa: Queen's Printer, 1954), 418–35. For a summary of the complex jurisdictional questions related to fisheries, see Gerald La Forest, *Natural Resources and Public Property under the Canadian Constitution* (Toronto: University of Toronto Press, 1967), 77–79; 157–60; 165–66; and 176–82.

21. See the summary of correspondence 1884 and 1885 re: Fishing Stations, RG 10, vol. 3755, file 30979–1 pt. 2; and Depy Min. of Fisheries to Vankoughnet, Oct. 27, 1888, RG 10, vol. 3788, file 43856.

22. Depy Min. of Fisheries to Vankoughnet, Sept. 11, 1889, RG 10, vol. 3755, file 30979–1 pt. 1.

23. OIC 4 Jan. 1892, RG 23, vol. 241, file 1509 pt. 1. Copy found in RG 10, vol. 3755, file 30979–4.

24. Hayter Reed to A. E. Forget, Nov. 20, 1893 and Forget, circular letter, Nov. 24, 1893, RG 10, vol. 3581, file 878 pt A.

25. Dep. Min. of Fisheries to D.S.G.I.A., Jan. 3, 1894, RG 23, vol. 126, file 170 pt. 1.

26. S.G.I.A. to Minister of Marine and Fisheries, Jan. 29, 1894, RG 23, vol. 126, file 170 pt. 1.

27. S.G.I.A. to Minister of Marine and Fisheries, May 11, 1894, RG 23, vol. 126, file 170 pt. 1. Fisheries officers and members of the NWMP surveyed by the Department of Marine and Fisheries had argued that Indians should pay for licenses and that the DIA should feed Indians rather than allow them to fish in the closed season. See Comptroller of NWMP to Minister of Marine and Fisheries, Feb. 22, 1894, Jan. 29, 1894, RG 23, vol. 126, file 170 pt. 1.

28. Hayter Reed, "Memorandum for the Information of the Minister re Fishing Privileges Claimed by Indians," Nov. 18, 1895, RG 23, vol. 126, file 170 pt. 1. All quotes including the added emphasis are from the Fisheries Department copy. This memorandum follows a lengthy undated memorandum on Ontario, British Columbia, Manitoba, and the North-West Territories prepared by S. Stewart, "Fishing Privileges Claimed by Indians," RG 10, vol. 3908, file 107,297–1.

29. E.E. Prince, Dominion Commissioner of Fisheries to Reed, July 27, 1896; Reed to Prince, July 30, 1896; Prince to Inspector G.S. Davidson, Sept. 10, 1896; Dep. Min. of Fisheries to D.S.G.I.A., Sept. 10, 1896, RG 23, vol. 126, file 170 pt. 1.

30. Dep. Min. of Marine and Fisheries to Secretary, Indian Affairs, Nov. 22, 1897, RG 23, vol. 126, file 170 pt. 1. The regulations for 1897 reflected this pattern. Particular lakes and specific opportunities for Indian subsistence fishing were identified: Indians and Half-breeds were allowed to fish for 10 days during the closed season at Lac La Biche; Indians only had the privilege at Lac Ste. Anne; Indians, Half-breeds, and white settlers at Pigeon Lake, White Whale Lake, and Big Lake. OIC, 5 Oct. 1897, RG 23, vol. 126, file 170 pt. 1.

31. E.E. Prince, Memorandum, April 5, 1898; J.D. McLean to Dep. Min. of Marine and Fisheries, July 20, 1898; Dep. Min. of Fisheries to McLean, Aug. 4, 1898, RG 23, vol. 306, file 2445 pt. 1; J.D. McLean, Memorandum, June 7, 1898, RG 10, vol. 3908, file 107,297-3; J.D. McLean to Dep. Min. of Marine and Fisheries, June 23, 1900; D.S.G.I.A. to Dep. Min. of Marine and Fisheries, Nov. 17, 1908; G.J. Desberats to D.S.G.I.A., Nov. 26, 1908, RG 23, vol. 126, file 170 pt. 2; D.S.G.I.A. to David Laird, Feb. 8, 1906, RG 10, vol. 6972, file 774/20-2 pt. 1.

32. See *Ordinances of the Northwest Territories*, 1898, c. 85, sec. 2 and *Ordinances of the Northwest Territories*, 1903, c. 29, sec. 2 and 17. For a discussion of the important place given to hunting for food in the structure of early game regulations and the rise of sport hunting in Western Canada generally consult George Colpitts, *Game in the Garden: A Human History of Wildlife in Western Canada to 1940* (Vancouver: UBC Press, 2002), 63–102.

33. *Statutes of Alberta, 1907*, c. 14, sec. 28.

34. Colpitts, *Game in the Garden*, 86–87.

35. Frank Pedley to Dep. Attorney General (AB), Dec. 16, 1907, RG 10, vol. 6732, file 420-2.

36. Dep. Attorney General to S.G.I.A., Jan. 2, 1908, RG 10, vol. 6732, file 420-2.

37. Oliver to Dep. Attorney General, Jan. 22, 1908, RG 10, vol. 6732, file 420-2. The reference to the terms of the treaty is unclear. Oliver may have been so unaware of the terms of the various treaties that he believed the "subject to regulations" provisions were unique to Treaty 8. It is possible that his comment is related to the change in the regulatory authority specified in the text of Treaty 8. In Treaty 6, the regulatory authority is "Her Government of Her Dominion of Canada," while in Treaty 8, the regulatory authority is "the Government of the Country." If that is the case, it appears that the federal government understood that under Treaty 6 only the federal government could regulate the treaty privilege, but that under Treaty 8, the Provincial regulations were applicable.

38. James Campbell, Memorandum to Dep. Minister, Nov. 30, 1908; David Laird to Secretary, Dec. 16, 1908; Campbell Memorandum, Jan. 4, 1909; Pedley to Laird, Jan. 12, 1909; S. Stewart to Pedley, Feb. 25, 1909, RG 10, vol. 6737, file 420-4 pt. 1.

39. P.L. Grasse to Assistant Commissioner, May 17, 1894; Forget to Grasse, June 11, 1894, RG 10, vol. 3581, file 878 pt. A. A summary of some of the problems related to the Stony Indians and game laws is S. Stewart, "Memorandum Re: Destruction of Game," Dec. 17, 1903; Sibbald to D.S.G.I.A., Dec. 23, 1903, RG 10, vol. 6732, file 420-2.

40. Peter Wesley, Moses Bearspaw to Government of Canada, April 9, 1907, RG 10, vol. 6732, file 420-2. The Stoney were not alone in claiming that the regulations violated the treaty see Chiefs of Swan River Agency to D.S.G.I.A., Sept. 21, 1907, RG 10, vol. 6732, file 420-2 and Chief James Sennum to Minister of Interior, May 3, 1909, RG 10, vol. 6732, file 420-2A.

41. See RG 10, vol. 6732, file 420-2A for a copy of the decision. Stuart's position with regard to Dominion legislation prevailing over the Province is consistent with the logic of *G.T.R. v. A. G. for Canada* [1907] A.C. 65 in Olmsted, arr. *Judicial Decisions of the Privy Council*, 530. Stuart's position with respect to Indians having to comply with Provincial laws in the absence of

federal legislation is consistent with *R. v. Hill* [1907] 15 O.L.R. 406, reprinted in B. Slatery and L. Charlton, comps., *Canadian Native Law Cases*, vol. 3 (Saskatoon: Native Law Centre, 1985).

42. For some of the difficulties interpreting the decision see David Laird, "Memorandum for the Secretary," Dec. 1, 1910, RG 10, vol. 6732, file 420–2A.

43. Benjamin Lawton (AB Game Guardian) to D.S.G.I.A., Mar. 28, 1912, RG 10, vol. 6732, file 420–2A. *Statutes of Alberta*, 1911–1912, c. 4, s. 25(4).

44. See for example McLean to Samuel Wolf (Muskeg Lake), Apr. 11, 1914; McLean to Thomas Muchoow, George Turner, and Jacob Badger (Mistawasis), May 7, 1914; McLean to Henry Twobears, Jan. 24, 1916, RG 10, vol. 6756, file 420–11 pt. 1; and McLean to Chief Francis Alexis (Lac Ste. Anne), Aug. 10, 1918, RG 10, vol. 6732, file 420–2A.

45. *Dominion Alberta Saskatchewan Fisheries Commission, 1910–11* (Ottawa: Government Printer, 1912), 22 and 31; Dep. Min. of Fisheries to D.S.G.I.A., April 18, 1914; and D.S.G.I.A. to Dep. Min. of Fisheries, April 25, 1914, RG 23, vol. 999, file 721–4–37[1].

46. Charles Barber (MB Game Guardian) to McLean, Oct. 4, 1918; S. Stewart to Barber, Oct. 29, 1918; and Minister of Agriculture to Arthur Meighen, Oct. 21, 1918.

47. Opinion 1447/17, W. Stuart Edwards to D.C. Scott, Oct. 5, 1917, RG 10, vol. 6731, file 420–1. This position was later quoted in the context of the NRTA discussions. Memorandum, Feb. 6, 1925, RG 10, vol. 6820, file 492–4–2 pt. 1. Lord Watson's reference is in *St. Catherines Milling and Lumber vs. The Queen* [1888] 14 A.C. 46 at 60, in Slatery and Charlton, comps. *Canadian Native Law Cases*, 555.

48. Scott, Memorandum to Minister, Mar. 15, 1919, RG 10, vol. 6731, file 420–1.

49. Notice, Feb. 1, 1909 (Manitoba Indians), RG 10, vol. 6737, file 420–4 pt. 1; Notice, Mar. 10, 1919 (numerous bands), RG 10, vol. 6731, file 420–1.

50. Canada, *Debates of the House of Commons*, 1920, 3379.

51. *R. v. Rogers* [1923] 2 W.W.R. 353 at 359. Dennistoun dissented from the decision to not enforce provincial game laws on reserves, but is in concurrence with the position that game laws would apply off reserve.

52. *R. v. Hill* [1907] 15 O.L.R. 406 and *R. v. Martin* [1917] 39 D.L.R. 635.

53. Commission of Conservation, Canada, *National Conference on Conservation of Game, Fur Bearing Animals and Other Wildlife*, (Ottawa: J.de L.Tache, printer, 1919), 19–38. Fred Bradshaw, SK Game Guardian, delivered a stinging critique of the Department's assistance and Indian hunting habits at the conference.

54. Circular Letter, J.D. McLean to Agents, Apr. 26, 1926, RG 10, vol. 6732, file 420–2B.

55. D.C. Scott to Lt.-Governor of Manitoba, Feb. 5, 1922, RG 10, vol. 6737, file 420–4 pt. 2.

56. John A. Reid, "Memorandum Re: Administration of Certain Natural Resources of the Prairie Provinces," submitted to Arthur Meighen, April 18, 1921, RG 15, D-II-1, vol. 1163, file 5308722; D.C. Scott, Memorandum to Charles Stewart, March 9, 1922, RG 10, vol. 6820, file 492–4–2 pt. 1.

57. Memorandum, January 29, 1925, RG 10, vol. 6820, file 492–4–2 pt. 1.

58. Biggar, Memorandum, January 30, 1925, RG 10, vol. 6820, file 492–4–2 pt. 1.

59. Appendix H: Indian Lands in a Memorandum to Prime Minister by Biggar (copy to Scott, 17 Feb. 1925), RG 10, vol. 6820, file 492–4–2 pt. 1.

60. Draft Alberta Agreement sent to D.C. Scott, May–June 1925 in RG 10, vol. 6820, file 492–4–2 pt. 1.

61. Brownlee to King, Apr. 7, 1926, *Unpublished Sessional Papers, 1926–27*, Paper No. 84a, RG 14, D 2, vol. 157.

62. Chisholm to Scott, Aug. 22, 1929; Scott to Chisholm, Sept. 4, 1929, RG 10, vol. 6820, file 492–4–2 pt. 1.

63. Explanatory Memorandum RE Manitoba Resources Agreement, RG 22, vol. 3, file 6.

64. RG 22, vol. 3, file 6.

65. W. Stuart Edwards to Duncan Campbell Scott, Feb. 12, 1931, RG 22, vol. 22, file 91; W. Stuart Edwards to Harold McGill, Aug. 30, 1933, RG 10, vol. 6820, file 492–4–2. For a discussion of this opinion and others see Frank Tough, "Introduction to Documents: Indian Hunting Rights, Natural Resource Transfer Agreements and Legal Opinions from the Department of Justice," *Native Studies Review* 10, no. 2 (1995): 121–67.

66. O.M. Biggar, Draft Letter, Indian Affairs to C.F. Newell (Edmonton Fish and Game Association), Mar. 3, 1930, RG 10, vol. 6820, file 492–4–2 pt. 1. See Solicitor to Deputy Minister of Interior, Dec. 2, 1932, RG 22, vol. 22, file 91 for similar conclusions.

67. *Daniels v. White* [1968] S.C.R. 517. See also Dep. Min of Interior to Edwards, Nov. 12, 1931, RG 22, vol. 22, file 91; and Dan Gottesman, "Native Hunting and the Migratory Birds Convention Act: Historical, Political, and Ideological Perspectives," *Journal of Canadian Studies* 18, no. 3 (1983): 67–89.

68. *Sero v. Gault* [1921] 50 O.L.R. 27, in Slatery and Charlton, comps., *Canadian Native Law Cases*, 468. See also Lise Hansen, "Treaty Fishing Rights and the Development of Fisheries Legislation in Ontario: A Primer," *Native Studies Review* 10, no. 2 (1995): 121–67.

69. Circular Letter, D.C. Scott to Agents, May 30, 1931, RG 10, vol. 8860, file 1/18–11–2 pt. 1; Memorandum H.H. Rowatt to Department solicitor, Jan. 23, 1933, RG 22, vol. 22, file 91.

70. *Alberta Scrapbook Hansard*, 50, *Edmonton Bulletin* Feb. 20, 1930.

71. *R. v. Wesley* [1932], 2 W.W.R. 337; *R. v. Smith* [1935] 2 W.W.R. 433. Justice Hall also noted that the NRTA continued and protected the treaty right in his dissent in *Daniels v. White* [1968] S.C.R. 517. In *Frank v. The Queen* [1978] 1 S.C.R. 95, the Court recognized that the NRTA right was significantly different than the treaty right.

72. *R. v. Horseman* [1990] 1 S.C.R. 901 and *R. v. Badger* [1996] 1 S.C.R. 771.

73. Noel Lyon, "Constitutional Issues in Native Law," in Bradford Morse, ed. *Aboriginal Peoples and the Law* (Ottawa: Carleton University Press, 1989), 429–31.

74. Clem Chartier, "Indian: An Analysis of the Term as used in Section 91(24) of the British North America Act," *Saskatchewan Law Review* 43 (1978–79): 38–80.

75. *R. v. Ferguson* [1993] 2 C.N.L.R. 148; aff'd [1994] 1 C.N.L.R. 117 (Alta. Q. B.); *R. v. Grumbo* [1998] 3 C.N.L.R. 172; *R. v. Blais* [2003] 2 S.C.R. 236.

76. The important decisions are *Calder v. Attorney General of British Columbia* [1973] S.C.R. 313; *Nowegijick v. The Queen* [1983] 1 S.C.R. 29; *Simon v. The Queen* [1985] 2 S.C.R. 387; *R. v. Sioui* [1990] 1 S.C.R. 1025; *R. v. Sparrow* [1990] 1075; *R. v. Badger* [1996] 1 S.C.R. 771; and *R. v. Marshall* [1999] 3 S.C.R. 456.

77. [1996] 1 S.C.R. 771, at 778.

78. For a discussion of the increasing scope of treaty rights and the government's obligation to uphold the "honour and integrity" of the Crown, see Robert Mainville, *An Overview of Aboriginal and Treaty Rights and Compensation for Their Breach* (Saskatoon: Purich Publishing, 2001), 34–52. In the recent *Marshall* decision, Justice (now Chief Justice) McLachlin expressed some concern regarding the scope of treaty rights in the modern context. She concluded that they should be read in the context within which they were made. *R. v. Marshall* [1999] 3 S.C.R. 456 at 513–15.

79. *R. v. Sundown* [1999] 1 S.C.R. 393; *R. v. Catarat* [2001] 2 CNLR 158.

80. *Halfway River First Nation v. BC* [1999] 64 B.C.L.R. (3rd) 206; *Whitefish Lake First Nation v. Director, Northwest Boreal Region, Alberta Environment*, re: Tri Link Resources Ltd., EAB Appeal No. 99–009.

Nine

Justices of the Peace in Alberta

ROD MACLEOD AND NANCY PARKER

As the Justice of the Peace is required to act not only ministerially, but judicially, he ought in all his acts to avoid whatever may lead to the appearance of partiality in his opinions and judgments. The impression that he who is raised to the seat of Justice, leans in his decisions to the side of friendship, or to that of a political party, is destructive of all confidence, and alienates the minds of men from that obedience to the laws, and that respect for justice, which are so essential for the support of good order in society.[1]

The office of justice of the peace is ubiquitous in common law jurisdictions. Ancient and protean, it has developed in very different ways even within a single country like Canada. It is one of those parts of the provincial constitutions that, under Section 92 (1) of the Constitution Act 1867, may be amended unilaterally by the provincial legislatures and that has largely been ignored by constitutional scholars. Perhaps this lack of attention is because so much of our history has been consumed by fierce constitutional fights over education—an area of exclusive provincial jurisdiction but with special safeguards for religious minorities included in the Constitution Act, 1867. If there is no jurisdictional conflict, even very fundamental changes can pass with little notice. Few people now realize, for example, that for most of the period since Confederation, the Quebec legislature included an appointed upper house analogous to the Senate of Canada. It vanished without a ripple in the 1960s. Changes to the provincial court systems, which were assumed not to be included in the guarantees of judicial independence covering the superior courts, have likewise attracted little attention, in spite of the fact that those courts handle the great majority of the country's judicial business.

That was the case, at least, until the mid-1990s when several provincial governments, including Alberta, affected by the financial stringency of the times, attempted to reduce the salaries of Provincial Court judges as an economy measure. In Alberta, the government by regulation in 1994 reduced the salaries of Provincial Court judges by 5%. When some judges intimated that they would refuse to sit in protest against the move, Premier Klein during a radio interview said that any judge who refused to sit should be, "very, very quickly fired."[2] This was far too good an opportunity to pass up and several lawyers with cases being heard in Provincial Court immediately filed motions arguing that these events demonstrated that those courts did not meet the Charter requirement for independent and impartial tribunals. These cases made their way up the appeal ladder and were combined with cases from Manitoba and Prince Edward Island that raised the same issues.

The *Provincial Court Judges Reference* (1997) extended the independent and impartial requirement to judges of the provincial courts in a way that strongly suggested that justices of the peace would also be included if the issue came before the courts. It did so in the case of *Ell v. Alberta* decided by the Supreme Court in 2003.[3] The Ell case grew directly out of reforms begun by the Alberta government in the 1980s, reforms that made greater changes to the office of justice of the peace in the province than had taken place over the previous century. These changes were undoubtedly driven by the Supreme Court's interpretation of the Charter. They represent, as Justice La Forest pointed out in his dissenting opinion in the *Provincial Court Judges Reference*, a significant usurpation of provincial powers.[4] The road to the changed situation of justices of the peace at the beginning of the 21st century is one that goes back long before the creation of the Province of Alberta in 1905.

The office of justice of the peace in Alberta has existed since the creation of the province in 1905. Alberta inherited the system of appointing and using justices from the North-West Territories; a system that was already significantly different from those in other parts of Canada. The territorial system was in some important respects more modern and professionalized than those of the older provinces. Specifically, the existence of a full-time police force in the form of the North West Mounted Police and the early appointment of stipendiary magistrates meant that the justices in the North-West Territories had a more restricted role than their contemporaries in, for example, Ontario or Quebec. The Canadian government in the late nineteenth century tended to regard the North West Territories as an area where it could try out simpler and more efficient approaches to the administration of justice. The Mounted

Police were one example of this experimentation and the elimination of the grand jury was another.

The new province of Alberta immediately passed legislation to continue the territorial system.[5] The fact that the same statute made provision for both police magistrates and justices of the peace was an indication of how closely integrated the two offices were seen to be. The province often preferred to appoint magistrates who had the power of two justices sitting together, particularly in remote areas where travel difficulties and sparse populations made it difficult to arrange sessions. The provincial government appointed unpaid magistrates who were as inexpensive as justices and seem in the early part of the century to have heard very much the same kind of cases. Salaried magistrates in the larger centres handled more serious cases. In Alberta, from the 1920s to the 1970s, the role of magistrates expanded to meet the needs of the growing population of the province. During the same period, justices of the peace continued to be appointed and while their role in trying cases waned, their role in such activities as taking informations and issuing warrants remained constant.

By the 1950s there was a growing number of different kinds of justice of the peace in Alberta. In addition to the traditional lay justices of the peace (fee justices) and senior RCMP officers, there were two new categories. A number of RCMP constables and non-commissioned officers assigned to traffic duties were appointed justices of the peace, with functions limited to signing traffic tickets issued by members of the force. Some civil servants, known as staff justices of the peace, were also appointed. In 1978 the province created a new category of staff justices of the peace known as hearing officers. These individuals worked in Calgary and Edmonton, dealing mainly with first appearances in traffic and municipal by-law cases and hearing bail applications. The creation of traffic commissioners (sitting justices of the peace) in 1991 continued the process of specialization and professionalization of justices of the peace by requiring legal training.

The office of justice of the peace is one of the most ancient of the institutions that characterize the English system of Common Law. It is also one of the most distinctive; none of the civil law systems of Europe had officials remotely like the unpaid, locally based, English Justices. The powers and duties entrusted to justices of the peace have waxed and waned enormously over the centuries, both in Britain and in her former colonies around the world. The diversity of the office across the various provincial and territorial jurisdictions in Canada in the 21st century is an indication that it is still being adapted to changing circumstances.

Although some medievalists claim to find the roots of the justices of the peace in the Anglo-Saxon kingdoms, it was in the unique circumstances of the 13th and 14th centuries that the office took permanent shape. Unlike France and the other continental kingdoms, England was relatively free from the threat of external attack. The English kings could thus delegate powers to the local elites without having to fear that in doing so they were compromising the integrity of their kingdom. Throughout this period, the English kings were intent on maintaining control of their continental lands in Normandy. This required money and men, both of which could most efficiently be obtained with the support of the country gentry. Given commissions as justices of the peace, they became unpaid local agents of the crown with extensive judicial and administrative powers. In return they got the opportunity to become participants in the governance of the country. As the historian Norma Landau, author of the most sophisticated study of the subject, puts it:

> So the justices were the premier exemplars of two traditions of govern-
> ment which the English considered unique to their island; the practice
> of self-government at the king's command and the acceptance of respon-
> sibility by the elite. On the Continent, the elite fled from their estates,
> preferring the pleasures of the court to the burdens of local leadership.
> In England, the elite accepted the obligations inherent in their social
> status.... Of all the European landed elites, only the English captured
> the central government. Only in England did the state not develop into
> an entity separate from the elite and in conflict with it. In England the
> landed elite monopolized government, and the justices therefore embod-
> ied the peculiarly English union of social and official power.[6]

The Statute of Winchester of 1361 regularized the office by requiring the appointment of justices in every shire and defining their powers and duties. Another statute the following year required the justices of the county to meet quarterly to hear all but the most serious cases (Quarter Sessions). Two or more justices could sit at any time (Petty Sessions). Quarter Sessions and Petty Sessions had the power to hear and determine all felonies short of treason, but as Sir Thomas Skyrme points out, they generally preferred to send cases of murder and other serious crimes to the assizes.[7] Justices acting alone had substantial powers to investigate complaints and either release suspects on bail or commit them to prison to await trial.[8] They could impose fines for minor offences. In their judicial role, however, the emphasis was on the collectivity of the commission of the peace rather than the individuals who made it up.

In an age before the development of police forces and modern institutions of local government, the justices carried out both these functions. They were responsible for regulating weights and measures, for licensing alehouses, for setting local tax rates and a host of other duties. As the name implies, justices of the peace were primarily responsible for maintaining order in their communities. They were charged with mobilizing whatever community resources existed to deal with riots and other disturbances and they could arrest suspected criminals on suspicion. Obviously, there was little room among these multiple roles for the modern concept of judicial independence. The same individual would very often hear a complaint, make the arrest, decide on bail and sit in judgement. The medieval and early modern mentality would have considered the notion that the last of these functions should be separate from the previous ones to be both odd and unworkable. The ideal was instead the paternalistic community leader who knew the history and reputations of everyone in his area and was responsible for overseeing every aspect of their daily existence. He performed these duties without pay because it was expected of those with high social standing. The few JP's who processed large numbers of cases for the sake of the fees attached were known contemptuously as "trading justices."

Historians agree that the justices reached the height of their powers in England in the eighteenth century. Thereafter, the rapid growth of large cities, especially London, made necessary new and more specialized political and administrative structures, such as police forces and elected municipal governments that took over many of the functions of the justices. It was just at this time that the office of justice made the trans-Atlantic journey to Canada.

The powers of justices of the peace in the British North American colonies, and later in the provinces of Canada, variously included civil, criminal and administrative duties, as well as commonly civic or municipal government.[9] While over the course of the late-eighteenth and early-nineteenth centuries a large body of statute law developed concerning jurisdiction over specific activities, some of the most significant powers of justices of the peace still rested on the traditional responsibilities associated with their individual commissions. Specifically, the powers of two justices of the peace sitting together in petty sessions and of those in the county-wide meeting of justices of the peace sitting with juries at Quarter Sessions of the Peace rested with the commissions rather than legislation. Some of the English traditions regarding justices of the peace did not make an easy translation to the Colonies. Most particularly, the standard property qualifications were designed to ensure that the "most worthy men in the county" were appointed, posed difficulties for earlier Governors.[10] The absence of a class of gentry who might be expected to fulfill the roles of magistrates on a largely volunteer basis prompted the creation of salaried (or stipendiary) magistrates at a relatively early stage in most colonies. A number of cities instituted Mayor's courts where, with the assistance of Recorders, a range of summary offences could be tried. Over time the Recorders were acknowledged as having the powers of petty sessions, which evolved in similar terms and duties as police or stipendiary magistrates courts.

When examining the eighteenth and nineteenth century inferior courts, it is important to note that the separation of legislative and judicial branches of government, now constitutionally entrenched, was not at all traditional. Indeed, it would have been a surprising concept in British North America, where judges of the Superior Courts sat on the Governor's Legislative Councils and routinely drafted legislation, where Mayors or Reeves presided over municipal courts, and where justices of the peace administered many aspects of local government. It is also fair to say that well past the Confederation era, patronage was the rule, rather than the exception, in judicial appointments at all levels of the courts.

Under English law as it was received in the colonies, one justice sitting alone (out of sessions), could: issue warrants, conduct preliminary inquiries, investigate misdemeanours, try a variety of summary offences, and bind those accused of more serious offences on recognizances (or sureties for good behaviour) or commit them to gaol to await trial. Two or more justices sitting together (petty sessions) had more extensive summary powers and, depending on local circumstances, performed an array of administrative duties related to the poor laws and to licensing. Together with the grand jurors sitting at the quarter or general sessions of the peace, magistrates were the heart of local government. The criminal jurisdiction of this court was extensive: it included powers to hear appeals from some convictions by justices of the peace out of sessions,[11] and, in theory, the same authority to hear and determine serious criminal cases as the assizes (the judges of the superior courts on circuit). In practice, however, capital offences were sent to the higher court.[12] These general powers accompanied English law to the colonies and were then subject to local amendments.

Local changes were extensive. For example, in Quebec between 1764 and 1836, "some 300 separate pieces of colonial legislation modified the powers of justice of the peace and their various courts."[13] The jurisdictions of the Courts were extended by statutes for specific offences. Generally, if the new offence was felony it would fall in the jurisdiction of the Quarter or General Sessions of the Peace and higher criminal courts. For misdemeanours, the jurisdiction was usually specified to one, two, or more justices of the peace.[14]

Like Lower Canada, the laws defining the jurisdiction of magistrates in Upper Canada were in a constant state of flux, and the reform decade of the 1830s brought a number of significant changes.[15] A general form for convictions by justices of the peace was provided in 1832, and the same legislation declared that any defects in form could not be a basis for appeal.[16] The following year the bail proceedings were adjusted and then amended further in the next session.[17] Also in 1834, summary powers in cases of common assaults and petty trespasses were granted to justices of the peace sitting alone, with appeals from such convictions to be heard at the quarter sessions.[18] After the rebellions of 1837–1838, justices of the peace were empowered to seize and detain arms "collected or kept for purposes dangerous to the public peace."[19] These powers were in addition to the traditional authority of justices of the peace to "read the riot act," which turned participation in a disorderly crowd into a felonious offence.[20]

After the union of the colonies of Upper and Lower Canada (renamed Canada East, and Canada West) in 1841, the measures taken to provide more uniform criminal laws for the provinces essentially imported the consolidations provided by Peel's Acts in Britain.[21] The amendments to summary and pre-trial criminal procedures contained in Jervis' Acts were enacted in 1851.[22] Further amendments came with the Consolidated Statutes in 1859 and included "An Act respecting the prompt and summary administration of Criminal Justice in certain cases."[23] That Act provided for summary trials, with the consent of the accused, by the "Recorder in any City," in cases of larceny where the property was valued at less than one dollar, attempted larceny, including larceny from the person, aggravated assault, assault on females or male children, and assault on peace officers. Under this jurisdiction, the maximum punishments were restricted to three months imprisonment for larceny, and six months imprisonment and/or a fine of not more than one hundred dollars for assaults. The consent of the accused was not required for summary trials of prostitution offences, which carried the same maximum penalties as assaults. Under this Act all of the police magistrates in Upper Canada were granted the same authority as city recorders.

Among the changes following the union of the Canadas in the 1840s were first the District Council Bill, and then the *Municipal Corporations Act*, which put most of the administrative duties of the quarter sessions into the hands of incorporated councils.[24] It has been claimed that this deviation from English traditions was welcomed because Upper Canada had neither the number nor quality of justices of the peace to allow for effective local government.[25] Concern over the quality of justices of the peace led to increased property qualifications, which by 1859 were: "possession of absolute property...of or above the value of one thousand two hundred dollars."[26] This remedy could not guarantee that those who were qualified, and had accepted their commission by swearing an oath, would actually perform their duties. The potential difficulties of a weak inferior court could be circumvented in incorporated towns or cities because the 1849 Municipal Corporations Act made provisions for the appointment of stipendiary police magistrates.[27] After Confederation, the same solution would be offered to Ontario counties, but that proposal generated as much controversy as the ongoing disputes over the incumbent justices of the peace.

In 1859 in the provinces of Canada the territorial jurisdiction of justices of the peace was first limited by separating cities and towns where there was a sitting police magistrate from the adjoining county. In other words, the "justices of the peace for a county in which a city [separated for judicial purposes] lies," had "no jurisdiction over offences committed in the city."[28] The police magistrates in those cities were made *ex officio* justices of the peace for both the city and surrounding county.[29] This grant of a monopoly over the criminal business within cities to police magistrates followed similar English provisions that were "probably introduced to prevent unseemly squabbling between magistrates having concurrent jurisdiction."[30] Eventually it also gave rise to appeals from convictions by justices of the peace sitting instead of, or in conjunction with, city stipendiaries.[31] Similar provisions for exclusive criminal jurisdiction for paid magistrates were granted to rural counties in Ontario in 1892.[32]

The general pattern of transferring administrative and judicial duties from lay justices of the peace to salaried professionals was also followed in other provinces. In British Columbia, the first commissions of the peace were issued without property qualifications and allowances were made for the magistrates to "make charge for their services."[33] The first stipendiary magistrate was appointed in Victoria in 1858 and on the mainland the same jurisdiction was put in the hands of the gold commissioners. By 1866 the united colonies had eleven stipendiary magistrates, and of those, six were selected to serve as County Court judges. The combination of administrative and judicial functions of these appointees created difficulties when attempts were made to install professionals with legal training in the inferior courts after Confederation.[34]

Nova Scotia took considerably longer than other provinces to restrict both the civil and administrative functions and criminal jurisdiction of its justice of the peace. Although the first stipendiary magistrate was appointed in Halifax in 1815, there was a hiatus in that office after the Mayor's court was created in 1841. At Confederation, the stipendiary magistrate's court was reinstated in Halifax and that court was granted a monopoly over minor criminal proceedings in the city.[35] Such changes were slower in the rest of the province. Justices of the peace sitting at quarter sessions kept their civic administrative duties until 1879 and exclusive criminal jurisdiction provisions were not enacted for municipal magistrates until 1888.[36]

Even though there was considerable local variation among the provinces in the powers, functions and duties of justices of the peace before and after Confederation, there were common themes in their selection and qualifications. Generally, following from the English tradition, barristers and solicitors could not be appointed justices of the peace while they continued to practice.[37] Although not specified by legislation or individual commissions, available rolls of justices of the peace in the provinces of British Columbia, Ontario and Nova Scotia suggest that there were three functional categories of appointments. First, there were *ex officio* office holders like mayors and reeves who might continue to hold their commission after they had left elected office. Second, there were a number of government employees, like Indian Agents, who were normally issued commissions to aid them in the execution of their duties. Third, a large number of appointees had their standing in the community, more specifically their political party, recognized with a commission. The provincial returns from justices of the peace suggest that for the most part these were honorific, rather than active appointments. The tenure of most of the justices of the peace also suggests that it was far easier to appoint than to dismiss these local notables. The most common reasons for names to be dropped from the consolidated lists of justices of the peace in nineteenth century Ontario were that the justice had moved out of the judicial district or had died in office.[38]

Having a large number of inactive justices of the peace created problems for provincial governments trying to keep track of appointments. Nova Scotia's remedy was to have a standing provision requiring all justices of the peace to produce their commissions and qualifications so that the county wardens could draw up new rolls.[39] Similarly, in 1891, Ontario implemented an Act that required all the justices of the peace who wanted to keep their commissions to renew their oaths of office and provide renewed evidence of their property qualification.[40] By containing a provision that cancelled all previous commissions of the peace when a new one was issued, Manitoba legislation allowed for sweeping overhauls of the benches of the inferior courts.[41] As a patronage position, an appointment as justice of the peace offered more potential for community status than direct profit. Despite occasional complaints about individual justices having a financial motive in promoting litigation, it is important to note that fixed fees were not high. For most of the nineteenth century the fees ranged from ten cents for every subpoena to fifty cents for taking information and issuing warrants in Ontario.[42] A very similar schedule of fees in summary trials was included in the Canadian Criminal Code.[43] At these restricted rates it is fair to say that justices of the peace were rendering largely voluntary service. There was a much wider range in the remuneration of stipendiary magistrates. Generally, salaries were negotiated with their respective municipalities, but some provinces found it necessary to set maximum or minimum amounts payable to magistrates.

The nineteenth century evolution of the inferior courts in Canada was thus marked by the rise of the office of stipendiary magistrate and, in the second half of the century, by a general decline in the powers, functions and duties of the office of justice of the peace. While justices of the peace lost powers, stipendiary magistrates were granted increasing summary powers, and eventually the authority, with the consent of the accused, to try most indictable offences.[44] According to the published national statistics, the number of indictable offences tried by magistrates increased from 3,224 in 1885 to 8,116 in 1905.[45] During the same period there were roughly 10 times the number of convictions for summary offences as for indictable offences. In this context, it is not surprising to find a law journal commentary in 1892 arguing that since the "Police Court occupies the position of a Criminal Court for the relief of higher Courts and the speedy disposition of business,...it is essential in the public interest that a professional man should perform the duties of magistrate."[46]

Justices of the peace made their appearance in what was to become Western Canada decades before Confederation was achieved in 1867. Reports of violence arising from competition between rival Montreal fur traders in the west led the British government to pass the *Canada Jurisdiction Act* in 1803.[47] This statute permitted the governor of Lower Canada to appoint justices in the "Indian Territories." This seems to have included both the Hudson's Bay Company's territories (Rupert's Land) and the rest of British territory west of Upper Canada. Even so, it failed entirely as a remedy for violence in the fur trade. In fact, the next two decades were marked by an even more serious conflict between the Montreal interests amalgamated into the North West Company and the Hudson's Bay Company under new and aggressive leadership. Both companies contrived to have their senior employees appointed justices of the peace, who then used their powers to harass the opposition by arresting them and sending them off on the year-long journey to Montreal for trial.

The situation was finally resolved when the British government imposed a merger of the two companies in 1821. Under the statute that formalized the merger, the Hudson's Bay Company had the responsibility for the administration of justice.[48] It did almost nothing to exercise its judicial powers until 1835, when Parliament's consideration of the renewal of the company's monopoly produced a show of activity. In that year, the company attempted to prosecute three of its employees for the murder of 11 Hare Indians on the Mackenzie River.[49] In a more substantial move, it created four judicial districts in the Red River settlement in what is now southern Manitoba and appointed a justice of the peace in each one.[50] The justices heard minor civil and criminal cases and sent more serious matters to a General Quarterly Court consisting of the governor of Assiniboia and his Council. In 1839, a professionally trained Recorder was added to the latter body.[51]

This remained the situation until the Canadian takeover of the HBC territories in 1870. For the first few years afterward, the Canadian government focused mainly on the fledgling province of Manitoba. In the North-West Territories, Ottawa merely passed legislation that allowed the existing laws and judicial appointments to continue in force.[52] In 1870, an Order-in-Council under this legislation empowered the lieutenant-governor of the North-West Territories to appoint justices of the peace. As in the other parts of Canada at this time, the legislation did not specify the terms of appointment. Without examining each individual commission, it would be impossible to say with absolute certainty that all appointments were at pleasure, but this seems to have been the case. In August of 1870, Lieutenant-Governor Adams G. Archibald appointed the first six justices under the new government.[53] Who these individuals were and whether or not they tried any cases is unknown. In the early 1870s, several reports commissioned by the Canadian authorities on the state of affairs in the North-West Territories, most notably those by Captain William F. Butler and Colonel Patrick Robertson-Ross, convinced Ottawa that more sophisticated provisions for the administration of justice were necessary.[54]

The result in 1873 was "An act respecting the Administration of Justice and for the establishment of a Police Force in the North-West Territories."[55] Often referred to as the "Mounted Police Act," this legislation was a good deal more than that. It in fact created an integrated system of police and courts that was to become one of the defining features of the Canadian prairies. The lieutenant-governor retained his power to appoint justices and now had the authority to appoint one or more stipendiary magistrates with the powers of two justices of the peace. The magistrates held office "during pleasure" and received the very substantial salary of $3,000.00 annually for the period. More serious cases were to be sent to the Manitoba Court of Queen's Bench. The commissioner and all superintendents of the NWMP were *ex officio* justices of the peace. In 1874, the assistant commissioner and inspectors were added to the list of *ex officio* justices and the commissioner was given the powers of a stipendiary magistrate, although of course he did not receive any extra remuneration for those duties.[56] Thus began the practice of conferring judicial powers on police officers, a practice that would continue in the province of Alberta (and in Saskatchewan) after its creation in 1905 and would ultimately last well over a century.

Appointing police as justices of the peace with the power to preside over trials is obviously deeply offensive to modern notions of the independence of the judiciary, but it does not seem to have bothered either the legal profession or the general public very much at the time. In the North-West Territories in the late nineteenth century, police justices tried cases alone, sitting together with another police or civilian JP and occasionally with a stipendiary magistrate (from 1877 a stipendiary magistrate sitting with two justices and a jury could try capital cases).[57] A recent study of all criminal cases tried in the NWT before 1885 found no differences in sentencing patterns between police and civilian justices.[58] By 1886 the government of the North-West Territories had lost track of the justices holding commissions. Accordingly, the lieutenant-governor cancelled all appointments except those for justices living north of 55° latitude and reappointed those who were alive, still resident in the Territories, and willing to serve.[59] This process was repeated in 1892.[60]

The primary motivation for these wholesale purges of the justice list seems to have been administrative efficiency. There can be no doubt, however, that political concerns also played a role, and that the lieutenant-governor used the opportunity to cleanse the ranks of known supporters of the opposition.[61] Appointments as justices were subject to the same considerations of party patronage as all other government appointments in Canada in this period. It was considered a normal and legitimate part of the governing process for the party in power to reward its supporters with positions under its control. There were different rules for various kinds of government appointments. Most administrative positions in the civil service were subject to change at the whim of the government in power. That is, political appointees could expect that they might lose their jobs and be replaced when a new party took office, although this did not invariably happen.[62] Judges and mounted policemen, on the other hand, were all subject to political nomination, but were never fired on grounds of political affiliation. The same was true for justices, at least on an individual basis.[63]

Unlike the magistrates (who were invariably referred to as "judges" in the territorial press) and policemen, justices of the peace were unpaid. They were entitled to fees, but these were not high enough to be a motivating factor. They were not even sufficient to cover the cost of justices' handbooks and copies of the statutes. There was a prolonged battle between the territorial and federal governments over who should pay for supplying the necessary law books.[64] By the mid-1880s there were approximately 100 justices in the North-West Territories who were trying 60 to 70 cases a year in total, an average of less than one per justice. In their capacity as *ex officio* justices of the peace, the much smaller number of NWMP inspectors and superintendents were trying several hundred cases annually.[65]

The new province of Alberta that came into existence in September of 1905 inherited the Territorial system of appointing justices and made few significant changes over the next half century, the main one being that the terms of appointment were codified in a statute that covered both magistrates and justices. While magistrates were appointed at pleasure, justices from 1906 onward were appointed for the duration of the commission of the peace.[66] The issuance of a new commission automatically cancelled all existing appointments, but since this was never done, justices in Alberta effectively held office for life until an age limit of 75 was introduced in 1955.[67] Mounted policemen continued to constitute a significant percentage of the justices in the province in the first half of the 20th century. Their judicial activities were not, as might be expected, confined to remote rural areas of the province.[68] In the 1950s, the Alberta government began appointing police officers as justices of the peace with powers restricted to accepting affidavits for the issuance of traffic tickets.[69] In 1987, a total of 584 of the 972 justices in the province fell into this category.[70] Interestingly, at this late date there were still 8 to 10 RCMP inspectors with unrestricted JP appointments, as well as two members of the force who were appointed as fee justices.[71] The system finally came to an end in January of 1990 when all police justice of the peace appointments were cancelled.[72]

Civilian justices were appointed in response to perceived demand. Often the local police would write to the Attorney General to complain that their work was being hampered by the inability to find a justice or magistrate.[73] After some years experience, the Attorney General's department began to rely on magistrates whenever possible. In 1922, the *Magistrates and Justices Act* was amended to eliminate the requirement that magistrates have three years' experience at the bar.[74] This enabled the Alberta government to appoint a large number of unpaid police magistrates in addition to the salaried ones.[75] This was clearly an alternative to appointing more justices and having them sit together in the traditional English manner. Thus, for example, Francois Adam was appointed as an unpaid magistrate in the northern community of Hythe on June 8, 1928. He typically heard 5 to 10 cases a month, the great majority of which were *Highway Traffic Act*, *Motor Vehicle Act* and minor liquor offences. Although he had the authority to try quite serious criminal offences, he dealt only with minor assaults, petty thefts and vagrancy, and sent all others to the stipendiary magistrate's court at Peace River. The heaviest sentence he imposed was 60 days and by far the majority were small fines.[76]

In 1938 a group of businessmen in Didsbury began to lobby the government for the appointment of a magistrate. After two years of letters and petitions, the Attorney General finally agreed and on May 22, 1940 appointed David N. McDonald, who listed his occupation as "gardener." McDonald remained a magistrate until the mid-1950s, never hearing more than a dozen cases a month. As with Francois Adam, the great bulk of his work involved traffic matters and liquor offences, although on one occasion he imposed a sentence of 18 months for theft.[77] John Chalmers Duguid was clerk of the Calgary Police Court in the late 1940s. He was appointed justice of the peace on December 9, 1949 and occasionally substituted for the regular magistrates if they were ill or on leave. In 1954, Duguid was appointed police magistrate in the Calgary suburb of Forest Lawn, where he heard from 10 to 30 cases a month. Like his rural counterparts, traffic and liquor cases made up by far the greatest part of his work. It is apparent that by the 1950s in the larger cities in the province, higher volumes of cases were creating pressures for a more differentiated and specialized system of inferior courts.

The fees that justices and unpaid magistrates were entitled to provided some economic incentive for doing the job in 1905, but they completely failed to keep pace with inflation during the 20th century. In 1905 the average annual wage for production workers in Canada was $375.00.[78] Justices and unpaid magistrates that year received fifty cents for hearing a case and a dollar if the case lasted more than two hours.[79] By 1927, average wages had almost tripled to $994.00.[80] Fees had increased to 75c cents for a case and $1.50 if it went over two hours.[81] By the mid-1960s, the average wage was $4,492.00, approximately 15 times that of 1905 levels.[82] Fees for justices in 1965 were a dollar for hearing a case and two dollars if it lasted more than two hours.[83] It is obvious that as early as the 1920s there was no possibility of using the income from a justice's fees as a meaningful supplement to one's income. By the 1960s, the fees were inconsequential and for all intents and purposes, anyone who has been appointed as a fee justice of the peace in Alberta since the middle of the 20th century has been volunteering his or her time for the good of the community.

One of the striking features of the history of justices of the peace in Alberta is that the government rarely, if ever, exercised its power to remove justices from office except when they no longer met the eligibility requirements. The most common reason for cancelling commissions was that the individual in question had moved out of the province. However, there were other reasons: Alfred J. Thomas of Sundre decided in 1966 to leave his insurance agency and become a lay minister. Ministers and priests were among those excluded from eligibility, so his service as justice came to an end.[84] Complaints from the public sometimes led to reprimands, but the Attorney General's department preferred explaining errors in law to the drastic step of dismissing justices. The department seems to have been reluctant to dismiss justices even when it was clear that they were not carrying out any of the functions of their office. Robert Andison of Edmonton was appointed justice of the peace in 1922 and over the next 43 years he faithfully filled out the required semi-annual returns showing no activity. He was finally removed from the list of justices in 1965 after a revision in the legislation introduced compulsory retirement at age 75 for provincial judges and justices.[85] This may be evidence that vestiges of the old social prestige attached to the office survived into the late 20th century.

As a result of the oil boom, the 25 years between 1950 and 1975 represented a period of very rapid population growth in Alberta and the number of people in the province doubled during that quarter century.[86] The workload of the courts increased even more rapidly. In Canada between 1962 and 1975, the number of Criminal Code cases coming before the courts approximately tripled, while provincial statute offences doubled.[87] In Alberta, the response to these developments was to transform the police magistrates into provincial court judges. (Most other Canadian provinces were faced with the same problems around this time and created similar institutions.) The provincial court almost immediately became the workhorse of the judicial system. By 1973, the provincial courts were not only handling the great majority of minor traffic and other offences, but were hearing 93 per cent of the 23,916 indictable offences tried in the province that year.[88] The expansion of the jurisdiction of the provincial court judges in Alberta, as in other provinces, has continued into the new millennium. In criminal law there has been a steady increase in the number of offences over which the provincial court judges have absolute jurisdiction. Provincial court judges have been given more responsibility in family law and many provinces have raised the limits on small claims.[89]

The powers and responsibilities of justices of the peace in the same period underwent no similar expansion. The number of civilian justices in Alberta in 1987 was 386, only a few more than the province had in 1905. Their capacity to preside over trials remained as restricted as it had always been, both in law and practice. One result of the change from magistrates to provincial court judges was a steady decrease in the percentage of cases tried by justices of the peace. The big change for justices of the peace came with the creation in 1991 of the office of sitting justice of the peace to preside over traffic courts. This reorganization of the Alberta courts was designed to solve the problem of the huge backlog of cases that had built up in the provincial courts by giving concurrent jurisdiction to sitting justices of the peace to try traffic and bylaw offences. The sitting justices of the peace or traffic commissioners were appointed for a fixed term and had to be lawyers with at least five years' experience. Traffic commissioners represent a major step in the direction of professionalization of justices. But in spite of their legal training and full-time, salaried employment, their powers to preside over trials were more restricted than those of their earlier, more generic, counterparts since criminal offences were specifically excluded from the list of their responsibilities.[90] In practice, their trial jurisdiction was even more restricted than the regulation setting out their jurisdiction suggests.

As the scope of their jurisdiction shrank and qualifications for holding the office were raised, the quantity of work increased dramatically. The average number of cases commenced in Calgary Traffic Court for the years 1992/3 through 1997/8 was 184,775, while the average for Adult Provincial Court was 36, 970.[91] On average, over the fiscal years 1992/3 through 1997/8 almost five times the number of cases were commenced in Traffic Court as compared with Adult Provincial Court in Calgary. During this period, the most frequent type of cases commenced in the Calgary Traffic Court were Highway Traffic and Motor Vehicle offences. In the five years before 1997/8, these cases accounted for approximately two thirds of the total handled by the Calgary Traffic Court (67.5 per cent in 1992/3 and 64.9 per cent in 1997/8). Most of the other third of the court's business consisted of municipal by-law offences, that is, traffic offences from within the City of Calgary (29.9 per cent in 1992/3 and 32.5 per cent in 1997/8). There were a minuscule number of federal offences, usually 30 to 40 a year and reaching a high figure of 221 in 1996/7 (in percentage terms these are negligible numbers, and the 221 cases in 1996/7 represent just over one-tenth of a percentage point).[92] The category of other provincial offences was stable at just over 2.5 per cent for the period. In 1992/3, the great majority of these other provincial offences (85 per cent) were liquor cases. In the 1990s, in other words, more than 99 per cent of the cases handled by the Calgary Traffic Court were traffic cases.[93]

It would be tempting to see the quite dramatic alterations in the office of justice of the peace in Alberta in the late 20th century as just another example of change being imposed by the Supreme Court and the Charter. Some Western separatists will undoubtedly argue that local powers are being eroded by Ottawa's centralizing project and there is, in fact, a small degree of fact in such an assertion. The traditional justice of the peace of the kind that still exists in England and in which office local elites exercise a significant degree of responsibility for solving community problems and maintaining order, has disappeared altogether in Alberta. The process of change, however, began in the 1970s under the Lougheed government, almost a decade before the Charter came into existence. The Kirby Report of 1975 had a centralizing influence on all the inferior courts of the province. In 1984 a report to the Alberta Branch of the Canadian Bar Association (the Irving Report) carried the process further by recommending the placement of justices of the peace under the supervision of the Chief Judge of the Provincial Court.[94] The Irving Report came after the Charter, but before *Re Currie and the Niagara Escarpment Commission* (1985) and *Valente v. The Queen* (1986), the first two Charter cases dealing with judicial independence.[95] Those cases unquestionably speeded up the reform of the system that had begun in the 1970s. By the end of the century, the small handful of remaining justices of the peace were all in Edmonton and Calgary.

The complete elimination of community-based justices of the peace was certainly in line with the Alberta government's general policy of shifting power to the centre. Public school boards lost their independent taxing power at about the same time and hospital boards were replaced by unelected regional health authorities. There are signs, however, that centralized efficiency may have its limits. In November of 2003, a dozen towns in central Alberta passed resolutions calling on the government to appoint a sitting justice of the peace in the area. After the Central Alberta Bar Association had passed a similar resolution, a member of the executive of the was quoted in the press as saying: "Do we have equal access to justice in central Alberta? I think not. Our concern is that the citizens of central Alberta don't have the same access to justice that the citizens in Edmonton and Calgary do."[96] Alberta Justice responded that it is reviewing the matter.

Acknowledgement

The authors would like to thank Alberta Justice for permission to use parts of reports originally produced in connection with the cases of *R. v. Airth* and *Ell v. Alberta*.

Notes

1. Hugh Taylor, *Manual of the Offices, Duties, and Liabilities of a Justice of the Peace, with Practical Forms, for the Use of Magistrates Out of Session* (Montreal: Armour and Ramsay, 1843), 27.
2. *Reference re Remuneration of Judges of the Provincial Court* (P.E.I.), [1997] 3 S.C.R., p. 42.
3. *Ell v. Alberta* [2003] 1 S.C.R.
4. *Reference re Remuneration of Judges of the Provincial Court* (P.E.I.), [1997] 3 S.C.R., p. 23.
5. *An Act Respecting Police Magistrates and Justices of the Peace* 1906, Cap.13.
6. Norma Landau, *The Justices of the Peace, 1679–1760* (Berkeley: University of California Press, 1984), 1–2.
7. Sir Thomas Skyrme, *History of the Justices of the Peace: Volume I, England to 1689* (Chichester: Barry Rose, 1991), 31–38.

8. Where these sessions met every three months they were termed Quarter Sessions, otherwise they were properly referred to as General Sessions of the Peace. If circumstances demanded, an interim meeting of these could be termed Special Sessions of the Peace.

9. For a sample of an annotated Commission explaining these duties see: John George Marshall, *The Justice of the Peace and County and Township Officer in the Province of Nova Scotia being a Guide to such Justice and Officers in the Discharge of their Official Duties* (Halifax: Gossip and Coade, 1846), 292–302.

10. The "most worthy" definition was provided by (1361) 34 Edw. III, c. 1 cited by William Blackstone, *Commentaries on the Laws of England*, vol. I, A facsimile of the first edition, (1765; Chicago: University of Chicago Press, 1979), 340. The property qualifications instituted under (1439) 18 Henry VI, c. 11, were £20; under (1732) 5 Geo. II, c. 11, that amount was raised to £100 per annum.

11. Joseph E. McDougall, "General Sessions of the Peace," *Canada Law Journal* (1900): 10–16.

12. John Beattie, *Crime and the Courts in England, 1660–1880* (Princeton: Princeton University Press, 1986), 283.

13. Donald Fyson, et al. *The Court Structure of Quebec and Lower Canada 1764 to 1860* (Montreal: McGill University, Montreal History Group, 1994), 43.

14. See: Fyson, et al., *The Court Structure of Quebec*; and G.W. Wicksteed, *Table of the Provincial Statutes and Ordinances in Force or Which Have Been in Force in Lower Canada: in their chronological order, shewing which of them, or what parts of any of them, are now in force with a continuation of the Index to the statutes in force, &c.: prepared by order of the Legislative Assembly, on motion of J.W. Gamble* (Toronto: S. Derbishire & G. Desbarats, 1857).

15. John D. Blackwell, "Crime in the London District, 1828–1837: A Case Study on the Effect of the 1833 Reform in Upper Canadian Penal Law," *Queen's Law Journal* 6 (1981): 528–59.

16. (1832) 2 William IV, c. 2 (UC).

17. (1833) 3 William IV, c. 2; and (1834) 4 William IV, c. 5 (UC).

18. (1834) 4 William IV, c. 4 (UC).

19. (1838) 1 Vict., c. 11; and c. 12 (UC).

20. (1714) 1 Geo I, stat. 2, c. 5 (Eng); William Blackstone, *Commentaries on the Laws of England*, Vol. 4, *Of Public Wrongs*, A facsimile of the first edition (1769; Chicago: University of Chicago Press, 1979), 142; and G.W. Keeton, *Keeping the Peace* (Chichester and London: Barry Rose Publishers, 1975), 48–89.

21. (1841) 4&5 Vict., c. 25; c. 26; c. 27 (PC); cited by Desmond Brown, *The Genesis of the Canadian Criminal Code of 1892* (Toronto: The Osgoode Society, 1989), 57.

22. (1848) 11&12 Vict., c. 42, 43, 44 (Eng); see Wesley Pue, "The Criminal Twilight Zone: Pre-Trial Procedures in the 1840s," 11 *Alberta Law Review* 2 (1983): 335–63.

23. CSC [1859], c. 105.

24. (1841) 4&5 Vict., c. 10; and (1849) 12 Vict., c. 81 (PC).

25. J.A. Aitchison, "The Municipal Corporations Act of 1849," *Canadian Historical Review* 30 (1949): 110.

26. C.S.C. [1859], c. 100, s. 3.

27. (1849) 12 Vict., c. 81 (PC); also see: Paul Craven, "Law and Ideology: The Toronto Police Court 1850–80" in David H. Flaherty, ed. *Essays in the History of Canadian Law*, vol. 2 (Toronto: Osgoode Society, 1983), 261–62.

28. C.S.U.C. [1859], c. 54, ss. 361, 365.

29. C.S.U.C. [1859], c. 54, s. 369.

30. 28 Geo. III, c. 49 (Eng); and *The King v. Sainsbury*, 4 T.R. 451, cited *Regina v. Riley* (1884), 12 OPR 104.

31. *Regina v. Gordon* (1888) 16 OR 64; and *Regina v. Lynch* (1890) 19 OR 664.

32. (1892) 55 Vict., c. 16, s. 5 (ON).

33. Douglas to Newcastle, 11 April, 1853, cited in David M.L. Farr, "The Organization of the Judicial System in the Colonies of Vancouver Island and British Columbia, 1849–1871," 3 *U.B.C. Law Review* 1 (March, 1967): 4.

34. Hamar Foster, "The Struggle for the Supreme Court: Law and Politics in British Columbia, 1871–1885," in Louis Knafla, ed., *Law and Justice in a New Land: Essays in Western Canadian Legal History* (Toronto: Carswell, 1986), 174–79.

35. Phillip Gerard, "The Rise and Fall of Urban Justice in Halifax, 1815–1886," *Nova Scotia Historical Review* 8, no. 2 (1988): 58.

36. "Municipal Corporations Act" 42 Vict. (1879), c. 1 (NS); and 51 Vict. (1888), c. 1 (NS).

37. The exceptions to this rule were the chairmen of the Courts of Quarter Sessions in Lower Canada who had to be barristers of at least five years' standing and who did not have to meet property requirements. 13 & 14 Vict., c. 35, s. 9 also as C.S.L.C. [1861], c.97.

38. Nancy Parker, "Reaching a Verdict: The Changing Structure of Decision-Making in the Canadian Criminal Courts, 1867–1905" (PhD Diss., York University, 1998), 186–231.

39. R.S.N.S. [1888], c. 101, s. 8.

40. *Disqualification of Justices of the Peace Act*, 54 Vict. (1891), c. 16 (ON).

41. *Public Officers Act*, R.S.M. [1880–1], c. 7, s. 18.

42. The fees were consistent between 22 Vict. (1859), c. 119 and R.S.O. [1897], c. 95.

43. 55–56 Vict. (1892), c. 29, s. 871 (Can.).

44. The authority to hear "Speedy Trials" was first granted to stipendiary magistrates in Ontario under 38 Vict. (1875), c. 47 (Can.) and offered to all provinces under 63 & 64 Vict. (1900), c.46, s. 785 (Can.).

45. Canada, *Sessional Papers*, "Appendix to the Report of the Minister of Agriculture for the year 1885: Criminal Statistics for the Year 1885" (49 Vict., No. 10A, 1886) and "Report of Criminal Statistics for the Year Ended 30th September 1905," (5–6 Edward VII, No. 17A, 1906).

46. "Police Magistrates," *Canadian Law Times* 12 (1892): 218.

47. 43 Geo. III (1803), c. 138.

48. 1 & 2 Geo. IV (1821), c. 66.

49. Hamar Foster, "Sins Against the Great Spirit: The Law, the Hudson's Bay Company, and the Mackenzie's River Murders, 1835–1839," *Criminal Justice History: An International Annual* 10 (1989): 23–74.

50. Kathryn M. Bindon, "Hudson's Bay Company Law: Adam Thom and the Institution of Order in Rupert's Land 1839–54," in David H. Flaherty, ed., *Essays in the History of Canadian Law*, vol. I (Toronto: The Osgoode Society, 1981), 43–87.

51. Ibid.

52. "An Act for the Temporary Government of Rupert's Land and the North Western Territory when united with Canada," 32 & 33 Vict., c. 3. This legislation was extended in 1870 to 1871 (33 Vict. c. 3) and indefinitely the following year (34 Vict. c. 16).

53. W.P. Ward, "The Administration of Justice in the North-West Territories, 1870–1887" (M.A. Diss, University of Alberta, 1966), 14–15.

54. R.C. Macleod, *The North-West Mounted Police and Law Enforcement 1873–1905* (Toronto: University of Toronto Press, 1976), 3–20.

55. 36 Vict., c. 35. Indian agents were also *ex officio* justices, but only for matters arising from the *Indian Act*.

56. 37 Vict., c.22.

57. Ward, "The Administration of Justice," 49.

58. R.C. Macleod and Heather Rollason, "'Restrain the Lawless Savages': Native Defendants in the Criminal Courts of the North West Territories, 1878–1885," *Journal of Historical Sociology* 10, no. 2 (June 1997): 157–83.

59. Ward, "The Administration of Justice," 96–97.

60. Thomas Michael Reynolds, "Justices of the Peace in the North-West Territories, 1870–1905" (MA Diss., University of Regina, 1978), 32.

61. Ibid., Chapter II.

62. J.E. Hodgetts, William McCloskey, Reginald Whitaker and V. Seymour Wilson, *The Biography of an Institution: The Civil Service Commission of Canada 1908–1967* (Montreal: McGill-Queen's University Press, 1972), Chapter 1.

63. Reynolds, "Justices in the North-West Territories," Chapter 2.

64. Ibid., 67.

65. Database of Criminal Cases Tried in the NWT 1878–1885, compiled by R.C. Macleod and Heather Rollason.

66. *An Act Respecting Police Magistrates and Justices of the Peace*, RSA, 1906, c. 13.

67. RSA, 1955, c. 186. Justices could, of course, be removed if they left the province or failed to complete the monthly returns of cases tried. The age limit was reduced to 70 in 1971, *The Justices of the Peace Act*, 1971, c. 57.

68. Provincial Archives of Alberta, Attorney General's Department; Magistrate, Provincial Judge and Justice of the Peace Files, 1897–1975. 79.105, JP316, F.W. Hancock. Hancock was first appointed JP while he was an inspector in the Alberta Provincial Police in Peace River, 8 July, 1920. In 1928 he was transferred to Edmonton to command "A" Division of the APP, where he continued to try cases, mainly traffic and liquor offences, on a regular basis. When the RCMP replaced the APP in 1932, he transferred to the new force and was promoted to assistant superintendent the following year. He retired from the RCMP in 1954 and put his judicial experience to use by becoming a magistrate in the Edmonton Traffic Court in 1956. In 1960 he was appointed magistrate at Stony Plain.

69. See, for example, PAA, JP files, 79.105, JP4010, RCMP Corporal Donald William Callbeck. D.L. Paul, Administration Officer, Attorney General's Department to Commanding Officer, RCMP "K" Division, August 16, 1968.

70. *R. v. Grant David Magee*, transcript of testimony of Joyce Topilko November 24, 1987, 49.

71. Ibid., 367, 371.

72. Order-in-Council 704/89, December 7, 1989.

73. A good example of this is to be found in PAA, JP files, 79.105, JP1737, Alfred J. Thomas. Thomas was appointed JP July 8, 1959, after Sundre police constable Fred Bainton pointed out that the nearest magistrate was in Olds, 40 km away.

74. R.S.A. 1922, c. 78.

75. Magistrates, like justices, were entitled to fees for specific services.

76. PAA, JP Files, 79.105, JP2, Francois Adam.

77. PAA, JP Files, 79.105, JP1155, David N. McDonald.

78. M.C. Urquhart and K.A.H. Buckley, *Historical Statistics of Canada,* 2nd ed. (Ottawa: Statistics Canada, 1983), E44.

79. *The Criminal Code*, R.S.C. 1907, Cap. 146, s. 770.

80. Urquhart and Buckley, Ibid.

81. *The Criminal Code*, R.S.C., 1927, Cap. 36, s. 770.

82. Urquhart and Buckley, Ibid.

The hereditary monarch, Her Majesty Queen Elizabeth II, Queen of Canada, embodies Canada and is the Canadian Head of State. To Canadians, Queen Elizabeth is an international symbol and her "appeal is to values that burst beyond the limits of nationality."[3] Representing the Queen for all Canadians is the governor-general, who is really "the principal symbol of unity and continuity in the country."[4]

Since the time of contact with the First Nations, Canadians have always lived under a monarchical system of government and the Office of governor-general is an uninterrupted, continuous institution that dates back to those early beginnings. From the time of Confederation, the lieutenant-governors were to participate in the provincial aspects of the Crown's sovereignty.

In 1867, there was much ambiguity about the Office of lieutenant-governor. The Fathers of Confederation first agreed that the lieutenant-governor was to be a "federal officer," that is, a representative of the federal government who would act as intermediary between Ottawa and provincial administrations. The lieutenant-governor is therefore appointed by the governor-general, not the Monarch, and the federal government pays the lieutenant-governor's salary.[5] However, all other aspects of the Office, such as the residence, support staff and supplies, are the responsibility of each provincial government. This subordination of Office is revealed in the manner in which the lieutenant-governor is addressed: since the time of Lord Dufferin, lieutenant-governors have been addressed as "Your Honour" rather than as "Your Excellency," as is the case with the governor-general. To ensure the dominance of the federal government within Confederation, the lieutenant-governors were given authority to veto or to reserve for the federal government's consideration any bills that the lieutenant-governor, acting as a federal watchdog, did not consider to be in the national interest.[6]

Over time, the Office of the lieutenant-governor has evolved from that of being a servant of the federal government to being the direct representative of the Monarch within the provincial sphere of jurisdiction. This evolution has strengthened the role of the lieutenant-governor *vis-à-vis* the federal government and has thus enhanced the provincial prerogatives and power of the Office. One of the notable constitutional squabbles that marked the transformation of the lieutenant-governor from a federal official to a direct representative of the Queen within the provincial sphere centred on the lieutenant-governor of Alberta. In 1937, His Honour, John Bowen, refused Royal Assent to three Social Credit Bills and asked the governor-general for guidance because he believed the legislation was unconstitutional. The refusal to accept Premier Aberhart's advice caused a constitutional crisis that ended in the clarification of the role and exercise of power of lieutenant-governors within the Canadian system of constitutional Monarchy.

The whole crisis began rather innocuously when, in October 1937, the lieutenant-governor neglected the protocol of asking Ottawa's guidance and "reserved" the Social Credit legislation for the federal government's approval. The personal enmity between Lieutenant-Governor John Bowen and Premier William Aberhart had been exacerbated by Aberhart's failure to enact "Social Credit" legislation at the outset of his administration. At one point, several caucus members circulated a petition to His Honour, requesting Aberhart's replacement.[7] The friction then worsened when Aberhart attempted to quell rebellion within Social Credit ranks by proposing legislation that was designed to keep the legislative caucus loyal to him. For example, in a brief session that opened on August 3, 1937 and ended three days later, the Aberhart government brought in what was supposedly "Social Credit" legislation—two bills concerning banks and one dealing with civil rights, which prevented an appeal to the courts questioning the validity of provincial legislation.[8] Although these bills snuffed out the back-bench revolt for Aberhart, they raised important constitutional issues such as the freedom of the press and whether provinces had jurisdiction over banking matters within the Canadian federal system of government. These were the matters that the lieutenant-governor queried. Before signing these bills, the lieutenant-governor requested that the premier and the Attorney General, John Hugill, come to his office for consultation. Speculation arose in the Alberta press as to whether the lieutenant-governor would employ his very-seldom-used prerogative powers and reserve these bills for the pleasure of the governor-general.

When His Honour asked the Attorney General for his opinion of the bills, Aberhart expected Hugill to assure the lieutenant-governor that he approved of them. Instead, the Attorney General confided to His Honour that they were unconstitutional and advised him to reserve the bills. Aberhart broke into the conversation and insisted that His Honour sign the bills. Since the premier was willing to take responsibility for this action, Bowen signed.[9] J.R. Mallory, a political scientist from the University of Toronto, later wrote that he doubted the wisdom of Hugill's advice to the lieutenant-governor. He noted that the rules governing the use of the reserve powers were laid down by Sir John A. Macdonald in 1882 when Macdonald told lieutenant-governors that they should only use the reserve power in their capacity as Dominion officers and only on explicit instructions from the governor-general.[10]

Although the questionable bills became law through lieutenant-governor Bowen's signature, within 10 days they were disallowed by the governor-general.[11] When Aberhart refused to allow His Honour to publish the proclamation of disallowance in the *Alberta Gazette,* the federal government had them published in the *Canada Gazette.*[12] The bills were reintroduced at a subsequent session of the Alberta Legislature in revised form, but on this occasion, the lieutenant-governor reserved them for the pleasure of the federal authorities[13] without instructions or advice from the federal government.[14] Needless to say, Aberhart was angered and determined to retaliate against the lieutenant-governor. As a response to Bowen's actions, Aberhart challenged the "reserve" power of the lieutenant-governor before the courts, but the Supreme Court found that the power of reservation existed and was "subject to no limitation or restriction."[15] Despite this unambiguous ruling, the reserve power of the lieutenant-governor was nevertheless becoming an anachronistic power.

As John Diefenbaker noted in his memoirs, the lieutenant-governor was originally "the principal federal check on provincial government, but this is no longer so."[16] The last time a lieutenant-governor "exceeded his authority," according to John Diefenbaker, was when the lieutenant-governor of Saskatchewan, the Honourable Frank L. Bastedo, reserved the 1961 *Mineral Contracts Alteration Act*. Like Bowen years earlier in Alberta, Bastedo considered this legislation *ultra vires* of provincial jurisdiction and contrary to the national interest.[17] Diefenbaker believed that no provincial Act should be reserved except on the explicit request of the federal government and made reference to the 1882 Macdonald statement in making his own opinion known in the House of Commons.[18] This was the last time any lieutenant-governor reserved a provincial bill for the pleasure of the governor-general. Thus, although the power to reserve exists as a convention, tradition has led to its disuse. The breaking of the tie between the lieutenant-governor and the federal authority in Canada, which is what the reserve power represented, has consequently increased the stature of the lieutenant-governor, who now has come to represent the Queen more directly within the provincial sphere of jurisdiction without any reference to Ottawa.

While the reserve power of the lieutenant-governor has fallen into disuse, the lieutenant-governors still do not automatically sign bills, or, more particularly, Orders-in-Council, that are placed before them. Again in Alberta, this royal prerogative has made newspaper headlines. During his term as lieutenant-governor, His Honour, Gordon Towers, blocked a $1.5-million grant from The Honourable Ken Kowalski's department because he considered it inappropriate. This matter involved the bailout by the Alberta Opportunity Company of the Dunvegan Motor Inn in Fairview, which went into receivership in 1992. Towers demanded that the Order-in-Council be written in such a way that the Department of Economic Development keep control of the funds.[19] After a five-day dispute, Kowalski backed down and the lieutenant-governor signed the Order-in-Council.[20] This confrontation, correctly, allowed Towers to claim that his actions proved that the lieutenant-governor "is not just a rubber stamp."[21]

Besides such noted clashes between the lieutenant-governor and premier, there have been other celebrated differences between the lieutenant-governor and the premier that have caught the public's attention. From the outset of taking office, Premier Ralph Klein clashed with His Honour Gordon Towers. Their first disagreement occurred over the logistics of the swearing-in ceremony of Klein's first cabinet upon his election as leader of the Conservative Party in December 1992. The lieutenant-governor wanted the swearing-in to take place at Government House, while Klein wanted a public ceremony at the Legislature Building, to which more people could be invited. As a saw-off, there was a small formal ceremony at Government House to satisfy the lieutenant-governor, followed by a major event for 2,500 at the Legislature Building.[22] In order to demonstrate his annoyance, in April 1993 Premier Klein did not have a grand "Speech from the Throne" to re-open the Legislature. In rather curt fashion, the lieutenant-governor opened the Legislative Session, which was immediately followed by a rather grandiose "state of the province address" given by the premier.[23]

Shortly after this episode, His Honour Gordon Towers told reporters of an election call that would occur in June 1993, about which the premier had informed the lieutenant-governor in confidence. Because of this indiscretion, Klein snubbed His Honour when requesting a dissolution of the Legislature by sending the deputy premier, Ken Kowalski, to ask for the dissolution and the official calling of the election. Some authorities called the premier's actions "astound[ing]" and "highly unusual" and most agreed that "it could be seen as a snub."[24]

More recently, on the Ides of March, March 15, 2000, Her Honour, the Honourable Lois Hole stepped into the centre of political controversy over the infamous Bill 11, the Health Care legislation proposed by the provincial government. This bill caused much controversy and debate throughout the province. Opponents claimed the bill would enable the establishment of a two-tier hospital system in Alberta. While this heated public discussion was in full swing, Her Honour stated at a meeting in Red Deer that she wanted to chat with Premier Klein before giving final assent to this piece of legislation. Hole explained that while she was not supposed to take a political stance, she made her remarks because Bill 11 was on everyone's mind. She explained that "I'm hearing things and I will tell...[the premier] what I'm hearing, and I hope it will help him."[25]

Even the Leader of Her Majesty's Official Opposition called the remarks "highly unusual" because although the lieutenant-governor has the right to warn and advise the premier, she must do so in private and out of the glare of public scrutiny, just as she stated at her Installation: "she won't hesitate to offer Premier Ralph Klein advice if she thinks the government is headed in the wrong direction, although she'll be careful about making public statements."[26] According to the constitutional expert, Allan Tupper, the lieutenant-governor does have the legal right under the constitution to refuse assent even if the premier advises her to sign, yet this aspect of the constitution has become inoperative in modern times, especially when the premier is supported by a majority in the Assembly.[27] It came as no surprise that Her Honour clarified her position in a terse press release and without comment: Her Honour confirmed that she would not use her authority and decline Royal Assent to the controversial private health care bill before the Legislature. She explained: "*For the record, I will fulfill the duty of my office recognizing the role of elected representatives in the democratic process if and when Royal Assent is sought...I have confirmed this to Premier Klein.*"[28] In effect, the lieutenant-governor who holds all power in Alberta must be careful to remain above the political fray and allow the premier to exercise the Crown's power on behalf of all Albertans.

Nevertheless, three years later, Her Honour again came perilously close to the line separating pageantry from politics. On Friday evening, June 6, 2003, Her Honour Lois Hole attended the Edmonton Symphony Orchestra's commemoration of the 50th anniversary of the Coronation of Her Majesty, Queen Elizabeth II, for the purpose of presenting the members of the orchestra with Queen's Jubilee medals. Addressing the orchestra and audience from a podium on stage, Her Honour praised public education, public libraries and the need for the arts and criticized those who placed them in jeopardy. Newspaper accounts reported that, although Her Honour named no names, "the audience recognized the target of her admonitions as the philistines who run the provincial government."[29] Paula Simons, a columnist for the *Edmonton Journal*, reminded her readers and Her Honour that a lieutenant-governor is not supposed to criticize the policies of Her Majesty's government but is supposed to remain apolitical. She noted that the Honourable Lois Hole's speech at the Winspear Centre "gave a gentle but decided push to the edge of that envelope."[30] Explaining her remarks later, Her Honour said that she now had "a clearer sense of what's important"[31] because of the death of her husband, Ted, just a few months previously, and her own fight with cancer. She explained that her comments were merely "a call to all Albertans to support education."[32] Despite this explanation, some observers questioned whether Her Honour had "ventured beyond what we customarily expect lieutenant-governors to be involved in."[33] Undoubtedly, because of her popularity amongst the Albertan population, the premier and the minister of learning's spokesman could only agree with Her Honour "on the importance of public education."[34] The Honourable Lois Hole appeared to have great self-knowledge in assessing how close she could approach the political realm.

Now and again Lois Hole could not refrain from dipping into the political sphere, and in fact, became what one commentator called the "social conscience" of the province. In September 2004, at a ceremony on the steps of the Legislature to kick off the countdown to the province's centennial, she encouraged Albertans to celebrate "'our anniversary by working together to build an even greater Alberta, with the world's best schools and libraries, a revitalized artistic community, more effective help for the poor and disenfranchised in Alberta with a new spirit of community and caring.'"[35] She later told reporters that "'we didn't put the oil in the ground' and 'it wouldn't hurt to share with some of the others.'"[36] Again, in her last public appearance as lieutenant-governor and in the presence of the premier, Her Honour Lois Hole stated that "Albertans from all walks of life have made it abundantly clear that first-class pubic health care is a top priority." In her speech on this occasion of the announcement that the Lois Hole Hospital for Women would be built within the existing Royal Alexandra Hospital, Her Honour told the assembled guests that the building was a "sign that Albertans remain committed to public health care."[37] Although clearly a political statement, the premier, realizing the popularity of Lois Hole, ignored the comment and was forced to admit that the new hospital for women was "named after someone who is a model for the very best our province has to offer."[38] Yet again, the lieutenant-governor knew how far she could dabble in the political realm.

In the early years of Alberta, the lieutenant-governor meddled in politics too, even more so than would be acceptable today. Alberta's first lieutenant-governor, George Bulyea, was a key figure in keeping the Liberals in power by ensuring not only that Premier Rutherford resigned, but that he was succeeded by someone His Honour George Bulyea wanted as his successor. In part, His Honour's actions flowed from his constitutional responsibility to ensure that there is always a first minister, a premier. This individual is the person who commands the support of the majority in the Legislative Assembly. Because there has never been a party in a minority position in the Assembly in the history of Alberta, one would think that the lieutenant-governor's choice of premier would be straightforward. Yet, this was not the case in our province in 1910. The Honourable George Bulyea was a staunch Liberal who had been appointed by the governor-general on the advice of the Liberal prime minister of Canada, Sir Wilfrid Laurier. In order to keep the Liberals in power in Alberta in the midst of the Alberta and Great Waterways Railway Scandal, which raised unfounded charges of corruption against Premier Rutherford,[39] the lieutenant-governor helped to engineer his premier's dismissal and eventual replacement by the lieutenant-governor's personal choice, the chief justice of Alberta, Arthur Sifton. There was much behind-the-scenes manoeuvring by His Honour George Bulyea and the federal minister for Alberta, Frank Oliver, to replace Rutherford with one of their own supporters rather than the Rutherford opponent and apparent natural choice for the job, William Cushing of Calgary. Unaware of the machinations within Liberal ranks, the public was caught by surprise by the announcement of Rutherford's removal and his successor's appointment. Bulyea's actions on May 26, 1910, when he dashed to the Legislature dressed "in a tweed suit and bowler hat" not only scandalized the *Edmonton Journal* because he was wearing apparel deemed inappropriate for a representative of the King, but also left the impression with the public that he had hastily decided to fire Rutherford in a fit of moral conscience.[40] It is unclear whether the clothes worn by the lieutenant-governor in announcing Rutherford's resignation to the Assembly or the resignation itself caused more chatter amongst Albertans!

At any rate, Lieutenant-Governor Bulyea made certain that Arthur Sifton had the support of the majority in the Legislative Assembly when he took the oath of office as premier of the province. This constitutional custom guided all lieutenant-governors in appointing premiers. When Premier Brownlee became caught up in a nasty civil action in late June 1934 as a defendant in the alleged seduction of a young woman, Vivian MacMillan, his political position as government leader was jeopardized amid rumours and gossip, fired by Alberta newspaper titillation.[41] Immediately following his trial on the evening of June 30, Brownlee visited the lieutenant-governor at Government House to inform him that he intended to resign, but would await until a successor was chosen.[42] An Edmonton caucus meeting was called after the Dominion Day holiday and by July 5 the caucus had settled on Gavin Reid as Brownlee's successor. Satisfied with the decision, Brownlee officially tendered his resignation to Lieutenant-Governor Walsh. He advised His Honour that Reid was the choice of the majority of the Assembly. However, the lieutenant-governor refused Brownlee's resignation until he was certain a new government could be formed. Thus, when Gavin Reid arrived at Government House, the lieutenant-governor refused to swear him in as premier until he was ready to present His Honour with a complete cabinet.[43] Finally, on July 10, 1934, Gavin Reid became premier of Alberta and the new ministry was sworn in at the same time.[44] The lieutenant-governor had ensured the province had a premier and government. Reid would remain in office until William Aberhart and his Social Credit followers defeated the United Farmers of Alberta in the general election of August 1935.

When the Social Credit Party won the election of August 22, 1935, William Aberhart, although leader of the Party, had not sought election personally. Thus, without a seat in the Legislative Assembly, the lieutenant-governor had to be assured that Aberhart was his Party's choice for premier. When he was satisfied that this was indeed the Party's wishes, His Honour William Walsh swore Aberhart and his government into office and because of a pre-arranged resignation by a newly-elected member from the Social Credit Party, he also set in motion procedures for Aberhart to run in a by-election. Since Aberhart was duly elected in the by-election, he could remain as premier.

When Ernest Manning succeeded William Aberhart a premier after the latter died in office on May 23, 1943, the public focused on the lieutenant-governor's role once again. After the spring session of the Legislature, Aberhart had gone to Vancouver to study French and visit his daughter. While he was out of the province, Ernest Manning acted as premier, but that was a customary arrangement of convenience and not intended as a formal sign of succession. Immediately after Aberhart's funeral, Lieutenant-Governor Bowen therefore turned to Manning to submit a name as premier to him. The Social Credit members of the Assembly met in caucus and unanimously chose Ernest Manning as their new leader.[45] When Manning informed the lieutenant-governor of his mandate to form a government, His Honour swore Manning in as premier on May 31, 1943.[46]

Since the death of Aberhart in office, the transition from one premier to another has been more routine: either elections have determined the choice of premier or political conventions have chosen a party leader before a premier officially resigns office. The lieutenant-governor, while always accepting the advice of the outgoing premier, makes certain that the nominee has the support of the majority in the Assembly.[47]

The Alberta lieutenant-governor has a particular relationship with the premier of the province that is based on custom and constitutional convention rather than any written constitutional document. The Crown holds all power in the province but exercises none; the premier holds no power in Alberta, but exercises all power in the province. Sometimes this symbiotic relationship leads to friction between the lieutenant-governor and his premier. If a premier sometimes displays arrogance, the Crown's representative is there to deflate a premier's swollen ego, since nothing can occur without the agreement of the lieutenant-governor. His Honour Ralph Steinhauer once remarked on the pre-eminent position of the lieutenant-governor within the province when a prominent politician squeezed ahead of him in a line-up. His Honour commented nonchalantly: "Go ahead, I don't have to fight for my position."[48] On the other hand, the lieutenant-governor must always be aware that his Office "is no place for self-aggrandizement or private hobby horses"[49] because he must act only upon the advice of the premier.

His Honour Frank Lynch-Staunton found that Premier Peter Lougheed was very much in control. When the premier wanted something done, he demanded action immediately. On one occasion when His Honour was at a dinner at the Mayfair Golf Club in Edmonton, he received word that the premier wanted some bills signed that very night. The premier had sent a driver to fetch the lieutenant-governor. On reading the bills, His Honour could see no reason for the hurry, but the premier got his way in that instance.[50]

Not surprisingly, on a subsequent occasion, a different scenario occurred. His Honour Frank Lynch-Staunton was at Banff to open and speak at a convention. The premier wanted to adjourn the session of the Legislative Assembly the very night the lieutenant-governor was supposed to speak. The premier asked His Honour to return to Edmonton immediately as only the lieutenant-governor can perform that task. As was his right, and with experience gleaned from other occasions, the lieutenant-governor pulled his weight a bit, finished his part at the convention, gave his excuses to the brass and left. He had kept the Members of the Legislative Assembly waiting until 11:30 P.M. before setting them free, but could not understand why prorogation had to occur that very evening instead of noon the next day![51] The mere presence of the lieutenant-governor within the parliamentary system makes the premier think twice before acting hastily and without the public's interest at heart. The lieutenant-governors of Alberta have often forced their premiers to ponder anew hastily-proposed schemes in order that they might serve the public interest better.

Lieutenant-Governors have not always been as observant in ensuring that the premiers understand that the lieutenant-governor is, constitutionally, number one in the province. Although terminally ill, Her Honour Lois Hole could be faulted for signing the election writ in October 2004. Although suffering from the gnawing pain of cancer, Her Honour went to her office in the Legislature Building to greet the premier whom she assumed would be coming to visit her to ask that the Legislature be dissolved. On that day, October 25, she was frail but was determined to do her duty. However, the premier did not arrive and the writ she was required to sign was delivered by the premier's assistant chief of staff! Her Honour should have sent the political aide back to the premier with the message that Her Honour awaited her premier's arrival. Instead, she signed the document, contradicting a tradition of our parliamentary system.[52] If lieutenant-governors do not insist that the premier come in person to ask for a dissolution of the Legislature, the constitutional relevance and role of the Crown's provincial representative is diminished.

Another area where lieutenant-governors should insist that their proper position as an integral part of the Canadian Crown be enhanced is with respect to the Order of Precedence for Canada. In 1867, the lieutenant-governor ranked immediately behind the Queen, the governor-general and the senior officer commanding British military forces. With the demise of this latter office, lieutenant-governors should rank immediately behind the Queen and governor-general; the Canadian Crown should be placed in all its three aspects before any other office. Over time, however, lieutenant-governors have fallen in the table of precedence for Canada. Since the Royal Visit of King George VI and Queen Elizabeth in 1939, on all occasions the Canadian prime minister and federal cabinet ministers take precedence over lieutenant-governors at all federal functions.[53]

Nevertheless, since Confederation the lieutenant-governor has gradually come to exercise almost all of the Queen's powers as Head of State within provincial jurisdiction. This transformation of the Office of lieutenant-governor seemed to be presaged by the Fathers of Confederation, who granted the lieutenant-governors a great seal, which is the main instrument and symbol of sovereign authority, by which they are authorized to act "in the Queen's name."[54] The lieutenant-governors of Alberta have taken this responsibility to heart.

Besides ensuring that there is always a premier in office from whom to take advice, another important function of the lieutenant-governor is to give Royal Assent to all bills passed by the Legislature. The lieutenant-governor gives Royal Assent in the Queen's name to all legislation as the final, formal step in the legislative process. This is why bills always contain the introductory phrase: " Her Majesty, by and with the advice and consent of the Legislative Assembly of Alberta, enacts as follows."

In Alberta, Royal Assent is generally given in the Legislative Assembly. The lieutenant-governor arrives, is escorted into the Assembly, and sits on the Throne. The Clerk Assistant then reads all the Bills at once, giving the number of each Bill and its title before asking Royal Assent, which the lieutenant-governor gives by nodding her or his head. In the past, when a lieutenant-governor was always male, he wore a hat, which, as one reporter noted, "certainly makes the lieutenant-governor different from all others present in the House and thus enables him to approve of the work of his officers by tipping his hat."[55] Once the gesture of signifying approval of the legislation passed by the Legislature has been completed, the lieutenant-governor rises and leaves the Assembly without ceremony.

Just as the power of the premier has increased within Confederation along with the powers of provincial governments, so too the position of lieutenant-governor has strengthened. As stated at the outset, the lieutenant-governor has gradually shed the role of federal representative in the province and has instead enhanced the office's status as the Monarch's representative at the provincial level in the same manner as the governor-general represents the Monarch at the pan-Canadian level of our Confederation. However, the new position of the lieutenant-governor did not occur without a struggle.

From 1867 onwards, Oliver Mowat, the premier of Ontario, attempted to change the notion of the subordination of the lieutenant-governor (and thus also of the provinces) to the governor-general and to the federal government. He initiated a series of court cases that eventually brought the Judicial Committee of the Privy Council in 1892 to recognize the lieutenant-governors as full representatives of the Crown for all purposes of provincial jurisdiction.[56] Because of this decision, the vast majority of Queen's Counsel are appointed by the lieutenant-governor on the advice of the premier and not the governor-general. Since the Queen reigns in right of each province as well as of Canada as a whole, the phrase "Her Majesty (or the Crown) in right of Alberta" frequently occurs in the constitutional and legal documents of the province. This link between the Monarch and the lieutenant-governor has over the years been reinforced through ritual and ceremony at the provincial level.

For example, although both London and Ottawa attempted to prevent the playing of "God Save the Queen" for the lieutenant-governor during the early years of Confederation,[57] their views were thwarted by wily provincial administrations. By the time Alberta became a province in 1905, permission was granted to fire a 15-gun salute when the provincial Legislature was opened and closed, "not as a personal honour to the Lieutenant Governor" but rather "as a ceremonial observance emphasizing the importance of the event."[58] Presently, a 15-gun vice-regal salute is appropriate on the assembling and closing of a provincial Legislature. In addition, in the last half century, the Alberta lieutenant-governor has set the precedent of visiting the Monarch. In June 1956, His Honour J.J. Bowlen was in London and was invited to Buckingham Palace for a private audience with the Queen.[59] This was the first time that a lieutenant-governor from a Dominion had ever received such an invitation.[60] Since that time, this visiting privilege has become a custom, and all provincial representatives of the Monarch in Canada meet the Sovereign in private audience in Britain.

In 1983, the Honourable Frank Lynch-Staunton decided to pay his visit to the Queen. His Honour and his two daughters were not only invited to Windsor Castle for lunch, but also to Kensington Palace for lunch with Princess Margaret. Frank Lynch-Staunton made the trip with the lieutenant-governor of Saskatchewan and thus sat on the Queen's left while his colleague sat on her right. This seating arrangement followed strict protocol that dictated that since Saskatchewan was one week older than Alberta, the lieutenant-governor from Saskatchewan sat on the Queen's right.[61] Her Honour Louis Hole visited the Queen in London in November 2000 and was granted an audience of over half an hour, with the subjects of discussion ranging from gardening to important affairs of state.[62]

Besides the development of a more direct relationship between the lieutenant-governors and the Monarch, the bonds between the lieutenant-governors and the governor-general have also been strengthened. Until very recent times, lieutenant-governors dealt mainly through the federal Secretary of State. When His Excellency Roland Michener was nearing the end of his term of office as governor-general in the early 1970s, he proposed that the governor-general and lieutenant-governors should meet on a regular basis. Therefore, in November 1973 he invited all lieutenant-governors to a conference at Rideau Hall. All the lieutenant-governors came except Grant MacEwan from Alberta, who had a prior commitment. At this meeting, the lieutenant-governors discussed their constitutional responsibilities as well as the way in which to discharge their unofficial and ceremonial functions. Michener saw that papers and documents were prepared for the meeting and that constitutional authorities came to talk to the group.[63] This conference, instituted at the very end of Michener's term, became a biennial affair and subsequently, because of its usefulness, has become an annual ritual.[64] On these occasions, the lieutenant-governors learn a great deal about the conduct of their offices from each other, the governor-general, and from the constitutional experts.

One of these meetings also led to the indecorous spat between His Honour "Bud" Olson and his predecessor, the Honourable Gordon Towers, over the moving of the New Year Levee from Edmonton to Medicine Hat on January 1, 1997. At their annual get-together in the fall of 1996, the governor-general and lieutenant-governors had decided that moving the New Year Levee from the capital city in each jurisdiction to another city in that jurisdiction from time-to-time would allow the Crown to strengthen the personal and living bond with the people. Gordon Towers dismissed the move as a break with tradition and maintained that the Levee should remain in Edmonton.[65] He called the decision a silly move and offered to tackle Olson "any time, anywhere" over the issue. Olson replied in his best provincial "royal" dialect, saying that he did not "give a damn" what Towers thought.[66] In the end, the *Edmonton Journal* editorial writer suggested that "Any opportunity to enhance the profile of the lieutenant-governor by allowing for opportunities for Albertans to meet the incumbent should be welcomed." This move would serve to underscore the important position of our constitutional monarch. However, the writer continued, the lieutenant-governor should not tamper with the ritual of the Levee and its traditional link with Government House, but should establish a second annual ceremonial occasion, one that could move about the province from year to year.[67] Her Honour Lois Hole took this advice to heart and has held her New Year Levees at Government House in Edmonton[68] with the promise of other levees around the province on other occasions.[69]

Finally, distinctive symbols of office for lieutenant-governors have become more evident and reflect the constitutional importance of the lieutenant-governor within the provincial sphere. The most visible innovation is the lieutenant-governor's flag or standard. The original flag of the lieutenant-governor of Alberta followed the customary design for most of the Queen's provincial representatives, and consisted "of a Union Flag in the centre of which is placed a white disc, which in turn is charged with a shield of the arms for the province surrounded by a wreath of green maple leaves."[70] On September 28, 1981, all lieutenant-governors in Canada were granted new flags of office.[71] His Honour Frank Lynch-Staunton accepted the Alberta lieutenant-governor's flag at Government House.[72] Similar ceremonies were held across the country as lieutenant-governors officially received new flags with their provinces' shields centred on a royal blue background. Above the shield is a St. Edward's crown, signifying the sovereign's representative in the province. These flags were redesigned so that the lieutenant-governor's flags would correspond with the governor-general's flag, which has a royal blue background.[73] This is the flag which today flies over the lieutenant-governor's office above the main entrance of the Legislature Building.

More recently, the governor-general has granted lieutenant-governors a Badge of Office, for "shorn of the unique ceremonial garb that once clothed the figures of lieutenant-governors on special occasions, the vice-regal representatives of Canada's provincial governments can all too easily fade into the crowd" becoming nearly indistinguishable from others wearing tailored suits or gowns.[74] To signal their importance for constitutional or ceremonial roles, new badges of recognition, authorized and designed by the chancellery of the governor-general's office, have been designed. These badges consist of an attractive ray or star design comprised of four maple leaves with a central single maple leaf surmounted by a crown.[75]

Architecture has always played a major symbolic role in establishing the importance and legitimacy of the Crown in Canada. As the noted French novelist, Victor Hugo, wrote: "the greatest productions of architecture are not so much individual as social works,...the deposit left by a people."[76] In other words, structures capture the spirit of an age and represent the aspirations of a people.[77] Because the Crown represents all that is most cherished by a people, it is only natural that vice-regal architecture should reflect these characteristics back to a society. One of the main physical features of the Crown has been an official residence where the sovereign's representatives may entertain, greet visitors and carry out the responsibilities of the vice-regal office. At the time that Alberta entered Confederation as a province, a magnificent Government House was planned for the Crown's representative at the same time as the Legislature was being built. Because the edifice for the people's representatives had priority, the lieutenant-governor had to find an appropriate home until work could begin on Government House.

During the first years of Confederation, the province used the home of The Honourable Frank Oliver as the official residence of His Honour Lieutenant-Governor George Bulyea. This home was located on the southeast corner of 103 Street and 100 Avenue in Edmonton. With a commanding view of the river valley, this 12-room mansion served well as the lieutenant-governor's residence until 1913.[78] Many of the most famous functions in the social life of the early years of the province were held in this home.[79]

Government House eventually arose on the Groat Estates and was officially opened on October 7, 1913. The structure was designed by Allan M. Jeffers, a graduate of the Rhode Island School of Design in the United States, and the architect who designed the Legislature.[80] The impressive building stood on a high bluff with a commanding view of the North Saskatchewan River and was surrounded by 28 acres of trees and gardens. Government House was built with a steel-and-concrete frame that was covered with sandstone brought from a quarry near Calgary. The two-storey bay windows, mullioned windows and triangular gables are typical of the Jacobean Revival style, which, although very popular throughout North America at this time, is seldom found in Alberta. A magnificent conservatory filled with flowers and tropical plants adjoined the three-storey mansion and there was also a large stable for the horses and carriages of the lieutenant-governor.

The last chatelaine of Government House, Edith Bowen, described it as "homey," but a place of "quality and elegance."[81] It was beautifully furnished with many European pieces. There were antiques, "Queen Anne furniture, rich draperies and carpets, and stocks of crested china, silver services and candlesticks embossed with the crest of the Province of Alberta."[82] A ball-room wing was planned, but it was never built because the first resident, His Honour George Bulyea, did not approve of dancing. A reception hall, drawing room, grand dining room and music room were on the main floor. Visiting dignitaries were quartered on the second floor and the third floor contained the servant's quarters.[83]

Government House was to serve the same formal setting for public ceremonies and entertainment as Government House in Ottawa did. The highlight of the social season in Edmonton, the Opening of the Legislature, always had a social dimension to it, and this function was held at Government House. The event was a very formal white-tie affair to which all the members of the Legislature and their wives, as well as the president and faculty members of the University, the judiciary, clergy, police, military, and the various officers of the Legislature were invited. The lieutenant-governor wore his distinguished Windsor uniform and his wife a long evening gown. Guests were treated to refreshments, alcoholic or non-alcoholic, depending on the lieutenant-governor, and hors-d'oeuvres in the large Reception Room, the Billiards Room downstairs and the Conservatory at the side of the main structure. This mansion was certainly suitable for the representative of the Monarch in Alberta. However, in 1938, after a squabble between His Honour John Bowen and Premier William Aberhart, Government House ceased to be the residence of the lieutenant-governor of Alberta.

This conflict began when the lieutenant-governor neglected protocol in October 1937 and reserved the Social Credit legislation for the federal government's approval. When the Alberta premier lost the court battle over the right of the lieutenant-governor to reserve provincial legislation for the pleasure of the governor-general, he took other constitutional, though questionable, measures to express his anger with the lieutenant-governor.

The first public indication of what Aberhart proposed as punishment came in December of that year at the Social Credit Convention, when delegates voted to stop all provincial funding for the maintenance of the position of lieutenant-governor. The resolution included maintenance of Government House. Then in March 1938, the Alberta Legislature, sitting in committee of supply, instructed the government not to spend any money for either the maintenance of Government House or the office of the lieutenant-governor. Existing money for these purposes expired at the end of March (the fiscal year), and since the federal government only pays for the salary of the lieutenant-governor, His Honour faced problems with respect to accommodation, staff, transportation and all other ancillary services connected with his Office. Nevertheless, His Honour chose to ignore the Legislature's actions.

As the end of March approached and the Sovereign's representative gave no indication that he intended either to move or fire his staff, the government gave him one month's grace and expenditures were carried out by special warrant. As the end of April approached, the battle lines between the lieutenant-governor and the Social Credit government became clearer. Bowen claimed that he could vacate Government House only through "proper procedure," which for him meant by an Order-in-Council which he, as lieutenant-governor, would have to sign. The government, on the other hand, argued that an Order-in-Council was not necessary to close a building owned by the provincial government.[84] Thus was the nature of the impasse as midnight approached on 30 April.

Even though the government had issued orders to cut off all utilities, including water, lights, telephone and gas on April 30, the lieutenant-governor, his wife and staff remained held up in Government House. As the crisis deepened, the government decided on a new course of action. All staff, including the caretaker and secretary, were released from service and all office supplies were cut off.[85] At the last minute, Aberhart decided to grant Bowen another temporary extension of residence and to postpone the cutting off of utilities for 10 days.[86] However, his reprieve was not swift enough to prevent the ever-efficient city of Edmonton telephone company from cutting off all telephones throughout the mansion. By oversight, one telephone in the basement of the residence, formerly used by the now-released caretaker, remained functional and allowed the lieutenant-governor to communicate with the outside world. Fortunately for His Honour, the notice to cut off water, light and gas was cancelled in time.

His Honour and his wife, dignified refugees in the elegant setting of Government House, awaited the deadline of the 10-day extension. On Friday afternoon, May 6, 1938, Bowen finally signed an Order-in-Council formally closing Government House, with the Order to take effect on May 10.[87] On Monday May 9, just three hours before the deadline was to take effect at midnight, the vice-regal couple evacuated Government House and sought refuge in a federally-owned and operated building, the Canadian National Railway's Hotel Macdonald. They took up residence in a fifth-floor suite and hung the Union Jack on the flagpole to signify their presence.

The action taken by the Alberta premier embarrassed the federal government and forced the prime minister, Mackenzie King, to enter the fray as mediator. In response to the prime minister's call that the Crown be supplied with "essential services,"[88] the Alberta government refused His Honour's request for an office other than the one in the Legislature Building,[89] the permanent use of a car and chauffeur, secretary and supplies.[90] The lieutenant-governor was thus forced to use taxis and the secretarial pool to meet his needs.[91] Eventually, the Social Credit government provided stationery supplies and allowed His Honour to phone for a ride if he required transportation on official business. The government took an inventory of all furnishings in Government House[92] and subsequently auctioned them off.

After becoming a Veteran's Hospital and lying vacant, the Tory government of Peter Lougheed restored the building. Because some of the grounds had been severed for the building of a provincial Archives and Museum, today Government House remains a building for official functions, but is no longer the home of the lieutenant-governor. It stands, restored and elegant as ever, but crippled as a symbol of the Crown's presence, for all Albertans to contemplate. The Alberta government was finally shamed into action and bought an official residence for the lieutenant-governor in 1966 because the Calgarian, Grant MacEwan, and his family had no place to stay in Edmonton. The Manning government was so embarrassed by the lack of any accommodation for the vice-regal couple that the provincial government bought a bungalow at 58 St. George Crescent in the Glenora district that could function as the official residence of the Crown's representative in Alberta.[93] However, because of the neglect of the present provincial government, this residence was demolished on March 25, 2004, leaving the lieutenant-governor once again without an official residence on the eve of Alberta's centennial celebrations as a province.[94] Finally, in May 2005, the province announced that a new residence would be built on the site of the former one. Until the new residence is built, the lieutenant-governor will be housed at 50 St. George's crescent, a two-storey Georgian home located a few doors down the crescent from the former residence.[95] A spokesman for the government stated that the new building "will be fit for a Queen's representative—stately, secure, sound and accessible."[96]

Besides symbols such as a stately residence, ceremonies also reflect the constitutional power and authority of the lieutenant-governor as the Queen's representative in the province. The most important ceremony in our constitutional Monarchy in which the lieutenant-governor participates is the Opening of Sessions of the Provincial Legislature of Alberta. The Opening of a Session represents the supreme moment of our province's political life and the ritual takes place regularly in the capital when the Crown's representative in the province reads *The Speech from the Throne*. The lieutenant-governor arrives at the Legislature grounds, and as His Honour alights from a carriage or car, a 15-gun salute booms out over the river valley. Then the lieutenant-governor inspects the guard of honour (outside if the weather permits; otherwise inside the rotunda of the Legislature Building). Greeted by the gentlemen escort, the lieutenant-governor proceeds to the vice-regal offices on the third floor of the Legislature to prepare for the entry into the Legislative Chamber itself.

When the lieutenant-governor enters the Assembly Chamber, a trumpet fanfare sounds from the galleries to signal the beginning of this ceremony that is rooted in history, pomp and pageantry. Walking to the dais that is situated against the south wall of the Legislature Chamber, the lieutenant-governor takes her or his place on the throne and presides over the Crown's court in Alberta. The premier sits on the lieutenant-governor's right, and is flanked by members of the government in their places. The leader of Her Majesty's Loyal Opposition and other opposition members sit to the left. Facing the lieutenant-governor is the chief justice of the Alberta Court of Appeal and filling the Legislative Assembly Chamber are people in formal dress and varied uniforms, including members of the consular corps, bishops, and the president of the University of Alberta. Gathered around the throne and wearing their aquillettes and medals, are the gentlemen escorts, who historically have accompanied the sovereign to Parliament as protection. The escort includes senior officers of the Armed Forces, the assistant commissioner of K-Division of the Royal Canadian Mounted Police, the chief of the Edmonton Police Service, and the lieutenant-governor's aides-de-camp and private secretary. A little below, on His Honour's right, stands the Speaker of the Legislative Assembly, dressed in black robes and tricorn hat, and the Sergeant at Arms of the Legislature, who carries the Black Rod into the Assembly at the head of the vice-regal procession. All those with power and authority over us are gathered together before the throne to hear a message from the Queen's representative in Alberta. This ceremony reminds us that we live in a constitutional monarchy where the Sovereign "personifies the state and is the personal symbol of allegiance, unity and authority for all Canadians."[97]

All of these ceremonies and symbols of office have enhanced the status and importance of the Office of lieutenant-governor within the context of the Canadian Crown. The provincial manifestation of the Crown, the lieutenant-governor, has come to represent the Monarch within Alberta's jurisdiction in the same way that the governor-general represents the Monarch at the federal level of competence. The lieutenant-governor therefore acts with respect to the province just as the governor-general does for Canada, and exercises all of the Queen's powers within provincial jurisdiction. The lieutenant-governor, and the provincial Crown which the lieutenant-governor personifies, symbolizes the sovereignty of the provincial government within Confederation. The direct link with the Sovereign is essential to the constitutional status of the provinces in the federal state because the provinces derive sovereignty over their own constitutionally-allocated powers, not from the federal Parliament or the governor-general, but from the Crown and the Queen.[98] As her term of office was coming to an end, the former lieutenant-governor of Ontario, the Honourable Hilary M. Weston, defined this new reality. In a speech before the Canadian Club of Toronto, she noted that "Though we are appointed by Ottawa, we are no longer its agent nor some sort of local assistant to the governor-general. Rather, we are the legal personifications of jurisdictions, such as education and health, in which the provinces are autonomous and sovereign."[99] Under the terms of the *Constitution Act, 1867*, the lieutenant-governor is appointed for a minimum period of five years, which may be extended, and remains in office until a successor is appointed and installed.[100]

Authorization to make any changes regarding "the office of the Queen, the Governor General and the Lieutenant Governor of a province," can only be given through resolutions of the Senate and House of Commons and of the Legislative Assembly of each province.[101] This constitutional necessity means that Canada will remain a constitutional monarchy well into the foreseeable future and that the Queen will remain at the top of the tables of precedence for Canada and the provinces.

The Office of lieutenant-governor of Alberta is successful because it has been flexible and adaptable to change over time. The position of the lieutenant-governor of Alberta has increased in importance as part of the Maple Crown of Canada as the place and position of the province has become more vital to the Canadian Confederation. By playing a significant part in the functioning of the Maple Crown, the office of lieutenant-governor of Alberta has grown to embody the sovereignty of the province within the larger Canadian family and has taken its place as one of the brightest jewels in the Maple Crown. Indeed, the Crown is the lynchpin that holds our constitutional structure together and the Office of lieutenant-governor plays an essential role in that polity.

Notes

1. Jacques Monet, s.j., "The Queen Opens Parliament," in *The Silver Jubilee: Royal Visit to Canada* (Ottawa: Deneau & Greenberg, 1977), 38.
2. "Rallies, babies and hard advice to Indians cap remarkable MacEwan Vice-regency," *St. John's Edmonton Report*, 8 July 1974, 10.
3. Monet, "The Queen Opens Parliament," 38.
4. Ibid., 38.
5. *The Constitutions Acts, 1867–1982*, from J.L. Finlay and D.N. Sprague, *The Structure of Canadian History*, 5 ed. (Scarborough, Ontario: Prentice Hall Allyn and Bacon Canada, [1997]), s. 58, 618.
6. Ibid., ss. 59 and 60, 618; s. 55, 617; and s. 90, 624.
7. Norman Ward, "Hon. James Gardiner and the Liberal Party of Alberta, 1935–40," *Canadian Historical Review* 51, no. 3 (September 1975): 305–06.

8.	The Credit of Alberta Regulation Bill "enabled the province to regulate the credit policy of the chartered banks operating in Alberta." J.R. Mallory, *Social Credit and the Federal Power in Canada* (Toronto: University of Toronto Press, 1954), 73. This bill "required every bank and every bank employee to obtain a license from the provincial government. Upon being licensed each bank would have a local directorate appointed by the Social Credit Board to supervise all of its activities, thus giving the Social Credit Board complete control over their credit policies." See David R. Elliott and Iris Miller, *Bible Bill: A Biography of William Aberhart* ([Edmonton]: Reidmore Books, [1987]), 267. A second Bill, the Bank Employees Civil Rights Bill "prohibited any unlicensed bank or bank employee from having any access to the courts." See Elliott and Miller, *Bible Bill, 267.* The third Bill, the Judicature Act Amendment Bill, "prohibited any court action over the constitutionality of any enactment of the Alberta Legislature." See Elliott and Miller, *Bible Bill,* 267 and Mallory, *Social Credit and the Federal Power in Canada*, 73. The first two statutes contravened Section 91, subsection 15 whereby the federal government is given exclusive control over "Banking, Incorporation of Banks, and the Issue of Paper Money." See *The Constitution Acts, 1867–1982* from J.L. Finlay and D.N. Sprague, *The Structure of Canadian History*, 5th ed. (Scarborough, Ontario: Prentice Hall Allyn and Bacon Canada, [1997]), Section 91, 15, 625. These pieces of legislation were seen to be an attack against the banks and the federal government. Thus the federal government acted and disallowed all three bills. See Mallory, *Social Credit and the Federal Power in Canada*, 76–77.

9.	Elliott and Miller, *Bible Bill*, 268; Mallory, *Social Credit and the Federal Power*, 74–75.

10.	Mallory, *Social Credit and the Federal Power*, 75–76.

11.	Ibid., 76.

12.	John T. Saywell, "The Lieutenant-Governors," in David J. Bellamy, Jon H. Pammett, and Donald C. Rowat, eds., *The Provincial Political Systems, Comparative Essays* (Toronto: Methuen, [1976]), 305.

13.	Ibid., 307.

14.	Mallory, *Social Credit and the Federal Power in Canada*, 80.

15.	Saywell, "The Lieutenant-Governors," 307.

16.	John G. Diefenbaker, *One Canada. Memoirs of the Right Honourable John G. Diefenbaker: The Years of Achievement 1957–1962*, Vol. II (Toronto: Macmillan of Canada, [1976]), 56. This reserve power is contained in s. 90 of the *The Constitution Acts, 1867 to 1982 (The British North America Act)* in Finlay and Sprague, *The Structure of Canadian History*, 624.

17.	Ibid., 56.

18.	Ibid., 56–57.

19.	Joan Crockett, "Lt.-Gov. Wouldn't OK grant from Kowalski," *Edmonton Journal*, Friday, 23 December 1994, A1 & A4.

20.	Joan Crockett, "Loan was stalled for 5 days," *Edmonton Journal*, Wednesday, 11 January 1995, A5.

21.	Joan Crockett, "Lt.-Gov. Wouldn't OK grant from Kowalski," *Edmonton Journal*, Friday, 23 December 1994, A1 & A4.

22.	Joan Crockett, "Klein's 'snub' of Lt.-Gov. raises eyebrows," *Edmonton Journal*, Wednesday, 19 May 1993, A9.

23.	Ibid.

24.	Ibid.

25.	Ashley Geddes, "Lt.-Gov. Questions Health Bill: Lois Hole says she wants to chat with Klein before giving final assent to Bill," *Edmonton Journal*, Friday, 17 March 2000, A18.

26.	Larry Johnsrude, "New Lt.-Gov. Lois Hole will champion education: She'll be installed in wheelchair after breaking heel," *Edmonton Journal*, Thursday, 10 February 2000, A7.

27. Ashley Geddes, "Lt.-Gov. Questions Health Bill: Lois Hole says she wants to chat with Klein before giving final assent to Bill," *Edmonton Journal*, Friday, 17 March 2000, A18.

28. "Royal Round-up: news from the realms" Edmonton, March 28, *Canadian Monarchist News/Les Nouvelles Monarchiques du Canada*, 5, no. 2 (Spring/Summer 2000), 8.

29. Bill Rankin, "ESO's tribute to Her Majesty full of pomp, glory, *Edmonton Journal*, Sunday, 8 June 2003, B9.

30. Paula Simons, "Lois Hole pleads for public education," *Edmonton Journal*, Tuesday, 10 June 2003, A1.

31. Ibid.

32. Jeff Holubitsky, "Hole comments sting Tory MLAs," *Edmonton Journal*, Wednesday, 11 June 2003, B1.

33. Ibid., B7.

34. Ibid., B7.

35. Graham Thomson, "Alberta has lost its social conscience," *Edmonton Journal*, January 11, 2005, A10.

36. Ibid., A10.

37. Andy Ogle, "City women's hospital named after Lois Hole," *Edmonton Journal*, Wednesday, 17 November 2004, A1 and A14.

38. Ibid., A1 and A14.

39. L.G. Thomas, *The Liberal Party in Alberta: A History of Politics in the Province of Alberta 1905–1921* (Toronto: University of Toronto Press, 1959), 206.

40. Thomas, *The Liberal Party in Alberta*, 89–94.

41. Ernest Watkins, *The Golden Province: A Political History of Alberta* (Calgary: Sandstone Publishing Ltd., [1980]), 80–81.

42. "Brownlee, Cabinet Place Resignations in Hands of U.F.A. Party's Caucus," *Edmonton Journal*, Tuesday, 3 July 1934, 1.

43. "Hon. R.G. Reid named Premier-elect, cabinet selections in progress," *Edmonton Journal*, Thursday, 5 July 1934, 1.

44. "Reid Cabinet Takes Office Today," *Edmonton Journal*, Tuesday, 10 July 1934, 1.

45. Alfred J. Hooke, *30+5; I Know, I Was There* ([Edmonton]: [Institute of Applied Art], [1971]), 169.

46. Watkins, *Golden Province*, 141–43.

47. "Fathoming vice-regality takes trip into antiquity," *Edmonton Journal*, Friday, 12 July 1974, 39.

48. *Alberta Magazine*, July/August 1980, 34.

49. "Vice-Regal: 'This is a Fragile Institution'," *The National Post*, Monday, 10 December 2001, A4.

50. Frank Lynch-Staunton, *Greener Pastures: The Memoirs of F. Lynch-Staunton* (Edmonton: Jasper Printing Group, 1987), 41.

51. Ibid., 41–42.

52. Graham Thomson, "Alberta has lost its social conscience," *Edmonton Journal*, January 11, 2005, A10.

53. John T. Saywell, *The Office of Lieutenant-Governor: A Study in Canadian Government and Politics* (Toronto: University of Toronto Press, 1957), 17–18.

54. Conrad Swan, *Canada: Symbols of Sovereignty* (Toronto: University of Toronto Press, [1977]), 33, 212.

55. "Fathoming vice-regality takes trip into antiquity," *Edmonton Journal*, Friday, 12 July 1974, 39.

56. Saywell, *The Office of Lieutenant-Governor*, 14. Also see A. Margaret Evans, *Sir Oliver Mowat* (Toronto: University of Toronto Press, [1992]), 148, 154, 176, 178–79.

57. Swan, *Canada: Symbols of Sovereignty*, 16.

58. Ibid., 17.

59. Letter to His Honour John Bowlen from C. Stein, under-secretary of state, Ottawa, 4 April 1956, Provincial Archives of Alberta, lieutenant-governors private correspondence 1960–65, J. Percy Page, GS 84.464 A-1.

60. A.W. (Tony) Cashman, *The Vice-Regal Cowboy: Life and Times of Alberta's J.J. Bowlen* (Edmonton: The Institute of Applied Arts, 1957), 194.

61. "Court and Social: Court Circular," *London Times*, April 14, 1983, 16; and Lynch-Staunton, *Greener Pastures*, 42–43.

62. "Getting the Royal Treatment," *Edmonton Journal*, Thursday, 2 November 2000, A3.

63. Peter Stursberg, *Roland Michener: The Last Viceroy* (Toronto: McGraw-Hill Ryerson, [1989]), 202–03.

64. Ibid., 203.

65. Steve Chase, "This Bud's for them: Olson takes New Year's levee South," *Edmonton Sun*, Saturday, 30 November 1996, News 3.

66. Ibid.

67. Ashley Geddes, "Olson staying but levee moving," *Edmonton Journal*, Friday, 6 December 1996. A6.

68. Vicki Hall, "New Year's Day levee to stay in city after break from tradition," *Edmonton Journal*, Friday, 17 November 2000, A7.

69. Allan Chambers, "Lois Hole 'worth the wait', for folks in levee lineup," *Edmonton Journal*, Tuesday, 2 January 2001, B1.

70. Swan, *Canada: Symbols of Sovereignty*, 213.

71. Government of Alberta, *The Alberta Gazette*, Part I, Vol. 77, Wednesday, 30 September 1981, No. 18.

72. "New flag flies high at Government House," *Edmonton Journal*, Wednesday, 30 September 1981, J2.

73. Government of Canada, *Symbols of Canada* ([Ottawa]: [Canadian Government Publishing], [1999]), 8.

74. "Lieutenant-governors now have badge of office," *National Post*, Saturday, 17 February 2001, B6.

75. Ibid.

76. Victor Hugo, *The Hunchback of Notre Dame* (New York: [Random House], [1941]), 96.

77. Ibid., 116–17.

78. "First Government House Awaits Demolition Crews," *Edmonton Journal*, Thursday, 16 May 1957, 5.

79. "Oliver House is taken over as Defence H.Q.," *Edmonton Bulletin*, Thursday, 10 June 1943, 16.

80. D.R. Babcock, *A Gentleman of Strathcona, Alexander Cameron Rutherford* (Calgary: The Friends of Rutherford House and The University of Calgary Press, 1989), 172.

81. Provincial Archives of Alberta, recorded conversation with Mrs. J.C. (Oliver) Bowen on 27 March 1972, #72.128.

82. Lori Yanish and Shirley Lowe, *Edmonton's West Side Story: The History of the Original West End of Edmonton from 1870* [Edmonton: Jasper Printing Group, 1991], 96.

83. Ibid., 96.

84. "Lt.-Governor Given 10-day moving grace," *Edmonton Bulletin*, Wednesday, 4 May 1938, 1 and 2.

85. "Cabinet fires C.V. Dacre: Governor's Secretary is Dismissed with one Month's pay," *Edmonton Journal*, Wednesday, 4 May 1938, 1 & 2.

86. "Lt.-Governor Given 10-day moving grace," *Edmonton Bulletin*, Wednesday, 4 May 1938, 1 and 2.

87. "Governor Signs Own Ouster," *Edmonton Bulletin*, Saturday, 7 May 1938, 1 and 2.

88. "Bowen Moves Residence to C.N.R. Hotel," *Edmonton Bulletin*, Tuesday, 10 May 1938, 1 and 2.

89. "Government Sends Governor 'Notice'," *Edmonton Journal*, Monday, 2 May 1938, 1 and 2; "Cabinet Won't provide staff for Governor," *Edmonton Journal*, Monday, 16 May 1938, 1 and 3.

90. "Bowen Plans Change Home Monday Night," *Edmonton Bulletin*, Monday, 9 May 1938, 1.

91. Elliott and Miller, Bible Bill, 278.

92. "Government House Fixings get inventory," *Edmonton Bulletin*, Wednesday, 18 May 1938, 1.

93. Yardley Jones, "'Momma—a Mister J.W. Grant MacEwan's here....'," *Edmonton Journal*, Saturday, 8 January 1966, 4; and "MacEwan to Get Official Home," *Edmonton Journal*, Wednesday, 16 February 1966, 1.

94. Tom Barrett, "Buyers rush to bid on land next to lieutenant-governor's lot," *Edmonton Journal*, Tuesday, 1 June 2004, B2.

95. Vernon Clement Jones, "Lt.-Gov. gets temporary residence," *Edmonton Journal*, Saturday, 14 May 2005, B3.

96. Ibid., B3.

97. Letter from the Honourable Gordon Campbell to Lt (N) Gene Fedderly, June 28, 2001 as printed in *The Canadian Monarchist New/Les Nouvelles Monarchiques du Canada* 6, no. 1 (Summer 2001): 2.

98. Frank MacKinnon, *The Crown in Canada* ([Calgary]: Glenbow-Alberta Institute, McClelland and Stewart West, [1976]), 91.

99. "Vice-Regal: 'This is a Fragile Institution'," *National Post*, Monday, 10 December 2001, A4.

100. *The Constitution Act, 1867*, in Finlay and Sprague, s. 59, 618.

101. See the *Constitution Act, 1982*, s. 41.

Eleven

Federal-Provincial Tensions and the Evolution of a Province

PRESTON MANNING

Introduction

The constitutional and political evolution of Alberta is the story of the evolution of a territory and a province within the Canadian federal system. During the course of developments, there were several periods of serious tension between the government and politicians of Alberta and the government of Canada that had an impact on the evolution, present status, and future prospects of the province. The six periods of tension that form the focus of the current analysis are: (1) The Struggle for Provincehood (prior to 1905); (2) The Struggle for Control Over Natural Resources (1905–1930); (3) The Struggle for Survival (1939–1945); (4) The Struggle for Identity (particularly from 1965 forward); (5) The Struggle for Control of Petroleum Prices and Revenues (1973–1988); and (6) The Emergence of the New West (1987 to 2005).

The perspective from which these periods of tension are discussed is that of an Alberta-based politician[1]—a partisan participant in the affairs of the province as distinct from a detached observer. Each discussion commences with an anecdote relevant to the tensions of the period in question. The anecdotes chosen are those of which the author has personal knowledge. The evolution of Alberta as a province is, after all, a human story—a story of real people with all their strengths and faults, acting in specific circumstances often beyond their control, with real consequences for better and for worse; a story that should not be lost through the clinical presentation and analysis of historical facts and conclusions.

The Struggle for Provincehood

When Ernest C. Manning, my father, was first elected to the Alberta Legislature in 1935, he was appointed to the Cabinet as provincial secretary. At 27 years of age, he was the youngest minister in the government. But his deputy—a man named Eddie Trowbridge—was one of the oldest deputy ministers in the Alberta civil service. Eddie Trowbridge had begun his public service career as a clerk in the territorial government prior to Alberta's becoming a province. He had known and had carefully observed every premier of Alberta and of Saskatchewan from 1905 to 1935, and he never tired of telling my father that the best premier the West ever produced was F.W.G. Haultain.[2] Haultain, of course, had been premier of the old North-West Territories and had presided over the struggle to attain provincial status for those territories.

According to Trowbridge, Haultain's vision of the future was as big and expansive as the West itself—on a par with the Canada visions of Sir John A. Macdonald and Sir Wilfrid Laurier. At the heart of his vision was constitutional equality for the West with the older provinces of Canada, and the unification of the West into one big province—a province that would eventually be large and strong enough to counterbalance the weight of the large provinces of central Canada in directing the future course of Confederation. Haultain's ideas and principles entered the West's constitutional and political gene pool and profoundly affected the attitudes and actions of generations of politicians and citizens to come.

Haultain's principled quest for equality between East and West was rooted in practical concerns. The federal government had absolute power over collecting taxes, but expected the territories to pay for their infrastructure through a system of federal grants and a sparse power over fines and licenses. Nearing the turn of the century, the fiscal situation of the territories became acute due to pressures caused by the influx of immigrants into the territories. So, on May 2, 1900, Haultain stood up in the Territorial Legislature and put forward the reasons for provincehood. It was a three and a half hour speech that emphasized, more than anything else, equality and fairness between East and West.[3]

Haultain's principled insistence that the West should be reconstituted as one big province rather than allowing itself to be divided up into several provinces was also rooted in practical politics. Haultain knew that a united West would have more bargaining power—and it had precious little in any event—than a divided West. He argued this point vigorously in a famous debate with Manitoba Premier Rodman Roblin at Indian Head, Saskatchewan, on December 18, 1901. Haultain suspected that the federal government would pursue a "divide and conquer" strategy with respect to the western territories— playing one sectional interest off against another and thereby weakening the West's capacity to bargain for better terms and conditions of provincehood. Those territorial politicians who co-operated with this federal strategy, for parochial reasons or out of personal political ambition, he characterized as "Little Westerners." Manitoba's demands for better terms, he said, had been denied because they were made in isolation from the rest of the West. But, he continued, "some day not far distant the *joint demand of a united West* cannot be disregarded."[4]

In October of 1901 Haultain had met with a sub-committee of the Privy Council, including Laurier, to discuss the prospects for autonomy—autonomy with equality. However, the meetings turned out to be futile. In March 1902 the proposal for provincehood was rejected. But Haultain and his colleagues were persistent. They redoubled their efforts and in January 1905 negotiations on the granting of provincial powers to the territories began again in earnest. By this time, however, it had become apparent that if some measure of provincehood was to be granted, it was the intention of the federal government to divide the West into several provinces, and that it would find enough support to carry the day among territorial politicians anxious to be bigger fish in smaller ponds. It also became clear that any new western provinces would not enjoy the full entitlement of rights that genuine constitutional equality with the older provinces of Canada should have brought.

Alberta was therefore born on September 1, 1905,[5] as one of two new provinces (Saskatchewan being the other). Provincehood conferred upon Albertans a new status, with powers its people had never enjoyed before, but Alberta was also born with two huge handicaps—one constitutional and the other political.

Constitutionally, Alberta was "born unequal"—unequal to the founding provinces of Canada with respect to the control of its natural resources and the control of its schools. The federal government retained control of the province's natural resources, including public lands, and it imposed on the province a dual system of public and denominational schools. Thus the struggle for full constitutional equality, the priority that generations of Albertans have given to the principle of "equality in law" for both persons and provinces, as well as the sensitivities of Albertans to any federal policy that appears to detract from the equality principle, has characterized the political evolution of the province, its relations with its fellow provinces, and its relations with the federal government from that day to this.

This struggle for equality initially expressed itself in Herculean efforts to gain provincial control over natural resources[6] such as land and petroleum and culminated in the Natural Resources Transfer Agreement of 1930 (more on this in the next section). However, it also became the distinguishing feature of Alberta's approach to national politics and federal-provincial relations in the second half of the twentieth century, finding expression in Premier Lougheed's wars with Ottawa over petroleum pricing in the 1970s and early 1980s, the Reform Party's conceptualization of Canada[7] as a partnership of equal citizens and equal provinces in the 1990s, and a similar definition of Canada endorsed by the provincial premiers and territorial leaders in the Calgary Declaration of 1997.[8]

Politically, Alberta was also "born divided." It was now constitutionally divided from rather than united with its sister provinces on the prairies. It was divided community by community between Haultain's Big Westerners and the Liberals' Little Westerners, and it was increasingly divided north-south as Calgary and Edmonton bitterly competed to become its capital city. Some of those divisions remain in different forms, but still discernible and influential, to this very day in such issues as whether to build "firewalls" around the province to protect it from unwanted federal intrusions or to build "bridges" and strategic alliances with other provinces and Ottawa; whether to be Big Westerners, endeavouring to reform the federal system by winning seats in the federal Parliament, or Little Westerners gravitating to Edmonton and threatening separation as the best tactic for securing federal action on western discontents and alienation; or whether the Battle of Alberta will be won by the Edmonton Eskimos and Edmonton Oilers or the Calgary Stampeders and Calgary Flames—symbols of much more than football and hockey rivalries.

The Struggle for Control Over Natural Resources

On February 13, 1970, Alberta Provincial Treasurer A.O. Aalborg rose in his place in the Legislative Assembly to deliver the province's first "Billion Dollar Budget." It was a time of celebration for a province that, in the depths of the Depression, had been flat on its back with a total outstanding debt of $161 million and an annual provincial revenue of $15 million, of which over $8 million was allocated to debt service charges.[9]

Of the billion dollars of provincial revenue projected for the following year (1971), 26% or $258 million[10] was attributable to revenues from mines and minerals, with petroleum royalties alone amounting to $112 million.[11] Mr. Aalborg might well have paused before delivering that Budget to offer a brief prayer of thanksgiving for those revenues that made the dramatic difference between Alberta's being a "have" rather than a "have not" province. That those petroleum-based revenues flowed to the provincial treasury in Edmonton rather than to the federal treasury in Ottawa was the result of a 25-year struggle on the part of a previous generation of Alberta politicians and civil servants to wrest control of the province's natural resources from the federal government—a struggle that culminated in the Natural Resources Transfer Agreement of 1930.

The struggle for control of natural resources by the people of the prairie provinces began in earnest in 1869 when a young Métis, Louis Riel, placed his foot on a surveyor's chain that belonged to the federally-authorized Dominion Land Survey crew attempting to cross his uncle's land near the community of Red River. In doing so Riel declared "This is our land"—one of the first officially recorded confrontations between representatives of the federal government and the people of the West over natural resources.[12]

When Alberta achieved provincehood in 1905, it was not given control over its natural resources like the older provinces of Canada. For a short time, the federal Liberals were successful in persuading their provincial brethren—who formed Alberta's first provincial government under Premier Rutherford—that this was not a serious liability. Alberta was to be adequately compensated by a generous federal subsidy. Indeed, of the $2.5 million in revenues projected in Alberta's first budget as a province, almost half was to come from the federal subsidy.[13]

But the new provincial government committed itself to an ambitious—indeed foolhardy—railway building program and whereas the federal government had used generous land grants to induce railway development, the province was unable to do so. It was forced, by its lack of control of public lands, to rely primarily on offering cash subsidies and government guarantees of corporate bonds to railway developers in order to stimulate railway building in the province. This policy quickly proved to be disastrous. In particular, its mishandling of the development of the ill-conceived Alberta and Great Waterways Railroad forced the resignation of the Rutherford government in 1910. It was replaced by a reorganized Liberal administration under the leadership of Arthur Sifton.

The notable historian, L.G. Thomas, described the Alberta and Great Waterways Railway crisis of 1910—rooted in part in Alberta's inability to control its public lands—as "the critical episode" in the early political history of the province. It was "a political crisis which turned out one Liberal government and replaced it with another, very nearly produced a permanent schism in the provincial Liberal party, and severely shook the confidence of the Alberta public in old political parties."[14]

In reality, the willingness of both the provincial Liberals and the provincial Conservatives to pursue provincial control over natural resources for Alberta was compromised by the positions of their federal counterparts. The federal Liberals under Laurier had been opposed to such control from the outset, and their provincial brethren were reluctant to challenge them vigorously for fear of losing the benefits of federal patronage. In 1911, however, the Laurier Liberals in Ottawa were replaced by the Conservatives under Robert Borden and the prospects for a transfer of resource control looked brighter. The Borden Conservatives, however, were reluctant to move quickly on the issue while the principal beneficiary of such a policy would be the Liberal administration that was in power provincially. Managing Canada's role in World War I soon became (rightfully so) the principal preoccupation of the Borden administration and over the next decade little progress was made on the issue of transferring control of natural resources to Alberta.

By 1921, however, no Alberta-based politician—provincial or federal—could ignore or remain indifferent to the economic implications for the province of continued federal stewardship of the province's natural resources. From 1900 to 1905 alone, the federal government had alienated 6,400,000 acres of the most fertile land in Alberta to various eastern Canadian corporations as subsidies for the construction of railways, not in Alberta, but in British Columbia, Manitoba, and Ontario. Another 10 million acres had been granted to homesteaders without compensation to the province, while other huge tracts of land had gone for Indian reserves, forest reserves and national parks. (In its infancy as a province, Alberta provided 95% of the national park area in Canada.[15]) In addition to public lands, the federal government was awarding extensive mineral leases to various corporations, most of them based in the east. With the discovery of the Turner Valley oil field in 1912–1913, control over petroleum development and the revenues derived from this resource became a growing bone of contention.

In 1921 as well, a new alignment of the political stars—both federally and provincially—gave new impetus to the quest for provincial control. As Alberta's governing Liberal party became weaker and less effective, the people of the province began to look for economic and political leadership, not to the opposition Conservatives, who were also declining in effectiveness and influence, but to organizations outside the formal political arena altogether. In Alberta, the most prominent of these was the United Farmers of Alberta, then under the leadership of Henry Wise Wood and its very able legal counsel, John E. Brownlee. While Wood preferred to keep the UFA out of provincial and federal politics and to bring the influence of the UFA to bear on whoever formed the government, his members increasingly favoured direct political action. The UFA developed a provincial election platform that included a strong commitment to agricultural reforms, social reforms, and securing provincial control of natural resources. It ran candidates under its own banner in the Alberta provincial election of July 1921. When the smoke cleared, it had elected 38 members to the 61-seat provincial assembly and had replaced the Liberals as the government of Alberta.

It was the beginning of what L.G. Thomas called the "pattern" of provincial politics in Alberta: "a pattern of sweeping victory [by a new party in a provincial election], succeeded by long tenure of office with only ineffective opposition...[then] virtual annihilation [not at the hands of its traditional opposition, but] at the hands of a young rival of unexpected vigour, and a sudden decline into political obscurity, if not complete extinction."[16]

Meanwhile on the federal front, the farmers' movement, of which the UFA was a part, had brought into being the Progressive Party of Canada. It startled the political establishment of central and eastern Canada, first by unexpectedly winning (by a large margin) a federal by-election in Medicine Hat in 1921 and then later in the year electing 65 members to the House of Commons in the general election. Although the Progressives now formed the second largest group of members in the Commons, they did not like the "party" concept and refused to take the position of official opposition. Most importantly for the West and for Alberta, the Progressives were a reform-oriented party that was deeply committed to systemic change in trade policy (abolition of the tariff), agricultural policy, transportation policy, political institutions, and the constitutional arrangements that denied Alberta and the other prairie provinces control over their lands and other natural resources.[17]

Mackenzie King's Liberals, who formed a minority federal government in 1921, needed the support of the Progressives to govern and were thus more than amenable to responding to key elements of the Progressives' agenda. This was even more true after the 1925 federal election in which Liberal support declined, the Conservatives rebounded, and the Progressives held the balance of power even though their own representation was reduced to 24 seats. It was imperative throughout most of the decade that King assiduously court the Progressives—the objective being to absorb them into the Liberal fold by absorbing key elements of their platform. Thus it was that the election of the UFA government in Alberta and the presence of a strong Progressive element in Ottawa finally created the political conditions conducive to positive action on the issue of transferring control of natural resources to the prairie provinces.

The first UFA premier in Alberta, Herbert Greenfield, was the compromise choice of the UFA leadership. His Attorney General was the much more able John E. Brownlee, who made the natural resources transfer issue his own, and succeeded Greenfield as premier in 1926. In 1925, a special committee of Parliament had been formed to formally discuss the issue. Negotiations carried on for some time at the glacial pace that seems to characterize all federal-provincial negotiations in Canada, and it was not until December 11, 1929, that Premier Brownlee entered into final negotiations with Prime Minister King. Their first meeting was not cordial, ending with both King and Brownlee storming out of the meeting room through different doors.[18] Three days later, however, the two adversaries were able to reach an agreement. It was the Leader of the Opposition (and also a Calgarian), R.B. Bennett, who played a crucial role in coaxing the bitter negotiators back to the table,[19] as King was acutely aware that Bennett was quite prepared to promise the Prairie provinces whatever he (King) might deny them.

Finally, on Saturday, December 14, 1929 (the superstitious King did not want to sign anything on Friday the thirteenth) the historic National Resource Transfer Agreement was signed. It was formally passed into law as an amendment to the Canadian constitution the following year.[20]

By virtue of this agreement, Alberta was placed "in the same position as the original Provinces of Confederation are in virtue of section 109 of the British North America Act"—the section which provided that "The interest of the Crown in all Crown lands, mines, minerals (precious and base) and royalties derived therefrom within the Province, and all sums due and payable for such...shall, from and after the coming into force of this agreement...belong to the Province...and the said lands, mines, minerals, and royalties shall be administered by the Province for the purposes thereof...."[21]

Alberta, a province with immense natural resources, had finally achieved equality in law with the founding provinces of Canada with respect to provincial control of those resources. No wonder a crowd of more than 3,000 cheering citizens met Brownlee at the CPR station in Edmonton when he returned from Ottawa.

Subsequent provincial treasurers, such as Anders Aalborg, who would present Alberta's first billion-dollar budget 40 years later, had the Progressives, Mackenzie King, the UFA and especially Premier Brownlee to thank for the fact that the public portion of petroleum revenues generated by Alberta's oil and gas development flowed into the provincial treasury in Edmonton rather than into the coffers of the federal government in Ottawa.

The fact that the newly created province of Alberta spent the first 25 years of its life engaged in a struggle for control of its natural resources under the banner of "equality" refined and deepened Alberta's commitment to the equality principle and its desire to see that principle enshrined in constitutional law. That commitment, and the federal government's reactions to it, continued to shape Alberta-Ottawa relations through the oil and gas boom following the Leduc discoveries in 1947, the "energy wars" of the 1970s and early 1980s, and even the more recent debate over the Kyoto Accord in the 1990s.

The fact that Alberta eventually gained control of its natural resources, and that those resources included vast quantities of oil, natural gas, coal and oil sands, enormously strengthened the province economically, particularly in the latter half of the twentieth century. Alberta's growing economic strength within the federation, and the dependence of that strength on the petroleum industry, have made energy policy a driving force in provincial politics and a touchstone whereby Albertans judge federal politicians, parties and governments. The provincial revenues derived from petroleum resources have also made Alberta the largest contributor by far (on a per capita basis) to equalization and federal-provincial transfers to have-not provinces, giving the province and its people an understandably acute interest in how Ottawa handles public money and administers redistribution policies.

The fact that this momentous development in the life of the province—gaining control of its natural resources through a constitutional amendment negotiated with the federal government—was achieved largely by the efforts of a new political party also became embedded in the province's political consciousness. Contrary to the conventional political wisdom, there were other options besides going back and forth between the Liberals and Conservatives in order to achieve change. It was possible to achieve major changes—even to change the national agenda and the constitution—through third-party advocacy and the leverage that draining votes away from the traditional parties gave to those third parties. It was a lesson that Albertans would absorb and return to twice more before the end of the twentieth century. The willingness to accept "a new party" as an instrument of change entered the Alberta political psyche during the struggle for control over natural resources and became a distinguishing characteristic of Alberta's political culture from that day to this.

The Struggle for Survival

My parents' generation experienced the Great Depression and the Second World War. The struggle for survival that characterized that period affected their lives, their careers and their politics, and it is illustrated by some of the stories they would tell to illustrate the stress of those times—stories which they preferred to forget and which had to be coaxed out of them by their children and grandchildren.

There were my mother's stories of doing "relief work" in southern Alberta—visiting farm homes where the only meat dish was gopher stew and where the children wore clothes made from gunny sacks that once held binder twine. Relief work was still very much an activity of the churches and private charities, with governments only just beginning to lay the foundations of the modern welfare state.

My mother was already a concert pianist in her teens, and had been recruited by William Aberhart—principal of Crescent Heights High School in Calgary, pioneer Christian radio broadcaster, and destined to become Premier of Alberta in the heart of the Great Depression—to play the piano on his religious radio program. She was particularly familiar with William Aberhart's soup kitchen on 8th Avenue Southwest in Calgary, which he ran in connection with his Bible Institute. There, haggard men who had been riding the rails would line up for a meal after jumping off the trains at the western outskirts of Calgary to evade the CPR police. In her view, it was Aberhart's experience of walking up and down that line day after day and seeing the desperate condition of former students whom he had sent off to be doctors, teachers and lawyers, that ultimately drove him into political education and, eventually, politics. These were desperate times that made people and politicians willing to entertain desperate measures to secure and provide relief.

Then there were my father's stories of trying to run a cash-strapped, debt-ridden provincial government in that dark time—in particular meeting with treasury officials like Keith Huckvale (who later became Provincial Auditor) at the end of each month to see how much cash had come in from the few taxes (mainly sales taxes on fuel) that could still be collected, and then pro-rating civil servants' salaries and other required provincial payments on the basis of cash available. Many public servants would end up receiving only a portion of their salary, but few would quit because in those days a half-paid job was better than no job at all.

My father would also tell of the bitter, hard-edged speeches that charac-terized the politics of the day—speeches denouncing the capitalist interests whom the West blamed for the Depression and blasting the federal gov-ernment for its ineptitude in dealing with the crisis. At first it was the Conservative government of R.B. Bennett that bore the brunt of that anger. But when, in the federal election campaign of 1935, the Liberal, Mackenzie King, offered Alberta a helping hand (on the condition, of course, that Alberta vote Liberal), the province showed its contempt for that kind of patronizing condescension by electing Social Credit members to all its seats in the House of Commons. King's ultimate response to this rejection was to reject the Alberta government's request for federal aid to prevent it from defaulting on its provincial indebtedness, even though a Bank of Canada study commissioned in 1937 attributed most of this indebtedness to the mis-management of provincial railway development by the provincial Liberals during the first 16 years of the province's life.[22] Amicable federal-provincial relations were also a casualty of the politics of desperation that characterized the Depression years.

My father also remembered that day—September 10, 1939—when all those speeches blasting the national government and cursing the indifference or incompetence of Ottawa had to be substantially modified or even put away. They were suddenly inappropriate and out of place. An issue even larger than that of surviving the Depression now loomed on the horizon—the survival of democracy, the survival of freedom, the survival of the British Empire of which Canada still considered itself a part, from the threat of Hitler and the Nazis came to dominate the public consciousness and demanded co-operation rather than confrontation between the provincial and federal governments.

What impact did these struggles for survival presented by the Depression and the War have on the evolution, present status, and future prospects of the province? Volumes could be written in response to such a question, but the four impacts that appeared to register most strongly on the Alberta politicians I knew who lived through that period were as follows:

Once again, when Albertans became disillusioned with the political and economic status quo, they turned not to the traditional alternative—the official opposition party in their Legislature or in the federal Parliament—but to "something new." In the 1935 provincial election, every single member of the UFA government was thrown out of the Legislature. The government was replaced, not by the provincial Liberal Party, salivating as it was at the personal scandal that had discredited Premier Brownlee and desperate to return to power after 14 years in the wilderness, but by William Aberhart's radical and untried Social Credit party. And in the federal election that year, Albertans did the same thing, rejecting the overtures of Liberal leader Mackenzie King in favour of federal Social Credit candidates. Thus the acceptability of a new political party as a legitimate vehicle for expressing and acting upon the province's frustrations and aspirations became even more deeply embedded in Alberta's political culture. "The pattern," as L.G. Thomas would call it, was becoming more deeply entrenched.

Second, rightly or wrongly, many Albertans emerged from the Depression and War years with the conviction that when they and their province were in deep trouble they were largely on their own, but when the nation was in trouble, they were expected to come to its aid. They could not and did not deny their obligation to their country, but they must not neglect their obligation to their province. This one-way-street conception of how Canadian Confederation worked in practice became deeply seared into the provincial consciousness and fostered the attitude that Alberta had better take care of itself—especially when times are good—because in a real crisis the national government cannot be counted upon to do so.

A third unexpected impact of the Depression and the War on Alberta was the impact on the priority to be attached by future Legislatures to education, particularly higher education. As a result of the Depression and the War, many Albertans missed their opportunity for a higher education or had to defer it until much later in life. In my father's case, having been raised on a homestead in Saskatchewan, there was barely enough money in those Depression years to send one son (the oldest) to university. In the case of the thousands of young men who enlisted to fight in the war (my father was rejected for active military service because of tubercular lungs and so joined the reserves), the opportunity for higher education was either forfeited altogether or at best postponed. In any event, during the 1950s and 1960s the Alberta Legislature contained numerous people who attached a very high priority to higher education because of what they themselves had missed. Because of their near reverence for education, the easiest dollar to extract from the Alberta Legislature during that period was one designated for education. Ironically, in later years, when the Legislature came to be filled by people who had, for the most part, acquired the benefits of higher education for themselves, the bloom went off the higher-education rose, to be replaced by investments first in economic diversification and later in health care.

Fourth, for future politicians like myself, raised in a political home very much shaped by the Depression and the War years, there developed a distinct awareness of what I came to think of as "the tides." Beyond the immediate and particular concerns and issues of the day, there are great tides in the affairs of men, of provinces, and of federations—mega-forces far beyond the reach of political parties or public policies to halt or direct. During times of relative peace and prosperity, power flows out from the centre of the Canadian federation, strengthening provincial governments and regional political initiatives. But during times of economic and political insecurity—such as recession, depression, and war—the tide inexorably turns and power starts to flow back to the centre and national institutions. If one is launching a new political boat—a distinctive provincial policy initiative or a regional or national political initiative—it makes sense to first check the direction of the great tides and if possible time your launch to go with rather than against the tide.

The Struggle for Identity

One afternoon early in 1963 I dropped in at my father's office on the third floor of the Legislature in Edmonton to find him particularly perplexed. That morning he had received a telegram from then Prime Minister Pearson outlining draft terms of reference for a Royal Commission that Pearson proposed to form to address the issue of national unity.

The Commission was to be named the Royal Commission on Bilingualism and Biculturalism and its terms of reference contained a definition of Canadian identity that my father considered worse than misguided. In particular, it defined Canada as "an equal partnership between the two founding races" (the French and the English), while, in a subordinate clause, "taking into account the contributions made by other ethnic groups."[23]

My father's reaction to this was representative of the thinking of many Albertans and other western Canadians. First, he thought it extremely unwise for any twentieth-century country, particularly one as demographically diverse as Canada, to define itself in racial and ethnic terms. He considered such a racially-based definition a formula for national disunity of the most virulent kind—making Canada a country where it would become necessary to ask, in order to determine a citizen's constitutional standing and entitlements "Of which race are you? Are you one of the founding ones, or one of the others whom we must 'take into account'?"

Second, while the definition of Canada proposed by the prime minister may have had historical validity and, even in the 1960s, may have described the dominant constitutional and political reality of Central Canada, it was completely inadequate as a description of the twentieth-century demographic and political realities of Alberta, Western Canada, Atlantic Canada, or the North. As he once told Pearson, if you stood at the main downtown intersections of Alberta's largest cities—Jasper Avenue and 101st Street in Edmonton or 9th Avenue and 1st Street SW in Calgary—and shouted, "This is an equal partnership between two founding races, cultures, and languages— the English and the French," passers-by would probably suggest that you seek psychiatric help. Such a definition in no way described the present-day reality or identity of those particular parts of Canada.

From my father's perspective, living and working in Edmonton—at the time the most multicultural city in the country—the prime minister's definition of Canada also had one other great deficiency. By focusing on English and French roots and languages, by referring to "other ethnic groups" in a subordinate fashion, and by focusing only on the "cultural" contributions of those groups, it appeared to relegate millions of Canadians to second-class status, particularly those immigrants whose ethnic origins and mother tongues were neither French nor English and whose immense contribution to Canada was first and foremost economic.[24]

If you stopped one of those immigrants on the street and asked, "Why did you choose to come to Canada?" not one in a thousand would answer, "To get in on the great equal partnership between the French and the English." No, they would answer, "We came for economic opportunity, to get land or work. We came for personal political freedom and for personal safety. We came for the chance to better educate and care for our children.

These are the foundations of our conception of Canada—what Canada means to us."

The initial impact of what was regarded as yet another attempt by the federal government to impose a central Canadian definition of Canada on the country as a whole,[25] was to generate western resistance—in particular resistance to "official bilingualism." But the longer-range impact, which would manifest itself more strongly in the 1980s and 1990s, was to force westerners, and Albertans in particular, to think through and articulate their own definition of Canada more clearly. It was all very well for Albertans to say that the definition of Canada as an equal partnership between two founding races, languages, and cultures was inadequate and even pernicious, but what would Albertans propose to put in its place?

One answer to that question was provided by the Reform Party of Canada, strongly influenced by its Alberta roots, through its critique of the 1987 Meech Lake constitutional accord, its participation in the Charlottetown Referendum campaign of 1992,[26] and its contributions to the parliamentary debate preceding the 1995 Quebec referendum on secession.[27]

A similar answer was provided in the Calgary Declaration of 1997—a declaration endorsed by Alberta's Premier Klein, all of Alberta's Reform members of Parliament, and all the other provincial and territorial premiers (except, predictably, Premier Bouchard of Quebec).[28]

What both answers sought to articulate was the concept of Canada as a partnership, not between two founding races, languages, and cultures but among "equal citizens" and "equal provinces"—citizens and provinces "equal in law" and "equal in powers," notwithstanding all the other differences between them. It was a conception of Canada much more compatible with Alberta's congenital commitment to attaining "equality" than any conception of Canada or Canadian federalism emanating from Ottawa.

The Struggle for Control of Petroleum Prices and Revenues

Al (not his real name), an Alberta-based businessman engaged in providing consulting services to the energy industry, attended a downtown business forum in Edmonton sometime early in 1984. The guest speaker was a federal cabinet minister who took the occasion to announce some proposed federal expenditure in Alberta to the order of $200 million. The minister was of the old school of politicians (more prevalent in some parts of the country than others) who believe that the support of almost any community, voting bloc, or interest group is for sale, the only question being at what price. So confident was the minister in the validity of this assumption and the purchasing power of $200 million that he failed to notice the coolness with which his announcement was received by those present at the Edmonton meeting. Had he been able to follow Al back to his consulting office, the minister might have gained some insight into the source of that coolness. When Al returned to his office he threw down his brief case and marched into an adjoining meeting room. There on the wall was a white board, and written near the top of it in bold red figures was a number—"$100 billion."[29] Al seized the red marker pen, wrote down "$200 million," and made the subtraction, declaring loudly to no one in particular: "$100 billion minus $200 million. Big deal! The feds still owe us $99.8 billion." The scene in Al's meeting room was repeated in various forms and with varying degrees of emotion in many board rooms, conference rooms, and meeting rooms across Alberta in those years. At its root was yet another struggle between Alberta and the federal government over natural resources, this time focused specifically on the control of petroleum prices and revenues and the challenge of the National Energy Program.

From 1947 to 1960, wellhead prices for Alberta oil were largely set by competitive forces in the international market and rarely exceeded $2.65 per barrel.[30] During this period, the biggest challenge facing the Alberta government and the province's petroleum producers, especially the smaller Canadian companies, was the marketing of Alberta oil and gas. At the beginning of this period, Ontario and Quebec were uninterested in purchasing Alberta oil as they could obtain cheaper supplies from offshore sources. Arguments that it would be "in the national interest" for Central Canadians to pay a small premium for Alberta oil in order to develop Canadian energy self-sufficiency fell on deaf ears. Also, during this period, the United States had imposed quotas on oil imported into that country in order to protect its producers from cheap offshore imports. These quotas applied to Canadian imports as well and when Alberta tried to persuade the American authorities to take a larger volume of Alberta oil, their predictable reply was, "Why should we cut back our oil production to take more of yours when your own people in eastern Canada are not willing to open up their markets to Alberta oil?"[31]

Eventually, as the supply of western Canadian petroleum and the demands of Central Canada increased, it became both politically expedient and economically feasible to bring the two together. The Interprovincial Pipeline (oil) from Alberta to Sarnia was completed in 1953.[32] The controversial TransCanada

Pipeline (gas), subject of the famous "pipeline debate" in the House of Commons that contributed to the defeat of the St. Laurent government in 1957, was completed that same year.[33] In addition, the Borden Commission, established by the Diefenbaker government in 1959, recommended an extension of the use of western Canadian oil as far as the "Ottawa Valley line"—the point in Canada where the cost of Alberta oil coming east equated the cost of offshore oil coming west from eastern Canada. This arrangement, while indirectly insulating Canadian oil prices from world oil prices, did not upset the existing oil price regime in Canada to any significant degree for the next decade.

Then in 1973, following the Arab-Israeli War, everything changed. Government price regulation became the principal determinant of oil prices internationally and domestically, once again putting the Government of Canada and the Government of Alberta on a collision-course with respect to the management and pricing of Alberta's most valuable natural resource.

Immediately after the Arab-Israeli War, the Organization of Petroleum Exporting Countries (OPEC) cut off oil supplies to western nations. From October 1973 to June 1974, world oil prices rose from $2.75 per barrel to $11.75 per barrel. Oil consumers who prior to 1973 had railed against alleged price-fixing by multinational oil companies now got their first taste of "political price-fixing" by governments—a 300% increase in oil prices in less than nine months. This immediately raised the question, what should happen to the price of domestic crude oil sold in Canada, in the light of this hike in international prices?

Here in effect is what happened—a story[34] of increasing intervention by the federal government in the pricing and management of Alberta's most valuable natural resource:

• In 1973–1974, the federal government froze the price of oil within Canada and imposed an export tax on oil exported to the United States. This was the first time that such a tax had ever been imposed on the export of any Canadian natural resource.
• In 1976, an agreement was reached at a federal-provincial energy conference to establish a price of $6.50 per barrel for all Canadian domestic oil, this price to increase at the rate of 1$ per barrel per year toward the world price. Alberta and Saskatchewan then dramatically increased their royalty rates; Ottawa refused to let oil companies continue to deduct these royalties from operating income before taxes, and Canadian oil exploration and development activity plummeted.

• By 1977, both levels of government were forced to make major concessions in taxation, depletion allowances and royalties to reverse the decline in exploration and development. Activity dramatically increased and was stimulated further by rising international prices.

• By 1979, world prices (having absorbed the initial OPEC intervention and now reflecting real world supply, demand and replacement costs) were at $25.70 per barrel, with the Canadian domestic price being held at $15.63 per barrel—more than $10 per barrel under the prevailing world price.

•By 1980, the federal government was becoming increasingly alarmed by the continued escalation in world price, the political necessity of protecting the big consuming provinces from increasing domestic prices, and the growing revenues and economic clout of the oil-producing provinces, especially Alberta.

•On October 28, 1980, the Trudeau government introduced its National Energy Program (NEP) as part of its first budget following the 1980 federal election. Through the NEP, the federal government unilaterally intervened once again in the management and pricing of Canadian petroleum resources, on a massive and unprecedented scale. Alberta, as the largest petroleum producing province by far, bore the brunt of this intervention.

The National Energy Program of 1980 was primarily an attempt to protect Canadian energy consumers, particularly those of the large energy-consuming provinces of central Canada, from rising petroleum prices by imposing price controls on domestic petroleum production and imposing new taxes on petroleum-based revenues to finance refiner and consumer subsidies.[35] The NEP rejected tying domestic prices to world market prices and instead substituted a federal government-established schedule of prices for domestic oil production, a new price system for "blending" the costs of different sources of oil into one weighted-average price to consumers, and a federal government-established city-gate price for natural gas shipped inter-provincially. At the same time, the NEP imposed a Petroleum Compensation Charge to reduce the federal government's import subsidy burden, a new natural gas and gas liquids tax applicable to gas exports as well as to all gas produced and consumed in Canada, the continuation of the oil export tax but a sharing of the revenue therefrom with the producing provinces, a federal tax on natural gas exports, and a new Petroleum Gas Revenue Tax (a tax, not on the net incomes of petroleum producers, but on gross revenues). The NEP also purported to be concerned with increasing Canadian energy security and Canadian ownership of the petroleum industry, although in the end its price controls and taxation measures had the opposite effect.

Many westerners, and Albertans especially, viewed federal intervention in the energy sector after 1973, and particularly through the NEP, as rank discrimination that subjected Alberta's most valuable natural resource and industry to grossly inequitable treatment in comparison with federal treatment of the natural resources and industries of central Canada.

Thus, as Ernest C. Manning (now a Senator) would explain it,[36] people in southern Alberta would drive down to Butte or Billings, Montana, and see in the stores all kinds of manufactured goods selling at prices significantly lower than those at which comparable products could be purchased in Lethbridge just a few hundred miles to the north. When those Albertans would ask why they could not buy those same products at home at the same low prices, they would be told by their federal government that the higher prices charged in Canada were necessary in the national interest to develop and support a strong Canadian manufacturing sector. And so the Alberta family returning home from Montana would swallow hard, sing "O Canada," and shell out the higher prices—all in support of the national interest as Ottawa defined it.

But after 1973 and the rapid rise in international oil prices, a different philosophy began to emanate from Ottawa that struck Albertans as both contradictory and discriminatory. Not only did "the national interest" require Albertans to pay prices equal to or *substantially more* than international prices for much of the industrial output of central Canada, but now it would also required them to sell their most precious natural resource to refiners in central Canada at *substantially less* than the international price.

When Albertans bought British Columbia salmon, the price they paid was the price the canneries could get in the international market. When Albertans bought gold produced in Ontario, they were not quoted a special discount price because they were Canadians and the gold was mined in Canada. The price they were quoted was the price in London, Tokyo, New York or Zurich—the international price for gold. The same was true of Ontario nickel, Quebec iron ore, and so on. All were sold at the international price. But now, by virtue of the NEP, western oil was to be treated differently and subjected to a different set of rules.

Western oil after 1973–1974 was to be subject to an export tax—a tax the like of which had never been imposed on exports of B.C. lumber or salmon, or on exports of Ontario gold or nickel, or on exports of Quebec iron ore or pulp—a tax that would enable Ottawa to collect twice as much revenue as Alberta was collecting on every barrel of oil exported. After 1980 and the institution of the NEP, Western oil and gas was to be subjected to a regime of price controls and extraordinary taxes the like of which had never been imposed on any other resource industry in Canada—price controls that would compel the sale of enormous volumes of western oil and gas to users in the large consuming provinces at prices far below world price, and extraordinary taxes that would result in a massive transfer or wealth from the oil-producing provinces to the federal treasury. The impacts of these measures would be both economic and political, reshaping the relations of Alberta to the federal Liberal and Conservative parties, the institutions of the federal government, and even the United States, for decades to come.

By 1985, figures compiled by economist Robert Mansell at the University of Calgary[37] showed that the NEP and related tax policies had resulted in a net transfer of wealth from the producing provinces to the federal treasury and the energy consumers of central and eastern Canada to the amount of approximately *$100 billion*—the largest inter-regional transfer of wealth in the history of the country. About 60% of this figure represented wealth transferred through the sale of western oil and gas below the world price as a result of federal regulation and pricing policies. The other 40%, or $40 billion, represented transfers from federal taxes on western energy resources and producers. When, as a result, the Alberta oil patch went into the inevitable tail spin—with an immediate loss of some 60,000 jobs in the oil industry service sector alone—there was no "reverse flow" from the federal treasury, only a slight decrease in the rate of exploitation.

The political impacts of the NEP and related legislation were not long in manifesting themselves either. Western separatism reared its head. The Western Canada Concept Party (WCC) was founded in 1980 to promote the separation of the western provinces and territories from Canada. WCC member Gordon Kesler was elected to the Alberta Legislature in a 1982 by-election in Olds-Didsbury. Later that same year, the party took 11.8 per cent of the vote in a general election (although Kesler himself lost his seat).[38] Ways and means of getting more regional fairness in large federations through institutional reform also became hot topics of discussion, particularly in Alberta. In 1981 the Canada West Foundation published its seminal study[39] on Senate reform as an effective way of safeguarding regional interests through more effective regional representation in the Canadian Parliament. Two years later (August 1983), the Canadian Committee for a Triple-E Senate[40] was founded by an

Alberta farmer, Bert Brown, and others calling for a Senate that was Elected, Equal, and Effective at representing and safeguarding regional interests.

By calling for institutional reform in response to the regional discrimination inherent in the NEP, Albertans were being both realistic and national in their thinking. Of course Albertans realized that the rapid escalation of petroleum prices after 1973 was bound to create national problems, in particular major conflicts between the interests of the consuming and producing provinces. And of course Albertans expected the federal government to be active in reconciling those conflicts "in the national interest." However, from Alberta's perspective that reconciliation would have been much more fair and genuine if Canada had a Parliament where regional interests were truly and vigorously represented in an effective and accountable upper chamber, where representation by population was vigorously adhered to in the lower chamber, and where measures to address conflicting interests did not become law until those measures carried the judgement of a majority in both chambers.

In the Canada of 1973, the only effective representatives of regional interests were the provincial governments. No effective *federal* institution dedicated to this purpose existed—certainly not the un-elected, patronage-appointed, "unequal" Senate of the day. If Canada had had a Triple-E Senate at the time of the OPEC crisis, Parliament might still have been obliged to enact a National Energy Program, but, Albertans argued, it would have achieved a fairer balance between consuming and producing interests than that which was unilaterally imposed by the federal executive via the National Energy Program. Thus Alberta politicians, both provincial and federal, became increasingly committed to working for a Triple-E Senate—institutional reform aimed at improving regional representation in Ottawa—as a direct result of the NEP and related federal energy policies perceived as discriminating against the province.

But the search for greater institutional and legal protection from federal raids on the natural resource wealth of the province did not stop with Senate reform. Westerners had always had an interest in the potential of free trade to liberate captive markets from central authority ever since the day Louis Riel's father led the first free-trade rally in western Canada in 1846.[41] But after the NEP, interest in a Canada-U.S. Free Trade Agreement—one which would guarantee free trade in energy and prohibit NEP-style price and tax discrimination[42]—returned to the political front burner with a vengeance. Westerners, especially Albertans, and Quebec business interests, combined forces to persuade Brian Mulroney and the hierarchy of the Conservative Party (once the great bastion of protectionism) to embrace the concept of Canada-U.S. Free Trade and eventually to make it the centrepiece of their successful 1988 election campaign. Nevertheless, it struck many Albertans as ironic and sad that Alberta was able to secure greater protection of its right to manage and price its most precious natural resource through an international treaty with the United States than it could through any of the provisions of the Canadian Constitution or the institutions of Canadian federalism.[43]

As previously mentioned, the effect of the National Energy Program on so many western Canadians led some to question the equity of the whole federal system and the benefits of confederation itself. What type of a system, they asked, would permit a hundred-billion-dollar raid on the resource wealth of one region by the federal government in the name of the national interest? Where was the equity, particularly for the private investor, in a federal economic regime that lets market forces allocate resources *when market prices are low*, but insists on government intervention in the market place when prices are high? Why was it acceptable national policy to impose a special revenue tax on companies engaged in developing the petroleum resources of western Canada, while exempting the largest (at the time) energy companies in the country, Ontario Hydro and Hydro-Quebec, from taxation altogether? Why was the accumulation of capital in Alberta's Heritage Trust Fund a menace to Confederation, while the accumulation of similar amounts of capital in the depreciation accounts of Ontario Hydro and Hydro-Quebec was completely acceptable? How could federal politicians who were always talking about the need for justice and equity in federal-provincial relations explain the fiscal inequities in the regional distribution of federal fiscal balances in Canada?

The inability of representatives of the federal Liberal Party to answer these questions in the 1970s and 1980s, combined with the Quebec-centric nature of Liberal constitutional policies, virtually destroyed the federal Liberals in western Canada. These concerns and the fact that the federal Conservatives would be the immediate beneficiaries of the Liberal collapse without themselves having to seriously address these questions meant that any western support for the Conservatives might be relatively short-lived. Predictably, in 1984, the Liberal government was swept from office and the Mulroney Conservatives, with strong support from the West, were swept in.[44] When the smoke cleared, there were only two Liberal members of Parliament left west of the Lakehead—one each in Manitoba and British Columbia, but none whatsoever in Alberta and Saskatchewan. The political fallout from the NEP was driving Alberta back to its political roots—a reawakened concern with constitutional "equality," a growing mistrust of any federal politician or party who defined "the national interest" exclusively in central-Canadian terms, and a new interest in the potential of political action outside the traditional party structures altogether.

The Emergence of the New West

On October 17, 1986, five Albertans met in a boardroom in Calgary to talk about what could be done to protect and advance the interests of the province and the West under the prevailing circumstances. Those circumstances included wholesale alienation from the federal Liberal Party, growing disillusionment with the Mulroney Conservatives,[45] and a rising tide of separatist sentiment not only in Quebec but also in the West.

The five Albertans present were senior gas executive and tireless promoter of the Triple-E Senate, Jim Gray; Dr. David Elton, political scientist, pollster, and president of a respected public policy think-tank, the Canada West Foundation; Bob Muir, who had been senior legal counsel for Dome Petroleum; Doug Hilland, a corporate director and lawyer with strong oil-patch connections; and myself.

By the time the meeting concluded we had resolved to hold—in co-operation with like-minded friends such as Edmonton businessman Francis Winspear, former Canada West President Stan Roberts, and western magazine publisher Ted Byfield—a big public "assembly" in Vancouver to produce a Western Agenda for Change and to decide upon the best political vehicle to advance it. Six months later that assembly concluded with a 75% vote in favour of creating a new, broadly-based federal political party with its roots in the West—the Reform Party of Canada.[46]

Ten years later that western-based Reform Party, with its national headquarters in Calgary and holding 24 out of 26 of Alberta's federal seats, became the Official Opposition in the Parliament of Canada. Immediately after attaining this position, its annual convention then passed a resolution calling for the building of "a United Alternative" to the federal Liberals—a bigger, broader political tent embracing fiscal conservatives, social conservatives, small-d democrats, and reform-oriented federalists across the country regardless of their former political affiliations. Eventually this initiative was to result in the creation of the Canadian Conservative Reform Alliance

(Canadian Alliance, for short) which formed the Official Opposition in the 37th Parliament following the 2000 federal election. After a brief period of internal turmoil under new leader Stockwell Day, the building of the bigger broader tent continued through the union of the Alliance and the Progressive Conservatives to form the Conservative Party of Canada under the leadership of Calgary MP Stephen Harper. In the 2004 federal election that party won 99 seats, including 26 out of Alberta's 28 federal seats, and may well become the governing party of Canada in the 39th Parliament.

The confidence that a western-based political initiative with its origins in Alberta could successfully bring about major changes in the national agenda and the positions and structures of the traditional federal parties came, in part, from the knowledge that the West had done something similar before.[47] But it also came from a growing awareness of the West's increasing demographic and economic strength. Within a few short years, western-based think-tanks like the Calgary-based Canada West Foundation would be predicting that the New West of the twenty-first century would be home to at least one-third of all Canadians, produce one-third of the GNP, be responsible for almost fifty per cent of Canada's exports, and hold close to one-third of the seats in the House of Commons. Such a region, with Alberta at its heart, should have the will and the strength not just to address and redress its own regional concerns, but to reshape national policies and institutions in the interests of the West and all Canadians. And if that New West—given its projected resources and strengths—could not simultaneously advance its own interests and reshape the federation, then the fault would lie with westerners themselves and western-based political leaders rather than with the inertia and deficiencies of Canadian federalism.

The emergence of the New West, with Alberta at its heart, will no doubt result in new tensions (many of them productive) between the province and the federal government, with further impacts on the province and the federation. As Alberta celebrates its 100th anniversary as a province, it is fitting to speculate on the nature of those new tensions and how the province might most appropriately meet them.

In the past, the federal government has responded to the needs and challenges represented by Alberta:

• By at first denying Alberta's desire for a change in its constitutional status, but then acceding to it, at least in part, by granting it limited provincehood.

• By at first denying the province's desire for constitutional equality, particularly full control of its natural resources, but then acceding to it, at least in part, via a constitutional amendment.

• By at first ignoring Alberta's equality-based conceptions of national identity and seeking to impose central-Canadian definitions on the province, but then grudgingly conceding adjustments more acceptable to the West.

• By attempting to reassert federal control over the pricing and allocation of Alberta's petroleum resources after the OPEC-initiated price hikes of the 1970s and 1980s, but then ceding much of that control to an international Free Trade Agreement that offered Alberta more price protection than did Canada's federal constitution or institutions.

• By bitterly resisting western-based political initiatives in the form of new parties with new ideas, but then gradually accepting the necessity of recognizing both.

How will central Canada, the federal government, and the federal system respond to the challenges of the New West with Alberta at its heart? Most likely in the same way as in the past—by first denying the reality of the New West, but then gradually acceding, at least in part, to its demands and aspirations as the growing weight of its demographic, economic, and political influence becomes impossible to ignore. The more willing Alberta is to play a leadership role in helping to formulate those demands and in uniting the West rather than pushing its demands unilaterally, the greater the influence of the New West and Alberta will be on the rest of the federation. As F.W.G. Haultain put it so many years ago, "the joint demand of a united west cannot be disregarded."[48]

At the federal level, acceding to the realities of the New West means recognizing that in the future no truly national government can be formed that does not include strong representation from the West and Alberta; that in the future no truly national policy—economic, social, cultural, or constitutional—can be adopted and implemented without western input and concurrence; that in the future no foreign or trade policy, in particular policies affecting Canada-U.S. relations, can be adopted or pursued without taking into account western interests and perspectives; and that in the future no conception of Canadian identity can be considered truly national and contemporary unless it incorporates western perspectives and aspirations.

Will Albertans in future years turn increasingly inward or outward? Will Albertans in future years continue to support political innovation both federally and provincially? The answers to these questions will determine to a large degree the nature and extent of the leadership which Alberta will exert in helping the New West to define and strengthen itself and to shape its future relations with Ottawa and the rest of the federation.

More specifically, will Alberta use its growing strength to focus primarily on itself and to distance itself from national programs and institutions? Or will it lever its growing strength through the formation of strategic regional and national alliances with like-minded others in other parts of the country to change national policies and institutions for the benefit of all Canadians? In other words, will the Alberta of the twenty-first century dedicate itself to building firewalls[49] or bridges?[50] Or in the language of F.W.G. Haultain—the champion of constitutional equality and a united West—will Albertans choose to act as "Big Westerners" or "Little Westerners"?

And equally important, will Albertans continue to support political innovation, federally and provincially?

In 1989, Albertans elected the first Reformer ever to sit in the national Parliament. Seven months later, 620,000 Albertans went to the polls to vote in Canada's first-ever Senate Nominee Election. In 1993, 629,402 Albertans marked an X on a federal ballot beside the name of a political party that had not even existed six years before. In 2000, 739,514 Albertans marked an X on a federal ballot beside the name of a political party that had not existed one year before. And in 2004, 783,131 Albertans marked an X on a federal ballot beside the name of a political party that had been in existence less than seven months. This is a remarkable record—unequalled anywhere else in Canada—of supporting and encouraging political innovation at the federal level—a record that needs to be continued if Alberta is to continue to exercise national political leadership.

What about continued political innovation at the provincial level? The "pattern," as L.G. Thomas called it, involves long periods of one-party government (29 years on average) with periodic upheavals in which the long-time governing party is replaced, not by its traditional opposition but by a new group with a big new idea—more specifically, replacement of the provincial Liberals in 1921 by the UFA with its new ideas on democratic governance and agricultural reform; replacement of the UFA in 1935 by Social Credit with its radical ideas on monetary reform; and replacement of Social Credit in 1971 by the Lougheed Conservatives with new ideas on modernization and economic diversification. Will the pattern repeat itself in the decade of Alberta's centenary? If so, what will be the next big idea to energize Alberta provincial politics and who will be its champions?

The next 10 years will most likely provide definitive answers to all these questions. And like Haultain's challenge to think big not small, and the efforts of Alberta reformers to break the mould of traditional two-party politics and traditional national policy, those answers will shape the evolution of Alberta and its relations with the rest of Canada for the next hundred years.

Acknowledgement

The author wishes to express appreciation to Jean Marie Clemenger, my secretary and research assistant, and Michael Jankovic, a political science student at the University of Calgary, for their assistance in fact-finding and providing background research materials for this paper.

Notes

1. The Manning family has been actively involved in Alberta politics for 72 of the 100 years that Alberta has been a province. Ernest C. Manning participated in the founding of the Alberta Social Credit Party in 1933, was elected to the Provincial Legislature in 1935 when he became a cabinet minister, and served as premier of the province from 1943 to 1968. He also represented Alberta in the Canadian Senate from 1970 to 1983. The author, Preston Manning, participated in the formation of the Alberta-based federal Reform Party in 1987, became its first Leader in 1988, was elected to Parliament to represent the constituency of Calgary Southwest in 1993, was re-elected in 1997 and 2000, served as Leader of the Official Opposition from 1997 to 2000, and participated in the formation of the Canadian Alliance, which also became the Official Opposition in the Canadian Parliament.

2. Despite his outstanding abilities and achievements—as a lawyer in Fort McLeod, Alberta, as premier of the old North-West Territories, as leader of the Opposition in the Saskatchewan Legislature, as chief justice of Saskatchewan, and as chancellor of the University of Saskatchewan—Haultain is little known or remembered by most Canadians. Two books that tell his story well are Grant MacEwan's *Frederick Haultain: Frontier Statesman of the Canadian Northwest* (Saskatoon: Western Producer Prairie Books, 1985) and C. Cecil Lingard, *Territorial Government in Canada* (Toronto: University of Toronto Press, 1946), which is a more scholarly study.

3. Lingard, *Territorial Government in Canada*, 27–31.

4. Lingard, *Territorial Government in Canada*, 46.

5. Canada, *The Alberta Act: An Act to establish and provide for the Government of the Province of Alberta*, S.C.1905, c.3, reprinted in RSC 1985, App. 2.

6. Lingard, *Territorial Government in Canada*, 244–46.

7. Section 3 of Reform's *New Canada Act* (Reform Collection, University of Calgary Archives).

8. Articles 2 and 6 of the Framework for Discussion on Canadian Unity contained in the *Calgary Declaration* are especially useful. News release and text can be found at http://www.gov.nf.ca/currentevents/unity/unity1.htm.

9. These figures are for the fiscal year ending March 31, 1935, and are taken from a summary of Alberta's Public Finances (1931–1938) contained in a "Report on the Financial Position of the Province of Alberta" prepared by the Bank of Canada, April 1937, at the request of the premier of Alberta.

10. Legislative Assembly of Alberta, *Budget Speech of Hon. A.O. Aalborg* (Edmonton: L.S. Wall, Queen's Printer for Alberta, 1970).

11. Don Sellar, "Budget Finishes, Pay as You Go," *Calgary Herald*, February 14, 1970, 1–2.

12. Thomas Flanagan, *Louis Riel* (Ottawa: Canadian Historical Association, 1992), 6–10. See also The Heritage Centre site's biography, *Louis Riel: One Life, One Vision*, available at http://www.shsb.mb.ca/Riel/indexenglish.htm.

13. L.G. Thomas, *The Liberal Party in Alberta, A History of Politics in the Province of Alberta 1905–1921* (Toronto: University of Toronto Press, 1959).

14. Thomas, *The Liberal Party in Alberta*, 58, 60.

15. Franklin L. Foster, *John E. Brownlee: A Biography* (Lloydminster, Alberta: Foster Learning Inc., 1981), 86–87.

16. Thomas, *The Liberal Party in Alberta*, Introduction, xi.

17. W.L. Morton, *The Progressive Party in Canada* (Toronto: University of Toronto Press, 1950, reprinted 1971), 306.

18. Foster, *John E. Brownlee*, 166–67.

19. Canada's Digital Collections, "Brownlee and the Natural Resources Transfer Agreement," at http://collections.ic.gc.ca/abpolitics/events/issues_resources.html.

20. Canada, *The British North America Act, 1930*, Enactment No. 16.

21. For a brief but excellent description of the final negotiation between Brownlee and King and the resulting agreement, see Foster, *John E. Brownlee*, 165–70.

22. *Report on the Financial Position of the Province of Alberta* (Bank of Canada, April 1937).

23. Canada, Royal Commission on Bilingualism and Biculturalism, *Report of the Royal Commission on Bilingualism and Biculturalism* (Ottawa: Queen's Printer, 1967–1970), 173–74. The terms of reference of the B&B Commission, issued on July 19, 1963, required it "to inquire into and report upon the existing state of bilingualism and biculturalism in Canada and to recommend what steps should be taken to develop the Canadian Confederation on the basis of an equal partnership between the two founding races, taking into account the contribution made by the other ethnic groups to the cultural enrichment of Canada and the measures that should be taken to safeguard that contribution...."

24. This was the one major criticism of the original terms of reference of the Bilingualism and Biculturalism Commission to which Pearson responded. When it became clear to the federal Liberals that if they persisted with the "biculturalism" emphasis, a majority of the non-French, non-English elements of the population would oppose any special status for Quebec, the emphasis was shifted to "multiculturalism" and the importance of recognizing its contribution to the Canadian identity.

25. Previous attempts, from the perspective of westerners who thought about such things, would include the attempt by Ontario and Quebec media and politicians to conceptualize the first Riel Rebellion as some western re-enactment of the Battle of the Plains of Abraham on the banks of the Red River, and the attempt of Macdonald's National Policy to forever cast western Canada as a hewer of wood and drawer of water for central Canadian industries and a captive market for their goods.

26. It was Reform's position that both the Meech Lake and Charlottetown accords perpetuated and further entrenched the "two nations" model of Canada. As a constructive alternative, Reform proposed a vision of Canada in which all citizens and provinces would be treated equally in law *regardless* of their race, culture, and language, rather than a Canada where some citizens and provinces would possess special entitlements *because* of their race, culture, and language. To the charge that Reform and Albertans were unwilling to recognize the cultural and linguistic uniqueness of Quebec, we answered that we were quite prepared to recognize Quebec's distinctiveness provided that such recognition did not confer on the government of Quebec constitutional powers not granted to the other provinces. To the charge that our western concept of equality implied "treating all provinces the same regardless of the differences between them," we emphasized that we were advocating "equal treatment *in law*." Give all the provinces of Canada exactly the same set of tools (powers) to fashion their particular space in the national house. Obviously, Quebec would use those powers differently than would Alberta, and Prince Edward Island's use of those powers would be different in focus and scale from that of British Columbia. Under Reform's western-inspired model of federalism, *both* equality and diversity would be recognized and strengthened.

27. In the year preceding the 1995 Quebec referendum on secession, Reform tried again and again to get the Chrétien government to define a "fresh vision of Canada" and a "better federalism" to compete more effectively with Lucien Bouchard's vision of a sovereign Quebec and the sovereignists' withering attacks on "status quo federalism." Reform offered its own ideas as to the nature of that New Canada, at the heart of which was again the concept of equality of citizens and provinces in law. On June 7, 1995, the House of Commons spent a full day debating a motion embodying this concept. The motion, put forward by the author, read in part, "That this House strongly affirm and support the desire of Canadians to remain federally united as one People...affirming the equality and uniqueness of all our citizens and provinces." The Chrétien government, using its majority, amended the original motion to completely exclude the equality reference, so that the truncated motion eventually passed by the House simply read "That this House strongly affirm and support the desire of Canadians to live together in a federation." (See *Hansard Debates, Canadian House of Commons*, June 7, 1995.)

28. The Calgary Declaration of September 14, 1997, set forth guidelines, agreed to by all the provincial and territorial premiers except Quebec's, for consulting the public on seven principles for strengthening Canadian federalism. Those principles included recognition of the equality of citizens and provinces in law; recognition of the value of diversity, including the uniqueness of Quebec and the role of its government in protecting and developing that unique character within Canada; and the principle that constitutional amendments conferring powers on one province must make those same powers available to all provinces (the equality in law principle, stated once again). On September 24, the prime minister spoke in the House on the Calgary Declaration, strongly emphasizing its recognition of Quebec's uniqueness but completely ignoring its declaration of the equality of all citizens and provinces in law. See Preston Manning, *Think Big: My Adventures in Life and Democracy* (Toronto: McClelland and Stewart, 2002), 204.

29. Figures in the order of $100-billion with respect to the fiscal impact on Alberta of the National Energy Program and related legislation are derived from the fiscal balance studies conducted by Dr. Robert Mansell and his colleagues at the University of Calgary. See for example, Robert Mansell and Ronald Schlenker, "The Provincial Distribution of Federal Fiscal Imbalances," *Canadian Business Economics* (Winter 1995): 3–22.

30. G. Campbell Watkins, "Canadian Oil and Gas Pricing," *Oil in the Seventies: Essays on Energy Policy* (Fraser Institute, 1977), 96–99.

31. Taken from Ernest C. Manning's recollections of the period as recounted in a speech in the Canadian Senate, November 21, 1979. See *Debates of the Senate*, November 21, 1979, especially pp. 386–89.

32. For more details see Robert Bott, *Mileposts: The Story of the World's Longest Petroleum Pipeline* (Edmonton: Interprovincial Pipeline Company, 1989).

33. For more on this stormy period in Canadian history, see William Kilbourn, *Pipeline: Transcanada and the Great Debate, a History of Business and Politics* (Toronto: Clarke, Irwin & Co., 1970).

34. For a more detailed description and analysis of the struggle between the Lougheed administration of Alberta and the federal administration of Pierre Trudeau over the control of petroleum pricing during this period, see the chapter by Douglas Owram in this volume.

35. *The National Energy Program,* Report EP 80-4E (Ministry of Energy, Mines, and Resources Canada, 1980).

36. The following five paragraphs are paraphrased from a number of speeches given on this subject during the period by Senator E.C. Manning, including the Senate speech on November 21, 1979. See *Debates of the Senate*, November 21, 1979, pp. 386–89.

37. See Mansell and Schlenker, "The Provincial Distribution of Federal Fiscal Imbalances" for updated figures.

38. Bob Bragg, "Confederation gets boos," *Calgary Herald*, November 20, 1980, A1; Bruce Winning, "Separatist wins," *Calgary Herald*, February 18, 1982, A1; Yvonne Zacharias, "Smashing win, voters say: Lougheed for Alberta," *Calgary Herald*, November 3, 1982, A1.

39. *Regional Representation: The Canadian Partnership;* the report of a Canada West Foundation task force comprising Dr. Peter McCormick, Ernest C. Manning, and Gordon Gibson (Canada West Foundation, September 1981).

40. Source: Personal conversation with Bert Brown.

41. For a very brief description of the petition in 1846 and the protest in 1848, see Douglas Hill, *The Opening of the Canadian West* (New York: John Day, 1967), 54–55.

42. *Canada–US Free Trade Agreement* (1989), Chapter 9, "Energy."

43. By the 1990s, of course, Albertans would learn that International Treaties could cut both ways with respect to the protection of natural resources when the Chrétien government entered into the Kyoto Accord and threatened to impose carbon taxes on Alberta hydrocarbon production in the name of its international commitments to greenhouse gas emission reductions.

44. The Conservatives' total of 211 seats included 58 seats in the four western provinces.

45. Preston Manning, *Think Big*, 25–27.

46. For the full story of the birth and development of the Reform Party see Preston Manning, *The New Canada* (Toronto : Macmillan, 1992) and the same author's *Think Big*.

47. The western-based Progressive Party of Canada forced major changes in the platform and positions of the federal Liberal Party and a realignment of national politics in the 1920s. The western-based Canadian Commonwealth Federation (CCF), which later became the New Democratic Party (NDP), later had a similar impact on federal politics in the 1960s and 1970s.

48. Lingard, *Territorial Government in Canada*, 46.

49. Stephen Harper, Tom Flanagan, Ted Morton, Rainer Knopff, Andrew Crooks, and Ken Boessenkool, "The Alberta Agenda," Open Letter to Premier Ralph Klein in the *National Post*, January 26, 2001, A14.

50. Preston Manning, "Four Bridges to Unity in the West," *Calgary Herald*, March 15, 2004, A11.

Twelve

Alberta's Métis Settlements
A Brief History
FRED V. MARTIN

Introduction

Alberta's centenary celebrations in 2005 will demonstrate great pride in the economic accomplishments of the province's first century. Given the extent to which these accomplishments are driven by oil and the luck of location, a greater source of pride should be the leadership it has shown in the recognition of the Métis—Alberta is still the only place in Canada with a land base the Métis can call their own. Legislation making possible that long-held dream was passed in 1938. A half-century later, in 1990, Alberta's constitution was amended to protect the land base and recognize the unique place of the Métis in Alberta's history. These are historical achievements of the province that are worthy of centenary pride.

In amending Alberta's constitution, the *Constitution of Alberta Amendment Act, 1990* recognized the historic and future status of the Métis in a preamble that began:

> WHEREAS the Metis were present when the province of Alberta was established and they and the land set aside for their use form a unique part of the history and culture of the province; and
>
> WHEREAS it is desired that the Metis should continue to have a land base to provide for the preservation and enhancement of Metis culture and identity and to enable the Metis to attain self-governance under the laws of Alberta and, to that end, Her Majesty in right of Alberta is granting title to land to the Metis Settlements General Council....

These constitutional clauses look back—recognizing the historical roots and contributions of the Métis, and look forward—expressing commitments to ensuring the Métis have a land base on which they can govern themselves and preserve their culture.

The constitutional amendment was part of a legislative package that protected the Métis land base, known as "Metis Settlement Areas," and created a new framework for self-government on the lands. On the economic side, it enabled management- and benefits-sharing for the oil and gas found there, and provided 17-year funding to help the Métis Settlements "catch up and keep up" with their neighbours. These Alberta initiatives predate by many years the recent decisions of the Supreme Court of Canada that provide national recognition of Métis rights. The fact that "redneck" Alberta provided this kind of leadership often surprises the rest of Canada. How did it happen?

The short answer is common sense and courage. Leaders of the Métis and of the province were pragmatic, were able to agree on the shape of a mutually desirable future, and were prepared to take the risks needed to get there. In doing so they showed the vision, responsibility and mutual respect that is too often missing from the relationship between governments and aboriginal communities.

Alberta has been different. The roots of the difference appear in the approach taken to develop the first Métis Settlements legislation in 1938, and a half-century later to implement *Alberta-Metis Settlements Accord* of 1989. The original legislation made it possible for today's Métis to govern eight Métis Settlements—6,000 people on more than 1.25 million acres of land in northern Alberta. How these lands came to be set aside and governed by Métis is a story of determined leadership more focused on strategic results than on a general recognition of rights. The recognition has come, however. The right to survival as a people, rooted in British and Canadian history, is now recognized in the constitutions of Canada and Alberta. It was not, however, the cornerstone of the Métis leadership's survival strategy. That strategy focused on provincial acceptance of specific results that would create a foundation for survival. It first became evident in the events of the "Dirty Thirties" when the desperate depression conditions of Alberta's Métis, dramatized by their leaders, raised government concerns. A joint effort to address the situation led to the pragmatic solution of self-help on a land base, and consequently to the creation of the Métis Settlements. A half-century later, a similar approach produced the *Alberta-Metis Settlements Accord* of 1989—the basis of today's legislative framework for the Settlements.

That is a snapshot of the history of Alberta's Métis Settlements legislation. To put this snapshot into context, we need to go back to the origins of Canada and the western provinces, and at the role aboriginal rights played in their development.

Aboriginal Rights and Confederation
The Context of Aboriginal Rights

The foundations of aboriginal rights have been explored in innumerable scholarly papers and court decisions. For our purposes it is sufficient to quote from Brian Slattery's landmark study on this topic:

> A review of the Crown's historical relations with aboriginal peoples supports the conclusion that the Crown, in offering its protection to such peoples, accepted that they would retain their lands, as well as their political and cultural institutions and customary laws, unless the terms of treaties ruled this out or legislation was enacted to the contrary. Native groups would retain a measure of internal autonomy, allowing them to govern their own affairs as they found convenient, subject to the overriding authority of the Crown in Parliament. The Crown assumed a general obligation to protect aboriginal peoples and their lands and generally to look out for their best interests—what the judges have described as a fiduciary or rust-like obligation. In return, native peoples were required to maintained [sic] allegiance to the Crown, to abide by her laws, and to keep the peace.[1]

The underlying principle was that when exercising its dominion over new lands, the Crown established a legal framework recognizing and respecting the right of indigenous peoples to maintain their identity as a people.[2]

The principle was followed in the formation of Canada. The *British North America Act* of 1867 (now the *Constitution Act, 1867*) established the country of Canada. It combined existing provinces and peoples. In other words, the Act operated in two dimensions—a horizontal dimension relating to government, and a vertical dimension relating to nation-building. The horizontal dimension contained the components of the new government, the institutions and systems that provided a framework for future political life. The vertical dimension contained the components of the new nation, the recognition of the indigenous peoples that comprised the new nation. As an act of the British Parliament, the recognition of the "indigenous" British citizens was implicit. However the Act also recognized the two other indigenous peoples of the confederation provinces—the French and the First Nations. The French "nation" was recognized and guaranteed cultural survival rights such as language and education. The First Nations were recognized by creating a unique relationship between "Indians"[3] and their lands and the new national government.

The next stage of confederation building, the creation of the province of Manitoba, provided further constitutional recognition of indigenous people. A Manitoba Court of Appeal decision in 1988 summarized the history:

Rupert's land was granted to the Hudson's Bay Company by Charles II in 1670. By 1867, the effective authority of the company in Rupert's Land was on the decline. The United Kingdom Parliament was thus able to foresee, and provide for, the eventual union of Rupert's Land with Canada. Provisions for this union are to be found in the *Constitution Act, 1867* and the *Rupert's Land Act, 1868*.

Included in Rupert's Land was the territory which was to become Manitoba. Many of those who lived in the territory in the years immediately preceding union were persons of mixed native and European blood, their European ancestors having come to North America after 1670. These persons were then known as "half-breeds." Some half-breeds occupied small areas of land and all used unoccupied land freely. The area of land used by them lacked definition.

In anticipation of the union of Rupert's Land with Canada, the Parliament of Canada enacted the *Rupert's Land Act*, S.C. 1869, c.3, by which it made provision for the future government of the territory. Also in anticipation of the union, the Government of Canada sent survey teams into the territory.

In August, 1869, a number of half-breeds, fearful of the effect the proposed union would have on their use of land, opposed the making of surveys. What followed was, from Canada's viewpoint, rebellion. A number of local inhabitants openly disputed Canada's right to annex the territory, although others were anxious for union. A state of unrest prevailed. The authority of the Company had been weakened by its own inaction. In the absence of an effective ruling power, a provisional government was formed by some of the people.

The Provisional Government (as it styled itself) sent delegates to Ottawa to negotiate the terms on which the territory might be united with Canada. A draft bill resulted from the negotiations. Before its enactment as the *Manitoba Act*, it was approved by what was known as the Assembly of the Provisional Government. This Act, assented to in May, 1870, preceded the effective date on which legislative authority for the government of the territory was vested in the Parliament of Canada by the Order of Her Majesty in Her Imperial Council dated June 23, 1870.[4]

The decision goes on to quote several sections of the *Manitoba Act* dealing with land, including sections 30 and 31. These sections provide that:

30. All ungranted or waste lands in the Province shall be...vested in the Crown, and administered by the Government of Canada for the purposes of the Dominion, subject to...the conditions and stipulation contained in the agreement for the surrender of Rupert's Land by the Hudson's Bay Company to Her Majesty.

31. And whereas, it is expedient, towards the extinguishment of the Indian title to the lands in the Province, to appropriate a portion of such ungranted lands, to the extent of one million four hundred thousand acres thereof, for the benefit of the families of the half-breed residents, it is hereby enacted, that, under regulations to be from time to time made by the Governor-General-in-Council, the Lieutenant-Governor shall select such lots or tracts in such parts of the Province as he may deem expedient, to the extent aforesaid, and divide the same among the children of the half-breed heads of families residing in the Province at the time of the said transfer to Canada, and the same shall be granted to the said children respectively, in such mode and on such conditions as to settlement and otherwise, as the Governor-General-in-Council may from time to time determine.

In short, the Dominion retained public lands and resources in Manitoba subject to the conditions of the surrender by the Hudson's Bay Company, and recognized the Métis as an indigenous people with unextinguished land rights. Thus in the first expansion beyond the founding provinces, Canada maintained the approach of nation building by recognizing the vertical component, indigenous peoples, as well as the horizontal component of political structures for the newly added territory.

Initially, the province of Manitoba was a small area of land about 100 miles by 140 miles. However, at the same time as Manitoba was added as a province, the vast area of land north and west to the boundary of British Columbia, known as Rupert's Land and the North-Western Territory, were transferred to Canada. The Order-in-Council that transferred the land provided that upon the transference of the territories in question to the Canadian Government, the claims of the Indian tribes to compensation for lands required for purposes of settlement will be considered and settled in conformity with the equitable principles which have uniformly governed the British Crown in its dealings with the aborigines.[5]

All of the land surrendered by the Hudson's Bay Company had been surrendered on the condition that

Any claims of Indians to compensation for lands required for purposes of settlement shall be disposed of by the Canadian Government in communication with the Imperial Government; and the Company shall be relieved of all responsibility in respect of them.[6]

Actions on the Plains

Following the creation of Manitoba on July 15, 1870, the Dominion government retained the public lands of Manitoba, as well as the lands that would later become Alberta and Saskatchewan. It held those lands subject to the commitments made to the Métis in the *Manitoba Act* and subject to the claims of the Indians.

Following its acquisition of the western territory, the Dominion government set out to sign treaties with the Indians and thereby resolve the claims problem. The government recognized that the Métis also had claims in this territory and developed a strategy of dealing with these claims concurrent with its efforts to negotiate treaties. To that end, in 1879 the *Dominion Lands Act* gave the governor-general-in-council authority

To satisfy any claims existing in connection with the extinguishment of the Indian title, preferred by half-breeds resident in the North-West Territories outside of the limits of Manitoba, on the fifteenth day of July, one thousand eight hundred and seventy, by granting land to such persons, to such extent and on such terms and conditions as may be deemed expedient.[7]

In other words, the federal government recognized that it had an obligation to satisfy Métis land claims not only in Manitoba, but also in what is now Alberta and Saskatchewan.

The situation was summarized in a memorandum dated October 4, 1934, prepared for the Alberta Resources Commission by Mr. Cohoon, a senior official in the Department of the Interior. The memorandum stated:

> The policy of issuing scrip to half-breeds was adopted in consideration of the interference with the aboriginal rights of this class by the extension of trade and settlement into the territories, and it was felt that an obligation devolved upon the State to properly and fully extinguish these rights to the entire satisfaction of the half-breeds.
>
> The rights of half-breeds were recognized by the Government by reason of their Indian blood. Indian and half-breed rights differed in degree, but they were obviously co-existent.
>
> The general policy was to extinguish the half-breed rights in any territory at the same time the Indian rights were extinguished....
>
> The claims were investigated by Commissioners appointed by the Governor in Council, and where allowed, scrip was issued under the authority of Orders in Council passed in pursuance of the statutes in that behalf.[8]

The memorandum goes on to give a synopsis of each of the relevant Orders-in-Council that provide for the issuance of Métis scrip and identify as nearly as possible from the records how much half-breed land scrip was still outstanding.

At the close of the nineteenth century, the west was undergoing a major transition. The Métis had established themselves as a people requiring recognition when the Red River settlement area joined Canada in 1870. The rest of the great plains had become part of Canada at the same time. A railway opened the area to new arrivals who were more interested in wheat than in buffalo. The flood of new arrivals led to the inevitable destruction of the old way of life for the Indians and Métis. The result was revolt. The "Northwest Rebellion" of 1885 saw major battles at Fort Pitt[9] in Saskatchewan near the border of Alberta and the Métis community at Fishing Lake. The "Frog Lake Massacre," a major event in that uprising, also occurred less than 20 miles from Fishing Lake.

The violent confrontations between the old and new powers on the plains were followed in Alberta by a more peaceful experiment at establishing a Métis land base. This was the Catholic church's effort to establish a Métis community on collectively-held lands at St. Paul, about 40 miles northwest of

Fishing Lake.[10] Ten years after the end of "The Rebellion," Father Albert Lacombe approached the federal government in an effort to set up a farming colony for the Métis. As a Catholic priest famous for his work in with native peoples in Alberta, Father Lacombe had some credibility. He also had a willing listener in A.M. Burgess, the deputy minister of the Department of the Interior, who had himself produced a report on the Métis in the North-West Territories in 1889.[11] The result was the creation in 1895 of the colony of St. Paul des Métis.

By 1898 there were 50 Métis families living on the colony. Control of the colony was in the hands of the Catholic Church, although two of the five members of the managing Board were federal politicians.[12] Along with training in agriculture, the major focus of the management appeared to be religious instruction and education.[13] After 10 years, the managing Board decided that the effort had been a failure and on April 10, 1909 the colony lands were opened to homesteading. On that day, in what was apparently an orchestrated effort, 250 French Canadian settlers registered claims on most of the land.[14] Most of the Métis left to find another home.[15]

Alberta and the Métis Settlements
Public Lands In Transition

The colony at St. Paul was established on public lands before the creation of the province. On the creation of Alberta in *The Alberta Act* of 1905, the Dominion, as it had in the case of Manitoba, kept the natural resources and public lands.[16] While apparently supporting the effort to eliminate communally-held lands at St. Paul des Métis, the federal government continued to encourage individual Métis land holdings by issuing scrip to half-breeds resident in Alberta in an effort to extinguish claims.[17] Individual claims were settled by grants from the retained lands.

The fact that the Dominion had retained Crown lands and resources galled the western provinces. They felt they were being treated as second-class citizens: the original parties to confederation had no such reservations. Pressure for equality led to the *Natural Resources Transfer Agreement* of December 14, 1929. By this agreement Alberta acquired the Crown lands and resources within its boundaries, "subject to any trusts existing in respect thereof, and to any interest other than that of the Crown in the same."[18] This agreement subsequently achieved constitutional status by being incorporated into *The British North America Act, 1930* and thereby into the *Constitution Act, 1982*.

While the government in Edmonton had been pressuring Ottawa for land, they had been receiving similar pressure from the province's Métis. The pressure began in the eastern part of central Alberta at the Métis community of Fishing Lake. That pressure for land and general assistance should be coming from this quarter is not surprising—many of the biggest events in the struggle to define Indian and Métis roles in the new Canada had happened within a 100-mile radius.

By the mid-1920s there was a fair-sized community of Métis on forest reserve lands retained by the Dominion at Fishing Lake. Many of the Métis had lived on the St. Paul des Métis Colony.[19] In 1929, the Métis, led by Charley Delorme, became concerned that the land was to be transferred to the province and opened for settlement.[20] Given the events of the previous 40 years in their general vicinity, it is not surprising that they began organizing to get the land protected before the transfer took place. That did not happen, but they continued to organize and lobby the federal and provincial governments for land and aid in general.

As the full force of the Depression hit the Métis, they began organizing throughout the province. They had the good fortune of attracting very capable leadership, the three best-known being Jim Brady, Malcolm Norris, and Joseph Dion.[21] By 1931 they were able to submit a petition of more than 500 names to the provincial government calling for land, education, health care and an unrestricted right to hunt and fish. This led to the circulation of a questionnaire among the Métis by the province's Department of Lands and Mines. The topics dealt with in the questionnaire hinted that the provincial government was already considering some kind of land scheme in response to Métis concerns.[22] By late in 1933 those concerns had made it to the Legislature, where the leader of the Conservatives moved a resolution that a special committee be appointed to investigate Métis concerns and consider "some plan of colonization of the half-breed population."[23]

Early in 1934, the provincial government began making arrangements for a committee to investigate "the half-breed question," and asked the federal government to participate. Ottawa refused. The scope of issues envisioned as part of the "half-breed question" is unknown. In public, the province made it clear that the proposed Commission would consider the "half-breed question" only from the perspective of the need for social relief. Land was relevant, only indirectly, as one component of relief. It may be legitimate, however, to question whether or not there was concern within the government as to a broader scope of land-related issues.

In the summer of 1934, Alberta's minister of railways and telephones, George Hoadley, planned a visit to Ottawa for talks with federal authorities. One of the topics for discussion was the "Half-Breed problem." On July 23, prior to his departure, his deputy minister, J. Harvie, sent him a memorandum stating:

> I am informed by the Premier it is your intention to discuss with the Federal authorities the question of representation by them on the Commission to be set up to investigate *the claims of the half-breeds*.[24] [emphasis added]

It is not clear whether the deputy minister was simply referring to the claims of poverty and destitution made by Métis leaders, or whether there was an intention to discuss broader land-related matters with federal authorities.

On returning to Edmonton, Hoadley sent a memorandum on September 7 to Premier Reid stating:

> RE: HALF-BREED PROBLEM
> I am returning your file in connection with the above subject.
> I took this matter up while I was in Ottawa and found that the Dominion Government declined to appoint a representative on the proposed Royal Commission to investigate this problem. They considered it wholly a matter for the Province to deal with, as all half-breeds are citizens and do not come under the Department of Indian Affairs or any other federal Department.[25]

The superintendent general of Indian affairs, T.G. Murphy, confirmed this in a letter to the provincial minister of telephones and public health, George Hoadley, on October 10, 1934. He referred to their telephone conversation that morning regarding "the appointment of a commission by the Government of Alberta to investigate the half-breed question." He indicated that under the provisions of the *Indian Act* the purview of his department was restricted to Indians as defined in that Act. He set out the definition and concluded:

> In these circumstances, it is my opinion that half-breeds are not the responsibility of the Dominion Government and that the problem of

relief for half-breed settlers is a matter for the consideration of the municipality or the Province concerned.[26]

Immediately following this, there was an exchange of correspondence between the premier of Alberta, R.G. Reid, and the member of Parliament for Athabasca, Percy Davies. Davies wrote the premier on October 18, 1934:

Replying to yours of the 12th instant, I understood that the Federal Government asked that the question of legal liability should be referred to the Courts for a decision before the Dominion would undertake any responsibility in respect of the Halfbreed population. Furthermore, I also understood that the Federal Government was willing to abide by the decision of the Courts and if the courts should find that there was any legal liability resting with the Dominion, that the Dominion would shoulder it.[27]

In short, the federal government was not prepared to assume any responsibility for the Métis unless ordered to do so by the Courts. Apparently the possibility of seeking such an order was discussed between the governments of Alberta and Saskatchewan, but it was never pursued.

Murphy and Hoadley had discussed the proposed Commission on the telephone on October 10. Whether they discussed a mandate for the commission that would deal with Métis issues beyond health and welfare is unknown. However, the briefing memorandum dated October 4, 1934, and prepared by A.A. Cohoon of Murphy's department, [28] certainly focused on the legal issues respecting responsibility for redeeming Métis land scrip. [29]

In his memorandum of October 4, 1934, Mr. Cohoon outlined what was, apparently, the federal government's viewpoint on the scrip issue—that prior to 1930 the Crown's duty to redeem Métis scrip was a trust encumbering Crown lands in Alberta. This duty arose by virtue of the conditions in the Hudson's Bay Company surrender and in the subsequent transfer of lands to the Dominion. However, clause 1 of the *Natural Resources Transfer Agreement* had provided that

In order that the Province may be in the same position as the original Provinces of Confederation are in by virtue of section one hundred and nine of the British North America Act, 1867, the interest of the Crown in all Crown lands,...shall...belong to the Province, subject to any trusts existing in respect thereof.[30]

The "subject to any trusts existing" component meant that the province was now responsible for those trusts. The Privy Council had considered the scope of the term "trusts" as used in section 109 in *Attorney General of Canada v. Attorney General of Ontario*.[31] In the Dominion's view that decision clearly implied that the existing trusts would include responsibility for redeeming Métis scrip.

By late in 1934, there were apparently two Métis land-related issues before the provincial government. It had to consider its responsibility for enabling individual Métis land ownership through scrip redemption. It also appeared ready to consider the possibility of enabling the Métis to exercise some form of "communal ownership" of land.

The first issue was dealt with by a provincial Order-in-Council on June 18, 1935. The Order began:

Whereas land scrip notes were issued from time to time by the Government of Canada to half-breed grantees properly entitled thereto, in satisfaction of their claims arising out of the extinguishment of the Indian title, and to be used in connection with vacant and available Dominion lands; and

Whereas there are no regulations providing for the redemption of any such scrip, which might be applicable to the Province; and

Whereas it is proper and convenient that regulations be established in respect thereto....[32]

The O.C. then went on to provide for the locating of land scrip "on any vacant and available Provincial lands."

To deal with the second issue, the Province established a Royal Commission on December 12, 1934, to look into "the problems of health, education and general welfare of the Half-breed population of the Province."[33] The Commission, headed by the Honourable A.F. Ewing, an Alberta Supreme Court Justice, came to be known as the Ewing Commission.

The Ewing Commission Searches for Solutions

By mid-1935 it appears that the Province had accepted total responsibility for the Métis. It had acted, from what it apparently considered a legal obligation, to enable the satisfaction of individual Métis land claims by redeeming land scrip with provincial Crown lands. Also, for what it apparently considered an obligation of conscience, it had set in motion a process to consider the propriety of protecting the Métis as a people by setting aside communal lands. Through all of this there is no indication of any concern that the Métis might be "Indians" for the purposes of section 91(24) of the *Constitution Act, 1867*, and consequently within "the exclusive Legislative Authority of the Parliament of Canada."[34]

The Ewing Commission held hearings throughout Alberta in 1935 and submitted its report on February 15, 1936.[35] To no one's surprise, the Commission recommended the establishment of Métis Colonies—lands to be held by the Crown but set aside for the exclusive use and occupation of associations of Métis. The Commission made it clear that in so doing they were not responding to Métis claims regarding rights to land. In its report the Commission briefly discussed the extinguishment of Indian title claims by "half-breeds" through the issuing of scrip and went on to say

> The story of this scrip and its final outcome is still vivid in living memory. The precautions of Parliament were easily circumvented and the scrip passed readily and cheaply into the hands of speculators. The resultant advantages to the half-breeds were negligible. The policy of the Federal Government, however, extending over a period of thirty years, and these issues of scrip, throw a strong light on the present problem.
>
> In the first place, the scrip was issued in extinguishment of any supposed right which the half-breed had to special consideration. But *the Government of this Province is now faced, not with a legal or contractual right, but with an actual condition of privation, penury and suffering.* The right to live cannot be extinguished and the situation as revealed to your Commission seems to call for Governmental guidance and assistance.[36] [emphasis added]

Two points are worth making with regard to this part of the report: the Commission made it clear that the rights issue was not on the table, and the Métis leadership did not insist that it be dealt with. The Commission had made it clear that it was not interested in discussing the issue of Métis land rights, and Métis leaders did not argue their case on the basis of rights. Rather they focused on Métis needs and on the economic advantages for the government of a self-supporting colony system—the approach was results rather than rights oriented.

Sanders makes the following comments in this regard:

The assumptions in Alberta in 1933 would seem to have been:
1. Métis claims to Indian title had been extinguished by the Half-breed grants under the *Manitoba Act* and the *Dominion Lands Act*.
2. Métis and non-status Indians were the responsibility of the provinces either because they were not "Indians" within the meaning of that term in the *British North America Act* of 1867, or because the federal government had chosen to exclude them from the exercise of federal legislative jurisdiction over "Indians."
3. The Métis of northern Alberta were not asserting rights but needs.
4. The understood response to the Métis situation in Alberta was going to be some kind of allocation of land (and land was now under provincial ownership and jurisdiction).

The Ewing Commission operated on these assumptions. The Métis colony system in Alberta has operated on them ever since. In contrast the Métis in Saskatchewan in the 1930s sought provincial support in order to present claims to the federal government. In response the Saskatchewan government commissioned the study by Hodges and Noonan which suggested that Métis claims were not of a legal character and, in any case, had been settled. Manitoba Métis in the same period also asserted land claims which would presumably have involved petitioning the federal government.[37]

From the vantage point of history, it now appears that the Métis leadership in Alberta better read the climate of the time, and consequently was able to employ a more effective strategy to achieve the common goal of securing a land base.

The Ewing Commission recommended setting aside land for the Métis. However, it might have been more accurate to describe the intended beneficiaries as landless natives rather than Métis. The Commission's mandate was with respect to the "Half-breed population of the Province," and it had a problem defining just who that was. The Commission's report stated:

It may be well to define here the term "half-breed" or "Metis." We are not concerned with a technically correct definition. We merely wish to give a clear meaning to the term as used in this report. By either term is meant a person of mixed blood, white and Indian, *who lives the life of the ordinary Indian*, and includes a non-treaty Indian. It is apparent to everyone that there are in this Province many persons of mixed blood (Indian and white) who have settled down as farmers, who are making a good living in that occupation and who do not need, nor do they desire, public assistance. The term as used in this report has no application to such men.[38] [emphasis added]

Although the Commission had difficulty defining "Métis," it recognized that these people formed an identifiable group linked by aboriginal ancestry and lifestyle. It refused to discuss the rights of the group, but recognized that some such rights might exist, for example by stating that "The Commission is of opinion that as the Metis were the original inhabitants of these great unsettled areas and are dependent on wild life and fish for their livelihood, they should be given preference over non-residents in respect of fur, game and fish."[39]

Pocklington comments as follows on the Commission's report:

The basic problem is that a fundamental ambiguity permeates the Commission's treatment of the relationship between the Métis and the government, and thereby the dominant society as a whole.

The core of the ambiguity has to do with the Commission's recognition of the uniqueness of the Métis. Throughout much of the report of the Commission the uniqueness of the Métis is seen to consist in their poverty, poor health, and lack of education. But of course the Métis were not really unique in these respects. On the one hand, plenty of white settlers shared these debilities. And on the other hand, many persons of mixed Indian and white ancestry did not. If the Métis were in fact just victims of the depression, they could have been dealt with by the same measures of relief granted to other citizens. That the Commission did not recommend that they be treated in the ordinary way of people ravaged by the Depression was at least an implicit recognition that the Métis had something else in common. Part of what they had in common is made explicit in the report. The Commissioners mention frequently the propensity of the Métis to pursue a common style of life. Only this commonality could justify the recommendation that colonies be established exclusively for the Métis. The striking ambiguity here is that the Métis are characterized as *both* ordinary *and* special. Clearly, the Commissioners, while steadfastly opposed to granting the Métis special status like that of the Indians, were constrained to admit that the Métis were unique. This ambiguity emerges most clearly in the recommendation that, while the Métis should not be compelled to join colonies, they would have no other claim to public assistance if they did not.[40]

In summary, the Ewing Commission focused on a social problem and recommended a pragmatic solution. It saw a group of suffering people of aboriginal ancestry and "Indian" lifestyle for whom the federal government disclaimed any responsibility. It recognized them as "Metis" and as "original inhabitants of these great unsettled areas." It concluded: "your Commissioners are of the opinion that some form of farm colonies is the most effective, and, ultimately, the cheapest method of dealing with the problem."[41]

The Ewing Commission did not concern itself with the question of whether or not the Métis had any legal right to demand such lands. From its perspective, the rights issue was simply not relevant. The Métis leaders did not demand that the rights issue be discussed. As a result, the work of the Ewing Commission is of historical and social interest, but probably of little significance in the discussion of the legal rights of the people who were the focus of its efforts.

Early Métis Settlements Legislation

The provincial government responded positively to the report of the Ewing Commission. The federal government had disclaimed any responsibility for the people whose needs the Commission sought to address. Probably because of its recent success in negotiating the Natural Resources Agreement, the province was unwilling to take the responsibility issue to the courts. Instead, it accepted what it saw as its social obligations and began setting up the machinery to reserve land for the Métis and to provide for a limited form of local government on the reserved areas.

In a rather unique co-operative approach, Métis leaders apparently prepared drafts of the enabling legislation[42] and worked with representatives of the provincial government on subsequent revisions until a mutually acceptable draft was complete.[43] *The Metis Population Betterment Act* was passed and received assent on November 22, 1938. A joint Métis-government committee was established to identify suitable Métis Settlement area sites and land areas were set aside by Orders-in-Council commencing late in 1938. By the end of the next year, Settlement Associations had held organizational meetings in eight of the areas and adopted a common constitution and bylaws.

The preamble to the Act had referred to the recommendations of the Ewing Commission and recognized the Métis role in developing the Act by acknowledging that it was in the public interest

> that the ways and means of giving effect to such recommendations should be arrived at by means of conferences and negotiations between the Government of the Province and representatives of the Métis population of the Province.[44]

The scheme agreed to in the Act and Settlement constitutions would certainly not satisfy any contemporary proponent of self-government. The Act was three short pages of bare-bones legislation. It made four key things possible: first, the minister could help the Métis organize Settlement Associations; second, by Order-in-Council unoccupied Provincial Lands could be set aside for settlement by the members of the Associations; third, the Associations could develop a constitution and bylaws providing the basic framework for local self-government; and fourth, the Associations and the minister could co-operatively formulate schemes for bettering the members and settling them on the reserved lands.

The only means of putting legislative flesh on these bare-bones principles appears to have been by co-operatively developing schemes for the betterment and settlement of members. That these schemes were intended to be something more than departmental programs is implied by the requirement in the Act that

> Every scheme formulated pursuant to this Act shall be submitted by the Minister to the Lieutenant Governor in Council for approval, and upon the same being so approved, shall be laid upon the table of the Legislative Assembly.[45]

From a legislative drafting viewpoint, the preferable approach today would probably be to enable the skeleton legislation to be filled out by regulations. In the original Act, however, the only regulation-making powers were with respect to hunting, fishing and trapping.

The Act provided a sparse framework for local government by stating that the "control of the business and affairs of the association shall be in a

Board,"[46] and by enabling the associations to develop constitutions and bylaws providing for "the election of the members of the Board."[47] The provisions of the original constitution, and all changes, were subject to ministerial approval and the aims and objects of the associations had to include co-operation with the minister.

The Constitution adopted by the Settlement Associations,[48] and approved by the minister, outlined minimal requirements for membership, elections, Board meetings, and other details of managing the Settlement Association. It provided a rather vague general bylaw-making power that enabled the Board to pass bylaws "pertaining to the management and governing of the Settlement Association and the reserved area occupied by their Settlement Association."[49] The bylaws had to be consistent with the provisions of the constitution and approved by the minister.

The bare-bones legislative framework provided by the original Act was adequate for the purpose at hand. It made it possible to set aside lands and established a means for residents to govern them, subject to the ultimate authority of the provincial government. The goal of Métis leaders such as Brady and Norris was to create a land base. They were prepared to make a few concessions to reach that goal. The legislation was adequate, and that was enough.

The Act was amended on February 16, 1940[50] to a form that was to remain essentially unchanged for 50 years. The preamble was dropped, but new provisions roughly tripled the size of the Act. The most significant new provisions enabled regulations governing most aspects of settlement life, particularly the allocation and use of land and resources, to be made by Order-in-Council. The new provisions also made it possible to convert Settlement Areas into Improvement Districts—the standard rural "local government" entities for non-natives—and enabled descent of an individual's interest in land to his family. Finally the provisions prohibited the use of a Settlement member's property as security.

The last substantive change to the Act, before the Alberta-Métis Settlements Accord, was made in 1952.[51] The original Act, and each subsequent version, had stated that the constitution and bylaws of a Settlement Association

> shall provide that the control of the business and affairs of the association shall be in a Board consisting of not more than five persons and shall make provision for election of the members of the Board.[52]

The 1952 amendment stripped the Settlements of any clear legal basis for self-government. The words "control of the business and affairs of the association shall be in a Board" were removed. The power to constitutionally provide for election of all five Board members was also removed. In its place were added two new sections:

(2a) A Settlement Association shall have a Local Board consisting of a chairman who shall be the local supervisor of the area appointed by the Metis Rehabilitation Branch of the Department of Public Welfare and four members who shall be *bona fide* members of the Settlement Association.
(2b) The Minister shall appoint two of the members of the Local Board and the members of the Settlement Association shall elect two of the members of the Local Board by secret ballot.[53]

In short, the Act was changed to weaken the mandate of the Board and to change it from an elected body to one that was mainly an appointed one.

This is one of many provisions that, as the first half-century of the Settlements progressed, made the Act and Regulations increasingly unworkable. In addition to becoming anachronistic and inadequate as Settlement government became more complex and sophisticated, the legislation had internal inconsistencies and uncertain legitimacy. For example, despite the wording of the Act, a regulation, *Regulations Governing the Constitution of Settlement Associations* (A.R. 56/66), was approved in 1966 that replaced previous regulations on the same topic.[54] It specified that "The affairs and business of an association shall be transacted by a Board consisting of 3 members" and "The Board shall consist of three members all of whom shall be elected by the members of the Colony."[55] These provisions clearly contradicted the Act's stipulation of a five-member Board.

The contradiction led to practical problems. Oil companies negotiating with Settlement Councils for access to Settlement lands questioned the legitimacy of the elected councils on the basis that the five-member elected council was not properly constituted under either the Act or the regulations. The issue never went to court, however. As with other parts of the Act and Regulations, the fact that the provisions were unworkable meant they were largely ignored by the Métis and the government. Settlement members continued to elect all five members of their Board, and the government and industry by and large dealt with the council as the proper representatives of the Settlement.

By the end of the 1960s, the focus of Settlement leaders began to change. For 30 years the leaders of each Settlement had concentrated primarily on the problems of survival on their particular Settlement. As the 1970s began, the focus began to shift outward and Settlement leaders became actively concerned about the collective interests of all the Settlements and their prospects for the future. The most significant event leading to this new focus on collective action was the loss of Wolf Lake.

Land surrounding Wolf Lake in northeastern Alberta was set aside for the Wolf Lake Settlement Association in 1939. By the late 1950s there were roughly a dozen families living on the Settlement area.[56] However, in 1960 a provincial Order-in-Council[57] was passed eliminating the Settlement area. The resident families were moved to nearby communities or to other Settlements. The Province's stated reason for the closing was that the area could not be adequately serviced. Others have expressed the view that a factor in the decision was the federal government's need for a bombing range for the nearby Cold Lake Air Force base.[58] Whatever the motivation, the legitimacy of the Province's action became the subject of litigation between the Métis Settlements and the Province.[59] Whatever the reason or legitimacy, the news that a Settlement area had been eliminated created concern throughout the remaining Settlements that they might be next.

This concern for land security was heightened by a review of the Settlement situation started in 1969. Prodded by the Métis Association of Alberta, the provincial government set up a Métis Task Force, including representatives of the Métis Association, to conduct a review of The *Metis Betterment Act*, the Métis Settlements and the Metis Rehabilitation Branch of the Department of Social Services. In 1972 the Task Force presented its report.[60] The report stated:

> it is incumbent upon the Committee to suggest it was not necessarily the feeling of the [Ewing] Commission that Crown lands for the Metis people should be a perpetual commitment.[61]

It went on to recommend considering the conversion of the Settlement Areas into Improvement Districts and the possibility of enabling individual settlers to own their own land. In fairness, it should be noted that the main thrust of the report was to create a better legislative and policy environment for community development. The report also envisioned a possible continuation of the communal approach by stating that "We can foresee that some or all of the Metis settlements could, if desirable, take over all the Crown Lands as corporate bodies under the Improvement Districts."[62] In spite of its apparent good intent, the report caused grave concern on the Settlements. There it was read as a sign the government wanted to "lift the boundaries."

A third significant event that occurred in the late 1960s also had to do with land. Regulations under the *Metis Betterment Act* provided for a common trust fund shared by all eight Settlements.[63] The regulations specified that the Trust Fund[64] was to be credited with "all moneys accrued or hereafter accruing from the sources hereinafter set out," and included in the list of sources:

> moneys received by way of compensation from oil companies for use of surface rights on unoccupied lands, and all moneys received from the sale or lease of any other of the natural resources of the said areas.[65]

During the 1960s, oil and gas resources began to be developed on a number of Settlements and Settlement leaders took the view that the mines and minerals were part of the land set aside for their benefit. In their view, oil and gas were "natural resources" of the Settlement areas and consequently that money from the sale of these resources should be going to the Trust Fund. The Province disagreed and Settlement leaders filed a statement of claim[66] demanding that the moneys be paid to the Trust Fund. Without ruling on the merits of the case, the Court rejected the claim on procedural grounds.[67]

When Settlement leaders in the early 1970s looked at their collective situation, they were concerned. The provincial cabinet, without involving the Legislature, had eliminated the Settlement at Wolf Lake. A government task force had raised fears that "lifting the boundaries" might be considered for other Settlements. An initial effort to secure the benefit of subsoil resources had failed. It became apparent to Settlement leaders that an ongoing co-ordinated effort was required to secure the developmental essentials of land security, legislative authority and adequate financing.

Brady had realized the need for an organized common front as early as 1940 and, working with Norris, had tried to establish a co-ordinating organization for the Settlements.[68] They were unsuccessful. Thirty years later, in 1971, Métis Settlement leaders again began an effort to "federate" the Settlements. A group of Settlement leaders[69] visited the Settlements, met with Settlement Councils and members and discussed the common concerns of the Settlements and the need for a body to co-ordinate Settlement efforts. In 1975, the eight

Settlement Councils created such a body by formally incorporating the Alberta Federation of Métis Settlement Associations (commonly referred to as the "Federation"). The governing Board of the Federation consisted of the chairperson of each Settlement Council and four executive members elected at large. The Federation's mandate was to provide the Settlement Councils with a means of sharing information, co-ordinating efforts, and developing policies on matters that required co-operation—such as the sharing of the common Trust Fund.

The 1970s—Settlement Leaders Organize

In essence, the goals of the Settlements were the same in 1975 as they had been in 1939, and still are today: land security, local legislative authority and adequate finances—land, power, and money. With the long-term achievement of the first and third goals in mind, the Federation immediately began work on the legal action to secure the revenue from oil and gas resource development in Settlement areas. A new statement of claim was filed in 1977.[70] The major short-term focus of the Federation's efforts, however, was on the second goal—developing local legislative authority.

The Métis Task Force had reported in 1972 that the function of the Settlement Councils was "more consultative than administrative." Some Settlements had no office and all administrative functions were handled by staff of the Metis Development Branch. All purchasing was done by purchase order, and wages on Settlement projects were paid for by the Branch. Settlement Councils generally had no bank accounts of their own and no direct financial authority. One of the top priorities of the Federation was to begin building real local governments with adequate administrative capability.

Although Settlement concerns about the Métis Task Force recommendations had helped create the Federation, the Task Force and the Federation agreed on the importance of developing local self-government. The Task Force had emphasized the importance of this goal in its report, which while recommending that the Settlements be established as Improvement Districts in the near future, went on to say of this approach that "It is not a final objective, but merely a transitional stage of development with some specific date in mind to move into complete self-government."[71]

The Task Force Report had also pointed out the problems created by having all programs for the Settlements delivered by one government agency—the

Metis Rehabilitation Branch.[72] The Federation also saw this as a problem. The single agency approach provided a single line of communication and program delivery between the Province and the Settlements. That channel could be easily blocked or overloaded, with the result that developmental efforts were stymied. The Settlements had to open new channels to those in power to communicate Settlement needs and establish new mechanisms to meet those needs.

The most important new channel was to the federal government. After disclaiming responsibility for the Métis in the 1930s, the federal government had finally begun reassessing its role in the 1960s and in the early 1970s it began assisting Métis organizations through the Department of the Secretary of State. There were no direct links with the Settlements, however, until the secretary of state agreed to participate with the province in a local govern-ment development effort spearheaded by the Federation. The effort involved a number of projects extending over three years from 1976 to 1979. The projects enabled the Federation to hire trained fieldworkers to help Settlement Councils get organized and do the kind of research and writing necessary to tap external development resources.

This effort was greatly helped by a change in policy by the Metis Development Branch in the early 1970s. The policy change aimed at reducing the Branch's administrative role and developing the capacity of Settlement administrations. In simple terms it meant that every Settlement would have an office, office equipment and a clerk. It also meant that some real decision-making would move from the Branch to the Council.

The new policy, combined with offices, information and support staff led to a rapid growth in Council responsibilities in the late 1970s. The Federation and individual Councils became directly involved with a broad range of federal, provincial and private agencies. Where in 1969 a Settlement turned to the Branch for information and development assistance, by 1979 many of the Settlements had direct contractual or program delivery links with several federal government departments, with half a dozen provincial departments and with corporations in the private sector.[73] Some Settlement Councils began to feel overwhelmed as the limitations of the single agency were replaced by the problem of managing links with a multitude of agencies.

The problems were exacerbated by anachronistic legislation and the para-noia surrounding the natural resources litigation. The courts had rejected the Settlements lawsuit over oil and gas revenues on the procedural ground that the permission of the Crown was required to sue the Crown. Lougheed secured legislation eliminating this provision, allowing the Settlements to re-launch their natural resources lawsuit. The government and the Settlements agreed that there should be no changes to the *Metis Betterment Act* or its regulations while the matter was before the courts. As a result, while the responsibilities of the Settlement Councils grew rapidly, the legislative framework in which they operated was frozen. The Task Force Report in 1972 had recommended that the Act be rewritten.[74] That was at a time when a Council's function was, "more consultative than administrative." By 1979, most Councils had major administrative responsibilities.

The Act had been essentially static since 1940. The amendments in 1952 that had replaced the elected Council by a mostly appointed board were unworkable and by the mid-1970s they were universally ignored. Settlement members continued to elect the council as they had under their original Constitution. By 1979, the legal system provided by the Act and Regulations, with its internal inconsistencies, uncertain legitimacy, anachronisms and inadequacies, was increasingly unworkable. As more parts of the system became unworkable, they were ignored; and the more parts were ignored, the more unclear the legal framework for local government became. The resulting uncertainty aggravated the friction inherent in the change in roles of the Settlement Councils and the Branch.

In addition to locking in existing legislation, the natural resources litigation contributed to other developmental problems by hampering innovation and undermining trust. Provincial employees had to constantly check with the Attorney General's department before agreeing with any proposal from the Settlements or undertaking any new initiative. There was a constant concern that some well-intentioned action would prejudice the Province's position in the litigation. Having taken the position in its Statement of Defence that the Settlement Associations were not "persons at law," the Province found itself unable to enter into normal contractual relations with the Settlements. That made it impossible to transfer funds to the Settlement Association to encourage the development of local administrations. With the increasing direct links between federal agencies and the Settlements, it also led to an interesting source of potential friction between the federal and provincial governments. Federal government departments had no qualms about entering into contracts with the Settlement Associations and did so regularly. The Province was faced with the argument that Her Majesty, having contracted with the Settlement Associations on behalf of Canada, could hardly deny that capacity when acting on behalf of Alberta.

In 1979, the paranoid atmosphere finally created a political fiasco. Early one morning, representatives of the Metis Development Branch and other departments simultaneously appeared at all Settlement offices, seized Settlement and government files that were, in their opinion, relevant to the natural resource litigation, and removed the files to Edmonton. The Métis and the public were incensed by the action. The story made the front pages and an embarrassed government sought talks with the Settlements. Negotiations between the Federation and the government led to an investigation by the Alberta Ombudsman. In his report, the Ombudsman recommended that a committee be established to review and recommend changes to the *Metis Betterment Act* and Regulations.

In a sense, the Ombudsman's Report marked the end of an era. To recap the decade, at the start most Settlement Councils had no staff, no offices and no administrative responsibility. In most cases the only channel for information and developmental resources was through the Branch. By decade's end, the councils had the offices, equipment and staff to administer local programs. They had established links with provincial government departments, federal government departments and private sector corporations and agencies. They had begun managing housing programs, economic development projects, and local educational and cultural projects. In short, the 1970s saw Settlement leaders realize the goal set by Brady and Norris—they had developed the capacity to co-ordinate their efforts province-wide. In the 1980s the scene became national.

The 1980s—Constitution and Crisis

The Provincial Ombudsman carried out an investigation of the "file raids" and tabled his report in the summer of 1979.[75] The report called for the creation of a joint committee of Settlement and government representatives to, among other things, review the *Metis Betterment Act*. It also recommended that responsibility for the Settlements be transferred from the Department of Social Services and Community Health to the Department of Municipal Affairs. The transfer took place in October of 1980,[76] but it was not until March 31, 1982 that the recommended committee was finally established.[77]

The Joint Committee was chaired by the Honourable Dr. Grant MacEwan—former lieutenant-governor of Alberta. It included the president and past president of the Federation,[78] a member of the Legislature and an assistant deputy minister of municipal affairs. The Committee's mandate was "to act in an advisory capacity and in particular to review the *Metis Betterment Act* and Regulations and make recommendations to the Minister of Municipal Affairs which would allow for political, social, cultural and economic development on Métis Settlements."[79] The Committee held hearings on the Settlements and, based on the concerns expressed in the communities, developed suggested provisions of a new "*Metis Settlements Act*." The Committee's report, consisting of the provisions and explanatory comments, was transmitted to the minister on July 12, 1984.[80]

The Committee carried out its work in the new legal environment created by the recognition of Métis aboriginal rights in the Constitution of Canada—a major accomplishment for the Métis. There had been no mention of Métis rights in the federal government's constitutional package proposed late in 1980. In January of 1981, a Special Joint Committee of the Senate and House of Commons unanimously agreed that recognition of Métis aboriginal rights should be included.[81] Alberta, and other provinces, objected to the patriation process, Prime Minister Trudeau threatened to proceed without their consent, and the legality of the unilateral approach was referred to the Supreme Court of Canada. The Court's decision forced a new round of negotiations between Ottawa and the provinces, resulting in an agreement on an amended package on November 5, 1981. The recognition of aboriginal rights had been removed from the new package, reportedly due to pressure from western premiers.

In Alberta, Settlement leaders were extremely upset by the prospect of a patriated constitution with no recognition of Métis aboriginal rights. The President of the Federation, Elmer Ghostkeeper, led a quiet protest that burned sweetgrass along with the permanent flame at the Alberta Legislature. As public pressure mounted, Premier Lougheed agreed to meet with Settlement leaders to discuss the matter. At the meeting, Ghostkeeper presented the argument that recognizing the Métis in the constitution was essential if there was to be real equality in Canada between the west and the east. He argued that in the east, the two existing "nations"—the French and the Indians— had received constitutional recognition when subsumed into Canada in 1867. The French were assured language protection and the Indians special status entailing federal fiduciary responsibilities. Canada now included the west, and its new constitution should accord the indigenous "nation" of the west, the Métis, the same recognition as had been given to the indigenous "nations" in the east. The premier was intrigued by the argument. Whether he was persuaded is not known, but he did begin supporting the recognition of the "existing aboriginal rights" of the Métis in the constitution.

In the end, the new Canadian Constitution recognized existing aboriginal rights and specifically named the Métis as one of the aboriginal peoples. It also required the first ministers to meet to define the scope of those rights. This led to considerable soul-searching by aboriginal groups in preparation for the First Ministers Conference. A topic of particular concern to the Métis was the question of whether they came under federal or provincial jurisdiction. National Métis organizations were pressing for recognition of Métis as included in the term "Indians" as used in section 91(24) of the BNA Act (Constitution Act, 1867) and consequently to be under federal jurisdiction.

The Settlements took a different view. The Federation prepared a position paper on aboriginal rights, "Métisism: A Canadian Identity," and presented it to Premier Lougheed on June 30, 1982. The paper noted that the Settlements might be better off under federal jurisdiction since the federal government did not contest the right of Indians to benefit from the subsurface resource revenues of their lands. The paper then went on to say:

> This is not to suggest that we are seeking an exclusive relationship with the federal government. We believe that the province can be more responsive to the needs and aspirations of Métis settlers than a distant federal government. A case in point is the establishment of the Settlements at a time of federal neglect and indifference towards the Métis people. Provincial jurisdiction over education, municipalities, and health and welfare, reinforces our need to deal with the province. Perhaps the most compelling reason for us opting out of an exclusive relationship with the federal government is that, while it might enhance our political status, it does not fit with the Métis way of doing things. More than any other Canadians, we recognize the importance of western provincial rights: our ancestors formed two provisional governments to defend them. We are proud to be western Canadians and proud to be Albertans.[82]

Since then, the Settlements have consistently maintained this preference for working with the Province. Certainly they were affected by the question of whether Métis are "Indians" under the Constitution Act, 1867. However, in talks between the Settlements and the Province the issue was generally ignored on the basis that it was a question for the courts and not something either party could do anything about.

The year after the presentation of the "Métisism" paper, the first First Ministers' Conference on Aboriginal Constitutional Matters was held in Ottawa in April of 1983. Federation representatives attended with the Alberta government delegation. By the standards of future such conferences, this one was a success, but Settlement leaders nonetheless left with a feeling of unease. Their goal was to constitutionally protect their existing land base. The national process was one strategy to accomplish that goal. It became clear in Ottawa, however, that getting agreement on any position further clarifying aboriginal rights would be extremely difficult. The Settlements began looking for other options.

One of the options they began to consider was the possibility of protecting Settlement lands in the constitution by an amendment to the *Alberta Act*.[83] It appeared legally possible to make such an amendment under section 43 of the *Canada Act, 1982* by a "made in Alberta" process involving simply the Settlements and the Province. The Federation proposed the idea to Premier Lougheed after the disastrous 1984 First Ministers' Conference. The premier was very interested and said he would look into it. There was no more communication with the Federation on the subject until the 1985 First Ministers' Conference. At that conference, Premier Lougheed would not support federal initiatives using undefined terms such as "self-government." The national media criticized Lougheed's position, insinuating he was a "redneck." He was understandably angry. Outside the meeting he spoke to Federation leaders and suggested a deal. He would proceed with the *Alberta Act* amendment approach if the Settlements would commit to adopting fair and democratic procedures for membership and land allocations.[84]

The premier's commitment was a tremendous boost for Settlement leaders. It meant that there was finally a realistic possibility of achieving the fundamental goal of constitutionally protecting their land base. Settlement Councils met on April 28, 1985 at Westlock, north of Edmonton. After much debate, they passed the "Westlock Resolution." It set out basic principles to govern the granting of membership and the allocation of interests in Métis Settlement lands. It also committed the Settlements to "continue to work with the Government of the Province of Alberta to complete and implement the recommendations of the Committee and the principles of this Resolution."[85]

The Province accepted the Westlock Resolution as meeting the "fair and democratic" condition, and on June 3, 1985, Premier Lougheed introduced "*A Resolution Concerning an Amendment to the Alberta Act*" to the Alberta Legislature.

It was passed unanimously. In supporting the resolution, the Legislature committed itself to

> ...introduce, once a revised Metis Betterment Act has been enacted, a resolution to amend the *Alberta Act* by proclamation issued by Her Excellency the Governor General under the Great Seal of Canada to grant an estate in fee simple in existing Metis Settlement lands to the Metis Settlement Associations or to such appropriate Metis corporate entities as may be determined on behalf of the Metis people of Alberta, in accordance with this resolution.[86]

This resolution firmly committed the Province to pursue two objectives—the entrenchment of Métis land through an amendment to the *Alberta Act*, and the passage of a new *Metis Settlements Act* that would provide a modern framework for local self-government on the Settlements.

On January 13, 1986, the Federation met with the new premier of Alberta, Don Getty, to discuss the possibility of a joint effort aimed at producing a new "*Metis Settlements Act*" and an amendment to the *Alberta Act* prior to the 1987 First Minister's Conference. Following meetings on all the Settlements, the Federation, in July 1986, presented a proposal for such legislation in a document entitled "*By Means of Conferences and Negotiations We Ensure Our Rights.*"[87]

Negotiations on the new legislation proceeded through the end of 1986 and into 1987. The basics of the self-governance structure were worked in innumerable meetings with members and councils of the Settlements. The result was the "Blue Book"—named by the colour of its cover—setting out draft legislation on Settlement government, membership, and land allocation.

The major obstacle to moving forward was disagreement on the principle of "territorial integrity." To the Métis, this principle was absolutely basic. In essence it meant that the Métis would own the surface[88] of all the land within a specified boundary. The Province was not prepared to concede ownership of the road allowances and the beds and shores of the lakes and rivers. The matter had still not been resolved when the First Ministers' Conference opened on March 26, 1987. However, in his opening statement, Premier Getty reported on the negotiations and surprised his Cabinet colleagues by stating that "with regard to outstanding matters, we understand and agree with the concept of territorial integrity."[89]

With that obstacle removed, discussions proceeded rapidly. On June 17, 1987, a discussion paper entitled "Implementation of Resolution 18" was tabled in the Legislature. This was the "Blue Book" in its final form. It included drafts of a *Metis Settlements Act*, a resolution calling for an amendment to the *Alberta Act*, and letters patent to transfer the Province's interest in Settlement lands.

The Accord Era
Developing the Alberta-Métis Settlements Accord

The package introduced to the Alberta Legislature in 1987 provided a comprehensive framework for local self-government for the Settlements. In concept, it established the existing Settlements as bodies corporate, gave Councils bylaw-making powers, created a central land-holding body with the power to make laws binding on Settlement Councils and created a tribunal to adjudicate disputes on land, membership, and other matters. It also provided criteria for membership and rules for land allocation. Compared to the sparse and inadequate 22 sections of the existing *Metis Betterment Act*, its 212 sections overwhelmed most Settlement members.

The Federation held community meetings to discuss the paper. Although there was general support for the proposals, there was also concern that it was too much too soon. After discussions with the Province, it was agreed to start with less comprehensive legislation and implement the rest of the package, as modified in consultation with the communities, over time. The result was the introduction to the Legislative Assembly on July 5, 1988, of Bill 64, *Metis Settlements Act*, and Bill 65, *Metis Settlements Land Act*, and the tabling of a resolution to amend the *Alberta Act*. Introduction was only the start—the minister made it clear some resolution of the natural resource litigation was needed before the Bills could be passed and the land entrenched.

The only way to get discussions going on the lawsuit was to talk about the financial needs of the Settlements. That meant more studies and community meetings. A joint committee of Federation and government representatives was set up and engineering consultants hired to do a study of community needs. After several months of working with government departments and Settlement Councils, the consultants submitted a report to the committee setting out what they considered would be required for the Settlements to "catch up and keep up" with their neighbours. The report formed the basis for negotiations leading to a Finance Package that would commit the government to more than $310 million in funding over 17 years.

Settlement representatives met with Premier Getty in March 1989 and reached an agreement in principle: the government would pass Bills 64 and 65, request the federal government to amend the *Alberta Act* so as to entrench the land in Canada's Constitution, and sign a commitment to the Finance Package. It would also agree to the co-management of oil and gas development on the Settlement areas, enabling both the General Council and Settlement Councils to benefit financially from extraction activities. In exchange the Settlements would end the lawsuit.

All of this was, of course, subject to approval at the local level. Meetings were held in all communities to review the financial and legislative proposals. A 10-year consultative process to develop a new framework for the Settlements finally reached its end with a referendum on the proposed package. The referendum passed overwhelmingly, endorsing the draft legislation and the financial package. These became part of an agreement between the leaders of the Settlements and the Province called the "Alberta-Metis Settlements Accord." On Canada Day, July 1, 1989, the Accord was signed by representatives of the Federation and Premier Getty at a ceremony on the Kikino Métis Settlement.

From Accord to Legislation

The Accord signed on July 1, 1989 contained draft legislation, resolutions and resource co-management principles. It would take 16 months to translate all this into a package of bills that could be passed by the Legislature. During that time it was necessary to negotiate the final drafts of the legislation, flesh out the details of the sub-surface resources Co-management Agreement, and get federal co-operation in amending the *Alberta Act*.

Work on the legislation and co-management agreement proceeded apace, but the effort to get federal help in amending the *Alberta Act* went nowhere. Ottawa refused to participate, citing concerns about creating a precedent for Quebec and questioning the legality of the proposed approach via section 43 of the *Canada Act, 1982*. The federal refusal to co-operate, reminiscent of its position on the Ewing Commission half a century earlier, created a significant problem. Protecting the land in the Constitution of Canada had been a key element of the Accord. The Métis could not accept the package without some form of constitutional protection. The solution was again a "made in Alberta" approach. Instead of amending the *Alberta Act*, legislation would be passed amending the constitution of Alberta. This posed a minor problem in that no one was sure exactly what the constitution of Alberta was, but as with many other issues, pragmatism carried the day and collaborative drafting began on the necessary constitutional amendment.

A second major unfinished task was agreement on co-managing resources. The Accord outlined the proposed arrangement, but this was a completely new concept for the Department of Energy. It would take a great deal of work to develop an approach compatible with its existing system of granting land rights and collecting royalties. A committee of representatives of the Federation and the affected departments got the job of working out a solution.

The starting point was a memorandum from Federation president, Randy Hardy, setting out the Federation's understanding of the general clauses in the Accord. The minister of energy, Myron Kanik, responded, indicating agreement with most of the memorandum and identifying a few areas where discussion was required. At the same time, the Federation developed a draft General Council Policy that would establish the Settlements' legislative framework for oil and gas development. By the summer of 1990, the details had been worked out and a Co-management Agreement drafted as a schedule to the *Metis Settlements Act*. Although the Province refused to share in the proceeds from land sales or royalties, the agreement was worth tens of millions of dollars to the Settlements because it would give General Council the power to negotiate overriding royalties and partial ownership of oil and gas wells with prospective developers. The draft General Council Policy set out how the money coming to the General Council from this resource activity would be shared among the Settlements.

The third unfinished task was to create something to manage the process of getting the new regime up and running. This would be a major undertaking. Under the old Act, the province's Metis Betterment Branch in Edmonton had essentially handled all of the planning, administration, and financial management for the Settlements. How would the Settlements set up their own administrations? How would they manage the millions of dollars flowing in under the Accord? How would they establish the governance practices needed for effective and efficient local governments? The answer to all these questions was the Métis Settlements Transition Commission— a concept drawn from the approach used to manage transition in the Ft. McMurray area at the start of the multi-billion dollar tar sands development. The problem for the Settlements was how to give the Settlement Councils and General Council the power to govern while also ensuring

Settlement members of proper management and financial practices during the ramp-up period. The arrangement that was finally worked out entailed a special piece of legislation—the *Metis Settlements Accord Implementation Act*. This Act set out the Province's 17-year funding obligations agreed to in the Accord and created the Métis Settlements Transition Commission to oversee the spending of the money for the first seven years. By the summer of 1990, the bills containing the Accord implementation legislation were ready for the Legislative Assembly. They were introduced and passed with great fanfare. On November 1, 1990, four new statutes were proclaimed in effect and a new era began for the Settlements.

An Overview of the Métis Settlements Legislation

The legislative package implementing the Accord consisted of the *Constitution of Alberta Amendment Act, 1990*, the *Metis Settlements Land Protection Act*, the *Metis Settlements Act*, and the *Métis Settlements Accord Implementation Act*. The first provided recognition for the Métis and protection for the land-holding system. The second protected the land. The third provided a framework for self-government, and the fourth provided the structure for transition. We will engage in a general overview of some of the key features of each and leave the in-depth analyses to others.[90]

The *Constitution of Alberta Amendment Act, 1990*, was the cornerstone of the legislative package. The preamble of the constitutional amendment recognized the history and contribution of the Métis in Alberta and expressed the desire that they should continue to have a land base on which to maintain their identity and culture and attain self-governance under the laws of Alberta. The body of the Act contained provisions protecting the land from seizure and prohibiting the Legislature from passing any bill that would jeopardize General Council's holding of the land or amend the *Metis Settlements Land Protection Act*. It then protected itself from change by requiring that any changes have the support of the majority of the members of each Settlement. There was one exception, which reflected the fact that this Act resulted from Ottawa's refusal to co-operate in the constitutional protection set out in the Accord. This exception, section 8 of the Act, allowed the Legislature to repeal the Act if the land is protected by the Constitution of Canada.

The *Metis Settlements Land Protection Act* was the second component of the land protection package. It prevented the alienation of any of the fee simple without the consent of a majority of Settlement members, prohibited the use of the fee simple for security of any kind, and established a special expropriation process. Most significantly, from an economic point of view, it also prohibited new mineral exploration and development in any Settlement area without the consent of the Settlement Council and the General Council. This gave the General Council and Settlements the leverage needed to negotiate the terms of future oil and gas development—a leverage potentially worth upwards of $100 million.

The *Metis Settlements Accord Implementation Act* legislated the financial commitments of the Accord, established and empowered a Transition Commission to oversee and assist in development for the first seven years, and "froze" the oil and gas lawsuit. The financial commitments, aimed at enabling the Settlements to "catch up and keep up" with their neighbours, totalled $310 million spread over 17 years. This was staged as $25 million of "catch up" money for each of the first seven years, followed by $10 million per year and matching grants for the next 10 years. The matching grants commitment encouraged Settlements to raise funds locally by promising to match such funds two-for-one during the first five years and one-for-one during the last five years.

The second function of this Act was transition management. To that end it constituted a Transition Commission and gave it responsibility for the task. The Commission consisted of the minister, the president of the General Council, and a commissioner appointed to manage the Commission's mandate. That mandate was sweeping. In the language of the time, the commissioner was a "cop, consultant and clerk." As a "cop," he monitored management practices and the administration of Accord funds; as a "consultant," he provided the advice and technical expertise needed to develop effective Settlement administrations; and as a "clerk," he was responsible for maintaining critical records such as the Métis Settlements Land Registry and the Members Register.

The third function of the *Accord Implementation Act* was to freeze the natural resources lawsuit. This was another compromise driven by Ottawa's refusal to co-operate in constitutionally entrenching the land. The Accord had been based on extinguishing the claims in the lawsuit in exchange for, among other things, the protection of the land in Canada's Constitution. When this became impossible, an interim approach was adopted. The *Accord Implementation Act* blocked any action on the existing litigation so long as the Legislature did not tamper with the *Constitution of Alberta Amendment Act, 1990*. Settlement leaders described this as "putting the lawsuit in the freezer." As a result, the litigation remains before the Courts in suspended animation, possibly in perpetuity. There is one way out, however—protection of the land in Canada's Constitution. If that happens, the Legislature can repeal the amendment to Alberta's constitution and, at that point the claims are extinguished. This limbo-like status has led to numerous efforts by the Métis and the province to complete the commitments of the Accord through Canadian constitutional protection. For example, this became part of the proposed amendment to the Constitution in the disastrous *Charlottetown Accord* process.

The new framework for self-governance was set out in the *Metis Settlements Act*. Given its significance, it is worth noting how it was developed. The draft included in the Accord was the product of hundreds of meetings between government representatives, Settlement members and Settlement Councils. Settlement members had been uneasy about the scope of the proposed changes. They wanted "evolution, not revolution." In response, leaders committed to making only those changes needed to achieve the primary goal—the land, power and money needed to build communities and preserve a Métis way of life. Given the antiquated nature of the old legislation, however, these changes were still far-reaching.

To reflect the evolutionary principle, the new legislation preserved the basic structure of the Settlement Council—five councillors with staggered terms to ensure continuity. The general assembly of councillors that had operated as the representative of the common interest of all Settlements was retained and given the name of "Métis Settlements General Council." As representative of the common interest, the General Council was given the task of holding the fee simple title to all Settlement lands, negotiating royalties and participation in oil and gas development, and passing "Policies"—laws applicable to all Settlements. To reduce transitional shock, existing regulations governing life on the Settlements were, as far as possible, carried over into the new regime as General Council Policies.

Community concerns about the complexity of initial drafts of the legislation led to a second guiding principle of the *Metis Settlements Act*: provide the tools, not the finished structure. The Act did not seek to establish a complete body of laws for self-government. Rather, it created a framework in which those laws could be developed, both "legislatively" and "judicially." The "legislative" component comes through the Policies passed by the General Council Assembly, and the Settlements bylaws passed in accordance with these Policies. The overarching nature of the Policies is made clear by stipulating that no bylaw can contravene a General Council Policy. In the draft legislation included in the Accord, Policies could be passed with the support of six Settlements. The Act passed in 1990, however, was different. It created a class of Policies—essentially everything important—that could only be made with the support of all eight Settlements. The resulting veto power eventually came to hamstring the General Council and make passage of effective legislation almost impossible. We will return to that later.

General Council law-making was also constrained by the need to consult with the minister when making a Policy and by a condition that the minister could, within a specified time, veto the Policy. This did not mean ministerial consent was needed—General Council Policies took effect unless the minister exercised a timely veto. As it happens, the ministerial veto power has never been used, largely because the consultation process and the threat of a possible veto is sufficient to generate a viable compromise.

The third constraint on creation of "legislative" law on the Settlements was the bylaw-making process. In municipalities, elected Councils pass bylaws. On the Settlements, however, ultimate democracy prevails. All bylaws must be approved at a general meeting of Settlement members. This requires a level of participation from Settlement members that is highly desirable in theory, but not always attainable in the day-to-day world of local government. Despite the inherent difficulties, and not without frustration, the Settlements appear to have made this level of democracy work.

The *Metis Settlements Act* also enabled the development of a "judicial" component of law-making—"Métis common law" arising from decisions of the Métis Settlements Appeal Tribunal. The Tribunal was one of the key elements of the self-governance structure created by the Act. The Act required most members of the Tribunal to be from the Settlements. The rationale was that their decisions would reflect a common sense and cultural perspective rooted in the experience of Settlement living—something not available in the regular court system. The Tribunal was given broad powers to resolve disputes on the Settlements. Although technically an administrative tribunal, its role in fleshing out the legislated framework made it more like a "Métis court." It was empowered to hear appeals from Council decisions on matters of land and membership. It could also, if parties agreed, resolve disputes on a wide range of matters affecting life in the Settlement areas. In the important area of oil and gas development, it could resolve disputes between oil companies, landowners, and the Settlement Council. In its first 14 years, the Tribunal has been called on to do all these things and more—resolving everything from builder's lien problems to disposition of estates. Appeals from the Tribunal are made to the Alberta Court of Appeal. Over the years it has almost always upheld Tribunal decisions.

Experience and Changes

Fourteen years have passed since the new era began on the Settlements. How well has it worked? That is a question the partners to the Accord are now working together to try to answer. A few preliminary results are clear. The land has been protected, although entrenchment in Canada's Constitution remains a mutual unrealized goal. The standard of living on the Settlements is markedly better. Housing and infrastructure—public buildings, roads, water, sewer, utilities—are roughly on par with neighbouring communities. That part of the "catch up" plan clearly worked. As for the goal of self-reliance, considerable progress has been made. The level of training and employment has improved significantly and paved roads into all Settlements have enabled many Settlement members to work in nearby towns or industry sites and still live on the Settlement. That said, the income and education levels still lag behind the provincial averages.

On the governance side, the Métis Settlements Appeals Tribunal has developed into a respected judicial body whose decisions have stood the test of community acceptance and challenges to the Alberta Court of Appeal. Based on the experience of the first nine years, in 1999 the General Council and the Province established a joint task force to determine if the jurisdiction of the Appeal Tribunal should be expanded. The task force, consisting of a Judge, a member of the Legislature, a Métis Elder, and others with experience in Settlement government, held hearings on all Settlements, with the oil and gas industry, and with members of the Tribunal and Settlement Councils. In June 1999, it presented its report to the minister and the president of the General Council.

The Task Force Report recommended changes that would significantly increase the role of the Tribunal as a court in the self-governance structure. It recommended that the Tribunal be given more powers, be made more independent, and have a larger share of Settlement members. The expanded powers would enable the Tribunal to deal with election disputes and councillor disqualifications. The *Metis Settlements Act* required these matters to be dealt with by the Courts, and this had created enormous costs for Settlements since council elections took place every year and many wound up in the Courts. To make the Tribunal more "court-like" the report recommended replacing the existing political appointment process by one in which a jointly constituted independent body would be responsible for appointing and removing Tribunal members. Finally the Report recommended the establishment of a form of Ombudsman to provide an outlet for Settlement member complaints about the practices of their local governments and administrations. The Report included draft amendments to the *Metis Settlements Act* to implement its recommendations. It would be almost five years, however, before the proposed amendments, essentially intact, were enacted.

On the legislative law-making front, the 1990s saw the General Council and Settlement Councils develop a broad range of Policies and bylaws—legislation covering the granting and managing of land interests, resource management, industrial taxation, public utilities, financial matters, and many other areas of collective and local government. After the initial progress, however, movement on the governance front began to bog down. It slowly became clear that the self-governance structure contained flaws that were hampering development. At the local level, the system of annually electing two of the five Settlement Councillors created constant political activity. And, as the makeup of the Council changed with elections, Settlement Council priorities shifted accordingly. This political instability made it difficult to carry out the long-term planning and management needed for orderly development.

At the collective level, there was an even more significant problem. The entire self-government structure was a hub-and-spoke design—the General Council being the "hub" that held the Settlement "spokes" together. The General Council held the land, managed the collective moneys and oil and gas rights, created the framework of laws for all Settlements, and represented the Settlements in dealing with the provincial and federal governments. For the model to work, the centre had to be strong and effective. That became increasingly difficult, since essentially all power resided in the Settlement Councils. They elected the president and executive of General Council and any Settlement could veto a proposed Policy. This meant the executive branch of the structure had to be careful not to offend its eight electors and the legislative branch could only pass legislation agreeable to all eight. The centre, created for leadership in the Act, was hamstrung and able to act only with heroic effort. It was sometimes even impossible to pass the Policies needed to transfer Accord funds received by General Council to the Settlements to meet their annual budgetary needs. In those cases, the minister was called on to pass a Regulation in place of the financial allocation Policy.

By 2003, it became clear to a number of Settlement leaders that changes were needed in the Act to address the structural problems. The minister,[91] herself an Aboriginal person from northern Alberta, was also anxious to solve the problems. She consequently initiated a process to propose amendments to the Act.

The Amendments in 2004

Although Settlement leaders generally accepted the need for changes in the Act, there was no consensus on how they would be generated. When the minister took the initiative of proposing a package of amendments, the immediate response was resistance. Although Settlement leaders could support most of the proposals, they were upset that the traditional process of developing new legislation "by means of conferences and negotiations" was not being followed. The minister had provided an opportunity for the General Council to respond to draft amendments, but this was not the old approach of jointly developing such proposals. Given the experience of the past several years, however, the minister was not optimistic about the success of such a process. When no clear response was forthcoming, she decided that, given the need for change, she would have to proceed without General Council support. The package of amendments, with the support of some individual Settlements, was introduced to the Legislature and given assent May 11, 2004.[92]

The amendments made significant changes to the Act. The requirement for unanimity in passing General Council Policies was removed and replaced by the "6 of 8" rule that had been in the Accord package. The minister was empowered to make temporary Regulations, replaceable by the General Council, in any area in which the General Council could make a Policy. The annual election of two councillors was gone, replaced by an election of the entire council every three years. The recommendations of the 1999 Task Force Report on the Appeals Tribunal were, by and large, implemented, although they have yet to be proclaimed. Some less significant amendments sought to improve clarity and resolve minor issues.

These amendments fixed the most obvious problems that had cropped up in translating the structure envisioned in the Accord into the real world of

Settlement governance. There were two other amendments, however, that addressed the bigger picture. The first was an introductory "purpose" section that provides a constitutional and historical context for the Act. Words from the preamble of the *Constitution of Alberta Amendment Act, 1990* are included that elevate the Act from the world of routine legislation and put it in its appropriate historical context. The second amendment addressed the process concerns raised by Settlement leaders. It created a mechanism for the General Council to make "self-governance advancement proposals"—proposals for restructuring the self-governance model to make it better able to meet Settlement needs. The General Council and the minister are currently engaged in a similar process to rethink those basic structures in preparation for the end of the Accord funding era in 2007.

Conclusion

In its centenary year, Alberta and its Métis citizens have reason to be proud of their history. The story of the Métis Settlements is one of the few lights in the dark landscape of government and aboriginal relations in Canada. It signals that a partnership approach can work where there is mutual respect and a shared commitment to pragmatic problem solving.

Alberta's Métis leaders in the 1930s were able to achieve what has proven impossible in all other provinces—a Métis land base. For 50 years after the 1938 legislation, the Settlements functioned in a way that met the primary objectives of the original founders. The land provided a base on which the Métis achieved a basic level of individual and collective economic security and the Act provided a legal framework in which elected Métis representatives carried out the basics of local self-government. Although short of the ideal, it was a first for Métis in Canada and it was a foundation on which to build.

Fifty years later, the Accord created a new and firmer foundation. The land is now protected in the Constitution of Alberta. The Settlements and their collective government pass laws governing the interests in land, the development of resources, the allocation of financial assets exceeding $100 million, and generally most aspects of Settlement life. The communities now have roads, services, and facilities on par with those of their neighbours. There are still economic and educational challenges that remain. The governance structures created in the Accord may need some work.

These are challenges, but certainly not as daunting as those faced by the "road allowance" people at the height of the great depression. The approach that worked then, and over the next half-century, can be expected to work again. "By means of conferences and negotiations," the leaders of the Province and the Settlements will address them and move on.

Notes

1. B. Slattery, "Understanding Aboriginal Rights," (1987) 66 *The Canadian Bar Review* 727 at 736.
2. In this context, "peoples" means an organized cultural group exercising some control over a geographically definable area.
3. In this paper the term "Indians" is often used instead of "First Nations peoples" because of the historical context.
4. *Dumont et al* v. *A. G. Canada*, [1988] 5 W.W.R. 193 (MCA).
5. Schedule 9, *Order of Her Majesty in Council Admitting Rupert's Land and the North-Western Territory into the Union*, June 23, 1870.
6. Paragraph 14 of the Imperial Order-in-Council of June 23, 1870.
7. *Dominion Lands Act* of 1879, s.125.
8. Document found in the Provincial Archives of Alberta. No specific identification available.
9. See for example B. Beal and R.C. Macleod, *Prairie Fire: The 1885 North-West Rebellion* (Edmonton: Hurtig Publishers, 1984).
10. For a detailed description of the St. Paul des Métis settlement see Joe Sawchuk, Patricia Sawchuk and Theresa Ferguson, *Métis Land Rights in Alberta: A Political History* (Edmonton: Metis Association of Alberta, 1981), ch.5.
11. Sawchuk, Sawchuk and Ferguson, *Métis Land Rights in Alberta*, 166.
12. Sawchuk, Sawchuk and Ferguson, *Métis Land Rights in Alberta*, 167.
13. Sawchuk, Sawchuk and Ferguson, *Métis Land Rights in Alberta*, 170. A large part of the colony's budget apparently went to building a Catholic boarding school, church and presbytery.
14. Sawchuk, Sawchuk and Ferguson, *Métis Land Rights in Alberta*, 178.
15. After the St. Paul des Métis experience, there appears to have been a shared wariness by Métis and provincial government leaders regarding the role of the church on future Métis colonies. As a result, when land was set aside under the *Metis Population Betterment Act* 30 years later, regulations were made (A.R. 110/60, s.13, 14) limiting the use of lands leased for church purposes and prohibiting the use of these lands for a school or residence.
16. Section 21 of the *Alberta Act*, S.C. 1905, c.3 provided: "All Crown lands, mines and minerals and royalties incidental thereto...shall continue to be vested in the Crown and administered by the Government of Canada for the purposes of Canada."
17. For example, in conjunction with negotiations on Treaty No.10, including land in Alberta, P.C. 1459 was issued on July 20, 1906 and P.C. 326 was issued on February 15, 1908. These

P.C.s are discussed in a report by one of the Claims Commissioners, N.O. Cote, dated December 3, 1929.

18. Clause 1 of the Memorandum of Agreement.

19. Sawchuk, Sawchuk and Ferguson, *Métis Land Rights in Alberta*, 187.

20. Sawchuk, Sawchuk and Ferguson, *Métis Land Rights in Alberta*, 187. The land at Fishing Lake was part of the Crown lands to be transferred to the Province under the *Natural Resources Transfer Agreement* of 1929.

21. For details of the lives and work of Brady and Norris, see Murray Dobbin, *The One-and-a-half Men* (Vancouver: New Star Books, 1981).

22. Sawchuk, Sawchuk and Ferguson, *Métis Land Rights in Alberta*, 187. For example, the questionnaire asked whether they owned livestock or machinery and whether they had ever received scrip or taken homestead.

23. See T. Pocklington, *Our Land—Our Culture—Our Future: The Government and Politics of the Alberta Métis Settlements*, unpublished manuscript, University of Alberta, 1988, p. 11.

24. These and other Alberta government documents referred to in this section are located in the Provincial Archives of Alberta.

25. Ibid.

26. Ibid.

27. Ibid.

28. Cohoon was a senior official in the Department of the Interior. It is not known if there is any connection between this memorandum, which is apparently a briefing memo, and the letter six days later from Murphy, the superintendent general of the Department of Indian Affairs.

29. See note 24.

30. See note 24.

31. (1897) AC 199 at 210.

32. Order-in-Council 706–35, Regulations Respecting the Locating of Half-Breed Land Scrip in the Province.

33. Judith Hill, "The Ewing Commission, 1935: A Case Study in Métis-Government Relations," (Honours Diss., Department of History, University of Alberta, 1977).

34. Section 91 of the *Constitution Act, 1867*.

35. A thorough discussion of the events surrounding the hearings is contained in the paper by Judith Hill, "The Ewing Commission." See also Sawchuk, Sawchuk and Ferguson, *Métis Land Rights in Alberta*, 190–96. For political aspects of the Commission's work see Pocklington, *Our Land—Our Culture—Our Future*. For a legal analysis see Douglas Sanders, "A Legal Analysis of the Ewing Commission and the Métis Colony System in Alberta," in H.W. Daniels, *The Forgotten People: Métis and Non-Status Indian Land Claims* (Ottawa: Native Council of Canada, 1978), 22.

36. Report of the Ewing Commission.

37. Douglas Sanders, *A Legal Analysis of the Ewing Commission and the Métis Colony System in Alberta* (Saskatoon: University of Saskatchewan Native Law Centre, 1978).

38. Report of the Ewing Commission. An interesting aspect of this definition is that it made lifestyle a factor in the definition of "Métis." This cultural identification approach was at one time adopted in the definition of "Métis" for national aboriginal rights discussions, and in the Métis Settlements legislation in Alberta. It was not present, however, in legislation passed as a result of the report, i.e., *The Metis Population Betterment Act*, S.A. 1938, ch. 6. There the definition adopted (s.2(a)) was: "Metis" means a person of mixed white and Indian blood but does not include either an Indian or a non-treaty Indian as defined in *The Indian Act*."

39. Report of the Ewing Commission, p. 13.

40. Pocklington, *Our Land—Our Culture—Our Future*.

41. Report of the Ewing Commission.

42. The original drafts of the Act were reportedly prepared by Métis leaders Pete Tompkins and Joe Dion.

43. Sawchuk, Sawchuk and Ferguson, *Métis Land Rights in Alberta*, 198. Other Métis elders confirmed this in discussions with the author.

44. *The Metis Population Betterment Act*, S.A. 1938, c.6.

45. *The Metis Population Betterment Act*, S.A. 1938, c.6, s.5.

46. *The Metis Population Betterment Act*, S.A. 1938, c.6, s.4.

47. *The Metis Population Betterment Act*, S.A. 1938, c.6, s.4.

48. This constitution and bylaws was adopted by the government as Order-in-Council 285/40. It was modified slightly by the Settlements shortly thereafter, and the modification adopted as Order-in-Council 947/41. These two Order-in-Councils became Alberta Regulation 634/57.

49. Ibid.

50. *The Metis Population Betterment Act, 1940*, S.A. 1940, c.6

51. *An Act to amend The Metis Population Betterment Act*, S.A. 1952, c.54

52. *The Metis Population Betterment Act*, S.A. 1938, c.6, s.4(2)

53. *An Act to amend The Metis Population Betterment Act*, S.A. 1952, c.54, s.2(b)

54. The Settlements and the government disagreed on the legitimacy of this Regulation. The Settlements maintained that the minister's powers were limited to approving or disapproving a change in a Settlement's constitution and bylaws once it has been approved by a Settlement. That was the process followed in the original "Constitution of Settlement Associations" adopted in 1940 (Order-in-Council 285–40), and an amendment approved in 1941 (Order-in-Council 947–41). The original Constitution as amended became A.R. 634/57. The Settlements said they were not consulted on the changes that led to A.R. 56/66.

55. *Regulations Governing the Constitution of Settlement Associations*, A.R. 56/66, s. 3.

56. Sawchuk, Sawchuk and Ferguson, *Métis Land Rights in Alberta*, 200.

57. Order-in-Council 192–60, dated February 10, 1960, rescinded the Order-in-Councils that had set aside land for the Wolf Lake Settlement Association. Most of the members were moved to other settlements, and many became members at Fishing Lake.

58. Sawchuk, Sawchuk and Ferguson, *Métis Land Rights in Alberta*, 200.

59. *Keg River Metis Settlement Association et al v. Her Majesty the Queen in Right of Alberta*, No. 83520, Court of Queen's Bench of Alberta, Judicial District of Edmonton. In their statement of claim the Métis maintained that the action was contrary to the wishes of the members of the Settlement Association and was not within the authority provided by the *Metis Betterment Act*, c.202, R.S.A. 1955, in force at the time. This was part of the litigation "suspended" in the 1990 legislation package.

60. *The Report of the Metis Task Force Upon The Metis Betterment Act, Metis Settlements and the Metis Rehabilitation Branch*, Research & Planning Division, Human Resources Development Authority, Province of Alberta, February 1972.

61. *Report of the Metis Task Force*, 8.

62. *Report of the Metis Task Force*, 13.

63. The enabling Regulation was A.R. 112/60.

64. The proper name for the fund under the Regulation was the "Métis Population Betterment Trust Account Part I." It was commonly referred to simply as the "Trust Fund."

65. A.R. 112/60, s.1(a).

66. The statement of claim in *Poitras et al.* v. *Attorney-General for Alberta* was filed on July 29, 1968.
67. *Poitras et al.* v. *Attorney-General for Alberta*, (1969) 7 D.L.R.(3d) 161 (A.S.C). The Court held that the plaintiff had not complied with the requirements of the *Proceedings Against the Crown Act*, 1959 that required that permission be obtained from the lieutenant-governor-in-council before an action could be brought. The judge was critical of this requirement and on taking power Premier Lougheed had the legislation changed.
68. Sawchuk, Sawchuk and Ferguson, *Métis Land Rights in Alberta*, 200.
69. The early leaders were Lawrence Desjarlais, Maurice L'Hirondelle, Adrian Hope, Sam Johnson, and Richard Poitras.
70. A statement of claim on behalf of the eight Settlement Associations was filed on February 5, 1974 in the Supreme Court of Alberta (*Keg River Métis Settlement Association et al* v. *Her Majesty the Queen in Right of Alberta*, Action No. 83520). On July 6, 1977, a second statement of claim was filed as a class action by Maurice L'Hirondelle on behalf of the Settlement Associations and their members (*Maurice L'Hirondelle et al* v. *Her Majesty the Queen in Right of Alberta*, Action No. 100945). The two actions were joined and amended several times after the initial filing.
71. *Report of the Metis Task Force*, 12.
72. The name of this agency was subsequently changed to the "Metis Development Branch," and then to the "Metis Settlements Branch." It has also made the transition from a branch of the Department of Social Services to the Department of Municipal Affairs and eventually to the Department of Aboriginal Affairs and Northern Development.
73. The main federal sources were the Department of Employment and Immigration and the Department of the Secretary of State. Most Settlements also worked directly with half a dozen provincial departments and agencies responsible for housing, for roads, for social services, for cultural development, for grade school education and for advanced education. In addition, most Settlements contracted directly with oil and gas companies for work related to oil and gas exploration and development in their Settlement areas.
74. In the Report's summary, the third recommendation was "Rewrite the *Metis Betterment Act* to emphasize development at all levels of Metis Society."
75. Alberta. Office of the Ombudsman, *Report by the Provincial Ombudsman, Dealing with the Removal of Files from Metis Settlements on Monday, June 18/1979* (Edmonton: Office of the Ombudsman, 1979). For more details on the Report see Sawchuk, Sawchuk and Ferguson, *Métis Land Rights in Alberta*, 209.
76. Order-in-Council 718/80.
77. Order-in-Council 422/82 established the "Joint Committee to Review the *Metis Betterment Act*," gave it a mandate, named the government's representatives and the Chairman, and specified that the "deliberations and recommendations of the Committee shall be without prejudice" to the Settlements-Province litigation.
78. The president of the Federation throughout the work of the Committee was Elmer Ghostkeeper. Although Mr. L'Hirondelle, the past president, served on the Committee for some time, he had other obligations as the chief witness for the Settlements in the litigation. Eventually, the next president of the Federation, Randall Hardy, took his place.
79. O.C 422/82.
80. *Foundations for the Future of Alberta's Métis Settlements*, Report of the MacEwan Joint Métis-Government Committee to Review *The Metis Betterment Act* and Regulations to the Honourable J.G.J. Koziak, Minister of Municipal Affairs, July 12, 1984.

81. The events relating to aboriginal rights and the patriation of the Constitution are well documented. See for example David C. Hawkes, *Negotiating Aboriginal Self-Government: Developments Surrounding the 1985 First Ministers' Conference*, Aboriginal Peoples and Constitutional Reform, Background Paper No. 7 (Kingston, ON: Institute of Intergovernmental Relations, 1985); or Douglas E. Sanders, "Aboriginal Peoples and the Constitution," *Alberta Law Review* XIX, no.3 (1981): 410.

82. *Métisism: A Canadian Identity*, p. 17.

83. Originally *The Alberta Act*, 1905, 4–5 Edw.VII, c.3, (Can.), this Act is identified as part of the Constitution of Canada by s.52(2)(b) of the *Canada Act, 1982*.

84. For details of the 1985 conference see Hawkes, *Negotiating Aboriginal Self-Government*. The comments regarding Premier Lougheed are based on personal discussions at the time with the president of the Federation, Joseph Courtepatte.

85. Document in the archives of the Métis Settlements General Council.

86. Alberta *Hansard*, June 3, 1985, p. 1288.

87. Archives of the Métis Settlements General Council.

88. Matters relating to the mines and minerals were to be left to the Court's decision in the natural resources litigation.

89. First Ministers' Conference, March 26, 1987, Proceedings transcript.

90. For a detailed analysis of the Métis Settlements legislation see Catherine Bell, "Métis Self-Government: The Alberta Settlement Model" in J. Hylton, *Aboriginal Self-Government in Canada*, 2nd ed. (Saskatoon: Purich Publishing, 1999), 329.

91. The Honourable Pearl Calahason.

92. *Metis Settlements Amendment Act, 2004*.

Thirteen

The Perfect Storm
The National Energy Program and the Failure of Federal-Provincial Relations

DOUGLAS OWRAM

> "Who speaks for Canada?" Mr. Trudeau asked rhetorically.... "We all do," replied Mr. Lougheed.[1]

The National Energy Program (NEP) occupies a central place in Alberta mythology. Together with the freight rates of the CPR, the failure to transfer Crown lands in 1905 and the use of disallowance in the 1930s, the NEP symbolizes eastern greed and the need for western vigilance. So powerful is the symbol that even on the day Pierre Trudeau died, the obituary in the Calgary Herald ignored the constitution, FLQ and 1980 referendum to focus on bitter memories of his "much reviled federalist foray into the oilpatch," a foray that "drained away billions of oil and gas coffers from the West into federal coffers."[2]

The commentary, some 20 years later, echoes the harsh debate of one of the most confrontational federal-provincial battles in the history of the country. When the NEP was introduced in late 1980, it was hailed in the east as a "comprehensive energy program that can pay enormous dividends for this nation in the years ahead. It deserves the support of all Canadians."[3] In the West, it was alternately attacked as a "nefarious conspiracy between Quebec, Ontario and the Liberals"[4] and lamented as an economic disaster. "The real gamble," warned the Edmonton *Journal* "is that given Ottawa's bent towards confiscation and nationalization, the industry and the investment community will still feel it is worthwhile to develop Canada's oil and gas."[5]

The subsequent collapse of oil exploration and the end of the Alberta boom only confirmed the dire predictions of disaster in the minds of Albertans. Not only was the east greedy, it was stupid. Yet from a federal perspective, the NEP was necessary in a time of energy crisis and a policy that was wrecked as much by Alberta greed as by the unpredictable trend of energy prices.

Some excellent work has been done on the policy development of the NEP. In particular, Doern and Toner's 1985 book, *The Politics of Energy*, traces in some detail the way in which both sides evolved policies and counter-policies.[6] However, it is useful to view the NEP from a different angle. Whether one thinks the NEP was reasonable or not, it marked, on all sides, a spectacular failure in process. The decision by the federal government to proceed unilaterally in October 1980 signalled failure after years of negotiations and marked a low point in Alberta-federal relations. Pierre Trudeau headed west to accuse westerners generally of "hysteria."[7] Peter Lougheed took to the airwaves and talked in home-spun fashion about the struggle of the "pioneers and fore-fathers who fought to have resource ownership rights."[8] Westerners wrote letters to the editor calling for separation as "inevitable" and before the confrontation, the first openly separatist MLA had been elected in Alberta.

This article will focus on the reasons for the collapse of federal-provincial negotiations up to the announcement of the NEP. The failure was a landmark, if a negative one, in the complex history of the relationships that mark our federal system. It marked a particular era in these relations and affected the way they were considered in the future. As the nation moves into increasingly loaded discussion on another important federal-provincial issue—health-care—it is worthwhile analyzing the forces that converged in the late 1970s to create what can only be described as "the perfect storm" of federal-provincial diplomacy.

Several forces converged to create the storm. Had any of them been absent, a different and less confrontational result might have been anticipated. These were: (i) the existing balance of power in federal-provincial relations, (ii) the related but more specific issue of constitutional ambiguity, (iii) the importance of the issue, (iv) the way in which energy became a symbol for broader interests and disagreements, (v) the personalities, and (vi) the political situation. As will be argued, in each case the ingredients worked against a negotiated solution.

Ingredient 1: Federal-Provincial Relationships on the Eve of the Energy Crisis

In its simplest form, federalism is a system in which layers of government divide authority and responsibility in such a way that the other level cannot unilaterally change that division. Federalism was a natural arrangement for

Canada. The fact that Confederation was a merging of existing colonies and the sheer size of what was about to be a transcontinental nation made such an arrangement natural. Most importantly, though, federalism was necessary in Canada to manage linguistic and cultural divisions. For the francophones of Canada East and the Anglophones of Canada West, Confederation and the federal system was in part an escape from each other. To put it more positively, both cultures were allowed some degree of local control that enhanced the opportunity to preserve cultural and linguistic characteristics. This would fit a classic definition of federalism's purpose: to allow minorities some degree of control within a national majoritarian system.[9]

Initially, the relations between provinces and federal government within this system seemed well-defined. A series of devices within the *British North America Act* gave the federal government the preponderance of power.[10] Clauses such as the ability to disallow any provincial act, the invocation of the national interest under varied circumstances and even the appointment of the lieutenant-governors demonstrated the federal power. This was deliberate at a time when the American civil war demonstrated to many the follies of excessive local power. Moreover, with the imperial ties inherent in dominion status, Great Britain was available to mediate disputes that might arise.

By the latter half of the twentieth century, however, the assumptions of 1867 were obsolete. Federal powers had been weakened by a series of court decisions. More importantly, changing expectations in key areas of provincial jurisdiction—education and health—made the provinces much more important than had been anticipated in 1867. The idea that the federal government could simply override provincial interests and areas of jurisdiction had, in the process, become more circumscribed. The power of disallowance was last used against the early Social Credit government in, significantly, Alberta. National emergencies like the war gave the federal government temporary authority that were more or less accepted by all. Generally, however, provincial legitimacy and provincial authority had gained considerable ground since Confederation.[11]

The new reality required new means for negotiating differences between the levels of government. However, federal-provincial diplomacy evolved in a particular manner for a couple of reasons. First, Canada as of the 1970s did not have an amending formula and therefore no certainty as to how constitutional ambiguities might be resolved.[12] Second, the idea of the intraparty resolution of issues (mediation between national and local issues at the federal level in this case) as the political scientists have termed it, had never fully developed. The Canadian senate was regionally based, but lacked legitimacy. Canadian federal parties did not operate as adjuncts of provincial parties and therefore were not well equipped to serve as mediators between levels of government. The absence of an effective system of regional balances at the federal level accentuated the role of the provinces as the guardians of the particular region or minority interest.[13]

Almost by default, therefore, direct negotiations between the provinces and the federal government became the standard means of mediating national and local interests. Further, though a secretariat was established under Edgar Gallant in the 1960s and though provinces began to develop versions of inter-governmental affairs units, the tendency of federal-provincial diplomacy was to move quickly to what has been termed executive federalism. Premiers and prime ministers kept a close watch on anything that might have significant policy or political implications.

These practices were more or less entrenched by the end of World War 2. However, there were also some recent trends that affected the way discussions on energy developed in the 1970s. First, federal-provincial diplomacy became a central feature of Canadian political life during the 1960s. The post-war growth of the welfare state required almost continuous federal-provincial discussions on the allocation of duties and resources. This was especially the case after 1960 when the Quiet Revolution in Quebec linked a growing sense of nationalism with a more activist state. Furthermore, Quebec nationalism soon generated a whole new federal-provincial industry—constitutional politics. Growing discontent in Quebec led Premier William Robarts of Ontario to break with precedent and call a "Confederation of Tomorrow" Conference in 1967. By 1968, Premier Daniel Johnson of Quebec was publicly calling for a new constitution for Canada.[14] The federal government was forced to respond and from 1968–1971 a fairly intense attempt to repatriate and restructure the Canadian constitution took place. The failure of the Victoria proposal in 1971 slowed events somewhat. Nonetheless, during the entire discussion around energy there was a parallel process that looked at fundamental law. Inevitably the two issues became intertwined.

Second, by the late 1960s, the provinces had asserted an unprecedented degree of authority and legitimacy. Speaking to the Canadian Political Science Association in 1967, federal Deputy Minister Al Johnson concluded that in recent years "the forces of diversity have gathered force relative to those of unity."[15] Practically every political scientist of these years agreed. As Donald Smiley wrote 10 years later, "The story of Canadian federalism from the late

1950s onward is that of the relative weakening of the power of the national government and the strengthening of that of the provinces."[16] The heady days of federal dominance that carried over from World War 2 were gone. The Quiet Revolution, affluence in western Canada and the importance of the provincial jurisdiction in health and welfare all pointed to the new importance of the provinces.

Underpinning this growing provincial weight was growing expertise. Until well after the war, the federal government had a civil service that in competence, scale and resources could rarely be matched by the provinces. That was changing however. A symbolic event occurred in 1964 during federal-provincial negotiations on a contributory pension plan. The federal officials flew off to Quebec City to meet with the Lesage government. Rather than being over-awed by the federal plans and expertise, however, the Lesage officials produced a plan that was "better in virtually all respects than Ottawa's."[17] Tense negotiations followed as federal civil servants struggled to regain some control of the plan and to ensure a semblance of national planning.[18]

The dramatic change in Quebec was mirrored to a greater or lesser degree in at least the larger provinces through the 1960s and 1970s. Nowhere outside of Quebec, however, was the change as dramatic as in Alberta. Both the size of the Alberta civil service and its ability to operate on national issue remained limited through the 1960s. Social Credit had competent individuals, but its populist and rural roots worked against any rapid expansion of a civil service elite. However, the election of the Lougheed government in 1971 marked a fundamental shift. In a manner reminiscent of the Quiet Revolution, Lougheed argued that Alberta needed a more sophisticated and systematic approach to planning. This meant that it needed an equally sophisticated and systematic civil service. Between 1969 and 1979 the Alberta public service expanded from just over 17,000 to some 32,300.[19] Even such dramatic growth understates the way in which a new, highly-educated and committed coterie of experts developed in what became known as the "province building" departments, including the creation of a Department of Federal and Intergovernmental Affairs in 1972.[20]

When oil prices climbed sharply in 1973, a new era opened in issues of resource control. It did so in an environment of federal-provincial relations that was not at all as they had been envisioned at the time of Confederation and very different than even 15 years before.

Ingredient 2: Constitutional Ambiguity

The debate around resource revenue would still have occurred had the constitution been clearer; however, the discussion would have been different. As it was, both sides believed their position had sufficient constitutional force to press the case. The reality, though, was that both sides had some ammunition but not enough to resolve matters. As John Helliwell and Anthony Scott warned at the time,

> the constitution gives both levels of government substantial regulatory and revenue-raising powers over natural resources. Each level has substantially enough power to thwart the other, and therefore has insufficient power to proceed independently.... Furthermore, each government has powers that look so strong in isolation that there is a temptation for each to adopt positions that are so polarized as to admit only defeat or victory, thus threatening the search for compromise.[21]

Alberta liked to believe that the issue was not ambiguous at all. First of all, the *British North America Act* had assigned the ownership of resources to the provinces under sections 109 and 92. Further, for Alberta the issue had tremendous symbolic importance. When the province was created in 1905 the federal government withheld control of resources. It was not until 1930, after most settlement had taken place, that the federal government conferred on Alberta and Saskatchewan ownership that had always existed in other provinces.[22] History meant that it was a matter of faith "among both young and old in Alberta that the natural resources belong to the province."[23]

With this history and constitutional grounding, Alberta took an uncompromising view of resource control through the 1970s. Thus, to Merv Leitch, the minister of energy, the matter was clear: "In my view the key to the answer to nearly all questions of jurisdiction over natural resources lies in the ownership given to the provinces by the *British North America Act*." This answer encompassed the provincial right to

> decide whether to develop them, decide by whom, when and how they are going to be developed, determine the degree of processing that's to take place within the province, dispose of them upon conditions that they only be used in a certain way, or in a certain place, or by certain

people, determine the price at which they or the products resulting from their processing will be sold.[24]

It was a comprehensive control that could be overridden only through the most draconian federal application of power. By the late 1970s, the province was recommending, further, that the constitution be amended to repeal most of those federal overriding powers.[25]

The federal government, not surprisingly, saw the issue as more ambiguous. Though all administrations recognized provincial ownership of resources, there was also a counter-argument that rested on more general federal powers to legislate for the well-being of all Canadians. In the broadest sense, the federal government could appeal to such overriding clauses as "peace, order and good government" under Section 91 of the *British North America Act* or even to powers of disallowance. More specifically, however, federal power to regulate interprovincial and international trade under Section 91.3 gave sufficient room to intervene without resorting to such highly contentious powers.

There was one issue that was on the boundary between the constitution and politics. Alberta continually asked why energy should be the focus of federal intervention when other natural resources were left in the hands of the provinces. If federal power existed for oil, suggested Leitch, then it also implied the right to intervene in all resources: "If that [export] tax is valid for oil then there is no reason why it isn't valid with respect to timber leaving British Columbia, [or] iron, copper and other minerals leaving Quebec and Ontario."[26]

The federal government, for its part, was sensitive to this notion that one province was being singled out in a discriminatory fashion. It also believed, however, that petroleum was so essential that it was different and thus justified the overriding of provincial control in the name of Canada. As federal minister Donald Macdonald put it in 1975, the federal government was "exercising the right of all Canadians to a share in what is provincial but also Canadian wealth."[27] When the Department of Energy, Mines and Resources released its NEP program, it repeatedly returned to the notion that "energy has always been a special case" and that energy is a "national patrimony."[28]

Ingredient 3: Importance

The federal argument about the unique importance of energy was relevant. It was also an obstacle to any solution. The stakes were simply too high.

This had not always been the case. Until 1973, cheap oil was the norm and Canadian oil was barely competitive with the large reservoirs in the Middle East and the United States. Delivery systems were just being developed. Overall, there was much reason for federal-provincial co-operation. The Social Credit government needed federal assistance in developing delivery systems and the federal government wanted to encourage Canadian oil development. As for natural gas, it was barely relevant outside of western Canada. Once again, delivery was a problem and the price of the product did not justify the investment.

In this atmosphere, the constitutional ambiguities were manageable. The Social Credit government in Alberta took comfortable royalties off the production of oil and worked with the federal government to develop a national plan. In 1961 the result was the creation of the National Oil Policy and the famous two-tiered system. The West and Ontario got (slightly) higher priced western oil and the east got the cheaper imported oil. Both sides had as their main goal the production of an oil industry. Neither conservation nor price were primary issues.[29]

Everything changed in the 1970s. First, in 1973 the Arab states responded to the Yom Kippur war by putting new life into OPEC. International prices, long stagnant in real terms, rose from $2.50 a barrel in 1972 to $5.00 a barrel by 1974 and to $15 by 1978. Then, in 1979 the Iranian revolution drove prices to $20 a barrel and by the time the NEP was implemented, they were on their way to $40. In seven years, the price of oil had increased 15-fold and, even in the inflationary decade of the 1970s, had increased in real terms three and a half times.

There was also a sense that the rising prices foreshadowed a long-term problem. Though the prices were, in retrospect, driven by short term events, the sense of concern was pervasive by the latter part of the decade. Both oil companies and the federal government argued the point vigorously. In 1977, for example, the Department of Energy, Mines and Resources was arguing that "the world energy situation could well enter an extremely critical phase within the next ten or fifteen years."[30] By 1980 the same department foresaw $60 oil by 1990.[31] By the late 1970s, every speech, political position and revenue forecast presumed, at the very least, constant prices in real terms.[32] In such a scenario the long-term implications of resource control became central to the thinking of both federal and provincial governments.

Adding to the impact of the price change was the fact that Canadian energy consumption had also changed. Well into the post-war years, coal had been

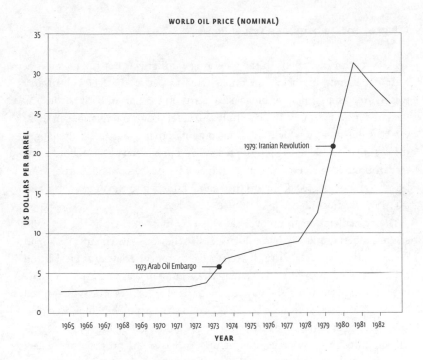

WORLD OIL PRICE (NOMINAL)

1979: Iranian Revolution

1973 Arab Oil Embargo

the most important source of energy. However, by the time energy prices had begun to increase, changes in technology and low prices meant that petroleum and natural gas between them accounted for approximately 60 per cent of Canadian energy consumption. By the time of the NEP, the percentage was closer to 70.[33]

The rise in prices changed the goals and perspectives of the various parties involved. There was no longer any need to nurture Canadian energy production. Demand was no longer the issue. Price and supply was. For governments the risks and rewards were now huge. In Alberta, the flow of revenue to the province increased from a little under a quarter billion dollars in 1968 to nearly four billion by the late 1970s, due both to higher prices and a more aggressive royalty regime.[34] Oil and natural gas royalties were far more important than provincial income tax to the provincial budget. The federal government's ability to gain access to petroleum and natural gas revenue was more limited and, indeed, was crucial to the evolution of the debate. Even the limited access it had through an export tax was persuasive of the potential importance to its own coffers. By 1978, oil and gas revenue to governments exceeded $5 billion a year. The financial stakes were enormous.

Ingredient 4: Energy as a Test of Power

Yet the central ingredient in the emerging conflict was not financial, or at least not merely financial. An understated aspect of the NEP controversy was its role as a symbol for broader concerns on the part of both parties. As Richard Simeon has noted in his study of federal-provincial relations in these years, the degree to which an issue contains other agendas often changes the nature of the debate. Both the federal and provincial governments made resource control a test of authority and, as with many symbolic battles, this led to a greater degree of importance being attached to the outcome. It also led to a win or lose mentality.

The symbolism on the provincial side was most explicit at the time. In essence Alberta, and to a lesser degree Saskatchewan, saw the increase in oil and gas prices as an opportunity to resolve historical grievances by shifting the balance of power within Canada. The argument was expressed in many forms through the 1970s but may be summarized as follows. The West evolved within a national political system that favoured the populous Ontario-Quebec axis. A sense of regional identity developed against a backdrop of grievances against railway development, freight rates, tariffs and a litany of other issues. Further, the small population of the West made it impossible to control federal institutions. The alternative was to look to the provincial power and provincial wealth as a buttress against the central Canadian majority.

These premises were well understood in Alberta even before the 1973 price shocks. Resources, however, became the perfect symbol of this broader sense of discrimination. The federal delay in transferring these resources to Alberta and Saskatchewan between 1905 and 1930 was one of the key historical mythologies of grievance. The fact that, once again, the federal government was eyeing western resources to protect eastern consumers linked the debate over natural resources to a much broader sense of western identity. In 1977, the sense of imbalance was summed up in an often-repeated passage by Premier Allan Blakeney of Saskatchewan: "We in the West find it passing strange that the national interest emerges only when we when we are talking about Western *resources* and Eastern *benefits*. If oil, why not iron ore and steel products? If natural gas, why not copper?"[35] In his television address after the imposition of the NEP, Premier Lougheed echoed the thought as a definite statement of western grievance: "If the oil was owned by the province of Ontario,...we would, in fact, in terms of the history of Canada, be paying world prices for our oil today."[36]

The struggle over resource control took on added importance because of a sense of urgency. By the late 1970s there a growing fear of impending scarcity added to the chorus of concern over high prices. Recurring forecasts by government, oil companies and conservationists all talked of a not-too-distant future when the world was going to run short of petroleum resources.[37] For many, a taste of this future was demonstrated by long gasoline line-ups south of the border and conservation measures both in North America and Europe. By 1979, a plurality of Canadians believed there would be a serious shortage of energy within five years.[38]

For the Alberta government, the assessments of declining oil reserves had a particular implication. As Lougheed put it to the Legislature in 1973, "For resource based Alberta, it is not an energy crisis, it is a time of energy opportunity."[39] However, it was an opportunity with a limited horizon. Somehow, before reserves declined and while massive funds continued to flow, Alberta had to restructure its economy, had to shift the fiscal balance within Confederation to ensure that in the future the province would be subject neither to the volatility of the natural resource sector nor the whims of economic policies designed by majorities elsewhere in Canada. For Albertans, fiscal invulnerability was an essential component in overcoming perceived regional discrimination.

To do this the Lougheed government embarked on an ambitious program of economic diversification. The principle was simple, though the achievement of it would prove difficult. As Lougheed emphasized in a 1974 federal-provincial conference:

> over the course of the next decade, Alberta must diversify and broaden the base of its economy and become less dependent upon the sale of unprocessed natural resources.... Take the economic rents created by rising oil prices and pour them into infrastructure, direct investments and tax reductions in order to move Alberta beyond a resource economy.[40]

It was not long before concrete examples started to appear. In 1974, for example, Alberta purchased controlling interest in Pacific Western Airlines. In 1976, one third of resource revenue was directed into the new Alberta Heritage fund with an explicit goal of working to diversify the Alberta economy.

From Alberta's perspective, therefore, the "excessive" flows of revenue seemed essential because they were limited in duration, because they were justified given past grievances and they were necessary given the provincial agenda. As Lougheed wrote to Trudeau in 1974, "we are concerned about a depleting—a rapidly depleting—resource. We view the proceeds from this resource as a capital asset, the proceeds of which must be reinvested if this province is to maintain its economic stability."[41] Winning the energy battle became nothing less than winning Alberta's rightful place within the future Canada.

The federal government talked less explicitly in terms of the "other agenda," preferring the rhetoric of equity to all Canadians. As Energy, Mines and Resources put it, "there must be recognition of a national claim—a claim by all Canadians—to a share in these revenues and benefits."[42] However, though this may be true, it is incomplete. For various reasons the federal government wanted to assert power and increase its revenue.

First, if Alberta was rich the federal government was increasingly poor. Beginning in the early 1970s federal expenditures had begun to outstrip revenues. Expensive welfare programs, politically based projects, inflation and a sluggish economy all contributed to a problem that was moving from incidental and intermittent to structural and recurrent. By the time of the NEP, the federal deficit was well over $9 billion.[43] There was, as yet, no public or political willingness to tackle the problem through expenditure reductions and an increase in revenue seemed the only way out. To make matters worse, the federal government was increasingly faced with additional costs brought on by the energy crisis itself. In such an atmosphere, it is not surprising that for the federal government revenue was as important as consumer prices. "The Government of Canada has a legitimate claim to a share of the energy industry's revenues, to support its energy initiatives, and its broad economic management responsibilities."[44]

Revenue is concrete and easy to explain. More abstract, but maybe more important, was the desire to reassert federal supremacy over a recalcitrant province. For several reasons, the federal government was fully aware of what political scientists were saying at the time—that provincial power was growing and that federal authority was weakening. Confederation seemed at stake.

Most importantly, Quebec nationalism had taken a new and dangerous turn in 1976 with the election of the Parti Quebecois as an avowedly separatist government. For Pierre Trudeau and his government, this threat to national unity was the single dominant issue facing the government. Between 1976 and 1980, as Alberta sparred on one side for greater provincial power and revenue, Quebec moved toward a referendum on sovereignty. The federal success in the referendum in May 1980 can be seen as one part of a two-step process to "rebalance" federalism. The second step came with the NEP in November.

Exacerbating the mood was the repeated failure of federal-provincial conferences to come up with a new constitution. The failure of the Victoria Charter in 1971 had led to many futile attempts to find a means by which all parties could move ahead. For the federal government, and particularly for Pierre Trudeau, the renewal of the constitution was both desirable in its own right and a vital weapon in the battle with Quebec separatism. By the late 1970s, the resistance of several premiers to change was beginning to be dismissed as mere obstinacy. The Liberals decided to take a harder line. "We have tried governing through consensus," complained Trudeau looking back on the NEP. "We have tried governing by being generous to the provinces...and that was never enough. So we have changed."[45]

In such an atmosphere the debate over energy took on symbolic connotations from the federal perspective as it had from the provincial. The NEP was not just a fiscal arrangement but, like the constitution and Quebec referendum, a vital test of federal power. As Trudeau noted shortly after the introduction of the program,

> There was a slippage of Canada towards, is it a community of communities or is it ten quasi-autonomous states? The slippage has been going on for a couple of decades now and I feel that they've [sic] had to be reversed and I think at least the swing of the pendulum has been stopped with the energy agreements, with the constitutional agreements.[46]

The specific agenda had become cluttered with wider issues, with symbolism and, indeed, to some degree became portrayed as a struggle about the very nature of Canada.

Ingredient 5: The Protagonists

Personalities intrude upon issues and the stronger the personalities, the more likely they will intrude strongly. Though Lougheed and Trudeau were far from the only actors in the NEP battles, their presence made the battle all the fiercer. Both had control over their own team, had strong personalities and, as we have seen, a strong sense of mission. In terms of their own experiences there were, on the surface, several similarities between the two. Both were well educated, from elite or near-elite families. Both shared the profession of law and were logical, determined and rational negotiators. Both had the reputations of being extremely intelligent and often faced accusations of arrogance.[47]

Yet for all these similarities there were also profound differences, especially in the way their personal experiences shaped their view of Canada. For if, as has been argued, Canada is a nation of "limited identities," both men reflected different parts of those multiple identities. Peter Lougheed's western roots were extremely deep. In a province with so much recent in-migration, Lougheed's family was exceptional. His grandfather had come West as the CPR was building across the prairies. On his grandmother's side the roots went even deeper. His grandmother was a Hardisty, a family with fur-trade and Métis roots. Lougheed's personal experiences accentuated his western perspective. Educated at the University of Alberta, he was a member of the Edmonton Eskimos football team and president of the Student Union. Unlike many of Alberta's elite, Lougheed's vantage point and his experience remained western and Albertan. A year spent obtaining a Harvard MBA did not fundamentally change that fact.[48]

There was one other way in which Lougheed was very much a westerner. His biography opens with the story of a young Peter observing the sale of goods from the home of his grandparents. "Beaulieu," as it was known, had once accommodated royalty, but was now sold off at low prices in the midst of economic collapse.[49] The economic volatility of the west was, to Peter Lougheed, very much a personal experience and added to his determination to take advantage of opportunity to change the underlying structures of Alberta.

Pierre Trudeau, in contrast, was very much a product of Montreal. Classically educated, from a bilingual and bicultural family and educated at the Université de Montreal, his own experiences reflected the interface of French and English cultures that typified that city. Unlike Lougheed, the younger Trudeau did spend considerable time outside his region, but his preference was to look outside the country rather than within it. Post-graduate study in Boston, Paris and London was supplemented by considerable travel. Trudeau was self-consciously an internationalist in the same way that Lougheed was self-consciously a westerner.

There was one thing they shared. Both were used to success. They had been exceptionally successful academically, athletically and socially. What was once said of Lougheed applied to both: "He was the golden boy."[50] Both were extremely competitive and neither accepted losing very readily. Given the other circumstances surrounding the energy debates of the 1970s, the two individuals were superb champions of their cause. Neither, however, was the sort to yield for the sake of peace.

Ingredient 6: The Political Situation

Politics, in the broadest sense, requires an eye on voter expectations, on party factions and on potential alliances. "Governments do not operate in a vacuum. They must bear in mind other groups—audiences—which form their environment and on which they depend for support."[51] In Canada, a tradition of brokerage politics has encouraged accommodation to different interests and therefore to the necessity of compromise. Observers of federal-provincial relations have emphasized that these characteristics apply to that arena as well. Multiple interests both within the federal government and between the provinces require flexibility. The result, to cite Simeon, is that "with some exceptions, the federal-provincial negotiations are conducted in a spirit of harmony. Seldom do policy differences become personal differences."[52] The NEP was one of those exceptions. Political forces, in this instance, worked against accommodation.

First, Alberta confronted not only the federal government but an hostile Ontario. The industrial heartland of Canada had been hard hit by rising energy prices and was increasingly strident in its demands that the economy be protected from price shocks. As early as 1976, Ontario's minister of energy, Dennis Timbrell, attacked both Alberta and the federal government for the "lemming-like March to international prices."[53] Frank Miller, Ontario treasurer, had even termed Lougheed a "greater threat to Confederation than Quebec's René Levesque."[54] Throughout the decade, Ontario's position was to resist "a seemingly unrelenting commitment to chase an artificial, erratic, and soaring world price—a price set by interests and circumstances foreign to Canada and our economic realities."[55]

From Alberta's perspective, the attitude of fellow Conservatives in Ontario was unfortunate but not surprising. It simply confirmed the suspicion that Ontario was clinging to privilege and resentful of the movement of wealth westward. When the Toronto *Star* worried that "so much of Canada's wealth is being siphoned into the coffers of a single province that the economic balance of Confederation will be threatened" it only confirmed the worst suspicion of Albertans.[56] Lougheed said as much at the August 1979 federal-provincial conference. Rejecting Ontario's position as "completely unacceptable," he accused Ontario of "a clear attempt to change the basic concept and arrangements of Confederation."[57]

The position of the federal government was, however, much more difficult. If it gave in to the West it faced a barrage of criticism from Ontario politicians and newspapers. As Dennis Timbrell unfairly complained, "the Government of Canada has abdicated its responsibility and the policy vacuum must be filled."[58] When the new Conservative government under Joe Clark tried a different approach, Premier Davis of Ontario complained that it was "an imprudent and excessive response to the claims of the producing provinces."[59] At times it seemed no stance was possible. Thus, when Trudeau took a strong stand during the election of 1979, Davis complained that the federal government was sowing disunity. As one biographer has noted wryly, that was "something Davis and Lougheed had been doing quite nicely by themselves for five years."[60] By the time Trudeau returned to power in 1980 he had reached a conclusion. His previous government had failed after repeated efforts to compromise. The Clark government had fallen in the face of intransigent Tory premiers in Ontario and Alberta. There was no chance of satisfying the critics so, as Marc Lalonde summed it up, it was time "the rules of the game were changed."[61]

Such an assertion had behind it some definitive arithmetic. The simple fact was that Ontario had more political clout in Ottawa. Ontario had 95 seats, easily overshadowing Alberta's 21.[62] Moreover, Ontario was a swing province. The loss of 23 seats in Ontario in 1979 was instrumental in the loss of power of Trudeau's Liberals. The failure of the Clark government to concern itself with Ontario concerns over oil was equally instrumental in the Liberal rebound in 1980. Throughout the 1970s, the Liberal cabinet had several Ontario members to reinforce the arguments of that province.

In contrast, the West was not fertile ground for the Liberals and Alberta in particular was hostile territory. Not one Liberal was elected from the province in any of the four elections between 1972 and 1980. Even more dramatically, the Liberals were eclipsed everywhere west of Ontario in the 1980 election.

This had two results. First, the national government lacked legitimacy in the West for any proposal, much less a unilateral one. In contrast, for example, the referendum battle in Quebec saw two sets of elected politicians—federal Liberals and provincial Parti Quebecois—each with a claim to represent the people. No such balance existed in 1980 in western Canada. Second, the absence of elected Albertans in government weakened the western perspective during energy discussions through the 1970s. The absence of any elected westerner in the 1980 government meant the national government devised a national plan by a party that was effectively regional.

Epilogue: Aftermath and Lessons Learned

On October 27, 1980 the Canadian government announced a comprehensive and interventionist energy program without the consent of the producing provinces. Though extremely complex in detail, the essence of the program was to maintain Canadian prices below the world market, provide direct incentives for certain types of oil exploration and production, and enhance Canadian ownership and control of oil and natural gas. The overall effect was to increase federal control and federal revenue while shielding, at least to a degree, consuming provinces. The federal-provincial process had failed and, whatever the merits of the program, they were lost in the anger over the unilateralism of the federal action.

However, as sometimes happens in history, the degree of failure helped the repair process. In the aftermath of the NEP announcement, the rhetoric escalated on both sides. Lougheed went on television to announce a 15 per cent cut-back in oil production. Other Alberta politicians mused openly about separatism. Trudeau scoffed both at threats of blackmail and at western "paranoia."[63] At the same time, however, an increasing number of voices in both the west and the east expressed unease at the confrontation. Before long, federal and provincial governments sat down to negotiate what had previously been un-negotiable. Less than a year after the proclamation of the NEP, a new deal was reached based on unrealistic amounts of money for all involved. However, by the time oil prices collapsed in 1982 the lessons of the NEP had been learned, though from differing perspectives. Future governments to date looked to compromise rather than confrontation, while the NEP became part of western mythology.

The NEP, though, is important because it is not typical of federal-provincial relations. Instead, as this paper has argued, an unusual conjunction of events was necessary in order to create the confrontation that had occurred. Had the constitution been clearer, had the issue been of less importance, had the leaders been different, or had the political representation in Ottawa been different, it is likely that the more normal trade-offs typical of federal-provincial diplomacy would have succeeded. As it is, the NEP stands as a test case of the range of forces that come into play in defining the outcomes of our complex federal system.

Notes

1. Cited in Richard Simeon, "Natural Resource Revenues and Canadian Federalism: A Survey of Issues," *Canadian Public Policy* 6, supplement (Winter 1980): 185.
2. Obituary, "NEP Tainted relationship with the West," *Calgary Herald*, September 29, 2000, A4.
3. Editorial, "But a superb energy plan," *Toronto Star*, October 29, 1980, A4.
4. E.A.E. Allard, letter to the editor, *Edmonton Journal*, November 4, 1980, A7.
5. Editorial, *Edmonton Journal*, November 3, 1980, A4.
6. G. Bruce Doern and Glen Toner, *The Politics of Energy: The Development and Implementation of the NEP* (Toronto: Methuen, 1985).
7. *Edmonton Journal*, November 4, 1980, A7.
8. "Transcript of Premier's Television address," *Calgary Herald*, October 31, 1980, A5.
9. Richard Simeon, *Federal-Provincial Diplomacy: The Making of Recent Policy in Canada* (Toronto: University of Toronto Press, 1972), 8–9.
10. For a classic centralist interpretation of the intent o the BNA Act see Donald Creighton, *The Road to Confederation: The Emergence of Canada, 1863–1867 Confederation* (Toronto: MacMillan, 1976).
11. David Cameron, "Whither Canadian Federalism? The Challenge of Regional Diversity and Maturity," in P. Meekison, ed., *Canadian Federalism: Myth or Reality*, 3rd ed. (Toronto: Methuen, 1977), 304–24.
12. As the passage of the new constitution soon after the NEP altered the fundamental law in some ways, this paper has assessed federal-provincial diplomacy of the pre-1980 period through the writings of that era. The key works of the time were Simeon, *Federal-Provincial Diplomacy*; Meekison, *Canadian Federalism*; Donald Smiley, *Canada in Question: Federalism in the Eighties* 3rd ed. (Toronto: McGraw-Hill/Ryerson, 1980); as well as several articles in the *Canadian Journal of Political Science* and *Canadian Public Policy*.
13. Donald Smiley, "Federal-Provincial Conflict in Canada," in Meekison, *Canadian Federalism*, 2–18.
14. Edward McWhinney, *Quebec and the Constitution 1960–1978* (Toronto: University of Toronto Press, 1979), 27.
15. A.W. Johnson, "The Dynamics of Federalism in Canada," *Canadian Journal of Political Science* 1, no. 1 (1968): 22; Donald Smiley, "Federal-Provincial Conflict in Canada," 3. See also, Alan Cairns, "The Governments and Societies of Canadian Federalism," *Canadian Journal of Political Science* X, no. 4 (1977): 695–726.
16. D. Smiley, "Territorialism and Canadian Institutions," *Canadian Public Policy* 3, no. 4 (Autumn 1977): 451
17. J.L.G. Granatstein, *Canada 1957–1967: The Years of Uncertainty and Innovation* (Toronto: McLelland and Stewart, 1986), 263. On the pension negotiations see Simeon, *Federal-Provincial Diplomacy*, Chap. 3.
18. John English, *The Worldly Years. The Life of Lester Pearson*, Vol. 2 1949–1972 (Toronto: Lester and Orpen and Dennis, 1992), 285–87.

19. Public Service Commissioner of Alberta, *Annual Report*, 1969, 13; Public Service Commissioner of Alberta, *Annual Report*, 1979, 18.

20. Cynthia Bojechko, "Lougheed's 'Energetic Bureaucrats': A Study of the Senior Civil Servants in Province-building Departments" (M.A. Diss., University of Alberta, 1982), 17, 119–20.

21. John Helliwell and Anthony Scott, *Canada in Fiscal Conflict: Resources and the West* ([Vancouver]: Pemberton Securities, 1981). See also W.D. Gainer and T.L. Powrie, "Public Revenue from Canadian Crude Petroleum Production," *Canadian Public Policy* 1, no. 1 (Winter 1975): 9.

22. Doern and Toner, *Politics of Energy*, 65–66.

23. Eric Hanson, "The Future of Western Canada: Economic, Social and Political," *Canadian Public Administration* 18, no. 1 (1975): 110.

24. Merv Leitch, "The Constitutional Position of Natural Resources: Notes for an Address given to the Canadian Council of Resource and Environment Ministers in Victoria, November 21st, 1974," in Meekison, *Canadian Federalism*, 172, 175–76.

25. Government of Alberta, *Harmony in Diversity: A New Federalism for Canada: Alberta Government Position Paper on Constitutional Change* (Edmonton: Government of Alberta, 1978), 6–7 and 13–14.

26. Leitch, "The Constitutional Position of Natural Resources," 172, 176

27. Statement by Donald MacDonald 1975 (opening remarks First Minister's Conference April 9–10, 1975). Cited in Meekison, *Canadian Federalism*, 405

28. Department of Energy, Mines and Resources, *The National Energy Program, 1980* (Ottawa: Supply and Services Canada, 1980), 11, 14.

29. Doern and Toner, *The Politics of Energy*, Part 2.

30. James E. Gander and Fred W. Belaire, *Energy Futures for Canadians: Long-Term Energy Assessment Program*, Report of a Study prepared for Energy Mines and Resources Canada (Ottawa: Energy, Mines and Resources Canada, 1978), 259.

31. EMR, *The National Energy Program*, 26.

32. For a contemporary assessment from a conservationist perspective see Jan Marmorek, *Over a Barrel: A Guide to the Canadian Energy Crisis* (Toronto: Doubleday, 1981), Chap. 1 and 2.

33. This is from Doern and Toner, *The Politics of Energy*, 86.

34. Province of Alberta, *Public Accounts for the Year Ended March 31 1968*, 38, 44; *Public Accounts for the Year Ended, March 31, 1980*, Vol. 1, 26.

35. "Notes for Remarks by Premier Blakeney, the Canadian Club, Toronto, January 4, 1977," in Meekison, *Canadian Federalism*, 179–88.

36. *Calgary Herald*, October 31, 1980, A4.

37. See, for example, Energy Mines and Resources Canada, *Canadian Oil and Gas Supply/Demand Overview* (Ottawa: The Division, 1979), Figures 14, 15.

38. Canadian Institute of Public Opinion, *The Gallup Report*, September 15, 1979.

39. Allan Hustak, *Peter Lougheed. A Biography* (Toronto: McLelland and Stewart, 1979), 160.

40. "'Energy Pricing,' Lougheed Opening Statement to Federal-Provincial Conference on Energy, January 22, 1974," in Meekison, *Canadian Federalism*, 397–403.

41. Hustak, *Lougheed*, 172.

42. EMR, *The National Energy Program*, 130.

43. *Canada Year Book*, 1988, Table 22.1.

44. EMR, The *National Energy Program*, 14.

45. Quoted in David Milne, *Tug of War. Ottawa and the Provinces Under Trudeau and Mulroney* (Toronto: J. Lorimer, 1986), 27.

46. Milne, *Tug of War*, 15.

47. Stephen Clarkson and Christina McCall, *Trudeau and our Times*, Vol. 1, *The Magnificent Obsession* (Toronto: McLelland and Stewart, 1990); Pierre Trudeau, *Memoirs* (Toronto: McLelland and Stewart, 1993).

48. Hustak, *Lougheed*, 30–48.

49. Hustak, *Lougheed*, 9–10.

50. Hustak, *Lougheed*, 38.

51. Simeon, *Federal-Provincial Diplomacy*, 13.

52. Simeon, *Federal-Provincial Diplomacy*, 13, 200.

53. Dennis Timbrell (Ontario Minister of Energy), "Speech to Queen's Park Press Gallery, February 7, 1976," in Meekison, *Canadian Federalism*, 411–12. See also Simeon, "Natural Resource Revenues," 182–91.

54. Clare Hoy, *Bill Davis: A Biography* (Toronto: Methuen, 1985), 323.

55. "Statement by the Hon. William Davis, Special First Ministers' Conference on Oil and Natural Gas Policy," November 12, 1979, in *Federal-Provincial Conference of First Ministers on Energy*, November 12, 1979 (Ottawa, 1979), 3.

56. Editorial, "Painful Clash with Alberta," *Toronto Star*, October 25, 1980, B2.

57. "Statement by Premier Lougheed of Alberta," August 15, 1979 in *Federal Provincial Conference of First Ministers on Energy*, November 12, 1979, 1

58. Dennis Timbrell, Speech to Queen's Park press gallery, February 7, 1976. Cited in Meekison, *Canadian Federalism*, 411–12.

59. "Statement by the Hon. William Davis, in *Federal-Provincial Conference of First Ministers on Energy*, November 12, 1979, 3.

60. Hoy, *Bill Davis*, 338.

61. Marc Lalonde, "Riding the Storm: Energy Policy, 1968–1984," in Thomas Axworthy and Pierre Elliott Trudeau, *Towards a Just Society: The Trudeau Years* (Markham, ON: Viking, 1990), 49–77, 63.

62. Even if Saskatchewan is included as a natural resource ally of Alberta, the numbers in the 1980 election were Ontario 95 to Alberta and Saskatchewan's 35.

63. "West warned against separatism 'blackmail,'" *Calgary Herald*, October 31, 1980, A3.

Fourteen

Premier Peter Lougheed, Alberta and the Transformation of Constitutionalism in Canada, 1971–1985

MICHAEL D. BEHIELS

What was Premier Peter Lougheed's major contribution to the transformation of constitutionalism in Canada? Lougheed's role in the transformation of the British North America Act, 1867 is analogous to the role played by Ontario's Premier Oliver Mowat in the late nineteenth century. In the Mowat tradition, Lougheed preached and practiced the gospel of provincial rights. Mowat, with the help of the Judicial Committee of the Privy Council, transformed John A. Macdonald's highly centralist quasi-federation into a classical federal system of co-ordinate sovereign powers—Ottawa versus the provinces.[1] Like Mowat, Lougheed understood that his primary role as premier was to defend and promote the economic, political and constitutional interests of his province. Lougheed used Alberta's highly profitable natural resources—oil and gas—to establish a powerful adversarial position vis-à-vis Prime Minister Pierre Elliott Trudeau's Liberal government. This strategy enabled Lougheed and his government to formulate and entrench a contemporary version of the provincial compact conception of Confederation. To this equality of the province's model, Lougheed grafted the notion of provincial diversity—an informal, functional system of asymmetrical federalism. Lougheed was highly successful in selling his vision of province-building to Albertans, to his fellow premiers, and to many Canadians. To achieve his constitutional objectives, Lougheed practiced the arts of an astute Machiavellian negotiator. Contrary to the public perception that he was intransigent, Lougheed, at crucial moments, proved capable of compromise, notably on the crucial issue of the Canadian Charter of Rights and Freedoms.

Lougheed, as an Albertan and as a Western Canadian, never subscribed to the two founding peoples or two nations theory of Confederation. Like many Albertans, he only reluctantly supported the entrenchment of the Official Languages at the federal level and would never consent to making Alberta officially bilingual. But, neither did Lougheed buy in to the contemporary Québécois neo-nationalists' territorial conception of duality—a bi-national Quebec/Canada restructured federation whereby an enhanced Quebec state would become the exclusive home of Canada's francophone minority. A resolute proponent of what John George Diefenbaker called "One Canada," Lougheed put all his political energy into entrenching the compact of provinces theory of Confederation. Alberta, in his view, was a fully sovereign entity within all areas of its jurisdiction. Ottawa's attempts to tamper with Alberta's prerogatives, especially in the areas of taxation and resource development, were tantamount to a declaration of constitutional warfare. Lougheed, backed by other premiers, saw to it that the principle of the equality of the provinces was entrenched in the very fabric of Canadian constitutionalism via the Alberta amending formula. Indeed, Mowat would have applauded!

Alberta Confronts Mega-constitutional Politics

Premier Lougheed altered, in stages, the Alberta government's approach to both the process and substance of constitutional renewal. During the protracted negotiations leading up to the failed Victoria Charter of 1971, the . Social Credit government's approach was very traditional. Then leader of the Official Opposition, Lougheed derided the Social Credit government for not obtaining "a mandate to make commitments regarding the Constitution on behalf of the people of Alberta."[2] Elected premier in 1971, Lougheed made effective use of Alberta's Legislative Assembly to strengthen his bargaining power *vis-à-vis* the Canadian government. Lougheed's position on the substantive matters of constitutional renewal evolved considerably after he created an advisory Ministry of Federal and Intergovernmental Affairs (FIGA) in June 1972. FIGA quickly became the war room for the political battles involving all aspects of federal-provincial relations. Driving the premier to reconsider Alberta's role in the federation and his approach to constitutional renewal was the political conflict with the Trudeau government over energy policy, particularly Ottawa's decision to impose an export tax on Alberta oil in the wake of the OPEC oil crisis. During a heated Federal-Provincial Conference on Energy in Ottawa on January 22, 1974, Lougheed expressed his government's rejection of Trudeau's centralist conception of the federation and his failure to consult with the producing provinces. "We view the federal export tax on

Alberta oil as contrary to both the spirit and the intent of Confederation. ... It is not just an export tax—it is also a price freeze on all of Alberta's oil production at immense cost to Albertans."[3] Lougheed's decision to alter fundamentally the political economy of Alberta by implementing a range of policies that would expand and diversify manufacturing in the province set the stage for a dramatic showdown with Trudeau over the renewal of the Constitution.

On April 9, 1975 Trudeau met with the premiers to discuss reopening negotiations on the constitution and proposed that they limit themselves to "patriation" of the BNA Act with the Victoria Charter amending formula. Premier Robert Bourassa demurred and insisted that "constitutional guarantees" for the French language and culture be included. When the prime minister's emissary, Gordon Robertson, toured the provincial capitals to discuss Trudeau's proposal and Bourassa's "constitutional guarantees," Alberta took the lead in the discussions.[4] Lou Hyndman, appointed Minister of FIGA in March 1975, warned the premier that "Alberta's influence in Confederation in decades ahead may be at stake; resource jurisdiction and Supreme Court appointments important side issues." A year later Hyndman informed Lougheed that FIGA had "increased Alberta's reputation as a province with a strong voice in federal-provincial relations. ... Increasingly we are looked upon as leaders in major Canadian decision-making."[5]

Following Lougheed's lead, the premiers at their annual conference in St. John's, Newfoundland in August 21–22, 1975 upped the ante. They agreed that patriation was a desirable goal but "should be dealt with in the context of a general review of the distribution of powers, control of resources, duplication of programs, and other related matters."[6] Following protracted discussions with Quebec government officials to ascertain what was meant by "constitutional guarantees" for the French language and culture, in late March 1976 Trudeau sent the premiers a revised version of the Draft Proclamation of the governor-general.[7] To make the constitutional reform more appealing to Western and Atlantic premiers, Trudeau outlined provisions for consultation with the provinces about appointments to the Supreme Court, the reduction of regional disparities, and indicated that he was open to altering the Victoria amending formula to accommodate Western premiers if they could arrive at an agreement on deletion of the population provision. Trudeau informed the premiers that Bourassa considered the "constitutional guarantees" for language and culture a bare minimum and that he would be looking for a redistribution of powers. Trudeau indicated that his government had no intention of discussing the distribution of powers and offered the provinces three options: simple patriation that Ottawa could achieve on its own since it did not affect ss. 91 and 92; patriation with the Victoria amending formula that would come into effect only when ratified by all the provincial Legislatures; and patriation with the entirety of Ottawa's Draft Proclamation comprising the 1976 version of the Victoria Charter. If unanimity was not possible on any of the three options, Trudeau informed the premiers, the federal government would decide if and when to proceed unilaterally with patriation and what to include in its package. Trudeau was inclined to include the Victoria amending formula on condition that it come into force upon ratification by all provincial Legislatures.[8]

Trudeau's letter, tabled in the House on April 9, set off a firestorm within the Lougheed government. Hyndman, convinced that Trudeau was determined to patriate the Constitution with or without the provinces, encouraged Lougheed to get in touch with his fellow premiers and go on the offensive.[9] Peter Meekison, FIGA deputy minister, dissected Trudeau's letter for Hyndman. He noted that the premiers, at their meeting with Trudeau in April 1975, had never agreed to patriation with the Victoria amending formula. At the heart of Bourassa's "constitutional guarantees," was the Quebec government's insistence upon a new distribution of powers, including areas such as social policy, communications and immigration. Trudeau's proposal offered only the possibility of administrative agreements with Quebec not a transfer of powers. Meekison suggested that Alberta should not oppose patriation but should reject the Victoria amending formula since the Lougheed government had not participated in the negotiations leading up to it. Ottawa's approach ignored the established conventions surrounding patriation that require consultation with, and unanimous approval by, the provincial governments. Meekison recommended that the Alberta government reject Trudeau's options and develop its own approach.[10]

Taking FIGA's advice to heart, Lougheed went on the offensive immediately. "The Government of Alberta," he declared in a telex to Trudeau,

> feels strongly that any unilateral move by Parliament, on the federal government's initiative, to remove the Constitution from Westminster would be a clear violation of the historical precedent of Canadian constitutional development and the conventions and customs which have grown up over past decades concerning provincial participation in this very important matter. It is our firm view that such a major move should not be done unilaterally at the initiative of the federal government, but should be carried

out by the consent of the provinces, who are full partners in Confederation. The maintenance of the legitimate and historical powers (of the provinces) may be at stake if patriation is carried forward unilaterally.[11]

Lougheed's epic war with Trudeau over the renewal of Canada's constitution was underway. Its many battles would continue unabated until Queen Elizabeth II gave Royal Assent to the *Constitution Act, 1982* on April 17, 1982. Lougheed was pleased to witness the historic event.

The premiers, during the First Ministers' meeting in May and in private conversations with Trudeau on June 14, 1976, asked for several months to consider his proposals. Trudeau agreed to wait until mid-September and promised to consider any proposals that had unanimous provincial approval.[12] Lougheed, as chair of the 17th Annual Premiers' Conference in Edmonton in late August, was well placed to influence the agenda and the outcome of their deliberations. Hyndman, chair of the mid-August Conference of Intergovernmental Ministers and Attorneys General urged his premier and the cabinet to develop a general position on the constitution and decide what amending formula the government would support. He suggested that Alberta "introduce for discussion purposes a clause guaranteeing provincial ownership of resources," because it "may be desirable to have at least one province other than Quebec with a specific demand."[13] FIGA officials discovered that Quebec had an extensive list of demands: the curtailing Ottawa's spending, declaratory and residual powers, the entrenchment of equalization with a precise formula, and concurrent jurisdiction over cultural with provincial paramountcy. Quebec supported Alberta's position on the amending formula, the residual clause, a guarantee of provincial jurisdiction over resources and provincial input into Supreme Court appointments. Meekison opined that Quebec officials were looking for an ally and were pleased that Alberta was making specific demands. He suggested that Hyndman encourage Lougheed to pursue closer ties with Premier Bourassa. FIGA officials were apprised of Quebec's meetings with Ontario and British Columbia officials, learning that Ontario approved of Alberta's proposals while British Columbia appeared only interested in simple patriation.[14]

Prior to the meeting of the Attorneys General and Intergovernmental Ministers on August 13–15, Hyndman informed his Attorney General, Jim Foster, about Alberta's tentative position on Trudeau's three options. Option #3, patriation, amending formula, and substantive amendments to the Constitution, was considered too impractical given the political climate.

Option #2, patriation with the Victoria formula, could only be considered if it could be altered to make the region-based formula fairer to every western province. Alberta might possibly support Option #1, simple patriation with a guarantee that all aspects pertaining to the division of powers and other provincial rights could not be altered without unanimous provincial consent, if it could be drafted in such a way as to prevent Ottawa from abusing its amending powers.[15]

The premier and his cabinet inquired whether "it was *legally* possible for the Parliament of Canada, after patriation, to unilaterally amend the new 'Canadian Constitution' to reduce provincial powers." The Attorney General obtained legal advice from seven experts on Trudeau's options one and two. Some of the experts opined that Confederation was a compact of provinces, therefore any guarantees to the provinces attached to patriation would have to be respected by the federal government. One expert suggested that Ottawa could legally proceed with unilateral patriation but it would be politically embarrassing, especially in the U.K., if provincial opposition was strong. Gerry Gall and Peter Costigan, who rejected the compact theory as legally untenable, argued that constitutional conventions inherent in the Canadian federal structure would ensure that the "guarantee" offered in Option #1 would prevent Ottawa from amending the distribution of powers without unanimous provincial consent.[16] It appeared that the only way to stop Trudeau's unilateral action on patriation, with or without an amending formula, was for the premiers to take powerful political action.

During the Edmonton Annual Premiers' Conference in August, with Lougheed in the Chair, the premiers began exploratory talks on the constitution, patriation and an amending formula, continuing their discussions in Toronto on October 1–2, 1976. On October 14, Lougheed informed Trudeau that the premiers agreed on patriation providing there were concurrent negotiations on the expansion of the role of the provinces and/or jurisdiction in several areas: the Supreme Court, Senate representation, spending powers, culture, communications, and regional disparities. Reminding Trudeau of his promise to accept proposals agreed to by all the premiers, Lougheed informed him that they unanimously approved an increased role for the provinces in immigration, the entrenchment of Canada's two official languages, a reaffirmation of provincial taxing powers over natural resources, provincial veto power over the use of Ottawa's declaratory power, annual First Ministers Conferences, and that the creation of new provinces be subject to the amending formula.

There was no agreement on an amending formula. All the premiers, except Lougheed and William R. Bennett, supported Trudeau's revised Victoria Charter amending formula. Bennett insisted on a veto for British Columbia based on a five region formula.[17] Lougheed, determined to defend provincial powers outlined in ss. 92, 93, and 109 of the *BNA Act*, argued that it was imperative that an amending formula "should not permit an amendment that would take away rights, proprietary interest or jurisdiction from any province without the concurrence of that province."[18]

Trudeau was greatly perturbed at the meagre results of the premiers' deliberations. "We had agreed in April 1975," he reminded Lougheed,

> that we would see if "patriation," with an amending formula, could be achieved without getting into the distribution of powers. Your letter suggests to me that the Premiers...seem to have turned the process upside down and to have concentrated on increasing provincial powers without agreeing either on a basis for "patriation" or on a procedure for amendment. Beyond saying that the objective of "patriation" is a desirable one, your letter merely states circumstances where "patriation" should not be undertaken.

Trudeau bluntly declared that his promise to accept any proposal unanimously agreed to by the premiers was conditional upon that proposal incorporating the central objective of the exercise, patriation with an amending formula.[19]

Lougheed Forges Alberta's Role in Canadian Constitutionalism

Convinced that Trudeau was going to proceed unilaterally, Lougheed's government clearly outlined its position and obtained the support of the Alberta Legislative Assembly. A resolution was passed with only one dissenting vote on November 4, 1976, stating:

> Be it resolved that, the Legislative Assembly, while supporting the objective of patriation of the Canadian Constitution, re-affirm the fundamental principle of Confederation and hence direct the Government that it should not agree to any revised amending formula for the Constitution which could allow for existing rights, proprietary interests or jurisdiction to be taken away from any province without the specific concurrence of

that province, *and that it should refuse to give its support to any patriation prior to obtaining the unanimous consent of all provinces for a proper amending formula.*[20]

Alberta's position on constitutional renewal, as Lougheed explained in a candid letter to Albertan MP Harvie Andre, was misrepresented by the media in central Canada. Alberta supported patriation and the entrenchment of rights for Canada's official language minorities. His government could not accept the Victoria Charter amending formula because Alberta's position was that "the provinces are equal partners within Confederation and should have equal rights with respect to any future amendments that would affect existing provincial rights, proprietary interests or jurisdiction." Alberta was not seeking a veto. It was simply returning to the 1964 Fulton-Favreau amending formula with one important modification. Alberta did not want to have two classes of amendments, those amendable via a general formula and those requiring unanimity since this was considered far too rigid. Instead, Alberta was proposing an opting-out right for matters relating to ss. 92, 93, and 109 of the *BNA Act* so as to guarantee provincial sovereignty. Reminding Andre that the Alberta Conservative Party supported his government's position, Lougheed urged the national Conservative Party and caucus to do the same.[21]

While Lougheed was firming up Alberta's position on constitutional renewal, René Lévesque's secessionist Parti Québécois defeated the inept Bourassa government in the November 1976. This forced Trudeau to hasten the pace of constitutional discussions in order to pre-empt the Parti Québécois's referendum on secession. Trudeau's January 19, 1977 response to Lougheed was a brilliant Cartesian gambit to check-mate Lougheed's and the other premiers' counter-proposal. He proposed a revised Draft Resolution to Patriate the Constitution. "It seems to me," Trudeau clarified,

that the results of the meetings of the Premiers...are, in a sense, either too much or too little. They are too much in relation to the limited exercise we embarked upon in April, 1975. That, as reflected in my letter of April 19th, 1975, was intended to accomplish "patriation" of our constitution from Britain with the amending clause agreed on at Victoria. During our discussions between April 1975 and early 1976 we agreed not to address the issue of the distribution of powers. Your letter of October 14th raises the matter of the distribution of powers. If this is to be done properly, I think our review and our changes should be much more extensive than those covered in your letter of October 14th.

Trudeau reiterated that his experience with constitutional renewal confirmed the need to proceed by stages—patriation with an amending formula and then the distribution of powers.[22]

Trudeau explained his revised Draft Resolution. Part I proposed the entrenchment of the Victoria Charter amending formula. The new Part II addressed Senate reform by offering Atlantic Canada four additional Senators—26 to 30—and the Western region 12 additional Senators—24 to 36 distributed as Manitoba 7, Saskatchewan 7, Alberta 10, and British Columbia 12. The Northwest Territories and Yukon would get one each. Part III on Language Rights called for entrenchment of the Official Languages provisions at federal level with an opting-in provision for provinces. Article 21 was revised to refer only to language and preservation of it rather than to culture and development. In Part IV on Regional Disparities, Trudeau noted the consensus of the premiers and clarified that Article 22(b) referred to equalization as now developed. Regarding Part V, which dealt with Federal-Provincial Consultation, Trudeau offered Annual First Ministers' Meetings but only to consult the premiers on the creation of new provinces. Ottawa agreed to consult on areas of concurrent power such as immigration but would not agree to create new areas of concurrent power such as culture and communications since this entailed the distribution of powers. Part VI Misc. proposed the need for an Official French-language text with full force and effect.

Trudeau addressed the other matters raised by Lougheed—the Supreme Court, provincial taxing powers in the areas of primary production, and the exercise of the federal spending power. The last two dealt with the distribution of powers and would be left to stage two. The federal government, having serious second thoughts about the Victoria Charter provisions dealing with the Supreme Court, decided to reconsider the matter. If Ottawa and the provinces agreed on appointment procedures to the Supreme Court, these could be added to a final package. If the revised Draft Resolution was unacceptable to the premiers, Trudeau proposed that they return to the original plan of April 1975, patriation with the Victoria amending formula. He closed, in a classical divide-and-rule strategy, by noting that Premiers Schreyer of Manitoba and Campbell of Prince Edward Island had informed him that they did not consider that "patriation" needed to be linked with all the other matters raised in Lougheed's letter of October 24th.[23]

Lougheed was not amused. In his replies of February 21 and March 7, 1977, he declared that patriation of the constitution was not Alberta's priority. Resolving more pressing economic issues would have a more positive impact on national unity than trying to patriate the constitution. Lougheed strongly disagreed that the results of Premiers' Conference were too much or too little, stating that Alberta was willing to accept some aspects of the Draft Resolution—language rights, regional disparities and annual meetings of First Ministers. The Alberta government's priority was the amending formula. Lougheed was not willing to accept the Victoria amending formula that was never approved by the Alberta Legislative Assembly. He reminded Trudeau that his government's position on constitutional renewal and the amending formula was clearly outlined in the Legislature's Resolution of November 4, 1976. Lougheed queried why Trudeau refused to allow for a provincial role in appointments to the Supreme Court in his revised Draft Resolution.[24]

At their May 5–6 Western Premiers' Conference, the premiers—rejecting both the status quo and the Parti Québécois's demand for an unworkable and unacceptable "independence with economic association," but hoping to capitalize on the emerging political crisis—agreed that it was time for a comprehensive reshaping of Confederation. The premiers favoured stronger provincial governments.[25] Trudeau had already committed his government to wholesale constitutional renewal and his officials were preparing a comprehensive agenda. In mid-August 1977, a senior Federal official, Frank Carter, informed Alberta officials that a comprehensive package of constitutional proposals and changes in federal-provincial relations had been sent to the prime minister for consideration by Cabinet. Meekison conjectured that if the constitutional proposals received a hostile reception from premiers, Trudeau might take them directly to the Canadian people in an election early in 1978 so as to be able to confront Lévesque with a strengthened mandate.[26] In mid-December Meekison informed Hyndman that Trudeau's Cabinet was about to approve the constitutional package and that a bill would be presented to the House of Commons in early March 1978. The bill would contain three elements: entrenchment of a Charter of rights including language rights, reform of the Senate, and reform of the Supreme Court.[27]

By the winter of 1978 Quebec secession was high on the agenda of all the premiers. Lougheed outlined his government's approach to the looming crisis. Albertans, he proclaimed, are Canadians first. Yet Albertans, as leaders in the New West, were eager to shape the New Canada by being part of Canada's political mainstream. His government would take whatever constructive steps needed to keep Quebec citizens in the federation short of agreeing to any form of "sovereignty association." Force should not be used to keep Quebec in the federation but it would be necessary to insist on guarantees for individual rights and liberties. Furthermore, no province should have special status in Confederation because all provinces are equal, a reality grounded in a Constitution based on a compact of provinces. This equality should be reflected in any amending formula. Rejecting the status quo, Lougheed favoured the "third option" or "new federalism"—buzz words for more decentralization—because it was in the provinces where the real policy and political action were taking place. Each province would have the option of using or not using their new powers. Federalism's strength resided in its flexibility that should be enhanced via delegation of powers from Ottawa to the provinces, the expansion of concurrent powers, provincial input over appointments to the Supreme Court, the creation of a constitutional court, and direct provincial appointments to key federal boards and agencies. Lougheed believed that he could mould Canada into a more decentralized and diversified federation.[28]

Lougheed was appalled when the federal PC party's White Paper on the Constitution failed to make the crucial distinction between Canada's "central government system (responsible for matters such as defence) and the governance of eleven governments in a federal system (responsible jointly for such things as communications, transportation and economic development policy)." Lougheed objected vigorously to the White Paper's denunciation of the First Ministers' Annual Conferences as an unacceptable "fourth level of government" and its proposal to replace them with a House of Provinces that would undermine and weaken the provincial governments. Lougheed urged that the White Paper be reconsidered taking into account his critique of its fundamental flaws.[29]

Trudeau's Renewed Initiative and the Premiers' Riposte

On June 12, 1978 the Trudeau government tabled *A Time For Action*, hoping it would stimulate widespread debate throughout the country. It recommended comprehensive renewal—including a re-allocation of the distribution of powers, entrenchment of the Supreme Court, and a House of the Federation—of Canada's outmoded Constitution based on two conditions. First, Canada must remain "a genuine Federation in which the Constitution establishes a federal Parliament with real powers which apply to all parts of the country, and provincial legislatures with equally real powers within their respective territories." Second, the new Constitution must include a Charter of Rights and Freedoms that applies to both orders of government. In phase I,

Parliament would proceed with those matters on which it had full capacity to act on its own following consultation with the provinces such as the House of Commons, the Monarchy and the Office of the governor-general, the Senate and the Supreme Court. Phase II would address all matters requiring joint action by federal and provincial authorities, essentially all matters pertaining to the division of powers and responsibilities between the two orders of government.[30]

Trudeau acknowledged Lougheed's concerns about protecting the rights, proprietary interests and jurisdiction of the provinces as well as his reluctance to support a House of the Federation. Trudeau, aware that Alberta wanted increased provincial powers to develop its economy, reminded Lougheed that "the federal government will have to ensure that economic decision-making powers are distributed so that all provinces can be protected as part of a prosperous national economy."[31] On June 20, Bill C-60, An Act to amend the Constitution of Canada, was given first reading in the House of Commons and referred to a Joint Parliamentary Committee for deliberation.[32] Trudeau proposed to Lougheed and the other premiers that an open federal-provincial conference be held in mid-September for in-depth discussions on Bill C-60 and any alternative proposals.[33]

Lougheed took his time in responding to Trudeau's overtures. He wanted to know how Premier Lévesque—who received a letter from Trudeau emphasizing that "everything is negotiable"—was going to respond before agreeing to negotiations on Trudeau's constitutional proposals and their timing. Lévesque reminded Trudeau that his government was committed to holding a referendum on sovereignty-association but would not stand in the way of the modernization of Canada's outmoded constitution.[34] Clearly, the Parti Québécois government was not going to be co-operative. Backed by Hyndman and Meekison, Lougheed opted for a hard-line approach and informed the co-chairs, Maurice Lamontagne and Mark MacGuigan, of the Special Joint Committee of Parliament on the Constitution of Canada, that it was not the appropriate form for him to present Alberta's views on constitutional renewal.[35]

Alberta's hard-line stance was strongly influenced by the legal advice it received on Bill C-60. Peter M. Owen maintained that the Bill significantly weakened Alberta's control of its natural resources because it eliminated s. 109 of the BNA Act. He reiterated his November 19, 1976 opinion that the Bill enhanced Ottawa's "Peace, Order and Good Government" power, its declaratory power, and disallowance power. Since many aspects of the Bill were imprecise, convoluted and unclear, the Courts would play a much greater role in interpreting the renewed Constitution.[36] Alarmed by Ottawa's "hidden" intentions revealed in Owen's legal analysis, Hyndman informed Lougheed that Bill C-60 would "result in a massive transfer of power from the provinces to the Federal government."[37]

Brought up to speed on this interpretation by Lougheed at their August 9–10 annual meeting in Regina, the premiers went on the offensive on the process and substance of constitutional reform. Their strategy was to derail Trudeau's constitutional renewal initiative by making it inordinately time-consuming, impractical, and risky to national unity. Unanimously rejecting Trudeau's two-phase approach since institutional and jurisdictional problems were interrelated, they reiterated that the division of powers was the key issue in constitutional reform and should be addressed in conjunction with all other matters. The premiers maintained that substantive constitutional reforms concerning the Senate and the Monarchy, given the equality of the provinces, required the concurrence of all governments.[38]

On matters of substance, they insisted that the agenda must accommodate all proposals including those of the October 1976 Consensus of the premiers, the Task Force Report on Canadian Unity, and Ottawa's Bill C-60. The premiers, including Lévesque, added new areas of consensus: abolition of federal powers of reservation and disallowance, limitation on Ottawa's power to implement treaties, provincial jurisdiction over fisheries, confirmation and strengthening of provincial powers with respect to natural resources, consultation of provinces in appointments to Superior, District and County Courts, and provincial involvement in appointments to the Supreme Court. Other areas requiring attention included the federal emergency power, provincial access to indirect taxation, the federal residual power, the amending formula and patriation, and the delegation of powers between government. The premiers then critiqued Bill C-60. They denounced the constitutional changes that substituted a governor-general whose appointment and dismissal would be solely at the pleasure of the federal Cabinet, for the Queen as ultimate authority. They dismissed the House of the Federation as unworkable. Divided on the Charter, some premiers approved entrenchment while others argued that "under our parliamentary system, individual rights are better protected by basic constitutional traditions and the ordinary legislative process." They considered that the proposed language guarantees requiring the provinces to provide expensive and unnecessary public services for their linguistic minorities went too far. Supporting Lougheed's concern, the premiers insisted that s. 109 pertaining to natural resources should be carried over into the proposed new Constitution and they maintained that s. 32 was an attempt to usurp provincial control over offshore territories and resources.[39]

Lougheed Counter-Attacks Trudeau's Diplomatic Manoeuvring

Clearly, the premiers believed they, not Trudeau, were in control. Trying to regain the initiative, Marc Lalonde, the minister of state for federal-provincial relations, in his statement to the Joint Parliamentary Committee on the Constitution studying Bill C-60, reminded everyone of the damage that was being done to the economy and to national unity by the secessionist Parti Québécois government. Lalonde informed the Committee and Canadians that Ottawa's approach was one of flexibility—he did not ask for the House to approve Bill C-60 in principle before sending it to committee for study. Ottawa opted to kick-start the process by amending purely "federal" parts of the Constitution because Premier Lévesque's secessionist government would object to any and all "constitutional changes for which a major objective is to keep Quebec a part of Canada." Lalonde warned: "This time we *cannot* fail. There is too much at stake."[40]

Trudeau responded in a conciliatory yet firm tone and in great detail to the premiers' communiqué on constitutional reform. Trudeau emphasized that there were substantial areas of agreement between the position of the premiers and Ottawa on all eleven subjects listed in their 1976 Consensus. Ottawa was willing to address the six areas of consensus and he agreed that the "other subjects" required early consideration. Trudeau reiterated that discussion of matters pertaining to phases I and II could proceed simultaneously since institutional and jurisdictional issues interact as long as phase I was completed before Quebec's referendum. Trudeau reaffirmed Ottawa's competence, under s. 91(1), to amend the BNA *Act* in areas of federal concern. He took umbrage with the premiers' expressed doubt that the federal government had the legal authority to act alone within the jurisdiction of Parliament under s. 91(1). The premiers criticized federal intrusions into areas of their jurisdiction, yet it was ironic, Trudeau declared, that they refused to acknowledge their intrusion into federal jurisdiction in their Regina communiqué. Trudeau made it clear that "Parliament itself must decide whether the national interest requires it to exercise the powers it possesses. And the federal government does not accept the proposition that the power of Parliament under section 91(1) can only be exercised with the approval of each provincial government."[41]

Hoping to undermine the growing controversy over his reform proposals concerning the Crown and Senate, Trudeau made two overtures. First, he reiterated Lalonde's comments that the Queen would remain the "sovereign head" of Canada. His government had no intention of altering the constitutional status of the Crown and the governor-general but rather embed the current status in the Constitution. Given the premiers' and the Joint Parliamentary Committee's concerns regarding the legality of his government's proposals to replace the Senate with a House of the Federation, Trudeau referred the matter to the Supreme Court.[42] The Supreme Court reference on whether the federal government had the constitutional authority to proceed unilaterally with changes to the Senate was made in late November 1978.[43] In its December 21, 1979 landmark decision, the Court sided with the premiers. Senate reform could not proceed without substantial provincial consent.[44]

Given Trudeau's determination to proceed without provincial approval for what he considered crucial aspects of the Constitution, Lougheed further clarified Alberta's position on an amending formula in advance of the late October constitutional conference. Ottawa argued that Alberta favoured the more rigid principle of the 1964 Fulton-Favreau formula that granted each province a veto.[45] In fact, Lougheed opposed a veto because it was too rigid. Meekison suggested supplementing the Fulton-Favreau formula, one requiring the approval of Parliament and the Legislative Assemblies in two-thirds of the provinces with 50 per cent of the population in Canada, with an opting-out clause on "matters coming within sections 92, 93, 94(a) and 109 of BNA Act." This approach gave all provinces an equal say in amendments, avoided rigidity, did away with the outmoded regional approach of Victoria, and allowed for greater diversity within the federal system.[46] Lougheed, concerned that Premier Bennett's drive for a five-region amending formula and Senate reform would undermine provincial control over resources, tried to convince him that "amendments to overcome the impact of the decisions of the Supreme Court of Canada in both the 'CIGOL' and 'Potash' cases" were far more important than items on the agenda for the October First Ministers' Conference, especially the entrenchment of a bill of rights. He pleaded with Bennett to join Alberta's drive to preserve provincial ownership rights of their natural resources.[47]

Lougheed led the fight against Bill C-60 which, in his view, entailed Trudeau's overly centralist vision. On October 19,[48] he tabled in the Legislature a document, *Harmony in Diversity: A New Federalism for Canada*, outlining Alberta's far more decentralist vision of a restructured federation.[49] Alberta's priority was the distribution of powers, especially the need to strengthen the provinces' ownership of resources, the restructuring of the Supreme Court of Canada to make it more representative, and more provincial control over federal boards and agencies. Neither Senate reform nor the Charter were priorities since they were not considered relevant to the new federalism of powerful provinces that Alberta envisaged for the future. When asked how Alberta's position compared with the Parti Québécois's sovereignty-association, Lougheed replied that Quebecers—as distinguished from the Parti Québécois—shared Albertans' desire for greater control over their affairs.[50]

During his opening address at the October, 1978 First Ministers' Conference Lougheed, determined to undermine Trudeau's vision, declared that all the first ministers—the premiers and the prime minister—spoke for Canada. He reiterated that Confederation was a partnership between provinces, one that entailed responsibilities but also provided benefits. It was time to rearrange the federal system—one dominated by the economic decision-makers in the "golden triangle" and backed by Ottawa's so-called "national policies"—to ensure that all its benefits were shared more equitably. Provincial governments, with exclusive control over their economies and natural resources, had to be strong enough to function as counterweights to the political power in the House of Commons.[51]

Throughout the proceedings Trudeau kept his cool. He succeeded in getting the premiers to agree on a wide-ranging, ambitious agenda: resource ownership and inter-provincial trade, indirect taxation, communications, Senate, Supreme Court of Canada, unification of family law, fisheries, offshore resources, equalization and regional development, Charter of Rights, spending power, declaratory power, amending formula, "Patriation" and delegation of legislative authority and monarchy. A Continuing Committee of Ministers on the Constitution (CCMC) was set up to prepare reports on all the agenda items before the next First Ministers' meeting on February 5–6, 1979. Lougheed, reasonably pleased that the premiers had managed to expand the agenda to suit their interests, remained skeptical of the entire process and mistrusted Trudeau's intentions.[52]

Alberta was determined to be fully prepared for the conference. At FIGA, the minister and his officials followed closely the Task Force on National Unity to ascertain what sort of recommendations on constitutional reform it would make. In November 1978, Hyndman met with its co-chair, Jean-Luc Pépin, and reported to the premier that Pépin did not understand Alberta's concerns.[53] Hyndman and Lougheed were well-briefed on the amending formula, the Charter, language rights, and natural resources by FIGA's Deputy Minister Meekison.[54] The premier and his FIGA minister had already gained Ottawa's and many of the premiers' support on the crucial issue of natural resources. Nevertheless, Lougheed was not satisfied with Ottawa's proposal because the term "compelling national interest" was too imprecise and would allow Ottawa to legislate in areas of provincial jurisdiction by simply adding the term in the preamble to any Act.[55] It remained for Lougheed to lobby hard to get Trudeau and his fellow premiers to accept Alberta's amending formula— 7/50 with the opting-out clause pertaining to all amendments affecting provincial rights, proprietary interests and jurisdictions. He argued that no province should have a veto since that would all but guarantee the impossibility of constitutional renewal. To those critics who maintained that Alberta's formula would ensure over time that different parts of the Constitution would be applied differently in Canada, Lougheed responded that such diversity—later called asymmetrical federalism—was the reality and the practice in Canada's longstanding federal system. Because of its equality provision and its flexibility, Lougheed concluded that Alberta's amending formula "is the most reasonable and practical one which can be developed at this time."[56]

On the Charter, Lougheed went on the offensive to protect the parliamentary supremacy of the Alberta Legislative Assembly. He forcefully reminded Trudeau that Alberta's major concern was not with rights but rather with their entrenchment because entrenchment "has the effect *not* of transferring rights to *people*, but rather of transferring powers from the political arena to the judiciary. Entrenchment constitutes an abdication of the accountability by elected legislatures to appointed courts." Legislators would be incapable of responding to the evolving needs of Canadian society thereby alienating citizens from their political institutions.[57] Lougheed revealed that his government would consider entrenching a limited number of rights— fundamental rights, democratic and language rights excluding language of education rights—with a notwithstanding provision. Alberta, with the backing of Quebec, British Columbia, Manitoba and Nova Scotia, rejected Trudeau's proposal that Official Language Minority children be granted freedom of choice in education. According to Lougheed the conference had failed to address Alberta's concerns. Adding insult to injury, Trudeau sent the premiers a list of additional demands over the national economy.[58]

On February 28, 1979 Marc Lalonde sent Roy Romanow, co-chairman of the steering committee of the CCMC, a letter imploring him to set up an agenda to analyse both the provincial and federal lists of demands. He hoped the CCMC's work could be completed in time for a First Ministers' Conference slated for the end of the year.[59] The Committee's work ended abruptly when Trudeau issued a call for a federal election in May. The CCMC resumed its work in the fall of 1979 but had little time to consider the sub-committee reports before its task was halted once again. In hindsight, it is evident that the October–November 1978 conference was the turning point in constitutional negotiations. The premiers, aware that the Trudeau government could not remain in office beyond the normal four-year term, had increased their demands and adopted a stalling tactic at the February 1979 conference. They believed that a federal election would bring Joe Clark's Progressive Conservative Party into office. Clark, who preached his "community of communities" conception of Canada and was sympathetic to Québécois neo-nationalism, was perceived as being far more accommodating to the premiers' demands for a devolution of powers to provincial governments.[60]

Clark's Conservative Party won the election of May 22, 1979. But Prime Minister Clark presided over a minority government because he had failed to make an expected breakthrough in Quebec. Lacking a clear constitutional agenda beyond a vague sympathy for the decentralist philosophy of the Task Force Report on National Unity, Clark appointed a Québécois neo-nationalist, Arthur Tremblay, to the Senate and made him head of a special constitutional research group. Tremblay's task remained largely incomplete when the Clark government was defeated in the House in December on its budget.[61] Trudeau became prime minister once again following the Liberal Party's victory in the February 18, 1980 federal election. Trudeau had been enticed back to carry out his goal of patriating the *BNA Act* with a comprehensive Charter of Rights and Freedoms protecting and promoting both individual and minority rights— with or without the support of the premiers.

A Constitutional Showdown:
Trudeau and the People Versus the Premiers

Once again the premiers had to confront Trudeau, a formidable political foe when it came to matters of national unity and constitutional reform. Lougheed was well-prepared to deal with a revitalized Trudeau government.[62]

Step by step, he laid out Alberta's ground rules for the inevitable constitutional showdown with Trudeau. During his June 1979 interview with Laurier La Pierre of Radio Canada, Lougheed expressed his determination to protect Alberta's constitutional rights if the Parti Québécois government won the referendum. The central government was not the "federal" government and did not have the authority on its own to negotiate the secession of a province. Any negotiations would have to involve all the provincial legislatures and their governments.[63] Determined not to be labelled soft on separatism, Lougheed, following the advice of Meekison, convinced his fellow premiers at their 20th Annual Meeting in August 1979 to make it very clear that progress on matters of interprovincial agreements did not signal their willingness to negotiate economic association with an independent Quebec.[64] Lougheed also decided to support the People to People Petition for Canadian Unity by designating February 3–9, 1980 as Canadian Unity Week in Alberta.[65]

Lougheed supported the Quebec Liberal Party's *A New Canadian Federation* constitutional proposals, except for the Council of the Federation, because they dovetailed with Alberta's *Harmony in Diversity's* decentralist vision.[66] Lougheed took advantage of the Western Premiers' Conference in Lethbridge to reinforce the premiers' negotiating power in any post-referendum constitutional negotiations. The premiers, rejecting the status quo, declared in their April 23 communiqué that changes within the federation were essential for Western Canada to achieve its full potential. Their priorities were enhanced provincial control over natural resources and communications and the restructuring of national institutions. They declared that they would interpret a "no" vote in the Quebec referendum as a vote against separation and a vote in favour of intensive negotiations for constitutional change.[67]

Ottawa and Quebec federalist forces, marshalled by the Trudeau government, handily defeated the Parti Québécois in the May referendum by a margin of 20 points. Trudeau went into action immediately to bring about constitutional renewal he had been seeking since 1968. The provinces could hop on Ottawa's constitutional train or watch from the sidelines as Trudeau proceeded with constitutional reforms comprising patriation, an amending formula, and a uniquely Canadian Charter of Rights and Freedoms. The minister of justice, Jean Chrétien, held bilateral meetings with each of the premiers to ascertain where they stood on Trudeau's limited package. He did not raise the issue of the division of powers so central to the premiers.[68] During an initial First Ministers' Conference on June 9, 1980, Trudeau proposed two shortlists of reforms. The first, dubbed the "People's Package," included a Charter, equalization and patriation with an amending formula. The second, called the "Governments' List," included resource ownership (offshore resources and fisheries) and interprovincial trade, communications, family law, the economic union, Senate reform, and entrenchment of the Supreme Court. Intensive summer-long negotiations would culminate in a constitutional conference in Ottawa on September 8–12.[69]

Knowing all too well that there was little chance of achieving agreement, Lougheed adopted an intertwined set of constitutional priorities. His first goal was to prevent any unilateral move by Trudeau to patriate the *BNA Act*. His second goal was to hold out for an amending formula based on the principle of the equality of the provinces, the only formula that would guarantee his third objective, enhanced protection for provincial jurisdiction over natural resources including taxing powers.[70] His fourth objective was to limit the Charter to a very basic list of fundamental rights, one that would not include entrenchment of language of education rights for the official language minorities.[71]

Early in 1979 Trudeau added a controversial dimension to constitutional negotiations. He invited the National Indian Brotherhood (NIB), the Native Council of Canada, and the Inuit Tapirisat leaders to present their constitutional aspirations to the First Ministers. He promised them a role at the table on matters affecting their communities following Patriation.[72] Meekison informed his minister of the NIB's contention that Indians constitute a sovereign people with the right to equality of status with the First Ministers in constitutional talks.[73] Western premiers were concerned that Trudeau intended to use constitutional negotiations to transfer Ottawa's fiduciary responsibilities for Indians to the provinces.[74] While agreeing that the Aboriginal groups should be invited to present their views to the First Ministers, Lougheed insisted that they not be granted the right to have formal representation at the negotiating table.[75] When constitutional discussions resumed in the summer of 1980, national and provincial Aboriginal organizations lobbied hard for direct participation. In June, the Indian Association of Alberta (IAA) met with Lougheed's caucus and Cabinet to demand direct and ongoing participation in the constitutional renewal process. Concerned, Lougheed's goal was to restrict the Aboriginal organizations to the role of observers in the negotiating process so as to thwart any constitutional recognition of an Aboriginal inherent right to self-government. He and his government were determined to prevent the creation of a Third Order of government within the federation since this development would entail the transfer of natural resources and taxing powers to Alberta's expanding Indian and Métis communities.[76]

By the end of July, Roy Romanow, chair of the CCMC, announced that there was slim hope of achieving a consensus either on the "People's Package" or the "Governments' list." He blamed the breakdown in discussions on Ottawa's refusal, at the insistence of the Western premiers, to amend its overly intrusive proposals for an economic union that extended the federal power to regulate trade and commerce.[77] Any possibility of the First Ministers salvaging the faltering negotiations at their September meeting ended abruptly when the premiers got their hands on an explosive confidential Report to Cabinet on Constitutional Discussions dated August 30, 1980. The Report, authored by Michael Kirby, a senior official in the Privy Council Office, outlined a range of strategies that Ottawa could use to best its provincial opponents. Kirby outlined how Ottawa could proceed unilaterally by exploiting growing public support for the "People's Package" and warned that the ensuing political struggle would be very tough.[78]

Lougheed, with the backing of several premiers who had different but complementary agendas, led the counter-charge to derail Trudeau's constitutional reform train. Since it was clear that the September Conference would fail, Lougheed took the opportunity in his opening statement to reiterate his watertight compartments conception of Canadian federalism, one that was being threatened by Trudeau's hasty unilateral approach to constitutional renewal. The crisis facing Canada resided in the "interpretation of and the attitudes towards the Confederation-arrangement displayed by the central government. From our perspective it seems to us the central government has consistently interpreted the arrangement in their favour and relied more extensively upon their overriding powers than is appropriate in a true federal system."[79]

In an interesting turn of events, Lougheed became a strategic proponent of asymmetrical federalism. His critics were quick to point out the contradiction between Lougheed's insistence on the equality of provinces in any amending formula and his support for asymmetry. Nonetheless, Lougheed was willing to live with the contradiction if he could build a powerful provincial alliance, including Quebec's Premier Lévesque, capable of preventing Trudeau's unilateral initiative. Lougheed returned to his conception of classic federalism incorporating powerful, sovereign provinces. He argued that the premiers had done their level best to arrive at a consensus and expressed disappointment that Trudeau said no to the premiers' consensus. Concluding that this was inevitable given that there were two fundamentally different views about Canada, he declared that his approach to Constitutional renewal was just as Canadian as Trudeau's. He contended that the provincial governments are closer to the people and should have more say in how they are governed, especially when dealing with human rights and civil liberties. He wondered why Trudeau rejected out of hand the Vancouver Consensus on the amending formula—Alberta's amending formula—since it was flexible and avoided the problems of unanimity. He reiterated that exclusive provincial control over resources was crucial and insisted that attention be given to the economy, especially energy development. The existing constitution could be made to work if only Ottawa would change its attitude toward the provinces. He warned Trudeau not to take unilateral action on patriation because it would damage federalism.[80]

The "Gang of Eight" Counter-Attacks Trudeau's Unilateralism

It was time for bold and decisive action. On October 2, 1980 Trudeau announced a Proposed Resolution for a Joint Address to the Queen Respecting the Constitution of Canada. He contended that the First Ministers had failed because the "historic" unanimity rule had given each First Minister a veto that was used to "bargain freedom against fish, fundamental rights against oil." The premiers' insistence on an outmoded and undemocratic veto created "a radically new concept of Canada, one in which the national good was merely the sum total of provincial demands, one where the division of powers upon which our federation traditionally rests, could be altered for no other reason than that Provinces agreed amongst themselves that it should be altered."[81] The Resolution was put before a Special Joint Committee of the Senate and the House headed up by Senator Harry Hays and Liberal MP Serge Joyal. Its televised hearings galvanized support in favour of the "People's Package."

The September conference precipitated a round of finger-pointing and recriminations. The premiers were angry that they were left to announce the failure and patch up their differences. Lougheed was furious at Premier Bill Davis for placing most of the blame on the premiers, namely himself. Premier Lyon invited Lougheed to lunch with him and Davis so that they could work out a common strategy against Trudeau's decision to move forward unilaterally.[82] Countering the media claim that a group of difficult and parochial premiers were to blame, Lougheed decided to blame Ottawa for the failure of the Conference because Trudeau had adopted the hard-line strategy outlined in the infamous Kirby Report.[83]

Determined to derail the Resolution or have it amended to suit Alberta's conception of Canadian federalism, Lougheed set in motion a comprehensive counter-attack on several fronts. On October 14, 1980, he managed to convince five premiers—Manitoba, Newfoundland, British Columbia, Prince Edward Island, and Quebec—to join him in a powerful provincial alliance. They would be joined by the premiers of Nova Scotia and Saskatchewan in February 1981. For Lougheed, this strategic alliance had two goals: first, to derail Trudeau's unilateral train, and, second, to force Trudeau back to the bargaining table. Separatist Premier Lévesque was one of the staunchest members of the alliance. Following the Patriation decision, Lougheed began to understand that Lévesque's only goal was to derail the constitutional renewal process. On October 23,1980, the Attorneys General and ministers of justice of the six dissident provinces decided to launch references on Trudeau's resolution in the Courts of Appeal in Quebec, Manitoba and Newfoundland.[84] Lougheed turned to Alberta's Legislature for political support. It approved a Resolution that proclaimed that Alberta supported patriation on three conditions: there be safeguards for the protection of provincial rights, proprietary interests and jurisdictions; there were no amendments diminishing these rights; and that the government of Canada not proceed unilaterally.[85] The Lougheed government boycotted parliamentary hearings. Dick Johnston, FIGA minister, informed the co-chairs of the Special Joint Committee and Chrétien that Alberta objected in the strongest terms to the manner in which the Committee was struck and to its method of seeking provincial government input.[86]

Second, Lougheed and Johnston set out to explain why the Alberta government was determined to derail or amend in a substantive manner Trudeau's unilateral Resolution. Lougheed was emboldened by the Supreme Court's December 21, 1979 decision on the Ottawa's reference regarding the constitutionality of Bill C-60's proposed House of Provinces as a replacement for the Senate. The Supreme Court ruled unanimously that the Canadian Parliament could not use its amending authority under Section 91(1) to alter unilaterally the essential nature of the Senate.[87] Why? Because the "Senate has a vital rôle as an institution forming part of the federal system created by the (BNA) Act," and could not be altered without provincial consent. Emboldened by this decision, Lougheed and Johnston characterized Trudeau's Resolution as "nothing short of a constitutional revolution." Patriation must be linked to an acceptable amending formula—the Alberta formula—to ensure a smooth transition of sovereignty from Westminster to Canada thereby protecting the federal nature of Canada's Constitution. Alberta joined five other provinces in a legal challenge of the constitutionality of Trudeau's unilateral Resolution. Lougheed warned Trudeau not to proceed with parliamentary approval of the Resolution until the Supreme Court had decided on its constitutionality. To do so would seriously imperil national unity.[88]

The third dimension of Alberta's counter-attack involved taking the battle to the Parliament and media of the United Kingdom. Johnston was authorized to make a formal submission to, and a request to be heard by, the Select Committee on Foreign Affairs, called the Anthony Kershaw Committee, of the U.K. House of Commons. Alberta made it clear that it opposed unilateral action by the federal government because it "violates a number of important principles of federalism and recognized conventions of the Canadian Constitution." The Canadian Parliament under Section 91(1) did not have the authority to amend the *BNA Act* "in cases affecting federal-provincial relationships and the legislative powers, rights and proprietary interests of the provinces." Under section 7 of the *Statute of Westminster* there is a duty attached to the United Kingdom's responsibility to amend the *BNA Act*. The United Kingdom, as trustee of both the Parliament of Canada and the provincial Legislatures, can only enact a constitutional amendment by Canada if it is "properly requested," that is, constitutionally valid.[89]

Following the release of his Committee's First Report, MP Kershaw spoke to the Edmonton Chamber of Commerce on February 6. He declared: "All we can do, all we should do, indeed all we must do, is to check whether what we are asked to do is constitutionally correct for the British Parliament....to guarantee that amendments to the Canadian constitution are brought about in a manner consistent with the federal nature of the Canadian constitution; in that sense, as guardian of the federal nature of the Canadian constitution." The U.K. Parliament would support a Resolution of the Parliament of Canada if it had "all or nearly all of the Provinces. We do not insist that the request be unanimous." He warned that before the matter was resolved there would be, metaphorically-speaking, blood on the floor of the U.K. Parliament.[90] Lougheed and Johnston met with Kershaw the following day. They asked if the United Kingdom government accepted the interpretation of its role and responsibilities outlined in the Report and discussed the reaction in the U.K. to the debate over the Resolution in the Canadian Parliament and to the Manitoba Court's decision on the constitutionality of the Resolution.

Lougheed's U.K. informants told him that British MPs and a few constitutional experts now "recognize that Westminster has a 'trusteeship function' relative to the fulfillment of section 7 of the Statute of Westminster," but that Prime Minister Thatcher and her government, generally supported by the British press, were reluctant to interfere in Canadian affairs. The most effective response was for Alberta to convince the Thatcher government that Canada was a federation and not a unitary state. It was likely the U.K. Parliament would go along with the ruling of Canada's Supreme Court, a ruling that was eagerly awaited.[91] This assessment of the situation was confirmed by James Horsman, Alberta's minister of advanced education and manpower. He strongly urged Lougheed to visit the U.K. and make Alberta's position clear to the MPs and Lords as well as the informed British public.[92]

A crucial dimension of the Alberta government's counter-attack was to support co-ordinated legal and political challenges by several provinces against the Resolution.[93] Following the acceptance of several minor amendments proposed by Chrétien, the Hays-Joyal Special Joint Committee endorsed the Resolution in its Report released in early February.[94] Lougheed immediately demanded a legal opinion on the Resolution's amended section dealing with natural resources. The amendment was first proposed by the federal NDP Party and drafted by Premier Blakeney of Saskatchewan but Lougheed did not find it protected Alberta's interests.[95] The Consolidated Resolution was approved by the House of Commons on April 23 and the next day by the Senate. Trudeau assured smooth passage by agreeing in early April to refer the Resolution to the Supreme Court when in late March the Newfoundland Court of Appeal ruled unanimously that the Resolution was unconstitutional. Given that the Manitoba Court of Appeal ruled against the provinces in early February and the Quebec Court of Appeal would do so in mid-April, Trudeau believed that his government stood at least a fifty-fifty chance of obtaining a positive ruling from the Supreme Court.[96]

Premier Sterling Lyon proposed to Lougheed that eight premiers—New Brunswick and Ontario excepted—weaken the political legitimacy of Trudeau's unilateral Resolution by agreeing to an amending formula and presenting it to the public in a dramatic manner.[97] On April 3, Lyon urged Trudeau to suspend Parliament's deliberation and vote on the Resolution and indicated that the premiers would agree on an amending formula during their April 16 meeting. Trudeau replied that Parliament had unanimously agreed to complete debate and the vote by April 23 so that the Supreme Court would know the final content of the Resolution. He hoped the premiers could agree upon an amending formula—he doubted that Ontario and New Brunswick premiers, who represented nearly 40 per cent of the Canada's population, would support it.[98]

FIGA prepared an extensive briefing book for Lougheed's meeting with seven of his fellow premiers to hammer out a consensus on the amending formula.[99] On April 16 the premiers— dubbed the "Gang of Eight" by the media—released their Canadian patriation plan including, at the insistence of Lévesque, a slightly modified "Vancouver Consensus" 7/50 amending formula. If the Trudeau government withdrew its Resolution and agreed to a full constitutional conference based on their plan and their previous constitutional agendas, the premiers would discontinue all court action.[100]

Meekison, convinced that Trudeau would not accept the premiers' offer, expected that he might make a counter-offer involving the Charter or resort to a divide and conquer strategy. He advised that the premiers should stick by their accord until it was no longer politically useful.[101] The Official Opposition criticized Lougheed for signing an Accord that violated the November 4, 1976 Resolution of the Alberta Legislature requiring "unanimous consent of all provinces for a proper amending formula." Johnston assured Lougheed that the government had lived up to the letter and the spirit of Resolution since it was still possible that Ontario and New Brunswick would sign on since they had, in the past, agreed to the amending formula. In the interim, Alberta pursued the battle against Trudeau's unconstitutional Resolution at home and in the U.K.[102] Dennis Anderson, a government MLA, gathered further intelligence in the U.K., concluding that the British Government would comply with the Supreme Court ruling but it could take up to a year. He advised Lougheed and the other premiers to increase their lobbying efforts to counteract Ottawa's extensive and effective lobbing campaign.[103] Between July 20 and 25, Jeremy Akerman, working through Alberta's agent general, Jim MacKibben, met with Conservative and Labour MPs and other provincial agents general. He was convinced that Alberta's battle could be won in the U.K. Parliament if it could convince MPs and Lords that supporting Trudeau's unilateral Resolution entailed greater intervention in Canadian affairs than amending or rejection. The provinces' lobbying efforts would be enhanced greatly by a supportive Supreme Court decision, especially if the premiers and Intergovernmental Affairs Deputies joined the lobbying in the U.K.[104]

The Supreme Court's Patriation Decision

The Supreme Court rendered its controversial decision in the *Patriation Reference* case on September 28, 1981. The decision dramatically altered the dynamic of the ongoing mega-constitutional negotiations. The Court reviewed the three central questions addressed in the Manitoba, Quebec and Newfoundland court cases: First, did the *Constitution Act, 1981* affect the federal-provincial relationship or provincial powers? Second, was there a constitutional convention necessitating provincial consent for such an amendment? Third, was this provincial consent a constitutional requirement? All the judges answered the first question in the affirmative without explanation. On the second question, the court ruled, six to three, in a convoluted and questionable fashion that there was a "constitutional convention" obliging Ottawa to obtain "a substantial degree of provincial consent" before proceeding with an amendment affecting federal-provincial relations or provincial powers. Underlying the convention was the principle of federalism. Yet, since conventions by nature are political and evolve, the Court's role was limited to one of recognition and not enforcement. Chief Justice Bora Laskin, ostensibly writing for dissent, concluded that there was no discernable constitutional convention requiring the consent of *all* the provinces. By a majority of seven to two—four roving judges played a role in both majorities—on the third question the Court ruled (again with Laskin ostensibly holding the pen), that it was constitutionally legal for Parliament to proceed unilaterally with its Resolution. The alleged constitutional convention had never been transformed by statute into a binding legal requirement enforceable by the Courts. Finally, the overriding powers granted to the central government under the *BNA Act* undermined the majority's use of the federal principle to buttress its case for a constitutionally binding convention.[105]

The Patriation decision was interpreted as a "politically correct" ruling, which perhaps explains why political leaders and the general public found it too complex and ambiguous to understand. Given the decision's juxtaposition of legal opinion and political *obiter dicta*, the dispute between the Resolution's advocates and critics would have to be resolved in the political arena.[106] The decision paradoxically reinforced both Trudeau's legal and political bargaining positions. The government's Resolution was constitutionally legal and it could be forwarded to the U.K. with the support of some but not *all* of the premiers. Trudeau concluded that it was politically advantageous to meet the premiers to see if he could obtain the support of several provinces. While undermining the legal position of the "Gang of Eight" premiers, the convoluted decision allowed the group to proclaim a major political victory. The Court unanimously supported their claim that the Resolution affected provincial jurisdiction and then ruled, six to three, that there was a constitutional convention requiring consent of a substantial number but not all of the provinces for its approval. Unfortunately, this convention could not be enforced by the Courts. Nonetheless, the dissident premiers, led by Lougheed, spun the ruling in their favour by stressing almost exclusively the Court's recognition of a politically binding constitutional convention that was on par with the legal dimension. Lougheed was determined to force Trudeau back to the bargaining table. As a last resort it was important to attempt to stop Patriation in the U.K.[107]

The Alberta government stressed the historic nature of the Patriation ruling as well as its profound and enduring impact on the evolution of Canada's constitutional development. The Supreme Court recognized and affirmed the legitimacy of the Alberta government's and Legislature's contention that the Resolution offended the federal principle at the heart of the Canada's federal system, thereby threatening rather than strengthening national unity. Alberta's Attorney General and its FIGA minister urged the prime minister to convene a constitutional conference so that negotiations could be resumed so that Canadians could obtain a truly Canadian Constitution.[108] Concerned that Trudeau might orchestrate another failed constitutional conference or obtain the support of more provinces and forward Parliament's Resolution directly to the U.K., Lougheed wanted to know what impact the Supreme Court's decision might have on the U.K. government and Parliament. He was advised by the Deputy Attorney General that the Supreme Court ruling left untouched the legislative authority of the U.K. Parliament while "the provinces' internal sovereignty does not authorize extra-territorial provincial sovereignty to impair the U.K. Parliament's right to change the BNA Act or the Federal Government's right to request such change."[109] Convinced of a convergence between the Kershaw Report and the Supreme Court decision,[110] Premier Lougheed paid a visit to the U.K. in early October to enhance his government's lobby efforts.[111] A brochure, The Canadian Constitutional Resolution: A Decision for the United Kingdom, was distributed to U.K. politicians and the media in which the dissident premiers emphasized their interpretation of the Supreme Court decision and called upon the U.K. Parliament not to pass an unconstitutional Resolution. In doing so, it would force a negotiated political settlement in Canada, that is, "a made-in-Canada Constitution, having the support of both the provinces and people of Canada." The Alberta government also prepared a Petition for its agent general to present to the U.K. Parliament that made the same request·[112]

Alberta's Amending Formula for the Charter

Lougheed had done everything he could to strengthen Alberta's bargaining position. The dissident premiers issued a communiqué on October 19 urging the prime minister to convene a constitutional conference during the first week of November with an advance meeting the week of October 26 of ministers responsible for the constitution. Trudeau, in his response to Premier Bennett, reminded him that the premiers had turned down his invitation for a First Minister's meeting six times since the Supreme Court decision. Trudeau expressed disappointment that Bennett had refused to reveal whether the dissident premiers were willing to compromise. Nevertheless, Trudeau agreed to convene a First Minister's meeting on November 2 and to continue the meeting until a consensus was reached or it became clear that an agreement was not possible. Trudeau believed that if they all approached the meeting in good faith and determination it was possible to produce a national consensus on a constitutional resolution.[113]

Building on his reputation as a successful negotiator, Lougheed reaffirmed his hard-line strategic approach during his opening remarks at the Constitutional Conference. He reminded Canadians that he had just signed an energy accord with Ottawa on September 1, 1981. Why is it not possible, he asked, to make a deal on the Constitution? Despite the premiers' agreement in principle on the "Vancouver Consensus Amending Formula" of September 1980, Trudeau said no and embarked on a "reckless" and "divisive" unilateral course of action that violates the federal nature of Canada. The Supreme Court's Patriation decision reaffirmed once again the Federal Principle when it recognized that not only was there an established constitutional convention requiring provincial consent to amendments affecting provincial rights, but that it would be unconstitutional for Parliament to proceed unilaterally without substantial provincial support. He reminded Trudeau that the Supreme Court "did not say that what the federal government is proposing is legal but rather that there is nothing in law to prevent the passage of the Federal Resolution, which is an entirely different thing." Contending that Canadians wanted a "Made in Canada" constitution not a "Made in Britain" constitution," Lougheed urged Trudeau, Davis, and Hatfield to support the April 16 Constitutional Accord hammered out by the dissident premiers. That Accord's amending formula reflected the equality of provinces principle while respecting the federal principle. Lougheed's highly provocative proposal meant that deliberations on the Charter would be deferred to the second phase of constitutional renewal, after patriation and the Alberta amending formula had been achieved.[114] Clearly Lougheed realized that Trudeau would never agree to relinquish his Charter, the *raison d'être* and essence of Parliament's Constitutional Resolution, but it was the dissident premiers' strongest and most effective opening gambit.

During the first three days of the Conference, it seemed that the dissident premiers' hard-line approach would fail, thereby giving political legitimacy to Trudeau's unilateral Resolution.[115] A cagey and wizened Trudeau set out to crack the "Gang of Eight" using his most effective ploy. He made Premier Lévesque an offer he could not refuse—a referendum on the amending formula, which Lévesque, after promising his fellow premiers that he would not, quickly accepted. As events rapidly unfolded he would regret his hasty decision. The other premiers were dead set against referenda because they eroded their power as well as the sovereignty of their Legislatures. For Lougheed, Lévesque's acceptance signalled that he had abandoned the Premiers' Accord. He and they were now free to explore their respective constitutional compromises with Trudeau and his chief negotiator, Jean Chrétien. Roy McMurtry and Roy Romanow, Attorneys General of Ontario and Saskatchewan, joined Chrétien in the kitchen of the Government Conference Centre to explore possible elements of a compromise deal. They fashioned the "kitchen accord" comprising two fundamental elements: Alberta's "Vancouver Consensus" amending formula without fiscal compensation for provinces opting out would displace the Victoria amending formula, and a notwithstanding clause, s. 33, would be added to the Charter to guarantee the sovereignty of the Legislatures. Premier Blakeney took on the arduous task of selling the deal to his fellow premiers. Chrétien conveyed the "kitchen accord" to the prime minister at 24 Sussex. Late into the night of November 4–5, Trudeau, pressured by his close ally, Premier Davis, reluctantly agreed to the compromise deal based on the following conditions. The notwithstanding clause, with a five-year statutory limit, would apply to Fundamental Freedoms, Legal Rights and Equality Rights but not to official language rights, ss. 16–22, nor to s. 23 on Minority Language Education Rights on which the "kitchen deal" had called for provincial referenda. The provinces agreed to accept Ottawa's equalization and regional disparities clause as well as the holding of a constitutional conference dealing with Aboriginal issues, including the definition of their rights to be included in the constitution. During the morning session of November 5, all the First Ministers—except a shocked Lévesque who learned of the potential deal when he arrived late—signed an accord comprising the agreed-upon amendments to Trudeau's Parliamentary Resolution.[116]

Lougheed could afford to be magnanimous in his closing remarks since he believed that the final Resolution reflected his and Albertans' conception of federalism. Lougheed was most pleased that Alberta got its amending formula, one that entrenched the equality of the provinces. Alberta had insisted on the notwithstanding clause for the Charter, a condition he believed was necessary for the preservation of provincial rights and British Parliamentary democracy in Canada. Lougheed contended that the amended Resolution, by recognizing the Supreme Court of Canada's decision regarding constitutional conventions, entrenched the equality of the provinces in Canada's federal system of governance. Finally, Alberta helped the provinces avoid a referendum on the constitution since referenda are divisive and undermine political leadership. He called on Ottawa to make overtures to Quebec on the issue of full financial compensation for opting out of amendments pertaining to programs in areas of exclusive provincial jurisdiction. Canada could and should accommodate a certain degree of informal asymmetry in the way which federalism functioned.[117] Aware of the contradictions, Lougheed did not elaborate on how asymmetry jived with the principle and practice of the equality of provinces. Neither did he state publicly that he believed that s. 92A, reaffirming provincial control over non-renewable resources, could only be guaranteed because he obtained his Alberta amending formula.[118]

Lougheed and his fellow premiers immediately faced an unrelenting barrage of criticism from Premier Lévesque, his minister in charge of Constitutional negotiations, Claude Morin, and the entire Francophone media. In a letter dated November 6 and later in his book,[119] Morin argued that the premiers, led by Lougheed, had betrayed Premier Lévesque and the people of Quebec by violating the Provincial Accord of April 16, 1981, which Lévesque, at great political risk, had very reluctantly given up Quebec's historic veto over constitutional change in exchange for the premiers' agreement to derail Trudeau's unilateral resolution.[120] Lougheed believed otherwise. Once the Supreme Court Patriation decision had derailed Trudeau's unilateral Resolution and forced him back to the table, the April 16 Accord had accomplished its primary objective. Stung by the harsh criticism emanating from Quebec, on March 8, 1982

Lougheed explained to Lévesque how and why the April 16 Accord had been set aside by the dissident premiers during the evening and night of November 4–5. He argued that Lévesque understood from the outset that once Trudeau had been stopped by the Supreme Court from taking unilateral action and was compelled to hold a final conference, each of the premiers was on his own to seek whatever deal he could get. Lévesque in his blunt reply of May 5, 1982 indicated that the premiers had taken advantage of his "Catch 22" predicament.[121] Clearly there was no possible meeting of minds on how to interpret the unravelling of the dissident premiers.

Trudeau and the premiers faced a national firestorm of political criticism from several women's organizations for dropping s. 28, reaffirming gender rights, as well as all the radicalized national and provincial Aboriginal organizations for dropping s. 34 on Aboriginal rights. Lougheed did not, for reasons of *real politique*, oppose the restitution of s. 28 since polls showed that Albertans favoured this affirmation of gender rights. It was an entirely different matter for Aboriginal rights. Premier Lougheed, backed by British Columbia's Premier Bennett, who demanded that Ottawa provide full financial compensation for any and all Aboriginal land claims, was the most vociferous opponent of the reinstitution of s. 34 (s. 35 in the final deal). The Lougheed government was dealing with an increasingly radicalized IAA after the Trudeau government allowed national Aboriginal leaders to present their views on the constitution to the First Ministers in 1978. In its submission to the Special Joint Committee on the Trudeau Resolution, the IAA demanded the entrenchment of full native self-government—a Third Order of Indian government in a sovereignty-association arrangement with Canada—in the Constitution before accepting Patriation.[122]

When Trudeau informed the Aboriginal organizations that their concerns would be addressed following the successful completion of the Patriation round, they received as *quid pro quo* a guarantee, stated in s. 25, that the *Charter* "shall not be construed so as to abrogate or derogate from any aboriginal, treaty or other rights or freedoms that pertain to aboriginal peoples of Canada." Aboriginal leaders insisted on and obtained s. 35 of the *Constitution Act* recognizing and affirming their aboriginal and treaty rights and defining "aboriginal peoples of Canada" to include the Indian, Inuit and Métis peoples. As part of the November 5 deal, Lougheed and the other Western premiers insisted that s. 35 be dropped from the amended Consolidated Resolution. Lougheed argued that the jurisprudence on aboriginal rights remained "relatively undeveloped" so it was impossible to predict the impact of s. 35. It was prudent that the definition of Aboriginal rights be left to a future constitutional conference.[123]

As Trudeau had done with the women's organizations, he urged all the Aboriginal organizations to pressure the recalcitrant premiers to reinstate s. 35. The IAA, in tandem with NIB, launched a vociferous provincial campaign to get Lougheed to support full reinstatement of s. 35, urging Albertans to pressure Lougheed, Trudeau and their provincial MLAs and federal MPs to support the entrenchment of Indian Treaties and Treaty rights in the Constitution before Patriation.[124] Lougheed and his minister of Native affairs tried desperately to counter the campaign by arguing that E. Steinhauer was misinforming Albertans about the Alberta government's position which fully supported the protection of Aboriginal and Treaty rights under s. 25. The premiers were not party to the negotiations between the Trudeau government and the national Aboriginal organizations on s. 35 and did not consider themselves bound by clause. Lougheed assured Albertans that his government would never accept a Third Order of government for its Aboriginal peoples.[125]

A growing public outcry forced Lougheed and his fellow Western premiers to back down and reinstate s. 35. Nevertheless, Lougheed, ever the hard liner, insisted that the term "existing" be inserted before "aboriginal and Treaty rights" in s. 35(1). All premiers agreed and the revised s. 35 was accepted by Ottawa on 24 November.[126] Consequently, both the IAA and the NIB leaders denounced the revised s. 35 as completely unsatisfactory, urged that Trudeau not proceed with his amended Consolidated Resolution, and promised that he would encounter a phalanx of Aboriginal opposition in the U.K.[127] Fearful that the ongoing negotiations involving several amendments, including ss. 28 and 35, could derail their November 5 accord, the premiers urged Trudeau on November 30 to end the process and get on with Parliament's ratification of the amended Consolidated Resolution.[128] On December 9, the day after Parliament passed the Resolution, Lougheed declared in the Alberta Legislature that the Patriation Resolution with Alberta's amending formula and the circumscribed Trudeau Charter was "a momentous occasion in Canada's constitutional development. ... Through democratic transition, Canadians will have achieved full and complete sovereignty—a made in Canada Constitution."[129]

Promoting and Defending the *Constitution Act, 1982*

Even before the Queen arrived in Canada on April 17, 1982 to give Royal Assent to the *Constitution Act, 1982*, Lougheed had to defend his constitutional handiwork against a nascent Alberta separatist movement. The separatists charged that the Constitution weakened property rights because these were not entrenched in the Charter. Lougheed argued that this was not so, but clearly his government would have to do a much better job of communicating Alberta's gains in the *Constitution Act, 1982*.[130] A pamphlet, entitled *Canada's New Constitution and What it Means to Albertans*, explained the 7/50 amending formula—Alberta's proposal—that entrenched the equality of the provinces and guaranteed provincial autonomy, especially over resources. It emphasized that the Charter protected women's rights in s. 28 and Aboriginal Rights in ss. 25 and 35 while s. 33 affirmed the continued supremacy of the Alberta Legislature. On the controversial matter of property rights, it stated that s. 26 guaranteed that other rights and freedoms are not affected by the Charter, and reminded Albertans that s. 1 of the Alberta Bill of Rights protected property rights as did the common law traditions of the province.[131]

The more serious constitutional challenge facing Lougheed's government was the controversial and complex issue of Aboriginal self-government. Michael Kirby proposed two meetings of government officials in September and December and a meeting of First Ministers and the leaders of the Aboriginal organizations in January to set the agenda for the April 1983 Aboriginal Conference required by the *Constitution Act, 1982*. The AFN rejected the proposed meetings on the grounds that the First Nations must negotiate a nation to nation bilateral agreement with Canada on their relationship with Canada before they would participate in the Conference. The AFN was determined to guarantee that Canada did not transfer any of its fiduciary responsibilities to the provinces, so it did not want the premiers involved in any of the preliminary negotiations.[132] AFN and federal officials held seven bilateral meetings between June 22 and November 29. AFN Chief, David Ahenakew, requested an exchange of letters acknowledging the formal establishment of this bilateral political process. As long as the process continued, he indicated that the AFN was willing to participate in the Aboriginal Conference.[133] Trudeau disagreed with Ahenakew's claim that the purpose of bilateral discussions was to "facilitate recognition of aboriginal title and Indian rights in the Canadian Constitution." These goals could only be achieved via the 7/50 amending formula following a successful Aboriginal

Conference. Discussion of these matters at the official level was preparatory work and "should in no way be taken as agreement that the specific matters listed do in fact, in our view, constitute aboriginal rights."[134]

Alberta was also embroiled in this dispute over protocol. Dick Johnston, Alberta's FIGA minister, acknowledging AFN Chief Ahenakew's preference for bilateral negotiations with Ottawa, reminded him that "provincial legislatures as well as the federal Parliament must, under the terms of *The Constitution Act, 1982*, approve any constitutional amendments related to the rights of aboriginal peoples." He urged the Chief to participate in the preparatory process along with representatives of the other two Aboriginal organizations, the Inuit Committee on National Issues and the Native Council of Canada.[135] The AFN's hard-line position had originated within a radicalized IAA and its new president, Charles Wood. This development caused a serious rift between it and the Alberta government that prompted the cancellation of their annual June meeting.[136] Alberta continued its discussions with individual Indian Chiefs as well as with the moderate leaders of the Métis Association of Alberta (MAA) and the Federation of Métis Settlements (FMS).[137] IAA President Wood was furious at this tactic of divide and rule. He insisted that Alberta's Aboriginal people be given the right to veto any policies or legislation that threatened their longstanding Treaty and Aboriginal Rights. He called upon the Alberta government to stop "politically seducing individual Chiefs" and to "enter into constructive diplomacy with the collective Treaty Indian Chiefs inside Alberta." Lougheed rejected the charge of political interference while assuring President Wood that his government would take no actions that might threaten or diminish the Treaty rights guaranteed Alberta's Indian people.[138] Many Alberta Chiefs and the IAA—staunch advocates of independence for Indian nations—joined other western Chiefs to form the Coalition of First Nations. This AFN splinter group rejected the legitimacy of the *Constitution Act, 1982* as well as its multilateral negotiating s. 37 process and boycotted all the conferences devoted to Aboriginal matters.[139]

By December, the Lougheed government was also questioning its ongoing negotiations with the MAA. This was made evident by FMS's decision to pursue a lawsuit against the government. Alberta's Attorney General obtained an in-house legal opinion on Alberta's constitutional responsibilities towards its Métis peoples. Solicitor Susan Carter concluded that the Métis peoples did not have any "existing" aboriginal rights since they only became "aboriginal peoples" by virtue of s. 35(2) of the *Constitution Act, 1982*. They may acquire aboriginal rights that relate to land and resources through the Aboriginal

Conference process and these rights may have some effect upon their present lawsuit or future lawsuits. Negotiations between the government and the Métis associations came to an abrupt halt, prompting their leaders to complain bitterly to the premier. Lougheed responded that his government would take as much time as it needed to formulate new positions in preparation for the Aboriginal conference.[140]

In response to the constitutional demands of Alberta's Métis associations and the three national Aboriginal organizations as set out in the First Ministers' Conference Working Agenda, James Horsman, FIGA minister, presented his hard-line recommendations to the Cabinet/Caucus Committees on Native Land Claims and Native Affairs. Alberta should support entrenching a statement of principles on Aboriginal rights, social and cultural rights, family law, and education rights rather than constitutionally-binding guarantees. The same approach should be adopted concerning the proposed Charter of Rights for Aboriginal Peoples. Alberta proposed granting aboriginal people a constitutional requirement to be consulted—no formal consent—in advance of constitutional amendments affecting ss. 25 of the Charter, s. 35 of the *Constitution Act, 1982* and s. 91(24) of the *Constitution Act, 1867*. Alberta was willing to consider a constitutional amendment to guarantee gender equality for Native women. But, Alberta was not prepared to endorse the entrenchment of self-government, collective ownership of land and resources, hunting and fishing rights, aboriginal title or a land base for Métis, or guaranteed representation in political institutions for Canada's Aboriginal peoples.[141] On February 21, 1983 Alberta's responses to the Aboriginal peoples constitutional demands were relayed by the FIGA and Native Affairs Minister to the Alberta Métis associations. The presidents of the MAA and the FMS were shocked to learn that their good faith bargaining with Alberta officials had come to naught. The Alberta government had decided to pursue a non-constitutional, "made-in-Alberta" process and agreement to resolve Métis rights. The Métis associations queried whether government's positions on aboriginal rights in the constitution were open to revision before the March 15–16 conference. Lougheed, replying in a diplomatic yet firm manner, restated Alberta's position on Aboriginal constitutional issues, outlined in some detail what the government had accomplished for Alberta's Métis and what it hoped to do in the future. He did not anticipate any major revisions to Alberta's aboriginal policies prior to the conference.[142]

At the Aboriginal constitutional conference, to the surprise of the premiers and many observers, Trudeau set aside his long-standing opposition to the

Aboriginal organizations' demand for self-government. Seeking middle ground between the polar positions of integration/assimilation or segregation/independence, Trudeau proposed a model of semi-autonomous, self-governing Aboriginal communities within the Canadian federation. The premiers, especially Lougheed,[143] remained wary and critical of the Aboriginal organizations' demand for unfettered self-government and hoped that the conference would fail. Bowing to public pressure, they reluctantly agreed to three important amendments. The first, demanded by Aboriginal women's organizations, entailed a gender equality clause, s. 35(4), that obliged Ottawa to delete the discriminatory article from the Indian Act in 1985. The second, intended to legitimize ongoing land claims negotiations and agreements, comprised a new s. 35(3) stating that "For greater certainty, in subsection (1) 'treaty rights' includes rights that now exist by way of land claims agreements or may be so acquired." The premiers felt obliged to accept a revised s. 37(1) mandating three more conferences dedicated to Aboriginal matters.[144]

Aboriginal nationalists garnered considerable support from the House of Commons Special Committee on Indian Self-Government. Its November 1983 Report, Indian Self-Government in Canada, called the Penner Report, embraced the two-row wampum model of separate and equal nations, that is, the Aboriginal First Nations and the Canadian nation moving in tandem canoes down the river toward their separate futures.[145] The Penner Committee concluded that "it is quite possible that Indian governments may already have the right to self-government, for any rights or freedoms recognized by the Royal Proclamation of 1763 are now guaranteed in the Constitution Act, 1982, Section 25."[146] The Report recommended that the federal government recognize and entrench Indian self-government in the Constitution of Canada as a Third Order of government with control over "virtually the entire range of law-making, policy, program delivery, law enforcement and adjudication powers would be available to an Indian First Nation government within its territory."[147] AFN leaders developed a series of composite amendments that "included a clear recognition of the right of self-government, supplemented by a process to agree on specific powers and financial arrangements. The right, however was free standing. It was not dependent on agreements, though it could be defined by a process of negotiation."[148]

Trudeau and the premiers were extremely wary of the radical nature of the Penner Report and the impact it was having on Aboriginal leaders. On March 5, 1984 John Munro, federal minister of Indian Affairs and Northern Development, indicated that Ottawa was considering a bottom-up legislative approach to the achievement of negotiated self-governments with certain mature Indian nations. The government proposal, outlined in Bill C-52, entailed a modified form of the Penner Report's legislative approach to negotiating self-government with individual bands.[149] Trudeau, in his opening remarks to the March 8–9, 1984 Constitutional Conference of First Ministers' on the Rights of Aboriginal Peoples, reiterated that his government did not support entrenchment of Aboriginal First Nation's governments since a Third Order of government would drastically alter the authority and rights of Parliament and the provincial Legislatures while undermining Aboriginals' sense of Canadian identity and citizenship. Ottawa, characterizing s. 35 as an "empty box," proposed a more cautious, evolutionary process of building democratic self-government institutions for selected Aboriginal communities through a careful "delegation of federal powers" sanctioned by Parliament and the provincial Legislatures.[150]

Since it was unlikely that Ottawa and the premiers would ever consent to a Third Order of government for the Aboriginal communities, Lougheed's primary concern was with the claim made by Métis National Council at the Conference that there existed thanks to ss. 91(24), 25, and 35 a joint federal and provincial responsibility for Métis people.[151] If this dual jurisdiction was affirmed, what claims, Lougheed asked, "would be made for land within Alberta by the federal government to meet their responsibilities?" Clearly, Alberta had no intention of sharing jurisdiction over its Métis communities with Ottawa since that might entail transferring extensive tracts of land—including their resources—already set aside for Métis settlements to the federal government.[152]

Trudeau retired from office and Brian Mulroney, the leader of the Conservative Party, won the September 1984 federal election against the leader of the Liberal Party, John Turner. Prime Minister Mulroney, eager to demonstrate his skills as a negotiator, decided to disclose the federal government's proposal in advance of the 1985 Aboriginal conference. Based on the concept of delegated aboriginal self-government as per the 1984 federal draft, Mulroney's initial proposal was rejected unceremoniously by the premiers of British Columbia, Alberta, Saskatchewan and Nova Scotia for going too far. When Ottawa removed the provincial requirement to become involved in negotiations, the revised resolution won the support of eight premiers—only seven were required under the amending formula. The premiers of Alberta and British Columbia refused to accept the revised proposal because they believed it established a Third Order of government. The AFN rejected the federal proposals outright since there was no recognition of an inherent right to self-government and the provinces had both a role in, and a veto over, the negotiations leading to self-government. Nonetheless, it appeared that Mulroney had the required support of the other national Aboriginal organization leaders—the Métis National Council, the Native Council of Canada, and the newly-formed Prairie Treaty Nations Alliance. Mulroney was unable to obtain the support of the Inuit Committee on National Issues despite consultation with their communities. At the Toronto conference in June, New Brunswick and Ontario—having received negative feedback—also withdrew their support.[153] Provincial autonomy was safe from the threat of a Third Order of government. Lougheed's government was able to get on with negotiating a made-in-Alberta agreement with the Métis communities and their leaders.[154]

Conspicuous by its absence from Lougheed government's constitutional agenda prior to November 1982 was Senate reform. Lougheed steadfastly opposed all proposals—emanating from Trudeau, Clark, the Task Force on National Unity, and Western Canadian organizations—for a House of Provinces. He consistently rejected calls for an elected Senate because it would weaken the provincial governments and the First Ministers conferences. Gordon Kesler, an elected MLA for the Western Canada Concept party, and his secessionist followers promoted a Triple "E" Senate—equal, elected, efficient—as the only alternative to independence. They denounced Lougheed's unwarranted compromises on energy matters, his acceptance of a Charter that did not entrench property rights and Alberta's lack of political clout in Ottawa. Lougheed first ignored the movement and then tried to ride the wave by blaming Ottawa for Alberta's economic woes while dramatically increasing government spending on a whole range of programs in the lead-up to the November 2, 1982 provincial election. Lougheed, ignoring the secessionists, received an overwhelming mandate, 75 of 79 seats with 62 per cent of the vote.[155]

The Lougheed government quietly took up the issue of Senate reform, hoping to undermine the secessionist movement's strongest argument— Alberta's lack of political clout in Ottawa that reinforced Albertan's sense of alienation. Lougheed preferred a provincially-appointed Senate with dramatically enhanced powers because it would act as a powerful tool of the provincial governments at the heart of the Canadian Parliamentary system. The government's ill-conceived discussion paper, A Provincially-Appointed Senate: A New Federalism for Canada,[156] was criticized and ridiculed by the opposition parties and the media as a bald-face attempt to replace an outmoded, undemocratic prime minister's House of Patronage with a premiers' House of Patronage. Politically embarrassed, Lougheed attempted to co-opt the growing Western Canadian movement for Senate reform based on the Triple "E" model, elected, equal, and effective.[157] The Triple "E" Senate, if ever implemented, would accelerate Alberta's transformation of constitutionalism in Canada.

Lougheed's Constitutional Legacy

In the fall of 1985, after a decade of fierce mega-constitutional political battles, Lougheed announced his decision to retire. He fortuitously avoided the abject failure of the fourth constitutional conference on Aboriginal matters in 1987 and the crises over the Meech Lake and Charlottetown Accords. Paradoxically, Lougheed's significant and far-reaching role in the transformation of Canadian constitutionalism was neither fully understood nor appreciated by most Albertans and Canadians. In retrospect, with the help of perceptive advisors, FIGA ministers and mandarins, and his own keen grasp of the essence of provincial rights in the tradition of Oliver Mowat, Lougheed made a tremendous contribution to the renewal, informally and formally, of Canada's Constitution. He did so by incessantly promoting and enhancing provincial autonomy, especially in the area of resource development and taxation, and by holding out for the Alberta amending formula, one based on the equality of the provinces.

The political and constitutional shift away from the traditional conception of a Canada, one based on four regions and two founding nationalities as reflected in a region-based amending formula, was very controversial and highly destabilizing. Both Lougheed and Trudeau were able to capitalize on Canadians' desire for constitutional renewal. They channelled the tension created by the election of a Quebec separatist government in 1976 to obtain the *Constitution Act, 1982*, one comprising their respective transformational constitutional visions. During his last administration, Lougheed promoted his vision of provincial equality within an informal asymmetrical federation. When required, he defended executive federalism and elite accommodation by ensuring that a Triple "E" Senate be made to work in harmony with an entrenched system of First Ministers Conferences. Paradoxically, Mulroney's and Bourassa's failed attempts to weaken the *Constitution Act, 1982* and the Charter via the Meech Lake and Charlottetown Constitutional accords infused new life into the moribund Québécois secessionist movement. The Parti Québécois, re-elected in 1994, held a second referendum on the secession of Quebec in 1995 which came extremely close to destroying Canada. Thanks to the vigilance of Canadians who jealously defended the Canadian Charter of Rights and Freedoms and spoke up loud and clear for Canada, the remarkable constitutional legacies of both Lougheed and Trudeau remained intact for future generations to enjoy.

Notes

1. Christopher Armstrong, *The Politics of Federalism: Ontario's Relations with the Federal Government, 1867–1942* (Toronto: University of Toronto Press, 1981); John T. Saywell, *The Lawmakers: Judicial Power and the Shaping of Canadian Federalism* (Toronto: University of Toronto Press, 2002).

2. Progressive Conservative Association of Alberta, New Release, June 11, 1971, p. 1. Public Archives of Alberta (PAA), Peter Lougheed Papers, 85.401/142/11.

3. Alberta, FIGA, *First Report to March 31, 1974* (Edmonton: FIGA, 1974), 32.

4. J. Peter Meekison, ADM, to Hyndman. "Prime Minister's Letter, March 31 on Patriation and the Amending Formula," PAA, 85.401/274/17.

5. Hyndman to Lougheed, July 8, 1975; Hyndman to Lougheed, September 13, 1976, PAA, 85.401/59/1058.

6. Alberta, FIGA, "Communiqué from the Sixteenth Annual Conference of Premiers, St. John's Newfoundland, August 21–22, 1975," *Third Annual Report 1975–76* (Edmonton: FIGA, 1976), 36.

7. Trudeau to Lougheed, March 31, 1976, PAA, 85.401/678/39. A copy of the letter and the Draft Proclamation can be found in Alberta, FIGA, *Fourth Annual Report to March 31, 1977* (Edmonton: FIGA, 1977), 55–62.

8. Alberta, FIGA, *Fourth Annual Report*, 1–10.

9. Hyndman to Lougheed, April 5, 1976. "BNA Act—"Patriation"—April 9th deadline," PAA, 85.401/274/17.

10. Meekison to Hyndman, April 7, 1976, "Memo: Prime Minister's letter, March 30 [sic] on patriation and the amending formula," PAA, 85.401/274/17, quote at 7.

11. TELEX from Lougheed to Trudeau, April 7, 1976. Re: Trudeau's letter of March 31, 1976, PAA, 85.401/678/39.

12. Meekison to Hyndman, July 8, 1976, Notes on a meeting with Gordon Robertson, Ottawa, Ontario, July 6, 1976, PAA, 85.401/276/18.

13. Meekison to Deputy Minister Harold S. Millican, June 27, 1976; and Hyndman to Lougheed, June 30, 1976, RE: Progress Report, PAA, 85.401/276/18.

14. Meekison to Hyndman, July 8, 1976, Notes on meeting of Alberta and Quebec Officials, Quebec City, July 5, 1976; Barbara Anderson and Oryssia Lennie to Meekison, July 21, 1976, Notes on a second meeting of Alberta and Quebec officials, Edmonton, July 21, 1976, PAA, 85.401/276/18.

15. Hyndman to Jim Foster, August 4, 1976, Constitutional Meeting—Attorneys General—August 13–15, PAA, 85.401/276/18.

16. Ibid., Attachment: Legal Opinions, 1–7.

17. Premier William R. Bennett, *What is British Columbia's position on the Constitution of Canada* (Victoria: Government of British Columbia, November 1976).

18. Premier Lougheed to Prime Minister Trudeau, October 14, 1976, PAA, 85.401/276/18. Also in Alberta, FIGA, *Fourth Annual Report*, 63–64.

19. Prime Minister Trudeau to Premier Lougheed, October 18, 1976, Alberta, FIGA, *Fourth Annual Report*, 65.

20. *Alberta Hansard*, 1 and 4 November, 1976, 1772 and 1782. The underlined section was an amendment proposed by the opposition.

21. Lougheed to Dr. Harvie Andre, M.P. November 12, 1976, PAA, 85.401/275/18.

22. Prime Minister Trudeau to Premier Peter Lougheed, January 19, 1977. Alberta, FIGA, *Fourth Annual Report*, 66–69.

23. Alberta, FIGA, *Fourth Annual Report*, Attached: Draft Resolution Respecting the Constitution of Canada, 70–75.

24. Premier Lougheed to Prime Minister Trudeau, February 21 and March 7, 1977. Alberta, FIGA, *Fourth Annual Report*, 75–77.

25. Communiqués from Western Premiers' Conference, May 5–6, 1977, Brandon, Manitoba. State of Confederation Alberta, FIGA, *Fifth Annual Report to March 31, 1978* (Edmonton: FIGA, 1978), 46–47.

26. Meekison to Hyndman, August 17, 1977. Notes from a meeting with Frank Carter, August 16, 1977, PAA, 85.401/272/17, 1–3.

27. Meekison to Hyndman, December 12, 1977, Federal Initiatives in 1978, PAA, 85.401/272/17, 1–2. Hyndman, in remarks on the memo, indicated that Trudeau intended to move unilaterally since he maintained that his proposals did not impinge upon provincial jurisdiction.

28. Honourable Peter Lougheed, Premier, to Government MLA's, January 4, 1978, PAA, 85.64/7/ National Unity, 1–6; Peter Lougheed, "Address to the Canadian Unity Conference sponsored by the Canada West Foundation," Banff, March 29, 1978, PAA, 85.401/272/17, 1–14.

29. Lougheed to Flora Macdonald, MP, House of Commons, March 30, 1978, PAA 85.64/7/ National Unity, 2; Hyndman to Lougheed, "P.C. 'White Paper' #1 Revisions," April 4, 1978, PAA, 85.401/292/19. Hyndman advised the premier to tell Clark to drop the paper since it presented an unnecessary target for the Trudeau government.

30. Pierre Elliott Trudeau, *A Time For Action: Toward the Renewal of the Canadian Federation* (Ottawa: Minister of Supply and Services Canada, 1979), 1–26.

31. Trudeau to Lougheed, June 12, 1978, PAA, 85.401/272/17, 6.

32. The House of Commons of Canada, Bill C-60, An Act to amend the Constitution of Canada. Third Session, Thirteenth Parliament, 26–27 Elizabeth II, 1977–78, p. 1–77.

33. Trudeau to Lougheed, July 7, 1978, PAA, 85.401/272/17, p. 1–5.

34. Lévesque to Trudeau, July 14, 1978, PAA, 85.401/272/17, p. 2.

35. Lamontagne and MacGuigan to Lougheed, July 25, 1978; Meekison to Hyndman, July 4, 1978, PAA, 85.401/272/17, p. 8; Lougheed to Lamontagne and MacGuigan, August 3, 1978, PAA, 85.401/277/18.

36. Peter M. Owen, Q.C. to Hyndman, July 25, 1978, PAA, 85.401/277/18, p. 1–10.

37. Hyndman to Lougheed, July 27, 1978, PAA, 85.401/277/18.

38. Alberta, FIGA, *Sixth Annual Report to March 31, 1979* (Edmonton: FIGA, 1979), 43.

39. Alberta, FIGA, *Sixth Annual Report*, 44–46.

40. Marc Lalonde, Minister of State for Federal-Provincial Relations, Statement to the Joint

Parliamentary Committee on the Constitution, 15 August 1978, PAA, 85.401/279/18, p. 4 mimeo.

41. Trudeau to Alan Blakeney, September 13, 1978, PAA, 85.401/277/18, p.5.

42. Trudeau to Alan Blakeney, September 13, 1978, PAA, 85.401/277/18, pp. 3 and 6.

43. Alberta, FIGA, *Sixth Annual Report*, 18.

44. Reference Re Legislative Authority of Parliament to Alter or Replace the Senate [1980] 1 S.C.R. 54.

45. Lalonde to Hyndman, September 25, 1978, PAA, 85.401/275/18.

46. Hyndman to Lougheed, October 2, 1978, PAA, 85.401/277/18.

47. Quote from Lougheed to Bennett, October 10, 1978, PAA, 85.401/274/18. See Meekison to Hyndman, October 6, 1978, Memo on British Columbia's position, PAA, 85.401/277/18.

48. Trudeau to Lougheed, October 18, 1978; Lougheed to Trudeau, October 20, 1978, PAA, 85.401/277/18.

49. Alberta, *Harmony in Diversity: A New Federalism for Canada* (Edmonton: Government of Alberta, October 1978), 1–24.

50. Press Conference—Constitution (Alberta Position Paper), October 19, 1978, PAA, 85.401/277/18, pp. 1–20.

51. Statement by Premier Peter Lougheed to the First Ministers' Conference on the Constitution, October 30, 1978, Ottawa, PAA, 85.401/275/18, pp. 1–7, quote at 7.

52. Jack O'Neill to Hyndman, November 10, 1978. PAA, 85.401/277/18.

53. Hyndman to Lougheed, January 11, 1979, Re: Meeting with Jean-Luc Pépin and Muriel Kovitz Task Force on National Unity, Nov. 15, 1978, PAA, 85/64/National Unity.

54. Meekison to Hyndman, January 26, 1979, "The Task Force on Canadian Unity: A Future Together," PAA, 85/64/National Unity, pp. 1–6; Meekison to Hyndman, January 29, 1979, PAA, 85.64/6/Constition. Four memos on amending formula, Charter of Rights, language rights, and natural resources.

55. Premier Lougheed, "Charter of Rights (speaking notes), February 1979," PAA, 85. 401/266/18, p. 4.

56. "Alberta Proposal. Amending Formula for the Canadian Constitution, Ottawa, 5 February 1979," PAA, 85.401/681/39, p. 1–5.

57. Premier Lougheed, "Charter of Rights (speaking notes), February 1979," PAA, 85.401/266/18, p. 1–2.

58. Transcript of Premier Lougheed's Press Conference on the Constitution, February 7, 1979, PAA, 85.64/6/Constitution, p. 1–6; Gail Armitage (FIGA) to Meekison, February 19, 1979, "The Constitutional Process: Phases I and II," PAA, 85.64/5/Constitution-Ministerial, 1979–1980.

59. Lalonde to Romanow, February 28, 1979, PAA, 85.64/6/Constitution.

60. Progressive Conservative Party, *Discussion Paper, The Constitution and National Unity* (Ottawa: Progressive Conservative Party, 1978).

61. Edward McWhinney, *Canada and the Constitution 1979–1982: Patriation and the Charter of Rights* (Toronto: University of Toronto Press, 1982), 12–13.

62. Meekison to Johnston, January 30, 1980, Re: Terms of Reference for the Task Force on the Renewal of the Federation, PAA, 85.64/7.

63. Interview—Premier Lougheed and Laurier La Pierre of C.B.C. French Network Calgary, Alberta, Thursday, June 21, 1979, PAA, 85.401/711/41, p. 6–9.

64. Meekison to Johnston, June 12, 1979, PAA, 85.64/6/Constitution.

65. Johnston to Lougheed, January 28, 1980, Re: Alberta's Role in the National Unity Debate, PAA, 85.64/7.

66. Alberta, FIGA, *Seventh Annual Report to March 31, 1980* (Edmonton: FIGA, 1980), 43.

67. Alberta, FIGA, *Eighth Annual Report to March 31, 1981* (Edmonton: FIGA, 1981), 45.

68. Meekison to Johnston, RE: Meeting between Tom Wells and Honourable Jean Chrétien, May 20, 1980, PAA, 85.64/5/Constitution-Ministerial, 1979–Oct. 1980.

69. McWhinney, *Canada and the Constitution*, 42–44.

70. Meekison to Johnston, Re: Meeting with Honourable Jean Chrétien, May 22, 1980, PAA, 85.64/5/Constitution-Ministerial, 1979–Oct. 1980.

71. Meekison to Johnston, Re: Alberta's Language Policy, June 2, 1980; July 11, 1980; Dick Johnston, Minister of FIGA, to Caucus Members, July 11, 1980, Re: Language Policy, PAA, 85.64/7/Alberta's Position on Language Rights.

72. Meekison to Johnston, Re: Natives and the Constitution, April 10, 1979; Johnston to Crawford, Att. Gen. and McCrimmon, Native Affairs, April 11, 1979, Re: Natives and the Constitution, PAA, 85.64/5/Constitution-Ministerial, 1979–Oct. 1980; and Trudeau to Starblanket, August 11, 1980, PAA, 85.401/50/898.

73. Meekison to Johnston, June 5, 1979 and Johnston to Lougheed, June 6, 1979, Re: Indian Participation in Discussions on Constitution, PAA, 85.64/6/Constitution.

74. Don McCrimmon, minister responsible for Native Affairs, to his fellow provincial ministers, Report of the Ministers' three meetings on Indian Matters since April 1976, PAA, 85.401/50/892.

75. Noel Starblanket, NIB President, to Lougheed, January 19, 1979; Lougheed to Starblanket, March 8, 1979; Starblanket to Lougheed, March 28, 1979; Starblanket to Lougheed, August 28, 1979, PAA, 85.64/6/Constitution.

76. Native Secretariat, RE: Briefing material. Indian Association—All Chiefs Annual Delegation to the Economic Affairs Caucus Committee, June 18, 1980; Native Secretariat, RE: Minutes. Delegation to the Economic Affairs Caucus Committee Indian Association of Alberta, June 18, 1980; Native Secretariat, RE: Meeting of Alberta Premier/Cabinet Members and Alberta Chiefs, June 18, 1980, PAA, 85.401/50/894 & 898 & 900.

77. Government of Saskatchewan, Intergovernmental Affairs, News Release, July 17, 1980. Romanow Issues Statement at Constitutional Conference; News Release, July 28, 1980, Optimism by Romanow shaken after Vancouver, PAA, 85.64/5/Constitution-Ministerial, 1979–Oct. 1980.

78. Ottawa, Federal-Provincial Relations Office and Department of Justice, *Report to Cabinet on Constitutional Discussions, Summer 1980, and the Outlook for the First Ministers Conference and Beyond*. August 30, 1980, *Ministers' Eyes Only*, PAA 85.401/279/18, p. 43–60, quote at 43.

79. "Opening Remarks by Premier Peter Lougheed. First Ministers' Conference on the Constitution, September 8, 1980," Alberta, FIGA, *Eighth Annual Report*, 57–58.

80. "Closing Statement by the Honourable Peter Lougheed, Premier of Alberta. First Ministers' Conference on the Constitution, September 8, 1980," Alberta, FIGA, *Eighth Annual Report*, 59–62.

81. Office of the Prime Minister, Release. "Statement By the Prime Minister. Ottawa, October 2, 1980," PAA 85.401/278/18, p. 3.

82. Sterling Lyon to Peter Lougheed and Bill Davis to Lougheed, September 13, 1980, PAA, 85.401/113/2023.

83. Excerpts of Premier Peter Lougheed's Address to the Canada West Foundation Conference, Banff, Alberta, Saturday, November 29, 1980, PAA, 85.401/302/19, 3–4.

84. "Lougheed to Lévesque, March 8, 1982," in J. Peter Meekison, intr., *Constitutional Patriation: The Lougheed-Lévesque Correspondence* (Kingston, ON: Institute of Intergovernmental Relations, Queen's University and Canada West Foundation, 1999), 16–18.

85. Johnston to Chrétien, December 4, 1980, PAA, 85.401/289/39.

86. Johnson to Hays and Joyal, November 26, 1980 and Johnson to Chrétien, November 25, 1980, PAA, 85.401/289/39.

87. Reference Re Legislative Authority of Parliament to Alter or Replace the Senate [1980] 1 S.C.R. 54.

88. Johnston to Chrétien, December 4, 1980, PAA, 85.401/289/39, p. 1–4; Excerpts of Premier Peter Lougheed's Address to the Canada West Foundation Conference, Banff, Alberta, Saturday, November 29, 1980, PAA, 85.401/302/19, p. 5–10.

89. Submission by the Government of Alberta to the Select Committee on Foreign Affairs, House of Commons, Parliament of the United Kingdom, November 26, 1980; Dick Johnston to Mr. Anthony Kershaw, MP, Chairman, November 26, 1980, PAA, 85.401/306/19.

90. Speech by Sir Anthony Kershaw, M.C., M.P., to the Edmonton Chamber of Commerce on Friday, February 6, 1981, PAA, 85.401/306/19, p. 1–8.

91. Scott Schlosser and Tory Kirby, Christ Church, Oxford to Lougheed, January 20, 1981; Lougheed's reply, April 13, 1981; Scott Schlosser to Lougheed, May 19, 1981, PAA, 85.401/695/40.

92. James D. Horsman to Lougheed, February 10, 1981, PAA, 85.401/306/19.

93. Lyon to Lougheed, February 16, 1981, PAA, 85.401/273/17.

94. Minister of Justice and Attorney General of Canada, News Release: Communiqué, January 12, 1981; Minutes of Proceedings and Evidence of the Special Joint Committee of the Senate and of the House of Commons on the Constitution of Canada, *Report to Parliament* 57 (Friday, February 13, 1981), 1–43.

95. Broadbent to Trudeau, October 20, 1980; Trudeau to Broadbent, October 21, 1980; Johnston to Lougheed, February 13 and 20, 1981, with annotations by Lougheed, PAA 85. 401/273/17 & 299/19.

96. McWhinney, *Canada and the Constitution*, 65–79.

97. Lyon to Lougheed, February 16, 1981, PAA, 85.401/273/17.

98. Lyon to Trudeau, April 3, 1981 and Trudeau to Lyon, April13, 1981, PAA, 85.401/273/17.

99. Alberta, FIGA, Briefing Material: Meeting of Provincial Premiers, April 15–16, 1981, Ottawa, Table of Contents, Confidential, PAA, 85.401/114/2047.

100. Constitutional Accord, Canadian Patriation Plan, April 16, 1981. Alberta, FIGA, *Ninth Annual Report to March 31, 1982* (Edmonton: FIGA, 1982), 65–66; Premiers, News Release and Amending Formula for the Constitution of Canada, April 16, 1981, PAA, 85.401/693/39.

101. Meekison to Johnston, April 13, 1981, PAA, 85.401/114/2047.

102. Johnston to Lougheed, April 23, 1981, Comparison of the 1976 Alberta Legislative Resolution and the 1981 Constitutional Accord, PAA, 85.401/262/17.

103. Dennis Anderson, MLA, to Lougheed and Johnston, May 25, 1981, Re: London Visit and the Constitution, May 8–22, 1981, PAA, 85.401/306/19.

104. Jeremy Akerman, FIGA London, to Lougheed and Edmund L. Morris, August 10, 1981, Report on Activities in London Relative to the Constitutional Review, July 20–25 inclusive, PAA, 85.401/695/40.

105. Re Resolution to Amend the Constitution [1981] 1 S.C.R. 753.

106. Peter H. Russell, "The Supreme Court Decision: Bold Statescraft Based on Questionable Jurisprudence," in Peter H. Russell, Robert Decary, et al., *The Court and the Constitution: Comments on the Supreme Court Reference on Constitutional Amendment, 1982* (Kingston, ON: Institute of Intergovernmental Relations, Queen's University, 1982), 1–12.

107. Dissenting Premiers, "Analysis of Supreme Court of Canada Decision on the Canadian Constitution," PAA, 85.410/694/39.

108. Statement by Honourable Neil Crawford, Attorney General, and Honourable Dick Johnston, Minister of Federal and Intergovernmental Affairs, Tuesday, September 29, 1981, PAA, 85.401/273/17.

109. Mr. Ross W. Paisley, Deputy Attorney General to The Hon. Neil Crawford, Attorney General, September 29, 1981, PAA, 85.401/694/39.

110. Meekison to Johnston, September 30, 1981, Implications of the Supreme Court Decision on the Kershaw Report, PAA, 85.401/305/19.

111. Lougheed to Edward Du Cann, October 20, 1981; Lougheed to Sir Bernard Braine, MP, October 22, 1981, PAA, 85.401/695/40. Two of many letters acknowledging his meetings with senior British politicians whom he thanked for supporting the existence of a Canadian constitutional convention and the crisis that would be create if the U.K. Parliament flouted the convention recognized by Canada's Supreme Court.

112. Msg for the Agent General from Michael Pritchard, Re: Petition on Canadian Constitutional Proposals, October 6, 1981, PAA, 85.401/305/19.

113. Premiers, Communiqué, Montreal, October 19, 1981; Prime Minister Trudeau, Office of the Prime Minister, Release, October 20, 1981, PAA, 85.401/303/19.

114. Opening Statement by Honourable Peter Lougheed, Premier of Alberta, to the First Ministers' Conference on the Constitution, November 2, 1981. Reproduced in Alberta, FIGA, *Ninth Annual Report*, 68–70.

115. For a detailed account of the conference consult Roy Romanow, John Whyte and Howard Leeson, *Canada...Notwithstanding: The Making of the Constitution 1976–1982* (Toronto: Carswell/Methuen, 1984), 188–214. Lougheed, through his representative Peter Meekison, insisted that s. 33 apply to Fundamental Freedoms (see p. 209).

116. "Accord of 5 November 1981," in McWhinney, *Canada and the Constitution*, 165–66.

117. Closing Remarks by Premier Peter Lougheed, First Ministers' Conference on the Constitution, November 2–5, 1981. Reproduced in Alberta, FIGA, *Ninth Annual Report*, 73–74.

118. Meekison to Lougheed, October 22, 1980, "The Constitution—Resources," PAA, 85.401/299/19.

119. Claude Morin, *Lendemains piégés: Du referendum à la nuit des longs couteaux* (Montréal: Boréal, 1988).

120. Claude Morin to Dick Johnston, November 6, 1981, in Meekison, *Constitutional Patriation*, 13–14.

121. Meekison, *Constitutional Patriation*, 15–30.

122. E. Steinhauer, President, IAA, Brief on Treaty Indian Concerns on the Process of Constitutional Renewal in Canada, September 8, 1980, PAA, 85.64/5/Native Affairs; Presentation by the Indian Association of Alberta to the Special Joint Committee of the Senate and House of Commons on Patriation of the Canadian Constitution, December 18, 1980, PAA, 85.401/50/887; Briefing Note: Natives and the Constitution—June 17 meeting with the Indian Association of Alberta, June 1981, PAA, 85.401/50/887.

123. Meekison to Johnston, November 12, 1981, Re: Natives and the Constitution, PAA, 85.401/684/39.

124. Steinhauer, President, IAA. Memo to all P.T.O's, November 16, 1981; Steinhauer, President of IAA. Telex to All Members of Parliament, November 16, 1981, PAA, 85.401/50/903; Steinhauer, President of IAA, Statement on Treaty Indian Position of the Alberta Government, November 19, 1981, PAA, 85.401/50/894.

125. Lougheed to Steinhauer, November 16, 1981, Re: Misinformation, PAA, 85.401/50/903; Minister of Native Affairs, Statement to Representatives of the Indian Association of Alberta at the Legislative Building Steps, Edmonton, November 19, 1981, PAA, 85.401/50/894.

126. Alberta, Government of Alberta, Statement by Premier Lougheed, Re: Constitutional Resolution and Native Rights, November 20, 1981; Lougheed to Sam Sinclair, President, Métis Association of Alberta, November 20, 1981, PAA, 85.401/50/897 and 903.

127. Steinhauer to Lougheed, November 20, 1981; November 21, 1981. Steinhauer to Trudeau, copy to Lougheed, November 21, 1981; Roger Tassé, Deputy Minister of Justice to Meekison, November 24, 1981, PAA, 85.401/50/903; Aboriginal Rights Coalition to the Prime Minister and all Provincial Premiers, November 25, 1981, Re: Reinstatement of a revised Section 35 as Part II of the Constitutional Resolution, PAA, 85.401/50/897.

128. Premier Bennett to Trudeau, November 30, 1981; Trudeau to Bennett, November 30, 1981, PAA 85.401/303/19.

129. Ministerial Statement by the Honourable Peter Lougheed, Premier of Alberta, December 9, 1981, PAA, 85.401/680/39.

130. Transcript of media briefing with Premier Lougheed, February 18, 1982, Re: By-election victory for the Alberta separatist candidate, PAA, 85.401/44/792.

131. Alberta, Government of Alberta, *Canada's New Constitution and what it means to Albertans* (Edmonton: Government of Alberta, April 1982).

132. Trudeau to David Ahenakew, National Chief, AFN, May 10, 1982; Statement by Dr. D. Ahenakew to Trudeau, June 22, 1982; Michael Kirby to Ahenakew, June 23, 1982, Re: Negotiating process; Ahenakew to Lougheed and Trudeau, August 19 and September 9, 1982, Re: Section 37 Conference, PAA, 85.401/50/907.

133. Ahenakew to Trudeau, November 29, 1982, PAA, 85.401/118/2181.

134. Trudeau to Ahenakew, December 20, 1982., PAA, 85.401/118/2181.

135. Johnston to Ahenakew, October 12, 1982, Re: S. 37 Conference, PAA, 85.401/50/907.

136. Don McCrimmon, Minister of Native Affairs, to Charles Wood, President, IAA, October 21, 1982, PAA, 85.401/118/2181.

137. Sam Sinclair, President MAA and Elmer Ghostkeeper, President FMS to Lougheed, June 14, 1982, PAA, 85.401/51/911. With attached briefs to the Alberta Government dated June 9, 1982; Lougheed to Sinclair and Ghostkeeper, July 28, 1982; Sinclair and Ghostkeeper to Lougheed, August 11, 1982, PAA, 85.401/51/911.

138. Charles Wood, Pres. IAA to Lougheed, November 25 and 30, 1982; Lougheed to Wood, December 23, 1982, PAA, 85.401/118/2181.

139. Eric Robinson and Henry Bird Quinney, *The Infested Blanket: Canada's Constitutional Genocide of Indian Nations* (Winnipeg: Queenston House, 1985), xxiii, 58, 72,102–04.

140. Susan G. Cartier, Att. Gen's Office, to D.G. Rae, Att. Gen's office, December 1, 1982, Metis and the Constitution; Neil Crawford, Attorney General to Lougheed, December 8, 1982; Sinclair and Ghostkeeper to Lougheed, December 13, 1982; Lougheed to Sinclair and Ghostkeeper, December 23, 1982, PAA, 85.401/51/907.

141. James D. Horsman, FIGA Minister, to Cabinet/Caucus Committee on Native Land Claims and Cabinet/Caucus Committee on Native Affairs, January 26, 1983, with attached document Natives and the Constitution, First Ministers' Conference Working Agenda, PAA, 85.401/51/907.

142. Sinclair and Ghostkeeper to Lougheed, March 2, 1983; Lougheed to Sinclair and Ghostkeeper, March 4, 1983, PAA, 85,401/51/907.

143. Opening Statement by Premier P. Lougheed, First Ministers' Conference on Aboriginal Constitutional Matters, March 15–16, 1983, Ottawa. Doc. 800-17/011, PAA, 85.401/118/2182. Lougheed insisted on a made-in-Alberta solution.

144. David C. Hawkes, *Negotiating Aboriginal Self-Government* (Kingston, Ontario: Institute of Intergovernmental Relations, 1985), 8–9.
145. Canada, "Indian Self-Government in Canada," *Minutes and Proceedings of the Special Committee on Indian Self-Government*, no. 40, October 12 and 20, 1983. Referred to as the *Penner Report*.
146. *Penner Report*, 112.
147. *Penner Report*, 63.
148. Douglas E. Sanders, "An Uncertain Path: The Aboriginal Constitutional Conferences," in Joseph M. Weiler and Robin M. Elliot, eds., *Litigating the Values of a Nation: The Canadian Charter of Rights and Freedoms* (Toronto: Carswell, 1986), 68.
149. Canada, Minister of Indian Affairs and Northern Development, *Response of the Government to the Report of the Special Committee on Indian Self-Government* (Ottawa: Minister of Supply and Services, March 5 1984), 1–7.
150. P.E. Trudeau, "Statement by the Prime Minister of Canada to the Conference of First Ministers on Aboriginal Constitutional Matters, 8–9 March 1984," in Menno Boldt and J. Anthony Long, eds., *The Quest for Justice. Aboriginal Peoples and Aboriginal Rights* (Toronto: University of Toronto Press, 1985), 148–56, quote 152.
151. Métis National Council, Opening Remarks, and Métis National Council Draft Constitutional Accords on Métis Self-Identification and Enumeration, First Ministers' Conference on Aboriginal Constitutional Matters 8–9 March 8, 1984, PAA, 85.401/51/910.
152. Lougheed to Pahl, March 12, 1984, Re: Meeting, Metis Association of Alberta, April 28, 1984, PAA, 85.401/51/910. Lougheed's inquiry prompted a memo to the Attorney General's ADM requesting legal advice on the Métis jurisdictional issue. H.W. Thiessen, Alberta Native Secretariat, to D.G. Rae, Ass. DM, Civil Division, March 21, 1984, PAA, 85.401/51/910.
153. Sanders, "An Uncertain Path," 70–71.
154. Alberta, Ministry of Municipal Affairs, *Report of the MacEwan Joint Metis-Government Committee to Review the Metis Betterment Act and Regulations* (Edmonton: Government of Alberta, 1984).
155. Faron Ellis, "A dream of independence rises out of the post-NEP carnage," In Paul Bunner, ed., *Lougheed and the War with Ottawa, 1971–1981* (Edmonton: History Book Publications, 2003), 260–69.
156. Alberta, Government of Alberta, *A Provincially-Appointed Senate: A New Federalism for Canada* (Edmonton: Government of Alberta, August 1982).
157. Report of the Alberta Select Special Committee on Upper House Reform, *Strengthening Canada: Reform of Canada's Senate* (Edmonton: Plains Publishing Inc., March 1985; Second Printing, January 1988).

Fifteen

Equality and Women's Political Identity in Post-1970s Alberta

LOIS HARDER

As a key and founding constituent among democratic values, it might be presumed that equality would be a touchstone for the legislative and administrative practices of contemporary government. However, as both the recent history of public policy and of women's organizing in Alberta reveal, equality is complex, defined in multiple ways, profoundly disputed and, as I will argue, increasingly ephemeral. The shifting meaning of the term is directly correlated to the context in which it is used. One might consider, for example, the contrast between Alberta's demands for equality within Confederation and its resistance to the extension of equality rights to gay men and lesbians. In addition to the understanding of equality that is operative in any specific situation, it is also important to consider the broader context of governance, i.e. the prevailing thinking about the relationship between the state and citizens in a given period.

In the 1970s and 1980s, when state intervention into the economy was an acceptable practice, equality was often expressed in demands and justifications for redistributive policies: from higher to lower income earners and from the strong to the vulnerable. Even then, however, women struggled mightily for recognition of the political, economic and social implications of gender inequity. With the onset of neo-liberal governance in the 1990s, freedom largely displaced equality. Both the right and the left of the political spectrum were dissatisfied with the practice of politics that had prevailed in the post-war era, but the right was particularly successful at galvanizing public opinion around the fiscal crisis of the state. In adopting neo-liberalism, the state's role in providing the foundation for a thriving economy was to be accomplished through deregulation, privatization, self-reliance and individual responsibility. As the Alberta government's 1993 Speech from the Throne declared: "this government has stayed true to the philosophy

459

that government should get out of rather than into the lives of Albertans. People in this province know that more government and more laws mean more expense, red tape and confusion and less freedom."[1] Moreover, the previous decades' claims for social rights and redistribution—claims that were often cast in the language of demands for equality—were deemed selfish and outdated. Again, the 1993 Throne Speech declared that "this government is confident that Albertans have the strength and the courage to make the tough decisions, for when it comes to the quality of our lives and our future, there is no place for the kind of self-interest that has surfaced across this country in the past."[2]

This essay will explore the concept of equality as it has been variously manifested in the political struggles of Alberta's women's groups and the policy initiatives undertaken by Progressive Conservative administrations. The women's movements have been a central voice in the struggle for social rights, social justice and equality. Hence, their efforts to implement and change public policy in the interests of gender equity provide a rich source through which to explore the complexities of equality as a democratic value and the implications of how we define equality for how we understand ourselves, our relationships to each other and our identities as citizens. After briefly outlining five general articulations of equality that have been variously and sometimes simultaneously mobilized by feminist groups and offices of the Alberta state since the 1970s, I will offer a series of illustrative examples. The essay will conclude with some thoughts on the consequences of the displacement of "equality" by "freedom" for gender equality and for the contemporary condition of governance in Alberta.

Meanings of Equality

In her comparative study, *Gender, Equality and Welfare States*, Diane Sainsbury outlines five conceptions of equality that commingle in contemporary industrial democracies.[3] Formal equality is the simplest conception, asserting that all citizens are equal and hence should be treated in precisely the same way. According to this understanding, a maternity leave policy would be considered discriminatory, since it would only apply to women and thus would not treat men and women the same way.[4] A second conception of equality asserts that while people are not the same, they should share the same opportunities to realize their talents and fulfil their aspirations. Providing these opportunities may thus require treating people differently, depending on their relative advantages. In the context of feminist debates, this understanding of equality has often been used in proposals to create more equitable workplaces.

Equality as difference has also been advanced in situations in which overcoming the significance of difference is not the immediate objective. Rather, the goal of such equality-based initiatives is to acknowledge gender difference as it operates in the present context. In this articulation of equality, instead of asserting that men and women are equal and hence the same, proponents acknowledge the differing social responsibilities that are ascribed to men and women. The consequences of these differing social responsibilities thus become the desired object of policy. In Alberta, protection against domestic violence is, arguably, the most significant feminist example of this understanding of equality. As well, recognition of the unpaid caring work that women perform in the home has also become a subject of some interest in this context. Of course, feminist adherents of this view might argue that the recognition of unpaid work is a means to increase its social worth and, potentially, to entice more men to do more of it. Others might assert that regardless of whether or not domestic labour can be sold to men, at present women are more inclined to undertake caring work, hence it is a matter of social justice that the value of that work and the women who perform it, be recognized.

A fourth understanding of gender equality, this one articulated by moral- or neo-conservatives, also takes gender difference as its starting point, but this position diverges from that of many feminists in the assertion that "biology is destiny" and hence that men and women may be equal, but they have separate and sustaining gender roles to fulfil.[5] The similarities between the neo-conservative and the feminist understanding of difference is apparent and creates a situation in which both positions may claim a victory when policy initiatives recognizing unpaid labour, for example, are undertaken in the name of equality. As we will see, however, the Alberta government's initiatives around unpaid labour have been considerably more neo-conservative than feminist. The neo-conservative vision of gender equality has also been mobilized to justify the gendered wage gap and to oppose pay and employment equity policies. In this view, gender inequality in the workplace is the product of women's preference to curb their employment ambitions in the service of their families rather than a structural feature of a labour market that is unwilling to accommodate familial obligations.

A final understanding of equality, and one that is most prevalent in the contemporary moment, emphasizes the individual and might be described as the elision of equality with freedom. This conception bears some similarities to formal equality in the sense that all citizens are understood to have a foundational sameness, but the weight here is placed much more on an expectation that an individual must take responsibility for reaching his or her aspirations. Rather than a right to state protection against discrimination, the state ensures the freedom to pursue one's aspirations, largely through its minimal presence and an emphasis on the market as the vehicle for individual fulfilment and expression. Opportunity plays an important role here, but opportunity is only manifested in the provision of substantive programs and services in the cases of children and, occasionally, the disabled and Aboriginal peoples. Gender inequality is simply a non-issue.

On the basis of this five-part schematic of equality definitions, we will now explore their iterations over the decades of Progressive Conservative government. During the Lougheed years, and particularly during the oil boom, formal equality was often used as the government's defence against feminist demands for a recognition of women's difference and the need to account for that difference, whether to ameliorate it or support it, in public policy. However, as the example of matrimonial property will demonstrate, the Alberta state could also make use of an understanding of equality as difference when the political need arose. With the decline in oil prices and the onset of the fiscal crisis of the welfare state, equality as difference, in all its variations, became much more prominent and largely supplanted formal equality. Finally, with the onset of neo-liberal governance in the 1990s, equality/freedom and the neo-conservative understandings of gender equality have risen to prominence.

Formal Equality

The protection of individual rights was a central priority of the Lougheed Conservatives in their first term of office. Indeed, the first bill introduced by the new government was the *Alberta Bill of Rights Act*, followed shortly by the *Individual Rights Protection Act* (IRPA).[6] Under the terms of these acts, individuals were to be protected from both undue incursions by the state as well as from "discrimination by other citizens as a result of race, creed, colour, religion, national origin, sex or age."[7] But as the emerging second wave of the feminist movement would quickly discover, the vision of gender equality articulated in the IRPA was not one that they shared.

Perhaps the clearest statement of the government's position on gender equality was advanced by Deputy Premier Hugh Horner during the first annual meeting of the Alberta Status of Women Action Committee (ASWAC). ASWAC had prepared a detailed brief, entitled *Joint Initiatives: A Goal for Women and Government in Alberta*. Their recommendations included the establishment of a government office that would provide a gender-based analysis of proposed legislation as well as the appointment of a citizen's advisory council that would operate at arms-length from government and would communicate the priorities and concerns of women's groups to elected representatives and civil servants.[8] In responding to these recommendations, Horner asserted that the proposed measures were unnecessary and that they would constitute an act of discrimination against women. He stated that such initiatives "would suggest that women are incapable of looking after themselves and would suggest that they need special protection. My understanding of the aspirations of the women in Alberta is one which indicates to me that they do not want 'special status' but equality!"[9] For Horner and for his government, then, recognition of difference was antithetical to equality rather than essential to its realization.

This rigid adherence to equality as sameness was not sustained by the Alberta government in the context of matrimonial property legislation. While advocates for reform asserted that a new matrimonial property law should rest on the premise that marriage is an equal partnership between spouses, the Alberta government resisted this claim.

The issue of matrimonial property vaulted onto provincial political agendas across Canada in the early 1970s in response to a Supreme Court ruling involving an Alberta woman, Irene Murdoch. The court argued that "the work of an 'ordinary' ranch wife and of a homemaker and mother was not sufficient contribution to establish that she had a beneficial interest in the property."[10] In essence, the argument advanced by the Court was that Irene Murdoch could not claim a share of the property she had worked with her husband because her 20 years of labour did not constitute a financial investment. Even after extensive research by the Institute of Law Research and Reform and an unprecedented public awareness and lobbying campaign by women's groups, all of which recommended the drafting of legislation that recognized the equality of spouses as the starting point for the division of matrimonial property, the Alberta government steadfastly refused to consider equal partnership as the appropriate foundation for the law. Instead, matrimonial property legislation was passed that required judges to consider 19 criteria when dividing the possessions of divorcing spouses.[11]

The debate surrounding matrimonial property reveals the operation of three distinct notions of equality and demonstrates the flexibility with which these understandings of equality are mobilized by each of the parties to the debate. In advocating for the recognition of marriage as an equal partnership, feminists, who are generally less amenable to the formal equality position, nonetheless staked their claim to this perspective. Or did they? In fact, deferred sharing might be understood as recognizing equality as difference, since spouses may not make the same *financial* contribution to a marriage, but nonetheless, the unpaid work of many women entails the care and maintenance of the property and the well-being of the breadwinner, thus enabling him to engage in paid work and acquire the financial wherewithal to acquire property. On the one hand, the concept of equal sharing does advance an understanding of strict equality between men and women, but when the circumstances through which people live their married lives are brought into consideration, the understanding of equality that is operating is considerably more complex. In fact, we can observe two instances of the "equality as difference" formulation here: one that emphasizes the "productive" work of an "ordinary ranch wife," or work that directly contributes to getting the goods to market, and a second instance that emphasizes the "reproductive" work, or the significance of the "ranch wife's" unpaid domestic labour to the integrity of the ranch operation.

For its part, the Alberta government appeared to be uncharacteristically resistant to the notion of formal equality advanced in the proposal for equal sharing. Instead, the government passed legislation that enabled judges to take gender differences into account, though not necessarily in the service of ensuring an equitable outcome for men and women. Moreover, this acknowledgement of difference was rather opportunistically framed in terms of the need to secure the gains that "liberated" women were making in the workplace. Al "Boomer" Adair advanced this view in a letter to the Calgary Status of Women Action Committee. He observed that "an arbitrary fifty-fifty split would cause varying degrees of injustice in most cases. For example...an industrious woman married for years to an alcoholic who did not work at all and had accumulated nothing would be forced to give him one half of her property."[12] But tellingly, the social climber who only married a man in order to divorce him for his money was also described in the letter.[13] Confronted with a situation in which adherence to the formal equality of men and women might pose a threat to men's historic claims to property, the Alberta government deviated from its standard position. Not surprisingly, feminists concluded that formal equality was only worth upholding when its consequences did not disrupt the status quo.

It is important to note that while the Alberta government of the 1970s was resistant to demands for gender equality, it was considerably more responsive to the social justice claims of disabled children and adults, seniors and low-income Albertans. Virtually every throne and budget speech throughout the decade remarks on the need to address the well-being of people who, through no fault of their own, were unable to share in Alberta's growing prosperity.[14] Obviously such sentiments, particularly when they are manifested in substantive programs and spending commitments, provide a meaningful enhancement of people's lives, and as such, would be initiatives that feminist groups would support as part of a broader equity agenda. However, the contrast between the generosity on the part of the Alberta state towards "the vulnerable" and its intransigence in the face of feminist demands for equality calls for explanation.

This disjuncture can be understood as a straightforward rejection of the idea that women collectively constitute a disadvantaged group. Obviously there are disabled women, low income women, and women who are subject to racial oppression, but in this view, the social harm that these people confront comes by virtue of disability, poverty and race. Gender in itself is not a source of inequity. After all, this position suggests, most women, like most men, live in relative comfort. And certainly in the 1970s, when the profound restructuring of the labour market was not yet widely appreciated, middle class women might appear highly advantaged, having had the opportunity to seek postsecondary education, but having a choice as to whether they engaged in paid labour or were supported by their husbands while they raised their children.[15] Indeed, this perception was used to justify paying women less than men, even for the same job, since men were understood to be working to support their families, whereas women, especially married women, were presumed to be working for their personal fulfilment or for a bit of extra cash.

The fact that women's well-being was directly linked to the beneficence of a spouse was not, and, indeed, is not, widely understood as a source of vulnerability or as an unacceptable form of dependency. Women's subservience within the family is seen as natural rather than as the outcome of a series of both covert and overt regulative practices. As a result, the precarious conditions of women's lives are largely invisible, obscured by the contradictory assertions that formal equality guaranteed everyone access to opportunities and the gendered assumptions that hardwire women's subordination into our social order. Hence, when Alberta's elected officials were confronted by highly articulate, well-spoken women who nonetheless asserted that they faced systemic disadvantage, the legitimacy of the feminist case for ameliorative action to ensure equality was not immediately apparent.

Equality as Difference

The 1980s brought a series of disruptions and challenges to the Conservative government's approach to governance. After a decade in which public coffers were vastly enriched by resource royalties, the price of oil declined dramatically. While the Alberta government had largely circumvented the fiscal crises that had befallen their provincial compatriots as well as the federal government during the 1970s, the combination of reduced natural resource revenues, federal efforts to forestall economic decline in central Canada through the implementation of the National Energy Program, and a generalized crisis in governance among industrialized nations all cast a long shadow on Alberta's prospects for the 1980s.

The tumult in Alberta's political economy as well as the patriation of the Constitution and the inclusion of the Charter of Rights within the *Constitution Act* of 1982 provided a unique opportunity for the province's women's groups to advance their claims to gender equality. The language of equality was pervasive, whether it was expressed in terms of Alberta's place within Confederation or in the equality rights section of the Charter. Moreover, with the election of the Mulroney Conservatives to Parliament in 1984 and their pro-western policy platform, the provincial government was less able to insist that Albertans maintain a united front in order to "fight the feds."[16] As well, the 1984 election had witnessed the first federal leaders' debate on women's issues, an event that clearly acknowledged the significance of the women's movement on the Canadian political landscape and contrasted quite sharply with the denials and foot-dragging of the Alberta government. It was in this context that the Alberta government released its grasp on formal equality. But even as it established a number of offices designed to address women's needs, thus expressing an understanding of equality that suggested that equality necessitated different treatment, it also came upon two new tactics for containing women's demands: procedural fairness and the juxtaposition of women's rights with the invocation of the traditional family. In embracing these strategies of containment, all women's groups, whether they were feminist, neo-conservative or somewhere in-between, were to be granted equal voice within the Alberta state's machinery for the representation of women. Despite, or perhaps because of, the fiscal crises of the Canadian and Alberta states that marked the decade, the 1980s witnessed the most significant institutional achievements for women's gender equality demands, but these achievements would prove to be bittersweet.

The story of women's efforts to advance gender equality rights and, ultimately, to shield gender equality from the notwithstanding clause of the 1982 *Constitution Act*, has been comprehensively documented by Alexandra Dobrowolsky in *The Politics of Pragmatism*.[17] The Alberta government was strongly committed to the notwithstanding clause (section 33), which was enacted as a means to protect provincial autonomy but also enabled governments to enact laws, for a period of five years, that contravene the fundamental freedoms, civil rights and equality rights outlined in sections 2 and 7–15 of the *Charter*. In the original agreement, a series of interpretive clauses, including section 28, which states that "the rights and freedoms referred to in [the *Charter*] are guaranteed equally to male and female persons" were also subject to the notwithstanding clause. However, in a flurry of organizing, Alberta women's groups and their national and provincial counterparts were successful in persuading the prime minister and their respective premiers to release section 28 from the notwithstanding clause.

Another important victory for women *vis-à-vis* the *Charter* was the inclusion, in section 15, of a subsection that allowed for the development of affirmative action, or employment equity programs. As countless examples had demonstrated, without explicit provision for such programs, their existence could be challenged as an act of discrimination. In the context of the *Charter*, then, feminist initiatives laid claim to equality guarantees that understood this value in terms of both sameness and difference.

With regard to women's ongoing efforts to advance gender equality within Alberta's law, public policy and administration, their most obvious successes lay in the establishment of the Women's Secretariat and the Alberta Advisory Council on Women's Issues (AACWI). In establishing these bodies, the Alberta government abandoned its claim that such offices would represent an abrogation of formal equality. However, in both the expectations regarding the work that these offices would undertake and in the appointments to the Advisory Council, the Alberta government loudly broadcast their wariness of feminist understandings of equality.

Efforts to secure an Advisory Council had begun in the 1970s, with ASWAC's *Joint Initiatives* proposal being among the earliest articulations of the need for such an office. However, as the years went by and the Alberta government steadfastly refused to consider such a Council, ASWAC became convinced that pressing the issue would be fruitless. Even if an Advisory Council was to be established, its powers would likely be so circumscribed as to render the agency ineffective and, further, the government would be able to trade on the symbolic value of an Advisory Council, dismissing any criticisms of the council as evidence that the women's movement was impossible to satisfy. But ASWAC's skepticism was not shared by a coalition of women's groups that formed in the early 1980s, the Provincial Committee for a Council on Women's Affairs. The Committee, which sought to distance itself from the radicalism of explicitly feminist organizations, felt confident that its conciliatory, reasoned and non-threatening approach to its negotiations with elected officials and government representatives would ensure its success.[18] Indeed, in response to the minister of labour's observation that an "Advisory Council" would imply an unwanted duty, on the part of the government, to consider the council's advice, the coalition agreed to drop the term "advisory" from its name.[19]

Despite the Coalition's optimism and accommodations, they too, grew increasingly skeptical about the viability of a Council. Although their tactics did produce some response, these were really half measures—an attempt to include the functions of an Advisory Council into the Women's Secretariat and the Interdepartmental Committee on Women's Affairs and the appointment of a Cabinet Committee on Women's Issues.[20]

The Women's Secretariat was established in 1984 with a mandate to promote the consideration of gender equality issues in the formulation of legislation and public policy and to serve as a liaison between the Alberta government and the province's women's groups. Its establishment, which coincided with the appointment of both Cabinet and Interdepartmental Committees on Women's Issues, represented a departure from the government's position in the previous decade that had insisted that government offices for women would constitute "special status" rather than equality. But the shift was quite subtle, as evidenced by the appeal to procedural fairness in the face of the establishment of the conservative women's movement, primarily represented by the Alberta Federation of Women United for Families (AFWUF).

AFWUF was established in the early 1980s in order to curb what it viewed as the undue influence of feminist groups on public policy. The organization advanced a neo-conservative view of gender equality; a view that sought to maintain women's domesticity, to safeguard heterosexual marriage and to preserve the single income, two-parent nuclear family. And while this set of objectives could not logically co-exist with feminist aspirations, AFWUF, nonetheless, insisted that both the federal and provincial governments should give their organization the same level of support that was provided to feminist groups. The federal Secretary of State Women's Program initially rejected this claim, insisting that a commitment to improving the status of women was necessary in order to be eligible for funding,[21] but the Alberta government, with its ambivalent history of responsiveness to feminist demands, was more inclined to avoid a potential showdown with its neo-conservative supporters by acquiescing to AFWUF's request.[22] Again, this recommendation suggested a notion of procedural fairness that had more to do with the appearance of inclusiveness than with developing policies that positively affect the conditions of women's lives. Thus, distinct understandings of equality as difference came to be equated for the purposes of funding Alberta's women's groups.

The consequences of this decision to ignore the normative underpinnings of Alberta's various women's groups posed considerable difficulties for the Women's Secretariat. The Secretariat's staff understood the political logic of the government's position, but they also felt that their efforts to encourage departments to apply gender-based analysis to policy development would be fruitless in the absence of a coherent articulation of gender equality. The neo-conservative vision of "separate but equal" was not one they shared. Thus, when the Secretariat was asked by Premier Lougheed to facilitate a meeting between the Interdepartmental Committee on Women's Issues and AFWUF, they faced the complex challenge of walking the line between the government's commitment to procedural fairness and their own feminist proclivities.

For its part, AFWUF did little to ease the Secretariat's discomfort. In its presentation to the Interdepartmental Committee, AFWUF representatives declared their disapproval of the Women's Secretariat by insisting that the Secretariat could not represent the concerns of all Alberta women and that feminists were over-represented in government appointments.[23] Following the meeting, AFWUF asserted that the Secretariat had agreed to reproduce and distribute its resolution book to all elected representatives. The Secretariat rejected this claim, but after being pressured by the minister responsible for women's issues, they provided the material to members of the Cabinet Committee on Women's Issues and selected MLAs.

Subsequently, the Secretariat encouraged presentations to the Interdepartmental Committee from Planned Parenthood, the Provincial Coalition for a Council on Women's Affairs, ASWAC and a number of other women's groups. But because the Interdepartmental Committee had no decision-making authority, it soon became apparent that it would not provide an adequate venue for managing the relationship between the Alberta state and women's groups. As with the assertion of formal equality, the government was ultimately forced to recognize that political obligations are bred of rights and institutions. Particularly at a time of economic downturn and growing electoral discontent, a bolder gesture to Alberta's women was required. This gesture came in the establishment of the Alberta Advisory Council on Women's Issues (AACWI). However, the absence of any women's movement activists on the Council, the appointment of a chair with no knowledge of women's issues and no capacity to publish research apart from that under the auspices of the minister responsible for women's issues indicated the Alberta government's ongoing resistance to even moderate gender equality initiatives.

In addition to the ambivalence that framed the Alberta government's approach to the representation of gender equity concerns in the machinery of government, a distinct hostility towards feminist equality claims would be registered in the Getty government's celebration of the traditional family. The establishment of Family Day as a statutory holiday, the appointment of the Premier's Council in Support of Alberta Families, the development of a Family Policy Grid that was to inform the policy-making process, and a plethora of sentimental references to "the family" during legislative debates were notable features of Alberta's governance in the late 1980s. The form of the family that was being invoked in these initiatives was the two-parent, single-earner, heterosexual variety; a family form that was decreasingly representative of the organization of most households and that was also the object of substantial feminist critique. Nonetheless, feminist antipathy towards "traditional" notions of domesticity did not preclude feminists' recognition that caring work was profoundly meaningful to women, as witnessed in the variations of equality as difference discussed earlier.

The emphasis on the family in the political discourse of the late 1980s was not solely the result of a strategy to discount feminist equality demands, although it did have this effect. Rather, in the context of Alberta's intensifying fiscal crisis and increasing pressure on social service budgets, the family represented a means to offload state responsibilities to the private sphere of the home. Increasingly, hospitals, schools and nursing homes were relying on the family to take up where their budgets left off. Tellingly, this invocation of the family was often made in concert with calls to self-reliance; calls that would only be comprehensible if "the self" was, in fact, the corporate unit of the family and if women were prepared to conflate their personal desires with the needs of their spouses and children. This engulfing of women by their families would subsequently be reinforced with the elision of equality and freedom in the neo-liberal era. But in the late 1980s, when the Family Policy Grid shared space with the Plan for Action for Alberta Women as well as the Women's Secretariat and the AACWI, a notion of gender equality that included women's roles within both the public and private realms was still operative. As long as the prevailing view of governance included a legitimate role for the state in securing people's life chances, feminists would be able to use this professed commitment to secure at least some symbolic recognition of gender equality. It would take neo-liberalism's disdain for government and celebration of the market to resolve, or at least thoroughly obscure, the growing contradictions in the Alberta state's stance on gender equality.

Neo-liberalism and Equality

As Canada slid into economic recession in the early 1990s and concern intensified around the fiscal crises of the national and provincial governments, Alberta embarked on a bold initiative to fundamentally restructure the relationships among the state, the market and citizens. Democratic rhetoric was prominently featured in this re-making of government and, particularly in the Klein government's first term of office, restructuring efforts were framed in terms of returning government to the people. In the 1993 Throne Speech, for example, the government announced that one of its key commitments was "to listen to the people it is privileged to serve, to consult with them, and to be as open, compassionate, and fair as possible in reflecting their wishes, their hopes, and their dreams."[24] Thus the government's program of far-reaching budget cuts was justified as a response to the expressed wishes of Albertans: "in the recent election Albertans gave a loud and clear message of support for this government's commitment to put our financial house in order. Albertans want good government at a cost they can afford."[25] As well, the government's program was described in the language of freedom; precisely, negative freedom, or the ability to live one's life with as little interference from the state as possible. In the 1996 Throne Speech, for example, the government declared that "central to all of the government's efforts is its commitment to provide services that reflect Albertans' desire to take more responsibility for their lives in the workplace, in the marketplace and in the community."[26]

In this context, the democratic value of equality became highly circumscribed. Progressive conceptions of equality as difference, generally associated with claims for ameliorative action and the investment of state resources, were virtually to disappear from political discourse. Indeed, such conceptions were cast as antithetical to democracy. As the Alberta government declared in its 1998 Budget Speech:

> There are those who believe we should have an all-powerful government providing for every need in every facet of life. Their vision means government must plan the lives of citizens.... [T]he more government tries to unnecessarily interfere [sic] in the lives of its citizens, the more it will stifle initiative and growth as people become weary under the weight of excessive government and taxation.[27]

Thus, the combination of a desire to limit spending and an ideological commitment to reducing the role of the state in people's lives led to the Klein government's decision to abolish the Women's Secretariat and the AACWI—moves that were officially justified in the language of open, democratic discourse: "Times have changed, women's groups have multiplied and grown in strength, and they can and want to speak for themselves to government without a publicly funded intermediary."[28] Further, the appointment of women to key cabinet positions, including the Ministry of Finance, gave some credence to the claim that the only barriers facing women were the ones that they imagined.

Rhetoric and symbolism aside, however, the adoption of neo-liberal government, with its emphasis on maximizing the freedom of the market and minimizing the role of the state in people's lives, had significant gendered consequences. A reduction in kindergarten funding from 400 to 200 hours indicated the government's assumption that families, but particularly women, would be able to fill in the gap with either their time or with money for alternative care arrangements. Cuts to health care budgets and the ensuing reductions in nursing staff placed additional burdens on women to meet the care needs of their ailing family members. In addition, a concerted attack on the Alberta Human Rights Commission, launched in reaction to the Commission's decision to include discrimination on the basis of sexual orientation within its investigatory purview, revealed the government's ambivalence regarding its obligation to protect Albertans in the event that their rights and, indeed, freedoms were abrogated.[29]

Once the language of freedom drowns out the legitimacy of claims to equality, the capacity of equality-seeking groups to argue that particular policy initiatives have a disproportionate effect on their members' lives becomes increasingly difficult. After all, the government might argue, families can decide amongst themselves who cares for the children and for the sick. Moreover, because this capacity for choice is precisely what women have demanded and because neo-liberal governments impose fewer explicit regulative strictures on their citizens, policy-makers might readily assert that individual preference and initiative rather than structural impediments determine who meets the caring needs that the state no longer provides.

What this send-up of freedom obscures, however, is the extent to which the passive state also governs. It is profoundly disingenuous to insist that a long-established gender order might suddenly be overwhelmed by individuals recently awakened to their new-found autonomy. It is also disingenuous to disavow the extent to which public policy has both reinforced the gender order and, indeed, continues to actively rely upon it in order to ensure that its political program succeeds.

There are two notable exceptions to the erasure of equality from the Alberta state's official political discourse. These claims are manifested in the characterization of the province's place within Confederation and in the government's tax reform initiatives. With regard to Alberta's place in Canada, the government asserted that

> Albertans want to be full and equal partners in Canada, but true partnership is only possible when all parties are respected and valued for what they bring to the table. Alberta's ability to be a partner in Canada is compromised by the current federal government, which often does not listen to the people of this province.[30]

The degree to which the form of this call for equality repeats the claims of virtually every equality-seeking group is both striking and ironic.[31]

Equality also makes an appearance in the context of tax reform, where neo-conservative calls to treat equal-earning families equally have been realized in the adoption of a flat tax at the provincial level and in the provision of the same basic deduction for dependent spouses as for wage earners. Central to the equal-earning families argument is the claim that the tax system should provide horizontal equity—that people in like situations should be treated the same way.[32] According to this logic, a father who supports his family on an income of $60,000 should not have to pay higher taxes than a family in which the husband and wife each earn $30,000. However, due to progressive tax rates at the federal level (i.e., those who make more money are taxed at a higher rate) and the use of the individual as the basic unit of taxation, higher income earners pay more tax.[33]

The claim that "equal earning families should be treated equally" is deceptive in its simplicity. First, to the extent that equality continues to define liberal democracies, that equality is understood in terms of individuals, not families. There is no guarantee that all family members, or even the adults in a family, will have equal access to the finances or control over financial decision-making. In making the claim that families rather than individuals should be equated, the neo-conservative position invokes a Lockean notion of man's legal personality residing in his ownership of property and control over his household. As such, the family is subsumed in its patriarch.

Even if one does not object to the use of family rather than individual income as the basis for determining horizontal equity, it might also be noted that the equal-earning families argument rests on the presumption that the single-earner and dual-earner families have the same ability to pay. This presumption ignores both the extra expenses that people in the paid work force incur as a result of their need for transportation, appropriate attire and child care, and the benefits that accrue to the two-parent, single-earner family from the care provided by the spouse, generally, the wife, who is not employed in the paid labour force. As a parliamentary subcommittee discovered when investigating the equal-earning family argument, while the single-earner two-parent family may pay more in taxes, they nonetheless have more disposable income.[34]

In extending the basic personal deduction to dependent spouses, Alberta's tax reform initiatives appear to grant equality to all couple relationships, regardless of whether both partners earned income.[35] But again, the result of this reform was to provide a disproportionate benefit to high-earners in sole breadwinner, two-parent families. Indeed, as the Alberta Treasury's figures demonstrated, the people who would enjoy the greatest benefit from the reforms were those who constituted the "traditional" family and earned more than $100,000 annually. Moreover, their tax savings would be $1,535 more than a two-earner family in the same tax bracket, largely because of the extension of the basic personal amount to dependent spouses.[36] When one considers that the single-earner family already had more disposable income before the reform, this was quite an advantage.

Of course, one might assert that the extension of the basic personal amount to dependent spouses acknowledges the value of unpaid labour and, as such, would meet feminists' demands for recognizing the caring work that women disproportionately provide. Again, however, there was no certainty that women would be the direct beneficiaries of this tax break, nor has the government articulated the recognition of women's unpaid labour as the objective of its reform initiatives. In fact, the primary motivations for tax reform were to ensure Alberta's attractiveness as a location for capital investment and an ideological antipathy to taxation in general.[37] The advancement of the equal-earning families argument as part of this initiative appears to have been a secondary objective.

The simultaneous erasure of explicit references to gender equality from the province's political discourse and the continued reliance on an unequal gender order as a central enabling condition for the operation of neo-liberal governance has posed considerable difficulties for feminists. The assertion that government policies and programs treat men and women differently is greeted with reactions usually reserved for claims of spectral sightings. It is not surprising, given this hostility, that many feminist groups have simply given up on the Alberta government, preferring to direct their energies and resources to more local and more global struggles. The question thus becomes, to what extent do feminist iterations of gender equality continue to matter in Alberta? The evidence suggests that they matter very little at the level of public policy, but in the context of the everyday lives of Alberta women, they matter more than ever.

Conclusion

This chapter has drawn on the relationship between the Alberta state and the province's women's groups to explore the multiple and shifting meanings of equality. During the years of the oil boom and the early days of feminism's second wave, gender equality was variously construed as meaning that men and women should be treated in precisely the same way; or that women would require specifically-designed measures in order to attain the same social and economic stature as men. Tellingly, the Alberta state and women's groups made use of both meanings, depending on their respective readings of a particular political situation. Nonetheless, formal equality tended to be deployed by the province, while equality as difference was more widely adopted by women's groups. As the provincial economy weakened through the 1980s, formal equality was largely abandoned. Instead, the province acknowledged the legitimacy of women's demands for recognition but did so in contradictory ways. On the one hand, the province appeared to heed feminist claims for women's autonomy, while on the other, the province embraced neo-conservative notions of separate spheres as it heralded the virtues of the traditional family. Finally, with the adoption of neo-liberal governance in the 1990s, equality was relegated to a residual democratic virtue and replaced by freedom. In this context, an individual's life chances are claimed to be the product of her initiative, entrepreneurialism and resourcefulness. Whatever disadvantages a person faced were to be overcome through perseverance or by acceptance. As the social theorist, Nikolas Rose, asserts,

> Modern individuals are not merely "free to choose," but *obliged to be free*, to understand and enact their lives in terms of choice. They must interpret their past and dream their future as outcomes of choices made or choices still to make. Their choices are, in their turn, seen as realizations of the attributes of the choosing person—expressions of personality—and reflect back upon the person who has made them.[38]

In those moments when equality was mobilized, it was primarily used to emphasize the importance of treating entities in the same way. However, as we observed in the context of tax reform, formal equality can also disguise the promotion of a neo-conservative gender order.

Equality, then, is a contingent concept whose meaning relies on the intentions of the actors who mobilize it and the context in which it is manifested. Yet its power as a democratic virtue rests in its promise, a promise of the life we should be living and the goal of particular political struggles. To the extent that equality has fallen out of favour in the contemporary moment, we might query whether this is because we have developed a preference for freedom, or because it has become increasingly difficult to define the standard to which we would be equal. Nonetheless, for those who have yet to experience the advantages of Alberta's opportunities, many women among them, the promise of equality will continue to beckon.

Notes

1. Alberta Legislative Assembly, *Debates* (31 August 1993), p. 10.
2. Ibid.
3. Diane Sainsbury, *Gender, Equality and Welfare States* (Cambridge: Cambridge University Press, 1996), 173–74. I have adapted Sainsbury's discussion to more aptly fit the Alberta situation. Where she downplays the neo-conservative mobilization of gender difference, I assert that this vision has had a strong presence in the province.
4. Indeed, this situation arose in Alberta. After the passage of the *Individual Rights Protection Act*, the province's Industrial Relations Board was forbidden from compelling private sector employers to implement maternity leave provisions since they would be discriminatory and hence contravene the IRPA. Ultimately, the government reversed its stance but it did so by creating an exemption to the IRPA. See Lois Harder, *State of Struggle: Feminism and Politics in Alberta* (Edmonton: University of Alberta Press, 2003), 26–28.
5. There are also feminists who adhere to the view that "biology is destiny." But rather than maintaining a world of separate spheres, their political program envisions a world in which female characteristics receive greater social value and political power.
6. The Bill of Rights focused on the relationship between citizens and the state and was replaced in 1982 by the Canadian Charter of Rights and Freedoms. The *Individual Rights Protection Act* concerned private relationships between employers and workers, landlords and tenants, and service providers and consumers.
7. Alberta Legislative Assembly, *Debates* (2 March 1972), p. 6.
8. Alberta Status of Women Action Committee, *Joint Initiatives. A Goal for Women and Government in Alberta* (Edmonton: Alberta Status of Women Action Committee, 1976), 4–5.
9. Hugh Horner, "An Address by Hon. Dr. Hugh M. Horner, Deputy Premier and Minister of Transportation, Government of Alberta to Alberta Status of Women Action Committee," 29 October 1976.
10. *Alberta Women's Newsletter* 1 (Spring 1974): 4.
11. Harder, *State of Struggle*, 34.
12. Al "Boomer" Adair to CSWAC, 13 December 1977, CSWAC Collection, Glenbow Archives, Calgary.
13. Ibid.
14. See, for example, Alberta Legislative Assembly, *Debates* (23 January 1975), p. 1; (2 March 1978), p. 1.
15. The view of social order that I am sketching takes heterosexuality and marriage as standard features. As with gender, however, the alleged self-evidence of these features merits critical reflection.
16. Linda Trimble, "The Politics of Gender in Modern Alberta," in Allan Tupper and Roger Gibbins, eds. *Government and Politics in Alberta* (Edmonton: University of Alberta Press, 1992), 224 and 233.
17. Alexandra Dobrowolsky, *The Politics of Pragmatism: Women, Representation and Constitutionalism in Canada* (Toronto: Oxford University Press, 2000).
18. Harder, *State of Struggle*, 59.
19. Julie Anne LeGras, "Council on Women's Affairs, Background Paper," 15 January 1983, Provincial Archives of Alberta, Edmonton, 2.
20. Interdepartmental Committee on Women's Issues, minutes, 29 October 1984, Women's Bureau Collection, Provincial Archives of Alberta, Edmonton.

21. See Kim Macleod, "Balance views, Real Women told," *Edmonton Journal* 28 November 1987: B5.

22. In fact, the initial reaction from the minister responsible for women's issues to AFWUF's demands was to suggest the withdrawal of funding from all women's groups. His colleagues and ministerial staff ultimately persuaded him to rethink this position. See Harder, *State of Struggle*, 56.

23. Alberta Women's Secretariat, "Summary of AFWUF's Presentation to the Interdepartmental Committee on Women's Issues," 27 March 1985, Women's Bureau Collection, Provincial Archives of Alberta, Edmonton. For a more detailed discussion of this meeting see Harder, *State of Struggle*, 75–77.

24. Alberta Legislative Assembly, *Debates* (31 August 1993), p. 8.

25. Alberta Legislative Assembly, *Debates* (31 August, 1993), p. 8.

26. Alberta Legislative Assembly, *Debates* (13 February 1996), p. 2.

27. Alberta Legislative Assembly, *Debates* (12 February 1998), p.355.

28. Alberta Legislative Assembly, *Debates* (27 March 1995), p. 839.

29. See Harder, *State of Struggle*, esp. 130–33 and 143–50.

30. Alberta Legislative Assembly, *Debates* (18 February 2003), p. 4.

31. It is not clear precisely what form of equality is being demanded here. While formal equality has appeared in assertions that Canada is a country of ten equal provinces, equality as difference is also apparent in demands for the opportunity to opt out of federal-provincial programs, with compensation. Further, in reflecting on Alberta's recent forays in the federal-provincial arena, one might query at what point the demand for equality becomes a demand for autonomy or freedom. Here, one might consider Alberta's desire to pursue health reforms that might abrogate the *Canada Health Act* or to consider the construction of a "firewall" to protect the province from federal intervention.

32. The discussion on the taxation of equal-earning families is drawn from Lois Harder, "Child Care, Taxation and Normative Commitments: Excavating the Child Care Expense Deduction Debate," *Studies in Political Economy* 73 (2004): 97–99.

33. Progressive tax rates are justified in terms of "vertical equity"—the principle that the more affluent should provide a greater amount of their income to taxes in order to offset income disparities. This principle has been justified in various ways, including that it buys social peace by reducing the desperation of the poor and that society has a moral obligation to provide for the less fortunate.

34. Canada, House of Commons, Sub-Committee on Tax Equity, "For the Benefit of Our Children." Figures provided by the Federal Department of Finance to the Sub-Committee demonstrated that while a single-earner family making $60,000 paid $5,874 more in income tax than a dual-earner family with the same total income, the dual-earner family had $4,704 less in disposable income after tax.

35. As of 2000, married couples as well as opposite and same-sex common-law partners are required to declare their relationship for the purposes of the *Income Tax Act*.

36. Alberta, "Tax Plan Savings for Albertans" 2001. Online. www.finance.gov.ab.ca/whatsnew/newsreel/2001/n010103a.pdf.

37. The 1997 Budget Speech provides an especially colourful articulation of this view in the form of a parable about slavery. See Alberta Legislative Assembly, *Debates*, 21 April 1997, 83.

38. Nikolas Rose, *Powers of Freedom: Reframing Political Thought* (Cambridge: Cambridge University Press, 1999), 87.

Sixteen

Uncertain Future
Alberta in the Canadian Community
ALLAN TUPPER

As Alberta begins its second century, its place in Canada remains a topic of debate. The province's recent constitutional and intergovernmental experience under the leadership of Ralph Klein, Alberta's twelfth premier, has presented new ways of looking at Alberta's contemporary constitutional and intergovernmental dynamics and raises several possibilities for the future.

Contrary to political and journalistic rhetoric, Alberta exerts a strong influence on national affairs and its portrayal of itself as an oppressed, ignored and misunderstood hinterland is no longer convincing. Under Premier Klein, Alberta's intergovernmental relations have been rhetorically critical of national policies and institutions, but substantively, they have been unexceptional in content and process. This "normalization" of Alberta's intergovernmental politics has complex sources. In fact, it is possible to see the Klein governments as transitional ones in Alberta's quest for a stable place in Canada. Peter Lougheed, Alberta's premier from 1971 to 1985, established Alberta as a powerful force in Canada with decisive new constitutional and intergovernmental priorities.[1] His positions continue to prevail in many areas, but they are in need of an overhaul that the Klein government has not undertaken for several reasons.

Alberta is increasingly being shaped by broader forces in Canada and the world. In 2005, the confluence of several such forces suggests that Alberta's position in Canada must be recast if the province is to retain its influence. Alberta's internal politics are also growing more complex in ways that demand changes in the province's national role. Tentative indications are that a "Big Western" perspective, as analyzed by Preston Manning in his contribution to this volume, will emerge and that Alberta's position in Canada will change notably. In making this claim, I recognize that a powerful provincialism animates Alberta society, but that broader forces will redefine such provincialism. Alberta's second century will likely see a warmer embrace of the national community.

There are three major dynamics that emerge from an investigation of the Klein years: (1) Alberta's continuing commitment to intergovernmental relations as the principal vehicle for undertaking its national agenda, (2) the implications of the changing international order, and (3) the impact of the Charter of Rights and Freedoms on Alberta's provincial politics and place in Canada. Each of these subjects is complex in its own right and I knowingly sacrifice nuance in favour of presenting the larger picture here.

In probing Alberta's place within Canada, no obvious trajectory presents itself. The Klein years, let alone Alberta's first century, are multifaceted.[2] The first Klein government, 1993–1997, was consumed by the goal of restructuring Alberta's public finances. After 1997, the province's fiscal and economic situation improved dramatically. With renewed affluence, the province embarked on new intergovernmental initiatives and became somewhat more confrontational with the Government of Canada. In the new millennium, Premier Klein appeared disinterested. Observers noted uncharacteristically erratic and ill-conceived Alberta positions on national issues. Regardless, the Conservatives were again re-elected in the 2004 general election on the basis of a promise of new plans for the investment of Alberta's budget surpluses.

Alberta's centenary is a fitting time to reflect on the province's past, on its potential and on its strengths and weaknesses as a society. It is also a time to think about neglected aspects of Alberta's experience, especially the "national" side of Alberta's constitutional and intergovernmental history. With few exceptions, scholarship, public debate and, self-evidently, provincial governments, emphasize provincial dimensions of Albertans' identities and shared experiences. Alberta's distinctiveness, political alienation and quest for a larger national voice are major themes. The dominant image is that of a restless, wealthy province whose well-being and ambitions are frustrated by an unfair national political system and constitutional order.

The dominant provincial story is incomplete. Alberta's experience is also a part of a complex national history with many positive features. Remarkably little is said about the substantial benefits that accrue to Alberta from its participation in the Canadian experience. The idea that Alberta's prosperity and strengths as a society are attributable to its existence in a larger national community is seldom acknowledged. Federal-provincial co-operation, by far the norm, is ignored at the expense of spectacular instances of intergovernmental conflict. The attitudes, aspirations and careers of Albertans who achieve national influence are overlooked compared to those on the provincial stage.

More importantly, the impressive durability, flexibility and responsiveness of the Canadian constitution are lost in the barrage of complaint. The constitutional and intergovernmental order, while certainly an obstacle to some Alberta interests, has facilitated remarkable transformations in Alberta society. Such transformations include the successful establishment of a complex welfare state, the orderly transition of a rural, agrarian society into an urbanized one and most importantly, the maintenance (certainly not perfection), of a tolerant, open society. As Alan C. Cairns has argued about the Canadian constitution,

> the dustbin of recent history is littered with discarded constitutions cast aside after brief and withering exposure to reality. Constitutions capable of responding and adapting to the perils of change have sufficient scarcity value to be treated with the deference appropriate to rare achievements. All the more curious, therefore, has been the detached, unappreciative Canadian attitude to one of the most durable and successful constitutions in the world.[3]

Alberta's centenary should certainly celebrate Alberta's distinct history. Equally, it should acknowledge the beneficial impact of participation in a larger national community.

Intergovernmental Relations in the Klein Years

In 1992 when Ralph Klein became premier, Alberta was a troubled province. It was amassing substantial budgetary deficits, the Conservative provincial government was adrift and both major opposition parties, the Liberals and New Democrats, were growing in popularity. Outside of Calgary, Ralph Klein was not well known in Alberta, nor had he developed a noteworthy national presence. To many observers, Klein was an enigma. On the one hand, he portrayed himself as a "severely normal" Albertan well attuned to the rigours of everyday life. On the other hand, his populism was tempered by the need to secure elite support. His program, which stressed public finance reform, envisioned no radical changes to Alberta's power structures.

Unlike his Conservative predecessors, Peter Lougheed and Don Getty, Klein came to office lacking well-known views about intergovernmental relations, constitutional reform or Alberta's role in Canada. He certainly had no public persona as an "alienated" westerner with strong views about past injustices suffered by Albertans. Moreover, the energy and constitutional struggles that preoccupied Peter Lougheed had waned and they no longer galvanized provincial and national opinion. For his part, Don Getty had presided over the demanding Meech Lake and Charlottetown negotiations. Klein had played no major role in these national debates and came to office with a relatively clean slate. He sensed that Canadians had tired of formal constitutional change as a mechanism for national rejuvenation.

Klein relied heavily on "executive federalism"—negotiations between the political executive and senior appointed officials of the provinces, territories and federal government—as the key vehicle for Alberta's intergovernmental agenda. Executive federalism with its emphasis on secrecy, specialized language and complex policy debate seemed an unusual priority for a new premier with a populist image and a reputed impatience for policy discussions. But as Roger Gibbins has argued, executive federalism was a natural choice for Klein. It was almost a "philosophy of government" in Alberta where Peter Lougheed had cultivated public opinion about the province's structural weakness in national politics and the need for a strong provincial government as advocate of Alberta's interests.[4] Alberta elites, still angry about the National Energy Program, remained vigilant against "unilateral" federal actions. Moreover, Klein inherited substantial policy capacity and expertise in the provincial Department of Federal and Intergovernmental Affairs (FIGA) whose role was to devise government-wide strategies for intergovernmental relations. Executive federalism also provided the obvious vehicle for intergovernmental relations in a country preoccupied by budget deficits and weary of constitutional negotiations. Finally, Klein spoke about giving his backbenchers greater involvement policy-making. The reality was a government, like those of the other Canadian provinces, dominated by its premier. Executive federalism demanded Klein's participation and reinforced his dominance.

Klein's intergovernmental agenda was an interesting one. He articulated Alberta's commitment to "equality of the provinces" as a foundation. He also supported, although with little obvious enthusiasm, Premier Getty's pursuit of an elected Senate. His ideas implied a classical view of federalism as a political system where government authority was divided into compartments with, ideally, little overlap in functions or responsibilities. He spoke strongly about the need to avoid "duplication and overlap" in intergovernmental relations. He argued that Ottawa should respect provincial constitutional responsibilities for health, education and social assistance. He became a vigorous critic of some federal actions justified under the spending power. Klein also supported the idea of a "fiscal imbalance" that saw a mismatch between governments' responsibilities and financial resources in Canadian federalism. In his view, Ottawa had substantial financial resources and light expenditure responsibilities while provinces struggled with onerous expenditures. As Alberta amassed substantial budget surpluses in the late 1990s, this line of reasoning was much better advocated by Quebec, whose provincial government developed a coherent analysis.

Klein led the charge against the emerging trend whereby Ottawa required provincial governments to account for their "performance" in certain policy areas and for their expenditure of federal transfers. Standards for program delivery and accountability, if really necessary, were to be "national," that is negotiated jointly by the provinces, territories and federal government, not "federal," that is, determined by Ottawa alone. Finally, Alberta under Klein was more committed to interprovincial accords as a priority than either Getty or Lougheed had been. Klein's position was simple. If Ottawa was to be restrained, provincial governments would have to demonstrate that co-operative provincial action could meet the needs of a mobile, interdependent society.

Klein learned intergovernmental politics quickly. Alberta played important roles in the complex negotiations leading to both the Social Union Framework Agreement and a stronger agreement on Internal Trade. The province consistently advocated the need for an explicit provincial role in the negotiation and implementation of international agreements, especially when such agreements had demonstrable implications for provincial governments. During the 1995 referendum debate in Quebec, Klein spoke frequently about the need for accommodation in the interests of national unity. And in the complex area of Aboriginal policy, Klein's government advanced an innovative Aboriginal Policy Framework.[5] It argued that the economic and social well-being of Aboriginal peoples should be the primary public policy goal. Constitutional and intergovernmental issues should not deter governments from substantive policy changes.

As its budget surpluses grew, Alberta became rhetorically strident about health care as an intergovernmental issue. The province complained about the *Canada Health Act* as a constraint on provincial activity. The act allegedly restricted provincial innovation but Ottawa only paid for 15 per cent of

Alberta's total health care budget. The 2004 report by Alberta Conservative MLAs on *Strengthening Alberta's Role in Confederation* again claimed that the *Canada Health Act*, notably its seldom-used capacity to withhold funding to provincial governments, somehow impeded provincial government policy innovation.[6] Under Premier Klein, Alberta's position on this matter became nationally controversial at various times. In the 2004 general election campaign, Klein harmed the federal Conservatives by musing about the need for more private health care. Alberta's intentions became more confused when Premier Klein cut short his participation in the First Ministers meeting on Health Care in September 2004. Alberta's stance led the *National Post* to complain in an editorial, entitled "All Talk, No Action," that "For the past decade, Mr. Klein has teased medical reform advocates by flirting with challenging the Canada Health Act—and each time, he has backed off at the first sign of resistance."[7]

Alberta failed to generate substantial enthusiasm among other provinces for Senate reform. Provincial interests diverge considerably on this matter, making common cause difficult. Public opinion seems indifferent. Interestingly, Alberta ran elections for "Senators-in-waiting" coincident with the 2004 Alberta general election. The logic was to pressure the prime minister to accede to the Alberta *vox populi* and to appoint the winners in the Alberta election to vacant Senate seats. The Alberta elections are seen as preparatory to a major constitutional change. Interestingly, turnout in the Alberta general election in 2004 was a meagre 44.8 per cent. Only 28.6 percent of eligible voters cast ballots for the Senators-in-waiting.

Under Premier Klein, Alberta's grievances with Ottawa have been selective. For example, Alberta was silent about the major expansion of federal government authority in Canadian universities after 1997. Several substantial federal expenditure programs reshaped higher education and moved universities, a key force in Canada's economic future, into the federal orbit. As Ottawa spent large amounts on student financial assistance, on university infrastructure and on university research, Alberta and other provinces allowed tuitions to rise and were stingy with operating funds. Ottawa's role in higher education was justified by virtue of its commitment to advanced research, but many federal programs shifted provincial priorities. No evidence suggests any unhappiness with this state of affairs among Alberta students or university leaders.

Under Premier Jean Charest, Quebec is now the province most adept at achieving its interests. Charest was the architect of the Council of the Federation, a new interprovincial body that provides support, policy capacity and focus to the annual Premiers Meeting. The Council seeks common interprovincial cause on major national initiatives and is an important new element in Canadian executive federalism. Charest has vigorously advanced Quebec positions on Ottawa's agenda for cities, on health care and on intergovernmental finances. He has built alliances with federal opposition parties and other provincial governments. In this changing environment, Alberta is responding rather than leading. Alberta has sought a variety of allies, but no strong new alliances have been struck. During the 1990s, Klein worked with Michael Harris, the like-minded Conservative premier of Ontario. Recently, British Columbia and Alberta have begun to work together.[8] This alliance has interesting implications as two prosperous provinces co-operate to increase their national impact. It also makes obvious the increasing heterogeneity of western Canada. Alberta and British Columbia appear different from Saskatchewan and Manitoba, provinces whose populations are stagnant or declining and whose interests often differ from those of their two more prosperous western neighbours.

Ralph Klein has added colour and, sometimes, humour to national debate. However, his distinctive style and sometimes spontaneous remarks should not deflect attention from the conventional tenor of Alberta's intergovernmental relations under his leadership. What accounts for the recent "normalization" of Alberta's intergovernmental strategy? Doug Owram's perceptive analysis in this volume of the Alberta-Ottawa energy disputes is suggestive. First, health care, social assistance and urban issues, for example, do not lend themselves to distinctive provincial government positions. Albertans' interests in these matters do not differ greatly from those of British Columbians or Ontarians. Provincial governments that have themselves defined funding in these areas as a major problem cannot easily resist federal money. Moreover, health care, Canadians' pre-eminent concern, is not easily related to provincial history, to provincial distinctiveness or to a vision of provincial citizenship. To the degree that powerful symbols are involved, health care is seen as an element of Canadian citizenship, a theme that resonates in Alberta as elsewhere. These circumstances make anti-Ottawa crusades difficult in the millennium.

In the energy struggles of the 1970s, Pierre Trudeau and Peter Lougheed clashed intellectually and by dint of personality over major matters of policy and federalism. Both advocated imperialistic policy agendas that sought to extend their respective governments' powers. No powerful differences of vision, ideology or even personality shape federal provincial relations under Premier Klein, Prime Minister Chretien or Paul Martin. In the 1993–1997 period, both federal and provincial governments cut public expenditures and restructured their operations. Canadian federalism accommodated these objectives with surprising ease. When the federal and Alberta budgets went into surplus, both governments articulated common goals—a desire to pay down debt, to lower taxes and to "reinvest" in vital public services. Third, and implicit in the first explanation, Alberta has not developed a coherent alternative to federal plans. In many areas where Ottawa is ambitious—higher education and grants to municipal governments for example—Alberta has cut expenditures and unconsciously provided a foundation for federal ambitions. Under these circumstances, Alberta's position, despite its wealth, is like that of the other provinces. It can either increase provincial spending or rhetorically resist federal "intrusions."

The Changing International Order

An abiding theme in Alberta's history is the impact of the larger world. The United Kingdom, continental and Eastern Europe, the United States and now Asia exert strong influences on Alberta. Major themes are the impact of international forces on Alberta's "open," resource-based economy and the influence of immigration on Alberta society.

Less attention has been paid to the impact of a changing world on Alberta's constitutional position. Ralph Klein is Alberta's first premier to govern in a world shaped, not loosely by broad international forces, but directly by emergent supranational organizations and by international agreements that circumscribe governments' options. The influence of new international bodies and agreements is most evident in the Business Plan of Alberta's Department of International and Intergovernmental Relations, formerly the Department of Federal and Intergovernmental Affairs. The department notes three "core businesses"—Canadian Intergovernmental Relations, International Relations and Trade Policy.

In a persuasive analysis, Stephen McBride examines how new international organizations and agreements are radically changing democratic politics. He refers to a process of "quiet constitutionalism."[9] New international institutions and agreements are constitutional because they are extraordinarily important, difficult to change and pervasive in impact. They are "quiet" because they are not normally seen as constitutional in impact or design. McBride challenges the view that, since the failed Charlottetown Accord,

Canada has not experienced formal constitutional change. To the contrary, the growing power of international bodies and agreements has substantially changed the Canadian constitution. The subtlety of the process and a narrow, formal sense of constitutionalism blind us to the reality. McBride describes the impact of agreements like NAFTA and the power of supranational organizations like the WTO in these terms: "Thus negotiation and ratification of such agreements are part of a process that can be termed 'quiet constitutionalism' which produces constitutional change without overtly engaging in constitutional reform. The impact of quiet constitutionalism is ongoing and far-reaching. Fundamental changes have occurred affecting Canadian sovereignty and the degree to which democracy matters."[10]

In the 1980s, many influential Canadians became convinced that Canada must establish a free trade agreement with the United States. Several forceful Albertans, notably Peter Lougheed, led the national cause. Advocates of bilateral free trade advanced many arguments. One idea that attracted attention in Alberta was the notion that a bilateral free trade agreement, while limiting the capacity of governments to shape their economies, was worth the risk. The precise argument was that Alberta's "province-building" ambitions might be curtailed but the federal government would be restrained even more. In Alberta, a province whose elites were profoundly distressed by the National Energy Program, this appeal of bilateral free trade had great purchase. A long-standing western ambition would be achieved. As a major bonus, the capacity of an insensitive national government to harm Alberta would be curtailed.

As Alberta begins its second century, we are reminded of the old adage: "Be careful what you wish for!" The impact of international agreements on Alberta is becoming evident and worrisome. The capacity of democratic governments to shape their societies is certainly circumscribed by the new international order. Whether a liberal economic order is in the long-term interest of an open, geographically isolated and sparsely-populated province like Alberta remains to be seen. Moreover, the federal government, while impaired to a degree by new international agreements, exerts substantial and undisputed authority over international relations in all its dimensions. This results in a situation where provincial governments are bound by agreements that they do not directly negotiate or implement and as a result, "the provinces are increasingly bound by outcomes into which they had little input and, in some ways, are placed by the agreements under the supervision of federal authorities."[11] The new international order indirectly places Alberta in a subordinate position that, ironically, it has long struggled to avoid in relations with the federal government. Finally, the new international order exerts a further constitutional impact by enhancing the already substantial power of political executives in Canadian government. Like executive federalism, the negotiation and implementation of international agreements engage citizens at best indirectly, a fact that animates the anti-globalization movement. Heads of government and senior appointed officials, not legislatures or mechanisms of citizen engagement, are the principal actors. This development is worrisome in Alberta, whose politics are already characterized by extraordinary executive dominance.

The Charter of Rights and Freedoms

The Charter of Rights and Freedom profoundly altered the Canadian constitution in 1982. The Charter transformed constitutional politics from the exclusive domain of governments into a complex democratic process involving many organizations and citizens. It established new identities for Canadians. The Charter defined Canadians as equal citizens whose constitutional and political life rested on a pan-Canadian floor of shared rights. The Charter's ideal of "equality of citizens" rested uneasily with federalism's notion of "equality of provinces." As Alan Cairns put it: "For its Anglophone supporters, the Charter fosters a conception of citizenship that defines Canadians as equal bearers of rights independent of provincial location. This legitimates a citizen concern for the treatment of fellow Canadians by other than one's own provincial government."[12] Pierre Trudeau, a forceful Charter advocate, recognized the Charter's capacity to weaken provincial identities and provincial governments.

In 1982, Alberta was a lukewarm supporter of the Charter. The province prized its autonomy and defended provincial constitutional prerogatives, both of which were threatened by the Charter. And the Charter, with its potential for "judicial activism," worried a province with complaints about the Supreme Court as a "federal" institution. Alberta supported the notwithstanding clause as a limit on the Charter.

Under Premier Klein, Alberta gained a national reputation as a province ill at ease with the Charter. In several hotly-debated circumstances, Klein threatened to employ section 33 to thwart the Charter's impact or to achieve provincial government objectives. Yet the provincial government has still not used the notwithstanding clause. In every instance it has backed down from its threat. As a result, Alberta probably strikes many Canadians as a constitutional outsider. The province's distance from the mainstream is exaggerated by its government's rhetoric about the Charter.

Three recent controversies highlight Alberta's stance on the Charter. In 1998, a major dispute erupted about the province's treatment of mentally challenged persons in provincial facilities. For a time, Alberta, like other democratic governments, condoned the sterilization of mentally challenged persons in provincial institutions. Several victims of such practices sued the provincial government for compensation. The province responded with legislation that mandated a settlement and, by reference to section 33, limited victims' capacity to appeal to the courts. Alberta opposition parties sensed that the government was misreading public opinion and attacked. Many Albertans saw the sterilizations as repugnant and criticized the government. The government's response was also seen as offensive in a rights-conscious society. The government quickly retreated and put in a place a different process for dealing with the issue.

A second case gained greater national attention. Delwin Vriend, an employee at a religious college in Edmonton, believed that he had been dismissed because he was a homosexual and that his dismissal was illegal. However, Alberta's provincial human rights act, the *Individual Rights Protection Act*, unlike those in other provinces, did not enumerate sexual preference as a prohibited ground of discrimination. Vriend challenged this omission as contrary to the Charter's equality guarantees. The case ultimately went to the Supreme Court of Canada which "read in" sexual preference to the Alberta act and thereby sustained Vriend's case.

A controversy immediately erupted when members of the provincial government mused that the circumstances warranted use of the notwithstanding clause. Critics of the decision employed two principal arguments. First, the *Individual Rights Protection Act* consciously excluded sexual preference and, as such, was a legitimate reflection of public opinion that should prevail. Second, politicians, not courts, properly decided such matters. After heated public debate, Premier Klein announced that section 33 would not be used and that Alberta would take no further action on the matter. National media paid extraordinary attention to the views of religious minorities and to homophobic sentiment in Alberta. Much less attention was paid to widely-expressed support for both the Vriend decision and for the extension of the coverage of the *Individual Rights Protection Act*. Alberta embraced the Canadian norm in this regard but only its differences were highlighted.[13]

At time of writing in late 2004, Canadians are debating same-sex marriage, an issue that raises strong emotions. However, same-sex marriage has not dominated national politics as some had predicted prior to the 2004 general election. It highlights the genre of "lifestyle" issues that characterize affluent democracies.

A majority of Canadians appears to accept same-sex marriages, although support varies by province—with larger majorities in Quebec and British Columbia than elsewhere. However, the constitutional and political dimensions of the issue are confused and confusing. Six provincial governments, often prompted by courts, accept that the Charter demands marriage between persons of the same sex. The government of Canada referred the matter to the Supreme Court in an effort to gain clarity. As anticipated, the Supreme Court ruled that the Charter demanded that same-sex couples be allowed to marry legally, although its complex ruling gave ammunition to all sides. At time of writing, the federal government is preparing legislation that seeks a national resolution. Alberta is one of the four provinces not yet to come to terms with the issue.

The debate about same-sex marriage has intergovernmental, partisan and constitutional dimensions. Its entanglement with three significant matters of democratic procedure adds greater complexity. One procedural matter, articulated principally by the federal Conservative party, debates whether Parliament or the courts should resolve the matter. A second debate concerns the rules by which the House of Commons should decide. Should members be allowed to vote as they see fit? Finally, same-sex marriage raises use of the Charter's notwithstanding clause to somehow enshrine a "traditional" view of marriage as a union between a man and a woman.

In early 2005, Parliament passed legislation that provides legal sanction to same-sex marriage in Canada. Only the federal Conservative Party seems strongly opposed, although its position is complex. Premier Klein, prior to seeing Ottawa's proposed legislation, called for a national referendum and later urged use of the notwithstanding clause. He asserted that Alberta will employ all "political and legal" means to block same-sex marriage.

Klein's strategy is to position himself as a rhetorical leader among defenders of "traditional" marriage. At the same time, he can predictably lament that federal legislation imposes the will of a national majority on Albertans. Better still, he can then conveniently withdraw reference to the use of the notwithstanding clause. A drawback of this perhaps too clever strategy is to reinforce Alberta's unflattering stereotype as a narrow-minded province with minimal rights consciousness.

This brief analysis leads to three major conclusions. First, Alberta's recent political history explains its uneasiness with the Charter. Alberta's political leadership was suspicious of the Charter and the Supreme Court from the outset. As a province jealous of its autonomy, Alberta feared the nationalizing impact of the Charter and its potential restraints on provincial policy-making. On the other hand, no evidence suggests that Albertans are either less committed to the Charter than other Canadians or conversely that Charter critics are less prevalent in other provinces. Second, Alberta's intermittent rhetoric about using the notwithstanding clause to thwart the Charter has stimulated negative conceptions about Alberta as a society. The other side of the story—the weight of provincial public opinion against the government's use of the notwithstanding clause—has received little national attention. Popular opinion urges the provincial government to join the national consensus on major issues. Third, Alberta, like the rest of Canada, is now home to interest groups, citizens' movements and non-governmental organizations that animate a rights consciousness, that demand government response, and that join with like-minded groups in other parts of Canada and the world. "Charter Canadians" and their spokespersons populate Alberta just as they do other parts of the country.

Alberta's Second Century

Under Ralph Klein's leadership, Alberta has presented itself as a wealthy, yet discontented province. In the dominant view, Alberta must undertake intergovernmental policies that preserve the province's wealth, defend its constitutional prerogatives and extend its capacity for autonomous action. In practice, Alberta's opposition to federal policies, and in the case of the Charter, to the constitutional order, has been primarily rhetorical. Unlike the 1970s and the 1980s, no major intergovernmental issue has galvanized public opinion and animated the provincial government. Alberta certainly remains an anxious society, but perhaps its place in Canada seems more secure to the citizens than to its provincial politicians.

In January 2001, Stephen Harper, now leader of the Conservative Party of Canada, and several colleagues, wrote an "open" letter to Premier Klein. It argued that Alberta must defend itself from a hostile national government, that "it is imperative to take the initiative, to build firewalls around Alberta, to limit the extent to which an aggressive and hostile federal government can encroach upon legitimate provincial jurisdiction."[14] The authors advocated such immediate actions as withdrawal from the Canada Pension Plan, the establishment of a provincial police force to replace the RCMP and the replacement of the Canada Health and Social Transfer's cash portion with tax points so that Alberta could run its health care system free of federal constraints. From these and other reforms, Albertans would benefit considerably.

The "firewall" proposal was skilfully crafted to appeal to Albertans' pride, to their anxieties about their future and to their tradition of political protest. It portrayed Albertans as a united people with an identifiable common interest in reducing Ottawa's authority. It characterized federal policy as animated by ideals that were alien to Alberta's traditions and political culture. The authors warned of Ottawa's predatory instincts when it came to Alberta's resource wealth. Finally, a more autonomous Alberta government would creatively respond to Albertans' distinct needs and interests. In short, the firewall idea was a carefully-designed call to arms.

The firewall idea received little public support in Alberta, a province reputed to be a hotbed of angry provincialism. No major group publicly endorsed either its premises or specific recommendations. Three years later, the provincial government commissioned a committee of its backbenchers to examine citizens' views about Alberta's place in Canada. The committee's report was tepid in tone and devoid of rhetoric about an ominous federal government. It was at best lukewarm about specific firewall proposals. Albertans' disinterest in the firewall idea made little impression on media, who continue to cast Alberta as Canada's constitutional *enfant terrible*.

Alberta's considerably changed circumstances in Canada suggest major changes in its intergovernmental relations. The classic image of western alienation, modernized and politically perfected by Peter Lougheed, has little resonance in the new millennium. Alberta cannot easily be portrayed as a resource-rich colony of central Canada whose ambitions are thwarted by a national government dominated by Ontario and Quebec. Alberta's economic prosperity, modern infrastructure and substantial urbanization make implausible the role of exploited hinterland. Alberta's more diversified economy generates a wider range of interests and policy objectives, many of which are better served by federal than provincial policy. Common Alberta positions are harder to define as the province grows more complex.

Major issues of the day—the quality of education and health care for example—are defined as national problems that demand intergovernmental co-operation for their resolution. Distinctive Alberta positions and interests are hard to define under these circumstances. Finally, Alberta's influence on the national stage, although recently surpassed by Quebec, is undeniable. The province was instrumental in shaping the 1982 constitutional settlement, particularly the amending formula. Albertans played a major role in the debate about a bilateral free trade agreement with the United States. Moreover, its achievement and extension to the current NAFTA agreement remove a perennial western Canadian grievance. While unsuccessful to date, Alberta's actions have kept alive the perennial issue of Senate reform.

Other forces weigh on the provincial government. Over the last decade, Canadian provincial governments, including Alberta, have transformed their roles. The "province building" activities of the 1960s and 1970s with their ambitious expansion of civic works, schools and health care facilities were replaced, under the pressure of budget deficits, by expenditure cuts and provincial government restructuring. Provincial governments became stern and frugal. Privatization and other management changes frequently removed provincial governments from direct contact with citizens. Balanced provincial budgets were achieved by a redistribution of the costs of public services to municipal governments, non-government agencies and citizens themselves through increased user fees, higher tuitions at educational institutions and other devices. These changes are substantial in impact. Arguably, they are particularly important in Alberta where, under the Lougheed governments, extraordinary efforts were made to establish the provincial government as the primary source of citizen allegiance. Often controversially and sometimes ineffectively, the federal government entered areas where the provinces have changed their tune. Post-secondary education and health care have already been mentioned. Current federal efforts to establish direct links with urban governments are another example of Ottawa's efforts to increase its presence in the daily lives of Canadians. Finally, Alberta will likely face strong pressures to modernize its own political structures rather than demand changes in Ottawa. Other provinces, notably British Columbia, are debating electoral system and other democratic changes. Alberta's reputation as an innovative province will be sorely tested by the competition.

In this millennium, Canada, like the world, is manifestly more interdependent. Alberta elites, in resource, scientific and commercial spheres, are comfortable on the larger stage of Ottawa, North America and the broader world. As Albertans become more cosmopolitan, the federal government and international bodies assume greater importance and the provincial government less importance. The government of Canada is indisputably the lead source of foreign policy, with the provinces playing catch-up in many important areas. Tumultuous events abroad heighten Albertans' consciousness about the world beyond their borders. And the impact of advanced computer technology, while not yet fully understood, will likely weaken Albertans' identifications with the provincial government. As Roger Gibbins has argued, information technology is implicitly hostile to federalism. As a form of government, federalism stresses jurisdiction and territory. On the other hand, advanced communications technologies underscore membership in non-territorial communities and indifference to boundaries and borders. Advanced technologies may also weaken federalism by providing easy access to government services. Over time, citizens will likely demand "seamless" access to all government services in one place. Federalism and its ideas about provincial distinctiveness will be dealt another blow and "...as more and more government activities go on line there is a strong possibility that e democracy will be *less federal* than current democratic practices. Whether this loss will be mourned is another matter. My guess is that most Canadians would happily trade in sections 91 and 92 of the *Constitution Act* for a single portal on all government activities touching their lives."[15]

The Klein years are transitional ones as Alberta adapts to new circumstances. In the 1970s, Peter Lougheed's governments modernized Alberta's public services, established the province as a national force and advocated forceful constitutional positions. The Klein and Getty governments inherited and maintained this legacy. But circumstances now demand a rethinking of traditional assumptions and a new vision. As a result, the Klein governments are in a no-man's land between a clear past and an uncertain future. These circumstances help explain Alberta's primarily rhetorical opposition to the Charter of Rights and Freedoms and other national policies. Alberta's government knows what it dislikes but has no positive alternative. Alberta faces substantial changes. The "quiet constitutionalism" of a new international order weakens provinces' capacity to shape their societies. In an interdependent world, the national side of the Albertans' identities will be stimulated as the province recedes as a force in their lives. The provincial government has itself pursued policies that remove it from pride of place in citizens' minds. These and other forces demand a rethinking of Alberta's place in Canada. A "Big Western" perspective that sees Alberta as a positive force in national and international affairs will likely be required.

Two concluding cautions are required. First, since the 1930s many observers of Canadian society have predicted the weakening of provincial identities. Moreover, they have noted some of the same forces—the national focus of elites, advanced communications and international interdependence—that I have mentioned. Yet provincialism, while currently muted, remains a potent force in Alberta and other parts of Canada. It cannot be wished or analyzed away. Second, the power of provincial governments to create and maintain provincial identities, to defend provincial prerogatives and to articulate provincial visions is remarkable. As Alan Cairns has reminded us, provincial governments exert profound impacts on their provinces in the absence of any deeper sociological sense of community or identity:

> The sociological perspective pays inadequate attention to the possibility that the support for powerful, independent provincial governments is the product of the political system itself, that it is fostered and created by provincial government elites employing the policy-making apparatus of their jurisdictions, and that such support need not take the form of a distinct culture, society, or nation as these are conventionally understood.[16]

Alberta's provincial government will not quietly preside over a drift to its own obsolescence.

Notes

1. For an overview of the Lougheed years, see Allan Tupper, "Peter Lougheed, 1971–1985," in Bradford J. Rennie, ed., *Alberta Premiers of the Twentieth Century* (Regina: Canadian Plains Research Centre, 2004), 204–28.
2. For an overview of the Klein years, see Doreen Barrie, "Ralph Klein 1992–," in Rennie, ed. *Alberta Premiers*, 256–79. See also Mark Lisac's thoughtful and critical overview, *Alberta Politics Uncovered: Taking Back our Province* (Edmonton: NeWest Press, 2004).
3. Alan C. Cairns, "The Living Canadian Constitution," in Douglas E. Williams, ed., *Constitution and Government in Canada: Selected Essays by Alan C. Cairns* (Toronto: McClelland and Stewart, 1988), 27.
4. Roger Gibbins, "Alberta's Intergovernmental Relations Experience," in Harvey Lazar, ed., *Canada: The State of the Federation, 1997: Non-Constitutional Renewal* (Kingston, ON: Institute of Intergovernmental Relations 1998), 247–70. Gibbins's article is an invaluable overview.

5.   Government of Alberta, Department of Aboriginal Affairs and Northern Development, *Strengthening Relationships: The Government of Alberta's Aboriginal Policy Framework* (Edmonton: Government of Alberta, 2000).

6.   Government of Alberta, MLA Committee on Strengthening Alberta's Role in Confederation, *Final Report*, 2004, especially pp. 31–35.

7.   "All talk, no action," *National Post*, 28 December 2004, A-15.

8.   For an interesting analysis of Alberta's relations with British Columbia, see Gibbins, "Alberta's Intergovernmental Relations Experience," especially pp. 259–60.

9.   Stephen McBride, "Quiet Constitutionalism in Canada: The International Political Economy of Domestic Institutional Change," *Canadian Journal of Political Science* 36, no. 2 (June 2003): 251–74.

10. McBride, "Quiet Constitutionalism," 253–54.

11. McBride, "Quiet Constitutionalism," 260.

12. Alan C. Cairns, "Constitutional Change and the Three Equalities," in Douglas E. Williams, ed., *Reconfigurations: Canadian Citizenship and Constitutional Change, Selected Essays by Alan C. Cairns* (Toronto: McClelland and Stewart, 1995), 218.

13. Mark Lisac stresses this theme in *Alberta Politics Uncovered*, especially in his analysis of Alberta's "secret federalists."

14. "An Open Letter to Ralph Klein," *National Post*, January 24, 2001, A-14.

15. Roger Gibbins, "Federalism in a Digital World," *Canadian Journal of Political Science* 33, no. 4 (2000): 684.

16. Alan C. Cairns, "The Governments and Societies of Canadian Federalism," in Williams, ed., *Constitution and Government in Canada*, 145.

Selected Bibliography

Books

Aberhart, William. *Social Credit Manual: Social Credit as Applied to the Province of Alberta: Puzzling Questions and Their Answers*. Calgary: Western Print and Litho Co., 1935.

Allan, T.R.S. *Constitutional Justice: A Liberal Theory of the Rule of Law*. Oxford: Oxford University Press, 2001.

Armstrong, Christopher. *The Politics of Federalism: Ontario's Relations with the Federal Government, 1867–1942*. Ontario Historical Studies Series. Toronto: University of Toronto Press, 1981.

Ascah, Robert L. *Politics and Public Debt: The Dominion, the Banks and Alberta's Social Credit*. Edmonton: University of Alberta Press, 1999.

Asch, Michael. *Aboriginal and Treaty Rights in Canada: Essays on Law, Equity, and Respect for Difference*. Vancouver: University of British Columbia Press, 1997.

Backhouse, C. and Swainger, J., eds. *People and Places: Historical Influences on Legal Culture*. Vancouver: University of British Columbia Press, 2003.

Baker, H. Robert. "Law Transplanted, Justice Invented: Sources of Law for the Hudson's Bay Company in Rupert's Land, 1670–1870." M.A. Diss. University of Manitoba, 1996.

Baker, John Hamilton, and Louis A. Knafla. *Crime and Criminal Justice in Europe and Canada*. Waterloo: Wilfrid Laurier University Press, 1981.

Ball, Terence, and J.G.A. Pocock. *Conceptual Change and the Constitution*. Lawrence, KS: University Press of Kansas, 1988.

Beal, Bob, and R.C. Macleod. *Prairie Fire: The 1885 North-West Rebellion*. Edmonton: Hurtig, 1984.

Beatty, David M. *Constitutional Law in Theory and Practice*. Toronto: University of Toronto Press, 1995.

Beaudin, G.-A. *La constitution du Canada: Institutions, partage des pouvoir, droits et libertes*. Montreal: Wilson and Lafleur, 1990.

Begg, Alexander. *History of the North-West*. 3 vols. Toronto: Hunter, Rose and Co., 1894.

Behiels, Michael D. *The Meech Lake Primer: Conflicting Views of the 1987 Constitutional Accord*. Ottawa: University of Ottawa Press, 1989.

Berger, Thomas R. *A Long and Terrible Shadow: White Values and Native Rights in the Americas since 1492*. 2nd ed. Vancouver: Douglas and McIntyre, 1999.

Binnema, Theodore, Gerhard John Ens, R.C. Macleod, and John Elgin Foster. *From Rupert's Land to Canada: Essays in Honour of John E. Foster*. Edmonton: University of Alberta Press, 2001.

Bojechko, Cynthia. "Lougheed's 'Energetic Bureaucrats': a Study of the Senior Civil Servants in Province-Building Departments." M.A. Diss., University of Alberta, 1982.

Boldt, Menno, J. Anthony Long, and Leroy Little Bear. *The Quest for Justice: Aboriginal Peoples and Aboriginal Rights*. Toronto: University of Toronto Press, 1985.

Borrows, John. *Recovering Canada: The Resurgence of Indigenous Law*. Toronto: University of Toronto Press, 2002.

Bramley-Moore, A., *Canada and Her Colonies; or, Home Rule for Alberta*. London: W. Stewart, 1911.

Braz, Albert Raimundo. *The False Traitor: Louis Riel in Canadian Culture*. Toronto: University of Toronto Press, 2003.

Breen, David H. *The Canadian Prairie West and the Ranching Frontier 1874–1924*. Toronto: University of Toronto Press, 1982.

Brown, Desmond Haldane. *The Genesis of the Canadian Criminal Code of 1892*. Toronto: University of Toronto Press, 1989.

Brown, Jennifer S.H. *Strangers in Blood: Fur Trade Company Families in Indian Country*. Vancouver: University of British Columbia Press, 1980.

Buckley, K.A.H., F.H. Leacy, and M.C. Urquhart, *Historical Statistics of Canada*. 2nd ed. Ottawa: Statistics Canada, 1983.

Buckner, Phillip A., and John G. Reid. *The Atlantic Region to Confederation: A History*. Toronto: University of Toronto Press, 1994.

Bumsted, J.M., ed. *The Collected Writings of Lord Selkirk*. 2 vols. Winnipeg: Manitoba Record Society, 1998.

———. *Fur Trade Wars: The Founding of Western Canada*. Winnipeg: Great Plains Publications, 1999.

———. *Louis Riel v. Canada: The Making of a Rebel*. Winnipeg: Great Plains Publications, 2001.

Burley, Edith. *Servants of the Honourable Company: Work, Discipline, and Conflict in the Hudson's Bay Company, 1770–1870*. Canadian Social History Series. Toronto: Oxford University Press, 1997.

Burnet, Jean R., Howard Palmer, and Canada Multiculturalism Directorate. *Coming Canadians: An Introduction to a History of Canada's Peoples, Generations, a History of Canada's Peoples*. Toronto: McClelland and Stewart, 1988.

Byfield, Ted, ed. *Alberta in the 20th Century*. Vol. 5, *Brownlee and the Triumph of Populism 1920–1930*. Edmonton: United Western Communication, 1996.

Byrne, Timothy C. *Alberta's Revolutionary Leaders*. Calgary: Detselig Enterprises, 1991.

Cairns, A.C. *Charter Verses Federalism: The Dilemmas of Constitutional Reform*. Montreal: McGill Queen's University Press, 1992.

Cairns, Alan C., and Douglas E. Williams. *Constitution, Government and Society in Canada: Selected Essays*. Toronto: McClelland and Stewart, 1988.

———. *Disruptions: Constitutional Struggles from the Charter to Meech Lake*. Toronto: McClelland and Stewart, 1991.

Calvet, Louis Jean. *La guerre des langues et les politiques linguistiques*. Paris: Hachette Littératures, 1999.

Cassidy, Frank, and Institute for Research on Public Policy. *Aboriginal Self-Determination: Proceedings of a Conference Held September 30–October 3, 1990*. Lantzville: Oolichan Books, 1991.

Chalmers, John West, and Alberta Teachers' Association. *Schools of the Foothills Province: The Story of Public Education in Alberta* Toronto: University of Toronto Press, 1967.

Cleverdon, Catherine Lyle. *The Woman Suffrage Movement in Canada*. Toronto: University of Toronto Press, 1950.

Coates, Colin MacMillan, and Cecilia Louise Morgan. *Heroines and History: Representations of Madeleine De Verchères and Laura Secord*. Toronto: University of Toronto Press, 2002.

Colbourne, Maurice Dale. *Unemployment or War*. New York: Coward-McCann, 1928.

Colpitts, George. *Game in the Garden: A Human History of Wildlife in Western Canada to 1940*. Vancouver: UBC Press, 2002.

Cook, Ramsay. *The Maple Leaf Forever: Essays on Nationalism and Politics in Canada*. Toronto: Macmillan, 1971.

Creighton, Donald Grant. *The Road to Confederation: The Emergence of Canada, 1863–1867*. Toronto: Macmillan, 1964.

Cronkite, Frederick Clinton, and Otto E. Lang. *Contemporary Problems of Public Law in Canada: Essays in Honour of Dean F.C. Cronkite*. Toronto: University of Toronto Press, 1968.

Culhane, Dara, and Canada Council. *The Pleasure of the Crown: Anthropology, Law, and First Nations*. Burnaby: Talonbooks, 1998.

Dafoe, John Wesley. *Laurier: A Study in Canadian Politics*. Toronto: McClelland and Stewart, 1963.

Dawson, R. MacGregor. *The Government of Canada*. 5th ed. Toronto: University of Toronto Press, 1970.

DeCoste, Frederick Charles. *On Coming to Law: An Introduction to Law in Liberal Societies*. Markham: Butterworths, 2001.

Dempsey, Hugh Aylmer. *The CPR West: The Iron Road and the Making of a Nation*. Vancouver: Douglas and McIntyre, 1984.

Dickason, Olive Patricia. *Canada's First Nations: A History of Founding Peoples from Earliest Times*. Toronto: McClelland and Stewart, 1992.

Dobbin, Murray. *The One-and-a-Half Men: The Story of Jim Brady and Malcolm Norris, Metis Patriots of the Twentieth Century*. Vancouver: New Star Books, 1981.

Dobrowolsky, Alexandra Z. *The Politics of Pragmatism: Women, Representation, and Constitutionalism in Canada*. Don Mills: Oxford University Press, 2000.

Doern, G. Bruce, and Glen B. Toner. *The Politics of Energy: The Development and Implementation of the NEP*. Toronto: Methuen, 1985.

Donnelly, Murray Samuel. *The Government of Manitoba*. Toronto: University of Toronto Press, 1963.

Douglas, C.H. *The Alberta Experiment: An Interim Survey*. London: Eyre and Spottiswoode, 1937.

Drieksen, P. *We Are Métis: The Ethnography of a Halfbreed Community in Northern Alberta*. New York: AMS Press, 1985.

Eager, Evelyn. *Saskatchewan Government: Politics and Pragmatism*. Saskatoon: Western Producer Prairie Books, 1980.

Elliott, David Raymond, and Iris Miller. *Bible Bill: A Biography of William Aberhart*. Edmonton: Reidmore Books, 1987.

English, John. *The Life of Lester Pearson*. Vol. 2, *The Worldly Years, 1949–1972*. 1st ed. Toronto: A.A. Knopf Canada, 1992.

Ens, Gerhard John. *Homeland to Hinterland: The Changing Worlds of the Red River Metis in the Nineteenth Century*. Toronto: University of Toronto Press, 1996.

Evans, A. Margaret. *Sir Oliver Mowat*. Ontario Historical Studies Series. Toronto: University of Toronto Press, 1992.

Finkel, A., and M. Conrad. *History of the Canadian Peoples: Beginnings to 1867*. 2 vols. Toronto: Copp Clark Ltd, 1998.

Flaherty, David H. *Essays in the History of Canadian Law*. Toronto: University of Toronto Press, 1981.

Flanagan, Thomas. *Louis Riel*. Ottawa: Canadian Historical Association, 1992.

———. *Riel and the Rebellion: 1885 Reconsidered*. 2nd ed. Toronto: University of Toronto Press, 2000.

Forsey, Eugene A. *Freedom and Order*. Toronto: McClelland and Stewart, 1974.

Foster, Franklin Lloyd. *John E. Brownlee: A Biography*. Lloydminster: Foster Learning, 1996.

Foster, Hamar, John McLaren, Chet Orloff, eds. *Law for the Elephant, Law for the Beaver: Essays in the Legal History of the North American West*. Regina: Canadian Plains Research Center, 1992.

Fowke, Vernon C. *The National Policy and the Wheat Economy*. Social Credit in Alberta: Its Background and Development 7. Toronto: University of Toronto Press, 1973.

Francis, Daniel. *Battle for the West: Fur Traders and the Birth of Western Canada*. Edmonton: Hurtig, 1982.

Freeman, Edward A. *Comparative Politics*. 2nd ed. London: Macmillan, 1896.

Friesen, Gerald. *The Canadian Prairies: A History*. Toronto: University of Toronto Press, 1987.

Fumoleau, René. *As Long as This Land Shall Last: A History of Treaty 8 and Treaty 11, 1870–1939*. Toronto: McClelland and Stewart, 1975.

Galbraith, John S. *The Hudson's Bay Company as an Imperial Factor, 1821–1869*. Toronto: University of Toronto Press, 1957.

Getty, Ian A.L., and Antoine S. Lussier. *As Long as the Sun Shines and Water Flows: A Reader in Canadian Native Studies*. Vancouver: University of British Columbia Press, 1983.

Gibson, Ronald Dale, and Lee Gibson. *Substantial Justice: Law and Lawyers in Manitoba, 1670–1970*. Winnipeg: Peguis, 1972.

Gidney, R.D., and W.P.J. Millar. *Inventing Secondary Education: The Rise of the High School in Nineteenth-Century Ontario*. Kingston: McGill-Queen's University Press, 1990.

Granatstein, J.L. *Canada 1957–1967: The Years of Uncertainty and Innovation*. Canadian Centenary Series 19. Toronto: McClelland and Stewart, 1986.

Gray, James Henry. *Men against the Desert*. Saskatoon: Modern Press, 1967.

———. *The Winter Years: The Depression on the Prairies*. Toronto: Macmillan, 1966.

Green, L.C., and Olive Patricia Dickason. *The Law of Nations and the New World*. Edmonton: University of Alberta Press, 1989.

Griffon, Éric Batalla and Sandrine. *Écoles francophones, Alberta*. Edmonton: Le Franco et La Fédération des conseils scolaires francophones de l'Alberta, 2003.

Harder, Lois. *State of Struggle: Feminism and Politics in Alberta*. Edmonton: University of Alberta Press, 2003.

Hardy, W.G. *Alberta, a Natural History*. 1st ed. Edmonton: Hurtig, 1967.

Harring, Sidney L. *White Man's Law: Native People in Nineteenth-Century Canadian Jurisprudence*. Toronto: University of Toronto Press, 1998.

Hawkes, David C., and Queen's University Kingston, Ont. Institute of Intergovernmental Relations. *Negotiating Aboriginal Self-Government: Developments Surrounding the 1985 First Ministers' Conference*. Aboriginal Peoples and Constitutional Reform. Background Paper. No. 7. Kingston, ON: Institute of Intergovernmental Relations, 1985.

Helliwell, John F., Anthony Scott, and Pemberton Securities Limited. *Canada in Fiscal Conflict: Resources and the West: Summary Version*. Vancouver: Pemberton Securities Limited, 1981.

Hill, Douglas Arthur. *The Opening of the Canadian West: Where Strong Men Gathered*. 1st American ed. New York: J. Day, 1967.

Hogg, Peter W. *Constitutional Law of Canada*. Student ed. Scarborough: Carswell, 2001.

Horn, Michiel. *The Dirty Thirties: Canadians in the Great Depression*. Toronto: Copp Clark Pub. Co., 1972.

Hustak, Alan. *Peter Lougheed: A Biography*. Toronto: McClelland and Stewart, 1979.

Ilbert, Courtenay. *Legislative Methods and Forms*. Oxford: Clarendon Press, 1901.

Innis, Harold Adams, and Arthur J. Ray. *The Fur Trade in Canada: An Introduction to Canadian Economic History*. Toronto: University of Toronto Press, 1999.

Innis, Mary Quayle, and Canadian Federation of University Women. *The Clear Spirit: Twenty Canadian Women and Their Times*. Toronto: University of Toronto Press, 1966.

Irving, John Allan. *The Social Credit Movement in Alberta*. Social Credit in Alberta: Its Background and Development 10. Toronto: University of Toronto Press, 1959.

Johnston, Darlene, *The Taking of Indian Lands in Canada: Consent or Coercion?* Saskatoon: University of Saskatchewan Native Law Centre, 1989.

Jones, David C. *Empire of Dust: Settling and Abandoning the Prairie Dry Belt*. Calgary: University of Calgary Press, 2000.

Keeton, G.W. *Keeping the Peace*. London: Barry Rose Publishers, 1975.

Kilbourn, William. *Pipeline: Transcanada and the Great Debate, a History of Business and Politics*. Toronto: Clarke, Irwin, 1970.

Klassen, Henry C., ed. *The Canadian West: Social Change and Economic Development*. Calgary: Comprint, 1977.

Kymlicka, Will. *Finding Our Way: Rethinking Ethnocultural Relations in Canada*. Toronto: Oxford University Press, 1998.

___. *Multicultural Citizenship: A Liberal Theory of Minority Rights*. Oxford: Clarendon Press, 1995.

La Forest, G.V., *Natural Resources and Public Property under the Canadian Constitution*. Toronto: University of Toronto Press, 1967.

Lamoureux, P. *Bilingual Schooling in Alberta*. Edmonton: Alberta Education, 1984.

Laponce, J.A. *Languages and Their Territories*. Toronto: University of Toronto Press, 1987.

Laponce, J.A., and Université Laval Centre international de recherches sur le bilinguisme. *Langue et territoire*. Québec: Presses de l'Université Laval, 1984.

Lazar, Harvey. *Canada: The State of the Federation: 1997*. Kingston: Institute of Intergovernmental Relations, Queen's University, 1998.

Leduc, H. *Hostility Unmasked School Ordinance of 1892 of the North-West Territories and Its Disastrous Results*. Montreal: C.O. Beauchemin, 1896.

Lingard, Charles Cecil. *Territorial Government in Canada: The Autonomy Question in the Old North-West Territories*. Toronto: University of Toronto Press, 1946.

Lisac, Mark. *Alberta Politics Uncovered: Taking Back Our Province*. Edmonton: NeWest Press, 2004.

Lougheed, P. and Levesque, R., *Constitutional Patriation: The Lougheed-Levesque Correspondence*. Kingston: Institute of Intergovernmental Relations, 1999.

Lupul, Manoly R. *The Roman Catholic Church and the North-West School Question: A Study in Church-State Relations in Western Canada, 1875–1905*. Toronto: University of Toronto Press, 1974.

Lynch-Staunton, Frank. *Greener Pastures: The Memories of F. Lynch-Staunton*. Edmonton: Jasper Printing Group, 1987.

MacEwan, Grant. *Frederick Haultain: Frontier Statesman of the Canadian Northwest*. Saskatoon: Western Producer Prairie Books, 1985.

MacGregor, James G. *A History of Alberta*. Edmonton: Hurtig, 1972.

MacKinnon, Frank. *The Crown in Canada*. Calgary: McClelland and Stewart, 1976.

Macklem, Patrick. *Indigenous Difference and the Constitution of Canada*. Toronto: University of Toronto Press, 2001.

Macleod, R.C. *The N.W.M.P. and Law Enforcement, 1873–1905*. Toronto: University of Toronto Press, 1976.

Macleod, R.C., and Doug Owram. *The Formation of Alberta: A Documentary History*. Calgary: Alberta Records Publication Board, 1979.

MacPherson, C.B. *Democracy in Alberta: Social Credit and the Party System*. 2nd ed. Social Credit in Alberta: Its Background and Development 4. Toronto: University of Toronto Press, 1962.

Magnet, Joseph Eliot. *Official Languages of Canada: Perspectives from Law, Policy and the Future*. Cowansville: Éditions Y. Blais, 1995.

Mainville, Robert. *An Overview of Aboriginal and Treaty Rights and Compensation for Their Breach*. Saskatoon: Purich, 2001.

Mallory, J.R., *The Structure of Canadian Government*. rev. ed. Toronto: Gage, 1984.

Mancke, Elizabeth, and Rupert's Land Research Centre. *A Company of Businessmen: The Hudson's Bay Company and Long-Distance Trade, 1670–1730*. Winnipeg: Rupert's Land Research Centre, 1988.

Manfredi, Christopher P. *Judicial Power and the Charter: Canada and the Paradox of Liberal Constitutionalism*. Toronto: McClelland and Stewart, 1993.

Manning, Preston. *The New Canada*. Toronto: Macmillan, 1992.

———. *Think Big: My Adventures in Life and Democracy*. Toronto: McClelland and Stewart, 2002.

Marmorek, Jan, and Energy Probe. *Over a Barrel: A Guide to the Canadian Energy Crisis*. Toronto: Doubleday Canada, 1981.

Marsh, James H., ed. *The Canadian Encyclopedia*. 3 vols. Edmonton: Hurtig, 1985.

McWhinney, Edward. *Canada and the Constitution, 1979–1982: Patriation and the Charter of Rights*. Toronto: University of Toronto Press, 1982.

Meekison, J. Peter. *Canadian Federalism: Myth or Reality*. 3rd ed. Toronto: Methuen, 1977.

Miller, J.R. *Skyscrapers Hide the Heavens: A History of Indian-White Relations in Canada*. 3rd ed. Toronto: University of Toronto Press, 2000.

Miller, Jim, Arthur Ray, and Frank Tough. *Bounty and Benevolence: A History of the Saskatchewan Treaties*. Kingston: McGill-Queen's University Press, 2000.

Milne, David. *Tug of War: Ottawa and the Provinces under Trudeau and Mulroney*.
Toronto: Lorimer, 1986.

Milton W. Hamilton, et. al, eds. *The Papers of Sir William Johnson*. 14 vols.
Albany: University of New York, 1965.

Morin, Claude. *Lendemains piéges: Du référendum à la "nuit des longs couteaux."*
Montréal: Boréal, 1988.

Morris, Alexander. *The Treaties of Canada with the Indians of Manitoba and the North-
West Territories Including the Negotiations on Which They Were Based, and Other
Information Relating Thereto*. Toronto: Willing and Williamson, 1880.

Morrison, R. Bruce, and C. Roderick Wilson. *Native Peoples: The Canadian
Experience*. 2nd ed. Toronto: McClelland and Stewart, 1995.

Morton, Arthur S. *A History of the Canadian West to 1870–71; Being a History of Rupert's
Land the Hudson's Bay Company's Territory and of the North-West Territory Including
the Pacific Slope*. 2nd ed. Toronto: University of Toronto Press, 1973.

Morton, D. *The Queen V. Louis Riel*. Toronto: University of Toronto Press, 1974.

Morton, W.L. *The Progressive Party in Canada*. Social Credit in Alberta: Its
Background and Development 1. Toronto: University of Toronto
Press, 1950.

Nelles, H.V. *A Little History of Canada*. Toronto: Oxford University Press, 2004.

Nigol, P.C. "Discipline, Discretion and Control: The Private Justice System of
the Hudson's Bay Company in Rupert's Land, 1670–1770." Ph.D. Diss.,
University of Calgary, 2001.

Nikiforuk, A. *The Land before Us: A Geological History of Alberta*. Red Deer: Red Deer
College Press, 1994.

Oliver, Edmund Henry. *The Canadian North-West, Its Early Development and
Legislative Records*. Vol. 2. Ottawa: Govt. Print. Bureau, 1915.

Otter, A.A. den. *Civilizing the West: The Galts and the Development of Western Canada*.
Edmonton: University of Alberta Press, 1982.

Owram, Doug. *Promise of Eden: The Canadian Expansionist Movement and the Idea of the
West, 1856–1900*. Toronto: University of Toronto Press, 1980.

Palmer, Howard. *The Settlement of the West*. Calgary: University of Calgary
Press, 1977.

Palmer, Howard, and Tamara Jeppson Palmer. *Alberta: A New History*.
Edmonton: Hurtig, 1990.

———. *Peoples of Alberta: Portraits of Cultural Diversity*. Saskatoon: Western
Producer Prairie Books, 1985.

Pannekoek, Frits. *A Snug Little Flock: The Social Origins of the Riel Resistance of 1869–
1870*. Winnipeg: Watson and Dwyer, 1991.

Pannekoek, Frits, and Canadian Historical Association. *The Fur Trade and the Western Canadian Society*. Ottawa: Canadian Historical Association, 1987.

Parker, Nancy. "Reaching a Verdict: The Changing Structure of Decision-Making in the Canadian Criminal Courts, 1867–1905." Ph.D Diss., York University, 1998.

Patterson, Robert Steven. "F.W.G. Haultain and Education in the Early West." M.Ed. Diss., University of Alberta, 1961.

Persky, Stan, and David Suzuki Foundation. *Delgamuukw: The Supreme Court of Canada Decision on Aboriginal Title*. Vancouver: Greystone Books, 1998.

Piggot, F.T. *Imperial Statutes Applicable to the Colonies*. London: William Clowes, 1902.

Pocklington, T. "Our Land—Our Culture—Our Future: The Government and Politics of the Alberta Métis Settlements." Unpublished Manuscript, University of Alberta, Edmonton, 1988.

Price, Richard. *The Spirit of the Alberta Indian Treaties*. 3rd ed. Edmonton: University of Alberta Press, 2000.

Promislow, J. B. "Towards a Legal History of the Fur Trade: Looking for Law at York Factory, 1714–1763." LL.M. Diss., York University, 2004.

Public Archives of Canada, Adam Shortt, and Arthur G. Doughty. *Documents Relating to the Constitutional History of Canada*. 2nd and rev. ed. Ottawa: King's Printer, 1918.

Ramrattan, Annette. "The Theory of Catholic Schooling in the Archdiocese of Edmonton, 1884–1960." M.Ed. Diss., University of Alberta, 1982.

Rawls, John. *A Theory of Justice*. Oxford: Clarendon Press, 1972.

Ray, Arthur J. *I Have Lived Here since the World Began: An Illustrated History of Canada's Native Peoples*. Toronto: Key Porter Books, 1996.

___. *Indians in the Fur Trade: Their Role as Trappers, Hunters, and Middlemen in the Lands Southwest of Hudson Bay, 1660–1870*. Toronto: University of Toronto Press, 1974.

Ray, Arthur J., and Donald B. Freeman. *"Give Us Good Measure": An Economic Analysis of Relations between the Indians and the Hudson's Bay Company before 1763*. Toronto: University of Toronto Press, 1978.

Reynolds, Thomas Michael. "Justices of the Peace in the North-West Territories 1870–1905." M.A. Diss., University of Regina, 1978.

Rich, E.E. *The Fur Trade and the Northwest to 1857*. Toronto: McClelland and Stewart, 1967.

___. *The History of the Hudson's Bay Company 1670–1770*, ed. 2 vols. London: Hudson's Bay Record Society, 1959.

Rich, E.E., and Winston Churchill. *Hudson's Bay Company, 1670–1870*. 1st. ed. 3 vols. Toronto: McClelland and Stewart, 1960.

Robinson, Eric, and Henry Bird Quinney. *The Infested Blanket: Canada's Constitution-Genocide of Indian Nations*. Winnipeg: Queenston House, 1985.

Romanow, Roy J., John D. Whyte, and Howard A. Leeson. *Canada... Notwithstanding: The Making of the Constitution, 1976–1982*. Toronto: Carswell/Methuen, 1984.

Romney, Paul. *Getting It Wrong: How Canadians Forgot Their Past and Imperilled Confederation*. Toronto: University of Toronto Press, 1999.

Rusak, S.T. "Relations in Education between Bishop Legal and the Alberta Government, 1905–1920." M.Ed. Diss., University of Alberta, 1966.

Russell, P.H. *Federalism and the Charter: Leading Constitutional Decisions: A New Edition*. Montreal: McGill-Queen's University Press, 2003.

—— -. *Constitutional Odyssey: Can Canadians Become a Sovereign People?* 3rd ed. Toronto: University of Toronto Press, 2004.

——. *Recognizing Aboriginal Title: The Mabo Case and Indigenous Resistance to English-Settler Colonialism*. Toronto: University of Toronto Press, 2005.

Russell, Peter H., Rainer Knopff, and F.L. Morton. *Federalism and the Charter: Leading Constitutional Decisions*. New ed. Ottawa: Carleton University Press, 1989.

Sanders, Byrne Hope. *Emily Murphy, Crusader ("Janey Canuck")*. Toronto: Macmillan, 1945.

Sawchuk, Joe, Patricia Sawchuk, and Theresa A. Ferguson. *Métis Land Rights in Alberta: A Political History*, 1981.

Saywell, John. *The Lawmakers: Judicial Power and the Shaping of Canadian Federalism*. Toronto: University of Toronto Press, 2002.

Schneiderman, David, and Kate Sutherland. *Charting the Consequences: The Impact of Charter Rights on Canadian Law and Politics*. Toronto: University of Toronto Press, 1997.

Seager, J.H., and A. Thompson. *Canada 1922–39: Decades of Discord*. Toronto: McClelland and Stewart, 1985.

Silver, A.I. *The French-Canadian Idea of Confederation, 1864–1900*. Toronto: University of Toronto Press, 1982.

Simeon, Richard. *Federal-Provincial Diplomacy: The Making of Recent Policy in Canada*. Studies in the Structure of Power. Decision Making in Canada 5. Toronto: University of Toronto Press, 1972.

Sissons, C.B. *Church and State in Canadian Education: An Historical Study*. Toronto: Ryerson Press, 1959.

Skyrme, Thomas. *History of the Justices of the Peace*. 3 vols. Chichester: Barry
    Rose Publishers, 1991.

Smiley, Donald V. *Canada in Question: Federalism in the Eighties*. 3rd ed. Toronto:
    McGraw-Hill Ryerson, 1980.

———. *The Federal Condition in Canada*. Toronto: McGraw-Hill Ryerson, 1987.

Smiley, Donald V., and Ronald L. Watts. *Intrastate Federalism in Canada*.
    Toronto: University of Toronto Press, 1985.

Sprague, D.N. *Canada and the Métis, 1869–1885*. Waterloo: Wilfrid Laurier
    University Press, 1988.

Stursberg, Peter. *Roland Michener: The Last Viceroy*. Toronto: McGraw-Hill
    Ryerson, 1989.

Tarnopolsky, Walter Surma. *The Canadian Bill of Rights*. 2nd ed. Toronto:
    McClelland and Stewart, 1975.

Thomas, L.G. *The Liberal Party in Alberta: A History of Politics in the Province of Alberta:
    1905–1921*. Toronto: University of Toronto Press, 1959.

Thomas, Lewis Herbert. *The Struggle for Responsible Government in the North-West
    Territories, 1870–97*. 2nd ed. Toronto: University of Toronto Press, 1978.

Thompson, John Herd. *Forging the Prairie West*. Toronto: Oxford University
    Press, 1998.

Tomlins, Christopher L., and Bruce H. Mann. *The Many Legalities of Early
    America*. Chapel Hill: University of North Carolina Press, 2001.

Toombs, M.P. "The Control and Support of Public Education in Rupert's Land
    and the North-West Territories to 1905 and in Saskatchewan to 1960."
    Ph.D. Diss., University of Minnesota, 1962.

Trembley, Guy, and H. Brun. *Droit constitutionnelle*. 2nd ed. Cowansville: Yvon
    Blais, 1990.

Trigger, B. *Natives and Newcomers: Canada's "Heroic Age" Reconsidered*. Montreal:
    McGill-Queen's University Press, 1985.

Trudeau, Pierre Elliott. *Memoirs*. Toronto: McClelland and Stewart, 1993.

Van Herk, Aritha. *Mavericks: An Incorrigible History of Alberta*. Toronto: Viking, 2001.

Vaughan, Frederick. *The Canadian Federalist Experiment: From Defiant Monarchy to
    Reluctant Republic*. Montreal: McGill-Queen's University Press, 2003.

Ward, W.P. "The Administration of Justice in the North-West Territories,
    1870–1887." M.A. Diss., University of Alberta, 1966.

Watkins, Ernest. *The Golden Province: Political Alberta*. Calgary: Sandstone, 1980.

Whittington, Michael S., and Richard J. Van Loon. *Canadian Government and
    Politics: Institutions and Processes* Toronto: McGraw-Hill Ryerson, 1996.

Wood, David G. *The Lougheed Legacy*. Toronto: Key Porter Books, 1985.

Woodward, E.L. *The Age of Reform, 1815–1870.* 2nd ed. Oxford: Clarendon Press, 1954.

Journals and Articles

Aitchison, J.A. "The Municipal Corporations Act of 1849." *Canadian Historical Review* 30 (1949).

Anonymous. "Responsible Governance: The Implications of Judicial Independence for Policy and Practice in the Provincial Courts of Canada." *The Provincial Judges Journal* 20 (1997).

Aunger, Edmund A. "De la répression à la tolérance: Les contrariétés du néolibéralisme linguistique en Alberta." In *La gouvernance linguistique: le Canada en perspective*, edited by Jean-Pierre Wallot, 111–26. Ottawa: Presses de l'Université d'Ottawa, 2005.

———. "Justifying the End of Official Bilingualism: Canada's North-West Assembly and the Dual-Language Question, 1889–1892." *Canadian Journal of Political Science* 34 (2001): 451–86.

———. "Language and Law in the Province of Alberta." In *Language and Law*, edited by Paul Pupier and José Woehrling, 203–29. Montreal: Wilson & Lafleur, 1989.

———. "Legislating Language Use in Alberta: A Century of Incidental Provisions for a Fundamental Matter." *Alberta Law Review* 42 (2004): 463–97.

———. "The Mystery of the French Language Ordinances: An Investigation into Official Bilingualism and the Canadian North-West, 1870 to 1895." *Canadian Journal of Law and Society* 13 (1998): 89–124.

Baines, Beverly. "Law, Gender, Equality." In *Changing Patterns: Women in Canada*, edited by Sandra D. Burt, Lorraine Code and Lindsay Dorney, 243–78. Toronto: McClelland and Stewart, 1993.

Baker, H. Robert. "Creating Order in the Wilderness: Transplanting the English Law to Rupert's Land, 1835–51." *Law and History Review* 17 (1999): 209–46.

Barrie, Doreen. "Ralph Klein 1992–." In *Alberta Premiers of the Twentieth Century*, edited by Bradford J. Rennie, 204–28. Regina: Canadian Plains Research Center, 2004.

Bell, Catherine. "Metis Self-Government: The Alberta Settlement Model." In *Aboriginal Self-Government in Canada: Current Trends and Issues*, edited by John H. Hylton, 329–50. Saskatoon: Purich Pub., 1999.

Betke, C. "Pioneers and Police on the Canadian Prairies, 1885–1914." In *Lawful Authority: Readings on the History of Criminal Justice in Canada*, edited by R.C. Macleod, 98–119. Toronto: Copp Clark Pitman, 1988.

Bindon, K. "Hudson's Bay Company Law: Adam Thom and the Institution of Order in Rupert's Land, 1839–54." In *Essays in the History of Canadian Law*, edited by David H. Flaherty, 43–78. Toronto: University of Toronto Press, 1981.

Binnie, Susan W.S., and L.A. Knafla. "Beyond the State: Law and Legal Pluralism in the Making of Modern Societies." In *Law, Society, and the State: Essays in Modern Legal History*, edited by Louis A. Knafla and Susan W. S. Binnie, 3–33. Toronto: University of Toronto Press, 1995.

Borrows, J. "Constitutional Law from a First Nations Perspective: Self Government and the Royal Proclamation." *University of British Columbia Law Review* 28 (1994): 1–47.

———. "A Genealogy of Law: Inherent Sovereignty and First Nations Self-Government." *Osgoode Hall Law Journal* 30, no. 2 (1992): 291–353.

Bright, David. "The Other Woman: Lizzie Cyr and the Origins of the 'Persons' Case." *Canadian Journal of Legal Studies* 13, no. 2 (1998): 99–115.

Brown, D.H., "Unpredictable and Uncertain: Criminal Law in the Canadian Northwest before 1886." *Alberta Law Review* 17 (1979): 497–512.

___ "Abortive Efforts to Codify English Criminal Law." *Parliamentary History* 11, no. 1 (1992): 17–22.

Cairns, Alan. "The Governments and Societies of Canadian Federalism." *Canadian Journal of Political Science* 10, no. 4 (1977): 695–726.

———. "The Living Canadian Constitution." In *Constitution, Government and Society in Canada: Selected Essays*, edited by Alan C. Cairns and Douglas E. Williams. Toronto: McClelland and Stewart, 1988.

Cameron, David. "Whither Canadian Federalism? The Challenge of Regional Diversity and Maturity." In *Canadian Federalism: Myth or Reality*, edited by J. Peter Meekison, 304–24. Toronto: Methuen, 1977.

Chartier, Clem. "Indian: An Analysis of the Term as Used in Section 91(24) of the British North America Act." *Saskatchewan Law Review* 43 (1978–79): 37–80.

Clinton, R.N. "The Proclamation of 1763: Colonial Prelude to Two Centuries of Federal-State Management of Indian Affairs." *Boston University Law Review* 69 (1989): 329–85.

Colthart, James M. "Edward Ellice." In *Dictionary of Canadian Biography*, 233–39.
    Toronto: University of Toronto Press, 1976.

Cook, Ramsay. "Language Policy and the Glossophagic State." In *Language
    and the State*, edited by David Schneiderman. Cowansville, Québec:
    Éditions Yvon Blais, 1991.

Côté, Jean. "The Reception of English Law." *Alberta Law Review* 15 (1977): 29–92.

Denis, C. "The Nisga'a Treaty: What Future for the Inherent Right to Aboriginal
    Self Government." *Review of Constitutional Studies* 7 (2002): 35–54.

Eager, Evelyn. "Separate Schools and the Cabinet Crisis of 1905." *Lakehead
    University Review* 2, no. 2 (1969): 91–115.

Eccles, W.J. "Sovereignty-Association, 1500–1783." *Canadian Historical Review*
    LXV (1984): 475–510.

Ellis, Faron. "A Dream of Independence Rises out of the Post-Nep Carnage."
    In *Lougheed & the War with Ottawa, 1971–1981*, edited by Paul Bunner, 260–
    69. Edmonton: History Book Publications, 2003.

Foster, H. "Forgotten Arguments: Aboriginal Title and Sovereignty in Canada
    Jurisdiction Act Cases." *Manitoba Law Journal* 21 (1992): 343–45.

———. "Law and Necessity in Western Rupert's Land and Beyond, 1670–
    1870." In *Essays in the History of Canadian Law-the Middle Kingdom: The
    Northwest Territories and Prairie Provinces, 1670–1945*, edited by L.A. Knafla
    and J. Swainger. Vancouver: University of British Columbia Press,
    forthcoming.

———. "Long-Distance Justice: The Criminal Jurisdiction of Canadian Courts
    West of the Canadas, 1763–1859." *American Journal of Legal History* XXXIV
    (1990): 1–48.

———. "Sins against the Great Spirit: The Law, the Hudson's Bay Company,
    and the Mackenzie's River Murders, 1835–1839." *Criminal Justice History* X
    (1989): 23–76.

Foster, J. E, "Wintering, the Outsider Male and Ethnogenisis of the Western
    Plains Metis." *Prairie Forum* 19 (1994): 1–13.

Francis, R.D., and H. Ganzevoort, eds. *The Dirty Thirties in Prairie Canada: 11th
    Western Canada Studies Conference*. Vancouver: Tantalus Research, 1980.

Friesen, Jean. "Grant Me Wherewith to Make My Living." In *Aboriginal Resource
    Use in Canada*, edited by Kerry Abel and Jean Friesen, 141–55. Winnipeg:
    University of Manitoba Press, 1991.

———. "Magnificent Gifts: The Treaties of Canada with the Indians of the
    Northwest, 1869–76." *Transactions of the Royal Society of Canada* 5, no. 1
    (1986): 50.

Gibbins, Roger. "Alberta and the National Community." In *Government and Politics in Alberta*, edited by Roger Gibbins and Allan Tupper, 67–84. Edmonton: University of Alberta Press, 1992.

———. "Federalism in a Digital World." *Canadian Journal of Political Science* 33, no. 4 (Dec. 2000): 667–689.

Gibson, Dale. "Company Justice: Origins of Legal Institutions in Pre-Confederation Manitoba." *Manitoba Law Journal* 23, nos. 1&2 (1995): 247–92.

———. "The Real Laws of the Constitution." *Alberta Law Review* 28 (1990): 358–383.

———. "The Rule of Non-Law: Implications of the Manitoba Language Reference." *Transactions, Royal Society of Canada* 5, no. 1 (1986): 24.

Gidney, R.D. "Who Ran the Schools? Local Influence on Education Policy in Nineteenth Century Ontario." *Ontario History* LXXII, no. 2 (1980): 3–13.

Gottesman, Dan. "Native Hunting and the Migratory Birds Convention Act: Historical, Political, and Ideological Perspectives." *Journal of Canadian Studies* 18, no. 3 (1983): 67–89.

Hanson, Eric. "The Future of Western Canada: Economic, Social and Political." *Canadian Public Administration* 18, no. 1 (1975): 104–20.

Harder, Lois. "Child Care, Taxation and Normative Commitments: Excavating the Child Care Expense Deduction Debate." *Studies in Political Economy* 73 (2004): 97–99.

Harvey, H. "The Early Administration of Justice in the North West." *Alberta Law Quarterly* 1 (1934–1936): 1–15.

Hodgetts, J.E. "Constitution of Canada." In *The Oxford Companion to Canadian History*, edited by G. Hallowell, 152–53. Toronto: Oxford University Press, 2004.

Irwin, Robert. "A Clear Intention to Effect Such Modification: The Nrta and Treaty Hunting and Fishing Rights." *Native Studies Review* 13, no. 2 (2000): 43–80.

Johnson, A.W. "The Dynamics of Federalism in Canada." *Canadian Journal of Political Science* 1, no. 1 (1968): 18–39.

Lalonde, Marc. "Riding the Storm: Energy Policy, 1968-1984." In *Towards a Just Society*, edited by Thomas Axworthy and Pierre Elliott Trudeau, 49–77. Markham, ON: Viking, 1990.

Smandych, R., and R. Lindon. "Administering Justice without the State: A Study of the Private Justice System of the Hudson's Bay Company to 1800." *Canadian Journal of Law and Society* 11 (1996): 21–61.

Long, D.E.T. "The Elusive Mr. Ellice." *The Canadian Historical Review* XXIII, no. 1 (1942): 42–57.

Lyon, Noel. "Constitutional Issues in Native Law." In *Aboriginal Peoples and the Law: Indian, Metis and Inuit Rights in Canada*, edited by Bradford W. Morse, 429–31. Ottawa: Carleton University Press, 1989.

Asch, M., and P. Macklem. "Aboriginal Rights and Canadian Sovereignty: An Essay on R. vs. Sparrow." *Alberta Law Review* 29 (1991): 498–517.

Macleod, Kim. "Balance Views, Real Women Told." *Edmonton Journal* 28 November 1987, B5.

Marchildon, Ruby G. "The 'Persons' Controversy: The Legal Aspects of the Fight for Women Senators"." *Atlantis* 6, no. 2 (Spring 1981): 102–03.

Mayhall, Laura E. Nym. "Domesticating Emmeline: Representing the Suffragette, 1930–1993." *National Women's Studies Association Journal* 11, no. 2 (1999): 1–24.

McBride, Stephen. "Quiet Constitutionalism in Canada: The International Political Economy of Domestic Institutional Change." *Canadian Journal of Political Science* 36, no. 2 (2003): 251–74.

McCaul, C.C. "the Constitutional Status of the North-West Territories of Canada." *Canadian Law Times* 4 (1884): 49–61.

McConnell, W.H. "The Judicial Review of Prime Minister Bennett's New Deal." *Osgoode Hall Law Journal* 6, no. 1 (1968): 39–86.

McDonald, Neil. "Canadian Nationalism and North-West Schools, 1884–1905." In *Canadian Schools and Canadian Identity*, edited by Alf Chaiton and Neil McDonald. Toronto: Gage, 1977.

———. "David J. Goggin: Promoter of National Schools." In *Shaping the Schools of the Canadian West*, edited by David C. Jones, Nancy Mary Sheehan and Robert M. Stamp, 14–36. Calgary: Detselig, 1979.

McDonald, P.N. "The B.N.A. Act and near Banks: A Case Study on Federalism." *Alberta Law Review* 10, no. 2 (1972): 155–217.

McDougall, Joseph E. "General Sessions of the Peace." *Canada Law Journal* (1900): 10–16.

Meekison, Peter. "Alberta and the Constitution." In *Government and Politics in Alberta*, edited by Roger Gibbins and Allan Tupper, 247–68. Edmonton: University of Alberta Press, 1992.

———. "the Amending Formula." *Queen's Law Review* 8, no. 1–2 (Fall 1982/ Spring 1983): 99–112.

Morton, D. "Cavalry or Police: Keeping the Peace on Two Adjacent Frontiers, 1870–1900." *Journal of Canadian Studies* 12 (1977): 27–37.

Ogilvie, M.H. "Recent Developments in the History of Canadian Law: Legal History." *Ottawa Law Review* 19 (1987): 223–54.

Palmer, H. "Canadian Immigration and Ethnic History in the 1970s and 1980s." *Journal of Canadian Studies* 17, no. 1 (1982): 35–50.

Powrie, W.D., and T.L. Gainer. "Public Revenue from Canadian Crude Petroleum Production." *Canadian Public Policy* 1, no. 1 (Winter 1975): 1–12.

Pue, Wesley. "The Criminal Twilight Zone: Pre-Trial Procedures in the 1840s." *Alberta Law Review* 11, no. 2 (1983): 335–63.

Read, Frederick. "Early History of the Manitoba Courts." *Manitoba Bar News* 10, no. 2 (1937): 468–69.

Reid, J.P. "Early Provincial Constitutions." *Canadian Bar Review* 26 (1948): 621–70.

Rollason, Heather, and R.C. Macleod. "'Restrain the Lawless Savages': Native Defendants in the Criminal Courts of the North West Territories, 1878–1885." *Journal of Historical Sociology* 10, no. 2 (1997): 157–83.

Sanders, Douglas. "A Legal Analysis of the Ewing Commission and the Métis Colony System in Alberta." In *The Forgotten People: Metis and Non-Status Indian Land Claims*, edited by Harry W. Daniels. Ottawa: Native Council of Canada, 1979.

———. "An Uncertain Path: The Aboriginal Constitutional Conferences." In *Litigating the Values of a Nation: The Canadian Charter of Rights and Freedoms*, edited by Robin M. Elliot and Joseph M. Weiler. Toronto: Carswell, 1986.

Sanders, Douglas E. "Aboriginal Peoples and the Constitution." *Alberta Law Review* 19, no. 3 (1981): 410–427.

Schlenker, Robert Mansell and Ronald. "The Provincial Distribution of Federal Fiscal Imbalances." *Canadian Business Economics* (Winter 1995): 3–22.

Simeon, Richard. "Natural Resource Revenues and Canadian Federalism: A Survey of Issues." *Canadian Public Policy* 6, Supplement (Winter 1980): 182–91.

Slattery, B. "Aboriginal Sovereignty and Imperial Claims." *Osgoode Hall Law Journal* 29, no. 4 (1991): 681–703.

———. "Understanding Aboriginal Rights." *The Canadian Bar Review* 66 (1987): 727–83.

Smiley, Donald V. "Federal-Provincial Conflict in Canada." In *Canadian Federalism: Myth or Reality*, edited by J. Peter Meekison, 2–18. Toronto: Methuen, 1977.

———. "Territorialism and Canadian Institutions." *Canadian Public Policy* 3, no. 4 (Autumn 1977): 449–57.

Stone, Olive M. "Canadian Women as Legal Persons: How Alberta Combined Judicial Executive and Legislative Powers to Win Full Legal Personality for All Canadian Women." *Alberta Law Review* 17, no. 3 (1979): 331–71.

Trimble, Linda. "The Politics of Gender in Modern Alberta." In *Government and Politics in Alberta*, edited by Roger Gibbins and Allan Tupper, 219–45. Edmonton: University of Alberta Press, 1992.

Tupper, Allan. "Peter Lougheed, 1971–1985." In *Alberta Premiers of the Twentieth Century*, edited by Bradford J. Rennie, 204–28. Regina: Canadian Plains Research Center, 2004.

Walters, M. "British Imperial Constitutional Law and Aboriginal Rights: A Comment on Delgamuukw v. British Columbia." *Queen's Law Journal* 17 (1995): 350.

Ward, Norman. "Hon. James Gardiner and the Liberal Party of Alberta, 1935–40." *Canadian Historical Review* 51, no. 3 (Sept. 1975): 305–06.

Watkins, G. Campbell. "Canadian Oil and Gas Pricing." In *Oil in the Seventies: Essays on Energy Policy*, edited by James W. McKie, Walter J. Mead, Michael Walker, G. C. Watkins and G. David Quirin. Vancouver: Fraser Institute, 1977.

Wilson, Donald. "The Ryerson Years in Canada West." In *Canadian Education: A History*, edited by John Donald Wilson, Louis Philippe Audet and Robert M. Stamp, 214–40. Scarborough: Prentice-Hall of Canada, 1970.

Index

A Provincially-Appointed Senate: A New Federalism for Canada, 449–50

Aalborg, A.O., 318–19

Abbott, Douglas Charles, 223–24

Aberhart, William

  and lieutenant-governor, 290–92, 297, 305–6

  life of, 192–95, 324–25

  as premier, 195–205, 215, 228–29

  See also Social Credit government (1935–43), Aberhart

Aboriginal peoples

  HBC and, 29

  historical framework for rights, 347

  in early modern British legal culture, 10–16

  in patriation negotiations, 370–72, 430–31, 441–50; Aboriginal constitutional conferences, 371–72, 441, 443 51

  See also First Nations; Inuit people; Métis people

Accurate News and Information Act (Press Act), 201–5, 208–14, 220–29, 290–92

Act of 1821 for Regulating the Fur Trade, 37, 40–42, 47

Act of Union (1840), 166

Act to Amend and Consolidate the Laws Respecting the North-West Territories, 65–66

Act to Amend the Jury Act (1966), 50–51

Adair, Al "Boomer," 464

AFN. *See* Assembly of First Nations

AFWUF (Alberta Federation of Women United for Families), 468–71

Ahenakew, David, 444–45

Akerman, Jeremy, 436

Alberta, Ell v., 268

Alberta, Mahé v., 123, 127–31

Alberta, Public School Boards Association of Alberta v., 70, 84–86, 97n40, 97n50, 99n74

Alberta Act

  language provisions, 115–16

  Métis settlements and, 372–76

  natural resources in, 173–74

  NRTA negotiations, 180, 183

  separate schools issues, 83–86, 180–81

Alberta Advisory Council on Women's Issues (ASCWI), 467, 470–72

Alberta and Great Waterways Railway, 296, 319–20

Alberta Bill of Rights Act, 215–18, 444, 462, 477n6

Alberta Election Act, 117

Alberta Energy Company, 163n78

Alberta Federation of Métis Settlement Associations, 366–67, 370–76, 445–46

Alberta Federation of Women United for Families (AFWUF), 468–71

Alberta Game Act, 247–50

Alberta Human Rights Commission, 472–73

Alberta-Métis Settlements Accord (1989), 346, 373–79

Alberta Resources Transfer Agreement

  Indian hunting and fishing, 237, 242

  See also Natural Resource Transfer Agreement (NRTA)

Alberta Social Credit Act, 199, 206–7, 210, 213

Alberta Status of Women Action Committee (ASWAC), 463, 468

Alberta Transfer Act, 184

  See also Natural Resource Transfer Agreement (NRTA)

Alberta Treasury Branches
constitutionality of, 218, 228, 235n139
Alberta Women's Secretariat, 467–72
Alliance, Canadian, 336–37
An Act for the Temporary Government of Rupert's Land, 169
An Act to Amend the Constitution of Canada (Bill C-60), 422–27, 433–34
An Act to Amend the Factories Act, The Liquor Act, The Soldiers' Home Tax Exemption Act, 119
Anderson, Dennis, 436
Anderson, James, 183–84
Anderson, Sandra M.
on separate schools, 61–101
Andre, Harvie, 418
Anthony Kershaw Committee, 434, 438
Archibald, Adams G., 105, 239, 277–78
ASCWI (Alberta Advisory Council on Women's Issues), 467, 470–72
Assembly of First Nations, 444–48
Assiniboia, District of, 25–52
ambiguous authority in, 25–26, 38–48, 62
case citations in, 44–45
control by HBC after 1836, 42–45
General Court, 106
impact of *Act of 1821 for Regulating the Fur Trade*, 37, 40–42, 47
jury system in, 41–43, 48–52
justices of the peace and magistrates in, 37–38, 277
municipal codes, 42–43
See also Manitoba; Red River settlement
Attorney-General for Alberta, Poitras et al. v., 365, 388n67
Attorney-General for Canada, Henrietta Muir Edwards v. See Persons Case
Attorney-General of Canada, Dumont et al. v., 347–48
Attorney-General of Canada v. Attorney-General of Ontario, 356
Attorney-General of Canada v. Dupond, 226
Aunger, Edmund A.
on language legislation, 103–35

B & B Commission. *See* Royal Commission on Bilingualism and Biculturalism
Bagder, R. v., 259
Bank Employees Civil Rights Bill, 310n8

Bank Taxation Act
lieutenant-governor's reserve powers, 290–92, 310n8
Reference of, 201–8, 214, 220
Bastedo, Frank L., 292
Bathurst, Lord, 36–37, 39, 41
Baxter, John, 181
Beaudry, J. William, 121
Beetz, Jean, 226
Behiels, Michael D.
on Lougheed and patriation, 411–58
Bennett, R.B., 141, 174, 191–92, 219, 322
Bennett, William R., 417, 425, 439, 442
Biggar, O.M., 203–8, 210, 214, 253–57
bilingualism and biculturalism. *See* language rights; Royal Commission on Bilingualism and Biculturalism
Bill C-60 (*An Act to Amend the Constitution of Canada*), 422–26, 433–34
Birks and Sons v. Montreal, 222, 226
Blackstone, William, 13, 16
Blakeney, Allan, 400, 435, 440
Blatchford, K.A., 178
BNA Act
See *Constitution Act, 1867*
Borden, Sir Robert, 83, 141, 174–76, 320, 331
Bourassa, Robert, 413–15, 418
Bowen, Edith, 304
Bowen, John, 199, 202, 290–92, 305–6
Bowlen, J.J., 301
Bowman, Charles, 182–83
Boyle, John R., 119
Bracken, John, 178
Brady, Jim, 353, 362, 365, 369
Brandeis brief, 203, 219, 232n70
Breland, Pascal, 107
British Columbia
in *Constitution Act, 1867*, 167–68
in patriation negotiations, 415, 417, 419, 425, 427, 433, 442, 448; Gang of Eight, 432–40
justices of the peace and magistrates, 274–75
natural resources, 166–67
British Columbia, Delgamuukw v., xix, xxiv
British North America Act
See *Constitution Act, 1867*

Broadfoot, Barry, *Ten Lost Years*, 191, 196
Brown, Bert, 335
Brown, Desmond
  on development of criminal law, 25–60
Brown, George, 74, 76
Brownlee, John E.
  in NRTA negotiations, 179–80, 183, 258,
    322–23
  resignation of, 296–97
Budd, Gertrude E., 140
Bulyea, George, 295–96, 304
Burgess, A.M., 352
Business Corporations Act, 129
Byfield, Ted, 337

Cairns, Alan C., 481, 488, 495
Calder, Public Interest v., 44–45
Calgary Declaration, 318, 329, 343n28
Calgary Herald, 62, 113, 171–73, 201
Calgary Traffic Court, 269, 282–83
Canada Act, 1982 (U.K.), 372
  See also *Constitution Act, 1867*, patriation
    negotiations
Canada Health Act, 478n31, 483–84
Canada Jurisdiction Act
  HBC powers in Rupert's Land, 12–13
  jurisdictional ambiguity in, 25–26, 31–39
  justices of the peace and magistrates in,
    37–38, 277
  repeal of, 46
Canada West Foundation, 338
*Canada's New Constitution and What it Means to
    Albertans*, 444
Canadian Alliance party, 336–37
Canadian Bill of Rights, 1960, 208, 225
  implied rights principle, 213, 223–28
Canadian Charter of Rights and Freedoms, 1982, 488–91
  employment equity programs, 467
  equality rights in, 466
  freedom of the press, 208
  gender rights, 442, 444, 467
  impact of, 480, 488–91
  impact on implied rights principle, 225
  independent and impartial tribunals, 268
  language rights, 127
  notwithstanding clause, s.33, 131, 427,
    440–41, 488–91

patriation negotiations and, 411–12, 423,
    426–27, 430
  separate schools, 85–86
  sexual orientation, 489–90
Canadian Committee for a Triple-E Senate,
    334–35
Canadian Federation of Business and
    Professional Women's Club, 149–53
Canadian Press
  support for *Reference Re Alberta Statutes*, 202,
    209, 232n62
Cannon, Lawrence Arthur, 204–5, 208–11,
    219–20
Carter, Frank, 420
Carter, Susan, 445
Casgrain, Thérèse, 149
Catholic Church. *See* Roman Catholic Church
Catholic schools. *See* separate schools
Cavanaugh, Catherine
  on the Persons Case, 137–63
Cayley, Hugh, 111–13
CCMC (Continuing Committee of Ministers
    on the Constitution), 426, 428, 430
Charest, Jean, 484–85
Charlottetown Accord, 343n26, 450–51
Charter of Rights and Freedoms
  See *Canadian Charter of Rights and Freedoms,
    1982*
Chrétien, Jean, 429, 433, 435, 486
Clark, Joe, 428
Clarkson, Adrienne, 157–58
Coalition of First Nations, 445
Cohoon, A.A., 351, 355
Communistic Propaganda Act, 221
Connors, Richard
  on law in Rupert's Land, 1–23
  on legal and constitutional history of
    Alberta, xix–xxix
Conroy, H., 247
constitutions, xix–xxix
  as arena for conflict, xxix
  comparison of British and Canadian
    constitutions, 209–10, 223–25, 228
  as general principles, xxvi–xxvii
  as many legalities, xxii–xxiii, xxvi
  quiet constitutionalism and changing
    international order, 486–88, 493–94

as structure for powers of government,
xxvii
unwritten constitutional values, 227–29
See also federal/provincial relations
Constitution Act, 1867 (BNA Act)
amending authority, s.91(1), 424, 433–34
British disallowance of legislation, ss.55–
57, 199–202
comparison of British and Canadian
constitutions, 209–10, 223–25, 228
definition of Indians, 371
entry of new lands, s.146, 167–68
federal disallowance of provincial
legislation, s.90, 199–208
federal jurisdiction over Indian hunting
and fishing rights, s.91.12, 242, 257
implied rights principle, 213, 223–28
interpretation request by interested
persons, s.60, 141–42
jurisdiction over Indian peoples, s.91.24,
241–42
justices of the peace and magistrates, 267
natural resources and public lands,
s.109, 166, 322, 396–97, 417, 422, 424
parliamentary supremacy, 223–24
peace, order and good government, s.91,
209–12, 414, 422
persons, s.24, 137, 143–45
Preamble, 224
provincial taxation powers, s.92(2), 206,
414, 417
separate schools, s.93, 62–66, 71, 74,
76–81, 84, 417
Constitution Act, 1867, patriation negotiations,
411–58
Aboriginal rights, 370–72, 430–31,
441–51; Aboriginal constitutional
conferences, 371–72, 441, 443–51
amending formulas: 7/50 formula,
427, 436, 439–41, 444; amending
authority, 433–34; Fulton-Favreau,
418, 420, 425; Vancouver Consensus,
427, 430, 431, 432, 434–36, 439;
Victoria, 413–20, 425
at annual conferences of premiers: in
1975, 413–14, 417–18; in 1976, 415–17;
in 1977, 420; in 1978, 423, 426, 428,

442; in 1979, 426–32; in 1980, 429–30;
in 1981, 439–41
annual First Ministers Conferences as
issue, 416, 419–21
asymmetrical federalism, 411, 427, 431,
450
Bill C-60 (An Act to Amend the Constitution),
422–27, 433–34
British parliamentary response, 434–36,
438, 443
Charter of Rights, 420–23, 426–28, 430
compact of provinces theory, 411–12,
416, 421
continuing committee of ministers,
426, 428
division of powers as issue, 413–22, 426,
429
equalization payments, 415, 440–41
federalism White Paper (PC party,
federal), 421
gender rights, 442
immigration, 416, 419
Joint Parliamentary Committee, 370, 422,
424, 432–37
Kirby report on constitutional
discussions, 431–33
language provisions, 413, 416, 418–20,
423, 427, 430, 440
Monarchy reform, 423, 425
natural resources control, s.109, 413–16,
422, 424–27, 430, 450
A New Canadian Federation, 429
opting-out rights, 418, 425
People's Package, 429–32
political environment: in 1975, 413–15;
in 1976–1977, 415–20; in 1978–1979,
420–29, 442; in 1980–1981, 429–44; in
1982 and after, 444–51
property rights, 444
provincial alliances: Alberta and Quebec,
415; Gang of Eight, 432–40
Reference on Senate reform, 425, 433–34
References on patriation, 370, 433, 435–42
referendum on patriation, offer of,
440–41
regional disparities as issue, 413, 416,
419–20

Resolutions on, 417–18, 420, 433
Senate reform, 416, 419–26, 433–34; 449–
    50; House of Federation, 421–25
Special Joint Committee of Parliament,
    422, 424, 432
Supreme Court reform, 413, 415–16,
    419–21, 426
Task Force on National Unity, 426–28
A Time for Action, 421–22
veto powers for provinces, 416, 425, 427,
    432
See also *Canadian Charter of Rights and
    Freedoms, 1982;* Lougheed, Peter;
    Trudeau, Pierre; *and individual provinces*
Constitution Act, 1982
    interpretation of Preamble, 227
    language education rights for minorities,
        123, 130–31
    promotion and defense of, 444–51
    Royal Assent, 415
    unwritten constitutional values, 227–29
    See also *Canadian Charter of Rights and
        Freedoms; Constitution Act, 1867,*
        patriation negotiations
Constitution of Alberta Amendment Act (1990)
    recognition of Métis in, 345–46, 377–79,
        384
    See also Métis settlements
constitutions
    comparison of British and Canadian
        constitutions, 209–10, 223–25, 228
Continuing Committee of Ministers on the
    Constitution (CCMC), 426, 428, 430
Cook, Ramsay, 104
Cooperatives Act, 129
Coss, Peter, xxi
Costigan, Peter, 416
Coté, Louis, 152
Council of the Federation, 484–85
County Attorney Act, 49
Credit of Alberta Regulation Act
    lieutenant-governor's reserve powers,
        290–92, 310n8
    Reference re, 201–8, 213–14, 220
Cree language
    official language in Manitoba, 105
Crerar, T.A., 182–83

Crocket, Oswald Smith, 204, 208
Cushing, William, Calgary, 296
Cyr, Rex v., 138–39
    See also Persons Case

Dalhousie, Lord, 36–37
Daly, T. Mayne, 244–45
Davies, Percy, 355
Davis, Henry Hague, 208, 211
Davis, William G. (Bill), 406, 432, 440
Day, Stockwell, 338
Delaney, Kiki, 163n78
Delgamuukw v. British Columbia, xix, xxiv
Delorme, Charley, 353
denominational schools. *See* separate schools
Department of Federal and
    Intergovernmental Affairs (FIGA), in
        patriation negotiations
    Hyndman's role, 413–15, 420, 422–23,
        426–27
    Johnston's role, 433–34, 438, 445
    Meekison's role, 414–15, 420, 422, 425,
        427, 429, 430, 436
    role of FIGA, 395, 412–13; under Klein,
        482, 486
    See also Department of International and
        Intergovernmental Relations
Department of Indian Affairs (DIA)
    definition of Indians, 354–55, 358, 371
    federal/provincial conflicts on hunting
        and fishing regulations, 240–41
    pre-NRTA fishing conflicts with federal
        departments, 242–46
    pre-NRTA hunting regulation conflicts,
        246–55
Department of International and
    Intergovernmental Relations, in
        new international order, 486
Department of Marine and Fisheries, 242–47,
    257
Depression. *See* Great Depression
Dewdney, Edgar, 108–11
DIA. *See* Department of Indian Affairs
Dickson, Robert, 226
Diefenbaker, John, 292
Dion, Joseph, 353
Dobrowolsky, Alexandra, 467

Dominion Alberta Saskatchewan Fisheries Commission
(1910), 250
Dominion Lands Act
HBC and NRTA negotiations, 179, 184
Métis land claims, 350, 358
separate school issue, 81, 99n78
Dorchester, Lord, Montreal, 30
Douglas, C.H. *See* Social Credit government
(1935–43), Aberhart
Douglas, Ellen C., Winnipeg, 151
Ducharme, Denis, 126
Duff, Chief Justice Lyman Poore
Reference on Alberta Statutes, 204, 207–
14, 222–28, 234n99, 234n111, 234n113,
236n163
Dumont et al. v. A.G. Canada, 347–48
Duncan Commission, 181–82
Dunning, Charles, 177
Dunvegan Motor Inn controversy, 293
Dupond, Attorney-General of Canada v., 226

Eagle Lake fur trade dispute, 33–34
Edmonton Journal
demand for provincial status, 172
Reference of Press Act, 202–8, 220, 233n98
education
federal authority in post-secondary
education, 484
funding cutbacks and neo-liberalism, 472
need for intergovernmental co-
operation, 492
as post-Depression priority, 326–27
school lands, 176, 178, 180, 183–84
See also French language; language
rights; separate schools
Edwards, Henrietta Muir, 140, 142, 148, 150,
155, 157, 162n38
Edwards, William Stuart, 145, 257
Elbling, Switzman v. (Padlock Law case), 221–26
Elizabeth II, Queen of England
Royal Assent to *Constitution Act, 1982*, 415,
444
Ell v. Alberta, 268
Ellice, Edward, 39–40, 45, 52, 56n72
Elton, David, 337
England. *See* Great Britain
equality, 459–78

five concepts of, 460–62
equality (1) as sameness in treatment
(formal equality), 460–66, 467,
475–76
equality (2) as sameness in opportunity,
460–61
equality (3/4) as difference, 461, 464–72,
475–76
equality (5) as freedom, 461–62, 471–73,
476
equality for persons
gender equality, 459–61, 467–72
in *Charter of Rights*, 467, 488–91
matrimonial property law and, 462–65
neo-conservativism and, 461–62, 467,
469, 473–74, 476
neo-liberalism and, 462–63, 471–76
pay equity, 461, 465–66
persons as different from families, 474
procedural fairness, 466–68
redistributive policies and, 459–60, 465,
470–71, 478n33
sexual orientation and, 459–60, 473
traditional family and, 466–67, 470–75
See also Persons Case
equality for provinces
Haultain's vision for, 316–18
in Alberta's place in Canada, 459–60, 466,
473, 478n31
NEP as unequal intervention, 333–37, 397
NRTA as issue of, 323
power shifts as tides, 327, 338–39
Senate reform as, 334–35
equalization transfers
provincial interest in, 323, 415, 440–41
Eriksen, Maria, 163n78
Ewing Commission on Métis, 356–60, 364, 375
executive federalism
in NEP negotiations, 393–94, 482
in NRTA negotiations, 165
use by Klein, 485
use by Klein and Charest, 482

Fallis, Iva Campbell, 149–53
families
neo-liberalism and, 473–76
traditional forms, 466–67, 470–75

Famous Five Foundation, 154–58
Famous Five in Persons Case. *See* Persons Case
federal/provincial relations
    asymmetrical federalism, 411, 427, 431,
        441, 450
    Calgary Declaration on federalism, 318,
        329, 343n28
    compact of provinces theory, 411–12,
        416, 421
    equalization transfers: provincial
        interest in, 323
    executive federalism, 165, 393–94, 482
    impact of civil service expansion, 395
    impact of information technology on
        citizens and, 494
    in education and health care, 492–93
    interprovincial accords, 483
    NEP as atypical, 391–92, 407–8
    performance standards for provinces, 483
    personality issues, 403–5
    power shifts as tides, 327
    shifts to provincial power, 338–39, 394–95
    third-party advocacy, 324
    See also constitutions; Progressive
        Conservative government, (1992–),
        Klein
Federated Women's Institutes, 140
Federation of Métis Settlements (FMS)
    patriation negotiations, 445–46
    settlement negotiations, 366–76
Ferguson, William, 141
FIGA. *See* Department of Federal and
    Intergovernmental Affairs (FIGA)
First Nations
    Delgamuukw v. British Columbia, xix, xxiv
    gender rights for women, 446
    historical framework for rights, 347
    in patriation negotiations, 430–31,
        441–50; Aboriginal constitutional
        conferences, 372, 441, 443–51
    land claims under *Dominion Lands Act,*
        350–51
    policy framework for, 483
    reserves as NRTA issue, 253
    See also *Indian Act;* Indian Territories
First Nations hunting and fishing regulation,
    237–65

co-management of resources, 238, 260
commercial exchange rights, 238, 242–43,
    246, 258
comparison of hunting *vs.* fishing issues,
    242, 250
fishing: under NRTA, 257–60; pre-NRTA
    federal department conflicts, 237–38,
    242–46
hunting: under NRTA, 257–60; pre-NRTA
    regulation conflicts, 237–38, 246–56;
    under treaties, 248–55
in *Constitution Act, 1867,* ss.91.24; 92.13;
    92.16, 240–43
NRTA and, 237–38, 253–60
rights: under *Indian Act,* 241; of non-treaty
    aboriginal people, 238, 258–59; under
    NRTA, 237–38; under treaties, 248–55,
    259–60
treaty rights generally, 259–60
Treaty 1, 239, 245, 255
Treaty 2, 239, 245, 255
Treaty 3, 245, 255
Treaty 4, 239, 255
Treaty 5, 255
Treaty 6, 238–39, 242, 255, 260, 263n37
Treaty 7, 238, 240, 255
Treaty 8, 238, 240, 247–48, 255, 259, 263n37
fishing
    federal powers, 242–43
    provincial powers and NRTA, 242–43, 247
    See also Department of Marine and
        Fisheries; First Nations hunting and
        fishing; Métis people
Fishing Lake Métis community, 351, 353
Flanagan, Thomas
    on the NRTA, 165–89
FMS. *See* Federation of Métis Settlements
Fort Pitt, Saskatchewan, 351
Foster, Jim, 415
Frawley, J.J., 232n71
free trade
    agreement negotiations as quiet
        constitutionalism, 487, 494
    impact of NEP on, 335–36
freedom
    equality and, 461–62, 471–72, 476
    freedom of the press, 220–26

of language choice, 130–31
See also *Accurate News and Information Act*
(Press Act)
Freeman, Edward A., 112
French language
language of education (1905-88), 116–23
bilingualism in Alberta (1988–2005),
122–31
freedom of language choice, 130–31
in Manitoba, 103–6
in NWT school ordinances (1884–1901),
88–93, 101n111, 109, 111–12, 180
Manitoba Language Reference, 1985, 205, 227
by population (pre-1905), 103, 108
See also language rights; Royal
Commission on Bilingualism and
Biculturalism
Friesen, Jean, 238
Frog Lake Massacre, 351
Fulton-Favreau amending formula, 418,
420, 425

Gall, Gerry, 416
Gallant, Edgar, 394
game management
See *Alberta Game Act;* First Nations hunting
and fishing; Metis people
Gardiner, J.G., 182
gay and lesbian issues. *See* sexual orientation
gender issues
ASWAC recommendations on, 463
equality for Native women, 446
equality under *Charter of Rights*, 442, 444,
467
gender equity and equality, 459–61
matrimonial property law and, 462–65
neo-liberalism and, 462–63, 471–76
pay equity, 461, 465–66
same-sex marriage, 159, 490
tax reform issues, 473–75
Women's Secretariat, 467–72
See also equality; equality for persons;
Persons Case
Geoffrion, Aimé, 203–4, 206, 209–10, 214, 219
German language, 115, 122, 130
Getty, Don. *See* Progressive Conservative
government, (1985–92), Getty

Ghostkeeper, Elmer, 370
Gibbins, Roger, 482, 494
Gibson, Dale
on Social Credit court references, 191–236
Ginsberg, Rosa, Palestine, 147
Girard, Marc, 106
Goggin, David J., 67–68, 94n1, 96n32
Government House
ceremonies at, 293, 302
history of, 303-7
governor-general, office of
British disallowance of Canadian
legislation, 199–200
duty to appoint Senate, 145
and lieutenant-governors, 289–92, 301–2,
308–9
and Monarch, 289–90
as symbol, 289–90, 290
symbols of office, 303
See also individual governors-general
Grandin, Bishop Vital-Justin, 66
Gray, Jim, 337
Gray, W.S., 232n71
Great Britain, 1–16
colonial settlement patterns, 26–29, 35
colonial statutes, 45–52
colonialism and imperialism, 1, 5–9,
13–16, 26–29
comparison of British and Canadian
constitutions, 224–25, 228
early modern legal culture, 4–9, 12–16
early modern treatment of Aboriginal
peoples, 10–16, 26–27
patriation response, 434–39, 443
See also Judicial Committee of the Privy
Council (JCPC)
Great Depression
conditions in 1935, 191–97
post-Depression priorities, 326–27
relief efforts, 191–92, 324–25
relief for Métis people, 346, 353–55, 357–60
Greenfield, Herbert, 179

Haig, Margaret, Viscountess Rhondda, 146
Harder, Lois
on equality and women's political
identity, 459–78

Hardy, Randy, 376
Hargrave, John, 198
Harmony in Diversity, 426, 429
Harper, Stephen
  letter re firewall proposal, 491–92
Harris, Michael, 485
Harvie, J., 354
Haultain, Frederick W.
  against bilingualism, 109, 111, 113–14
  for constitutional equality, 316–18, 340
  for provincehood, 171, 173, 317, 339
  in NRTA negotiations, 174
  in separate schools negotiations, 67–70,
    74, 77–80, 94n1, 96n24
Hays, Harry, 432
HBC. *See* Hudson's Bay Company (HBC)
health care
  Canada Health Act, 478n31, 483–84
  cutbacks and neo-liberalism, 472
  federal/provincial relations, 492–93
  Klein's policies on, 295, 483, 485
  need for intergovernmental co-operation,
    492
  official languages, 121
  as symbol, 485
hearing officers, 269
  See also justices of the peace and magistrates
Helliwell, John, 396
Henrietta Muir Edwards v. Attorney-General for
  Canada. See Persons Case
Henry Birks and Sons v. Montreal, 222, 226
Hilland, Doug, 337
Hoadley, George, 354–55
Hole, Lois, 293–95, 299, 301–2, 302
Hole, Ted, 295
Horner, Hugh, 463
Horsman, James, 125–26, 435, 446
House of Federation (Senate reform), 421–25,
  433–34, 449
Hudson, Albert Blellock, 204, 208
Hudson's Bay Company (HBC), 1–16, 25–48
  Aboriginal people and, 29
  under *Act of 1821 for Regulating the Fur Trade*,
    37, 40–42, 47
  ambiguous authority in criminal law
    under, 25–26, 32–39, 45–46, 62
  British legal culture and, 26–32

Charter for Rupert's Land, 1, 4–5, 8–16,
  26, 28–29
  in NRTA negotiations, 179, 184
  justices of the peace and magistrates
    and, 34, 37–38
  map of forts in Rupert's Land, 2–3
  merger with North West Company, 33,
    39–40, 44, 277
  powers in Rupert's Land, 11–13, 16, 28–29,
    42–45, 48, 277
  rival companies and, 29–30, 33–37
  transfer of Rupert's Land, 168–70, 348–50,
    355
  See also Rupert's Land
Hugill, John, 197–200, 231n33, 290–92
hunting and game management
  See Alberta Game Act; First Nations hunting
    and fishing; Métis people
Hyndman, Lou, 413–15, 420, 422–23, 426–27

IAA. *See* Indian Association of Alberta (IAA)
identity, Canadian
  in B & B commission terms of reference,
    327–29, 342n23–24
  multiculturalism and, 327–29, 400
immigration
  Canadian identity and, 327–29
  impact on provincial resource rights,
    174, 176
  in patriation negotiations, 416, 419·
  language legislation and, 103
implied rights principle, 213, 223–28
income tax. *See* taxation
Indian Act
  application to Métis, 354–55, 358
  definition of *Indian*, 257–59, 371
  hunting and fishing under, 241, 247–52
  NRTA negotiations and, 253–56
  See also First Nations
Indian Association of Alberta (IAA), 430, 442–46
Indian Self-Government in Canada, 447–48
Indian Territories
  ambiguous authority in criminal law in,
    25–36, 45–48
  definition of, 32
  justices of the peace and magistrates in,
    32–33, 38, 41–42

merger of fur companies and, 40–41
Rupert's Land and, 25–26, 32–36
Individual Rights Protection Act (IRPA), 462, 477n4,
477n6, 489
Institute of Law Research and Reform
on matrimonial property law, 463
Interdepartmental Committee on Women's
Affairs, 468–70
Interpretation Act
language provisions, 118, 120, 124
Interprovincial Pipeline, 330
Inuit Committee on National Issues, 445, 449
Inuit people
in *Indian Act*, 259
in patriation negotiations, 430, 445,
449; Aboriginal constitutional
conferences, 371–72, 441, 443–51
Inuit Tapirisat, 430
IRPA, See *Individual Rights Protection Act* (IRPA)
Irving Report, 283
Irwin, Robert
on regulation of Indian hunting and
fishing, 237–65

Jamieson, Alice I., 138
JCPC. *See* Judicial Committee of the Privy
Council
Jeffers, Allan M., architect, 304
Johnson, Al, 394
Johnson, Daniel, 394
Johnston, Dick, 433–34, 438, 445
Joint Parliamentary Committee on the
Constitution, 370, 422, 424, 432–35
Joyal, Serge, 432
Judicature Act Amendment Bill, 310n8
Judicial Committee of the Privy Council
(JCPC), References to
on disallowance and reservation powers,
213
on Indian hunting and fishing
privileges, 251
on lieutenant-governors, 300
on Persons Case, 138, 145–46, 148
Reference Re Alberta Statutes, 213–19
on separate schools, 74, 181
Jury Act, 50–51
jury system, 41–43, 48–52

justices of the peace and magistrates, 267–88
before 1905, 12–13, 16, 37–38, 41, 48, 269–79
after 1905, 268–69, 279–84
categories of, 268–69, 275–76, 282
in *Canada Jurisdiction Act*, 37–38, 277
in *Constitution Act, 1867*, 267
independent and impartial requirement,
267–68, 278, 283–84
lieutenant-governor's power to appoint,
278–79
police magistrates, 268–69, 274, 278–80,
282, 287n68
powers and duties, 268–69, 275–76, 282–83
professionalization of justices, 269, 282–83
as provincial court judges, 282–84
salaries and fees for, 268–69, 276–79, 281
time in office, 275–77, 279, 281, 287n67
women's right to sit as magistrates, 138

Kanik, Myron, 376
*Keg River Métis Settlement Association et al. v. Her
Majesty the Queen in Right of Alberta*
natural resources and Métis settlements,
364, 367–69, 374–79, 387n59
Kenwood, Mrs. J.C., 150
Kershaw, Anthony, 434, 438
Kerwin, Patrick, 204, 208, 220
Kesler, Gordon, 334, 449
Killam, Albert, 25, 45
King, W.L. Mackenzie
on disallowance powers, 200
in NRTA negotiations, 177–80, 183–84, 321–22
Persons Case and, 141, 149–53
response to Depression, 325
Kirby, Michael, 431–33, 444
Kirby Report (1975), 283
Kirby Report (*Report to Cabinet on Constitutional
Discussions*), 431–33
Klein, Ralph. *See* Progressive Conservative
government, (1992–), Klein
Kopke, Brian, 159
Kowalski, Ken, 292–93
Kyoto Accord, 344n43

La Pierre, Laurier, 429
Lacombe, Father Albert, 352
Laird, David, 240

Lalonde, Marc, 406, 424, 425, 428
Lamer, Antonio, 227
Lamontagne, Maurice, 422
land claims. *See* First Nations; Métis
 settlements
Landau, Norma, 270
language rights, 103–35
 bilingualism in NWT, official
  (1870–1904), 104–9
 bilingualism in NWT as issue (1888–
  1904), 109–15, 124–26
 unilingualism in Alberta (1905–87), 115–24
 languages in Alberta (1988–2005), 122–31
 languages other than French or English,
  105, 115, 117, 122, 130
 for commerce, 118, 122, 129
 for court, 117, 119–20, 126–27
 for education, 69, 116–23, 126–27
 for elections, 117–19, 121, 124
 for municipal government, 117–18, 121
 freedom of language choice, 130–31
 in Manitoba, 103–6
 in patriation negotiations, 411–13, 416,
  418–20, 423, 427, 430, 440
 Mahé v. Alberta, 123, 127–31
 Manitoba Language Reference, 1985, 205, 227
 R. v. Mercure, 125–26
 school authorities for minority
  languages, 120, 123, 127–31
 unilingualism for nation-building, 103–
  4, 112, 129–30
 See also French language; Royal
  Commission on Bilingualism and
  Biculturalism
Languages Act, 125–26
Lapointe, Ernest, 143, 146
Laponce, Jean, 103–4, 129–30
Laskin, Bora, 226, 437
Laurier, Sir Wilfred, 171, 174–75
 in separate schools negotiations, 63,
  70–83, 98n62
Law, John M.
 on legal and constitutional history of
  Alberta, xix–xxix
Le Courrier de L'Ouest, 116
Leduc, Father Hippolyte, 68–69
Legal, Bishop, 69, 133n45

Legislative Assembly of Alberta
 ceremony to open, 301, 304–5, 307–8
 official languages, 116–17, 124–26
 speech from the throne, 293, 307
Legislature Building architect, 304
Leitch, Merv, 396–97
lesbian and gay issues. *See* sexual orientation
Lessard, Edmond P., 116, 162n57
Lethbridge News, 171
Lévesque, René
 in patriation negotiations, 418, 422–24,
  429, 431–42
Liberal Party (provincial) as government
  (1905–21), Rutherford, 296, 319–20
Liberal Party (federal) as government (1921–
  30), W.L.M. King
 King in NRTA negotiations, 177–80,
  183–84, 321–22
 King on disallowance powers, 200
 Persons Case and, 141, 149–53
 relations with Progressives, 321–22
Liberal Party (federal) government (1968–79;
  1980–84) Trudeau
 defeat and re-election (1979–80), 406, 428
 Trudeau in NEP negotiations, 391–92,
  402–7
 See also National Energy Program
  (NEP); Trudeau, Pierre Elliot;
  Trudeau, Pierre Elliot, in patriation
  negotiations
lieutenant-governor, office of, 289–313
 appointment of, 290, 309
 appointment of justices of the peace and
  magistrates, 278–79
 ceremonial duties, 289, 292–95, 300–303,
  307–8
 constitutional duties, 289–92, 294,
  298–300
 financial support for, 290, 305–6
 and governor-general, 289–92, 301–2,
  308–9
 manner of address to, 290
 and Monarchy, 289–90, 292, 299–301,
  308–9
 and premier, 293–99, 308
 rank of, 299, 301
 reserve powers, 290–94, 305–6, 310n16

Royal Assent ceremony, 300
as symbol, 289–90, 292, 309
symbols of office, 299–302, 308
See also Government House; *and specific
lieutenant-governors*
Loan and Trust Corporations Act, 129
Locke, John, *Two Treatises*, 1, 13–14, 16
Lougheed, Peter
and lieutenant-governor, 298
on minority language rights, 123
NEP negotiations, 391–92, 395, 400–407,
412–13
and pattern of new political parties, 340
personal background, 403–5
restoration of Government House, 306
See also Progressive Conservative
government, (1971–85), Lougheed
Lougheed, Peter, in patriation negotiations,
411–58
Aboriginal issues, 370–72, 430–31, 441–50
amending formulas: 7/50 modified
Vancouver formula, 436, 439–41, 444;
Fulton-Favreau variation, 418, 425
at annual conferences of premiers: in
1981, 439–41
British lobbying by, 438–39
Charter of Rights, 411–12, 427;
notwithstanding clause, 440–41
compact of provinces theory, 411–12, 416,
421
for asymmetrical federalism, 411–12, 427
for equality of provinces, 411–12, 418
for new federalism, 421
for province-building, 411–12
Gang of Eight counter-attack, 432–40
kitchen accord, 440–41
language rights, 411–12, 427, 440–41
Métis recognition, 370–72
natural resources, 413
promotion and defense of *Act*, 1982, 444–51
References on patriation, 433–42
Resolutions on patriation, 417, 420, 433, 436
response to Trudeau's drafts: in 1976, 414–
15, 424; in 1977, 419–20; in 1978 and
1979 (Bill C-60), 425–31; in 1980 (Gang
of Eight), 432–38; in 1980 (People's
Package), 429–32; in 1981, 439–43

Supreme Court appointments, 413
to Trudeau: on unilateral federal actions,
414–15
See also *Constitution Act, 1867*, patriation
negotiations; Department of
Federal and Intergovernmental
Affairs (FIGA), in patriation
negotiations
Lynch-Staunton, Frank, 298, 301, 303
Lyon, Sterling, 432, 435

MAA. *See* Métis Association of Alberta
MacAdams, Roberta, 139
MacBeth, Nancy, 126
Maccagno, Michael, 121
Macdonald, Donald, 397
Macdonald, Sir John A., 169–70, 240–41, 291
Macdonell, Aeneas and Miles, 33–35
MacEwan, Grant, 302, 307, 369–70
MacGuigan, Mark, 422
MacKibben, Jim, 436
Macleod, Rod
on justices of the peace, 267–88
The Macleod Gazette, 172
Macphail, Agnes, 148
Madden, A.F. McC., 4
magistrates. *See* justices of the peace and
magistrates
Magistrates and Justices Act (1922), 280
Magnet, Joseph Eliot, 104
Mahé v. Alberta, 123, 127–31
Mallory, J.R., 291
Manitoba
ambiguous authority in criminal law in,
25–26, 47–52
entry into confederation, 167–70, 348–50
in patriation negotiations, 419, 427; Gang
of Eight, 432–40
Indian hunting and fishing federal/
provincial conflicts, 240–42, 251–56
jury system, 60n151
justices of the peace and magistrates,
276, 277
Métis land rights, 348–50, 358
NRTA: negotiations and agreement, 174–
79, 181–85, 253–56; pre-NRTA natural
resources control, 167–71

official languages of, 103–6
Reference on languages, 205, 227
Reference on patriation, 433, 435, 437
Roblin and Haultain on provincehood, 317
separate schools in, 61, 66, 74, 76
See also Assiniboia, District of
Manitoba Act (1870)
Métis land rights, ss. 30–31, 348–50, 358
official languages, s.23, 104–5
public lands and natural resources, s.30, 169
Manitoba Language Reference, 1985, 205, 227
Manning, Ernest C. *See* Social Credit government (1943–68), Manning
Manning, Preston
on federal/provincial tensions, 315–44
founding of Reform party, 337–41, 341n1
Manolson, Ayala, 163n78
Mansell, Robert, 334
Martin, Fred V.
on Métis settlements, 345–89
Martin, Paul, 486
Martin, William Melville, 176
matrimonial property, 462–65
Maurice L'Hirondelle et al. v. The Queen
natural resources and Métis settlements, 367–69, 374–79, 388n70
McBride, Stephen, 486–87
McCaig, Ann, Roxanne and Jane, 163n78
McCarthy, D'Alton, 112
McCaul, C.C., 25, 45
McClung, Nellie, 139, 142, 148–53, 157
McDougall, William, 46
McKinney, Louise Crummy, 139, 142, 155
McPhail, Agnes, 139
McPherson, O.L., 192
Meech Lake Accord, 343n26, 450–51
Meekison, Peter, 414–15, 420, 422, 425, 427–30, 436
Meighen, Arthur, 141, 176–77, 252
Mercure, R. v., 125–26
Métis Association of Alberta (MAA), 364–66, 445–46
Métis Federation. *See* Alberta Federation of Métis Settlement Associations
Métis National Council, 448–49

Métis people
definition of *Métis* person, 354–55, 357–60, 371–72
early history in Manitoba, 348–51
Ewing Commission on, 356–60, 364, 375
federal and provincial relationships, 367–71, 375
historical framework for rights, 347
hunting and fishing, 353, 359, 361; pre-NRTA fishing regulations, 242–43, 250; trapping, 361
in *Alberta Act*, 372–76
in *Constitution Act, 1982*, 370–72, 445–46
in Manitoba, 348–51, 358
in patriation negotiations, 370–72, 430–31, 441–50; Aboriginal constitutional conferences, 371–72, 443–51
in Saskatchewan, 350, 358
and North-West Territories Council, 106–7
population, 346
provincial jurisdiction, 354–58
role in separate schools issue, 67
social relief in 1930s, 346, 353–60
See also Assiniboia, District of; Red River settlement
Métis Rehabilitation Branch, 366–67
Métis settlements, 345–89
Alberta-Métis Settlements Accord (1989), 346, 373–77; transition management, 376–79
Appeal Tribunal, 380–82
Ewing Commission on, 356–60, 364, 375
federation of settlement associations, 366–76, 445–46
in *Alberta Act*, 372–76
in *Constitution of Alberta Amendment Act* (1990), 345–46, 377–79, 384
in *Métis Population Betterment Act*, 360–66, 373–74; review of, 368–70
land rights: in *Dominion Lands Act*, 350, 358; in Manitoba, 170, 348–51, 358; in Saskatchewan, 350, 358; under NRTA, 355–56; private ownership of land, 362, 364; scrip policy and, 351–52, 355–57
lands for: area of land, 346; communal

lands for, 357–58, 365, 373–74;
Improvement District conversions,
362, 364–65; land allocation, 372–74
legal rights or social needs as issue,
357–60
natural resources: co-management and
revenues, 346, 365–71, 374–76, 382;
lawsuit (Keg River and Maurice
L'Hirondelle), 364, 367–69, 374–75,
378–79, 387n59; oil and gas industry,
363, 365, 376, 380, 388n73
provincial and federal relationships,
367–71, 375
provincial jurisdiction for, 354–58
report from Ombudsman, 369
self-government, 346, 366–68, 372–74,
377–84
task forces on (1972; 1999), 366–67, 381–84
trust fund for (*Poitras* case), 365, 388n67
Métis Settlements Accord Implementation Act, 377–
79, 383–84
Métis Settlements Act, 374, 379–81
Métis Settlements Branch, 367–69, 376,
388n72
Métis Settlements General Council, 345
Métis Settlements Land Act, 374
Métis Settlements Land Protection Act, 374, 376–78
Métis Task Force, 364–66
Métisism: A Canadian Identity, 371
Michener, Roland, 301–2
Milke, Mark
on the NRTA, 165–89
Millar, Nancy, 153
Miller, Frank, 405
Mills, David, 45, 47, 51
Milnes, Robert, 30–31
Montreal, Birks and Sons v., 222, 226
Montreal Women's Club, 140–41
Morin, Claude, 441
Morris, Alexander, 105, 239
"Mounted Police Act" (1873), 278
Mowat, Daniel, 114
Mowat, John, 33–34, 35
Mowat, Oliver, 49–50, 200, 300, 411, 450
Muir, Bob, 337
Mulligan, Sinclair v., 44
Mulroney, Brian, 448–49

multiculturalism
and B & B commission terms of
reference, 327–29
municipal governments
official languages, 117–18, 121, 124
Munro, John, 447–48
Munro, Kenneth
on the office of lieutenant-governor,
289–313
Murdoch, Irene, matrimonial property, 463
Murphy, Emily, 138, 140–48, 153, 162n57
Murphy, T.G., 354–55
Mutiny Act, 27–28

National Council of Women of Canada
(NCWC), 140, 147
National Energy Program (NEP), 329–37, 391–410
conditions before 1980: civil service
expansion, 395; economy, 330–33,
398–403; energy as special, 397–402;
energy consumption, 398–99;
political, 392–94, 402, 405–7
consequences of: economic, 329–30, 334,
407; political, 336–37, 412–13
constitutional ambiguity and, 392–93,
396–97
executive federalism, 393–94, 482
free trade promotion, 335–36
Lougheed's role, 391–92, 395, 400–407,
412–13
Ontario and, 330, 336, 391, 405–6
personalities of leaders, 392, 403–5
policies of: export taxes, 331–36, 412–13;
price controls, 332–34; summary,
332–33, 407–8
Quebec and, 330, 335–37, 391, 394–95,
402–3, 406
as symbol, 391–92, 400–403
Trudeau's role, 391–92, 402–7
as unequal intervention, 333–37, 397
Western identity and, 400
Western separatism and, 334–35, 392
National Indian Brotherhood (NIB), 430, 443
National Oil Policy, 398
national parks
NRTA negotiations, 179, 184, 320
Native Council of Canada, 430, 445, 449

Natural Resource Transfer Agreement
(NRTA), 165–89, 317–24
agreement terms, 184–85
Brownlee's role in negotiations, 179–80,
183, 258, 322–23
constitutional ambiguity, 396–97
constitutional equality through, 317–18,
323–24
constitutional status of, 322, 352
equality as issue, 323
executive federalism, 165
HBC interest in, 179, 184
impact of, 185, 400
Indian hunting and fishing rights,
253–60
King's role in negotiations, 177–80, 183–
84, 321–22
Métis land claims under, 355–56
national parks, 179, 184, 320
natural resources in *Constitution, 1867*,
s.109, 166, 372, 417, 422
negotiations for agreement, 174–84
pre-NRTA conditions, 165–74; federal use
of public lands, 320; homesteading,
170, 176, 177; immigration, 170,
174; political conditions, 321–22;
provincial budget shortfalls, 319–20;
railways, 170, 174, 181, 184; subsidies
to provinces, 169, 173–74, 178–79, 181,
183, 319
school lands, 176, 178, 180, 183–84
See also First Nations hunting and fishing
regulation
natural resources. *See* First Nations hunting
and fishing; fishing; Métis
people; National Energy Program
(NEP); Natural Resource Transfer
Agreement (NRTA); public lands
neo-liberalism
equality and, 459–60, 462–63, 471–76
NEP. *See* National Energy Program (NEP)
New Brunswick
gender rights, 139, 160n12
in patriation negotiations, 415, 435–36,
440, 449
natural resources control, 166, 181
NRTA negotiations, 181–82

as royal colony, 8
separate schools issue, 76
New Brunswick Broadcasting Co. v. Nova Scotia
(Speaker of the House of Assembly),
1993, 227
A New Canadian Federation, 429
Newcombe, Edmund Leslie, 139–40, 160n15
Newfoundland-Labrador
entry in *Constitution Act, 1867*, s.146, 167–68
Gang of Eight in patriation negotiations,
432–40
Reference on patriation, 433, 435, 437
Nicholas Flood Davin, 108
Norris, Malcolm, 353, 362, 365, 369
Norris, Tobias, 176–77
North West Company
administration of justice by, 277
ambiguous authority in criminal law
in, 36
conflicts with rival companies, 29–30, 33–37
merger with HBC, 33, 39–40, 44, 277
North West Mounted Police
impact on role of justices of the peace,
268–69
as justices of the peace and magistrates,
48, 278–80
See also Royal Canadian Mounted Police
North-West Rebellion
Manitoba's entry into confederation
and, 169
Provisional Government, 348–49
as response to rapid change, 351–52
as struggle for control of resources, 319
trial of Riel, 51–52
North-West Territories
ambiguous authority in criminal law in,
25–26, 45–52
bilingualism in NWT, official (1870–
1904), 103–10
bilingualism in NWT as issue (1888–
1904), 109–16, 124–26
unilingualism in Alberta (1905–2005),
115–19
common law, 48, 50–51
in *Constitution Act, 1867*, s.146, 167–68
Indian hunting and fishing federal/
provincial conflicts, 240–51

jury system, 41–43, 48–52
justices of the peace and magistrates in,
    36–38, 41, 48–50, 268–69, 277–79
legal culture in, 172–73
Legislative Assembly, 109–11
lieutenant-governor's powers, 173, 277–79
official languages: of Council, 105–6;
    language of education issues,
    114–17; language of publication for
    ordinances, 111–12, 115
provisional districts (Athabasca and
    Alberta), 171
school ordinances, 66–74, 82–93, 116–17, 180
separate school issues, 61–62
See also Haultain, Frederick W.; Rupert's
    Land
North-West Territories Act
amendment in 1886: official
    bilingualism, s.110, 106–8, 112, 116,
    125–26; statutes in force, 52
separate schools issues, s.11, 61–62, 65–
    66, 70, 79–83, 86
Northwest Territories
in patriation negotiations, 419
notwithstanding clause
    See Canadian Charter of Rights and Freedoms, 1982
Nova Scotia
Gang of Eight in patriation negotiations,
    432–40
justices of the peace and magistrates,
    275–76
natural resources control, 166, 181
NRTA negotiations, 181–82
as royal colony, 8
separate schools issue, 76
Nova Scotia Speaker's case, 227
NWT. See North-West Territories

Official Languages Act, 122
Oliver, Frank, 66, 83, 112, 248, 296, 304
Olson, "Bud," 302
Ontario
in patriation negotiations, 406, 415, 432,
    436, 440–41
justices of the peace and magistrates,
    274–76
natural resources control, 166, 182

NEP negotiations, 330–31, 336, 391, 405–6
separate schools and, 61–62, 66
Osborne, Fred, 183
Owen, Peter M., 422–23
Owram, Douglas
on NEP in federal/provincial relations,
    391–410

Padlock Law case, 221–26
PanCanadian Petroleum, 163n78
Parker, Nancy
on justices of the peace, 267–88
Parlby, Irene, 139, 142, 148, 153
Parti Québécois government
in patriation negotiations, 418, 420–26,
    431–42, 450
referendum on sovereignty, 418, 429
parties, political. See political parties, new
Paterson, Barbara, 156–57
Patriation Reference case, 370, 433, 435–42
Pearson, Lester B., 327–29, 342n23–24
Pedley, Frank, 247–48
Penner Report (Indian Self-Government in Canada),
    447–48
Pépin, Jean-Luc, 426–27
Perley, William, 110–11
Persons Case, 136–63
impact on interpretation, 138
in Constitution Act, 1867: interpretation,
    s.60, 141–42; persons, s.24, 137, 143–45
Lizzie Cyr case, 138–39
memorials to: plaque, 149–53; statues,
    136–37, 154–58
national women's networks and, 138–41,
    144–45
Quebec and, 139–40, 146, 148, 152
Reference to Supreme Court and Privy
    Council, 138, 141–46, 148
response to decision in, 146–50
as symbol, 137–38, 140, 158–59
W.L.M. King and, 141, 149–53
See also Edwards, Henrietta Muir;
    McClung, Nellie; McKinney, Louise;
    Murphy, Emily; Parlby, Irene
Petro-Canada, 163n78
Piquette, Leo, 124
Pocklington, T., 359–60

Poitras et al. v. Attorney-General for Alberta, 365,
    388n67
police magistrates. *See* justices of the peace
    and magistrates
political parties, new
    pattern of, 321–26, 340–41
    Progressive Party, 321
    Reform party, 337–41, 341n1
    Social Credit party, 192–96, 326, 340
    WCC party, 334
Pond, Peter, 29–30
Poy, Vivienne, 163n78
Prairie Treaty Nations Alliance, 449
premier, office of
    lieutenant-governor and, 293–99
Press Act. *See Accurate News and Information Act*
    (Press Act)
Prince, E.E., 246
Prince Edward Island
    in *Constitution Act, 1867*, s.146, 167–68
    in patriation negotiations, 419; Gang of
        Eight, 432–40
    NRTA negotiations, 181–82
    as royal colony, 8
Privy Council. *See* Judicial Committee of the
    Privy Council (JCPC)
Progressive Conservative government, (1971–
    85), Lougheed
    ASWAC recommendations to, 463
    bill of rights, 462
    civil service expansion, 395
    economic diversification, 401–2
    language rights, 123
    matrimonial property law, 462–65
    notwithstanding clause and gender
        rights, 467
    Resolution on patriation, 417, 420, 433, 436
    tabling of document on patriation
        (*Harmony in Diversity*), 426, 429
    Women's Secretariat, 467–72
    See also *Constitution Act, 1867*, patriation
        negotiations; Department of Federal
        and Intergovernmental Affairs
        (FIGA), in patriation negotiations;
        National Energy Program
Progressive Conservative government,
    (1985–92), Getty

family initiatives and equality, 470
language legislation and personal
    choice, 130
Métis settlements legislation, 373–77
Senate reform, 482
Progressive Conservative government,
    (1992–), Klein
    economic restructuring, 480–81
    executive federalism, 482
    firewall proposal to Klein, 491–92
    health care policies, 295, 483–85
    impact of budget cuts, 471–72
    impact of Charter of Rights, 480, 488–91
    intergovernmental relations, 479–86
    international forces, 480–81, 486–88
    Klein: on health care, 483–84; on judicial
        independence, 268; and lieutenant-
        governors, 293–94, 299
    lieutenant-governor's reserve powers,
        293–94, 299
    neo-liberalism and, 459–60, 471–76
    notwithstanding clause and language
        rights, 131
    provincialism of citizens, 479–80, 495
Progressive Conservative government
    (federal), (1979) Clark
    role in patriation of the constitution,
        428
Progressive Conservatives (federal)
    White Paper on patriation of
        constitution, 421
Progressive Party of Canada
    as reform-oriented party, 321
Proposed Resolution for a Joint Address to
    the Queen Respecting the
    Constitution, 432
Protestant school districts. *See* separate
    schools
Provincial Committee for a Council on
    Women's Affairs, 468
Provincial Court of Alberta
    Reference on independent and impartial
        requirement, 227, 267–68, 283–84
    See also justices of the peace and
        magistrates
provincial/federal relations. *See* federal/
    provincial relations

provincial/provincial relations
    pattern of interprovincial accords, 483, 485
Prowse, J. Harper, 121
Public Interest v. Calder, 44–45
public lands
    A & GW Railway crisis and, 296, 319–20
    federal control in *Alberta Act*, 352
    in *Constitution Act, 1867*, s.109, 166, 396–97,
        417, 422, 424
    national parks, 179, 184, 320
    school lands, 176, 178, 180, 183–84
    See also *Dominion Lands Act;* Métis
        settlements; Natural Resource
        Transfer Agreement (NRTA)
Public School Boards Association of Alberta v. Alberta,
        70, 84–86, 97n40, 97n50, 99n74

Quebec
    civil liberties cases, 220
    Council of the Federation, 484–85
    freedom of press (Padlock Law case), 221–26
    in patriation negotiations: Bourassa's
        role, 413–15; Gang of Eight, 432–41;
        Lévesque's role, 422–24, 431, 433,
        440–42; separatism and, 418, 420,
        424, 426, 451
    nationalism in 1970s, 394, 402
    natural resources control and NRTA,
        181–82
    Persons Case response, 139–40, 146, 148, 152
    pre-NEP import of oil and gas, 330–31
    Reference on patriation, 370, 433, 435, 437
    Reference on secession, 227–28
    referendum on sovereignty, 343n27,
        402–3, 418, 429
    separate schools and, 61, 66
    separatism and NEP, 402–3
    See also Parti Québécois
Quebec, Saumur v., 220
Quebec League for Women's Rights, 149

R. v. Bagder, 259
R. v. Mercure, 125–26
R. v. Stoney Joe, 249–52
Radcliffe, Cyril, 213
railways
    in NRTA negotiations, 170, 174, 181, 184

Ralston, J.L., 202–3, 208–10
Rand, Justice Ivan, 221–25
Re Currie and the Niagara Escarpment Commission
        (1985), 283–84
Re Fisheries, 242
Red River settlement
    ambiguous authority in criminal law in,
        34–39, 43–46, 62
    case citations in, 44–45
    jury system, 41–43, 48–52
    justices of the peace and magistrates in,
        34, 37–38, 48, 277
    settlement of, 34–35, 57n93
    See also Assiniboia, District of
Reed, Hayter, 245–46, 255
Reference Re Alberta Statutes, 1938, 204–14, 219–29
*Reference Re Legislative Authority of Parliament to
        Alter or Replace the Senate*, 425, 433–34
Reference Re Manitoba Languages 1985, 205, 227
*Reference Re Powers of Disallowance and Reservation,
        1938*, 202–8
Reform Party
    for constitutional equality, 318, 329,
        343n26
    founding of, 337–41, 341n1
    Persons Case monument and, 155–56
Regina Leader, 171–73
regionalism and identity, 400
*Regulations Governing the Constitution of Settlement
        Associations*, 363
Reid, R. Gavin, 296–97, 354–55
Reisman, Heather, 163n78
Report to Cabinet on Constitutional Discussions (Kirby
        Report), 431–33
Rex v. Cyr, 138–39
    See also Persons Case
Rich, E.E., 45
Richardson, John, 40
Riel, Louis. *See* North-West Rebellion
Robarts, William, 394
Roberts, Stan, 337
Robertson, Gordon, 413
Roblin, Sir Rodmond, 157, 174–75, 317
Roman Catholic Church
    Métis settlements, 351–52
    See also separate schools
Romanow, Roy, 428, 431

Rose, Nikolas, on freedom, 476
Ross, James, 110
Ross, John, 29–30
Rouleau, Charles, 107
Rowell, Newton Wesley, 144–45
Royal, Joseph, 110–11
Royal Canadian Mounted Police
    as justices of the peace, 269, 280, 287n68
    See also North West Mounted Police
Royal Commission on Bilingualism and
    Biculturalism, 327–29, 342n23–24
Royal Proclamation of 1763, 12, 27, 31, 447
Rupert's Land, 1–16, 25–52
    ambiguous authority in criminal law in,
        25–26, 32–39, 45–52, 62
    case citations, 44–45
    early British legal culture in, 12–16,
        26–28
    Ellice's role in legal ambiguities, 39–40,
        45, 52, 56n72
    entry in Constitution Act, 1867, s.146, 167–69
    entry into confederation, 348–50
    governor and council of, 29
    HBC Charter in, 1, 4–5, 8–16, 26, 28–29
    Indian Territories and, 25–26, 32–36
    indigenous people and HBC in, 29
    justices of the peace and magistrates in,
        34, 37–38
    map of, 2–3
    transfer to Canada, 168, 348–50, 355
    transport of accused out of, 27–30, 32–33
    See also Hudson's Bay Company (HBC)
Rupert's Land Act, 1868, 168, 348
Rutherford, Alexander, 295–96, 319–20

same-sex marriage, 159, 490
Sanders, Douglas, 358
Sankey, Lord Chancellor, 146
Saskatchewan
    Bill of Rights, 215, 218
    first women legislators in, 139
    in patriation negotiations, 419, 440–41,
        448; Gang of Eight, 432–40
    language rights, 125
    lieutenant-governor's roles and powers,
        292, 301
    Métis land claims, 350, 358

NRTA negotiations and agreement, 167,
    174–77, 182–86
population (1884), 108
separate school issues, 61–62, 67–68, 71,
    74–75, 77, 79
See also North-West Territories; Rupert's
    Land
Saskatchewan Act, 125, 174, 183–84
Saumur v. Quebec, 220
Sbaretti, Mgr. Donatus, 71–75
School Act
    minority language rights and regional
        authorities, 120, 123, 127–28, 130–31
    See also language rights
school lands, 176, 178, 180, 183–84
schools, separate. See separate schools
Scott, Anthony, 396
Scott, Duncan Campbell, 252–53, 255–56, 258
Scott, Isabella, 140–41, 146, 148
Scott, R.W., 72
Scott, Thomas Walter, 175
Secretary of State Women's Program, 469
Selkirk, Lord, 34–35, 39–40, 42
Senate
    exclusion of women from, 139–40
    Reference re Senate reform, 425, 433–34
    reform in patriation negotiations, 416,
        419–26, 433–34, 449–50; House of
        Federation, 421–25
    reform movements in 1920s, 143
    reforms for "Triple E," 334–35, 340, 449–
        50, 482–83
    See also Persons Case
separate schools, 61–101
    federal right to remedial legislation,
        64, 78
    funding for schools, 67–68, 77, 82–84
    Haultain's role in negotiations, 67–70,
        74, 77–80, 94n1, 96n24
    in Alberta Act, 83–86, 180–81
    in Autonomy Bill, 70–83, 98n62
    in Charter of Rights, 85–86
    in Constitution Act, 1867, s.93, 63–66, 71, 74,
        76–81, 84, 417
    in Dominion Lands Act, 81
    in North-West Territories Act, s.11, 61–62, 66,
        70, 79, 80, 82–83, 86

in NWT ordinances (1884–1901), 61–62,
66–74, 82–86, 88–93, 180
Laurier's role in negotiations, 70–83
local control, 84–86, 97n40, 97n50
local response to issue (1905), 62–63
Manitoba and, 61
minority rights, 64–66, 72–86, 97n50
minority rights and existing public
school system, 71–72, 82–86, 97n50
national schools *vs.* separate schools as
issue, 61–62, 67–70, 75, 83, 85, 94n1
Ontario and, 61–62, 66
population shifts, 67, 95n12, 95n22
provincial jurisdiction, 64–67, 71, 77–79,
83, 86
Quebec and, 61–62, 66
Reference to Privy Council, 74, 181
Reference to Supreme Court, 84–86, 96,
99n74, 180–81
Roman Catholic hierarchy, 61–62, 66–75,
82–83, 94n10, 95n12, 96n32, 100n107
school lands for, 81, 99n78
Sifton's role in negotiations, 63, 70–71,
80–83, 98n62
See also French language
separation, Western
constitutional inequalities and, 318
impact of NEP on, 334, 392
in 1980s, 449
letter re firewall proposal, 491–92
Seven Oaks fur trade murder case, 36
Sex Disqualification (Removal) Act, 147
sexual orientation
equality concepts and, 459
Human Rights Commission
investigations, 473
same-sex marriage, 159, 490
Vriend case, 489
Sherbrooke, Sir John, 36–37
Sifton, Arthur, 175, 296
Sifton, Clifford
in provincial status issue, 173–74
in separate schools negotiations, 63,
70–71, 80–83, 98n62
Simeon, Richard, 400
Simon, Viscount John A., 217
Simons, Paula, 294–95

Simpson, George, 42–44
Sinclair v. Mulligan, 44
Slattery, Brian, on aboriginal rights, 347
Smiley, Donald, 394–95
Social Credit government (1935–43), Aberhart,
191–236
Alberta Treasury Branches, 218, 228,
235n139
Bill of Rights, 215–18
closure of Government House, 305–6
Depression conditions, 192–94
disallowance of legislation generally,
199–200
Douglas: economic theories of, 192–95;
role in government, 196–200
federal disallowance of provincial
legislation, 199–200, 202–8
founding of Social Credit party, 192–96
legislation on policies generally (*Alberta
Social Credit Act*), 198–99, 206–7, 210,
213
monthly dividends to citizens, 195–96,
198
pattern of new political parties, 340
Reference of *Accurate News and Information
Act*, 201–5, 208–14, 220–29
Reference of *Bank Taxation Act*, 201–8, 214,
290–92, 310n8
Reference of *Credit of Alberta Regulation Act*,
201–8, 213–14, 290–92, 310n8
Reference to Privy Council, 213–19
References significance, 218–29
reserve powers of lieutenant-governor,
290–92
scrip (Prosperity Certificates), 197–98
Social Credit government (1943–68), Manning
in Depression era, 324–26
and lieutenant-governor, 297, 307
Manning: career and family, 316, 324–25,
341n1
on NEP, 333
Social Credit government (1968–71), Strom
budget, 318–19
Social Credit party
founding of, 192–96
Social Union Framework Agreement, 483
Sparrow test for treaty rights, 259–60

Special Joint Committee of Parliament on the
     Constitution of Canada, 370, 422,
     424, 432–37
Spence, Wishart Flett, 226
St. Catherines Milling v. The Queen, 251
St. Paul des Métis, 351–53
Statute of Westminster, 1930, 200, 434
Steinhauer, E., 443
Steinhauer, Ralph, 298
sterilization of mentally challenged persons,
     489
Stewart, Charles, 147, 176
stipendiaries. *See* justices of the peace and
     magistrates
Stoney Joe, R. v., 249–52
Stony Indians, Morley, 241–42, 249–51
Strengthening Alberta's Role in Confederation, 484
Supreme Court Act
     constitutional References to, 202
Supreme Court of Alberta
     constitutionality of ATBs, 218, 228,
          235n139
Supreme Court of Canada
     Brandeis briefs for, 203, 219
     constitutional validity of Alberta
          Treasury Branches, 218
     federal/provincial power shifts and
          references, 218–29
     freedom of discussion (Padlock Law
          case), 221–26
     language rights (Mahé), 127–28, 130–31
     lieutenant-governor's reserve powers, 292
     matrimonial property case (Murdoch),
          463
     patriation negotiations: appointment
          process as issue, 413, 415, 420
     Persons case, 141–42, 145–46
     power shift to federal government,
          218–20
     Reference re Alberta (Social Credit)
          statutes, 202, 205–14, 219–29
     Reference re independence of courts, 227
     Reference re languages of Manitoba
          statutes, 205, 227
     Reference re patriation, 370, 435–42
     Reference re powers of disallowance and
          reservation, 199–200, 202–8

Reference re Quebec secession, 227–28
Reference re same-sex marriage, 490
Reference re Senate reform, 425, 433–34
Reference re separate schools, 84–86, 96,
     99n74, 180–81
Vriend case, 489
Switzman v. Elbling (Padlock Law case), 221–26

Taché, Bishop Alexandre-Antonin, 66, 74
Task Force on National Unity, 426–28
taxation
     equality and tax reform, 473–75, 478n33
     export taxes in NEP, 331–36, 412–13
     as patriation issue, 431
     before provincehood, 166, 316
     provincial powers in *Constitution Act, 1867*,
          s.92(2), 206, 414, 417, 431
Taylor, Nick, 126
Temporary Government of Rupert's Land Act, 1869,
     64–65
Territories' Government Act, 47
Thatcher, Margaret, 435
The British North America Act, 1930, Enactment
          No. 16. *See* Natural Resource Transfer
          Agreement (NRTA)
The Queen, Maurice L'Hirondelle et al. v., 388n70
The Queen, St. Catherines Milling v., 251
The Queen, Valente v., 283–84
*The Queen in Right of Alberta, Keg River Métis
          Settlement Association et al. v.*, 387n59
Thom, Adam, 42–45, 48, 52
Thomas, L.G., 321, 326, 340
Thompson, John, 51, 112–13
Tilley, W.N., 202–4, 209–10
Timbrell, Dennis, 405–6
A Time for Action, 421–22
Towers, Gordon, 292–93, 302
Traffic Court
     justices of the peace duties in, 269, 282–83
TransCanada Pipeline, 331
treaties
     generally, 237, 259–60
     See also First Nations hunting and fishing
          regulation
Tremblay, Arthur, 428
Triple-E Senate, 334–35, 340, 449–50, 482–83
Trowbridge, Eddie, 316–18

Trudeau, Pierre Elliot
 defeat and re-election, 406, 428
 in NEP negotiations, 391–92, 402–7
 personal background, 403–5
Trudeau, Pierre Elliot, in patriation
   negotiations
 Aboriginal organizations and rights,
   430–31, 441–50
 at annual conferences of premiers: in
   1981, 439–41
 British parliamentary response, 434–36
 defeat and re-election, 428
 draft provisions: in 1976, 413–15, 424; in
   1977, 419–21; in 1978 (Bill C-60), 420–
   27; in 1979, 426–32; in 1980, 429–32
 gender rights, 442
 Kirby report on constitutional
   discussions, 431–33
 on patriation negotiations, 417
 promotion and defense of Act, 1982, 444–51
 proposed resolution for joint address to
   Queen, 432–33
 reopening of negotiations with three
   options, 413–16
 Resolution on unilateral patriation
   (1980), 432–36
 to Lougheed: on amending formula, 417–
   19; on division of powers, 422
 unilateral patriation, 413–18, 430–35
 See also Constitution Act, 1867, patriation
   negotiations
Tupper, Allan
 on future of Alberta, 479–95
 on lieutenant-governor's role, 294
Turgeon, W.F.A. and Turgeon Commission,
   182–84

Ukrainian language rights, 117, 122, 130
Union Act Amendment Act (1854), 166
United Farmers of Alberta, as government
   (1925–34), Brownlee

Brownlee's resignation, 296–97
 in 1935 election, 192, 194, 196
 in NRTA negotiations, 179–80, 183, 258,
   322–23
 as political pattern of new parties, 326, 340
United Farmers of Alberta, as government
   (1934–35), Reid, 296–97, 354–55
United States
 free trade, 335–36
 pre-NEP conditions, 330–31

Valente v. The Queen (1986), 283–84
Vancouver Consensus (on amending
   formula), 427, 430–36, 439
Vankoughnet, Lawrence, 240–41
Victoria Charter of 1971, 412–20, 425
Vriend, Delwin, 489

Walsh, William, 297
Waters, Lizzie, 138–39
 See also Persons Case
WCC. See Western Canada Concept Party
Weiler, Paul, 222
Western Canada Concept Party, 334, 449
Westlock Resolution on Métis settlements,
   372–73
Weston, Hilary M., 308–9
Wilson, Cairine, 149–53, 151, 162n57
Wilson, Mrs. J.A., 147
Winspear, Francis, 337
Wolf Lake Métis settlement, 364–65
Women's Christian Temperance Union, 140
women's issues. See equality; equality for
       persons; gender issues; Persons Case
Women's Secretariat, Alberta, 467–72
Wood, Charles, 445
Wright, Francis, 153–58

XY Company, 30

Yukon Territories, 419